A Cross Section of Educational Research

Journal Articles for Discussion and Evaluation

Fourth Edition

Lawrence S. Lyne

Editor

 Pyrczak Publishing

P.O. Box 250430 ♦ Glendale, CA 91225

"Pyrczak Publishing" is an imprint of Fred Pyrczak, Publisher, A California Corporation.

This edition was prepared in collaboration with Randall R. Bruce.

Although the editor and publisher have made every effort to ensure the accuracy and completeness of information contained in this book, we assume no responsibility for errors, inaccuracies, omissions, or any inconsistency herein. Any slights of people, places, or organizations are unintentional.

Project Director: Monica Lopez.

Editorial assistance provided by Cheryl Alcorn, Karen M. Disner, Jack Petit, Erica Simmons, Mel Yiasemide, and Sharon Young.

Printed in the United States of America by Malloy, Inc.

ISBN 1-884585-80-9

Contents

Continued →

Causal–Comparative Research

Program Evaluation

Qualitative Research

Continued →

Introduction to the Fourth Edition

This book is designed for students who are learning how to evaluate published educational research. The 38 research articles in this collection provide the stimulus material for such a course.

Selection of the Articles

Several criteria were used in the selection of the articles. The first criterion was that the articles needed to be comprehensible to students taking their first research methods course. Thus, to be selected, an article needed to illustrate straightforward designs and the use of only basic statistics.

Second, because most education majors become teachers, the articles needed to deal with topics of interest to classroom teachers. To test this criterion, students taking an educational research methods course were given the titles and abstracts (i.e., summaries) of a large number of articles to rate for interest. Only those that received moderate to high average ratings survived the screening of the initial pool of potential articles.

Third, the articles as a whole needed to illustrate a wide variety of approaches to research. You will notice in the table of contents that the articles represent 12 types of research, such as Qualitative Research, Quantitative Research, Content Analysis, Survey Research, Correlational Research, True Experimental Research, and so on.

Finally, the articles needed to be drawn from a large number of different journals. Because each journal has its own genre as well as criteria for the selection of submissions for publication, students can learn about the wide variations in educational research only by reading articles from a number of different journals. Application of this criterion resulted in 38 articles drawn from 22 different journals.

How to Use this Book

In the field tests, articles were assigned for homework at each class meeting. Students were required to read the articles and answer the questions at the end of each one. At the next class meeting, the articles were discussed with the instructor leading the discussion. Other arrangements are, of course, possible. For example, each student might be responsible for leading the discussion of one of the articles after all members of the class have read the article.

About the Questions at the End of Each Article

There are three types of questions at the end of each article. First, there are *Factual Questions*. The answers for these are explicitly stated in the articles. In addition to writing down the answers, students should record the line numbers where they found the answers. The line numbers will facilitate discussions if there are disagreements as to what constitutes a correct answer to a question.

Second, there are *Questions for Discussion*. Because these are designed to stimulate classroom discussions, most of these questions ask for students' opinions on various decisions made by the researchers in conducting and writing up their research. In the field tests, these questions led to lively classroom discussions. Because professional researchers often debate such issues with each other, students should not be surprised by such debates in their own classrooms.

Third, students are asked to make *Quality Ratings* for each article. This is done by the application of 13 fundamental criteria for evaluating research, using rating scale items that are repeated at the end of each article. These criteria may be supplemented by the more extensive list presented in Appendix A or with lists of criteria that are found in some research methods textbooks.

Reading the Statistics in this Book

Students who have taken a statistics class as a prerequisite to their research methods class should feel quite comfortable with the overwhelming majority of statistics found in this collection because articles that contained large numbers of obscure or highly advanced statistics were excluded from this book.

Students who are learning about statistics for the first time in the course in which they are using this book may need some additional help from their instructors. Keep in mind that it is not realistic to expect instructors of a research methods class to also teach a full-fledged course in statistical methods. Thus, there may be times when an instructor asks students to concentrate on the researcher's *interpretation* of statistics without extensive discussions of the theory underlying specific statistics.

The Classification of the Articles

Educational research methods textbooks vary somewhat in how various types of research are classified. While labels such as "true experiment," "qualitative research," and "survey" are common to almost all textbooks, others may be more idiosyncratic. In addition, some categories of research overlap each other. For instance, when analyzing the results of a survey, a researcher may compute correlation coefficients, making it unclear whether the research should be classified as survey research or as correlational research. An interesting classroom discussion topic is whether a given article can be classified as representing more than one type of research.

About the Fourth Edition

Many of the articles from the Third Edition were retained here. New to this edition are articles 1, 2, 3, 4, 7, 14, 16, 18, 19, 20, 21, 22, 26, 30, 31, 33, 34, 35, 36, and 37. In addition, Appendix B provides information that should be helpful in the evaluation of qualitative research.

Acknowledgments

I am grateful to Mildred L. Patten, who is the author of a similar collection titled *Educational and Psychological Research: A Cross Section of Journal Articles for Analysis and Evaluation*. Her collection emphasizes broad issues of interest to psychologists and educators, while this book emphasizes topics of interest to classroom teachers. Nevertheless, some structural elements of her book were employed in this one, such as the inclusion of three types of questions at the end of each article. She also provided me with advice on the criteria for selecting articles and numerous technical matters while I was preparing this book.

I also am indebted to the publishers who hold the copyrights to the articles in this book. Without their cooperation, it would not be possible to amass a collection such as the one found here.

Lawrence S. Lyne

Article 1

Involving Students in School Violence Prevention: Are They Willing to Help?

CHRISTY J. BRINKLEY
Arkansas State University

DAVID A. SAARNIO
Arkansas State University

ABSTRACT. Why are some students not willing to tell adults about a possibly violent situation in their school? In this study, 1,100 students in the Mid-South were surveyed on their knowledge of and willingness to tell about a possibly violent situation, their involvement in behaviors that are related to school violence, and their school's climate. About one-third of students knew of a potentially violent situation, and about three-fourths were willing to tell an adult. However, students who were involved in antecedents to violence and/or who had an unfavorable view of their school were much less likely to tell an adult about such situations. Efforts to prevent school violence should be designed with these factors in mind.

From *Journal of School Violence*, 5, 93–106. Copyright © 2006 by The Haworth Press, Inc. Reprinted with permission.

Involving Students in School Violence Prevention: Are They Willing to Help?

Violence in our nation's schools has become a focal point in our society over the past decade. Cities such as Jonesboro (Westside Middle School), Littleton (Columbine High School), and West Paducah (Heath High
5 School) have become well-known in the United States because of the shootings that have taken place there. Even though school violence actually declined in the 1990s (U.S. Surgeon General, 2001), it is clear that the school shootings that occurred in the same decade have
10 generated strong interest in the prevention of violence in schools. There is reason for concern. For example, although the number of students who reported carrying a weapon anywhere and at school has declined in recent years, 6% of students (over 900,000) report that
15 they have carried a weapon at least 1 day during the previous 30 days (National Center for Education Statistics, 2003). This is not something that should be ignored, especially because the presence of weapons can make students feel intimidated and threatened, and in
20 turn, make teaching and learning difficult (Ingersoll & LeBoeuf, 1997). Additionally, since 1992, at least 285 school-associated shooting deaths have occurred (National School Safety Center, 2004), suggesting that the threat of violence continues to exist.
25 In efforts to reduce the potential for school violence, a number of different programs have been im-

plemented. For example, metal detectors have been installed, school resource officers have been hired, mental health programs have been implemented, and
30 after-school programs have been instituted (e.g., through the Federal Safe Schools/Healthy Students Grant program). However, many such programs have been ineffective (Mendel, 2000).

Another approach has been suggested by a recent
35 collaboration by the United States Secret Service and United States Department of Education (Vossekuil, Fein, Reddy, Borum, & Modzeleski, 2002). Interviews were conducted with perpetrators of 37 incidents of targeted school violence (i.e., violence in which par-
40 ticular individuals were targeted) that occurred between December 1974 and June 2000. Important for our purposes, in over three-fourths of the attacks, at least one other person had prior knowledge of the attack. In almost two-thirds of the incidents, *more* than
45 one person had prior knowledge. The majority of those individuals who possessed knowledge of the impending attack were either a friend, schoolmate, or sibling of the attacker(s). Unfortunately, adults (e.g., school personnel) did not know about the impending attacks.
50 This suggests that those students who did have prior knowledge were not inclined to tell or warn an adult for one reason or another. If a warning had been given, perhaps many of the shootings could have been prevented. From this perspective, one approach to reduc-
55 ing school violence would be to create an atmosphere in which students feel comfortable "telling an adult whenever they hear about someone who is considering doing harm to another person" (Vossekuil et al., 2002, p. 42). In fact, Ronald Stephens (undated) of the Na-
60 tional School Safety Center suggested that "the best metal detector is the student" (cited in Cloud, 2001, and referred to by J. Arnette, personal communication, January 11, 2005).

If Vossekuil et al. (2002) and others (e.g., Stephens,
65 2001) are correct, students have the potential for reducing violence. However, an important issue that must be addressed is why students do not communicate with adults about an impending situation involving violence. Recent school-based (e.g., Halbig, 2000), popular (e.g.,
70 Fleishauer, 2001), and government (e.g., Fein et al.,

2002) sources have suggested that a "code of silence" exists in schools, which means that there is a lack of communication between students and adults. For example, Halbig (2000) pointed out that students have
75 learned that "tattling" on their peers is unacceptable, despite the consequences, because they fear being rejected by certain groups or being retaliated against by other students. Searches of the *ERIC* and *PsycInfo* databases indicate that very little academic research has
80 been conducted on the code of silence, suggesting that we do not have solid data on the nature or extent of this issue. In fact, we know of only one other research project focused directly on the code of silence. Over 2,000 7th- through 12th-grade students were asked (on an
85 online survey) whether they would tell an adult if they heard another student say he or she was going to shoot someone (Gaughan, Cerio, & Myers, 2001). The results indicated that 1 in 5 students had heard a rumor that a fellow student had a plan to shoot someone at school.
90 The same number of students reported that they had directly overheard another student talking about shooting someone at school. In all, 40% of students had heard another student talking about shooting someone, either directly or by rumor. However, only one-half of
95 students reported that they would tell an adult if they had prior knowledge of a potential shooting.

The primary purpose of the present study was to reexamine student willingness to communicate with adults about school violence. Because of the impor-
100 tance of and the paucity of studies on the topic, it is important to gain a clearer understanding of the extent to which there is a code of silence. Thus, this research builds upon and extends the work of Gaughan et al. (2001) to examine the code of silence and its corre-
105 lates.

A secondary purpose of the present study was to put the code of silence into a context of school climate, a critical area that the U.S. Department of Justice (2004) suggests should be considered in order to pre-
110 vent violence. In a position statement on school violence, the National Association of School Psychologists (2001) indicated that one major focus of violence prevention should be to "change the conditions that may be conducive to violent acts" (p. 2). This can be
115 done by enhancing school climate and promoting positive school support. Spitalli (2003) suggests that this should include trust among students and teachers, visibility of adults (students feel safe when adults are present), positive school climate, information hotlines, and
120 reinforced codes of discipline. Fein et al. (2004) made a similar suggestion in that the key components to creating a climate of school safety are fostering a culture of respect, creating connections between adults and students, and breaking the code of silence. Further,
125 Stephens (1998) suggested the need for students to be active in their safety, to feel welcome at school, and feel a sense of pride and ownership in their school. Thus, a positive school climate is essential. Schools

that have a positive climate of nurturance, inclusive-
130 ness, and community feeling have lower levels of violent behavior than schools that do not (Walker, 1995).

The present study is a descriptive one in which we address two questions: (1) Will students tell an adult if they know about possible antecedents to a violent at-
135 tack? For example, if a student brings a gun to school, will anyone tell an adult? If a student tells a friend that he or she is going to hurt someone with a weapon, will an adult know in time to prevent the attack? (2) What makes some students willing to tell and other students
140 not? Here we examine two different ideas. First, are the students who are NOT willing to tell possibly the ones who are exhibiting the antecedents of violent behavior (e.g., bringing guns to school)? Second, are there certain attributes of school climate that help determine
145 whether or not a student would tell? With answers to questions such as these, hopefully we can start to understand and find ways to diminish the code of silence.

Methods

Participants

The participants were 6th- through 11th-grade students in four school districts in the Mid-South (*N* =
150 1,198; *ns* varied across analyses because of missing data). Forty-eight percent of students were female (52% were male), 79% were white (13% were black), and 12% to 22% were from any given grade.

Procedures

As part of a larger survey, participants were asked
155 about four issues: (1) Their knowledge of violence-related antecedents in school (2 yes–no items: "I know of someone who has brought a gun or knife to school in the past 12 months" [also called below, "brought a weapon"] and "I have heard a student threaten to hurt
160 someone else with a weapon in the past 12 months" [also called below, "heard a threat"]); (2) Their willingness to tell about violence-related antecedents (2 yes–no items: "If I knew that someone brought a gun or knife to school, I would tell an adult" and "If I heard
165 a student threaten to hurt someone else with a weapon, I would tell an adult"); (3) Their participation in violence-related antecedent behaviors (3 items on a 5-point scale from "Never" to "10+ Times": How many times have you (a) "carried a knife to school in the past
170 6 months," (b) "carried a gun to school in the past 6 months," and (c) "threatened to hurt someone with a weapon"); (4) Their view of their school's climate (3 composite variables [all on a 5-point scale from "Strongly Disagree" to "Strongly Agree"]: Student–
175 Teacher Relationships, General School Atmosphere, and School Problems). The Appendix [at the end of this article] lists the individual school climate items. The composite variables were loosely based on Purkey and colleagues' Inviting School Safety Survey (e.g.,
180 Shoffner & Vacc, 1999).

2

Results

The results are organized based on the issues listed above. First, descriptive results for each of the four issues are provided. Second, analyses are used to examine what makes some students likely to tell and others not.

Descriptive Results

Knowledge of violence-related antecedents. About one-third of students reported that they knew of someone who had brought a weapon to school (28%) and/or had heard a threat (33%). Overall, males were more likely to report knowing about another student bringing a weapon to school (33%) or threatening someone with a weapon (38%) than females (23% and 29%, respectively), χ^2s (1) = 16.8 and 9.6, ps < .001. See Table 1.

A significant grade effect was found for knowing about weapons in school, χ^2 (5) = 76.7, p < .001 (see Table 1). Fewer 6th- and 7th-grade students (12% and 20%) reported knowing that someone brought a gun or knife to school than older students (32% to 43%). The grade effect indicates that as a student approaches or is in high school, he or she is more likely to know of weapons being brought to school. No significant differences with grade were found when students were asked if they had heard another student threaten someone with a weapon, χ^2 (5) = .26, p = .26 (see Table 1).

Willingness to tell about violence-related antecedents. About three-fourths of all students reported that they would tell an adult if they knew of someone who had brought a weapon to school (73%) and/or had heard a student threaten to hurt someone else with a weapon (74%). Overall, more females reported that they would tell an adult if they knew someone had brought a weapon to school (81%) or if they heard a student threaten someone else with a weapon (83%) than males (65% and 66%, respectively), χ^2s (1) = 37.2 and 41.6, ps < .001. Grade effects also were found (see Table 1). For example, 6th-grade students were much more likely to say that they would tell an adult about someone bringing a weapon than were 11th-grade students (91% of 6th-grade students said they would tell; only 59% of 11th-grade students say they would); in general, students in higher grades were less likely to say they would tell an adult, χ^2 (5) = 95.8, p < .001. A similar effect is found for students who are willing to report a threat, χ^2 (5) = 47.4, p < .001. The results show that from 8th grade on, only about two-thirds would report something as serious as the presence of a gun or knife at school. A few more students say they would report having heard a weapon-related threat, but even then, the percentage who would not tell is alarming (see Table 1).

Participation in violence-related antecedent behaviors. Violence-related antecedent behavior (e.g., bringing weapons to school) was not prevalent, but it was present. Of the over 1,100 students surveyed, 89 (8% of those who responded) reported having carried a knife to school in the past 6 months, 24 (2% of those who responded) reported having carried a gun to school in the past 6 months, and 87 (8% of those who responded) reported that they had threatened to harm someone with a weapon in the past 6 months. Males, overwhelmingly, were more likely to engage in any of the three behaviors than females: 77 males versus 12 females carried a knife, 22 males and 2 females carried a gun to school, and 71 males and 15 females threatened to hurt someone with a weapon. Frequencies by grade are presented in Table 2.

School climate. From 20 individual questions about school climate, three composite variables were created: Student–Teacher Relationships (9 items, such as teacher support and expectations), General School Atmosphere (6 items, such as student respect and safety), and School Problems (5 items, such as racism and drugs). Alphas for all composite variables were greater than .81. The Appendix presents a complete list of survey items pertaining to school climate. On average, students were neutral about their schools, with means of 3.3, 3.2, and 2.7 for student–teacher relationships, school atmosphere, and school problems, respectively (3 is the mid-point for each scale). Substantial variability was present, with standard deviations of .79, .77, and 1.03, respectively. An ANOVA for each composite variable by grade and sex indicated that the patterns for each variable were relatively similar. There were clear grades effects for each variable, all Fs > 6.4, ps < .001, with eta squares ranging from .03 to .32. Simply put, 6th- and 7th-graders reported more positive school climates than did older students, and the effect was largest for school problems (F = 110.6, eta squared = .32). Only one significant sex effect emerged, for student–teacher relationships, F(l, 1,167) = 16.3, p < .001, eta squared = .01. However, the male–female difference was not very large (means of 3.25 and 3.40, respectively) and will not be discussed further. No significant interactions emerged, all Fs < 2.1, ps > .05.

What Factors Make Students Willing to Tell?

Are knowing about possible violence and telling adults related? Conditional analyses indicated that those who knew of people bringing weapons to school or of threatening others with weapons were actually less likely to tell an adult than those who did not know of such situations, χ^2s (1) = 169.7 and 51.7, ps < .001. Thus, those who know of a potentially violent situation (weapons in school or threats) report that they are not as likely to tell an adult as are those who do not have this knowledge (see Table 3). For example, of the students who reported that they knew of someone who has brought a weapon to school, only 45% reported that they would tell an adult, considerably fewer than students who did not know of someone who brought a weapon to school (83%). However, of the students who reported that they have heard a student threaten to hurt someone else with a weapon, the majority (61%)

Table 1
Percentage of Students Answering "YES" to Knowing and Telling Survey Items

	Grade	Knowing items		Telling items	
		I know of someone who has brought a gun or knife to school in the past 12 months.	I have heard a student threaten to hurt someone else with a weapon in the past 12 months.	If I knew that someone brought a gun or knife to school, I would tell an adult.	If I heard a student threaten to hurt someone else with a weapon, I would tell an adult.
Male	6	12.4	30.1	88.2	80.6
	7	21.3	37.8	76.3	74.4
	8	43.4	39.4	60.6	64.3
	9	52.9	44.3	45.3	57.5
	10	44.1	40.3	45.6	47.0
	11	48.5	38.2	45.6	50.0
Female	6	10.7	26.4	93.3	90.9
	7	18.4	23.5	90.8	90.7
	8	26.5	26.5	74.0	79.2
	9	33.7	34.9	72.2	70.9
	10	22.0	32.2	73.9	82.0
	11	30.6	33.9	75.0	74.2

Table 2
Percentage of Students Who Have Engaged in Violence-Related Antecedents at Least Once

Grade	I've carried a knife to school in the past 6 months.	I've carried a gun to school in the past 6 months.	I've threatened to hurt someone with a weapon.
6	2.7	0.8	5.8
7	3.4	1.3	4.7
8	7.0	3.0	6.0
9	11.0	1.7	8.1
10	10.7	4.4	14.4
11	18.3	2.3	9.2

Table 3
Percentage of Students Who Know (or Do Not Know) of a Weapon in School and Who Would Tell an Adult

		If I knew that someone brought a gun or knife to school, I would tell an adult.	
		YES	NO
I know of someone who has brought a gun or knife to school in the past 12 months.	YES	44.6	**55.4**
	NO	**83.2**	16.8

Table 4
Percentage of Students Who Have Heard (or Have Not Heard) a Threat and Would Tell

		If I heard a student threaten to hurt someone else with a weapon, I would tell an adult.	
		YES	NO
I have heard a student threaten to hurt someone else with a weapon in the past 12 months.	YES	60.5	**39.5**
	NO	**80.4**	19.6

Table 5
Percentage of Students Who Have Carried a Gun and Would (or Would Not) Tell About Another Student Carrying a Weapon

		If I knew that someone brought a gun or knife to school, I would tell an adult.	
		YES	NO
I've carried a gun to school in the past 6 months.	YES	29.2	**70.8**
	NO	**73.7**	26.3

Table 6
Percentage of Students Who Have Threatened to Hurt Someone and Who Would (or Would Not) Tell About Another Student Threatening

		If I heard a student threaten to hurt someone else with a weapon, I would tell an adult.	
		YES	NO
I've threatened to hurt someone with a weapon.	YES	35.3	**64.7**
	NO	**77.1**	22.9

reported that they would tell someone (see Table 4); thus, threats are more likely to be reported than weapons. Nevertheless, about 40% of students reported that they would not tell an adult if they heard another student threaten someone with a weapon. This could imply that knowledge of weapons or threats stays within restricted groups (e.g., friends), or that the students who know of a threat may be the ones who are doing the threatening (but see above).

Relation between willingness to tell and violence-related antecedent behavior. Are students who will not tell about a potentially violent situation the same students who are bringing weapons to school and threatening others? Seventy-one percent of the students who *had* brought a gun to school reported that they *would not* tell an adult about someone else with a weapon, whereas 74% of those who *had not* brought a gun to school reported that they *would* tell an adult. Thus, the percentages are reversed, $\chi^2(1) = 23.53, p < .001$ (see Table 5). However, most students have not carried a gun (or knife) to school, and still 26% of those who *have not* carried a gun to school *would not* tell an adult if another student had a gun. Therefore, it is not only those students who carry weapons to school that will not talk to adults, but other students as well. The same results occurred for those who have (or have not) threatened someone with a weapon, $\chi^2(1) = 71.23, p < .001$ (see Table 6).

Relation Between School Climate and Willingness to Tell

The National Association of School Psychologists (2001) has suggested that school climate is an important factor in school violence. In the present study, we examined attributes of school climate that may be related to whether or not a student will tell. As discussed earlier, students were asked two questions about their willingness to tell an adult about antecedents to violent situations: "If I knew that someone brought a gun or knife to school, I would tell an adult" (also called "brought a weapon") and "If I heard a student threaten to hurt someone else with a weapon, I would tell an adult" (also called "heard a threat"). These two items served as the grouping variables for a discriminant analyses. The composite school climate variables (student–teacher relationships, general school atmosphere, and school problems) were used to discriminate stu-

dents who would and would not tell an adult about possible danger.

The discriminant analysis for "brought a weapon" yielded a single discriminant function (Wilks's Lambda, $p < .001$) and correctly classified 69% of the students. The Canonical Correlation was .35. Of the three composite variables, student–teacher relationships proved to be the most important, followed by school problems. The discriminant analysis for "heard a threat" yielded the same pattern of results, correctly classifying 69% of the students. Again, student–teacher relationships was the most important variable in the function.

Discussion

The results show that approximately one-third of students know about someone bringing weapons to school or threatening others with weapons. Although the majority of students are willing to tell an adult about these potentially dangerous situations, a meaningful number of students are not willing to tell. As would be expected, males are less likely to talk to an adult about threats (or weapons) than females, but even 1 in 6 females report that they would not tell an adult. Therefore, efforts to involve students in violence prevention, specifically by increasing trust and communication with teachers, should be designed with these differences in mind, but should not focus exclusively on either males or females. Also important, willingness to tell varies by grade, with younger students more likely to tell adults about potential violence. We do not know if this grade-related increase is because there are fewer secrets in school, there are more weapons being brought to school, or there is some other reason. Because many of the school shootings have taken place in the higher grades, it is especially important to increase communication in those grades in which it is less likely for communication to occur. These data also indicate that students may be less likely to tell if they actually know of someone bringing a weapon (or threatening) than if they do not know someone who brought a weapon (or threatened). Therefore, the code of silence does exist, especially for those who are more likely to know about weapons and threats.

Why does the code of silence exist? We cannot be certain, but we believe the current data provide a place to start. First, we know that those students who are most likely to engage in violence-related antecedent behavior (e.g., bringing weapons to school) are the ones that are least likely to tell adults about others' violence potential. However, those students are not the only ones who will not warn adults about potentially violent situations; about one-fourth of students who do not participate in antecedents of violent behavior still say that they would not tell an adult if they knew of a potentially violent situation.

Second, the way in which students view their school's climate, especially the relationships they have with their teachers, is related to their decision to communicate with adults about such critical situations. Therefore, it is likely that students who are involved in the violence-related behaviors (carrying weapons and threatening) do not have an adult with whom they have a positive and open relationship. In contrast, Halbig (2000) speculates that the reasons why students are reluctant to tell an adult if something is going to happen include the desire to be accepted socially—not be called a "narc" or "tattletale"—and the fear of retaliation. He suggests that a major area of focus in the schools needs to be on reducing the fear of consequences that might follow if a student speaks up. The data presented in this study and Halbig's hypothesis are not incompatible—we speculate that fear of consequences may be an element of school climate. In schools with a positive climate, social acceptance is based on respect and care for other individuals, so ostracism and retaliation are not prevalent. In this type of environment, students themselves help to maintain safety.

The data presented in this paper are not surprising. They confirm what most have already suspected and are similar to those of Gaughan et al. (2001), who found that only about one-half of students would tell an adult if they heard a student talking about shooting someone. As Gaughan et al. and others suggest, emphasis needs to be placed on communication between students and adults, and we need to recruit students themselves to be part of the solution to school violence. Unfortunately, we are not yet at the point that we can be sure that the students will help us. More work on student attitudes and culture, especially the code of silence, is needed.

References

Cloud, J. (2001, March 19). The Legacy of Columbine. *Time*, 32+.

Fein, R. A., Vossekuil, B., Pollack, W. S., Borum, R., Modzeleski, W., & Reddy, M. (2004). *Threat assessment in schools: A guide to managing threatening situations and to creating safe school climates.* Washington, DC: Education Publications Center.

Fleishauer, B. (2001). Breaking the code of silence. *NEA Today*, 20, 36.

Gaughan, E., Cerio, J. D., & Myers, R. A. (2001). *Lethal violence in schools: A national survey final report.* Alfred, NY: Alfred University.

Halbig, W. W. (2000). Breaking the code of silence [Electronic version]. *American School Board Journal*, 187, 34–36.

Ingersoll, S., & LeBoeuf, D. (1997). *Reaching Out to Youth Out of the Mainstream.* U.S. Department of Justice Juvenile Justice Bulletin (February). Washington, DC: U.S. Government Printing Office.

Mendel, R. A. (2000). *Less hype, more help: Reducing juvenile crime, what works—and what doesn't* [Electronic version]. American Youth Policy Forum, Washington, DC: Author.

National Association of School Psychologists. (2002). *Position statement on school violence.* Retrieved June 5, 2003, from http://www.nasponline.org/information/pospaper_violence.html

National Center for Education Statistics. (2003). *Indicators of school crime and safety, 2003.* Retrieved November 11, 2004, from http://nces.ed.gov/pubs2004/crime03/11.asp

National School Safety Center. (2004). *Report on school associated violent deaths.* Retrieved October 29, 2004, from www.nssc1.org/savd/savd.pdf

Shoffner, M. F., & Vacc, N. A. (1999). Psychometric Analysis of the Inviting School Safety Survey. *Measurement and Evaluation in Counseling and Development*, 32, 66–74.

Spitalli, S. J. (2003). Breaking the code of silence: How students can help keep school—and each other—safe. *American School Board Journal*, 190, 56–59.

Stephens, R. D. (1998). Statement made to subcommittee on early childhood, youth, and families, committee on education and the workforce, United States House of Representatives hearing on understanding violent children. Retrieved January 11, 2005, from http://www.nssc1.org/witness/testimon.htm

United States Department of Justice, Office of Justice Programs. (2004). Toward safe and orderly schools: The national study of delinquency prevention in schools (Research in Brief, NCJ 205005). Washington, DC: Author.

Walker, D. (1995). *School violence prevention. ERIC digest, Number 94.* Eugene, OR: *ERIC* Clearinghouse on Educational Management. (*ERIC* Document Reproduction Service No. ED379786). http://www.ericfacility.net/ericdigests/ed379786.html

Vossekuil, B., Fein, R. A., Reddy, M., Borum. R., & Modzeleski, W. (2002). The final report and findings of the Safe School Initiative. Washington, DC: U.S. Secret Service and U.S. Department of Education.

Acknowledgment: The authors wish to thank Wendy Christy for her help with the project.

About the authors: *Christy J. Brinkley* is school psychology specialist in Northeast Arkansas, and evaluation coordinator, Department of Psychology & Counseling, Arkansas State University, P.O. Box 1560, State University, AR 72467 (E-mail: christyjbrinkley @yahoo.com). *David A. Saarnio* is professor of psychology, Department of Psychology & Counseling, Arkansas State University, P.O. Box 1560, State University, AR 72467 (E-mail: dsaarnio@astate.edu).

Appendix

School Climate Items*

Student–Teacher Relationships (Alpha = .88)

Teachers develop caring relationships with students in my school.

Students are treated with warmth and respect by teachers and school staff.

The teachers and administrators in this school are fair in their discipline.

Teachers use a variety of methods to help students.

Teachers have reasonable goals for students.

Teachers value student effort rather than ability.

Teachers believe in rewarding students for a job well done.

All students are valued in this school.

When I am having problems, my teachers are supportive.

General School Atmosphere (Alpha = .81)

My school has a climate of kindness and encouragement.

Students get along well in my school.

As a whole, I am happy with my school.

I feel safe at school.

Most of the students in this school have respect for other students.

Most of the students in this school show respect for their teachers.

School Problems (Alpha = .85)

Racism is a problem in my school.

Drugs are a problem among students in my school.

Alcohol is a problem among students in my school.

Tobacco (cigarettes, chewing tobacco, etc.) is a problem among students in my school.

Gangs are a problem in this school.

* All items were rated on a 5-point scale from "Strongly Disagree" to "Strongly Agree."

Exercise for Article 1

Factual Questions

1. According to the researchers, has there been much academic research on the code of silence?

2. What is the primary purpose of this study?

3. What percentage of the participants was white?

4. Were older students "more" or "less" likely to know of weapons being brought to school (in comparison with younger students)?

5. What percentage of the 9th-grade students reported that they had carried a knife to school in the past six months?

Questions for Discussion

6. Would it be interesting to know whether the 1,198 students constituted the whole population (all students in grades 6 through 11) or were just a sample of all students? If they were a sample, would it be interesting to know how the sample was drawn? Explain. (See lines 148–153.)

7. The researchers present the wording of the questions. Is this important to you? Explain. (See lines 154–176 and the Appendix at the end of the article.)

8. The researchers state that the data they present are "not surprising." Are you surprised at any of the results? (See line 413.)

9. In your opinion, do the results of this study have important implications for helping to prevent school violence? Explain.

10. In your opinion, are the results of this study sufficiently promising to warrant conducting large-scale studies on this topic? Explain.

Quality Ratings

Directions: Indicate your level of agreement with each of the following statements by circling a number from 5 for strongly agree (SA) to 1 for strongly disagree (SD). If you believe an item is not applicable to this research article, leave it blank. Be prepared to explain your ratings. When responding to criteria A and B below, keep in mind that brief titles and abstracts are conventional in published research.

A. The title of the article is appropriate.

SA   5   4   3   2   1   SD

B. The abstract provides an effective overview of the research article.

SA   5   4   3   2   1   SD

C. The introduction establishes the importance of the study.

SA   5   4   3   2   1   SD

D. The literature review establishes the context for the study.

SA   5   4   3   2   1   SD

E. The research purpose, question, or hypothesis is clearly stated.

SA   5   4   3   2   1   SD

F. The method of sampling is sound.

SA   5   4   3   2   1   SD

G. Relevant demographics (for example, age, gender, and ethnicity) are described.

SA   5   4   3   2   1   SD

H. Measurement procedures are adequate.

SA   5   4   3   2   1   SD

I. All procedures have been described in sufficient detail to permit a replication of the study.

SA   5   4   3   2   1   SD

J. The participants have been adequately protected from potential harm.

SA   5   4   3   2   1   SD

K. The results are clearly described.

SA   5   4   3   2   1   SD

L. The discussion/conclusion is appropriate.

SA   5   4   3   2   1   SD

M. Despite any flaws, the report is worthy of publication.

SA   5   4   3   2   1   SD

Article 2

Retention Issues: A Study of Alabama Special Education Teachers

SHAWN PLASH
Baldwin County School System

CHRIS PIOTROWSKI
University of West Florida

ABSTRACT. This study investigated issues that impact attrition, migration, and retention of special education teachers in Alabama. The sample was composed of 70 teachers designated as *highly qualified* who responded to a job satisfaction instrument with a focus on retention issues developed by Levine (2001). The results indicated that the major reasons for either relocation or attrition were job conditions, occupational stress, demands of IDEA compliance, and increased caseload and class size. Other factors included the relocation of spouse's job and threat of litigation. Prior studies that corroborated the current findings were noted.

From *Education, 127*, 125–128. Copyright © 2006 by Project Innovation, Inc. Reprinted with permission.

It is projected that in the year 2010, there will be a need for 611,550 special education teachers in the U.S. Yet every year, about 13.2% of special education teachers leave their positions. Six percent leave the field altogether, while 7.2% of the special education teachers transfer to general education positions. Within the first 3 years of teaching, 29% of beginning teachers are projected to leave the profession; by the end of the 5th year, 39% leave the teaching field (see Billingsley, 2004, for a review). The purpose of the current study is to investigate issues that relate to the attrition, migration, and turnover of special education teachers in a county in southeast Alabama.

Causes of Attrition and Migration

Special education teachers are more vulnerable to stress or professional burnout than human service professionals (Nichols & Sosnowsky, 2002). This has contributed to feelings of emotional exhaustion and depersonalization and has threatened the special education teachers' sense of personal accomplishment. They tend to exhibit many of the same symptoms that are experienced by other human service professions, such as nurses, physicians, and police officers who are deeply involved with people who have physical, social, and emotional problems (Zabel & Zabel, 2001).

Embich (2001) contends that the four major problems associated with burnout are beyond the control of the special education teacher: role conflict, role ambiguity, perceived workload, and perceived principal support. Role conflict contributes to exhaustion by placing inconsistent, incompatible, or inappropriate demands on the instructor. Role ambiguity contributes to the majority of burnout. Moreover, special education teachers' responsibilities, rights, status and goals are often unclear (Piotrowski & Plash, 2006). Thus, the perceived workload of the special education teacher contributes to feelings of emotional exhaustion. This workload includes paperwork, attending parent conferences, planning, and participating in extracurricular activities. Furthermore, lack of administrative support contributes to elevated levels of emotional exhaustion and reduces the teachers' sense of accomplishment.

Miller, Brownell, and Smith (1999) conducted a study on the attrition of special education teachers and concluded that teachers leave the field primarily for four main reasons: (a) they do not possess the necessary certification; (b) they transfer to another school or district; (c) they dislike the school climate; and (d) they experience high levels of stress.

Methodology

This study was conducted in Baldwin County in southeast Alabama. All participants were teachers in the county school system and served special education students in their areas of expertise. A 63-item instrument was selected that would reflect specific issues relating to the retention and attrition of special education teachers. Dr. Berna Levine developed this measure in Cobb County, Georgia, for the purpose of determining why special education teachers leave the field of special education. The questionnaire assessed issues regarding job satisfaction, administration responsiveness, pre-employment preparation, and specific reasons for terminating employment (Levine, 2001).

In the year 2002, Dr. Ed Richardson, Alabama State Superintendent of Education, used guidelines set forth by NCLBA to develop a model for identifying *highly qualified teachers* in Alabama (Alabama Department of Education, 2003). *Highly qualified teachers* are defined as those teachers who hold full-state certification, possess solid content knowledge of specific instructional areas, and have received a bachelor's degree from a 4-year college or university (U.S. Department

of Education, 2002, 2003). *Highly qualified teachers* must teach core academic subjects such as English, reading or language arts, mathematics, science, foreign language, civics and government, economics, arts, his-
75 tory, and geography.

A packet was sent during the spring of 2004 through the school system's courier to each of the 260 special education teachers employed by the county. A total of 117 teachers agreed to participate in the survey.
80 Of these, 70 participants were rated as *highly qualified teachers* and served as the sample in this study.

Results

These results indicate that stress from demands of the job, inadequate planning time, wide diversity of student needs, class size/caseload size, excessive pa-
85 perwork, and demands associated with IDEA compliance are the major reasons that special education teachers acknowledge for leaving the workplace (Table 1). In addition, specific factors such as threats of litigation and spousal job relocation were noted as critical
90 concerns regarding retention in the field.

Table 1
Special Education Teachers' Major Reasons for Leaving the Workplace

Etiology factors	N	M	SD
Lack of administrative support	68	2.34	1.23
Lack of administrative knowledge	68	2.38	1.26
Lack of collegial support	68	1.96	1.07
Inadequate preparation or staff development	68	1.81	0.87
Limited opportunities to provide input	68	1.97	0.91
Excessive paperwork	68	2.99	1.07
Class size or caseload size	68	3.14	0.91
Inadequate planning time	68	2.66	1.16
Lack of parental or community support	68	2.34	1.00
Wide diversity of students	68	2.60	0.99
Demands associated with IDEA compliance	70	2.70	1.05

Note. Items were rated on a 4-point Likert scale: 1 = *not very important*, 2 = *somewhat important*, 3 = *very important*, 4 = *critical*. *N*s are different because some participants did not answer all of the questions. IDEA refers to Individuals with Disabilities Act.

Several issues seem to serve as a buffer for continued retention. Teachers in the current sample expressed the view that they have adequate staff development and are provided adequate opportunities for input. In addi-
95 tion, these respondents held very favorable views toward peer support.

Discussion and Implications

The *highly qualified* special education teachers in this study indicated that the two most important criteria contributing to a potential decision to leave the field
100 were excessive paperwork and stress created by demands of the job. These findings are consistent with the work of Gersten, Keating, and Yovanoff (2001), who found that stress due to job design is a critical factor that affects special education teachers' attrition
105 and retention. According to Gersten et al., teachers

believe they are hired to teach children with disabilities when in reality they spend the vast part of their day completing paperwork and attending meetings. Fur-
110 thermore, Brownell, Sindelar, Bishop, Lingley, and Seonjin (2002) and Singh and Billingsley (1996) reported that workplace conditions are one of three major areas that cause special education teachers to abandon careers.

The current sample also noted that the two most
115 important criteria if they were to consider leaving the school system or transferring to general education were: (a) care of children or family members, and (b) relocating due to a spouse's job opportunity. Ingersoll and Smith (2003) reported that personal factors are the
120 main reasons beginning teachers leave the field of education. Finally, in a recent study titled "Multitasking is multitaxing: Why special teachers are leaving the field" (2004), special education teachers reported that personal issues (e.g., retirement, family, and health fac-
125 tors, as well as stress and burnout) are one of the three areas of concern that impact their decision to leave the profession.

References

Alabama Department of Education. (2003). *The Alabama model for identifying highly qualified teachers*. Retrieved December 29, 2003, from ftp://ftp.alsde.edu/documents/66/SBE_Alabama_Model_for_Highly_Qualified_Teachers.pdf

Billingsley, B. S. (2004). Special education teacher retention and attrition: A critical analysis of the research literature. *Journal of Special Education, 38*, 39–55.

Brownell, M. T., Sindelar, P. T., Bishop, A. G., Lingley, L. K., & Seonjin, S. (2002). Special education teacher supply and teacher quality: The problems, the solution. *Focus on Exceptional Children, 35*, 1–16.

Embich, J. L. (2001). *The relationship of secondary special education teachers' roles and factors that lead to professional burnout*. Retrieved July 7, 2004, from http://80-vnweb.hwwilsonweb.com.ezproxy.lib.uwf.edu/hww/results/results_single.jhtml?

Gersten, R., Keating, T., & Yovanoff, P. (2001). Working in special education: Factors that enhance special teachers' intent to stay. *Exceptional Children, 67*, 549–567.

Ingersoll, R. M., & Smith, T. M. (2003). The wrong solution to the teacher shortage. *Educational Leadership, 60*, 2003.

Levine, B. S. (2001). *An examination of the factors related to the attrition and retention of special education teachers in Cobb County, Georgia*. Unpublished doctoral dissertation, University of Alabama.

Miller, M. D., Brownell, M. T., & Smith, S. W. (1999). Factors that predict teachers staying in, leaving, or transferring from the special education classroom. *Exceptional Children, 65*, 201–218.

Multitasking is multitaxing: Why special teachers are leaving the field. (2004). *Preventing School Failure, 48*, 1–9.

Nichols, A. S., & Sosnowsky, F. L. (2002). Burnout among special education teachers in self-contained cross-categorical classrooms. *Teacher Education and Special Education, 25*, 71–86.

Piotrowski, C., & Plash, S. H. (2006). Turnover and the educational consultant: An OD intervention perspective. *Organization Development Journal, 24*, 22–27.

Singh, K., & Billingsley, B. S. (1996). Intent to stay in teaching: Teachers of students with emotional disorders versus other special teachers. *Remedial and Special Education, 17*, 37–47.

U.S. Department of Education. (2002). *Meeting the highly qualified teachers challenge: The secretary's annual report on teacher quality*. Washington, DC: Author.

U.S. Department of Education. (2003). *Meeting the highly qualified teachers challenge: The secretary's annual report on teacher quality*. Washington, DC: Author.

Zabel, R. H., & Zabel, M. K. (2001). Revisiting burnout among special education teachers: Do age, experience, and preparation still matter? *Teacher Education and Special Education, 24*, 128–139.

Exercise for Article 2

Factual Questions

1. What is the explicitly stated purpose of the study?

2. This study had how many participants?

3. Which item had the highest mean score?

4. Which item had the lowest mean score?

5. Why do the numbers of cases (*N*) vary in Table 1?

Questions for Discussion

6. This study was conducted in a single county in Alabama. In your opinion, would it be worthwhile to replicate the study in other regions of the country? Explain. (See lines 49–50.)

7. What is your opinion of the definition of *highly qualified teachers*? (See lines 66–75.)

8. Do you think it was a good idea to study only *highly qualified teachers*? Explain.

9. Out of the 260 teachers contacted, 117 agreed to participate in this study. Does the failure of many of those contacted to participate affect the quality of this study? Explain. (See lines 76–79.)

10. In your opinion, do the results of this study have important implications for the retention of special education teachers? Explain.

11. If you were to conduct a study on the same topic, what changes, if any, would you make in the research methodology?

Quality Ratings

Directions: Indicate your level of agreement with each of the following statements by circling a number from 5 for strongly agree (SA) to 1 for strongly disagree (SD). If you believe an item is not applicable to this research article, leave it blank. Be prepared to explain your ratings. When responding to criteria A and B below, keep in mind that brief titles and abstracts are conventional in published research.

A. The title of the article is appropriate.
   SA   5   4   3   2   1   SD

B. The abstract provides an effective overview of the research article.
   SA   5   4   3   2   1   SD

C. The introduction establishes the importance of the study.
   SA   5   4   3   2   1   SD

D. The literature review establishes the context for the study.
   SA   5   4   3   2   1   SD

E. The research purpose, question, or hypothesis is clearly stated.
   SA   5   4   3   2   1   SD

F. The method of sampling is sound.
   SA   5   4   3   2   1   SD

G. Relevant demographics (for example, age, gender, and ethnicity) are described.
   SA   5   4   3   2   1   SD

H. Measurement procedures are adequate.
   SA   5   4   3   2   1   SD

I. All procedures have been described in sufficient detail to permit a replication of the study.
   SA   5   4   3   2   1   SD

J. The participants have been adequately protected from potential harm.
   SA   5   4   3   2   1   SD

K. The results are clearly described.
   SA   5   4   3   2   1   SD

L. The discussion/conclusion is appropriate.
   SA   5   4   3   2   1   SD

M. Despite any flaws, the report is worthy of publication.
   SA   5   4   3   2   1   SD

Article 3

To What Extent Are Literacy Initiatives Being Supported? Important Questions for Administrators

LESLIE MARLOW
Berry College

DUANE INMAN
Berry College

CRAIG SHWERY
University of Alabama

ABSTRACT. This study examined teachers' expressed perceptions of states' provisions for instructional materials and professional development opportunities related to state literacy initiatives for K–6 classroom teachers in 10 southeastern states. Approximately 400 teachers responded to a survey instrument that included the topics of materials and professional development. Generally, the survey results indicate that teachers did not express receipt of sufficient support in implementing a state/district-wide reading initiative to the extent one might deem desirable (or appropriate) by present agencies. It appears that responding teachers perceived themselves to be ill-prepared to meet accountability mandates associated with literacy and that participating teachers lacked training, had little access to sound instructional materials, and were unfamiliar with the state standards. This information results in questions that administrators must address if teachers are to effectively implement literacy initiatives proposed as a result of state mandates.

From *Reading Improvement, 42,* 179–186. Copyright © 2005 by Project Innovation, Inc. Reprinted with permission.

Literacy Initiative Support Systems Entering the 21st Century

The Elementary and Secondary Education Act (ESEA) (1965), Title 1, Part B (Reading Excellence Act, P. L. 105–277) was the first broad governmental initiative to address the literacy issue by advocating that all children would be able to read by the end of third grade. In 2002, ESEA was supplemented with the "No Child Left Behind Act." Similar to the Reading Excellence Act, the "No Child Left Behind Act" focuses on research-based methods, which some experts say will virtually guarantee a more structured, skills-based approach to the teaching of reading (Manzo, 2002; Ogle, 2002). This emphasis on research-based methods has led to increased attention regarding reading and literacy standards. National literacy standards suggested from both the International Reading Association (IRA) and the National Council of Teachers of English (NCTE) (1996) have provided the framework for states to develop their own literacy standards, including new state policy documentation intended to assist in bringing about positive literacy changes in teaching and learning for individual states (Kuder & Hasit, 2002; Wixson & Dutro, 1999).

While various states involved in redesigning their reading initiatives are enacting specific reading goals and standards for performance, many literacy educators, along with professional teaching organizations, have questioned the validity of many of the enacted reading measures (Block, Oaker, & Hurt, 2002; Block, Joyner, Joy, & Gaines, 2001; Hoffman et al. 1998; Allington, Guice, Michelson, Baker, & Li, 1996). Those involved with improving literacy instruction must provide ongoing staff development to ensure that implementation of reading reform models will be effective (Birman, Desimone, Porter, & Garet, 2000; Joyce, 1999; Darling-Hammond, 1995; Carter & Powell, 1992). Professional development is a powerful process for enhancing the knowledge base for teaching and the pedagogical skills needed to disseminate knowledge (Kraft, 1998; Hirsh, 1999; Joyce & Showers, 1983). Access to professional development opportunities provides teachers with an important link needed to successfully implement reading initiatives and is a useful tool for improving classroom instruction, curriculum design, and the effective use of primary teaching materials (Lieberman, 1999, 2001; Blair, 2003; Birman, 2000; Westchester Institute for Human Services Research, 1998).

Because state reading initiatives are relatively new components to teaching, there appears to be a dearth of research being done that examines state-mandated literacy professional opportunities and associated materials programs being used by the states. The purpose of this study was to examine teachers' expressed perceptions regarding their states' provisions for instructional materials and professional development opportunities related to state literacy initiatives for K–6 classroom teachers.

Population

Using the state's public school directory for each of several southern states, each school district within each state was assigned a number. Gay's Table of Random

Numbers (1996) was then used to identify 10 schools from each state. The principal of each selected school was contacted and requested to provide information from teachers who teach reading (K–6). Principals ran-
65 domly contacted 10 teachers who teach reading in their schools and obtained their participation in completing the surveys.

Instrumentation

The survey instrument was composed of four-point Likert Scale items ranging from Strongly Disagree to
70 Strongly Agree. The Likert Scale items fell into two categories: professional development and reading materials. Professional development items focused on the description of the state literacy initiative, provision by the school district to provide professional development
75 opportunities, and professional development opportunities provided by the state. The items focusing on materials targeted their appropriateness for the various grade levels, whether they effectively addressed the state's current assessment instrument, and whether
80 there were adequate supplemental reading materials available to accompany the mandated programs. Additionally, demographic items were included to provide background information on the respondents.

The pilot study of this instrument was conducted in
85 spring 2001. Test–retest stability was measured to determine the reliability of scores over time. A group of approximately 100 K–6 teachers completed the survey, once in January and once in April 2001. The scores from each were correlated and the coefficient of stabil-
90 ity was calculated to be 0.92. The pilot study results indicated the instrument to be reliable.

Procedures

One thousand surveys were sent out to participating teachers within the southern states. A packet of information was sent to the principal of each identified
95 school from the random sample. A cover letter and copy of the survey instrument were included in each packet. If the principal agreed to his/her faculty's participation in the study, the principal then distributed the survey instrument to the teachers who teach reading.
100 The teachers were to independently complete the surveys and return the self-addressed, stamped surveys. Only those interested participated. If a principal was unwilling to allow his/her teachers to participate, they were asked to return the surveys in the return envelope
105 to the researchers. These materials were submitted to a different school in the same geographic area. The return rate was approximately 40%.

For those participants or principals who wanted to know the results of the survey, such information was
110 requested by the individual providing their name and address. All information obtained by the survey was anonymously reported in group totals only.

Results

Demographics

As is evidenced in Table 1, the majority of the teachers were white, teaching in grades 1–4 in schools
115 with an enrollment between 251 and 1,000. There was a wide variety among the respondents' teaching experience, with the greatest response being 29% who had taught over 20 years.

Professional Development

Teacher responses indicated that 34% of the re-
120 spondents either agreed or strongly agreed that professional development opportunities from the school district were provided. Sixty-six percent of the respondents either disagreed or strongly disagreed that these opportunities were provided. Teachers' perceptions of
125 the provision for professional development opportunities from the state indicated that 31% of the respondents either agreed or strongly agreed that these development opportunities were provided. Fifty-nine percent of the respondents either disagreed or strongly dis-
130 agreed that these opportunities were provided. Ten percent expressed that they did not know. In addressing how thoroughly the literacy initiative of the district was described to the teachers of that district, responses were split, with 50% agreeing and 50% disagreeing that a
135 thorough description occurred. Therefore, while teachers indicated that they perceived themselves as being knowledgeable about state standards and the mandated literacy initiative based on the information that they were provided, the majority expressed their belief that
140 they were not provided with professional development opportunities in order to enhance their information about the reading knowledge base and pedagogy practices being used by the state and/or districts. Table 2 provides further description of the data.

Reading Materials

145 Eighty-seven percent agreed or strongly agreed that the primary reading materials available within their school were in accordance with the state literacy initiative and were appropriate for the specified grade levels. Six percent either disagreed or strongly disagreed, and
150 seven percent didn't know. When responding to the item regarding the availability of primary reading materials designed to meet the needs of specific grade levels, the majority, 87%, indicated the presence of such materials. Of those responding to the item ad-
155 dressing whether they perceived that the primary reading materials used by the school effectively addressed the standard evaluated by the required assessment instruments, 47% agreed or strongly agreed and 49% either disagreed or strongly disagreed. Four percent
160 didn't know. When queried regarding the availability of adequate supplemental reading materials to enhance state literacy initiatives, 15% agreed or strongly agreed that these materials were available, while 45% disagreed or strongly disagreed. The remaining 40% ex-

Table 1
Demographic Information

Ethnic origin		Years/classroom teaching		Current teaching placement		Perceived school student enrollment	
White	81%	1–5	11%	Pre-K/K	14%	<250	23%
African American	8%	6–10	15%	1–4	54%	251–499	43%
Hispanic	7%	11–20	17%	5–6	32%	500–1,000	27%
Native American/Asian	2%	Over 20	29%			Over 1,000	6%
No response	2%	No response	28%			No response	1%

Table 2
Responses to Likert Items Related to Professional Development Workshops

	Strongly Agree (4)	Agree (3)	Disagree (2)	Strongly Disagree (1)	Don't Know
Literacy initiative of the district was described to teachers	24%	26%	30%	20%	n/a
Workshops provided by school district	15%	19%	42%	24%	n/a
Workshops provided by state	11%	31%	10%		

Table 3
Responses to Likert Items Regarding Reading Materials

	Strongly Agree (4)	Agree (3)	Disagree (2)	Strongly Disagree (1)	Don't Know
Reading materials appropriate for specific grade levels	40%	47%	3%	3%	7%
Reading materials effectively address state assessment	21%	26%	30%	19%	4%
Adequate supplemental reading materials	4%	11%	27%	18%	40%

165 pressed that they were unaware if such materials were available. Table 3 provides additional description of the data.

Discussion

The majority of respondents indicated a concern re-
170 garding the adequacy of primary materials provided in addressing the standards, and teachers were evenly mixed in their opinions of the efficacy of these materials. However, perceptions of the adequacy of supplemental reading materials revealed only 15% of the respondents in agreement that their school provided ade-
175 quate supplementary reading materials, while three times as many teachers disagreed about the adequacy of such materials. Interestingly enough, 40% of the teachers expressed that they were not aware of the availability. While teachers can be unaware of informa-
180 tion and availability of materials for many reasons, a breakdown in communication among administration and teachers, perhaps even among colleagues, is a common reason. If a breakdown in communication

among the stakeholders does exist, administrators
185 should reflect upon several questions in an attempt to disseminate information more effectively: What media are being used to present the teachers with information about the district reading initiatives? Are multiple forms of media communication being used? Is there
190 ample opportunity for questions and responses in order for teachers to clarify their perceptions? If not, when can time be allocated to allow for clarification? Are teacher misconceptions about availability of materials addressed, and if so, how?
195 Only approximately 1/3 of teachers were in accord with the idea that workshops are provided. Approximately 2/3 disagreed that workshops are provided. If the lack of provision for workshops is indeed the case, administrators have some hard questions to which they
200 must respond: How are teachers to implement new reading programs without being trained? Is it the responsibility of the teacher to train him/herself, thereby providing students with the skills necessary to read

effectively and ultimately pass "the test?" If workshops were available, why did teachers select not to attend these workshops? Were the provided professional development opportunities required or optional? What motivation can be provided to encourage teachers to become more proactive learners?

In considering the broad topic of materials, participating teachers indicated that the primary materials are appropriate for the specific grade levels, yet only half expressed the belief that those same materials effectively address the standards. Does this indicate that perhaps the other half concluded that the primary materials were effective teaching tools, but they didn't address the state standards that are tested? Another possibility is that funding may have been available for primary materials, but perhaps there was a lack of funding for the supplemental materials. Was there the possibility that funding was not deemed necessary for supplemental materials? Since funds were spent for the primary programs, supplemental materials were not needed? An alternative explanation is that the comprehensive nature of new programs possibly precluded the necessity for the provision of supplemental materials. Teachers should be provided with specific information related to all materials and their relationship to state and national standards.

The information provided by the participating teachers raises additional questions for administrators when considering implementation of state/district-wide literacy initiatives: Was the issue of availability of supplemental materials addressed in the workshops at state and/or district levels? To what extent is collaboration occurring between the district schools and state agencies to ensure that teachers are adequately prepared for implementing district-wide literacy initiatives? How do districts ensure that schools have adequate teacher representation so that all schools will have a "specialist" with training available as a resource for other teachers—a local person to whom questions can be directed and immediately answered?

With the increasing focus on research-based methods intended to guarantee a more structured approach to the teaching of reading as well as the finances involved, administrators and their agencies need to ensure that teachers are adequately trained and supported for the implementation of these programs. The results of this survey indicated that teachers do not perceive that they are being supported in implementing state/district-wide reading initiatives to the extent one might deem desirable (or appropriate) by present agencies. Teachers indicate that they are ill-prepared to meet accountability mandates associated with literacy. They report that they have limited access to instructional materials and do not appear familiar with the standards themselves. The results also provided a number of additional questions that need to be addressed by administrators to further analyze educational circumstances and goals related to the state reading initiatives

between and among concerned stakeholders. The quality of literacy initiatives themselves can never be thoroughly investigated if the time is not taken to work through the implementation problems indicated by those involved in classroom presentation of the state literacy programs.

References

Allington, R., Guice, S., Michelson, N., Baker, K., & Li, S. (1996). Literature-based curriculum in high poverty schools. In Block, C., Oaker, M., & Hurt, N. (2002). The expertise of literacy teachers: A continuum from preschool to grade 5. *Reading Research Quarterly, 37,* 178–206.

Birman, B., Desimone, L., Porter, A., & Garet, M. (2000). Designing professional development that works. *Educational Leadership, 57,* 28–33.

Blair, J. (Feb. 5, 2003). With support, teachers would stay put, report finds. *Education Week,* Washington.

Block, C., Joyner, J., Joy, J., & Gaines, P. (2001). Process-based comprehension: Four educators' perspectives. In C. C. Block & M. Pressley (Eds.), *Research-based Comprehension Practices,* 119–134. NY: Guilford.

Block, C., Oaker, M., & Hurt, N. (2002). The expertise of literacy teachers: A continuum from preschool to grade 5. *Reading Research Quarterly, 37,* 178–206.

Carter, M., & Powell, D. (1992). Teacher leaders as staff developers. *Journal of Staff Development, 13,* 8–12.

Darling-Hammond, L., & McLaughlin, M. (1995). Policies that support professional development in an era of reform. *Phi Delta Kappa,* 597–604.

Elementary and Secondary Education Act (ESEA). www.ed.gov/offices/OESE/esea

Hirsh, S. (1999). Standards-based professional development. *High School Magazine, 7,* 31.

Hoffman, J. et al. (1998). The literature-based basals in first-grade classrooms: Savior, Satan, or same-old, same-old? *Reading Research Quarterly, 33,* 168–197.

Joyce, B. (1999). Reading about reading: Notes from a consumer to the scholars of literacy. *The Reading Teacher, 52,* 662–671.

Kraft, N. (1998). A New Model for Professional Development. rmcdenver.com/eetnet/alapp.htm

Kuder, S., & Hasit, C. (2002). *Enhancing literacy for all students.* Upper Saddle River, New Jersey: Merrill Prentice Hall.

Lieberman, A., & Miller, L. (Eds.) (2001). *Teachers caught in the action: Professional development that matters.* NY: Teachers College Press.

Manzo, K. (Feb. 20, 2002). Some educators see reading rules as too restrictive. *Education Week, 21,* 1–23.

Ogle, D. in Manzo, K. (Feb. 20, 2002). Some educators see reading rules as too restrictive. *Education Week, 21,* 1–23.

Sparks, D. (1999). Real-life view: An interview with Ann Lieberman. *Journal of Staff Development, 20.*

Westchester Institute for Human Services Research. (1998). *The Balanced View: Professional Development, 2.*

Wixson, K., & Dutro, E. (1999). Standards for primary-grade reading: An analysis of state frameworks. *The Elementary School Journal, 100,* 89–110.

Exercise for Article 3

Factual Questions

1. What is the explicitly stated "purpose" of this study?

2. The researchers state that they included "demographic items" in order to provide what?

3. What was the return rate?

4. What percentage of the respondents had 11 to 20 years of classroom teaching experience?

5. What percentage of the respondents strongly disagreed that they had adequate supplemental reading materials?

Questions for Discussion

6. The researchers state that they used a table of random numbers to select 10 schools. Is this important? Explain. (See lines 60–62.)

7. The researchers state that a pilot study of the instrument was conducted. Does this give you greater confidence in the results obtained by using the instrument? Explain. (See lines 84–91.)

8. The teachers were asked to "independently" complete the survey (i.e., complete it without consulting anyone else). Was this a good idea? Explain. (See lines 100–101.)

9. Are any of the results of this study especially interesting or surprising to you? Explain.

10. This study was conducted in several southern states. Do you think it would be valuable to replicate the study in other regions of the country? Explain.

Quality Ratings

Directions: Indicate your level of agreement with each of the following statements by circling a number from 5 for strongly agree (SA) to 1 for strongly disagree (SD). If you believe an item is not applicable to this research article, leave it blank. Be prepared to explain your ratings. When responding to criteria A and B below, keep in mind that brief titles and abstracts are conventional in published research.

A. The title of the article is appropriate.
SA   5   4   3   2   1   SD

B. The abstract provides an effective overview of the research article.
SA   5   4   3   2   1   SD

C. The introduction establishes the importance of the study.
SA   5   4   3   2   1   SD

D. The literature review establishes the context for the study.
SA   5   4   3   2   1   SD

E. The research purpose, question, or hypothesis is clearly stated.
SA   5   4   3   2   1   SD

F. The method of sampling is sound.
SA   5   4   3   2   1   SD

G. Relevant demographics (for example, age, gender, and ethnicity) are described.
SA   5   4   3   2   1   SD

H. Measurement procedures are adequate.
SA   5   4   3   2   1   SD

I. All procedures have been described in sufficient detail to permit a replication of the study.
SA   5   4   3   2   1   SD

J. The participants have been adequately protected from potential harm.
SA   5   4   3   2   1   SD

K. The results are clearly described.
SA   5   4   3   2   1   SD

L. The discussion/conclusion is appropriate.
SA   5   4   3   2   1   SD

M. Despite any flaws, the report is worthy of publication.
SA   5   4   3   2   1   SD

Article 4

Stalking and Related Harassment of Secondary School Counselors

JOHN S. C. ROMANS
Oklahoma State University

JONI R. HAYS
Oklahoma State University

CHRISTY PEARSON
Lookout Mountain Youth Services Center

L. CHRIS DuROY
Oklahoma Heart Hospital

BARBARA CARLOZZI
Oklahoma State University

ABSTRACT. In a study of stalking in secondary schools, 140 respondents reported they had been stalked, with perpetrators being evenly distributed between students and nonstudents. The largest nonstudent group of perpetrators was parents of students. Harassing phone calls and threatening correspondence constituted most of the stalking behaviors, but respondents also reported being followed, being watched, encountering a student with a weapon, and being victims of assault and property crimes. Although a number of negative consequences were reported to have resulted from the stalking incidents, most surprising—considering the amount of violence and threatening experiences reported—was that the majority of victims (57.9%) reported no concern for their safety. Prevention strategies for individuals and schools are suggested.

From *Journal of School Violence*, 5, 21–33. Copyright © 2006 by The Haworth Press, Inc. Reprinted with permission.

Stalking is a phenomenon that has recently become more familiar to researchers and the general public, unfortunately, often at the expense of traumatic experiences and lost lives. Tjaden and Thoennes (1998) esti-
5 mate that 1,006,970 women and 376,990 men are being stalked in the United States at any given time. Few of these instances are detailed to the media unless they involve someone of fame, or unless the victim dies. Only recently have governmental agencies focused on
10 the seriousness of stalking behaviors, and as a result, anti-stalking laws and ordinances have recently been enacted in all 50 states. Unfortunately, very little research had been done that defines stalking and the causes of this type of behavior.
15 One of the problems in researching stalking behavior is that no standard definition exists for stalking. Variations exist among countries in defining what behaviors constitute stalking and in identifying the number of occurrences required to identify a behavior as
20 stalking. Furthermore, some definitions consider the intent of the stalker, to inflict fear or concern for safety, while other definitions do not consider the stalker's intent. Some anti-stalking laws require a stalker to express a credible threat of harm before legal intervention

25 is possible. In other states, there does not have to be the presence of a credible threat for the unwanted behavior to be considered stalking. However, in a recent review of the literature on stalking, Sheridan, Blaauw, and Davies (2003) concluded that there is now a sufficient
30 research base to understand stalking behavior and, despite differing definitions, the behaviors of stalkers are fairly consistent across countries and across studies.

One of the most extensive reviews of stalking research reported by Sheridan, Blaauw, and Davies
35 (2003) was a study by Spitzberg (2002) involving 103 studies and 68,615 respondents. From that review, it was concluded that stalkers use a variety of methods, the most common being spying, telephoning, following the victim, and making actual contact with the victim.
40 Sheridan, Blaauw, and Davies (2003) also report that in representative samples, there is a fairly stable lifetime prevalence rate for stalking victimization, which ranges from approximately 12% to 16% among women and 4% to 7% for men. On the other hand, certain popula-
45 tions are most at risk for being victimized by stalkers, and those high-risk populations are people in highly visible jobs like politics, media, and public service; those who are frequently in contact with single people, such as students and young people; and those who have
50 prior histories of abuse.

In a comprehensive study sponsored by the National Institute of Justice (NIJ) and the National Center for Injury Prevention and Control (NCIPC), Tjaden and Thoennes (1998) interviewed 16,000 men and women
55 about their stalking experiences. They defined stalking as "a course of conduct directed at a specific person that involves repeated visual or physical proximity, nonconsensual communication of verbal, written, or implied threats, or a combination thereof, that would
60 cause a reasonable person fear" (p. 2). From the interviews, they found that stalking victims reported a "high level of fear" regardless of whether a direct credible threat of harm was made toward them. In phone interviews with participants, they found that 8% of women
65 and 2% of men had been stalked at some time. Of the stalking victims they interviewed, 78% were female

and 22% were male. Tjaden and Thoennes reported that 87% of the stalkers were men and 13% were women. They also found that more than half of the stalking victims were of age 18–29, suggesting a relationship between youth and the risk of being stalked.

Prior to the Tjaden and Thoennes (1998) study, there had been no wide-scale research done on stalking. The incidence of stalking had been explored in specific populations, including university counseling center professionals (Romans, Hays, & White, 1996), college students (Durant, Narston, & Eisenhandler, 1986; Fremouw, Westrup, & Pennypacker, 1997; Palmer, 1993; Rickgarn, 1989), clinical populations (Mullen & Pathé, 1994), and criminal populations (Harmon, Rosner, & Owens, 1995; Holmes, 1993; Leong, 1994). Additionally, other researchers are attempting to further understand the nature of stalking by formulating categories of stalkers, identifying characteristics of stalkers, and identifying the characteristics of stalking victims (Meloy, 1997; Meloy & Gothard, 1995; Pathé & Mullen, 1997; Roberts & Dziegielewski, 1996; Wright, Burgess, Burgess, Laszlo, McCrary, & Douglas, 1996; Zona, Sharma, & Lane, 1993).

A related term, "harassment," has been described as a "willful course of conduct directed at a specific person which seriously alarms or annoys the person, and which serves no legitimate purpose" (Henderson, 1992, p. 21). Other definitions of harassment ("Installing hidden," 2003) require proof that the perpetrator *intended* to provoke an emotional reaction in the victim. Differences between stalking and harassment include issues of repetition and intent, where stalking requires repeated or enduring incidents, and harassment may or may not require that the perpetrator intends to instill serious annoyance or alarm. Though both behaviors can have negative effects on the victim, stalking typically has more traumatic results, including physical harm and even death (Spearman, 1994).

Research regarding stalking and harassment behaviors has been conducted primarily with adult populations. There is little research regarding the incidence of stalking in the juvenile population, but there have been several extensive studies on sexual harassment in the schools. (See Kopels & Dupper, 1999; Lee, Croninger, Linn, & Chen, 1996; Yaffe, 1995.) A national study conducted by the American Association of University Women (in Kopels & Dupper, 1999; and Yaffe, 1995) reported on the results of 1,632 questionnaires received from students in grades 8 through 11. Between approximately 75% and 81% of the students reported being harassed. (The percentages varied according to sex, ethnicity, and whether or not they could name the place and surroundings where the incident occurred.) In this same study, 31% of the girls said they were harassed often.

Other studies were conducted by Roscoe et al. in the upper Midwest (Roscoe, Strouse, & Goodwin's study as cited in Kopels & Dupper, 1999), the NOW Legal Defense and Education Fund and Wellesley College Center for Research on Women (Stein, Marshall, & Tropp's study as cited in Kopels & Dupper, 1999), and the Connecticut Permanent Commission on Women and the School of Social Work at the University of Connecticut (Yaffe, 1995). These studies had sample sizes of 561, 4,200, and 543, respectively. In the Roscoe et al. study, 50% of the females and 37% of the males reported having been sexually harassed at least once; in the NOW study, 39% of the respondents (all female) reported being harassed at school daily during the last year; and in the Connecticut study, 92% of the girls and 57% of the boys reported being sexually harassed at least once during their high school years. Although the majority of sexual harassment was done by peers, the percentage of students reporting teacher-initiated sexual harassment ranged from 4% to approximately 18% of the students surveyed. In these and other studies (Lee, Croninger, Linn, & Chen, 1996; Fineran & Bennett, 1998), girls were more likely to be sexually harassed than boys, and older students were more likely to experience sexual harassment than younger students. Students evaluated their harassment as being unacceptable, embarrassing, making them self-conscious, less confident, decreasing their in-class participation and attention, and changing their behavior in the form of changing classes, seats, friends, routes home, and choosing to not attend school (Kopels & Dupper, 1999; Yaffe, 1995).

A related study focusing not on sexual harassment but rather on school violence and personal safety surveyed social workers working in a school setting (Astor, Behre, Wallace, & Fravil, 1998). The authors of this study asked social workers to address their concerns regarding their personal safety, which included estimating their level of fear, identifying perpetrators of violence, and describing precautions used in response to perceived violence. The respondents were also asked to provide information regarding violence prevention programs used in their schools and the need for training for school personnel. Social workers surveyed verified a fear for their personal safety, with many fearing for their personal safety at least once a month. Not surprisingly, inner-city school social workers reported fear significantly more than rural, urban, or suburban social workers. Over one-third of the respondents had been physically assaulted or threatened in the last year, and 77% of the perpetrators were students. Other perpetrators of violence included parents (49%) and student gang members (11%). Precautions taken by the school social workers included leaving their money at home, avoiding school after dark, staying in a group, avoiding the school parking lot, and taking special routes to school. Suggestions for training included a need for immediate in-service training regarding school violence and additional school violence education in graduate school programs in social work to help them prepare to enter the school setting. Pietr-

185 unk, Peterson, and Speaker (1998) examined perceptions of violence in school settings and found that school personnel fear violence from students and parents. They also found that school personnel thought that incidents of violence were increasing in the schools.

190 As noted earlier, two of the groups identified as high risk for being victimized by stalkers are students and those who work in public service. However, there is little information on the amount of stalking and stalking-related behavior that occurs in the secondary school. This information is needed in order to develop

195 interventions and policies designed to mitigate against these behaviors. This study was designed to address this gap in the literature.

Method

This study surveyed secondary school counselors on stalking and stalking-related behaviors within the

200 school setting. The purpose was to explore the incidence rate of stalking and stalking-related behaviors in an unresearched group.

Participants

Four hundred school counselors were randomly selected from a national school counselor mailing list and

205 were mailed the School Survey on Stalking, along with pre-stamped, addressed envelopes. Of the surveys mailed, 140 completed surveys from across the United States were returned, for a response rate of 36%. Thirty-two percent were completed by men, while

210 62.9% were completed by women. Ethnicity of respondents included 87.9% European American, 8.6% African American, 7% Asian American, 7% Hispanic American, and 2.1 % identified themselves as "other." The majority of respondents, 90.7%, had earned a mas-

215 ter's degree. The number of years respondents had worked as a school counselor ranged from 0 to 25 years. Approximately 21% had worked 0–5 years, 22.1% had worked 6–10 years, 18.6% had worked 11–15 years, 25% had worked 15–25 years, and 9.2% had

220 worked more than 25 years. Of the respondents participating in the survey, 21.4% were from school districts with fewer than 1,000 students, 31.4% were from districts with 1,000 to 4,999 students, 15% were from districts with 5,000 to 9,999 students, 5.7% were from

225 districts with 10,000 to 19,999 students, and 12% were from school districts larger than 20,000 students. Fourteen percent did not provide a number of students for their school district.

Instrument

The instrument titled "School Survey on Stalking"

230 was modified from a previous stalking instrument (Romans, Hays, & White, 1996). The questions on this survey were developed in consultation with school counseling personnel who had experience working with law enforcement and school issues. A panel of

235 four school counselors then reviewed and critiqued the instrument. Stalking was defined parallel to the Model Antistalking Code (1996) as the "willful, malicious, and repeated following and harassing of another person." Participants were asked how many times they had

240 been the targets of stalking by a current or former student. Participants were asked to describe the stalker in terms of age, gender, and any other dimensions they felt were important. Participants were also asked to report the number of times they had been stalked by a

245 nonstudent and the number of stalking incidences that had occurred to staff under their supervision. A section of the survey asked participants to note how many times they had experienced a variety of harassing and stalking-related events.

Results

250 Of the counselors surveyed, 12 respondents (8.5%) reported they had been stalked at least once. Overall, the 12 respondents who had been stalked reported 27 separate stalkers. The identities of the stalkers were evenly distributed between students and nonstudents,

255 with eight of the stalkers identified as current students, seven were former students, seven were parents of students, and five were identified as "other." In the other category, two stalkers were teachers, two were acquaintances, and one a stranger. All but one of the

260 stalkers were male. The youngest stalker was 15 years old and the oldest was 62 years old.

When asked for the types of stalking behaviors they had experienced, 8.5% of the respondents reported they had been followed, 11.2% said they were watched,

265 43.9% received harassing phone calls, and 20.8% received threatening correspondence. Reports of verbal assault (92.2%), physical assault (9.8%), stolen possessions (49%), and vandalism (30.2%) were also reported. In addition, 32.2% of the respondents had en-

270 countered a student with a weapon. Table 1 presents a breakdown of stalking-related events from current students, former students, parents, and others.

The respondents were also asked to report the number of incidences of stalking that have occurred to other

275 school personnel. The number of incidences reported ranged from 0 to 99, with three being the most frequently reported estimate of incidences of stalking occurring to other school personnel. Eight percent of the counselors reported that one student had been referred

280 to them for counseling because of stalking and/or harassing behaviors, 15% reported two students had been referred, 6.4% reported three had been referred, 4.3% reported four had been referred, and 11.4% reported five or more students had been referred for counseling.

285 Respondents had also reported many negative experiences as a result of being stalked. These experiences included stress/worry (17.9%), property damage (12.1%), financial loss (9.3%), concern for family/significant other (6.4%), psychological injury

290 (5.0%), physical injury (1.4%), and loss of time from work (1.4%). Table 2 reports the lifestyle changes

18

Table 1
Frequency of Stalking-Related Harassment

	Number of times event occurred					
	0	1	2	3	4	5+
Followed by						
Current student	139	1	0	0	0	0
Former student	136	2	2	0	0	0
Parent	138	1	1	0	0	0
Other	135	4	0	0	0	1
Watched by						
Current student	138	2	0	0	0	0
Former student	136	1	2	0	0	1
Parent	135	3	1	0	1	0
Other	135	2	1	0	0	2
Harassing phone calls by						
Current student	127	4	2	1	1	5
Former student	125	7	4	1	0	3
Parent	117	7	2	3	0	11
Other	129	3	3	1	1	3
Notes/e-mail by						
Current student	136	3	0	0	0	1
Former student	131	6	3	0	0	0
Parent	130	4	1	1	1	3
Other	133	2	3	0	0	2
Verbal assault by						
Current student	127	2	2	0	1	8
Former student	106	1	0	0	0	33
Parent	102	7	3	0	0	28
Other	92	1	0	0	0	47
Physical assault by						
Current student	136	3	1	0	0	0
Former student	135	3	1	1	0	0
Parent	138	2	0	0	0	0
Other	138	2	0	0	0	0
Possession taken by						
Current student	111	13	10	2	2	2
Former student	115	15	6	2	0	2
Parent	137	3	0	0	0	0
Other	134	2	4	0	0	0
Vandalism by						
Current student	127	9	3	0	1	0
Former student	121	16	1	2	0	0
Parent	136	3	1	0	0	0
Other	132	7	0	1	0	0

counselors have made as a result of their safety due to professional activity.

A somewhat surprising finding, given the amount of violence and threatening experiences reported by participants, was that few reported being very concerned for their personal safety (3.6%). The majority (57.9%) expressed no concern for their safety.

Discussion

The purpose of this study was to explore the incidence rate of stalking and stalking-related behaviors in an unresearched group. Thus, from the total number of counselors surveyed, 4.5% reported having been at some time a victim of stalking or harassment where the perpetrator was a school-related individual. Of the respondents who returned the survey, nearly 12% reported being the victim of school-related stalking or harassment. Verbal assaults were by far the most commonly reported behavior, followed by stolen possessions and harassing phone calls. Encountering students with weapons, vandalism, and receiving threatening correspondence were reported by approximately 20% to 30% of those who had been stalked; and being watched, physically assaulted, or followed were less likely to be reported by the respondents, with these latter behaviors reported by approximately 10% of those who reported being stalked. We do not know if fewer respondents reported being watched or followed because these behaviors actually occurred less often, or if they were reported less frequently because the victims were less likely to be aware of these behaviors. Almost 53% of the respondents were from school districts with less than 5,000 students, 15% came from

Table 2

Lifestyle Changes Made As a Result of Safety Concerns Related to Professional Activity

Change	*n*	Frequency (%)
Unlisted phone number	29	19
Installed security devices in office	2	1
Changed residence	4	3
Moved to new community	2	2
Installed security devices in home/apartment	7	5
Learned self-defense techniques	19	13
Reported suspicious activity to authorities	51	34
Purchased self-defense devices	20	13
Obtained restraining order	4	3
Instructed staff to restrict access to personal information	42	28

school districts with 5,000–10,000 students, and only about 18% were from districts with more than 10,000 students. (Fourteen percent did not identify the size of their school district.) The data from this study are therefore more representative of smaller school districts than of larger ones.

Limitations

The response rate to the survey for this research was relatively small (36%) and, as noted above, weighted in the direction of smaller school districts. Furthermore, the majority of respondents were European American. Therefore, we cannot say how well these data represent public schools in general in the United States. The data are also self-report and are based on retrospective behavior, which is more likely to lead to inaccuracies in reporting. Future research should include a broader range of school district sizes and more representation from minority populations. It would also be helpful to understand why the majority of respondents expressed no concern for their personal safety, especially considering the amount of violence and threatening behavior experienced by these respondents.

Conclusions and Recommendations

The data suggest that stalking of secondary school counselors occurs at a rate similar to that of other mental health professionals (Romans, Hays, & White, 1996). Future investigations that identify pre-stalking behaviors and stalker characteristics would likely have an impact on the effectiveness of risk-reduction initiatives. There is also a need for training on how to deal with potentially dangerous individuals. Training offered through professional development and academic preparation programs would likely contribute to a staff that is better equipped to deal with stalking behaviors, leading to safer school environments. Based on the first author's previous research and experience in university counseling centers, the following individual and school strategies are recommended for preventing the occurrence of stalking and dealing with stalking incidents.

Individual Strategies

1. Create clear and firm boundaries with students and parents.
2. Maintain an unlisted home telephone number.
3. Develop personal safety self-confidence by learning self-defense techniques and/or carrying defense devices.
4. Subscribe to caller identification, call tracing, call block, or other similar telephone safety enhancement options.
5. Use an answering machine to screen telephone calls at home.
6. Be aware that the nature of the school counselor's work places family members and significant others as potential targets of stalking.
7. Know applicable agency and institutional policies and local and state laws regarding harassment and stalking behaviors.
8. Guard against unwanted access to personal information, such as Social Security numbers, phone numbers, and e-mail addresses.
9. Early intervention is important. Intrusive behavior that continues beyond a couple of days, even behavior that is nonviolent and may appear relatively harmless, should be reported to the proper authorities. Self-protective behavior should be initiated immediately.

School Strategies

1. Create clear policies to facilitate the safety needs of all staff members.
2. Train individuals who have contact with students and parents to manage and control stalking and harassment behaviors.
3. Install "panic" buttons in counseling offices, similar to devices used by banks.
4. Develop clear policies for reporting dangerous student behaviors to specifically designated authorities.
5. Provide ongoing staff development training to deal strategically with potentially dangerous students.
6. Document details of possible stalking or other unwanted student behaviors with dates, times, tele-

phone calls, letters, and all incidences of harassment.

7. Utilize existing systems such as police departments, offices of student conduct, etc., when appropriate.

8. Encourage individual staff members to assume responsibility for taking personal safeguards at work and at home.

9. Include anti-stalking codes and policies in official school publications to educate parents and students about prohibited behaviors.

Similar to findings in previous studies, (Hays, Romans, Pearson, & Thayer, 1998), those who report they had experienced stalking and harassment in the schools also report overall minimal concern for their safety. This is interesting because those who may be at high risk for violence may not engage in prevention strategies to eliminate the behavior. Perpetrators of harassment may at times forewarn their victims of escalating potentially violent behavior, but the victims may be slow to act. In light of recent highly publicized episodes of violence in the schools, this lack of action or concern could become a serious form of negligence or an unnecessary opportunity for perpetrators to inflict emotional or physical harm on their victims. Recent research to differentiate stalking from intrusiveness suggests that a two-week duration may be a threshold beyond which perpetrators begin to feel a sense of entitlement to the victim (Purcell, Pathé, & Mullen, 2004). Stalking that continues beyond this two-week threshold appears to increase in seriousness and frequency, and to expand into more varied forms of pursuit (Purcell, Pathé, & Mullen, 2004). Further research that highlights the prevalence of stalking behavior in the school community would do much to increase attention to the need for appropriate action when stalking occurs or has been threatened, and attention to the above strategies for dealing with stalking might prevent undue injury.

References

Astor, R. A., Behre, W. J., Wallace, J. M., & Fravil, K. A. (1998). School social workers and school violence: Personal safety, training, and violence programs. *Social Work, 43*, 223–232.

Durant, C. E., Narston, L. L., & Eisenhandler, S. (1986). *Finding from the 1985 National R.A. Harassment Survey: Frequency and types of R.A. harassment and ways to deal with the problem.* University of Massachusetts: Amherst.

Fineran, S. & Bennett, L. (1998). Teenage peer sexual harassment: Implications for social work practice in education. *Social Work, 43*, 55–64.

Fremouw, W. J., Westrup, D., & Pennypacker, J. (1997). Stalking on campus: The prevalence and strategies for coping with stalking. *Journal of Forensic Sciences, 42*, 666–669.

Harmon, R. B., Rosner, R., & Owens, H. (1995). Obsessional harassment and erotomania in a criminal court population. *Journal of Forensic Sciences, 40*, 188–196.

Hays, J. R., Romans, J. S. C., Pearson, C. A., & Thayer, T. (1998). Stalking by residents: Experiences of residential life professionals. Unpublished manuscript.

Henderson, A. (1992). Stalking "stalkers" with tough new laws. *Governing, 5*, 20–21.

Holmes, R. M. (1993). Stalking in America: Types and methods of criminal stalkers. *Journal of Contemporary Criminal Justice, 9*, 317–327.

Installing hidden camera in bedroom was stalking, but not harassment. (2003). *American Journal of Family Law, 17*, 114–116.

Kopels, S. & Dupper, D. R. (1999). School-based peer sexual harassment. *Child Welfare, 78*, 435–461.

Lee, V. E., Croninger, R. G., Linn, E., & Chen, X. (1996). The culture of sexual harassment in secondary schools. *American Educational Research Journal, 33*, 383–417.

Leong, G. B. (1994). De Clerambault syndrome (Erotomania) in the criminal justice system: Another look at this recurring problem. *Journal of Forensic Sciences, 39*, 378–385.

Meloy, J. R. (1997). The clinical risk management of stalking: "Someone is watching over me...." *American Journal of Psychotherapy, 51*, 174–184.

Meloy, J. R. & Gothard, S. (1995). Demographic and clinical comparison of obsessional followers and offenders with mental disorders. *American Journal of Psychiatry, 152*, 258–263.

Mullen, P. E. & Pathé, M. (1994). The pathological extensions of love. *British Journal of Psychiatry, 165*, 614–623.

Palmer, C. J. (1993). *Violent crimes and other forms of victimization in residence halls.* College Administration Publications: Asheville, N.C.

Pathé, M., & Mullen, P. E. (1997). The impact of stalker on their victims. *British Journal of Psychiatry, 170*, 12–17.

Pietrzak, D., Peterson, G. J., & Speaker, K. M. (1998). Perceptions of school violence by elementary and middle school personnel. *Professional School Counseling, 1*, 23–29.

Purcell, R., Pathé, M., & Mullen, P .E. (2004). Editorial: When do repeated intrusions become stalking? *The Journal of Forensic Psychiatry & Psychology, 15*, 571–583.

Rickgarn, R. L. V. (1989). Violence in residence halls: Campus domestic violence. In J. M. Sherrill & D. G. Siegel (Eds.). *Responding to violence on campus (New Directions for Student Services).* Jossey-Bass: San Francisco.

Roberts, A. R., & Dziegielewski, S. F. (1996). Assessment typology and intervention with the survivors of stalking. *Aggression and Violent Behavior, 1*, 359–368.

Romans, J. S. C., Hays, J. R., & White, T. K. (1996). Stalking and related behaviors experienced by counseling center staff members from current or former clients. *Professional Psychology: Research and Practice, 27*, 595–599.

Sheridan, L. P., Blaauw, E., & Davies, G. M. (2003). Stalking. *Trauma, Violence, & Abuse, 4*, 148–162.

Spitzberg, B. H. (2002). The tactical topography of stalking victimization and management. *Trauma, Violence, & Abuse, 3*, 261–288.

Tjaden, P. & Thoennes, N. (1998). *Stalking in America: Findings from the National Violence Against Women Survey.* (NIJCDCP Publication, April). Washington, D.C.

Wright, J. A., Burgess, A. G., Burgess, A. W., Laszlo, A. T., McCrary, G. O., & Douglas, J. E. (1996). A typology of interpersonal stalking. *Journal of Interpersonal Violence, 11*, 487–502.

Yaffe, E. (1995). Expensive, illegal and wrong: Sexual harassment in our schools. *Phi Delta Kappan, 77*, 1–9.

Zona, M., Sharma, K., & Lane, J. A. (1993). A comparative study of erotomanic and obsessional subjects in a forensic sample. *Journal of Forensic Sciences, 38*, 894–903.

About the authors: *John S. C. Romans* (e-mail: John.Romans@ okstate.edu) is affiliated with the School of Applied Health and Educational Psychology, Oklahoma State University, Stillwater, OK. *Joni R. Hays* (e-mail: Joni.Hays@okstate.edu) is affiliated with University Counseling Services, Oklahoma State University, Stillwater, OK. *Christy Pearson* is affiliated with Lookout Mountain Youth Services Center, Golden, CO. *L. Chris DuRoy* is affiliated with Oklahoma Heart Hospital, Oklahoma City, OK. *Barbara Carlozzi* (e-mail: Barbara.Carlozzi@okstate.edu) is affiliated with the School of Applied Health and Educational Psychology, Oklahoma State University, Stillwater, OK.

Exercise for Article 4

Factual Questions

1. According to the researchers, is there a "standard" definition for stalking?

2. According to the researchers, are the terms "stalking" and "harassment" synonymous?

3. What percentage of the respondents was African American?

4. The questions on the survey were developed in consultation with whom?

5. How many of the counselors reported that they had been stalked at least once?

6. What was the most frequently reported "lifestyle change" made as a result of safety concerns?

Questions for Discussion

7. The researchers selected counselors at random. Is this important? Explain. (See lines 203–204.)

8. Does it surprise you that the response rate was only 36%? Explain. (See lines 206–208.)

9. The researchers describe one of their findings as "surprising." Does it also surprise you? (See lines 294–298.)

10. The researchers note that the results are more representative of smaller school districts than of larger ones. Do you regard this as a serious limitation of this study? Explain. (See lines 321–328.)

11. If you were to conduct a study on the same topic, what changes, if any, would you make in the research methodology?

12. In your opinion, are the results of this study sufficiently promising to warrant conducting large-scale studies on this topic? Explain.

Quality Ratings

Directions: Indicate your level of agreement with each of the following statements by circling a number from 5 for strongly agree (SA) to 1 for strongly disagree (SD). If you believe an item is not applicable to this research article, leave it blank. Be prepared to explain your ratings. When responding to criteria A and B below, keep in mind that brief titles and abstracts are conventional in published research.

A. The title of the article is appropriate.
   SA   5   4   3   2   1   SD

B. The abstract provides an effective overview of the research article.
   SA   5   4   3   2   1   SD

C. The introduction establishes the importance of the study.
   SA   5   4   3   2   1   SD

D. The literature review establishes the context for the study.
   SA   5   4   3   2   1   SD

E. The research purpose, question, or hypothesis is clearly stated.
   SA   5   4   3   2   1   SD

F. The method of sampling is sound.
   SA   5   4   3   2   1   SD

G. Relevant demographics (for example, age, gender, and ethnicity) are described.
   SA   5   4   3   2   1   SD

H. Measurement procedures are adequate.
   SA   5   4   3   2   1   SD

I. All procedures have been described in sufficient detail to permit a replication of the study.
   SA   5   4   3   2   1   SD

J. The participants have been adequately protected from potential harm.
   SA   5   4   3   2   1   SD

K. The results are clearly described.
   SA   5   4   3   2   1   SD

L. The discussion/conclusion is appropriate.
   SA   5   4   3   2   1   SD

M. Despite any flaws, the report is worthy of publication.
   SA   5   4   3   2   1   SD

Article 5

The "Nuts and Dolts" of Teacher Images in Children's Picture Storybooks: A Content Analysis

SARAH JO SANDEFUR
University of Tennessee, Chattanooga

LEANN MOORE
Texas A & M University, Commerce

ABSTRACT. Children's picture storybooks are rife with contradictory representations of teachers and school. Some of those images are fairly accurate. Some of those images are quite disparate from reality. These representations become subsumed into the collective consciousness of a society and shape expectations and behaviors of both students and teachers. Teachers cannot effectuate positive change in their profession unless and until they are aware of the internal and external influences that define and shape the educational institution. This ethnographic content analysis examines 62 titles and 96 images of teachers to probe the power of stereotypes/clichés. The authors found the following: The teacher in children's picture storybooks is overwhelmingly portrayed as a white, non-Hispanic woman. The teacher in picture storybooks who is sensitive, competent, and able to manage a classroom effectively is a minority. The negative images outnumbered the positive images. The teacher in children's picture storybooks is static, unchanging, and flat. The teacher is polarized and does not inspire in his or her students the pursuit of critical inquiry.

From *Education*, *125*, 41–55. Copyright © 2004 by Project Innovation, Inc. Reprinted with permission.

A recent children's book shares the story of a teacher. Miss Malarkey, home with the flu, narrates her concern about how her elementary students will behave with and be treated by the potential substitutes available to the school. Among the substitutes represented [5] are Mrs. Boba, a 20-something woman who is too busy painting her toenails to attend to Miss Malarkey's students. Mr. Doberman is a drill sergeant of a man who snarls at the children: "So ya think it's time for recess, [10] HUH?" Mr. Lemonjello, drawn as a small, bald, nervous man, is taunted by the students with the class iguana and is subsequently covered in paint at art time (*Miss Malarkey Won't Be In Today*, Finchler, 1998).

In this text, which is representative of many that [15] have been published with teachers as central characters, teachers are portrayed as insensitive, misguided, victimizing, or incompetent. We perceive these invalidating images as worthy of detailed analysis, based on a hypothesis that a propensity of images painting [20] teachers in an unflattering light may have broader consequences on cultural perceptions of teachers and schooling. Our ethnographic content analysis herein examines 96 images of teachers as they are found in 62 picture storybooks from 1965 to present. It is our per[25]spective that these images in part shape and define the idea of "Teacher" in the collective consciousness of a society.

Those of us in teacher education realize our students come to us with previously constructed images of [30] the profession. What is the origin of those images? When and how are these images formed and elaborated upon? It appears that the popular culture has done much to form or modify those images. Weber and Mitchell (1995) suggest that these multiple, often am[35]biguous, images are "…integral to the form and substance of our self-identities as teachers" (p. 32). They suggest that "…by studying images and probing their influence, teachers could play a more conscious and effective role in shaping their own and society's per[40]ceptions of teachers and their work" (p. 32). We have supported this "probing of images" by analyzing children's picture storybooks, examining their meanings and metaphors where they intersect with teachers and schooling. It is our intention that by sharing what we [45] have learned about the medium's responses to the profession, we will better serve teachers in playing that "conscious role" in defining their work.

We submit that children's picture storybooks are not benign. Although the illustrations of teachers are [50] often cartoon-like and at first glance fairly innocent, when taken as a whole they have power not just in teaching children and their parents about the culture of schooling, but in shaping it, as well. This is of concern particularly when the majority of the images of teach[55]ers are negative, mixed, or neutral as we have found in our research and will report herein. Gavriel Salomon, well known for his research in symbolic representations and their impact on children's learning and thinking, has this to say about the power of media:

[60] Media's symbolic forms of representation are clearly not neutral or indifferent packages that have no effect on the

represented information. Being part and parcel of the information itself, they influence the meanings one arrives at, the mental capacities that are called for, *and the ways one comes to view the world.* Perhaps more important, the culture that creates the media and develops their symbolic forms of representation also *opens the door for those forms to act on the minds of the young* in both more and less desirable ways. [italics added] (1997, p. 13).

We see Salomon's work here as foundational to our own in this way: If those images children and parents see of "teacher" are generally negative, then they will create a "world view" of "teacher" based upon stereotype. The many negative images of teachers in children's picture storybooks may be the message to readers that teachers are, at best, kind but uninspiring, and at worst, roadblocks to be torn down in order that children may move forward successfully.

Why Study Images of Teachers from Popular Culture?

As we were preparing to teach a graduate class titled "Portrayal of Teachers in Children's Literature and in Film," we began gathering a text set of picture storybooks that focused on teachers, teaching, and the school environment. We quickly became aware of the propensity of negative images of teachers, from witch to dragon, drill sergeant to milquetoast, incompetent fool to insensitive clod. We realized early in the graduate course that many teachers had not had the opportunity to critically examine images of their own profession in the popular media. They were unaware of the negative portrayals in existing texts, particularly in children's literature. Teachers may not have considered that the negative images of the teacher "may give the public further justification for a lack of support of education" (Crume, 1989, p. 36).

Children's literature is rife with contradictory representations of teachers and school. Some of those images are fairly accurate and some of those images are quite disparate from reality (Farber, Provenso, & Holm, 1994; Joseph & Burnaford, 1994; Knowles, Cole, & Presswood, 1994; Weber & Mitchell, 1995). These representations become subsumed into the collective consciousness of a society and shape expectations and behaviors of both students and teachers. They become a part of the images that children construct when they are invited to "draw a teacher" or "play school," and indeed the images that teachers draw of themselves. Consider, for example, the three-year-old boy with no prior schooling experience, who, in playing school, puts the dolls in straight rows, selects a domineering personality for a female teacher, and assigns homework (Weber & Mitchell, 1995).

This exploration into teacher images is a critical one at multiple levels of teacher education. Preservice teachers need to analyze via media images their personal motivations and expectations of the teaching profession and enter into teaching with clear understandings of how the broad culture perceives their work. Inservice teachers need to heighten their awareness of how children, parents, and community members perceive them. These perceptions may be in part media-induced and not based on the complex reality of a particular teacher. If information is indeed power, then perhaps those of us in the profession can better understand that popular images contribute to the public's frequent suspicion of our efficacy, and this heightened awareness can support us in addressing the negative images head on.

Research Perspectives

How do we as teachers, prospective teachers, and teacher educators come to so fully subscribe to the images we have both experienced and imagined? Have those images formed long before adulthood, perhaps even before the child enters school? Weber and Mitchell (1994) contend, "Even before children begin school, they have already been exposed to a myriad of images of teachers, classrooms and schools which have made strong and lasting impressions on them" (p. 2). Some of those images and attitudes form from direct experience with teachers. Barone, Meyerson, and Mallette (1995) explain, "When adults respond to the question of which person had the greatest impact on their lives, other than their immediate family, teachers are frequently mentioned" (p. 257). Those early images are not necessarily positive, often convey traditional teaching styles, and are marked with commonalities across the United States (Joseph & Burnaford, 1994; Weber & Mitchell, 1995).

In addition to the years of "on-the-job" experience with teaching and teachers that one acquires as a student sitting and observing "on the other side of the desk," a person has also acquired images and stereotypes of teaching and teachers from the person's experiences with literature and media. Lortie calls this "the apprenticeship-of-observation" (1975, p. 67). These forms of print media (literature) and visual media are part of "popular culture," which is inclusive of film, television, magazines, newspapers, music, video, books, cartoons, etc. In the past decade the literature on popular culture has grown dramatically as an increasing number of educators, social scientists, and other critical thinkers have begun to study the field (Daspit & Weaver, 1999; Giroux, 1994; Giroux, 1988; Giroux & Simon, 1989; McLaren, 1994; Trifonas, 2000; Weber & Mitchell, 1995). Weber and Mitchell (1994) explain, "So pervasive are teachers in popular culture that if you simply ask, as we have, schoolchildren and adults to name teachers they remember, not from school but from popular culture, a cast of fictionalized characters emerges that takes on larger-than-life proportions" (p. 14). These authors challenge us to examine how it is that children—even young children—would hold such strong images and that there be such similarity among the images they hold.

Studies of children's literature have previously examined issues of stereotyping (race, gender, ethnicity, age) as well as moral and ethical issues within stories (Dougherty & Engel, 1987; Hurley & Chadwick, 1998; Lamme, 1996). Recently, Barone, Meyerson, and Mallette (1995) examined the images of teachers in children's literature. They found a startling paradox: "On one hand, teachers are valued as contributing members of society; on the other hand, teachers are frequently portrayed in the media and literature as inept and not very bright" (p. 257).

Barone et al. (1995) found two types of teachers portrayed: traditional, non-child centered and nontraditional, more child-centered. The more prevalent type, the traditional teacher, was not usually liked nor respected by the students in the stories. The nontraditional teacher was seldom portrayed, but when the portrayal was presented, the teacher was shown to be valued and well liked. They contend that the reality of teaching is far too complex to fall into two such simple categories; that the act of teaching is complex. They point out that "…the authors of children's books often negate this complexity of teaching and learning, and classify teachers as those who care about students and those who are rigid or less sensitive to students' needs" (p. 260). Their study led to several disturbing conclusions: (a) the ubiquitous portrayal of traditional teachers as mean and strict make schools and schooling appear to be a dreadful experience, (b) the portrayal of teachers is frequently one in which the teacher is shown as having less intelligence than the students have, and (c) teachers are portrayed as having little or no confidence in their students and their abilities. Weber and Mitchell (1995) assert that "the stereotypes that are prevalent in the popular culture and experience of childhood play a formative role in the evolution of a teacher's identity and are part of the enculturation of teachers into their profession" (p. 27). Joseph and Burnaford (1994) address the numerous examples of caricatures or stereotypes as being somewhat different, but "…all are negative and all reduce the teacher to an object of scorn, disrespect, and sometimes fear" (p. 15).

What Research Framework Guided Our Study?

To answer our questions concerning the elements of the children's texts, we required a methodological framework from which we could examine the "character" of the texts. We found that framework in accessing research theories from anthropology and literary criticism, which suggested an appropriate approach to content analysis.

Submitting that all research directly or indirectly involves participant observation, David Altheide (1987) finds an ethnographic approach applicable to content analyses, in that the writings or electronic texts are ultimately products of social interaction. Ethnographic content analysis (ECA) requires a reflexive and highly interactive relationship between researcher and data with the objective of interpreting and verifying the communication of meaning. The meaning in the text message is assumed to be reflected in the multiple elements of form, content, context, and other nuances. The movement between researcher and data throughout the process of concept development, sampling, data collection, data analysis, and interpretation is systematic but not rigid, initially structured but receptive to emerging categories and concepts.

As we proceeded through the multiple readings of the picture storybooks, we attempted to foreground three main concepts: (a) to attempt to discover "meaning" is an attempt to include the multiple elements that make up the whole: appearance, language, subject taught, gender issues, racial/ethnic diversity, and other nuances as they became apparent; (b) the multiple readings of the selected sample of children's literature to understand and to interpret the structures of the texts are not to conform the texts to our analytic notions but to inform them; and (c) in the intimacy of our relationship with the data, we are acting on them and changing them, just as the data are changing us and the way we perceive past and present texts. As we encountered new texts, we attempted to consistently return to previous texts and to be receptive to new or revised interpretations that were revealed.

What Was Our Research Methodology?

We used Follett Library Resources' database to find titles addressing "teachers" and "schools." This resulted in a list of 62 titles and 96 teacher images published from 1965 to present (Appendix A at the end of this article). No chapter books or *Magic Schoolbus* series books were reviewed, as they did not qualify under the definition of "picture storybook" (Huck et al., 1997, p. 198). We specifically did not attend to publication dates or "in print/out of print" status, as many of these texts appear on school and public library shelves decades after they have gone out of print. Our approach provided us with the majority of children's picture storybooks available in the United States for purchase or available through public libraries.

To better guide our examinations about the images of teachers, ensure that we reviewed the titles consistently, and in order to record the details of the texts we reviewed, we noted details of each teacher representation in aspects of Appearance, Language, Subject, Approach, and Effectiveness. The specific details we were seeking under each category for each teacher represented in the sample literature are further described below:

Appearance: observable race, gender, approximate age, name, clothing, hairstyle, weight (thin, average, plump)

Language: representative utterances by the teacher represented in the book or as reported by the narrator of the book

285 *Subject*: the school subject(s) that the teacher was represented as teaching: reading/language arts, math, geography, history, etc.

Approach: any indicators of a teaching philosophy, including whether children were seated in rows, were working together in learning centers, were re-290 citing memorized material, whether the teacher was shown lecturing, etc.

Effectiveness: indicators included narrator's point of view, images or language about children's learn-ing from that teacher; images or language about 295 children's emotional response to the teacher, etc.

We also attempted to note the absence of data as well as the presence of data. For example, we noted the occurrences of a teacher remaining nameless through the book, of a teacher not being represented as teaching 300 any curriculum, or of a teacher failing to inspire any critical thinking in her students.

We entered data in the foregoing categories about each teacher representation onto forms, which we then reviewed in order to group the individually represented 305 teachers into four more specific categories: positive representations, negative representations, mixed re-view, and neutral. A teacher fitting into the category of "positive teacher" was represented as being sensitive to children's emotional needs, supportive of meaningful 310 learning, compassionate, warm, approachable, able to exercise classroom management skills without resort-ing to punitive measures or yelling, and was respectful and protective of children. A teacher would be classi-fied as a "negative teacher" if he or she were repre-315 sented as dictatorial, using harsh language, unable to manage classroom behavior, distant or removed, inat-tentive, unable to create a learning environment, allow-ing teasing or taunting among students, or unempa-thetic to students' diverse backgrounds. A teacher was 320 categorized as "mixed review" if they possessed char-acteristics that were both positive and negative: for example, if a teacher were otherwise represented as caring and effective in the classroom, but did nothing to halt the teasing of a child. The fourth category for 325 consideration was that of "neutral," in which a teacher was represented in the illustration of a text, but had neither a positive nor a negative effect on the children.

A doctoral student focusing on reading in the ele-mentary school and who is well versed in children's 330 literature served as an inter-rater for this part of the analysis. After having conferred on the characteristics of each category, she read each text independently of the researchers and categorized each teacher as "posi-tive," "negative," "mixed review," and "neutral." We 335 achieved 100% agreement in the category of "positive representations of teachers" and 93% agreement re-garding the "negative" images. We had 75% agreement on the "neutral" images and 100% agreement on the category of "mixed" images (two images). Upon fur-340 ther discussion of our qualifications for "neutral," we

were able to agree on all 14 images as having neither a positive nor negative impact on the children as repre-sented in the text.

What Were the Findings?

Our findings regarding the preponderance of the 345 images are detailed in the following paragraphs.

The teacher in children's picture storybooks is overwhelmingly portrayed as a white, non-Hispanic woman. There were only eight representations of Afri-can American teachers, and only three of them were 350 the protagonists of the books: *The Best Teacher in the World* (Chardiet & Maccarone, 1990); *Show and Tell* (Munsch, 1991); and *Will I Have a Friend?* (Cohen, 1967). Two Asians, no Native Americans, and no other persons of color are shown in the 96 teacher images, 355 making the total number of culturally diverse images represented at only 11% of the total.

The teacher in picture storybooks who is sensitive, competent, and able to manage a classroom effectively is a minority. The teacher who met the standards we 360 described for a "positive teacher," which include an ability to construct meaningful learning environments, compassion, respect, and management skills for a group of children, exists in only 42% of the teacher images in our sample. This means only 40 images out 365 of a total 96 images were demonstrative of teacher effi-cacy. Some examples of the "positive teacher" are found in Mr. Slingerland in *Lilly's Purple Plastic Purse* (Henkes, 1996), Mr. Falker in *Thank You, Mr. Falker* (Polacco, 1998), and Arizona Hughes in *My 370 Great-aunt Arizona* (Houston, 1992).

The negative images outnumbered the positive im-ages. Teachers who were dictatorial, used harsh lan-guage with children, were distant or removed, or al-lowed teasing among students comprised 42% of the 375 total number of 96 teacher representations. Examples of the "negative teacher" are found in the nameless teacher in *John Patrick Norman McHennessy—The Boy Who Was Always Late* (Burningham, 1987), Miss Tyler in *Today Was a Terrible Day* (Giff, 1980), and 380 Miss Landers in *The Art Lesson* (de Paola, 1989). There were only two teachers in the sample who re-ceived a "mixed review," which was by definition a generally positive teacher with some negative strate-gies, approaches, or statements (Mrs. Chud in *Chrysan-385 themum* [Henkes, 1991] and Mrs. Page in *Miss Alaineus: A Vocabulary Disaster* [Frasier, 2000]). Fourteen teacher images, or 15% of the total number, were represented as "neutral," meaning that the teacher in the text had neither a positive nor a negative impact 390 on the students. The nameless teachers in *Oliver Button Is a Sissy* (de Paola, 1979) and *Amazing Grace* (Hoff-man, 1991) are representative of "neutral" teacher im-ages.

The teacher in children's picture storybooks is 395 static, unchanging, and flat. An unexpected finding in this content analysis was that teachers in picture storybooks are never shown as learners themselves, never portrayed as moving from less effective to more effective. Like the nameless teacher in Miriam Cohen's *Welcome to First Grade!* series, if she is a paragon of kindness and patience, she will remain so unfailingly from the beginning of the text to its conclusion. If he is an incompetent novice, like Mr. Lemonjello in *Miss Malarkey Won't Be In Today* (Finchler, 1998), he will not be shown reflecting, learning, and reinventing himself into an informed and effective educator by book's end. Perhaps the evolution from mediocrity to effectiveness holds little in the way of entertainment value, but it could hold great value in the demonstration that teachers are complex human beings with a significant capacity for growth. The potential to paint realistic portraits of teachers is present, but we see little evidence of the medium's desire to construct such an image.

The teacher in children's picture books is polarized. Other researchers have also noted our concerns that we as teachers represented in picture storybooks are "healers or wounders…sensitive or callous, imaginative or repressive" (Joseph & Burnaford, 1994, p. 12). Only 15% of the teachers presented in our sample are neutral images, neither positively nor negatively impacting the children in the fictional classroom, and only two images out of the 96 examined qualified as a "mixed review" of mostly positive characteristics with some negative aspects of educational practice. Therefore, approximately 84% of the teachers represented in our sample are either very good or horrid. The teacher paragon in picture books "generally is a woman who never demonstrates the features of commonplace motherhood—impatience, frustration, or possibly interests in the world other than children themselves—demonstrates to children that the teacher is a wonderfully benign creature" (Joseph & Burnaford, 1994, p. 11). Ms. Darcy in *The Best Teacher in the World* (Chardiet & Maccarone, 1990), and Mrs. Beejorgenhoosen in *Rachel Parker, Kindergarten Show-off* (Martin, 1992) fit neatly into the mold of "paragon." They are not represented exhibiting any less-than-perfect, but realistic, characteristics of exhaustion, short-temperedness, or lapses in good judgment.

Several texts offer "over the top" representations of bad teachers. The often-reviewed *Black Lagoon* series depicts the teachers in children's imaginations as fire-breathing dragons or huge, green gorillas. The well-known *Miss Nelson* series (Allard) has created substitute teacher Viola Swamp in the likeness of a witch, complete with incredible bulk, large features, warts, and a perpetual bad hair day. The teachers in *The Big Box* (Morrison, 1999), put a child who "just can't handle her freedom" in a big, brown box. Other books offer slightly more subtle, but still alarming, representations of negative teaching practice. Consider Miss Tyler, the heavy-lidded, unsmiling teacher in *Today Was a Terrible Day* (Giff, 1980), who humiliates Ronald

five times in the course of the story; or Mrs. Bell, who in *Double Trouble in Walla-Walla* (Clements, 1997) takes a child to the principal for her unique language style. Even worse is the nameless teacher who repeatedly (and falsely) accuses a student of lying and threatens to strike him with a stick *(John Patrick Norman McHennessey—The Boy Who Was Always Late*, Burningham, 1987). In less drastic representations, but still of concern to those of us who believe that literature informs expectations about reality, teachers are represented as failing to protect children from their peers' taunts. Teachers are shown doing nothing to stop the teasing of children in *Chrysanthemum* (Henkes, 1991), *The Brand New Kid* (Couric, 2000), *Today Was a Terrible Day* (Giff, 1980), and *Miss Alaineus: A Vocabulary Disaster* (Frasier, 2000). If children are learning about teachers and school from the children's books read to them, we propose that there is cause for concern about the unrealistic expectations children could develop from such polarized and unrealistic images.

The teacher in children's picture books does not inspire in his or her students the pursuit of critical inquiry. The overwhelming majority of texts that represent teachers in a positive light—and these number in our sample only 42% of the total number of school-related children's literature—show them as kind caregivers who dry tears (Miss Hart in *Ruby the Copycat*, Rathmann, 1991), resolve jealousy between children (Mrs. Beejorgenhoosen in *Rachel Parker, Kindergarten Show-off*, Martin, 1992), restore self-esteem (Mrs. Twinkle in *Chrysanthemum*, Henkes, 1991), teach right from wrong (Ms. Darcy in *The Best Teacher in the World*, Chardiet & Maccarone, 1990). However, few teachers are represented as having a substantial impact on a child's learning. Joseph and Burnaford (1994) found that teachers are not seen "leading students toward intellectual pursuits—toward analyzing and challenging existing conditions of community and society…. The 'successful' teacher [in children's literature]…does not awaken students' intelligence. Such teachers value order; order is what they strive for, what they are paid for" (p. 16).

Our analysis confirms their findings. Examples are common in which teachers actually provide roadblocks to children's success. Tommy in *The Art Lesson* (de Paola, 1989) must wage battle to use his own crayons, use more than just one sheet of paper, and to create art based on his own vision and not the tired model of the art teacher. Miss Kincaid in *The Brand New Kid* (Couric, 2000) actually establishes the opportunity for children to tease the new boy who is an immigrant: "We have a new student…His name is a different one, Lazlo S. Gasky." Young Lazlo's mother must help him find his way into the culture of the school and community. In *David Goes to School* (Shannon, 1999), young David is met with negatively framed demands from his nameless and faceless teacher: "No, David!" "You're tardy!" "Keep your hands to yourself!" "Shhhhh!" and "You're staying after school!"

Only six books in our sample represent teachers as intellectually inspiring. Mr. Isobe in *Crow Boy* (Yashima, 1967) is represented as child-centered and appreciative of Chibi's knowledge of agriculture and botany, who values his drawings and stays after school to talk with young Chibi. He is represented as the catalyst for the crow imitations at the school talent show, which gain Chibi recognition and a newfound respect among his peers. In *Lilly's Purple Plastic Purse* (Henkes, 1996), Mr. Slingerland is such an effective teacher that he inspires Lilly to want to be a teacher (when she isn't wanting to be "a dancer or a surgeon or an ambulance driver or a diva..."). Mr. Cohen in *Creativity* (Steptoe, 1997) uses the arrival of a new immigrant in his class to teach about the history of immigration in this country and to deliver a message about tolerance and shared histories. Mrs. Hughes in *My Great-aunt Arizona* (Houston, 1992) teaches generations of children about "words and numbers and the faraway places they would visit someday." The nameless teacher in *When Will I Read?* (Cohen, 1977) helps young Jim come to the realization that he is a reader, and Mr. Falker in *Thank You, Mr. Falker* (Polacco, 1998) helps fifth-grader Trisha learn to read in three months and cries over her achievement when she reads her first book independently. Although these are excellent examples of how teachers can be represented as dedicated supporters of learning, only six texts out of the 62 in our sample construct images of teacher as an educated professional.

Discussion

Other researchers have found bias, prejudice, and stereotypical presentations of characters in children's books, and our study specifically about images of teachers does not dispute those findings (Barone, Meyerson, & Mallette, 1995; Hurley & Chadwick, 1998; Hurst, 1981). From our extensive 62-book sample of picture storybooks widely available to children, parents, and teachers, we have found a parade of teachers who discourage creativity, ignore teasing, and even threaten to hit children with sticks. We have also found teachers in children's literature who, in great devotion to the human good and the educative process, save children: from boredom, from illiteracy, and from the devastating effects of social isolation. Our deep concern is that the books in which the teacher is demonstrated as intelligent and inspiring (six in our 62-book sample) are dwarfed by the number of books in which the image of Teacher is one of daft incompetence, unreasonable anger, or rigid conformity.

We do not find images of teachers as transformative intellectuals, as educators, who "go beyond concern with forms of empowerment that promote individual achievement and traditional forms of academic success" (Giroux, 1989, p. 138). Instead, we find represen-

tations of teachers whose negatively metaphoric/derogatory surnames indicate the level of respect for the profession: Mr. Quackerbottom, Mrs. Nutty, Ima Berpur, Miss Bonkers, and Miss Malarkey.

Referring back to the graduate class we taught on representations of teachers in popular culture, we perceived a naïveté in these teachers as to the power of the media, to the power of stereotypes to shape the teaching profession, and the power that teachers have to combat the negative images. An overwhelming majority of our graduate students valued the traditional teacher who maintained order, was nurturing and caring, and whose focus was on the emotional well-being of the child. They failed to notice that it was an extremely rare image in picture storybooks that showed a teacher as an intellectually inspiring force.

Teachers cannot effectuate positive change in their profession unless and until they are aware of the internal and external influences that define and shape the educational institution. We want to encourage reflection and conversation about schooling and teaching, careful evaluation of extant images in popular culture in order to develop meaningful dialogue about the accuracy of those images, and to encourage teachers to examine their own memories of teachers and how they form current perceptions.

Implications for Future Research

Our explorations into the representations of teachers in picture storybooks have led to other and further questions regarding images that cultures create of its education professionals.

There is much information to be gleaned from a careful study of the portrayals of school administrators in picture storybooks. How are teachers and administrators represented in basal literature? How often do basal publishers select literature or write their own literature that has school as a setting and what is the ratio of positive representations to negative ones? Do children's authors in other cultures and countries create similar negative images of educators with the same frequency and ire as they do in the U.S.? How are teachers and administrators portrayed in literature for older children, as in beginning- and intermediate-chapter books, young adult novels? How have the images of teachers and administrators evolved over time in our culture? Was there a time in our history that teachers were consistently portrayed in a positive light, and was there perhaps a national event or series of events which caused the images to take on more negative characteristics?

Conclusion

Before we began this study, we came across a book titled *Through the Cracks* (Sollman, Emmons, & Paolini, 1994), which we decided not to include in our literature sample as we perceive this text to be more for teachers and teacher educators than children. The text now takes on new importance in light of our findings.

It chronicles change on one school campus through the eyes of an elementary-age student, Stella. Early in the story Stella and some of her peers begin to physically shrink and literally fall through the cracks of the classroom floor because of boredom—boredom with both the content and delivery of the school curriculum. The teachers initially are illustrated as lecturing to day-dreaming children, running off dittos, and grading papers during class time; one image even shows a teacher sharply reprimanding a child for painting her pig blue instead of the pink anticipated in the teacher's lesson plan. The children have become lost in a kind of academic purgatory under the floorboards. Here they remain until substantial changes are made on their campus. The children at first watch, then come up through the floor to become involved in a curriculum that has become relevant, child-centered, and integrative of the arts. Teachers are then represented as supporting children's learning through highly integrated explorations of Egypt, the American Revolution, geometry, life in a pond. Their images are shown guiding the children in recreating historical and social events; supporting student inquiry; exploring painting, building, drawing, dancing, and playing music as a way of knowing; cooking; becoming involved in community clean-up projects; interviewing experts; conducting science experiments; and more.

Linda Lamme (1996) concludes that "…children's literature is a resource with ample moral and ethical activity, that, when shared sensitively with children, can enhance their moral development and accomplish the lofty goals to which educators in a democracy aspire" (p. 412). Our point in sharing the contents of *Through the Cracks* is this: The picture storybook format has the potential to share with readers the reality of an effective and creative teacher. As opposed to an object of ridicule or scathing humor, a teacher can be represented as an intellectual who inspires children to stretch, grow, and explore previously unknown worlds and communicate that new knowledge through multiple communicative systems. The picture storybook has the potential to encourage a child to anticipate the valuable discoveries that are possible in the school setting; it can also demonstrate to parents how school ought to be and how teachers support children in cognitive and psychosocial ways. Children's literature can also provide positive enculturation for preservice teachers and validation for inservice teachers of the possibilities inherent in their social contributions. Positive representations of teachers have the potential to empower all the partners in the academic community: the children, their parents, teachers and administrators, and the community at large.

References

Altheide, D. (1987). Ethnographic content analysis. *Qualitative Sociology, 10,* 65–76.

Barone, D., Meyerson, M., & and Mallette, M. (1995). Images of teachers in children's literature. *The New Advocate, 8,* 257–270.

Crume, M. (1989). Images of teachers in films and literature. *Education Week,* October 4, 3.

Daspit, T., & Weaver, J. (1999). *Popular culture and critical pedagogy: Reading, constructing, connecting.* New York: Garland.

Dougherty, W., & Engle, R. (1987). An 80s look for sex equality in Caldecott winners and honor books. *The Reading Teacher, 40,* 394–398.

Farber, P., Provenzo, E., & Holm, G. (1994). *Schooling in the light of popular culture.* Albany, New York: State University of New York Press.

Giroux, H. (1988). *Teachers as intellectuals: Toward a critical pedagogy of learning.* Granby, MA: Bergin and Garvey.

Giroux, H. (1989). Schooling as a form of cultural politics: Toward a pedagogy of and for difference. In Henry A. Giroux & Peter L. McLaren (Eds.), *Critical pedagogy, the state and cultural struggle* (pp. 125–151). Albany, NY: SUNY Press.

Giroux, H. (1994). *Disturbing pleasures.* New York: Routledge.

Giroux, H., & Simon, R. (1989). *Popular culture, schooling and everyday life.* New York: Bergin & Garvey.

Huck, C., Hepler, S., Hickman, J., & Kiefer, B. (1997). *Children's literature in the elementary school* (6th ed.), Boston: McGraw.

Hurley, S., & Chadwick, C. (1998). The images of females, minorities, and the aged in Caldecott Award-winning picture books, 1958–1997. *Journal of Children's Literature, 24,* 58–66.

Hurst, J. B. (1981). Images in children's picture books. *Social Education, 45,* 138–143.

Joseph, P. B., & Burnaford, G. E. (1994). *Images of schoolteachers in Twentieth-Century America.* New York: St. Martin's Press.

Knowles, J. G., & Cole, A. L. (with Presswood, C. S.) (1994). *Through preservice teachers' eyes: Exploring field experiences through narrative and inquiry.* New York: Merrill.

Lamme, L. L. (1996). Digging deeply: Morals and ethics in children's literature. *Journal for a just and caring education, 2,* 411–419.

Leitch, V. B. (1988). *American literary criticism from the 30s to the 80s.* New York: Columbia UP.

Lepman, J. (Ed.). (1971). *How children see our world.* New York: Avon.

Lortie, D. C. (1975). *Schoolteacher: A sociological study.* Chicago: University of Chicago Press.

McLaren, P. (1994). *Life in schools: An introduction to critical pedagogy in the foundations of education.* White Plains, New York: Longman.

Salomon, G. (1997). Of mind and media: How culture's symbolic forms affect learning and thinking. *Phi Delta Kappan, 78,* 375–380.

Sollman, C., Emmons, B., & Paolini, J. (1994). *Through the cracks.* Worcester, MA: Davis Publications.

Trifonas, P. (2000). *Revolutionary pedagogies: Cultural politics, instituting education, and the discourse of theory.* New York: Routledge.

Weber, S., & Mitchell, C. (1995). *That's funny, you don't look like a teacher: Interrogating images and identity in popular culture.* Washington, DC: The Falmer Press.

Appendix A
Children's book references

Allard, H. (1985). *Miss Nelson has a field day.* Illustrated by James Marshall. New York: Scholastic.

Allard, H. (1982). *Miss Nelson is back.* Illustrated by James Marshall. Boston: Houghton Mifflin.

Allard, H. (1977). *Miss Nelson is missing.* Illustrated by James Marshall. Boston: Houghton Mifflin.

Burningham, J. (1987). *John Patrick Norman McHennessy—The boy who was always late.* New York: Crown.

Chardiet, B., & Maccarone, G. (1990). *The best teacher in the world.* Illustrated by G. Brian Karas. New York: Scholastic.

Clements, A. (1997). *Double trouble in Walla-Walla.* Illustrated by Sal Murdocca. Brookfield, CT: Millbrook.

Cohen, M. (1977). *When will I read?* Illustrated by Lillian Hoban. New York: Bantam.

Cohen, M. (1967). *Will I have a friend?* Illustrated by Lillian Hoban. New York: Aladdin.

Couric, K. (2000). *The brand new kid.* Illustrated by Majorie Priceman. New York: Doubleday.

de Paola, T. (1989). *The art lesson*. New York: Putnam.

de Paola, T. (1979). *Oliver Button is a sissy*. San Diego, CA: HBJ.

Finchler, J. (1995). *Miss Malarkey doesn't live in Room 10*. Illustrated by Kevin O'Malley. New York: Scholastic.

Finchler, J. (1998). *Miss Malarkey won't be in today*. Illustrated by Kevin O'Malley. New York: Walker.

Frasier, D. (2000). *Miss Alaineus*: *A vocabulary disaster*. San Diego, CA: Harcourt.

Giff, P. R. (1980). *Today was a terrible day*. New York: Puffin.

Hallinan, P. K. (1989). *My teacher's my friend*. Nashville, TN: Ideals.

Henkes, K. (1991). *Chrysanthemum*. New York: Greenwillow.

Henkes, K. (1996). *Lilly's purple plastic purse*. New York: Greenwillow.

Hoffman, M. (1991). *Amazing Grace*. Illustrated by Caroline Binch. New York: Scholastic.

Houston, G. (1992). *My great-aunt Arizona*. Illustrated by Susan Condie Lamb. New York: Harper-Collins.

Martin, A. M. (1992). *Rachel Parker, kindergarten show-off*. Illustrated by Nancy Poydar. New York: Holiday House.

McGovern, A. (1993). *Drop everything, it's D.E.A.R. time!* Illustrated by Anna DiVito. New York: Scholastic.

Morrison, T., & Morrison, S. (1999). *The big box*. Illustrated by Giselle Potter. New York: Hyperion.

Munsch, R. (1991). *Show and tell*. Illustrated by Michael Martchenko. Toronto, Canada: Annick.

Munsch, R. (1985). *Thomas' snowsuit*. Illustrated by Michael Martchenko. Toronto, Canada: Annick.

Polacco, P. (1998). *Thank you, Mr. Falker*. New York: Philomel.

Rathmann, P. (1991). *Ruby the copycat*. New York: Scholastic.

Schwartz, A. (1988). *Annabelle Swift, kindergartner*. New York: Orchard.

Seuss, Dr. (1978). *Gerald McBoing Boing*. New York: Random House.

Shannon, D. (1999). *David goes to school*. New York: Scholastic.

Yashima, T. (1965). *Crow Boy*. New York: Scholastic.

About the authors: *Sarah Jo Sandefur* is UTC Foundation assistant professor of literacy education, University of Tennessee, Chattanooga. *Leann Moore* is assistant dean, College of Education and Human Services, Texas A & M University, Commerce.

Address correspondence to: Dr. Sarah Jo Sandefur, UTC Teacher Preparation Academy, Dept. 4154, 203B Hunter Hall, 615 McCallie Avenue, Chattanooga, TN 37403.

Exercise for Article 5

Factual Questions

1. In the "Research Perspectives" section of this article, the researchers cite a "startling paradox." What is the paradox?

2. Which database did the researchers use to find the titles analyzed in this study?

3. The researchers noted details in five areas, including "Subject." To what does "Subject" refer?

4. What percentage of the 96 teacher images were culturally diverse images?

5. What was an "unexpected finding" of this study?

6. How many of the books represent teachers as intellectually inspiring?

Questions for Discussion

7. In your opinion, does the first paragraph provide convincing information? Explain. (See lines 1–13.)

8. The researchers attempted to note "the absence of data." In your opinion, is this important? Explain. (See lines 296–301.)

9. The researchers examined inter-rater agreement. Is this important? Why? Why not? (See lines 328–343.)

10. In the researchers' discussion of "Implications for Future Research," the researchers list a number of possible research questions. If you had to pick one to conduct a study on, which one would you pick? Explain the reason for your choice. (See lines 594–616.)

11. Overall, does this study convince you that images of teachers in children's picture storybooks influence the public's perceptions of the teaching profession? Explain.

12. Overall, what is your impression of content analysis as a method for obtaining important information on the education profession? How has this study influenced your answer?

Quality Ratings

Directions: Indicate your level of agreement with each of the following statements by circling a number from 5 for strongly agree (SA) to 1 for strongly disagree (SD). If you believe an item is not applicable to this research article, leave it blank. Be prepared to explain your ratings. When responding to criteria A and B below, keep in mind that brief titles and abstracts are conventional in published research.

A. The title of the article is appropriate.

    SA 5 4 3 2 1 SD

B. The abstract provides an effective overview of the research article.

    SA 5 4 3 2 1 SD

C. The introduction establishes the importance of the study.

    SA 5 4 3 2 1 SD

D. The literature review establishes the context for the study.

    SA 5 4 3 2 1 SD

E. The research purpose, question, or hypothesis is clearly stated.

    SA 5 4 3 2 1 SD

F. The method of sampling is sound.

    SA 5 4 3 2 1 SD

G. Relevant demographics (for example, age, gender, and ethnicity) are described.

    SA 5 4 3 2 1 SD

H. Measurement procedures are adequate.

    SA 5 4 3 2 1 SD

I. All procedures have been described in sufficient detail to permit a replication of the study.

    SA 5 4 3 2 1 SD

J. The participants have been adequately protected from potential harm.

    SA 5 4 3 2 1 SD

K. The results are clearly described.

    SA 5 4 3 2 1 SD

L. The discussion/conclusion is appropriate.

    SA 5 4 3 2 1 SD

M. Despite any flaws, the report is worthy of publication.

    SA 5 4 3 2 1 SD

Article 6

A Comparison of How Textbooks Teach Mathematical Problem Solving in Japan and the United States

RICHARD E. MAYER
University of California, Santa Barbara

VALERIE SIMS
University of California, Santa Barbara

HIDETSUGU TAJIKA
Aichi University of Education, Japan

ABSTRACT. This brief report compared the lesson on addition and subtraction of signed whole numbers in three seventh-grade Japanese mathematics textbooks with the corresponding lesson in four U.S. mathematics textbooks. The results indicated that Japanese books contained many more worked-out examples and relevant illustrations than did the U.S. books, whereas the U.S. books contained roughly as many exercises and many more irrelevant illustrations than did the Japanese books. The Japanese books devoted 81% of their space to explaining the solution procedure for worked-out examples compared to 36% in U.S. books; in contrast, the U.S. books devoted more space to unsolved exercises (45%) and interest-grabbing illustrations that are irrelevant to the lesson (19%) than did the Japanese books (19% and 0%, respectively). Finally, one of the U.S. books and all three Japanese books used meaningful instructional methods emphasizing (a) multiple representations of how to solve worked-out examples using words, symbols, and pictures and (b) inductive organization of material beginning with familiar situations and ending with formal statements of the solution rule. The results are consistent with classroom observations showing that Japanese mathematics instruction tends to emphasize the process of problem solving more effectively than does U.S. mathematics instruction (Stevenson & Stigler, 1992).

From *American Educational Research Journal*, *32*, 443–460. Copyright © 1995 by the American Educational Research Association. Reprinted with permission.

National and international assessments of mathematics achievement have consistently revealed that students in the United States perform more poorly than their cohorts in other industrialized nations, particularly students from Asian nations such as Japan (Robitaille & Garden, 1989; Stevenson, Lee, Chen, Stigler, Hsu, & Kitamura, 1990; Stevenson & Stigler, 1992; Stigler, Lee, & Stevenson, 1990). The relatively poor performance of U.S. students occurs not only on tests of basic computational skills but also on tests of mathematical problem solving.

Converging evidence suggests that an explanation for cross-national differences can be found in the *exposure hypothesis*: cross-national differences in mathematics achievement are related to differences in the quantity and quality of mathematics instruction (Mayer, Tajika, & Stanley, 1991; McKnight et al., 1987; Stevenson & Stigler, 1992). Stevenson, Stigler, Lee, Kitamura, Kimura, and Kato (1986) point out that Japanese students spend approximately twice as many hours per week on mathematics as U.S. students spend. Perhaps even more important, Stevenson and Stigler (1992) provide evidence that Japanese schools tend to emphasize the process of problem solving whereas U.S. schools tend to emphasize the mastery of facts and procedures for computing the correct answer. For example, compared to U.S. elementary school mathematics teachers, Japanese teachers provide more verbal explanations, engage students in more reflective discussion, are more likely to use concrete manipulatives to represent abstract concepts, are more likely to include a real-world problem in a lesson, present more coherent lessons, ask questions that require longer answers, provide more critical feedback, and focus on fewer problems in more depth (Stevenson & Stigler, 1992).

The present study compared how mathematical problem solving is taught in mathematics textbooks used in Japan and in the United States. In particular, we examined the hypothesis that a typical Japanese textbook is more oriented toward teaching conceptual understanding and problem-solving skills whereas typical U.S. textbooks are more oriented toward teaching isolated facts and rote computation. This study extends earlier research comparing how mathematical problem solving is taught in Japanese and U.S. classrooms (Stevenson & Stigler, 1992) and contributes to an emerging research base on cross-national comparisons of textbooks (Chambliss & Calfee, 1989; Okamoto, 1989; Stevenson & Bartsch, 1991).

Cross-national comparisons of mathematics textbooks are important in light of evidence that U.S. textbooks constitute a sort of de facto national curriculum. For example, Armbruster and Ostertag (1993, p. 69) assert that "the powerful role of textbooks in the American curriculum is by now well established."

Garner (1992, p. 53) notes that "textbooks serve as critical vehicles for knowledge acquisition in school" and can "replace teacher talk as the primary source of
60   information." Glynn, Andre, and Britton (1986, p. 245) propose that across many disciplines students experience "a heavy reliance on textual materials for a great deal of their knowledge." It follows that examining the content and teaching methods used in American and
65   Japanese mathematics textbooks provides a partial account of how mathematics is taught in the two nations.

Method

Materials

The data source consisted of lessons on addition and subtraction of signed whole numbers taken from three Japanese textbooks (Fukumori et al., 1992, pp.
70   19–25; Kodaira, 1992, pp. 27–32; Fujita & Maehara, 1992, pp. 17–25) and four U.S. textbooks (Bolster, Crown, Hamada et al., 1988, pp. 354–359; Fennell, Reys, Reys, & Webb, 1988, pp. 428–431; Rucker, Dilley, Lowry, & Ockenga, 1988, pp. 332–335; Wil-
75   loughby, Bereiter, Hilton, & Rubinstein, 1991, pp. 260–265) commonly used to teach seventh-grade mathematics. The number of pages for the lesson in the Japanese books ranged from 7 to 9 based on an average page size of 5.5 × 7.5 inches, and from 4 to 6 in the
80   U.S. books based on a page size averaging 7 × 9.5 inches. The Japanese books were approved by the Japanese Ministry of Education and were highly similar to one another because they conformed to detailed governmental specifications; the U.S. books were from
85   publishers' series that were approved for adoption by the California State Department of Education. The books were selected as typical based on consultations with teachers and school administrators in Japan and the United States. The lesson in all books described
90   how to add and subtract positive and negative whole numbers, such as $3 + 8 = \_, -3 + 8 = \_, 3 + -8 = \_, -3 + -8 = \_, 3 - 8 = \_, -3 - 8 = \_, 3 - -8 = \_$, and $-3 - -8 = \_$. In each of the Japanese books, the material was contained in the lesson titled, "Addition and Subtraction,"
95   taken from the chapter titled, "Positive and Negative Numbers" (Fujita & Maehara, 1992; Fukumori et al., 1992; Kodaira, 1992). In the U.S. books, the material was contained in lessons titled, "Adding and Subtracting Signed Numbers" (Willoughby, Bereiter, Hilton, &
100   Rubinstein, 1991); "Adding Integers" and "Subtracting Integers" (Fennell, Reys, Reys, & Webb, 1988; Rucker, Dilley, Lowry, & Ockenga, 1988); or "Adding Integers: Same Sign," "Adding Integers: Different Signs," and "Subtracting Integers" (Bolster, Crown,
105   Hamada et al., 1988). We also included the exercises involving addition and subtraction of signed integers in the end-of-the-chapter test. We did not include sections on addition and subtraction of signed fractions, signed decimals, or three or more signed numbers because this
110   material was not covered in all books. In short, the data source consisted of seven lessons on addition and sub-

traction of signed integers, ranging from 4 to 9 pages in length.

Procedure

To conduct a quantitative analysis of the instruc-
115   tional methods used for teaching students how to solve signed arithmetic problems, two independent raters broke each lesson into four parts—exercises, irrelevant illustrations, relevant illustrations, and explanation— and resolved conflicts by consensus. First, the raters
120   circled the exercise portions of each lesson using a colored marker. We defined an exercise as a symbol-based problem involving addition or subtraction of two signed integers for which no answer or explanation was provided, such as $-8 + 3 = \_$. In the Japanese
125   books, the exercises were labeled as "Problem" or "Exercise"; contained the instructions, "Calculate the following"; and were numbered consecutively. In the U.S. books, the exercises were presented under labels such as "Exercise" or "Practice"; contained instructions such
130   as, "Give each sum," "Give each difference," "Add," or "Subtract"; and were numbered consecutively. The raters counted the number of exercise problems involving addition or subtraction of two signed numbers in each lesson, including exercise problems given at the
135   end of the chapter. We did not include exercises involving fractions, decimals, or more than two numbers. There were no unresolved disagreements between the raters.

Second, the raters circled the irrelevant illustrations
140   in each lesson using a colored marker and circled the relevant illustrations using a different-colored marker. We defined an illustration as any line drawing, chart, picture, or photograph. Furthermore, we defined a relevant illustration as any line drawing or chart that repre-
145   sented the steps in the solution of a signed arithmetic problem and an irrelevant illustration as a picture or photograph that did not correspond to the steps in the solution of a signed arithmetic problem. To ensure consistency, the raters maintained a list of illustrations that
150   were classified as relevant and a list of illustrations that were classified as irrelevant. Relevant illustrations included line drawings showing changes in the water level of a water storage tank, changes in position on a number line, or changes in mixtures of negative and
155   positive ions in a beaker; irrelevant illustrations included a picture of a tape measure, a drawing of a ski village, a drawing of a mad scientist, a drawing of a submarine, a mural from an ancient Egyptian pyramid, a photo of a woman swinging a golf club, and a photo
160   of hockey players skating on ice. A series of line drawings about the same problem presented together on a page was counted as one illustration. The raters counted the number of relevant and irrelevant illustrations in each lesson. There were no unresolved dis-
165   agreements.

Third, the remaining portions of the lesson constituted the explanation and were circled with a colored marker designating explanation. Each rater counted the number of worked-out examples in the explanation portion of the lesson. A worked-out example was defined as a signed arithmetic problem in which the answer and verbal description of how it was generated were given. In most cases, the worked-out examples were presented under the heading, "Example." Each rater also counted the number of words in the explanation section of the lesson; words in headings and in relevant illustrations were included. A word was defined as any letter or letter group found in a dictionary. We did not include mathematical symbols such as numerals, +, −, or =. There were no unresolved disagreements between the raters.

One of the raters used a ruler to measure the space (in square inches) occupied by exercises, irrelevant illustrations, relevant illustrations, and explanation for each lesson. In measuring the areas, margin space was not included. Given the objective nature of these measurements, a second rater was not needed.

In sum, the quantitative data for each lesson included the number of exercises, the number of irrelevant illustrations, the number of relevant illustrations, the number of worked-out examples, the number of words, the area occupied by exercises, the area occupied by irrelevant illustrations, the area occupied by relevant illustrations, and the area occupied by explanation.

Results and Discussion

The instructional lesson is much longer in Japan than in the U.S., but the exercise set is about the same length in both nations. Research on instructional methods has emphasized the role of meaningful explanation rather than unguided hands-on symbol manipulating activities in promoting problem-solving competence (Mayer, 1987). The instructional part of the lesson— that is, the part of the lesson that did not contain to-be-solved exercises—was more than four times longer in the Japanese books than in the U.S. books: The mean number of words in the U.S. books was 208 compared to 925 in the Japanese books. However, the exercise part of the lesson, which emphasizes unguided symbol manipulation, was about the same in the two nations: The Japanese books contained an average of 63 exercises on addition and subtraction of signed numbers, whereas the U.S. books averaged 51 exercises. In both nations, additional worksheets and workbooks are available to supplement the textbook exercises. Overall, these data show a difference in the relative emphasis of Japanese and U.S. books: There were 14.7 words of instruction per exercise in the Japanese books compared to an average of 3.9 words of instruction per exercise in the U.S. books.

Worked-out examples and concrete analogies are more common in Japan than in the U.S. Research on multiple representations, case-based reasoning, and analogical reasoning has demonstrated the important role of worked-out examples and concrete analogies in helping students to improve their problem-solving skills (Mayer, 1987). Worked-out examples serve to model appropriate problem-solving processes, and concrete analogies provide a means for connecting procedures to familiar experience. On average, worked-out examples were three times more common in the Japanese textbooks than in the U.S. textbooks: U.S. books averaged approximately 4 worked-out examples compared to 15 in the Japanese lessons.

The Japanese books employed the same concrete analogy throughout the lesson on addition and subtraction of signed numbers. For example, one book presented a tank for storing water in which a rise in the water level is expressed by a positive number and a fall in the water level is expressed by a negative number. According to this analogy, addition of signed numbers occurs when the water level is changed twice—for example, a first change in the water level plus a second change in the water level produces a total change in the water level; subtraction of signed numbers occurs when one knows the total change and the second change but wants to find the first change. The analogy was represented in multiframe illustrations 9 times, indicating changes that corresponded to arithmetic operations. Another book used the analogy of walking east or west along a path, which was portrayed as arrows along a number line. The book contained 7 multiframe illustrations showing the process of taking two trips along the number line. For example, the problem $(+8) + (−3) =$ ___ was represented as two parts of a trip: an arrow from 0 to 8 (labeled as +8) and an arrow from 8 to 5 (labeled as −3). Below this figure, the solution was represented as an arrow from 0 to 5 (labeled as $+8 − 3$). A third book represented addition and subtraction of signed numbers as movement along a number line, including 6 sets of illustrations of number lines.

In contrast, the U.S. books used concrete analogies such as changes in temperature on a thermometer, keeping score in golf or hockey, matter and antimatter annihilation, and beakers containing positive and negative ions. However, in three out of four cases, the analogy used to represent addition was different from the analogy used to represent subtraction, and none of the analogies was represented in a multiframe illustration depicting changes that correspond to addition or subtraction. In the U.S. books, analogies used to describe addition of signed numbers were insufficient to describe subtraction of signed numbers. For example, in the matter/antimatter analogy, combining 5 bricks and 2 antibricks yielded 3 bricks (analogous to $5 + −2 = 3$). However, this analogy breaks down for situations in which a negative number is subtracted from another number (such as $5 − −2 = 7$), so the textbook used a different analogy, temperatures on a thermometer, to represent subtraction of signed numbers.

Relevant illustrations were more common in Japanese books than in U.S. books, but irrelevant illustra-

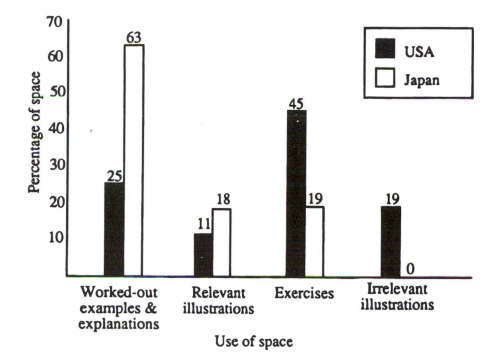

Figure 1. Proportion of page space devoted to explanations, relevant illustrations, exercises, and irrelevant illustrations in Japan and in the United States.

tions were more common in U.S. books than in Japanese books. Research on illustrations reveals that some
kinds of illustrations have more instructional value than
285 others (Levin & Mayer, 1993; Mayer, 1993). Illustrations that simply decorate the page are instructionally
irrelevant, whereas illustrations that explain the process
of signed arithmetic are instructionally relevant. Other
than the first page of the chapter, the Japanese books
290 contained more relevant and fewer irrelevant illustrations than U.S. books: The Japanese books contained
an average of 0 irrelevant and 11 relevant illustrations
compared to an average of 2 irrelevant and 4 relevant
illustrations in the U.S. books. The irrelevant illustra-
295 tions in U.S. textbooks may be intended to make the
material more interesting, but recent research on seductive details reveals that the addition of highly interesting and vivid material to a text often diminishes
students' recall of the important information (Garner,
300 Brown, Sanders, & Menke, 1992; Wade, 1992).

In summary, the foregoing analyses indicate that
the Japanese books contain far more worked-out examples and relevant illustrations than the U.S. books,
whereas U.S. books contain roughly as many exercises
305 and more irrelevant illustrations than Japanese books.
Another way to examine these kinds of differences is to
compare the allocation of page space in Japanese and
U.S. lessons, which is done in the next section.

Japanese books excel in devoting page space to ex-
310 *planation of problem-solving procedures, whereas U.S.*
books excel in devoting page space to unsolved exer-
cises and interest-grabbing illustrations. The allocation

of space in Japanese and U.S. textbooks represents the
values of the cultures that produced them. An emphasis
315 on understanding the process of problem solving is
reflected in the use of worked-out examples, which
model the problem-solving process in words, symbols,
and illustrations. Research on the teaching of problem-solving processes indicates that successful pro-
320 grams rely on the use of cognitive modeling techniques—such as detailed descriptions of worked-out
examples (Mayer, 1992). On average, 81% of the page
space in Japanese books was devoted to explanation of
problem-solving procedures (63% emphasizing
325 worked-out examples and 18% for corresponding illustrations) compared to 36% in U.S. books (25% emphasizing worked-out examples and 11% for corresponding illustrations).

In contrast, an emphasis on the product of problem
330 solving is reflected in the presentation of lists of
to-be-solved exercise problems. On average, 45% of
the page space in U.S. books was devoted to presenting
lists of exercise problems compared to 19% in Japanese books. Perhaps to compensate for what might be
335 considered the boring task of having to solve exercise
problems without guidance, authors of U.S. books
added interest-grabbing illustrations that were irrelevant to the problem-solving procedures. On average,
U.S. books devoted 19% of their space to irrelevant
340 illustrations compared to 0% in Japanese books. Figure
1 summarizes these differences in the use of space in
Japanese and U.S. textbooks.

2a. Excerpt from Japanese textbook that includes verbal, visual, and symbolic representations for each of three problem-solving steps.

We have a tank for storing water. If we put in or take out water, the water level in the tank goes up or down. If we express a change which raises the water level with a positive number, then we can express a change which lowers the water level with a negative number. If the water level rises 5 cm, the change in the water level is +5 cm. If the water level decreases 3 cm, the change in the water level is -3 cm...When the water level changes twice in succession we can express the change as:...

If the first change is: -3 cm
and the second change is: +8 cm
then the total change is: (-3) + (+8)
and this is +5 cm.   (-3) + (+8) = +5

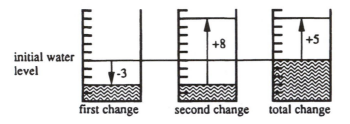

2b. Excerpt from Japanese textbook that includes verbal, visual, and symbolic representations for each of three problem-solving steps.

When you walk from A...you first walk 3 m to the east and then 5 m to the west. The two movements...will be expressed using positive and negative numbers. The first movement is +3 m, the second movement is -5 m, the result is -2 m... The calculation is expressed as follows: (+3) + (-5) = -2.

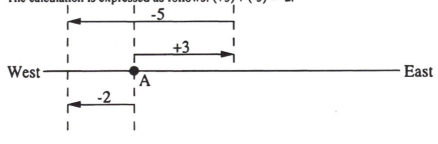

Figure 2. Representations used in Japanese textbooks to teach addition of numbers with different signs.

Note. 2a is adapted from Kodaira (1992); 2b is adapted from Fujita and Maehara (1992).

Meaningful instructional methods emphasizing the coordination of multiple representations were more 345 *common in Japanese books than in U.S. books.* Research in mathematics education emphasizes the importance of helping students build connections among multiple representations of a problem and of helping students induce solution rules based on experience with 350 familiar examples (Grouws, 1992; Hiebert, 1986). To analyze these aspects of meaningful instruction and to supplement the foregoing quantitative analyses, we analyzed the ways that the textbooks explained one type of signed arithmetic—namely, adding two num- 355 bers with different signs, such as $(+3) + (-8) = -5$ or $(-4) + (+3) = -1$. To assess the use of multiple representations in each lesson, we examined whether the lesson presented complete symbolic, verbal, and pictorial representations of a problem-solving procedure for 360 addition of integers with different signs. In particular, we evaluated whether or not the lesson included symbolic, verbal, and visual representations for the first

3a. Excerpt from U.S. textbook that includes visual and symbolic representations for some of three problem-solving steps.

Example. -5 + +1 = ?

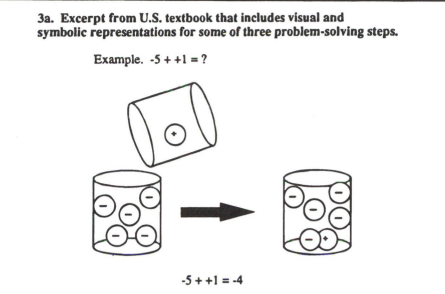

-5 + +1 = -4

3b. Excerpt from U.S. textbook that includes verbal, visual, and symbolic representations for each of three problem-solving steps.

Find 4 + (-7)

Starting at zero, move 4 units to the right.
From there, move 7 units to the left.

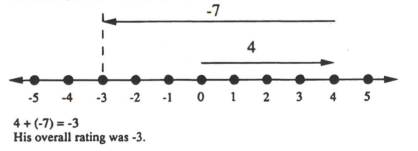

4 + (-7) = -3
His overall rating was -3.

Figure 3. Representations used in U.S. textbooks to teach addition of numbers with different signs.

Note. 3a is adapted from Rucker, Dilley, Lowry, and Ockenaga (1988); 3b is adapted from Bolster et al. (1988).

step (i.e., determining the value of the first number), the second step (i.e., adding the value of the second number), and the third step (i.e., using the resulting number as the final answer). To assess the use of an inductive method in each lesson, we determined whether or not the lesson progressed from familiar examples to a formal statement of the rule for addition of integers with different signs.

All three of the Japanese books systematically built connections among symbolic, verbal, and pictorial representations for each of three steps in solving the prob-

lem. In explaining how to add two numbers with different signs, one Japanese book (Kodaira, 1992) began by describing a water tank analogy in words. The book (p. 27) stated that "when the water level changes twice in succession, we can express the changes, starting with the first change as: (the first change) + (the second change)." In relating this analogy to addition of two numbers with different signs, the book (p. 28) described the situation in words: "If the first change is –3 cm and the second change is +8 cm, then the total change is (–3) + (+8), and this is +5

385 cm." Then the book presented the problem in symbolic form as "(−3) + (+8) = +5." Next to this was a pictorial representation of the problem consisting of three labeled frames, as shown in Figure 2a. Each step in the
390 problem was represented, starting with negative 3, adding positive 8, and ending with positive 5. At the end of a series of examples, the book presented a rule for addition of numbers with different signs (p. 30):

> In seeking the sum of two numbers with different signs,
395 > consider only their absolute values and subtract the smaller absolute value from the larger. Then assign to the sum the sign of the number with the larger absolute value. If the absolute values are equal, then the sum is 0.

Thus, the lesson was organized inductively, beginning with a familiar analogy and ending with a formal
400 statement of the solution rule.

A second Japanese book (Fujita & Maehara, 1992) began its discussion of addition of different-signed integers by describing a walk along a road (p. 17):

> Imagine that you are walking along a road which runs
405 > east and west in a straight line.... You first walk 3 meters to the east and then walk 5 meters to the west. Moving to the east will be used as the positive numbers and moving to the west will be used as the negative numbers.

Then, the book describes the computation in words and
410 symbols (p. 17): "Two movements and their results will be expressed as follows, when positive and negative numbers are used.... The first movement is +3 m, the second movement is −5 m, the result is −2 m." On the right, the book presented a number line with an
415 arrow from 0 to 3 corresponding to the first movement, from 3 to −2 corresponding to the second movement, and from 0 to −2 corresponding to the answer. This illustration is summarized in Figure 2b. Next, the example was expressed in symbolic form (p. 18):

420 > When moving twice in succession, the results...are expressed as follows by adding two numbers: (the first movement) + (the second movement). When the results are expressed like this, the calculation for the example is as follows: (+3) + (−5). The answer is −2, and so the
425 > computation is expressed as follows: (+3) + (−5) = −2.

Finally, after presenting several examples in verbal, visual, and symbolic forms, the section ended with a statement of the general principle (p. 20): "The sum of numbers with different signs: You can subtract the
430 smaller absolute value from the larger one and assign to the sum the sign of the number with the larger absolute value. When the absolute values are equal, the sum is 0." As in the other Japanese book, this lesson was organized inductively—beginning with a familiar
435 situation of walking east and west along a road and ending with a formal statement of the procedure for addition of numbers with different signs.

The third book (Fukumori et al., 1992, pp. 18–19) also used verbal, visual, and symbolic representations
440 to explain what to do "when you add a positive and negative number." The book connected symbols,

words, and pictures as follows. "(−7) + 5 means to get a number that is 5 larger than −7. A number 5 larger than −7 is the number −2, which is 2 smaller than 0, as
445 you can see on the number line below." Directly below was an illustration of a number line with an arrow from −7 to −2, and below that was the symbolic form of the problem, "(−7) + 5 = −2." After presenting several other examples of the same form in the same way, the
450 section ended with a statement of general principle: "Addition of a negative and positive number means subtraction of the negative number from the positive number... 3 + (−5) = 3 −5 = −2." Again, as in the other Japanese books, instruction moved from the familiar
455 statement of a problem in words and pictures to a formal statement of the solution procedure as a rule.

In contrast, only one of the four U.S. books contained symbolic, verbal, and pictorial representations of example problems involving addition of integers with
460 different signs. For example, one U.S. textbook (Willoughby, Bereiter, Hilton, & Rubinstein, 1991) began by presenting word problems about familiar analogies such as a thermometer: "The temperature is −4C. If it goes up 3C, what will it be?" For each word problem,
465 the book stated the problem in symbolic form but did not give an answer, such as "−4 + 3 = ?" Thus, the book presented only the first two steps in the problem—namely, starting at negative 4 and adding positive 3; it failed to describe the third step—namely, end-
470 ing at negative 1. The book also failed to connect the verbal and symbolic representation of the problem to a pictorial representation. In the next section of the chapter, titled "Adding and Subtracting Signed Numbers," the book (p. 263) listed rules such as: "To add 2 signed
475 numbers, if the signs are different, subtract the smaller absolute value from the larger and use the sign of the one with the larger absolute value." Then, the book provided exercises such as "(−8) + (+7) = n" along with instructions to use the above rule. This is a deductive
480 approach because it begins with stating a rule and then tells the learner to apply the rule to exercise problems.

In another U.S. textbook (Rucker, Dilley, Lowry, & Ockenga, 1988), the section on "Integers" began by representing positive and negative integers as beakers
485 containing positive and negative charges. Then, in the section on "Adding Integers," the book presented several examples. For each, there was a picture of one beaker containing positive or negative charges being poured into another beaker containing positive or nega-
490 tive charges and the resulting beaker; below the picture was a symbolic representation of the problem. For example, Figure 3a shows a beaker containing one positive charge being poured into a beaker containing 5 negative charges, and the result is a beaker containing
495 4 free negative charges. Directly under this picture was the equation, "−5 + +1 = −4." This lesson used symbols and pictures to present all three steps in the procedure—starting with negative 5, adding positive 1, and ending with negative 4—but failed to connect them to

words. There was no verbal description other than the general statement, "To understand how to add integers, you can think about putting charges together." The book then moved directly to exercises without ever presenting the solution rule.

Another book (Fennell, Reys, Reys, & Webb, 1988) used a creative analogy about annihilation of matter and antimatter to explain addition of signed integers (p. 428):

> In a galaxy totally different from our own, a scientist named Dr. Zarkov discovered antimatter. When he puts antimatter together with antimatter nothing happens. For example, if he puts 4 cups of antiwater together with 3 cups of antiwater, he gets 7 cups of antimatter. Strange as it may seem, however, when he puts equal amounts of matter and antimatter together, they both disappear. For example, if he puts 2 telephones and 2 antitelephones together, he is left with nothing. In his latest experiment, Dr. Zarkov added 2 antibricks to a box containing 5 bricks. There was a blinding flash of light. When the smoke cleared, he was left with 3 bricks.

There was no illustration for the bricks example, although there was an illustration depicting 2 light and 2 dark telephones being placed together, and then disappearing in a "poof." Later in the section, the bricks example was represented symbolically as, "2 antibricks + 5 bricks = 3 bricks," and as, "−2 + 5 = 3." In this case, the book described the three steps in the addition of signed integers within the context of an interesting situation and related them to a symbolic representation but failed to relate them to a pictorial representation. In addition, the book failed to state the solution rule in a formal way, but it asked the students to do so as an exercise (p. 429): "State rules for adding a positive integer and a negative integer."

Finally, the fourth U.S. book (Bolster et al., 1988) used a hockey analogy to explain addition of signed integers in a section titled "Adding Integers: Different Signs." The section (p. 356) started by describing a hockey-scoring procedure: "Angelo's hockey coach uses a plus/minus system to rate the performance of the players. If a player is on the ice when his team scores, he gets 1. If he is on the ice when the other team scores, he gets −1. For his first 10 games, Angelo's plus rating was 4, and his minus rating was −7. What was his overall rating?" Next, the book stated the problem symbolically: "Find 4 + (−7)." Finally, the book used a captioned number line illustration as shown in Figure 3b to represent the three steps in solving the problem. The caption described the steps: "Starting at zero, move 4 units to the right. From there, move 7 units to the left. His overall rating was −3." Although very short, this lesson makes connections among symbolic, verbal, and visual representations of all three steps in the example problem. Unlike the Japanese book, which included many complete examples, however, this book presented only one complete example. Finally, the lesson ended with a statement of the solu-

tion rule (p. 357): "To add two integers with different signs, consider the distance each integer is from zero. Subtract the shorter distance from the longer distance. In your answer, use the sign of the number farther from zero." Like the Japanese book, this textbook used an inductive approach, moving from familiar examples to a formal statement of the rule.

In summary, the books differed in their use of multiple representations to explain how to add a negative and positive integer and in their inclusion of a statement of the solution rule. The Japanese books presented complete explanations of at least two examples of addition of a positive and negative integer; in these examples, all three steps in the procedure were presented symbolically, verbally, and pictorially, and the solution rule was clearly stated at the end of the explanation. In contrast, one U.S. textbook presented a complete explanation of one example and a statement of the rule, one presented an explanation that lacked a pictorial representation and a statement of the rule, one presented an explanation that lacked a verbal representation and a statement of the rule, and one presented an explanation that lacked a pictorial representation and lacked portions of the symbolic and verbal representations. Overall, all of the Japanese books presented multiple representations of example problems and presented material in inductive order, whereas most of the U.S. books did not employ these meaningful instructional methods.

The lesson was better integrated into the Japanese books than into the U.S. books, and the U.S. books were much longer than the Japanese books. Research on text structure has highlighted the importance of organizing topics in a simple and coherent structure (Britton, Woodward, & Binkley, 1993; Jonassen, Beissner, & Yacci, 1993). The Japanese books, averaging less than 200 pages in length, contained an average of 7 chapters with each one divided into two or three coherent sections, whereas the U.S. textbooks, averaging 475 pages in length, contained an average of 12 chapters with each including approximately a dozen loosely related topics. For example, each of the Japanese books contained an entire chapter, titled "Positive and Negative Numbers," devoted exclusively to signed numbers. The chapter consisted of three related sections involving an introduction to signed numbers, addition/subtraction of signed numbers, and multiplication/division of signed numbers. In contrast, lessons on addition and subtraction of signed numbers were presented as short fragments within more diverse chapters throughout most of the U.S. books. In three U.S. books, material on addition and subtraction of signed numbers was in the same chapter as solving equations and coordinate graphing of equations; in another, it was taught in a chapter that included units of measure, mixed numbers, and improper fractions. Overall, compared to the U.S. textbooks, the Japanese textbooks were more

615 compact, presented a clearer structure, and covered fewer topics in more depth.

Conclusion

If textbooks serve as a sort of national curriculum, then international comparisons of textbook lessons can provide a partial picture of not only what is taught but 620 also how it is taught across nations. Two competing methods for teaching students how to solve mathematics problems are drill and practice—in which page space is devoted to unexplained exercises involving symbol manipulation—and cognitive modeling—in 625 which page space is devoted to presenting and connecting multiple representations of step-by-step problem-solving processes through worked-out examples. The drill-and-practice approach follows from a view of learning as knowledge acquisition that emphasizes the 630 *product of problem solving*—that is, getting the right answer; in contrast, the cognitive modeling approach follows from a view of learning as knowledge construction, which emphasizes *the process of problem solving*—that is, how to get the right answer (Mayer, 635 1989).

In this study, we are concerned with how much space in Japanese and U.S. mathematics textbooks is devoted to unexplained exercises consisting of symbol manipulation and how much space is devoted to build- 640 ing and connecting multiple representations for problem solving through worked-out example problems. Building on the exposure hypothesis, which originally focused on the allocation of instructional time (Mayer, Tajika, & Stanley, 1991; Stevenson & Stigler, 1992), 645 the amount of space in mathematics textbooks that is devoted to meaningful explanation of problem-solving strategies may be an important determinant of students' mathematical problem-solving competence.

If textbook page space is viewed as a limited re- 650 source, then the allocation of that space reflects the priorities of the cultures that produced them. In Japan, the major use of page space is to explain mathematical procedures and concepts in words, symbols, and graphics, with an emphasis on worked-out examples and 655 concrete analogies. In U.S. books, where the use of page space for explanation is minimized relative to Japanese books, the major use of page space is to present unexplained exercises in symbolic form for the students to solve on their own. These lessons are sup- 660 plemented with attention-grabbing graphics that, unlike those in the Japanese books, are interesting but irrelevant. Japanese textbooks devote over 80% of their space, and U.S. books devote less than 40% of their space to instruction in the process of problem solving 665 (i.e., words, pictures, and symbols that explain how to add and subtract signed numbers), whereas U.S. books devote over 60% of their space, and Japanese books devote less than 20% of their space to hands-on exercises without guidance and interesting-but-irrelevant 670 illustrations. A further analysis of lessons provides

converging evidence: All three of the Japanese books and only one of the four U.S. books presented worked-out examples that explained how to solve problems in words, symbols, and pictures.

675 In Japan, the textbooks provide worked-out examples that model successful problem-solving strategies for students; in the U.S., textbooks are more likely to provide lots of exercises for students to solve on their own without much guidance. In Japan, the textbooks 680 provide concrete analogies that help the student relate the concepts of addition and subtraction of signed numbers to a familiar situation; in the U.S., textbooks may give rules without much explanation. In Japan, the textbooks devote space to explaining mathematical 685 ideas in words, whereas U.S. textbooks devote relatively more space to manipulating symbols.

The picture that emerges from our study of mathematics textbooks is that cognitive modeling of problem-solving processes is emphasized more in Japan 690 than in the United States, whereas drill and practice on the product of problem solving is emphasized more in the United States than in Japan. Japanese textbooks seem to assume the learner is a cognitively active problem solver who seeks to understand the step-by-step 695 process for solving a class of problems. In contrast, U.S. textbooks seem to assume the learner is a behaviorally active knowledge acquisition machine who learns best from hands-on activity in solving problems with minimal guidance and who needs to be stimulated 700 by interesting decorative illustrations.

Our study is limited and should be interpreted as part of a converging set of research results. First, our data source involves only three Japanese and four U.S. books. Although we chose books that are widely used, 705 we did not exhaustively review other books and supplemental materials, such as workbooks. Second, we examined only one lesson—amounting to a few pages in each of the books in our sample. Although the material is a typical component of the mathematics curricu- 710 lum in both nations, we did not review other lessons. Furthermore, our subsequent analysis was even more restrictive, examining only addition of signed numbers with different signs. Finally, we focused on properties of the lessons that are related to problem-solving in- 715 struction, rather than other aspects of the text such as its readability. Ultimately, the practical goal of this study is to provide suggestions for the improvement of textbooks aimed at mathematical problem solving. The following suggestions need to be subjected to research 720 study: (a) present a few basic topics in depth, organized into coherent lessons, rather than a huge collection of fragments; (b) embed the lesson within a familiar situational context so that verbal, visual, and symbolic representations are interconnected; (c) use worked-out 725 examples to emphasize the process of problem solving; (d) present a verbal statement of the solution rule after presenting familiar worked-out examples. Finally, it should be noted that additional research is needed to

730 determine not only how to design effective textbooks but also how to use them successfully in classrooms (Driscoll, Moallem, Dick, & Kirby, 1994).

References

Armbruster, B., & Ostertag, J. (1993). Questions in elementary science and social studies textbooks. In B. K. Britton, A. Woodward, & M. Binkley (Eds.), *Learning from textbooks: Theory and practice* (pp. 69–94). Hillsdale, NJ: Erlbaum.

Bolster, L. C., Crown, W., Hamada, R., Hansen, V., Lindquist, M. M., McNerney, C., et al. (1988). *Invitation to mathematics* (7th grade). Glenview, IL: Scott, Foresman & Co.

Britton, B. K., Woodward, A., & Binkley, M. (Eds.) (1993). *Learning from textbooks: Theory and practice.* Hillsdale, NJ: Erlbaum.

Chambliss, M. J., & Calfee, R. C. (1989). Designing science textbooks to enhance student understanding. *Educational Psychologist, 24,* 307–322.

Driscoll, M. P., Moallem, M., Dick, W., & Kirby, E. (1994). How does the textbook contribute to learning in a middle school science class? *Contemporary Educational Psychology, 19,* 79–100.

Fennell, F., Reys, B. J., Reys, R. E., & Webb, A. W. (1988). *Mathematics unlimited* (7th grade). New York: Holt, Rinehart, & Winston.

Fujita, H., & Maehara, S. (Eds.) (1992). *New math* (in Japanese). Tokyo: Shoseki.

Fukumori, N., Kikuchi, H., Miwa, T., Iijima, Y., Igarashi, K., Iwai, S., et al. (1992). *Math 1* (in Japanese). Osaka, Japan: Keirinkan.

Garner, R. (1992). Learning from school texts. *Educational Psychologist, 27,* 53–63.

Garner, R., Brown, R., Sanders, S., & Menke, D. J. (1992). "Seductive details" and learning from text. In K. A. Renninger, S. Hidi, & A. Krapp (Eds.), *The role of interest in learning and development* (pp. 239–254). Hillsdale, NJ: Erlbaum.

Glynn, S. M., Andre, T., & Britton, B. K. (1986). The design of instructional text. *Educational Psychologist, 21,* 245–251.

Grouws, D. A. (Ed.) (1992). *Handbook of research on mathematics teaching and learning.* New York: Macmillan.

Hiebert, J. (Ed.) (1986). *Conceptual antiprocedural knowledge: The case of mathematics.* Hillsdale, NJ: Erlbaum.

Jonassen, D. H., Beissner, K., & Yacci, M. (1993). *Structural knowledge.* Hillsdale, NJ: Erlbaum.

Kodaira, K. (Ed.) (1992). *Japanese grade 7 mathematics* (H. Nagata, Trans.). Chicago: University of Chicago. (Original work published 1984)

Levin, J. R., & Mayer, R. E. (1993). Understanding illustrations in text. In B. Britton, A. Woodward, & M. Binkley (Eds.), *Learning from textbooks: Theory and practice* (pp. 95–113). Hillsdale, NJ: Erlbaum.

Mayer, R. E. (1987). *Educational psychology: A cognitive approach.* New York: Harper Collins.

Mayer, R. E. (1989). Cognition and instruction in mathematics. *Journal of Educational Psychology, 81,* 452–456.

Mayer, R. E. (1992). *Thinking, problem solving, cognition* (2nd ed.). New York: Freeman.

Mayer, R. E. (1993). Illustrations that instruct. In R. Glaser (Ed.), *Advances in instructional psychology* (Vol. 4, pp. 253–284). Hillsdale, NJ: Erlbaum.

Mayer, R. E., Tajika, H., & Stanley, C. (1991). Mathematical problem solving in Japan and the United States: A controlled comparison. *Journal of Educational Psychology, 83,* 69–72.

McKnight, C. C., Crosswhite, F. J., Dossey, J. A., Kifer, E., Swafford, J. O., Trayers, K. J., & Cooney, T. J. (1987). *The underachieving curriculum: Assessing U.S. school mathematics from an international perspective.* Champaign, IL: Stipes.

Okamoto, Y. (1989, April). *An analysis of addition and subtraction word problems in textbooks: An across national comparison.* Paper presented at the Annual Meeting of the American Educational Research Association, San Francisco.

Robitaille, D. F., & Garden, R. A. (1989). *The IEA study of mathematics II: Contexts and outcomes of school mathematics.* Oxford, England: Pergamon.

Rucker, W. E., Dilley, C. A., Lowry, D. W., & Ockenga, E. G. (1988). *Heath mathematics* (7th grade). Lexington, MA: D. C. Heath.

Stevenson, H. W., & Bartsch, K. (1991). An analysis of Japanese and American textbooks in mathematics. In R. Leetsma & H. Walberg (Eds.), *Japanese educational productivity.* Ann Arbor: Center for Japanese Studies.

Stevenson, H. W., Lee, S-Y., Chen, C., Stigler, J. W., Hsu, C-C., & Kitamura, S. (1990). Contexts of achievement: A study of American, Chinese, and Japanese children. *Monographs of the Society for Research in Child Development, 55* (1–2, Serial No. 221).

Stevenson, H. W., & Stigler, J. W. (1992). *The learning gap.* New York: Summit.

Stevenson, H. W., Stigler, J. W., Lee, S-Y., Kitamura, S., Kimura, S., & Kato, T. (1986). Achievement in mathematics. In H. Stevenson, H. Azuma, & K. Hakuta (Eds.), *Child development and education in Japan* (pp. 201–216). New York: Freeman.

Stigler, J. W., Lee, S-Y., & Stevenson, H. W. (1990). *Mathematical knowledge of Japanese, Chinese, and American elementary school children.* Reston, VA: National Council of Teachers of Mathematics.

Wade, S. E. (1992). How interest affects learning from text. In K. A. Renninger, S. Hidi, & A. Krapp (Eds.), *The role of interest in learning and development* (pp. 254–277). Hillsdale, NJ: Erlbaum.

Willoughby, S. S., Bereiter, C., Hilton, P., & Rubinstein, J. H. (1991). *Real math* (7th grade). La Salle, IL: Open Court.

Note: This project was supported by a grant from the Pacific Rim Research Program. Hidetsugu Tajika translated two of the Japanese textbook lessons into English.

About the authors: *Richard E. Mayer* is a professor of psychology and education, Department of Psychology, University of California, Santa Barbara, CA 93106. His specializations are educational and cognitive psychology. *Valerie Sims* is a Ph.D. candidate, Department of Psychology, University of California, Santa Barbara, CA 93106. Her specializations are cognitive and developmental psychology. *Hidetsugu Tajika* is an associate professor, Department of Psychology, Aichi University of Education, Kariya, Aichi 448 Japan. His specializations are memory and cognitive processes.

Exercise for Article 6

Factual Questions

1. The researchers explicitly state their research hypothesis for this study in which line(s)?

2. The lessons examined in this study ranged from a low of how many pages to a high of how many pages?

3. On the average, what percentage of the page space in Japanese textbooks is devoted to explanations of problem-solving procedures? What is the corresponding percentage for U.S. textbooks?

4. Which country's textbooks cover fewer topics?

5. According to the authors, which country's textbooks assume that students are "behaviorally active knowledge acquisition machines"?

6. The researchers note the need for research on how to use textbooks effectively in which lines?

Questions for Discussion

7. In lines 47–49, the researchers state that this study "contributes to an emerging research base on cross-national comparisons of textbooks" and cite three references for this statement. Would it have been appropriate for them to discuss this research base in more detail? Explain.

8. In lines 63–66, the researchers state that examining the content and teaching methods in textbooks "provides a partial account of how mathematics is taught…." Although it is partial, is it important?

What else might be examined to get a fuller account? Explain.

9. The researchers examined only one type of lesson in only five textbooks. Is this an important limitation? Is the study of value despite this limitation? Explain.

10. The researchers state that the selected textbooks were "typical." How did they determine this? How would you determine it? (See lines 86–89.)

11. The researchers used two "independent raters." Why did they bother to use two raters? What does "independent" mean? (See lines 114–138.)

12. Have these researchers demonstrated that differences between the two nations' textbooks are the *cause* of the differences in the mathematics achievement of the students in the two nations? Explain.

13. This study is an example of content analysis (also known as documentary analysis) in which the contents of documents are analyzed. Are there advantages and disadvantages to using content analysis as a research method for collecting information on problems in education? Explain.

Quality Ratings

Directions: Indicate your level of agreement with each of the following statements by circling a number from 5 for strongly agree (SA) to 1 for strongly disagree (SD). If you believe an item is not applicable to this research article, leave it blank. Be prepared to explain your ratings. When responding to criteria A and B below, keep in mind that brief titles and abstracts are conventional in published research.

A. The title of the article is appropriate.

SA   5   4   3   2   1   SD

B. The abstract provides an effective overview of the research article.

SA   5   4   3   2   1   SD

C. The introduction establishes the importance of the study.

SA   5   4   3   2   1   SD

D. The literature review establishes the context for the study.

SA   5   4   3   2   1   SD

E. The research purpose, question, or hypothesis is clearly stated.

SA   5   4   3   2   1   SD

F. The method of sampling is sound.

SA   5   4   3   2   1   SD

G. Relevant demographics (for example, age, gender, and ethnicity) are described.

SA   5   4   3   2   1   SD

H. Measurement procedures are adequate.

SA   5   4   3   2   1   SD

I. All procedures have been described in sufficient detail to permit a replication of the study.

SA   5   4   3   2   1   SD

J. The participants have been adequately protected from potential harm.

SA   5   4   3   2   1   SD

K. The results are clearly described.

SA   5   4   3   2   1   SD

L. The discussion/conclusion is appropriate.

SA   5   4   3   2   1   SD

M. Despite any flaws, the report is worthy of publication.

SA   5   4   3   2   1   SD

Article 7

Relation of Religiosity with Academic Dishonesty in a Sample of College Students

MELISSA A. HUELSMAN
Coastal Carolina University

JOAN PIROCH
Coastal Carolina University

DAVID WASIELESKI
Valdosta State University

ABSTRACT. This study was conducted to estimate the relationship between academic dishonesty and religiosity in a convenient sample of college students. Scores on the Santa Clara Strength of Religious Faith Questionnaire and the Academic Practices Survey were correlated for 70 undergraduate students. Overall, religiosity and academic dishonesty were not significantly related. However, follow-up analyses by sex indicated that this association was significant for women but not men. Research should be conducted to investigate whether this pattern is robust and indicates a differing role for religiosity as a standard for appropriate or inappropriate behavior.

From *Psychological Reports*, 99, 739–742. Copyright © 2006 by Psychological Reports. Reprinted with permission.

Academic dishonesty has long been a subject of empirical research given its effects on the learning community on college campuses. Scanlon and Neumann (2002) stated that 24.5% of their sampled students reported they plagiarized online at least sometimes, even while 89% of the students somewhat or strongly agreed that plagiarism was wrong. Most schools have policies designed to deter students from such misconduct, and many schools adopt honor codes specifically to address such dishonesty. Technological advances, such as the Internet and cell phones with cameras and text messaging capability, have opened up new vistas for the student willing to commit academic misconduct. Knowledge of the correlates of and reasons for academic dishonesty may help academicians and administrators discover ways to attenuate this problem.

To this end, researchers have examined personal and situational variables related to academic dishonesty. McCabe and Treviño (1997) indicated that demographic variables including but not limited to sex, age, and peer disapproval have been linked to academic dishonesty. Their strongest finding was that students engaged in less academic dishonesty when they believed that peers disapproved of this behavior. Honor codes, which provide a formal statement of the institution's, and by extension the students', disapproval of academic dishonesty, have also yielded an inverse relationship with incidence of academic misconduct (McCabe & Treviño, 2002).

In addition to such external standards that may influence students' behaviors, several studies have investigated whether internal standards of behavior may affect incidence of academic misconduct. One may anticipate that religiosity, for example, might provide a mitigating factor based on moral codes associated with most major religions. Unfortunately, few studies have been conducted to investigate the relationship between academic dishonesty and religiosity. However, previous research has supported an inverse relationship between religiosity and other objectionable behaviors. For example, Peltzer, Malaka, and Phaswana (2002) reported that low religiosity scores of college freshmen predicted recent alcohol, tobacco, and cannabis use.

Storch and Storch (2001) conducted a preliminary examination of the relationship between religiosity and academic dishonesty in college students. These researchers hypothesized an inverse relationship for the three domains of religiosity (organizational, nonorganizational, and intrinsic) and self-reported acts of academic dishonesty for 244 college students who completed a religiosity scale and nine questions designed to assess academic dishonesty. Analysis indicated that students who had high scores for nonorganizational and intrinsic religiosity reported the lowest rates of academic dishonesty regardless of sex (Storch & Storch, 2001). Of note is that these components of religiosity seem to focus much more on internal rather than external standards of behavior.

The current study seeks to follow up the Storch and Storch study (2001), using a unidimensional scale of religious faith, which better reflects the more internal (nonorganizational and intrinsic) aspects of religiosity, as well as a more detailed scale measuring academic practices. Based on previous results, an inverse relationship was hypothesized between self-reported academic dishonesty and religiosity.

Method

Participants

Participants (36 women and 34 men) were solicited from classes at a small university in the southeastern

70 U.S.A. The sample (M age = 19.1 yr.) included 17 freshmen, 15 sophomores, 16 juniors, and 22 seniors.

Procedure

All participants received a packet containing a demographic survey, the Academic Practices Survey (Roig & DeTommaso, 1995), and the Santa Clara
75 Strength of Religious Faith Questionnaire (Plante & Boccaccini, 1997). Data were collected during class sessions, and participation was voluntary.

Results and Discussion

Academic dishonesty was measured using the Academic Practices Survey. The possible range of scores is
80 4 to 120. High scores indicate greater frequency of participation in academic dishonest behaviors. The mean score for the sample was 41.2 ($SD = 1.62$). Religiosity was measured using the Santa Clara Strength of Religious Faith Questionnaire on which the possible
85 range of scores is 10 to 40. High scores indicate more agreement with items that measure religiosity (i.e., stronger religiosity). The mean score on the Santa Clara Strength of Religious Faith Questionnaire was 27.5 ($SD = 1.1$).
90 An alpha level of $p_{.05}$ was used for all statistical tests. The correlation between religiosity and academic dishonesty was not statistically significant ($r_{68} = -.13$, $p > .05$). This finding is inconsistent with results reported by Storch and Storch (2001).
95 Other studies suggested sex differences in the relationship between religiosity and both academic misconduct (Storch & Storch, 2001) and illegal behaviors (Peltzer et al., 2002). In the current study, men had a mean Academic Practices Survey score of 44.8 ($SD =$
100 7.9) and a mean score on the Santa Clara Strength of Religious Faith Questionnaire of 26.4 ($SD = 1.5$). The Pearson correlation between these scores was not significant ($r_{32} = .09$, $p > .05$). Women had a mean score on the Academic Practices Survey of 37.7 ($SD = 1.9$)
105 and a mean score on the Santa Clara Strength of Religious Faith Questionnaire of 28.6 ($SD = 1.4$). The Pearson correlation between these variables was statistically significant ($r_{34} = -.36$, $p < .05$) but modest.
Storch and Storch (2001) reported that men cheated
110 more than women. Given the differential relationship between academic misconduct and religiosity in the current study, independent t tests were calculated to investigate differences in scores between men and women for religiosity and academic dishonesty. There
115 were no significant differences in religiosity scores between men and women ($t_{68} = 1.07$, $p > .05$), but men and women did significantly differ in self-reported academic dishonesty ($t_{68} = -2.27$, $p < .05$). Men reported engaging more frequently in academically dis-
120 honest behaviors than women. Taken together, these results suggest that, while scores on religiosity were similar among these men and women, religiosity did not serve as a mitigating factor for the male students

but may have for the female students. Other studies
125 may assess this possibility.

The current study contained several methodological problems (such as the small sample size and somewhat nondiverse, predominantly Christian, sample), which suggest interpretations should be cautious. Neverthe-
130 less, these results support further directions for study, particularly regarding the potentially differing roles of religiosity as a standard of behavior for men and women.

References

McCabe, D. L., & Treviño, L. K. (1997). Individual and contextual influences on academic dishonesty: A multicampus investigation. *Research in Higher Education*, 38, 379–397.

McCabe, D. L., & Treviño, L. K. (2002). Honesty and honor codes. *Academe*, 88, 37–41.

Peltzer, K., Malaka, D. W., & Phaswana, N. (2002). Sociodemographic factors, religiosity, academic performance, and substance use among first-year university students in South Africa. *Psychological Reports*, 91, 105–113.

Plante, T. G., & Boccaccini, M. (1997). The Santa Clara Strength of Religious Faith Questionnaire. *Pastoral Psychology*, 45, 375–387.

Roig, M., & DeTommaso, L. (1995). Are college cheating and plagiarism related to academic procrastination? *Psychological Reports*, 77, 691–698.

Scanlon, P. M., & Neumann, D. R. (2002). Internet plagiarism among college students. *Journal of College Student Development*, 43, 374–385.

Storch, E. A., & Storch, J. B. (2001). Organizational, nonorganizational, and intrinsic religiosity and academic dishonesty. *Psychological Reports*, 88, 548–552.

Address correspondence to: Melissa Huelsman, 3715 North Valdosta Road, Apt. 109, Valdosta, GA 31602. E-mail: HuelsmanMA @aol.com

Exercise for Article 7

Factual Questions

1. What is the hypothesis for this study?

2. How many women participated in this study?

3. On the Academic Practices Survey, do "high scores" *or* "low scores" indicate greater frequency of participation in academic dishonest behaviors?

4. On the Santa Clara Strength of Religious Faith Questionnaire, do "high scores" *or* "low scores" indicate stronger religiosity?

5. For the total sample, what is the value of the correlation coefficient for the relationship between religiosity and academic dishonesty?

6. For the men, was the Pearson r statistically significant?

Questions for Discussion

7. At various points in the article, the researchers use the term "inverse relationship." (See, for example,

lines 65–67.) What is your understanding of the meaning of this term?

8. The researchers state that they used an "alpha level of $p_{.05}$." What is your understanding of the meaning of this term? (See lines 90–91.)

9. In your opinion, does the correlation coefficient of −.13 represent a strong relationship? Explain. (See lines 91–93.)

10. The researchers report three correlation coefficients (−.13, .09, and −.36). Which one indicates the strongest relationship? (See lines 90–108.)

11. The researchers mention two "methodological problems." In your opinion, how important are these problems? Explain. (See lines 126–129.)

12. If you were to conduct a study on the same topic, what changes, if any, would you make in the research methodology?

Quality Ratings

Directions: Indicate your level of agreement with each of the following statements by circling a number from 5 for strongly agree (SA) to 1 for strongly disagree (SD). If you believe an item is not applicable to this research article, leave it blank. Be prepared to explain your ratings. When responding to criteria A and B below, keep in mind that brief titles and abstracts are conventional in published research.

A. The title of the article is appropriate.

SA   5   4   3   2   1   SD

B. The abstract provides an effective overview of the research article.

SA   5   4   3   2   1   SD

C. The introduction establishes the importance of the study.

SA   5   4   3   2   1   SD

D. The literature review establishes the context for the study.

SA   5   4   3   2   1   SD

E. The research purpose, question, or hypothesis is clearly stated.

SA   5   4   3   2   1   SD

F. The method of sampling is sound.

SA   5   4   3   2   1   SD

G. Relevant demographics (for example, age, gender, and ethnicity) are described.

SA   5   4   3   2   1   SD

H. Measurement procedures are adequate.

SA   5   4   3   2   1   SD

I. All procedures have been described in sufficient detail to permit a replication of the study.

SA   5   4   3   2   1   SD

J. The participants have been adequately protected from potential harm.

SA   5   4   3   2   1   SD

K. The results are clearly described.

SA   5   4   3   2   1   SD

L. The discussion/conclusion is appropriate.

SA   5   4   3   2   1   SD

M. Despite any flaws, the report is worthy of publication.

SA   5   4   3   2   1   SD

Article 8

The Significance of Language and Cultural Education on Secondary Achievement: A Survey of Chinese-American and Korean-American Students

STEVEN K. LEE
California State University, Dominguez Hills

ABSTRACT. This study attempted to answer the question: What is the significance of language and cultural orientation on academic achievement? This study examined the relationship between the students' level of interest in maintaining their heritage language and culture and their achievement in school. The subjects for this study were 105 U.S.-born, Chinese-American and Korean-American students attending public high schools in Southern California. The study found that those who valued the acculturation process (adapting to the mainstream culture while preserving their language and culture) had superior academic achievement levels to those who were most interested in the assimilation process and who adopted the values and lifestyles of the dominant culture. In light of the implementation of the "English Only" policy in California's public schools, this study has important implications in public education—that curriculum and instruction should focus on helping language and cultural minority students to develop and maintain their heritage while exposing them to new ideas.

From *Bilingual Research Journal*, *26*, 213–224. Copyright © 2002 by National Association for Bilingual Education. Reprinted with permission.

There is a prevalent stereotype in the American society that Asian-American students are high achievers; hence, the term "model minority" is often used in reference to Asian-Americans. Such use emerged during
5 the 1960s in the midst of the civil rights movement (Osajima, 1988; Sue & Kitano, 1973). It was coined as a hegemonic device, attempting to divert attention away from the racial and ethnic tension of the period and laud the economic success of Asian-Americans
10 outside of the movement. Thus, the term was not really used to recognize the important contribution of Asian-Americans to American society. On the contrary, the model minority stereotype was propagated by the media to subdue growing demands from the African-
15 American and other minority groups for equal rights. The media often cited Asian-Americans as an example of a model group that achieved educational and social

prosperity in the absence of government assistance or intervention in schools and in employment, and who
20 were able to seek educational and employment opportunities—thereby delegitimizing the issue of racial inequality and suppressing public outcry for rectification and improvements in educational and social systems of the United States.
25 According to many scholars (e.g., Caplan, Choy, & Whitmore, 1991; Hsu, 1971; Kitano, 1969; Mordkowitz & Ginsberg, 1987; Sung, 1987) Asian-Americans are more successful in school because their culture emphasizes the value of education. In addition, the
30 family-oriented nature of Asian cultures, in which academic success is equated with upholding the family honor, is seen as facilitating conditions for educational success. Suzuki (1980), one of the first to examine educational achievement from a historical cultural per-
35 spective, posited that academic success of Asian-Americans was a reaction to social stratification that existed in the United States: Exclusion of Asian-Americans from social participation forced parents to push for education for their children to overcome the
40 social and political barriers. More recent studies (e.g., Hirschman & Wong, 1986; Mark & Chih, 1982; Sue & Okazaki, 1990) seem to support Suzuki's theory that perception of education as a key to social mobility is a contributing factor in academic achievement of Asian-
45 Americans. Stacey Lee (1996) found that among the different Asian-American student groups, the group that held the highest regard for education as the most essential for social mobility had superior academic achievement than those groups who did not see school
50 as the key to upward mobility in the society. Whereas the former group felt obligated to do their best in school, the latter group placed little interest in education.
55 In explaining the difference in academic achievement among minority groups, Ogbu (1989) distinguished between voluntary and involuntary minorities. According to this theory, voluntary immigrants do bet-

ter in school because they accept the host culture. This
theory also posits that voluntary immigrants believe
60   that their future is determined by their ability to overcome social and economic hurdles through academic
success. Studies by Mark and Chih (1982) and Lee
(1996) seem to support this theory: They found that
parents of Asian-American students often reminded
65   their children to excel in school to overcome racial
prejudice and discrimination. In other words, Asian-
Americans perceived education as the most important
form of empowerment for social mobility. Considering
that a relatively high percentage (5.3%) of Asian-
70   Americans enter colleges and universities, Asian-
American parents seem to have a great influence on
their children's educational interests. Involuntary immigrants are thought to reject the dominant culture
because they perceive the mainstream culture to be a
75   threat to their own identity. Thus, according to this
theory, involuntary immigrants may regard school success as giving up their culture at the expense of assimi-
lating to the dominant culture with which school is
associated.

80   Although it is true that Asian-Americans are generally more successful in education than other minority
groups—measured in terms of SAT scores and the percentage of Asian-Americans who have completed or
are currently enrolled in higher education—there is
85   growing evidence to suggest that not all Asian-
American students are doing well in school. Rumbaut
and Ima (1988) found that among the Southeast Asian
students, the Khmer and the Lao had a grade point average (GPA) below that of the majority (white) stu-
90   dents, whereas the GPA of the Vietnamese and Chi-
nese-Vietnamese students was well above the average
of the majority students. More recent studies (e.g.,
Trueba, Cheng, & Ima, 1993) seem to point in the direction that there is a need to clarify conceptual find-
95   ings by examining intra-group differences within the
Asian-American population. That is, academic
achievement of Asian-Americans can no longer be predicted based simply on the notion that all Asian-
Americans share a common culture. The implicit mes-
100 sage is that the socio- and psycho-cultural dynamics of
Asian-American students are as complex as any other
ethnic group's. As such, studies related to educational
achievement of Asian-American students must go beyond the rudimentary task of developing a conceptual
105 framework based on collective descriptions.

In explaining inter-group differences in academic
achievement, Ogbu (1989) classifies all Asian-
Americans as belonging to one group. That is, according to Ogbu's framework, fifth-generation Asian-
110 Americans are no different from recent immigrants—
both belong to the voluntary immigrant group. Although this framework provides an interesting and di-
chotomous view of the relationship between culture
and academic achievement, it fails to consider intra-
115 group and individual differences. That is, why are

some groups within the Asian-American population,
presumably who came to the United States voluntarily
to seek improved livelihood, doing better than others?
And why do some Asian-American students excel
120 while others barely make it through high school?

Caudill and De Vox (1956) were among the first to
examine educational achievement of Asian-Americans
from a cultural perspective. Based on their research on
Japanese-Americans, they reported that Japanese-
125 Americans are more successful because their cultural
characteristics are those highly regarded by mainstream
society. Kitano (1969) and Caplan, Choy, and Whitmore (1991) concluded that Asian-Americans are more
successful in the schools because of compatibility of
130 their culture with middle-class American culture. Although these postulations provide interesting perspectives, they seem to reinforce the "model minority"
stereotype by assuming that all Asian-Americans share
similar cultural backgrounds. For example, what does
135 Hmong culture have in common with Korean or Japanese culture? Or, do middle-class Americans really
hold high regard for Cambodian culture? Studies based
on the stereotypical treatment of Asian-Americans as a
homogeneous group ignore the importance of adaptive
140 strategies and other psychological and social variables
that may influence the learning experiences of Asian-
American students.

Gibson (1988) observed that among Punjabi students, there was a positive correlation between their
145 arrival in the United States and school success: The
longer the students have been in the United States, the
better their performance. Gibson's studies clearly suggest that appropriate behavior cannot be the most important determinant factor of academic achievement.
150 That is, assimilation is more likely for those students
who have been exposed longer to the dominant culture
than for those who have recently arrived in the United
States, so that there may be more cultural similarities
between mainstream students and those students who
155 have been in the United States longer than with the
newcomers. Considering this, theories based on behavior and cultural compatibility do not adequately explain
the educational achievement of Asian-American students. For example, if we were to accept the notion that
160 Asian-American students do better in school than other
minority students because there is "cultural match"
with the mainstream culture, it predicates not only that
Asian-American students share the same culture, but
also that there is no heuristic process within the Asian
165 and Asian-American culture.

The purpose of this study was to examine the significance of language and cultural identity on academic
achievement of Chinese-American and Korean-
American students in secondary schools. This study
170 was motivated by the emergence of studies that indicate that there is variation in academic achievement
among Asian-American students. This study attempted
to answer the question: Is there a correlation between

the students' level of interest in and awareness of cultural heritage and the level of academic achievement? This study investigated the possibility that educational achievement may be related to the students' involvement, interest, and awareness of their ancestral culture.

Method

Subjects

Subjects for this study were 105 male and female students of Chinese ($n = 57$) and Korean ($n = 48$) heritage enrolled in two high schools in an upper-middle-class community of Orange County, California. All the subjects, between the ages of 15 and 17, were enrolled in regular classes. Both schools offered courses in Chinese and Korean as foreign language classes. The two groups represented the largest minority group (approximately 20%) in the community. All subjects were born in the United States.

Instrument

The questionnaire, consisting of 10 closed-ended questions, was pretested on 23 high school students for clarification and appropriateness of the questions contained in the survey. The randomly selected students each received a questionnaire to be completed prior to beginning their class. Questions surveyed the subjects' background, interest, awareness, and views on cultural identity. They included:

1. Have you attended a Chinese or Korean language/culture school for more than one year while you were in middle or high school?
2. Do you know much about the history/culture of China or Korea?
3. Have you studied Chinese or Korean for more than one year at your high school?
4. Do you regularly attend (at least once a month) Chinese- or Korean-related cultural events/activities, including religious functions?
5. Do you speak Chinese or Korean in the home and/or with relatives/friends?
6. Are you interested in learning more about your cultural heritage?
7. Do you feel it is important for you to maintain your cultural identity?
8. Do you feel your culture/heritage contributes to the American culture/heritage?
9. Do you feel there should be diverse cultures represented in the United States?
10. Do you feel people should have a greater interest in their own ethnic culture/heritage than in the mainstream culture?

In addition to the questionnaire, Asian-American students were observed and interviewed during lunchtime for a total of approximately 20 hours.

Procedures

A research assistant distributed and collected the questionnaires. The research assistant also provided instructions prior to administering the questionnaire. The investigator personally observed and interviewed the students. Interviews were recorded on a cassette tape with the subjects' permission.

Results

Responding "yes" to the questions on the survey indicated orientation toward acculturation, an additive process of adapting to the mainstream culture while preserving the heritage culture. Conversely, responding "no" on the survey suggested orientation toward assimilation, toward adopting the values, behaviors, beliefs, and lifestyles of the dominant culture. The subjects' GPAs in relation to the number of affirmative responses were used to establish a correlation.

Although there was a wide range, 0 to 10, the majority of the subjects (about two-thirds) responded affirmatively to six to nine questions. The grade point average (GPA) ranged from 2.98 to 3.81 with a mean of 3.54. With the exception of two subjects who responded affirmatively to three questions, and who had a GPA of 2.98, there was a pattern in the relationship between the number of affirmative responses and the subjects' GPA; the subjects' GPA increased as the number of affirmative responses increased. Using the Pearson product-moment correlation coefficient (r) to find the strength of the relationship at the critical value of .05, 96 degrees of freedom (df), the correlation (r) was .94. Thus, the statistical analysis indicated that there was a strong correlation between the students' GPAs and the extent to which the subjects showed an interest in their cultural heritage. The level of significance for a two-tailed test at this level for a sample size of 105 is .201. Hence, the results revealed that students who had a greater awareness for and interest in developing biculturalism had superior grade point averages than their counterparts who had less interest in their heritage. The correlation was very significant, statistically.

Table 1

GPA in Relation to Number of Affirmative Responses

Subjects ($n = 105$)	No. of "Yes" Responses	GPA ($M = 3.54$)
2	0	3.17
2	3	2.98
6	4	3.19
10	5	3.25
17	6	3.27
23	7	3.58
19	8	3.76
17	9	3.78
9	10	3.81

It is interesting to note that only 38% indicated that they knew much about the history/culture of China or Korea. This is in sharp contrast to the 86% who responded that they were interested in learning more about their cultural heritage. This strongly suggests that

Asian-American students were not receiving an adequate amount of exposure to Asian history and culture in and outside the home. Also, while 81% of the subjects indicated that they have attended a Chinese or Korean language/culture school for at least a year, only 25% responded that they have studied Chinese or Korean at a high school. Thus, it seems most Chinese-American and Korean-American students are receiving educational language and cultural lessons at community-based private schools rather than at the public high schools. Considering the fact that both schools offered instructions in Chinese and Korean, the disparity between the two seems to suggest that the public schools may not be offering the kinds of instruction and experience students expect from the language classes.

Also worth noting is the great disparity between the percentage of subjects who indicated the importance of maintaining cultural identity (90%) and the percentage who thought their heritage contributed to American culture (41%). It seems the majority of the subjects perceived cultural heritage to be more important for personal identification than for actual contribution to United States culture. When subjects were asked this question during interviews, many thought that most Americans of different racial, ethnic, and/or cultural backgrounds did not recognize Chinese or Korean culture as part of U.S. culture. Therefore, it appears that for many, cultural contribution is based on their perception of the level of acceptance by other Americans. This was supported by 93% of the respondents, who indicated that cultural diversity should exist in the United States (see Table 2).

Table 2
Percentage of Affirmative Responses

Question	Percentage
1. Attended Chinese or Korean community school	81%
2. Knowledge about Chinese or Korean history/culture	38%
3. Studied Chinese or Korean at high school	25%
4. Attended Chinese- or Korean-related cultural activity	90%
5. Speak Chinese or Korean at home/with relatives/friends	78%
6. Interested in learning more about cultural heritage	86%
7. Important to maintain cultural identity	90%
8. Cultural heritage contributes to American culture	41%
9. Cultural diversity should exist in the United States	93%
10. Greater interest for own culture than mainstream culture	60%

Discussion

As one of the fastest growing minority groups in the United States, Asian-Americans are expected to account for 10% of the total population of the United States by 2040 (González, 1990). In California, Asian-American students already outnumber African-American students. Yet the model minority stereotype seems to have desensitized the need for inclusion of Asian-Americans on discussions of race and education; Asian-Americans are often treated as outsiders needing no special consideration. The results of this study seem to suggest that there are indeed intra-group and individual differences in academic achievement within the Chinese-American and Korean-American student populations. The study found that there was a strong correlation between the students' cultural interest/identity and their academic achievement.

Suzuki (1980) stated that Asian-American students receive favorable evaluations from their teachers due to compatibility between the Asian culture and the teachers' expectations. That is, certain Asian cultural characteristics, such as obedience, conformity, and respect for authority, were viewed favorably by teachers. In fact, Suzuki claimed that teachers may assign good grades to Asian-American students based on behavior rather than on academic performance. Both Goldstein (1985) and Lee (1996) reported that teachers' evaluation of Asian-American students was often based on observable characteristics and not on actual academic achievement. According to E. Lee and M. Lee (1980), acculturation vis-à-vis assimilation plays an important factor in academic achievement of Asian-American students because it allows them to exhibit those behaviors favored by teachers. Although these studies are helpful in understanding how behavior can influence teachers' assessment of students, they seem to discredit the achievement of Asian-American students by generating yet another overly simplified proposition—that behavior is what sets Asian-American students apart from other students. These findings do not substantiate (a) why some Asian-Americans fail while other Asian-Americans are successful, (b) why Asian-Americans generally score higher than other minority students on standardized tests in which observable behavior has no influence on the outcome, and (c) why grades based on behavior are Asian-American specific.

The results of this study have revealed that there are indeed intra-group differences among U.S.-born Chinese-American and Korean-American students. Those students who had had greater experience and interest in developing bilingualism and biculturalism enjoyed higher academic achievement than those who were less interested in their cultural heritage. Thus, this study not only invalidated the deeply rooted stereotype that Asian-Americans belong to a group that adheres to common cultural values and practices, but also that personal interest in bilingualism and biculturalism is related to academic achievement. The results revealed a positive correlation between the students' language and cultural identity and their academic achievement.

This study was an attempt to examine educational achievement of Chinese-Americans and Korean-

360 Americans from an intra-cultural perspective. That is, rather than attempting to devise an overly simplified concept based on collective treatment of Asian-Americans as a group, this study examined the issue of educational attainment from a psychocultural perspec-
365 tive of Chinese-Americans and Korean-Americans as individuals. This study has found that among Chinese-American and Korean-American students, the cultural interests and experiences of Asian-American students vary, and that these differences may influence their
370 academic performance. Thus, the implication from this study is that the educational community must recognize the significant contribution of education programs that promote heritage, language, and culture for language- and cultural-minority students.

There is no doubt that inclusion of Asian and
375 Asian-American experiences, as well as the recognition of the importance of their presence in schools, will empower Asian-American students to participate in the learning process. It is hypothesized that those students
380 who had greater interest in their language and cultural identity had superior academic achievement than their counterparts because they had greater motivation for a diversified learning experience and interest. That is, these students had superior cognitive, meta-cognitive,
385 and socioaffective strategies to help them do better in school. Hence, rather than emulating their peers to conform to the norm of the dominant culture (cultural compensatory strategy), these students were interested in empowering themselves by developing awareness
390 and pride in their heritage while undergoing personal experiences in the mainstream culture (cultural enrichment strategy). Thus, in this dichotomy, students who utilize the cultural enrichment strategy draw upon the positive qualities of at least two cultures from
395 which to adapt to the learning needs of the classroom. On the contrary, students applying the cultural compensatory strategy are at a disadvantaged position because their primary interest is to assimilate to the mainstream culture at the expense of losing their heritage.
400 Thus, cultural compensatory strategy tends to devalue one's ancestral culture while placing a high priority on adopting the mainstream culture.

As diversity within the Asian-American community increases, so is the likelihood that students will come to
405 school with varying interests in their cultural heritage. In 1992, approximately 41% of Asian-Americans were foreign born (Wong, 1992). By the year 2000, this percentage is projected to increase to about 50%. The increasing presence of Asian-American students in our
410 schools will inevitably demand that institutions of learning prepare themselves to be able to provide facilitative instruction in which bilingualism and biculturalism are encouraged and promoted for all students, including Asian-American students. This study has
415 shown that the issue of language and culture in academic achievement is more than a collective interpretation of similarities and differences between two cul-

tures: It is about accepting and supporting the students'
420 language and culture while allowing them the opportunity to experience diversity in thinking and practice. To this end, bilingual education programs in which the students' first language and culture are valued, respected, and encouraged—while students are exposed to a new language and culture—are invaluable to stu-
425 dents' eventual success in school.

References

Caplan, N., Choy, M. H., & Whitmore, J. K. (1991). *Children of the boat people: A study of educational success.* Ann Arbor, MI: University of Michigan Press.

Caudill, W., & De Vox, G. (1956). Achievement, culture and personality: The case of the Japanese Americans. *American Anthropologist, 58,* 1102–1127.

Gibson, M. (1988). *Accommodation without assimilation: Sikh immigrants in an American high school.* Ithaca, NY: Cornell University Press.

Goldstein, B. (1985). *Schooling for cultural transitions: Hmong girls and boys in American high schools.* Unpublished doctoral dissertation, University of Wisconsin, Madison.

González, R. (1990). When minority becomes majority: The challenging face of English classrooms. *English Journal, 79*(1), 16–23.

Hirschman, C., & Wong, M. G. (1986). The extraordinary educational attainment of Asian Americans: A search for historical evidence and explanations. *Social Forces, 65*(1), 1–27.

Hsu, F. L. K. (1971). *The challenge of the American dream: The Chinese in the United States.* Belmont, CA: Wadsworth.

Kitano, H. H. L. (1969). *Japanese Americans: The evolution of a subculture.* Englewood Cliffs, NJ: Prentice-Hall.

Lee, E., & Lee, M. (1980). *A study of classroom behaviors of Chinese American children and immigrant Chinese children in contrast to those of Black American children and White American children in an urban head start program.* Unpublished doctoral dissertation, University of San Francisco.

Lee, S. J. (1996). *Unraveling the model minority stereotype.* New York, NY: Teachers College Press.

Mark, D. M. L., & Chih, G. (1982). *A place called America.* Dubuque, IA: Kendall Hunt.

Mordkowitz, E. R., & Ginsberg, H. P. (1987). Early academic socialization of successful Asian-American college students. *Quarterly Newsletter of the Laboratory of Comparative Human Cognition, 9,* 85–91.

Ogbu, J. U. (1989). The individual in collective adaptation: A framework for focusing on academic underperformance and dropping out among involuntary minorities. In L. Weis, E. Farrar, & H. G. Petrie (Eds.), *Dropouts from school: Issues, dilemmas, and solutions* (pp. 181–204). Albany: State University of New York Press.

Osajima, K. (1988). Asian Americans as the model minority: An analysis of the popular press image in the 1960s and 1980s. In G. Y. Okihiro, S. Hune, A. A. Hansen, & J. M. Liu (Eds.), *Reflections on shattered windows: Promises and prospects for Asian American studies* (pp. 165–174). Pullman: Washington State University Press.

Rumbaut, R. G., & Ima, K. (1988). *The adaptation of Southwest Asian refugee youth: A comparative study.* Washington, DC: U.S. Office of Refugee Settlement.

Sue, S., & Kitano, H. H. L. (1973). Stereotypes as a measure of success. *Journal of Social Issues, 29*(2), 83–98.

Sue, S., & Okazaki, S. (1990). Asian-American educational achievements: A phenomenon in search of an explanation. *American Psychologist, 45*(8), 913–920.

Sung, B. L. (1987). *The adjustment experience of Chinese immigrant children in New York City.* New York: Center for Migration Studies.

Suzuki, R. H. (1980). Education and the socialization of Asian Americans: A revisionist analysis of the "model minority" thesis. In R. Endo, S. Sue, & N. N. Wagner (Eds.), *Asian-Americans: Social and psychological perspectives, Vol. 2* (pp. 155–175). Ben Lomond, CA: Science and Behavior Books.

Trueba, H. T., & Ima, K. (1993). *Myth or reality: Adaptive strategies of Asian Americans in California.* Washington, DC: The Farmer Press.

Wong, G. (1992). *California State University Asian Language BCLAD Consortium proposal.* Long Beach, CA: California State University Asian Language BCLAD Consortium.

Exercise for Article 8

Factual Questions

1. According to the literature review, Ogbu classifies Asian-Americans as belonging to how many groups?

2. How many of the subjects in this study were of Korean ancestry?

3. Responding "yes" to the questions on the survey indicated orientation toward
   A. acculturation.   B. assimilation.

4. In this report, what is the symbol for correlation?

5. What is the value of the correlation coefficient for the relationship between GPA and affirmative responses to the survey?

6. What was the GPA of the nine subjects who responded "yes" to all 10 survey questions?

7. Among all subjects, what percentage responded in the affirmative to studying Chinese or Korean at high school?

Questions for Discussion

8. The researcher states: "In addition to the questionnaire, Asian-American students were observed and interviewed during lunchtime for a total of approximately 20 hours." In your opinion, is this an important part of the study? Explain. (See lines 220–222.)

9. Would you characterize the correlation coefficient reported in this study as being "strong"? Explain. (See lines 247–261.)

10. In your opinion, does the correlation coefficient of .94 lend support to the possibility that acculturation *causes* higher achievement as indicated by students' GPAs? Does it indicate *proof of causation*? Explain.

11. In your opinion, to what extent do you think the results of this study support this implication stated by the researcher: "…the educational community must recognize the significant contribution of education programs that promote heritage, language, and culture for language- and cultural-minority students"? (See lines 371–374.)

Quality Ratings

Directions: Indicate your level of agreement with each of the following statements by circling a number from 5 for strongly agree (SA) to 1 for strongly disagree (SD). If you believe an item is not applicable to this research article, leave it blank. Be prepared to explain your ratings. When responding to criteria A and B below, keep in mind that brief titles and abstracts are conventional in published research.

A. The title of the article is appropriate.

   SA   5   4   3   2   1   SD

B. The abstract provides an effective overview of the research article.

   SA   5   4   3   2   1   SD

C. The introduction establishes the importance of the study.

   SA   5   4   3   2   1   SD

D. The literature review establishes the context for the study.

   SA   5   4   3   2   1   SD

E. The research purpose, question, or hypothesis is clearly stated.

   SA   5   4   3   2   1   SD

F. The method of sampling is sound.

   SA   5   4   3   2   1   SD

G. Relevant demographics (for example, age, gender, and ethnicity) are described.

   SA   5   4   3   2   1   SD

H. Measurement procedures are adequate.

   SA   5   4   3   2   1   SD

I. All procedures have been described in sufficient detail to permit a replication of the study.

   SA   5   4   3   2   1   SD

J. The participants have been adequately protected from potential harm.

   SA   5   4   3   2   1   SD

K. The results are clearly described.

   SA   5   4   3   2   1   SD

L. The discussion/conclusion is appropriate.

   SA   5   4   3   2   1   SD

M. Despite any flaws, the report is worthy of publication.

   SA   5   4   3   2   1   SD

Article 9

Test–Retest Reliability of the Self-Assessed Physical Activity Checklist

TRENT D. BROWN
RMIT University

BERNIE V. HOLLAND
RMIT University

SUMMARY. To estimate the test–retest reliability of a modified version of the Self-assessed Physical Activity Checklist, two administrations separated by five days were conducted for 52 boys and 51 girls in grade 6 in Australia. Intraclass correlation coefficients were calculated to assess the reliability. Similar test–retest reliabilities were found between boys and girls for light, moderate, and total physical activity, with the largest difference for vigorous physical activity (.44 vs. .12). The results suggest that the checklist is a more appropriate measure of boys' physical and sedentary activity, as boys reported higher reliability coefficients on all categories except for light physical activity and TV/video watching.

From *Perceptual and Motor Skills*, 99, 1099–1102. Copyright © 2004 by Perceptual and Motor Skills. Reprinted with permission.

Many physical activity questionnaires for children have been developed. Of those readily available, recall periods vary from one day to one year. Among these, one of the most commonly used physical activity sur-
5 veys is the Self-assessed Physical Activity Checklist (5, 11). This checklist is a 24-hr. recall scale which measures type, frequency, and intensity of physical and sedentary activity, is inexpensive, easy to administer, and has been validated (9). Furthermore, the scale uses
10 a segmented day for recall, so children recall physical activity before school, during school and after school, as this method is more accurate than reporting activity for the whole day (2). Despite the wide use of children's self-report surveys, little attention has been paid
15 to their test–retest reliabilities and in particular of the checklist (10).

The accuracy of self-report has been questioned, especially as recall periods lengthen, primarily because children are limited in their accurate recall of physical
20 activity (1). To overcome this limitation of memory, the use of the previous day has been suggested (4). In a recent review of such scales (8), only five of the 17 self-report scales examined used 24-hr. or previous-day recall and test–retest periods varied from 3 hr. to 4 wk.
25 Cale (4) reported a test–retest reliability coefficient over 4 wk. of .62 using a one-day recall administered for two weekdays and two weekend days by a sample of 12 children. In another study (12), for the test–retest

reliability of the Previous Day Physical Activity Re-
30 call, after 1 hr. the correlation was .98. In each study, coefficients were available for the overall sample, not for boys and girls separately.

Only a small number of studies could be located with sex-specific values of validation and reliability of
35 self-report scales by children and adolescents (3, 6) so the present purpose was to estimate the test–retest r of the Self-assessed Physical Activity Checklist protocol. Also, aims were to provide sex-specific reliability coefficients for light, moderate, vigorous, and total physical
40 activity and to examine the stability of two common sedentary activities: television viewing and computer/video game use.

Method

A total of 103 volunteers (52 boys and 51 girls) from five different grade 6 classes in physical educa-
45 tion from primary schools within the city of Melbourne were recruited. The M ± SD for subjects' ages were 11.7 ± .05 yr. for all 103; 11.8 ± 0.5 yr. for boys and 11.7 ± 0.5 yr. for girls. The RMIT University Human Research and Ethics Committee and Victorian Depart-
50 ment of Education and Training approved the study. Prior to participation, written approved consent was obtained from participants' parents or guardians.

A modified version of the Self-assessed Physical Activity Checklist was used to assess light, moderate,
55 vigorous, and total physical activity and the time engaged in sedentary activities of television viewing and computer use. The checklist was modified to include activities more common to the Australian lifestyle and context: cricket, Australian rules football and netball
60 replaced activities of ice hockey and American football. This provided a checklist of 24 physical activities to choose from, with three blank sections titled "other activities" so each participant could add an activity not on the checklist. Television viewing and computer use
65 were also listed and reported in hours and minutes engaged in each activity. The original checklist is a modified version of the Yesterday Activity Checklist (7) and is reliable and valid. Subjects completed the modified checklist twice with a minimum of five days between
70 administrations in the presence of the first author, who read the instructions. Participants were reminded to

52

Table 1

Means and Standard Deviations for Test and Retest and Intraclass Coefficients for Physical and Sedentary Activity

Measure	Boys (*n* = 52)					Girls (*n* = 51)				
	Test		Retest			Test		Retest		
	M	*SD*	*M*	*SD*	*r*	*M*	*SD*	*M*	*SD*	*r*
Physical activity (min./day)										
Light	78.4	58.7	57.4	44.6	.43	46.7	44.3	40.6	38.9	.47
Moderate	37.6	41.7	17.7	25.3	.36	20.7	28.4	25.3	25.0	.27
Vigorous	31.2	27.9	31.3	32.6	.44	50.7	52.2	30.6	43.8	.12
Total	147.1	71.1	106.4	47.0	.20	118.2	73.3	96.5	59.4	.19
Sedentary activity (min./day)										
TV/Video	105.5	88.7	73.1	60.8	.20	76.7	62.2	66.8	64.7	.38
Computer use	63.6	83.3	30.2	52.2	.40	30.3	46.9	24.2	46.9	.35
Total	169.1	125.0	103.3	82.6	.36	107.0	89.5	90.9	79.7	.34

recall physical or sedentary activity that lasted longer than 5 min.

Time in minutes spent performing each physical and sedentary activity were summed to provide a measure of total minutes in light, moderate, and vigorous physical activity. Activities have previously been classified as light, moderate, vigorous, and sedentary (5). Another category, total physical activity, was created by summing time in light, moderate, and vigorous activities. Minutes spent watching TV/video and playing video/computer games were summed for total sedentary activity. After an exploratory analysis, because data were skewed, a square root-transformation was used. The intraclass correlation coefficients were calculated based on a two-way mixed-effect analysis of variance.

Results and Discussion

Table 1 shows the means, standard deviations, and test–retest reliabilities for light, moderate, vigorous, and total physical activity, TV/video watching, playing computer/video games, and total sedentary activity. Mean times spent in physical and sedentary activities were greater for boys than for girls in all categories at both test times except for vigorous activity during the test and moderate activity during the retest. These results for physical activity are consistent with prior reports (5).

As shown in Table 1, the reliability coefficients for all categories varied from .12 to .47. Values were somewhat higher for boys than for girls, as in other studies of sex differences at test–retest of physical activity (6). Test–retest reliabilities were lower than previously reported for a number of reasons. Perhaps children cannot accurately recall their physical activity. For example, girls may report their physical activity behavior more accurately than boys (3); however, our results contradict this. Perhaps the difference then reflects types of activities participants remember. Second, improved reliability may be gained through the use of a 7-day as opposed to a 5-day test–retest format. As children's physical activity behavior is highly variable from day to day, recall error may be reduced by

using the same day during the retest as on the first day (8).

As no previous study has examined the test–retest scores of this checklist, the moderate reliabilities of light physical activity for both boys and girls and vigorous physical activity for boys are useful.

References

1. Baranowski, T. (1988). Validity and reliability of self-report measures of physical activity: An information-processing perspective. *Research Quarterly for Exercise and Sport, 59*, 314–327.
2. Baranowski, T., Dworkin, R. J., Cieslik, C. J., Hooks, P., Clearman, D. R., Ray, L., Dunn, J. K., & Nader, P. R. (1984). Reliability and validity of self-report of aerobic activity: Family health project. *Research Quarterly, 55*, 309–317.
3. Booth, M. L., Okely, A. D., Chey, T., & Bauman, A. (2002). The reliability and validity of the adolescent physical activity recall questionnaire. *Medicine and Science in Sports and Exercise, 34*, 1986–1995.
4. Cale, L. (1994). Self-report measures of children's physical activity: Recommendations for future development and a new alternative measure. *Health Education Journal, 53*, 439–453.
5. Myers, L., Strikmiller, P. K., Webber, L. S., & Berenson, G. S. (1996). Physical and sedentary activity in school children grades 5–8: The Bogalusa Heart Study. *Medicine and Science in Sports and Exercise, 28*, 852–859.
6. Sallis, J. F., Buono, M. J., Roby, J. J., Micale, F. G., & Nelson, J. A. (1993). Seven-day recall and other physical activity self-reports in children and adolescents. *Medicine and Science in Sports and Exercise, 25*, 99–108.
7. Sallis, J. F., Condon, S. A., Goggin, K. J., Roby, J. J., Kolody, B., & Alcaraz, J. E. (1993). The development of self-administered physical activity surveys for 4th grade students. *Research Quarterly for Exercise and Sport, 64*, 25–31.
8. Sallis, J. F. & Saelens, B. E. (2000). Assessment of physical activity by self-report: Status, limitations, and future directions. *Research Quarterly for Exercise and Sport, 71*, 1–14.
9. Sallis, J. F., Strikmiller, P. K., Harsha, D. W., Feldman, H. A., Ehlinger, S., Stone, E. J., Williston, J., & Woods, S. (1996). Validation of interviewer- and self-administered physical activity checklists for fifth grade students. *Medicine and Science in Sports and Exercise, 28*, 840–851.
10. Sirard, J. R., & Pate, R. R. (2001). Physical activity assessment in children and adolescents. *Sports Medicine, 31*, 439–454.
11. Treuth, M. S., Sherwood, N. E., Butte, N. F., McClanahan, B., Obarzanek, E., Zhou, A., Ayers, C., Adolph, A. L., Jordan, J., Jacobs, D. R., Jr., & Rochon, J. (2003). Validity and reliability of activity measures in African-American girls for GEMS. *Medicine and Science in Sports and Exercise, 35*, 532–539.
12. Weston, A. T, Petosa, R., & Pate, R. R. (1997). Validation of an instrument for measurement of physical activity in youth. *Medicine and Science in Sports and Exercise, 29*, 138–143.

Address correspondence to: Dr. Trent D. Brown, Monash University, Faculty of Education, Northways Road, Churchill, Victoria, Australia 3842. E-mail: trent.brown@education.monash.edu.au

Exercise for Article 9

Factual Questions

1. How many girls were included in this study?

2. What was the mean age for the boys in this study?

3. What was the mean number of minutes girls reported vigorous activity on the test? What was the mean number of minutes they reported vigorous activity on the retest?

4. What was the value of the test–retest correlation coefficient for vigorous activity reported by girls?

5. For girls, which physical activity was measured the most reliably? What is the value of the test–retest reliability coefficient (r) of this activity?

6. From test to retest, was the average number of minutes boys reported engaging in vigorous physical activities similar?

Questions for Discussion

7. The scale in this study asks children to recall activities separately during which three segments of a 24-hour day? In your opinion, is this important to know? (See lines 9–13.)

8. The researchers state that they used "volunteers." Is this important to know? Explain. (See line 43.)

9. The checklist was modified to include activities common to the Australian lifestyle. In your opinion, does this restrict the generalizability of the results to Americans? Explain. (See lines 57–61.)

10. The purpose of the checklist is to measure physical activity. Yet, items were included on sedentary activities. In your opinion, does the inclusion of items on sedentary activities provide important information? Explain. (See lines 53–57.)

11. The researchers state that the data were "skewed." What is your understanding of the meaning of this term? (See lines 83–84.)

12. Based on your knowledge of correlation coefficients and their application in assessing reliability, does the checklist appear to be reliable? Explain.

13. The researchers speculate that the reliabilities might have been higher if a 7-day instead of a 5-day test–retest format had been used (i.e., test twice on the same day of the week; for instance, test on one Friday and retest on the next Friday). Do you agree? Explain. (See lines 108–110.)

Quality Ratings

Directions: Indicate your level of agreement with each of the following statements by circling a number from 5 for strongly agree (SA) to 1 for strongly disagree (SD). If you believe an item is not applicable to this research article, leave it blank. Be prepared to explain your ratings. When responding to criteria A and B below, keep in mind that brief titles and abstracts are conventional in published research.

A. The title of the article is appropriate.

SA 5 4 3 2 1 SD

B. The abstract provides an effective overview of the research article.

SA 5 4 3 2 1 SD

C. The introduction establishes the importance of the study.

SA 5 4 3 2 1 SD

D. The literature review establishes the context for the study.

SA 5 4 3 2 1 SD

E. The research purpose, question, or hypothesis is clearly stated.

SA 5 4 3 2 1 SD

F. The method of sampling is sound.

SA 5 4 3 2 1 SD

G. Relevant demographics (for example, age, gender, and ethnicity) are described.

SA 5 4 3 2 1 SD

H. Measurement procedures are adequate.

SA 5 4 3 2 1 SD

I. All procedures have been described in sufficient detail to permit a replication of the study.

SA 5 4 3 2 1 SD

J. The participants have been adequately protected from potential harm.

SA 5 4 3 2 1 SD

K. The results are clearly described.

SA 5 4 3 2 1 SD

L. The discussion/conclusion is appropriate.

SA 5 4 3 2 1 SD

M. Despite any flaws, the report is worthy of publication.

SA 5 4 3 2 1 SD

Article 10

The Effects of Computer-Assisted Instruction on First-Grade Students' Vocabulary Development

CHARLOTTE BOLING
The University of West Florida

SARAH H. MARTIN
Eastern Kentucky University

MICHAEL A. MARTIN
Eastern Kentucky University

ABSTRACT. The purpose of the present study was to determine the effect of computer-assisted instruction on first-grade students' vocabulary development. Students participating in this study were randomly divided into experimental and control groups. The students in both groups were involved in DEAR (Drop Everything And Read) as part of their instruction in a balanced literacy program. During their normal DEAR time, the control group used a book and tape to explore stories. The experimental group explored stories using computerized storyboards. The results of the study show a significant difference for both groups on pre- and posttests. However, the mean difference demonstrates a much larger gain for students in the experimental group.

From *Reading Improvement*, 39, 79–88. Copyright © 2002 by Project Innovation, Inc. Reprinted with permission.

What can teachers do to ensure that the children they teach will develop into successful readers? This is a question that has puzzled the educational community for years. Most educators have their individual opinion as to how the reading process occurs. Morrow and Tracey (1997) state that some educators believe in a behaviorist approach, where reading is taught in a skills-based environment through a prescribed curriculum. Others believe in a more constructivist approach, where a relationship between the context and child must be developed where students build knowledge and gain skills through immersion in a literature-rich environment (Czubaj, 1997; Daniels & Zemelman, 1999). Whatever one believes, these approaches to reading instruction—behaviorist or constructivist—continue to be the subject of debates in our classrooms and communities.

The core beliefs that teachers possess have a great impact on students learning to read. Teachers' personal beliefs concerning the processes involved in learning to read greatly influence their instructional choices. A teacher's beliefs are based on his or her personal knowledge, experiences with instructional techniques, and the way students respond to the instructional strategies in classroom situations (Dillon, 2000; How-ard, McGee, Purcell, & Schwartz, 2000; Kinzer & Leu, 1999). Therefore, while teachers maintain their core beliefs about how children best learn to read, they are continuously striving to find the technique(s) that will have the greatest impact on their students.

Since the early 1920s, educators have used a multi-sensory approach to teaching reading by combining reading, writing, and speaking in a natural context and not through deliberate teaching (Chall, 1992). This has been particularly useful in the teaching of vocabulary. It stands to reason then that the most active vocabulary growth occurs in the early years of life. A child learns to connect an object with the sight, sound, smell, taste, and feel associated with the object. This experience is followed by certain sounds made to represent the object. Thus, communication begins and the concept associated with the object develops into vocabulary. For example, a child understands the physical properties of an apple. He knows how the object looks, tastes, feels, smells, and sounds. A loving parent then builds vocabulary in a natural context by adding the word associated to this object—apple. Then, this label is connected to the experience. "You are eating an apple."

As the vocabulary increases, children realize words are used in many contexts. Children must then reach beyond the actual word and activate their schema of the context in which the word is used to understand the meaning. For example, the word "mouse" can have different meanings, such as a small rodent or a computer device. A child needs to experience words being used in different contexts to understand the complexity of our language. The more children experience vocabulary in context, the sooner they will begin to realize that it is the concept of the word in question in the given context that provides meaning.

As a child progresses through the various aspects of literacy development (listening, speaking, reading, and writing), his/her communication skills become more interdependent upon vocabulary development. Vocabulary development involves understanding the "labeling" that goes with the "concept" that makes the word meaningful. It is acquired through direct experience, multiple exposure, content, association, and comprehension. As students become comfortable with new vocabulary words, they are more likely to use the words when communicating.

Elements of our "Technological Age" often influence the instructional decisions that teachers make in the classroom. One such decision is the role that computers will play in the reading development of the children one teaches. Computer-based teaching and learning have produced positive effects in the classroom. Students seem to be motivated by learning through this medium (Forcier, 1999). Therefore, it is essential that today's teachers change as our society changes (Hoffman & Pearson, 2000). Children who enter today's primary classrooms have been processing multisensory concepts for most of their young lives. Home computers, interactive games, television, the Internet, and software companies capitalize on this multisensory concept.

Software companies have developed many programs for beginning reading that appeal to the senses and interests of the young child who is learning to read. This multimedia concept stimulates the learner with sight, sound, and action while integrating skills necessary for language development. Instructional technology offers virtual multisensory perception that should provide meaningful instruction.

Teacher-centered instruction is one approach to the use of instructional technology in the classroom (Forcier, 1999). The teacher-centered approach is similar to the direct-instruction approach in that the teacher is directing the children through the learning in order to achieve the goals of the lesson. One category of the teacher-centered approach is computer-assisted instruction. When using computer-assisted instruction, the teacher organizes the learning situation. He/she selects the targeted learning goal, situates the learning environment, and then allows exploratory time as students engage in learning. The teacher then monitors the learning activities and modifies the instructional level as needed to meet the various needs of the children involved.

Classroom teachers have the unique opportunity to infuse a variety of technological components with multisensory learning while situating the learning situation. One area where this is especially true is in the teaching of reading to young children. The research study being reported employed a teacher-centered, computer-assisted instructional technique that situated progressive reading material in an attempt to answer the following question:

Will a computerized multisensory approach to the teaching of reading increase first graders' vocabulary development?

Review of Literature

Many software programs offer "read alongs" and "edutainment" that assist students as they learn letter sounds, vocabulary concepts, comprehension, and to enjoy literature. Interactive multimedia allows the printed word to take on sight, sound, and action, which visually and mentally stimulates the individual.

One such program is DaisyQuest I and II (Mitchell, Chad, & Stacy, 1984–2000). An in-depth study investigated the phonological awareness in preschool children utilizing this software (Brinkman & Torgesen, 1994). Each child in the treatment group interacted with a computerized story concerning "Daisy the friendly dragon." A computer, monitor, mouse, and standard headphone were provided to allow the child, as he/she listened to the story, to discover clues revealing where the dragon was hiding. The clues were revealed by correctly answering at least four correct answers in a row. The skills assessed were rhyming words, beginning sounds, ending sounds, middle sounds, and whether a word contained a given number of sounds. This study revealed that children in the treatment group responded at a higher and faster rate of reading readiness than children in the control group. Not only did the children in the treatment group gain knowledge to aid in their ability to read, these preschoolers had fun!

In another study, two literacy teachers (one a Reading Recovery teacher, the other a Title I reading teacher) wrote simple, predictable texts using the multimedia software HyperStudio (Wagner, 1978). These teachers created "talking books" for their students, with a focus on high-frequency words with graphics and animation to offer sight, sound, and movement. Students enjoyed experiencing the stories as the computer "read" the story to them as the cursor (pointing finger) touched each word. This process came full circle by the end of the school year, as these students were writing and reading their own stories. Students were then encouraged to use invented spelling, graphics, and sounds while they created their own stories using the Kid Pix software program (Hickman, 1984–2000). "The computer serves as a motivational tool in their journey to literacy" (Eisenwine & Hunt, 2000, p. 456).

There are many reasons why computer-assisted reading instruction has been effective. The computer provides immediate responses and practice for the child learning a skill. Struggling readers interface with the computer and practice a skill without embarrassing situations in the classroom. Interaction with a multisensory format provides motivation and a positive attitude toward reading and learning (Case & Truscott, 1999; Forcier, 1999).

A word of caution accompanies much of the literature, warning educators to focus on the targeted instructional goals and not be "enchanted" by the entertainment that makes software packages so appealing (Case & Truscott, 1999; Sherry, 1996). While this multisensory approach is highly motivating for young readers, the instructional purpose is to enable them to become better readers. Educators should choose the types of software and technological resources carefully in order to maximize learning without being entangled in the "bells and whistles."

185   The benefits of using instructional technology include "an intrinsic need to learn technology…motivation increases engagement time…students move beyond knowledge and comprehension and into application and analysis…and students develop computer literacy by applying various computer skills as part of the learning process" (Dockstader, 1999, p. 73). As Ray and Wepner (2000) suggest, the question as to whether or not technology is the valuable educational resource we think it is may be a moot point because it is such an integral part of our lives. However, the question concerning the most productive methods of using technology in the classroom still needs to be addressed. Therefore, the purpose of this study was to investigate the effects of computer-assisted instruction on first-grade students' vocabulary development. Specifically, this study investigated the impact of the WiggleWorks program (CAST & Scholastic, 1994–1996) on first-grade students' vocabulary development.

Method

Sample

A first-grade classroom at a mid-Atlantic elementary school was selected for this research project. The subjects were 21 first-grade students. There were 10 boys and 11 girls involved in this study. The ethnic background of this class was as follows: 13 Caucasian students, six African American students, one Hispanic student, and one Pakistani student. Students were from a lower socioeconomic status and had limited exposure to educational experiences outside the school. The subjects were assigned to either the control or experimental group by using a table of random numbers and applying those numbers to the students. Ten students were assigned to the control group and 11 to the experimental group.

Computer-Assisted Program

The WiggleWorks (1994–1996) software program was used in this study. Co-developed by CAST & Scholastic, Inc., this program offers a literacy curriculum based on a combination of speech, sounds, graphics, text, and customizable access features. The software program features 72 trade books, audiocassettes, and a variety of computer-based activities. Students use the trade books and audiocassettes to read independently with or without the support of the audiocassette. Using the software program, students may listen to a story, read along with a story, or read a story silently. As they read, students are encouraged to review the suggested vocabulary words by selecting My Words. Students may listen to a pronunciation of the word by clicking on it or hear the word contextually in the story. Students may add new words to their vocabulary list by clicking on the selected word and the plus sign or remove words by clicking on the subtraction sign. Stu-

dents may read and reread the story as they wish. Students may also create word families or practice spelling using a magnetic alphabet.

After listening to or reading a story, students have the option of composing their own stories. WiggleWorks provides a story starter, close-structured text, or free writing to help young students write their story. After composing a story, students may illustrate personal stories using basic drawing tools, stamps of the story characters, and/or story event backgrounds. Students may share their stories with others by recording their stories or printing the story and creating a book. These functions are available in a Read Aloud, Read, Write, My Book, and Magnet Board menu available to the individual user.

WiggleWorks is a managed instructional system. The management functions allow the teacher the opportunity to customize the computer-assisted instruction for each child. For instance, in Read Aloud, the settings can be adjusted so that the story is read to the student using a word-by-word, line-by-line, or whole-page approach. The management system also keeps a running log of individual and class activities. The Portfolio Management feature provides a reading record for each child (tracks the stories read, date and time individual stories were read, etc.), including reading and writing samples. The WiggleWorks software program provides a multimedia approach to literacy while supporting traditional methods with the accompanying trade books and audiocassettes.

Variables

The research project tested the independent variable of computer-assisted instruction on reading vocabulary development. Eleven students received the treatment monitored by one of the researchers. The dependent variable was a pre- and post-vocabulary test. The test was an independent word list administered by one of the researchers to the experimental and control groups at the beginning and end of each session.

Measurement

The instrument used to determine the effect of computer-assisted instruction on vocabulary was a pre- and posttest designed by one of the researchers. Six high-frequency vocabulary words from each of the seven stories were selected by the researcher and placed on an independent list. The independent list of words served as the pre- and post-vocabulary test for each. All results were compared to determine the effect the treatment had on these subjects.

Procedure

As a part of the regular curriculum, all students received reading vocabulary instruction. The teacher utilized the reading instructional curriculum adopted by the county, which consisted of reading textbooks, related materials, and charts provided by the publishing company. Students participated in daily reading in-

struction. Each student in the class was randomly assigned into two groups: a control group and an experimental group. In an attempt to limit extraneous learning, both groups continued to receive regular reading
instruction by the researcher/teacher. The regular reading curriculum had a 20-min time block, where students participated in a DEAR (Drop Everything And
Read) program. The researchers used this block of time
to implement this research project.

Seven predetermined stories were used for this research project. The stories were available on book and
tape as well as on interactive, computerized storyboards. The control group experienced the story in a
variety of ways. First, they listened to the assigned
story as the teacher/researcher read the story to them.
Next, students listened to the story on tape and read
along with an accompanying book. Last, students were
provided with an assortment of literature: library
books, classroom literature, or the students' personal
books to read at their leisure after the predetermined
book and tape assignment had been completed. During
that 20-min time span, the 10 students in the experimental group visited the media computer lab and explored the same story using the computerized storyboard. A computer, monitor, mouse, and headphone
were provided for each subject. During the first session, the teacher/researcher explained the working mechanics of the computer laboratory and answered any
questions from the students. Then, the lessons began as
students listened to enjoy the story. Next, the students
revisited and identified words unknown to them by
clicking on the word. The computerized storyboards
served as a remediator. These subjects saw the printed
word highlighted and heard it as the word was produced in sound. Students were required to listen to the
story once while reading along.

After completing those requirements, students
could listen to and/or read any story previously read or
any story at a lower level. Students were introduced to
a new WiggleWorks story every other day. During this
project, students experimented with seven different
stories that became progressively more challenging.
The ability levels of the stories ranged from kindergarten to second grade. The project continued for 6 weeks.

Results

The results were analyzed using a paired-samples t
test. An alpha level of .05 was set incorporating a two-
tailed significance level. The analyses showed significant positive changes for both groups. The mean scores
confirm that students using computerized storyboards
demonstrate significant gains in their ability to recall a
greater amount of new vocabulary words (see Table 1).
The pre- and posttest were analyzed using a paired-
samples t test. The results demonstrate a statistically
significant difference ($p < .002$) in the experimental
(computer) group. A significant difference ($p < .01$)

was also found (see Table 2) in the control group
(Book/Tape).

Table 1
Means and Standard Deviations

Group	Pretest		Posttest	
	M	SD	M	SD
Computer	3.7	4.37	16.9	13.17
Book/Tape	1.8	2.68	5.45	6.07

The mean scores of the pre- and post-vocabulary
tests indicate a significant gain in the experimental
(computer storyboard) group (MeanPre = 3.7; Mean-
Post = 16.9). A further analysis involving the reading
ability of the individual students demonstrated that
students with higher reading ability scored higher in
the experimental and control groups than average-
ability or low-ability students. Those students who
were performing successfully in their reading scored
significantly higher than those students who were performing at a lower level.

Table 2
Paired-Samples t Test

Group	df	t	p
Computer	9	4.18	0.002
Book/Tape	10	3.17	0.010

Discussion

The stories selected for this project were progressively more challenging so as to meet the needs of as
many young readers as possible. Students with greater
reading ability scored higher on the pretests and
showed greater improvement on the posttests. These
students seemed to possess a greater command of reading and technological skills required in maneuvering
the storyboards.

Students with less reading ability did not gain as
much from the experience. While they seemed to enjoy
the stories, they were greatly challenged by the pre-
and posttest. These students would have been more
successful with stories developmentally appropriate for
their reading ability. Overall, the ability level of the
students in the classroom seemed to mirror their performance in the computer-based reading instruction.
Strong readers worked somewhat independently, aver-
age-ability students were at an instructional level with
reading and technology skills, while students with less
reading ability needed assistance with reading and
technology. Students in the experimental group (computer storyboards) were greatly motivated by the use of
computers. They enjoyed the interactive, multisensory
aspect of learning. This was evidenced by the students'
request to spend more time listening to stories on the
computers. Multisensory teaching seemed to make
their learning fun.

Implications and Significance

This research project was designed to investigate the effects of computer-assisted instruction on first-grade students' vocabulary development. With the integration of sights, colors, sounds, actions, plus the printed word, vocabulary lessons took on a new meaning. Students recognized the word on sight, remembered the word through association and phonemes, and quite a few could use the word as a part of their spoken and written vocabulary. Students were able to recognize the words in isolation and in text.

Overall, implications of this research project are that a 20-min DEAR time using computerized storyboards directly results in improved vocabulary development among first-grade students. Learning new vocabulary words took place at a faster pace with greater accuracy than with the direct teaching format. "Technology brings to your classroom the capability of connecting dynamic, interactive vocabulary learning with reading, writing, spelling, and content learning" (Fox & Mitchell, 2000, p. 66).

Computerized classroom instruction does not imply inflated test scores or a magic potion for teaching. It is a motivating medium that enhances good teaching. The infusion of technology and literacy is a lifelong learning gift we create for our students.

Recommendations

Computer-assisted instruction has a positive influence on students' motivation, interest, and learning. This research project validates the effect that computer-assisted instruction has on first graders' vocabulary development during a crucial time when they are learning to read. To improve upon this study, a concentrated effort should be made to determine the developmental reading level of each student. Students could then receive more individualized instruction at their appropriate reading level. Additionally, teachers/researchers need to move students from dependent direct instruction to more independent learning. A natural follow-up to this study could be to see if this move to more independent learning is facilitated by differing uses of technology in the classroom.

References

Brinkman, D., & Torgeson, J. (1994). Computer administered instruction in phonological awareness: Evaluation of the DaisyQuest program. *The Journal of Research and Development in Education, 27*(2), 126–137.

Case, C., & Truscott, D. M. (1999). The lure of bells and whistles: Choosing the best software to support reading instruction. *Reading and Writing Quarterly, 15*(4), p. 361.

Chall, J. (1992). The new reading debates: Evidence from science, art, and ideology. *Teachers College Record, 94*(2), 315.

Czubaj, C. (1997). Whole language literature reading instruction. *Education, 117*(4), 538.

Daniels, H., & Zemelman, S. (1999). Whole language works: Sixty years of research. *Educational Research, 57*(2), 32.

Dillon, D. R. (2000). Identifying beliefs and knowledge, uncovering tensions, and solving problems. *Kids' insight: Reconsidering how to meet the literacy needs of all students* (pp. 72–79). Newark, DE: International Reading Association.

Dockstader, J. (1999). Teachers of the 21st century know the what, why, and how of technology integration. *T.H.E. Journal, 26*(6), 73–74.

Eisenwine, M. J., & Hunt, D. A. (2000). Using a computer in literacy groups with emergent readers. *The Reading Teacher, 53*(6), 456.

Forcier, R. C. (1999). Computer applications in education. *The computer as an educational tool* (pp. 60–93). Upper Saddle, NJ: Prentice-Hall, Inc.

Fox, B. J., & Mitchell, M. J. (2000). Using technology to support word recognition, spelling, and vocabulary acquisition. In R. Thurlow, W. J. Valmont, & S. B. Wepner (Eds.). *Linking Literacy and Technology*. Newark, DL: International Reading Association, Inc.

Hickman, C. (1984–2000). Kid Pix. Deluxe Version. [Unpublished computer software.] Available: http://www.pixelpoppin.com/kidpix/index.html

Hoffman, J., & Pearson, P. D. (2000). Reading teacher education in the next millennium: What your grandmother's teacher didn't know that your granddaughter's teacher should. *Reading Research Quarterly, 35*(1), 28–44.

Howard, B. C., McGee, S., Purcell, S., & Schwartz, N. (2000). The experience of constructivism: Transforming teacher epistemology. *Journal of Research on Computing in Education, 32*(4), 455–465.

Kinzer, C. K., & Leu, D. J. (1999). *Effective Literacy Instruction.* Upper Saddle River, NJ: Prentice-Hall, Inc.

Mitchell, C., & S. (1984–2000). DaisyQuest. [Unpublished computer software.] Available: http://www.greatwave.com/html/daisys.html

Morrow, L. M., & Tracey, D. H. (1997). Strategies used for phonics instruction in early childhood classrooms. *The Reading Teacher, 50*(8), 644.

Ray, L. C., & Wepner, S. B. (2000). Using technology for reading development. In R. Thurlow, W. J. Valmont, & S. B. Wepner (Eds.). *Linking Literacy and Technology*. Newark, DL: International Reading Association, Inc.

Sherry, L. (1996). Issues in distance learning. *International Journal of Educational Telecommunications, 1*(4), 337–365.

Wagner, R. (1978). HyperStudio. [Unpublished computer software.] Available: http://www.hyperstudio.com/

WiggleWorks [Computer Software]. (1994–1996.) New York: CAST & Scholastic, Inc.

Exercise for Article 10

Factual Questions

1. What is the research question explored by this study?

2. What "caution" is mentioned in the Review of Literature?

3. How many students participated in this study?

4. Who designed the instrument used in this study?

5. What is the value of the posttest mean for the book/tape group?

6. Were the gains by the experimental group statistically significant? If yes, at what probability level?

Questions for Discussion

7. The first five paragraphs provide a general background for the study. The use of computers is introduced in the sixth paragraph. In your opinion, how important are the first five paragraphs in establishing a context for the study?

8. The researchers state that the students were assigned at random to one of the two groups. How important is this? Would it be better to use a different method for assigning students? Explain. (See lines 212–215.)

9. In your opinion, is the procedure described in sufficient detail? Explain. (See lines 283–332.)

10. Has this study convinced you of the superiority of computer-assisted instruction for improving vocabulary development? Explain.

11. If you were conducting a study on the same topic, what changes in the research methodology, if any, would you make?

Quality Ratings

Directions: Indicate your level of agreement with each of the following statements by circling a number from 5 for strongly agree (SA) to 1 for strongly disagree (SD). If you believe an item is not applicable to this research article, leave it blank. Be prepared to explain your ratings. When responding to criteria A and B below, keep in mind that brief titles and abstracts are conventional in published research.

A. The title of the article is appropriate.

SA   5   4   3   2   1   SD

B. The abstract provides an effective overview of the research article.

SA   5   4   3   2   1   SD

C. The introduction establishes the importance of the study.

SA   5   4   3   2   1   SD

D. The literature review establishes the context for the study.

SA   5   4   3   2   1   SD

E. The research purpose, question, or hypothesis is clearly stated.

SA   5   4   3   2   1   SD

F. The method of sampling is sound.

SA   5   4   3   2   1   SD

G. Relevant demographics (for example, age, gender, and ethnicity) are described.

SA   5   4   3   2   1   SD

H. Measurement procedures are adequate.

SA   5   4   3   2   1   SD

I. All procedures have been described in sufficient detail to permit a replication of the study.

SA   5   4   3   2   1   SD

J. The participants have been adequately protected from potential harm.

SA   5   4   3   2   1   SD

K. The results are clearly described.

SA   5   4   3   2   1   SD

L. The discussion/conclusion is appropriate.

SA   5   4   3   2   1   SD

M. Despite any flaws, the report is worthy of publication.

SA   5   4   3   2   1   SD

Article 11

The Effect of a Computer Simulation Activity versus a Hands-on Activity on Product Creativity in Technology Education

KURT Y. MICHAEL
Central Shenandoah Valley Regional Governor's School, Virginia

Computer use in the classroom has become a popular method of instruction for many technology educators. This may be due to the fact that software programs have advanced beyond the early days of drill and practice instruction. With the introduction of the graphical user interface, increased processing speed, and affordability, computer use in education has finally come of age. Software designers are now able to design multidimensional educational programs that include high-quality graphics, stereo sound, and real time interaction (Bilan, 1992). One area of noticeable improvement is computer simulations.

Computer simulations are software programs that either replicate or mimic real world phenomena. If implemented correctly, computer simulations can help students learn about technological events and processes that may otherwise be unattainable due to cost, feasibility, or safety. Studies have shown that computer simulators can:

1. Be equally as effective as real life, hands-on laboratory experiences in teaching students scientific concepts (Choi & Gennaro, 1987).
2. Enhance the learning achievement levels of students (Betz, 1996).
3. Enhance the problem-solving skills of students (Gokhale, 1996).
4. Foster peer interaction (Bilan, 1992).

The educational benefits of computer simulations for learning are promising. Some researchers even suspect that computer simulations may enhance creativity (e.g., Betz, 1996; Gokhale, 1996; Harkow, 1996); however, after an extensive review of literature, no empirical research has been found to support this claim. For this reason, the following study was conducted to compare the effect of a computer simulation activity versus a traditional hands-on activity on students' product creativity.

Background

Product Creativity in Technology Education

Historically, technology educators have chosen the creation of products or projects as a means to teach technological concepts (Knoll, 1997). Olson (1973), in describing the important role projects play in the industrial arts/technology classroom, remarked, "The project represents human creative achievement with materials and ideas and results in an experience of self-fulfillment" (p. 21). Lewis (1999) reiterated this belief by stating, "Technology is in essence a manifestation of human creativity. Thus, an important way in which students can come to understand it would be by engaging in acts of technological creation" (p. 46). The result of technological creation is the creative product.

The creative product embodies the very essence of technology. The American Association for the Advancement of Science (Johnson, 1989) stated, "Technology is best described as a process, but is most commonly known by its products and their effects on society" (p. 1). A product can be described as a physical object, article, patent, theoretical system, an equation, or new technique (Brogden & Sprecher, 1964). A creative product is one that possesses some degree of unusualness (originality) and usefulness (Moss, 1966). When given the opportunity for self-expression, a student's project becomes nothing less than a creative product.

The creative product can be viewed as a physical representation of a person's "true" creative ability encapsulating both the creative person and process (Besemer & O'Quin, 1993). By examining the literature related to the creative person and process, technology educators may gain a deeper understanding of the creative product itself.

The Creative Person

Inventors such as Edison and Ford have been recognized as being highly creative. Why some people reach a level of creative genius while others do not is still unknown. However, Maslow (1962), after studying several of his subjects, determined that all people are

creative, not in the sense of creating great works, but rather, creative in a universal sense that attributes a portion of creative talent to every person. In trying to understand and predict a person's creative ability, two
80 factors have often been considered: intelligence and personality traits.

Intelligence

A frequently asked question among educators is "What is the relationship between creativity and intelligence?" Research has shown that there is no direct
85 correlation between creativity and intelligence quotient (I.Q.) (Edmunds, 1990; Hayes, 1990; Moss, 1966; Torrance, 1963). Edmunds (1990) conducted a study to determine whether there was a relationship between creativity and I.Q. Two hundred and eighty-one ran-
90 domly selected students, grades eight to eleven, from three different schools in New Brunswick, Canada, participated. The instruments used to collect data were the *Torrance Test of Creative Thinking* and the *Otis-Lennon School Ability Test*, used to test intellectual
95 ability. Based on a Pearson product moment analysis, results showed that I.Q. scores did not significantly correlate with creativity scores. The findings were consistent with the literature dealing with creativity and intelligence.
100   On a practical level, findings similar to the one above may explain why I.Q. measures have proven to be unsuccessful in predicting creative performance. Hayes (1990) pointed out that creative performance may be better predicted by isolating and investigating
105 personality traits.

Personality Traits

Researchers have shown that there are certain personality traits associated with creative people (e.g., DeVore, Horton, & Lawson, 1989; Hayes, 1990; Runco, Nemiro, & Walberg, 1998; Stein, 1974).
110 Runco, Nemiro, and Walberg (1998) identified and conducted a survey investigating personality traits associated with the creative person. The survey was mailed to 400 individuals who had submitted papers and/or published articles related to creativity. The re-
115 searchers asked participants to rate, in order of importance, various traits that they believed affected creative achievement. The survey contained 16 creative achievement clusters consisting of 141 items. One hundred and forty-three surveys were returned reflect-
120 ing a response of 35.8%. Results demonstrated that intrinsic motivation, problem finding, and questioning skills were considered the most important traits in predicting and identifying creative achievement. Though personality traits play an important part in understand-
125 ing creative ability, an equally important area of creativity theory lies in the identification of the creative process itself.

The Creative Process

Creativity is a process (Hayes, 1990; Stein, 1974;
130 Taylor, 1959; Torrance, 1963) that has been represented using various models. Wallas (1926) offered one of the earliest explanations of the creative process. His model consisted of four stages that are briefly described below:

1. Preparation: This is the first stage in which an in-
135   dividual identifies then investigates a problem from many different angles.
2. Incubation: At this stage, the individual stops all conscious work related to the problem.
3. Illumination: This stage is characterized by a sud-
140   den or immediate solution to the problem.
4. Verification: This is the last stage at which time the solution is tested.

Wallas' model has served as a foundation upon which other models have been built. Some researchers
145 have added the communication stage to the creative process (e.g., Stein, 1974; Taylor, 1959; Torrance, 1966). The communication stage is the final stage of the creative process. At this stage, the new idea confined to one's mind is transformed into a verbal or
150 nonverbal product. The product is then shared within a social context in order that others may react to and possibly accept or reject it. A more comprehensive description of the creative process is captured within a definition offered by Torrance (1966):

155   Creativity is a process of becoming sensitive to problems, deficiencies, gaps in knowledge, missing elements, disharmonies, and so on; identifying the difficult; searching for solutions, making guesses or formulating hypotheses about the deficiencies, testing and re-testing these hy-
160   potheses and possibly modifying and re-testing them, and finally communicating the results (p. 8).

Torrance's definition resembles what some have referred to as problem solving. For example, technology educators Savage and Sterry (1990), generalizing from
165 the work of several scholars, identified six steps to the problem-solving process:

- Defining the problem: Analyzing, gathering information, and establishing limitations that will isolate and identify the need or opportunity.
170 - Developing alternative solutions: Using principles, ideation, and brainstorming to develop alternate ways to meet the opportunity or solve the problem.
- Selecting a solution: Selecting the most plausi-
175   ble solution by identifying, modifying, and/or combining ideas from the group of possible solutions.
- Implementing and evaluating the solution: Modeling, operating, and assessing the effectiveness of the selected solution.
180 - Redesigning the solution: Incorporating improvements into the design of the solution that address needs identified during the evaluation phase.

185   • Interpreting the solution: Synthesizing and communicating the characteristics and operating parameters of the solution (p. 15).

By closely comparing Torrance's (1966) definition of creativity with that of Savage and Sterry's (1990)
190   problem-solving process, one can easily see similarities between the descriptions. Guilford (1976), a leading expert in the study of creativity, made a similar comparison between steps of the creative process offered by Wallas (1926) with those of the problem-solving
195   process proposed by the noted educational philosopher, John Dewey. In doing so, Guilford simply concluded that "Problem solving is creative; there is no other kind" (p. 98).

Hinton (1968) combined the creative process and
200   problem-solving process into what is now known as creative problem solving. He believed that creativity would be better understood if placed within a problem-solving structure. Creative problem solving is a subset of problem solving based on the assumption that not all
205   problems require a creative solution. He surmised that when a problem is solved with a learned response, no creativity has been expressed. However, when a simple problem is solved with an insightful response, a small measure of creativity has been expressed; when a com-
210   plex problem is solved with a novel solution, genuine creativity has occurred.

Genuine creativity is the result of the creative process that manifests itself into a creative product. Understanding the creative process as well as the creative
215   person may play an important role in realizing the true nature of the creative product. Though researchers have not reached a consensus as to what attributes make up the creative product (Besemer & Treffingger, 1981; Joram, Woodruff, Bryson, & Lindsay, 1992; Stein,
220   1974), identifying and evaluating the creative product has been a concern of some researchers. Notable is the work of Moss (1966) and Duenk (1966).

Evaluating the Creative Product in Industrial Arts/ Technology Education

Moss (1966) and Duenk (1966) have arguably conducted the most extensive research establishing criteria
225   for evaluating creative products within industrial arts/technology education. Moss (1966), in examining the criterion problem, concluded that unusualness (originality) and usefulness were the defining characteristics of the creative product produced by industrial
230   arts students. A description of his model is presented below:

1. Unusualness: To be creative, a product must possess some degree of unusualness [or originality]. The quality of unusualness may, theoretically, be
235   measured in terms of probability of occurrence; the less the probability of its occurrence, the more unusual the product (Moss, 1966, p. 7).

2. Usefulness: While some degree of unusualness is a necessary requirement for creative products, it is
240   not a sufficient condition. To be creative, an industrial arts student's product must also satisfy the minimal principle requirements of the problem situation; to some degree it must "work" or be potentially "workable." Completely ineffective, ir-
245   relevant solutions to teacher-imposed or student-initiated problems are not creative (Moss, 1966, p. 7).

3. Combining Unusualness and Usefulness: When a product possesses some degree of both unusual-
250   ness and usefulness, it is creative. But because these two criterion qualities are considered variables, the degree of creativity among products will also vary. The extent of each product's departure from the typical and its value as a problem solu-
255   tion will, in combination, determine the degree of creativity of each product. Giving the two qualities equal weight, as the unusualness and/or usefulness of a product increases so does its rated creativity; similarly, as the product approaches the conven-
260   tional and/or uselessness its rated creativity decreases (Moss, 1966, p. 8).

In establishing the construct validity of his theoretical model, Moss (1966) submitted his work for review to 57 industrial arts educators, two measurement spe-
265   cialists, and six educational psychologists. Results of the review found the proposed model was compatible with existing theory and practice of both creativity and industrial arts. No one disagreed with the major premise of using unusualness and usefulness as defining
270   characteristics for evaluating the creative products of industrial arts students.

To date, little additional research has been conducted to establish criteria for evaluating the creative products of industrial arts and/or technology education
275   students. If technology is best known by its creative products, then technology educators are obligated to identify characteristics that make a product more or less creative. Furthermore, educators must find ways to objectively measure these attributes and then teach
280   students in a manner that enhances the creativity of their products. A possible approach to enhancing product creativity is by incorporating computer simulation technology into the classroom. However, no research has been done in this area to measure the true effect of
285   computer simulation on product creativity. For that reason, other studies addressing computer use in general and product creativity will be explored.

Studies Related to Computers and the Creative Product

A study conducted by Joram, Woodruff, Bryson, and Lindsay (1992) found that average students pro-
290   duced their most creative work using word processors as compared to students using pencil and paper. The researchers hypothesized that word processing would hinder product creativity due to constant evaluation and

editing of their work. To test the hypothesis, average
295 and above-average eighth-grade writers were randomly
assigned to one of two groups. The first group was
asked to compose using word processors while the second group was asked to compose using pencil and paper. After collecting the compositions, both the word-
300 processed and handwritten texts were typed so that
they would be in the same format for the evaluators.
Based on the results, the researchers concluded that
word processing enhances the creative abilities of average writers. The researchers attributed this to the pros-
305 pect that word processing may allow the average writer
to generate a number of ideas, knowing that only a few
of them will be usable and the rest can be easily erased.
However, the researchers also found that word processing had a negative effect on the creativity of above-
310 average writers. These mixed results suggest that the
use of word processing may not be appropriate for all
students relative to creativity.

Similar to word processing, computer graphics programs may also help students improve the creativeness
315 of their products. In a study conducted by Howe
(1992), two advanced undergraduate classes in graphics design were assigned to one of two treatments. The
first treatment group was instructed to use a computer
graphic program to complete a design project whereas
320 the other group was asked to use conventional graphic
design equipment to design their product. Upon completion of the assignment, both groups' projects were
collected and photocopied so that they would be in the
same format before being evaluated. Based on the re-
325 sults, the researcher concluded that students using
computer graphics technology surpassed the conventional method in product creativity. The researcher
attributed this to the prospect that computer graphics
programs may enable graphic designers to generate an
330 abundance of ideas, then capture the most creative ones
and incorporate them into their designs. However, due
to a lack of random assignment, results of the study
should be generalized with caution.

Like word processing and computer graphics, simu-
335 lation technology is a type of computer application that
allows users to freely manipulate and edit virtual objects. Thus, it was surmised that computer simulation
may enhance creativity. This notion led to the development of the study reported herein.

Purpose of the Study

340 This study compared the effect of a computer simulation activity versus a traditional hands-on activity on
students' product creativity. A creative product was
defined as one that possesses some measure of both
unusualness (originality) and usefulness. The following
345 hypothesis and sub-hypotheses were examined.

Major Research Hypothesis

There is no difference in product *creativity* between
the computer simulation and traditional hands-on
groups.

Research Sub-Hypotheses

1. There is no difference in product *originality* be-
350   tween the computer simulation and traditional
   hands-on groups.
2. There is no difference in product *usefulness* between the computer simulation and traditional
   hands-on groups.

Method

Subjects

355 The subjects selected for this study were seventh-
grade technology education students from three different middle schools located in Northern Virginia, a
middle-to-upper-income suburb outside of Washington,
D.C. The school system's middle school technology
360 education programs provide learning situations that
allow the students to explore technology through problem-solving activities. The three participating schools
were chosen because of the teachers' willingness to
participate in the study.

Materials

365 Kits of *Classic Lego Bricks*™ were used with the
hands-on group. The demonstration version of *Gryphon Bricks*™ (Gryphon Software Corporation, 1996)
was used with the simulation group. This software allows students to assemble and disassemble computer-
370 generated Lego-type bricks in a virtual environment on
the screen of the computer. Subjects in the computer
simulation group were each assigned to a Macintosh
computer on which the *Gryphon Bricks* software was
installed. Each subject in the hands-on treatment group
375 was given a container of Lego bricks identical to those
available virtually in the Gryphon software.

Test Instrument

Products were evaluated based on a theoretical
model proposed by Moss (1966). Moss used the combination of *unusualness* (or originality) and *usefulness*
380 as criteria for determining product creativity. However,
Moss' actual instrument was not used in this study due
to low inter-rater reliability. Instead, a portion of the
Creative Product Semantic Scale or *CPSS* (Besemer &
O'Quin, 1989) was used to determine product creativ-
385 ity. Sub-scales "Original" and "Useful" from the *CPSS*
were chosen to be consistent with Moss' theoretical
model.

The *CPSS* has proven to be a reliable instrument in
evaluating a variety of creative products based on ob-
390 jective, analytical measures of creativity (Besemer &
O'Quin, 1986, 1987, 1989, 1993). This was accomplished by the use of a bipolar, semantic differential
scale. In general, semantic differential scales are good
for measuring mental concepts or images (Alreck,
395 1995). Because creativity is a mental concept, the semantic differential naturally lends itself to measuring
the creative product. Furthermore, the *CPSS* is flexible
enough to allow researchers to pick various subscales
based on the theoretical construct being investigated,

400 like the use of the "Original" and "Useful" subscales in this study. In support of this, Besemer and O'Quin (1986) stated, "… the subscale structure of the total scale lends itself to administration of relevant portions of the instrument rather than the whole" (p. 125).

405 The *CPSS* was used in a study conducted by Howe (1992). His reliability analysis, based on Cronbach's alpha coefficient, yielded good to high reliability across all subscales of the *CPSS*. Important to this study were the high reliability results for subscales 410 "Original" (.93) and "Useful" (.92). These high reliability coefficients are consistent with earlier studies conducted by Besemer and O'Quin (1986, 1987, 1989).

The Pilot Study

A pilot study was conducted in which a seventh-grade technology education class from a Southwest 415 Virginia middle school was selected. The pilot study consisted of 16 subjects who were randomly assigned to either a hands-on treatment group or a simulation treatment group. As a result of the pilot study, the time allocated for the students to assemble their creative 420 products was reduced from 30 minutes to 25 minutes because most of them had finished within the shorter time. Precedence for limiting the time needed to complete a creative task was found in Torrance's (1966) work in which 30 minutes was the time limit for a vari-425 ety of approaches to measuring creativity.

Procedure

One class from each of the three participating schools was selected for the study. Fifty-eight subjects participated, 21 females and 37 males, with an average age of 12.4 years. Subjects were given identification 430 numbers, then randomly assigned to either the hands-on or the computer simulation treatment group. The random assignment helped ensure the equivalence of groups and controlled for extraneous variables such as students' prior experience with open-ended problem-435 solving activities, use of Lego bricks and/or computer simulation programs, and other extraneous variables that may have confounded the results. The independent variable in this study was the instructional activity and the dependent variable was the subjects' creative prod-440 uct scores as determined by the combination of the "Original" and "Useful" subscales from the *CPSS* (Besemer & O'Quin, 1989).

Subjects in both the hands-on and the simulation groups were asked to construct a "creature" that they 445 believed would be found on a Lego planet. The "creature" scenario was chosen because it was an open-ended problem and possessed the greatest potential for imaginative student expression. The only difference in treatment between the two groups was that the hands-450 on group used real Lego bricks in constructing their products whereas the simulation treatment group used a computer simulator. Treatments were administered simultaneously and overall treatment time was the same for both groups. The hands-on treatment group

455 met in its regular classroom whereas the simulation treatment group met in a computer lab. The classroom teacher at each school proctored the hands-on treatment group and the researcher proctored the simulation treatment group.

460 The subjects in the hands-on treatment group were given five minutes to sort their bricks by color while subjects in the simulation treatment group watched a five-minute instructional video explaining how to use the simulation software. By having the students sort 465 their bricks for five minutes, the overall treatment time was the same for both groups, thus eliminating a variable that may otherwise influence the results. Then, the subjects in both groups were given the following scenario:

470 Pretend you are a toy designer working for the Lego Company. Your job is to create a "creature" using Lego bricks that will be used in a toy set called Lego Planet. What types of creatures might be found on a Lego planet? Use your creativity and make a creature that is 475 *original* in appearance yet *useful* to the toy manufacturer.

One more thing: The creature you construct must be able to fit within a five-inch cubed box. That means you must stay within the limits of your green base plate and make your creature no higher than 13 bricks.

480 You will have 25 minutes to complete this activity. If you finish early, spend more time thinking about how you can make your creature more creative. You must remain in your seat the whole time. If there are no questions, you may begin.

485 When the time was up, the subjects were asked to stop working. The hands-on treatment group's products were labeled, collected, and then reproduced in the computer simulation software by the researcher. This was done so that the raters could not distinguish from 490 which treatment group the products were created. Finally, the images of the products from both groups were printed using a color printer.

Product Evaluation

To evaluate the students' solutions, two raters were recruited: a middle school art teacher and a middle 495 school science teacher. The teachers were chosen because of their willingness to participate in the study and had a combined total of 36 years of teaching experience. To help establish inter-rater reliability, a rater training session was conducted during the pilot study. 500 The same teacher-raters used in the pilot study were used in the final study. The training session provided the teacher-raters with instructions on how to use the rating instrument and allowed them to practice rating sample products. During the session, disagreements on 505 product ratings were discussed and rules were developed by the raters to increase consistency. The pilot study confirmed that there was good inter-rater reliability across all the scales and thus the experimental procedures proceeded as designed. No significant differ-

510 ence in creativity, originality, or usefulness was found between the two treatment groups during the pilot study.

For the actual study, the teacher–raters were each given the printed images of the products from each of 515 the 58 subjects and were instructed to independently rate them using the "Original" and "Useful" subscales of the *CPSS* (Besemer & O'Quin, 1989). Three weeks were allowed for the rating process.

Findings

Once the ratings from the two raters had been ob-520 tained, an inter-rater reliability analysis, based on Cronbach's alpha coefficient, was conducted. Analysis yielded moderate to good inter-rater reliability (.74 to .88) across all the scales. The stated hypotheses were then tested using one-way analysis of variance 525 (ANOVA).

- No difference in product *Creativity* scores was found between the computer simulation group ($M = 41.7$, $SD = 7.67$) and the hands-on group ($M = 42.0$, $SD = 5.58$). Therefore, the null hy-530 pothesis was not rejected, $F(5,52) = 0.54$, $p = 0.75$.

- No difference in product *Originality* scores was found between the computer simulation group ($M = 20.59$, $SD = 4.44$) and the hands-on group 535 ($M = 21.10$, $SD = 3.10$). Thus, the null hypothesis was not rejected, $F(5,52) = 1.07$, $p = 0.39$.

- No difference in product *Usefulness* scores was found between the computer simulation group ($M = 21.15$, $SD = 4.17$) and the traditional 540 hands-on group ($M = 20.90$, $SD = 3.20$). Once again, the researcher failed to reject the null hypothesis, $F(5,52) = 0.49$, $p = 0.78$.

Conclusion

Though there are only a few empirical studies to support their claims, some researchers believe that 545 computers in general may improve student product creativity by allowing students to generate an abundance of ideas, capture the most creative ones, and incorporate them into their product (Howe, 1992; Joram, Woodruff, Bryson, & Lindsay, 1992). Similarly, some 550 researchers speculate that the use of computer simulations may enhance product creativity as well (Betz, 1996; Gokhale, 1996; Harkow, 1996). However, based on the results of this study, the use of computer simulation to enhance product creativity was not supported. 555 The creativity, usefulness, or originality of the resulting products appears to be the same whether students use a computer simulation of Lego bricks or whether they manipulated the actual bricks.

Because the simulation activity in this study was 560 nearly identical to the hands-on task, one might conclude that product creativity may be more reliant upon the individual's creative cognitive ability rather than the tools or means by which the product was created.

This would stand to reason based on Besemer and 565 O'Quin's (1993) belief that the creative product is unique in that it combines both the creative person and process into a tangible object representing the "true" measure of a person's creative ability. With this in mind, when studying a computer simulation's effect on 570 student product creativity, researchers may want to focus more attention on the creative person's traits and the cognitive process used to create the product rather than focusing on the tool or means by which the product was created. This approach to understanding stu-575 dent product creativity may lend itself more to qualitative rather than quantitative research.

If quantitative research is to continue in this area of study, researchers may wish to consider using a different theoretical model and instrument for measuring the 580 creative product. For example, if replicating this experiment, rather than using only the two subscales of the *Creative Product Semantic Scale* (Besemer & O'Quin, 1989), the complete instrument might be used, yielding additional dimensions of creativity. Additional 585 research regarding the various types of simulation programs is needed, along with the different effects they might have on student creativity in designing products. The use of computer simulations in technology education programs appears to be increasing with little re-590 search to support their effectiveness or viable use.

References

Alreck, T. L., & Settle, B. R. (1995). *The survey research handbook* (2nd Ed.). Chicago: Irwin Inc.

Besemer, S. P., & O'Quin, K. (1993). Assessing creative products: Progress and potentials. In S. G. Isaksen (Ed.), *Nurturing and developing creativity: The emergence of a discipline* (pp. 331–349). Norwood, New Jersey: Ablex Publishing Corp.

Besemer, S. P., & O'Quin, K. (1989). The development, reliability, and validity of the revised creative product semantic scale. *Creativity Research Journal*, 2, 268–279.

Besemer, S. P., & O'Quin, K. (1987). Creative product analysis: Testing a model by developing a judging instrument. In S. G. Isaksen, *Frontiers of creativity research: Beyond the basics.* (pp. 341–357). Buffalo, NY: Bearly Ltd.

Besemer, S. P., & O'Quin, K. (1986). Analysis of creative products: Refinement and test of a judging instrument. *Journal of Creative Behavior*, 20(2), 115–126.

Besemer, S. P., & Treffingger, D. (1981). Analysis of creative products: Review and synthesis. *Journal of Creative Behavior*, 15, 158–178.

Betz, J. A. (1996). Computer games: Increase learning in an interactive multi-disciplinary environment. *Journal of Technology Systems*, 24(2), 195–205.

Bilan, B. (1992). *Computer simulations: An integrated tool.* Paper presented at the SAGE/6th Canadian Symposium, The University of Calgary.

Brogden, H., & Sprecher, T. (1964). Criteria of creativity. In C. W. Taylor. *Creativity, progress and potential.* New York: McGraw Hill.

Choi, B., & Gennaro, E. (1987). The effectiveness of using computer simulated experiments on junior high students' understanding of the volume displacement concept. *Journal of Research in Science Teaching*, 24(6), 539–552.

DeVore, P., Horton, A., & Lawson, A. (1989). *Creativity, design, and technology.* Worcester, Massachusetts: Davis Publications, Inc.

Duenk, L. G. (1966). *A study of the concurrent validity of the Minnesota Test of Creative Thinking, Abbr. Form VII, for eighth-grade industrial arts students.* Minneapolis: Minnesota University. (Report No. BR-5-0113.)

Edmunds, A. L. (1990). Relationships among adolescent creativity, cognitive development, intelligence, and age. *Canadian Journal of Special Education*, 6(1), 61–71.

Gokhale, A. A. (1996). Effectiveness of computer simulation for enhancing higher order thinking. *Journal of Industrial Teacher Education*, 33(4), 36–46.

Gryphon Software Corporation (1996). *Gryphon Bricks Demo* (Version 1.0) [Computer Software]. Glendale, CA: Knowledge Adventure. [On-line] Available: http://www.kidsdomain.com/down/mac/bricksdemo.html

Guilford, J. (1976). Intellectual factors in productive thinking. In R. Mooney & T. Rayik (Eds.), *Explorations in creativity*. New York: Harper & Row.

Harkow, R. M. (1996). *Increasing creative thinking skills in second and third grade gifted students using imagery, computers, and creative problem solving*. Unpublished master's thesis, NOVA Southeastern University.

Hayes, J. R. (1990). *Cognitive processes in creativity*. (Paper No. 18). University of California, Berkeley.

Hinton, B. L. (1968, Spring). A model for the study of creative problem solving. *Journal of Creative Behavior, 2*(2), 133–142.

Howe, R. (1992). Uncovering the creative dimensions of computer-graphic design products. *Creativity Research Journal, 5*(3), 233–243.

Johnson, J. R. (1989). *Project 2061: Technology* (Association for the Advancement of Science Publication 89-06S). Washington, DC: American Association for the Advancement of Science.

Joram, E., Woodruff, E., Bryson, M., & Lindsay, P. (1992). The effects of revising with a word processor on writing composition. *Research in the Teaching of English, 26*(2), 167–192.

Knoll, M. (1997). The project method: Its vocational education origin and international development. *Journal of Industrial Teacher Education, 34*(3), 59–80.

Lewis, T. (1999). Research in technology education: Some areas of need. *Journal of Technology Education, 10*(2), 41–56.

Maslow, A. (1962). *Toward a psychology of being*. Princeton, NJ: Van Nostrand.

Moss, J. (1966). *Measuring creative abilities in junior high school industrial arts*. Washington, DC: American Council on Industrial Arts Teacher Education.

Olson, D. W. (1973). *Tecnol-o-gee*. Raleigh: North Carolina University School of Education, Office of Publications.

Runco, R. A., Nemiro, J., & Walberg, H. J. (1998). Personal explicit theories of creativity. *Journal of Creative Behavior, 32*(1), 1–17.

Savage, E., & Sterry, L. (1990). *A conceptual framework for technology education*. Reston, VA: International Technology Education Association.

Stein, M. (1974). *Stimulating creativity: Vol. 1. Individual procedures*. New York: Academic Press.

Taylor, I. A. (1959). The nature of the creative process. In P. Smith (Ed.), *Creativity: An examination of the creative process* (pp. 51–82). New York: Hastings House Publishers.

Torrance, E. P. (1966). *Torrance test on creative thinking: Norms-technical manual* (Research Edition). Lexington, MA: Personal Press.

Torrance, E. P. (1963). Creativity. In F. W. Hubbard (Ed.), *What research says to the teacher* (Number 28). Washington, DC: Department of Classroom Teachers American Educational Research Association of the National Education Association.

Wallas, G. (1926). *The art of thought*. New York: Harcourt, Brace and Company.

About the author: *Kurt Y. Michael* is a technology education teacher at Central Shenandoah Valley Regional Governor's School, Fishersville, Virginia. E-mail: michael@csvrgs.k12.va.us

Exercise for Article 11

Factual Questions

1. According to Moss (1966), a creative product is one that possesses what two things?

2. What two factors does the researcher mention as being often considered when trying to understand and predict creative ability?

3. The researcher cites a study in which the effects of word processors on creativity were evaluated. Were the results of this study conclusive? Explain.

4. The subjects were drawn from how many different middle schools?

5. *CPSS* stands for what words?

6. What does the researcher identify as "the independent variable in this study"?

7. ANOVA stands for what words?

8. What was the mean *Originality* score of the hands-on group?

Questions for Discussion

9. The researcher cites a reference published in 1926. Do you think this helps provide a historical context for this study? Do you think that providing a historical context is important? Explain. (See lines 130–144.)

10. The literature review is longer than those in many of the other research articles in this book. Do you think it is about the right length given the nature of this study? Explain.

11. The major research hypothesis and the research sub-hypotheses predict "no difference." Is this what you would have predicted in hypotheses if you had conducted the study? Explain. (See lines 346–354.)

12. In your opinion, are the materials used in this study described in sufficient detail? Explain. (See lines 365–376.)

13. To what extent does the fact that the researcher conducted a pilot study increase your overall evaluation of the study? (See lines 413–425.)

14. The researcher assigned students at random to the two groups. Do you agree with him that this was a desirable way to assign the students? Explain. (See lines 429–437.)

15. The researcher describes the inter-rater reliability as good. Do you agree? Explain. (See lines 506–509.)

16. Despite the findings of no differences between the groups, do you think that additional quantitative research should be conducted on this topic? Explain. (Consider the researcher's discussion of this issue in lines 519–542 before answering this question.)

Quality Ratings

Directions: Indicate your level of agreement with each of the following statements by circling a number from 5 for strongly agree (SA) to 1 for strongly disagree (SD). If you believe an item is not applicable to this research article, leave it blank. Be prepared to explain your ratings. When responding to criteria A and B below, keep in mind that brief titles and abstracts are conventional in published research.

A.   The title of the article is appropriate.

    SA   5   4   3   2   1   SD

B.   The abstract provides an effective overview of the research article.

    SA   5   4   3   2   1   SD

C.   The introduction establishes the importance of the study.

    SA   5   4   3   2   1   SD

D.   The literature review establishes the context for the study.

    SA   5   4   3   2   1   SD

E.   The research purpose, question, or hypothesis is clearly stated.

    SA   5   4   3   2   1   SD

F.   The method of sampling is sound.

    SA   5   4   3   2   1   SD

G.   Relevant demographics (for example, age, gender, and ethnicity) are described.

    SA   5   4   3   2   1   SD

H.   Measurement procedures are adequate.

    SA   5   4   3   2   1   SD

I.   All procedures have been described in sufficient detail to permit a replication of the study.

    SA   5   4   3   2   1   SD

J.   The participants have been adequately protected from potential harm.

    SA   5   4   3   2   1   SD

K.   The results are clearly described.

    SA   5   4   3   2   1   SD

L.   The discussion/conclusion is appropriate.

    SA   5   4   3   2   1   SD

M.   Despite any flaws, the report is worthy of publication.

    SA   5   4   3   2   1   SD

Article 12

Using Virtual Reality to Teach Disability Awareness

JAYNE PIVIK
University of Ottawa

IAN MACFARLANE
Nortel Networks

JOAN McCOMAS
University of Ottawa

MARC LAFLAMME
University of Ottawa

ABSTRACT. A desktop virtual reality (VR) program was designed and evaluated to teach children about the accessibility and attitudinal barriers encountered by their peers with mobility impairments. Within this software, children sitting in a virtual wheelchair experience obstacles such as stairs, narrow doors, objects too high to reach, and attitudinal barriers such as inappropriate comments. Using a collaborative research methodology, 15 youths with mobility impairments assisted in developing and beta-testing the software. The effectiveness of the program was then evaluated with 60 children in grades 4–6 using a controlled pretest/posttest design. The results indicated that the program was effective for increasing children's knowledge of accessibility barriers. Attitudes, grade level, familiarity with individuals with a disability, and gender were also investigated.

From *Journal of Educational Computing Research*, 26, 203–218.

Inclusive education of children with disabilities in public education institutions is now common in developed countries. In Canada, this means that 373,824 children with special needs between the ages of 5–14 years attend regular classes [1]. Inclusive education is considered by most as a positive experience for both children with and without disabilities and an important social policy toward ensuring full participation and accessibility for individuals with disabilities [2]. Theoretically, inclusive education allows children with disabilities the opportunity for "free and appropriate public education" as determined by the Education of the Handicapped Act (EHA) in the United States in 1975.

However, in reality, children with disabilities often have to contend with structural, physical, and attitudinal barriers for the 30 hours per week they spend at school. Examples of structural barriers include steep ramps, uncut sidewalk curbs, heavy doors, and one-inch thresholds [3, 4]. Stairs, narrow bathrooms, revolving doors, and turnstiles also have been reported as impediments that limit access and inclusion for individuals who use wheelchairs [5]. In addition to structural barriers, children with disabilities have to manage the physical limitations inherent to their disability. For example, a child with spina bifida may have to contend with poor upper extremity function (limiting fine motor skills such as writing), poor hand–eye coordination, potential neurological deficits, and difficulties with organizational skills [6].

Perhaps the most difficult type of barrier encountered by children with disabilities is negative attitudes expressed by their peers [7]. Attitudinal barriers experienced in educational integration, such as rejection and stereotyping [8, 9] or covert and overt bullying [10], can further isolate children with a disability and impact on their feelings of social acceptance and self-esteem. Social isolation has been linked to difficulty with future peer relations [4] and lower academic and cognitive development [11].

In order to increase social awareness, understanding, and acceptance toward children with disabilities by their nondisabled peers, disability awareness programs have been developed. Current methods of disability awareness programs for school children include: 1) simulating a disability (e.g., sitting in a wheelchair or wearing a blindfold), 2) providing information about disabilities, 3) live and video presentations/testimonials by individuals with disabilities, 4) pairing disabled and nondisabled children together in a buddy system, 5) group discussions about disability, and 6) a combination of the above methods [7]. Along with disability awareness, Roberts and Smith [12] recommend providing children without a disability with knowledge and practical skills that assist with social interactions with their disabled peers. Logic dictates that one of the most effective ways to impart knowledge about the realities for children with disabilities is to try to simulate the experience of the disability. In other words, to provide an opportunity where the child without a disability literally experiences different situations, viewpoints, perceptions, and interactions from the perspective of a child with a disability.

Simulation has been the cornerstone of virtual reality (VR), and in fact, the first uses of VR involved the

69

65 simulation of military experiences as noted by Kozak, Hancock, Arthur, and Chrysler [13]. VR is defined as a three-dimensional, participatory, computer-based simulation that occurs in real time and is often multisensory [14]. In other words, VR responds to the user's actions,
70 has real-time 3-D graphics, and provides a sense of immersion. There are many advantages to using VR for simulation. For example, VR provides a safe environment for practicing a skill, such as learning to cross street intersections [15–17]. Simulations using VR may
75 also be less costly than real-world simulations [18] and provide the user the opportunity for repetitive practice [19, 20]. Experiences that are not available in the real world can be simulated in a virtual environment, such as moving through a cellular structure or visiting his-
80 torical sites that are presently nonexistent or too far away to be accessible. Past experience has shown us that children using VR find it very interesting and stimulating, thus motivating the training experience [21]. Finally, desktop VR can provide a simulation that
85 can be made widely accessible through dissemination via the Internet.

The purpose of this project was to develop and evaluate a desktop VR program designed to teach children about the accessibility and attitudinal barriers
90 faced by children with mobility impairments. Desktop VR utilizes a personal computer, where the virtual environment is displayed on a conventional computer monitor and movement within the environment is effected through either a mouse, keyboard, or joystick.
95 Although less immersive than systems that use head-mounted display units, desktop VR systems have the advantages of being less expensive, more portable, and easier to use. The developed program, titled *Barriers: The Awareness Challenge*, used desktop VR to simu-
100 late the experiences of a child in a wheelchair in an environment familiar to most children—an elementary school. The specific objectives of this project were to examine the effectiveness of using a disability simulation with virtual reality to: 1) increase children's
105 knowledge of accessibility and attitudinal barriers that impact individuals with disabilities and 2) promote more positive attitudes toward children with disabilities.

Method

There were four phases to The Barriers Project. The
110 first was to utilize a collaborative research methodology, where youths with mobility impairments (our Disability Awareness Consultants) identified the barriers that would comprise the content of the software. The second phase was to develop the software, which in-
115 volved organizing the barriers into a script or storyboard, building the virtual environment, and then beta-testing it with our consultants. The third phase of the project involved evaluating the software to examine the impact of the program on youths without disabilities.
120 The final phase involved disseminating information about the program and providing free access to the software via the Internet.

Collaborative Software Development

In order to ensure that the software reflected the current status of accessibility and inclusion within an
125 elementary school setting, a collaborative research methodology was used. Fifteen Disability Awareness Consultants assisted in the content development and testing of the software. The consultants (aged 9–16 years) attended eight different schools on a full-time
130 basis and had either cerebral palsy ($n = 11$) or spina bifida ($n = 5$). Their mobility impairments ranged from difficulty walking (on uneven surfaces and/or for long periods of time) to constant use of an electric wheelchair for independent mobility. The barriers to full in-
135 clusion in their schools and the proposed solutions to these barriers were identified by these consultants during three focus group meetings. The final list of barriers and proposed solutions was then prioritized by the focus group participants, where each person was given
140 seven stickers and was asked to place one or more of the stickers on the barrier(s) they felt were necessary to include in the software. The barriers with the greatest number of stickers became the basis for the script or storyboard of the software program. Using this script, a
145 virtual elementary school was developed, which includes the exterior of a school, an outside playground, hallways, a classroom, a library, and two washrooms (one inaccessible). The children using the program were told that they were to travel in a "virtual wheel-
150 chair" and seek out all of the "building" and "bad attitude" barriers in the school. There are 24 barriers in the program, which include building barriers such as narrow hallways, crowded classrooms, a ramp that is too steep, a locker hook that is too high, and inaccessible
155 bathroom fixtures. The attitudinal barriers include comments from virtual students such as "Hey, look at the kid in the wheelchair!" or "Ha! Ha! You can't play here!"

The program presents a gaming style interface with
160 a first-person point of view during navigation through the world. The user moves within the virtual school using the cursor keys and can activate events such as opening doors or using the elevator by pressing the left button of the mouse. Two message areas are used: a
165 task message area and an information message area. The task messages instruct the child to complete specific tasks such as performing an action or going to a specific location. The information message center gives feedback to the child when barriers are identified. A
170 "wheelchair damage" display is used to encourage children to be careful as they navigate through the world and is activated when they bump into walls, objects, or people. As each barrier is correctly identified, the score is updated. A number of icons (such as a coat,
175 key, and book) are also displayed. The icons are added and removed as the student completes specific tasks. At

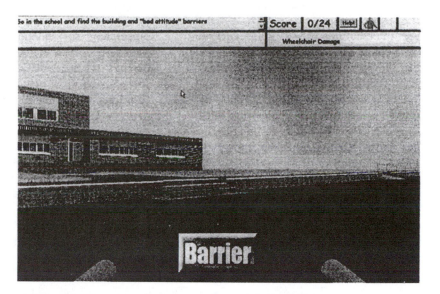

Figure 1. When first entering the world, the user is placed in the parking lot facing the school.

the end of the program, a results section is displayed listing all the barriers and each one is labeled as to whether it was found or not during the program.

180 The program was developed in VRML 2.0 (Virtual Reality Modeling Language) using CosmoWorlds. The CosmoPlayer 2.1 plug-in (for Netscape Navigator and Microsoft Internet Explorer) was used as the 3D viewer. The virtual school that was developed used the
185 scripting capabilities of VRML to control interactions with the virtual objects and people in the school. Fields, events, proximity nodes, and collision sensors are used extensively throughout the virtual world. Each barrier, whether it is structural or attitudinal, is acti-
190 vated by a proximity node. A number of fields are used to record the state of the world in relation to the location of the wheelchair and the interactions that have taken place. The child identifies a structural barrier by moving close to the barrier and clicking on the "Bar-
195 rier" button that floats just in front of the virtual wheelchair. For example, when first entering the world, the user is placed in the parking lot facing the school (Figure 1).

A proximity node surrounds the front steps that
200 lead up to the school. A number of fields indicate where the wheelchair is and which barriers have been found. For the front steps, the "atSidewalkSteps" field is initially "false" and the "SidewalkStepsIDed" field (which records whether the steps have been identified
205 as a barrier or not) is set to "false." If the "Barrier" button is clicked when the wheelchair is not at any of the barriers, an audio clip that indicates an incorrect choice is played. When the child navigates closer to the steps, the virtual wheelchair collides with the proximity
210 node that surrounds the steps. This collision triggers an event that sets the "atSidewalkSteps" field to "true." Now, if the "Barrier" button is clicked, a number of

events occur: 1) the number of correct barriers found is incremented, 2) an appropriate message is displayed in
215 the information message area (in this case, it informs the child that wheelchairs cannot go up stairs), 3) the "SidewalkStepsIDed" field is set to "true," which is used in the results section to indicate which barriers were found and which were not found, 4) the proximity
220 sensor is permanently disabled, and 5) an HTML page that corresponds to the current running total of the number of barriers found is loaded in the score frame. If the child navigates out of the proximity node without identifying the barrier, the value of the "atSidewalk-
225 Steps" field is toggled back to "false."

Attitudinal barriers are identified by clicking on the "Barrier" button after hearing an audio "bad attitude" comment. The script works in a manner similar to the structural barriers, except that an audio node is trig-
230 gered when a collision with the corresponding proximity node occurs. For example, when the child enters the classroom, a collision with a proximity node that is located just inside the door is triggered. This event triggers a sound node to play an audio clip "It's the kid
235 in the wheelchair" (said in a nasty, sarcastic tone indicating "a bad attitude"). While the wheelchair remains in the proximity node, the child can identify the attitudinal barrier (Figure 2). However, if the child moves farther into the classroom, they will leave the proximity
240 node and will be unable to identify the barrier unless they move back in (which will re-trigger the playing of the audio clip).

There are three distinct areas of the virtual world: outside the school, inside the school, and the results
245 section. The transition between the areas is accomplished by using a touch sensor to trigger an event that uses a switch node to change to the next "level." The touch sensor for the transition from the outside to the

Figure 2. While the wheelchair remains in the proximity node, the child can identify the attitudinal barrier.

inside is the automatic door opener, and the one that triggers the loading of the results is on the computer in the library. Once you have left an area, you cannot go back. The switch node is used so that the entire program can be implemented in a single VRML file that interacts with the HTML frames in which the world is loaded. The single file was necessary so that the running score for the entire world could be maintained without the need for applications, CGIs, or servlets running on a server. This permits schools and other users with slow Internet connections to download the entire set of files once and then run them locally on their machine whenever they want. Six of the Disability Awareness Consultants returned to the Rehabilitation Sciences Virtual Reality Lab at the University of Ottawa to beta-test the program for content validity and general usability. Modifications to the software were made based on their feedback.

Evaluation of the Software

Study Design

In order to evaluate the effectiveness of The Barriers software, a controlled pretest/posttest design was used. Using random assignment, half of the sample was given the VR intervention and the other half received an alternate desktop VR program—similar in length and based in a school setting, but without disability awareness information—in order to control for computer practice effects. The control program titled "Wheels," developed by R. J. Cooper & Associates, is an excellent desktop VR program designed to teach children how to use electric wheelchairs. Hence, the viewpoint of the control program is also from the first-person perspective at wheelchair height. As well, the control program also simulates wheelchair usage such as orienting oneself properly to enter doorways. The main difference between the two virtual environments is the presence of barriers (physical and attitudinal) in the intervention program. The hypotheses were that children receiving the Barriers Program would at posttest have: 1) a greater knowledge of barriers than the control group and 2) more positive attitudes toward peers with a disability compared to the control group.

Participants

Sixty youth (aged 9–11 years) participated in the study. All were from a local urban school and attended grade 4 ($n = 20$), grade 5 ($n = 19$), or grade 6 ($n = 21$). There were 24 males and 36 females in the sample. Half the sample ($n = 30$) received the Barriers intervention and the other half received the control program. Both programs took one-half hour to complete. Each child was tested individually and completed the program one time.

Measures

Two questionnaires were administered to the entire sample one week before and one week after the VR intervention. The Knowledge Questionnaire consisted of simply asking all the children to write out as many "building" and "people" barriers they could think of that might impact on children who use wheelchairs or crutches at school. Barriers were defined as "things that stop a person from doing what everybody else can do or cause people to be treated differently because of a disability." The building barrier example that was given was "smooth elevator buttons for people who are blind," and the people barrier example given was "someone who has a 'bad attitude' toward those who are different." Although this questionnaire was not a standardized measure, it was a simple, effective method for determining the youth's current knowledge of accessibility and attitudes within a school setting. For each accurate statement, the youth received one point.

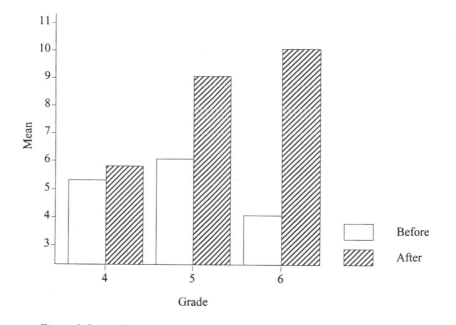

Figure 3. Pre- and postknowledge of barriers by grade for intervention group.

The attitude measure used was the Children's Social Distance from Handicapped Persons Scale, a scale developed specifically for school settings, which has 320 shown to be a quick, reliable measure of affective attitudes toward peers with a disability ($r = .78$) [22]. Concern over the word "handicapped" was allayed through conversations with experts in attitude measurement who indicated that the word "handicapped" is better 325 understood by children than the word "disabled" (Hazzard; Rosenbaum, personal communications, 1999). An example item of this measure is, "It would be okay if a handicapped kid sat next to me in class," to which the child could respond with "yes," "maybe yes," "maybe 330 no," or "no." Scores on this scale range from 0–30, with higher scores indicating more positive affective attitudes. The children also were asked to indicate whether they knew someone who was handicapped, to indicate what that handicap was, whether the person 335 was a friend, an acquaintance or a family member, and finally, how much they liked this person.

Results

Knowledge

The self-report Knowledge Scale was used to ascertain knowledge of both building or structural barriers and people or attitude barriers for both groups using 340 ANOVAs (group membership × time). Overall knowledge of barriers was examined by adding both the structural and attitude barriers together. Table 1 describes the building and attitudinal barriers for both groups before and after the intervention.

345 These results indicate that prior to the VR intervention, both the control group and the intervention group reported similar levels of knowledge within their school setting; however, following the intervention, the youth in the Barriers group reported a significantly 350 greater number of barriers than the control group, $F(1,57) = 5.35$, $p < .05$. When broken down by type (building or attitude barriers), there was a significant difference in post-reported barriers between the two groups for the building barriers, $F(1,56) = 11.27$, $p = $ 355 .001, with the Barriers group reporting more barriers.

Table 1
Mean (SD) Knowledge Scores Before and After VR Intervention

	Time	
Group	Before	After
Barriers		
Building	2.9 (1.9)	6.4 (3.9)
Attitude	2.2 (1.8)	3.2 (2.6)
Total	5.2 (3.3)	9.6 (6.0)
Control		
Building	2.5 (1.7)	3.4 (2.6)
Attitude	2.5 (1.4)	2.9 (2.1)
Total	5.0 (2.7)	6.4 (4.2)

There were no differences between groups for knowledge of attitudinal barriers, which was not unexpected because only 4 of the 24 barriers in the program were "bad attitude" barriers. Gender was also not a 360 significant factor for knowledge of barriers. There was a significant difference for children receiving the Barriers intervention by grade level on the total barriers reported following the VR intervention, $F(2,57) = 3.26$, $p < .05$, with grades 5 and 6 showing the greatest learn- 365 ing curve (see Figure 3).

Attitude and Previous Experience

No differences were found between the two groups or within groups for affective attitude measured with the Children's Social Distance from Handicapped Per-

370 sons Scale [22]. However, there was a significant difference between males and females on the post-attitude scale, $F(1,57) = 4.68$, $p < .05$, with males reporting higher affective attitudes than females. Previous experience of knowing someone with a disability has been shown to impact on attitude scores. In this study,
375 neither knowledge nor attitude scores showed differences for children who knew: 1) someone with a disability, 2) the type of disability of that person, 3) whether that person was a friend, an acquaintance, or a family member, or 4) how much they liked that person.
380 Interestingly, 54 of the 60 children reported they knew someone with a disability.

Discussion

Based on the results of this study, *Barriers: The Awareness Challenge* software was effective for increasing the knowledge of barriers within a familiar
385 setting for children in grades 4, 5, and 6. Building barriers were remembered most often, with grades 5 and 6 showing the greatest change. It is unclear whether the older children remembered more of the program at the posttest or whether their greater change in scores re-
390 flected previous findings that older children are more knowledgeable about disabilities [22] and are more accepting of their peers with a disability [23]. Regardless, sensitizing individuals to the difficulties associated with accessibility in public buildings remains an
395 important component to disability awareness promotion. Rowley-Kelly provides an excellent checklist of potential accessibility barriers that school administrators can use to evaluate their structural resources for all different types of disabilities [24]. Examples include
400 the need for wider aisles for access by people who use wheelchairs, tactile markings for individuals with visual impairments, flashing lights for fire alarms for individuals who are hearing impaired, and pictorial signage for those who have difficulty reading.
405 Although it has been 25 years since the precedent-setting Education of Handicapped Act, our children's schools are still riddled with accessibility barriers that serve to further isolate them from full participation and inclusion. More resources need to be allocated to im-
410 prove accessibility in schools and attention paid to making adjustments to existing provisions [25, 26]. Another recommendation for school resource allocation that arose from the focus groups with our Disability Awareness Consultants was the necessity for ensur-
415 ing that teachers and support staff have disability awareness training. This suggestion has been reinforced in the literature and specifically recommends that teachers be provided with training, sufficient materials, and on-site assistance [27, 28].
420 The lack of differences in attitude scores between the control and experimental groups was in all likelihood a function of the very high attitude scores of all the students participating in the study. On both the pretest and posttest scores, both groups had attitude scores

425 just under 90%; thus, either the measure was not sensitive enough and/or a ceiling effect occurred. Other factors that have been shown to impact the effectiveness of disability awareness programs include gender, where females report more positive attitudes, and familiarity,
430 where knowing someone with a disability positively influences knowledge of and attitudes toward persons with disabilities [29]. In our study, gender did not differentiate the two groups on knowledge of barriers or attitude before the VR intervention; however, males
435 did report a significantly higher posttest attitude score. This result is inconsistent with the literature [30, 31]. One possible explanation is that males were more familiar with the interactive gaming aspect of the VR program, as indicated by their higher game scores dur-
440 ing the program ($M = 16.5$, $SD = 4.56$) vs. females ($M = 14.39$, $SD = 3.57$). This gaming familiarity may have allowed the males to focus on the educational material being presented vs. maneuverability and orientation.

Regarding familiarity with disability issues, the
445 high attitude scores were most likely influenced by the great number of children in the study who knew someone with a disability [29]; in this case, 90% of the total sample. As such, knowledge and attitude scores showed no differences for children who knew someone
450 with a disability, the type of disability of that person, whether that person was a friend, acquaintance or family member, or how much they liked them. However, in evaluating the effectiveness of the software, even though most of the study sample knew someone with a
455 disability, and, as a group had very positive attitudes, they were still able to learn about accessibility barriers. This is important because increased knowledge about disabilities is believed to be necessary for creating a lasting influence on positive attitudes [32].
460 The authors realize that no simulation program will ever be able to truly describe the experiences and perceptions associated with having a disability. The concern expressed by French is that simulation programs trivialize the cumulative social and psychological ef-
465 fects of a disability and that they do not address the environmental and social barriers associated with a disability [33]. On the other hand, a lack of knowledge and understanding about issues related to a disability has been shown to lead to discrimination and isolation
470 in schools [8, 24]. The Barriers Project was designed with these concerns and issues in mind. The collaboration of youth with disabilities in the design of the program provided assurances of content validity as well as support for the concept of using VR to impart knowl-
475 edge to their peers. As well, the focus of the program is not based on simulating a sense of the physical limitations associated with a disability, but rather on the environmental and social barriers encountered by persons with a disability. Utilizing the social–political model of
480 disability, the Barriers Project revolved around the impact of the environment (both physical and social) on the experiences of a person using a wheelchair [2].

Every effort was made to accurately design a program that simulates maneuverability in a wheelchair in order
485 to highlight structural barriers such as narrow aisles, doorways, washroom stalls, and crowded classrooms. Although this provided a sense of frustration for the children tested on the program, it served to provide a sense of environmental constraints as well as to high-
490 light the capabilities of their peers who use a wheelchair.

The program also attempted to provide facilitated learning by using a problem-solving approach. In designing an environment that required active exploration
495 for solutions, we anticipated that the children would remember more barriers—a recommendation suggested by previous researchers [34–36]. However, during the beta-testing phase, when the entire VR school was open to exploration, we found that the children missed
500 many areas important to the learning objective. It appeared that in providing a totally unstructured environment, the children focused on exploration vs. barrier identification. Thus, the program was modified to be semi-structured (i.e., where the children were directed
505 to different areas, such as the library, where they could search and identify the barriers specific to that location). Overall, this was found to be an effective strategy based on the results and the anecdotal comments reported by the students testing the program. The anecdo-
510 tal comments included that: 1) it gave them a better understanding of the accessibility barriers that are all around them that they had not previously noticed, 2) "bad attitudes" are just as difficult as, if not more difficult than, building barriers, 3) the VR program was
515 good at simulating maneuverability in a wheelchair and could be extremely frustrating at times, 4) they had a new appreciation of the capabilities of people who use wheelchairs, and 5) the program was very motivating and they were interested in trying it again.

Limitations and Recommendations
520 The most obvious limitation of this study is the lack of effect of attitudinal change. This was probably due to positive attitudes of the students toward peers with a disability before the intervention as well as the relatively few attitudinal barriers in the program. The
525 school that agreed to be in the study is one of eight schools out of 128 that is identified as "accessible" by the school board. From a structural point of view, however, the school had all the accessibility barriers that were identified in the program. As part of the "accessi-
530 ble distinction," it is likely that there is a greater incidence of children with disabilities in this school (however, there were no children who used wheelchairs or crutches in the three classes tested), and, thus, greater disability awareness. For future studies, we would rec-
535 ommend controlling for place effects by testing the program in settings with and without previous awareness and sensitivity training.

Another likely influence that impacted on attitudi-
540 nal scores was the small percentage of attitudinal barriers presented in the program (4 of 24). Poor attitudes were depicted as nasty or sarcastic comments by virtual students. The use of these students or avatars in the program uses up a considerable amount of memory, which in turn slows down the program. For ease of use,
545 we decided to include as few avatars as possible. However, as both the hardware and software capabilities improve in the future, more avatars can be used to depict attitudinal barriers. The content of the attitudinal barriers also posed difficulties. Many of the statements
550 that our Disability Awareness Consultants proposed (such as the word "crip") were not included for fear of promoting or teaching negative attitudes. For that reason, this program could serve as a jump start for discussing negative attitudes toward people who are dif-
555 ferent.

VR was chosen as a teaching medium for a number of reasons: 1) it provided first-person simulation effects, 2) allowed us to control the environment (e.g., define and place barriers where we chose), 3) is acces-
560 sible to many individuals if distributed over the Internet, and 4) has shown to be an enjoyable experience for children. However, because this is the first VR program that provides disability awareness, we would recommend future studies compare it to traditional forms
565 of disability awareness training such as real-world wheelchair simulation, presentations, testimonials, and videos.

As well, because this project is the first of its kind to use VR to promote disability awareness, in this case,
570 for mobility impairments, it would be interesting to develop and test the effectiveness of VR for simulating other types of disabilities. It also would be interesting to give the user the opportunity to make modifications that would erase barriers within the virtual environ-
575 ment. For example, the user could widen aisles or lower drinking fountains in order to make them more accessible.

Even in a school whose students had very positive attitudes about peers with disabilities, they were still
580 able to learn about structural barriers in their environment that negatively impact the lives of individuals with disabilities. Hence, *Barriers: The Awareness Challenge* was considered successful in teaching about the environmental conditions faced by individuals with
585 mobility limitations and, thus, was made available free of charge via the Internet at http:/www.health. uottawa.ca/vrlab. We hope that along with children utilizing the program, teachers, staff, and parents also try the software. Along with raising awareness about
590 structural and attitudinal barriers, we hope this program will serve to initiate further discussions about disabilities, highlight how environmental constraints and attitudes impact society's views toward their members with a disability, and provide a forum that emphasizes
595 the capabilities of individuals who have disabilities.

References

1. Statistics Canada, *1991 Canadian Census*, Statistics Canada, Ottawa, Ontario, 1992.
2. M. Law and W. Dunn, Perspectives on Understanding and Changing the Environments of Children with Disabilities, *Physical & Occupational Therapy in Pediatrics*, *13*:3, pp. 10–17, 1993.
3. M. Law, Changing Disabling Environments through Participatory Research, *Canadian Journal of Rehabilitation*, *7*:1, pp. 22–23, 1993.
4. S. R. Asher and A. R. Taylor, Social Outcomes of Mainstreaming: Sociometric Assessment and Beyond, in *Social Development of Exceptional Children*, P. Strain (Ed.), Aspen Systems, Rockville, Maryland, pp. 1–18, 1982.
5. S. B. Baker and M. A. Rogosky-Grassi, Access to the School, in *Teaching the Student with Spina Bifida*, L. Fern, F. Rowley-Kelly, and D. H. Reigel (Eds.), Paul H. Brooks Publishing, Baltimore, pp. 31–70, 1993.
6. M. Rogosky-Grassi, Working with Perceptual-Motor Skills, in *Teaching the Student with Spina Bifida*, L. Fern, F. Rowley-Kelly, and D. H. Reigel (Eds.), Paul H. Brooks Publishing, Baltimore, pp. 193–209, 1993.
7. J. Donaldson, Changing Attitudes toward Handicapped Persons: A Review and Analyses of Research, *Exceptional Children*, *46*:7, pp. 504–513, 1980.
8. J. Gottlieb, Attitudes toward Retarded Children: Effects of Labeling and Academic Performance, *American Journal of Mental Deficiency*, *78*, pp. 15–19, 1980.
9. J. Gottlieb, L. Cohen, and L. Goldstein, Social Contact and Personal Adjustment as Variables Relating to Attitudes toward EMR Children, *Training School Bulletin*, *71*, pp. 9–16, 1974.
10. A. Llewellyn, The Abuse of Children with Physical Disabilities in Mainstream Schooling, *Developmental Medicine and Child Neurology*, *37*, pp. 740–743, 1995.
11. H. Gardner, Relations with Other Selves, in *Developmental Psychology* (2nd Edition), M. H. Bornstein and M. Lamb (Eds.), Lawrence Erlbaum Associates, Hillsdale, New Jersey, pp. 72–98, 1982.
12. C. Roberts and P. Smith, Attitudes and Behavior of Children toward Peers with Disabilities, *International Journal of Disability, Development and Education*, *46*:1, pp. 35–50, 1999.
13. J. J. Kozak, P. A. Hancock, E. J. Arthur, and S. T. Chrysler, Transfer of Training from Virtual Reality, *Ergonomics*, *36*, pp. 777–784, 1993.
14. K. Pimentel and K. Teixeiera, *Virtual Reality: Through the New Looking Glass*, McGraw-Hill, Toronto, 1995.
15. D. P. Inman and K. Loge, Teaching Motorized Wheelchair Operation in Virtual Reality, in *Proceedings of the 1995 CSUN Virtual Reality Conference*, California State University, Northridge, 1995.
16. D. Strickland, L. M. Marcus, G. B. Mesibov, and K. Hogan, Brief Report: Two Case Studies Using Virtual Reality as a Learning Tool for Autistic Children, *Journal of Autism and Developmental Disorders*, *26*:6, pp. 651–659, 1996.
17. F. D. Rusch, R. E. Cimera, D. L. Shelden, U. Thakkar, D. A. Chapman, Y. H. Khan, D. D. Moore, and J. S. LeBoy, Crossing Streets: A K–12 Virtual Reality Application for Understanding Knowledge Acquisition, in *Proceedings of the IEEE Virtual Reality Annual International Symposium*, IEEE Press, New York, 1997.
18. J. W. Regian, W. L. Shebilske, and J. M. Monk, Virtual Reality: An Instructional Medium for Visual-Spatial Tasks, *Journal of Communication*, *42*, pp. 136–149, 1992.
19. P. N. Wilson, N. Foreman, and D. Stanton, Virtual Reality, Disability and Rehabilitation, *Disability and Rehabilitation*, *19*:6, pp. 213–220, 1997.
20. B. R. Lowery and F. G. Knirk, Micro-Computer Video Games and Spatial Visualization Acquisition, *Journal of Educational Technology Systems*, *11*, pp. 155–166, 1982.
21. J. McComas, J. Pivik, and M. Laflamme, Children's Transfer of Spatial Learning from Virtual Reality to Real Environments, *CyberPsychology & Behavior*, *1*:2, pp. 115–122, 1998.
22. A. Hazzard, Children's Experience with Knowledge of and Attitude toward Disabled Persons, *Journal of Special Education*, *17*:2, pp. 131–139, 1983.
23. G. Royal and M. Roberts, Students' Perceptions of and Attitudes toward Disabilities: A Comparison of Twenty Conditions, *Journal of Clinical Child Psychology*, *16*:2, pp. 122–132, 1987.
24. F. Rowley-Kelly, Social Acceptance and Disability Awareness, in *Teaching the Student with Spina Bifida*, L. Fern, F. Rowley-Kelly, and D. H. Reigel (Eds.), Paul H. Brooks Publishing, Baltimore, pp. 245–250, 1993.
25. S. B. Baker and M. A. Rogosky-Grassi, Access to the School, in *Teaching the Student with Spina Bifida*, L. Fern, F. Rowley-Kelly, and D. H. Reigel (Eds.), Paul H. Brooks Publishing, Baltimore, pp. 31–70, 1993.
26. G. Clunies-Ross and K. O'Meara, Changing the Attitudes of Students toward Peers with Disabilities, *Australian Psychologist*, *24*:2, pp. 273–284, 1989.
27. A. Hazzard and B. Baker, Enhancing Children's Attitudes toward Disabled Peers Using a Multi-Media Intervention, *Journal of Applied Developmental Psychology*, *3*, pp. 247–262, 1982.
28. W. Henderson, Recommendations of Program Presenters about the Design and Implementation of Disability Awareness Programs for Elementary Students, doctoral dissertation, University of Massachusetts, 1987, *Dissertation Abstracts International*, *48*:09, p. 153, 1988.
29. P. L. Rosenbaum, R. W., Armstrong, and S. M. King, Determinants of Children's Attitudes toward Disability: A Review of Evidence, *Children's Health Care*, *17*:1, pp. 32–39, 1988.
30. Y. Leyser, C. Cumblad, and D. Strickman, Direct Intervention to Modify Attitudes toward the Handicapped by Community Volunteers: The Learning about Handicaps Programme, *Educational Review*, *38*:3, pp. 229–236, 1986.
31. A. Tripp, R. French, and C. Sherrill, Contact Theory and Attitudes of Children in Physical Education and Programs toward Peers with Disabilities, *Adapted Physical Activity Quarterly*, *12*, pp. 323–332, 1995.
32. M. Karniski, The Effect of Increased Knowledge of Body Systems and Functions on Attitudes toward the Disabled, *Rehabilitation Counseling Bulletin*, *22*, pp. 16–20, 1978.
33. S. French, Simulation Exercises in Disability Awareness Training: A Critique, in *Beyond Disability: Towards an Enabling Society*, G. Hales (Ed.), The Open University, Bristol, Pennsylvania, pp. 114–123, 1996.
34. K. Diamond, Factors in Preschool Children's Social Problem-Solving Strategies for Peers With and Without Disabilities, *Early Childhood Research Quarterly*, *9*:2, pp. 195–205, 1994.
35. J. Kilburn, Changing Attitudes, *Teaching Exceptional Children*, *16*, pp. 124–127, 1984.
36. S. Thurston, R. Wideman, M. Wideman, and P. Willet, Promoting Positive Attitudes on the Disabled, *History and Social Science Teacher*, *21*, pp. 39–43, 1985.

Acknowledgments: This project was funded by Human Resources Development Canada and Nortel Networks. The authors would like to thank our Disability Awareness Consultants, The Ottawa Children's Treatment Centre, The Canadian Paraplegic Association, Jason Odin, and Corpus Christi School for their assistance in this project.

Address correspondence to: Dr. Jayne Pivik, School of Rehabilitation Sciences, University of Ottawa, 451 Smyth Road, Ottawa, Ontario, Canada K1H 8M5.

Exercise for Article 12

Factual Questions

1. How is VR defined in this article?

2. What was the age range of the Disability Awareness Consultants?

3. What type of assignment was used to place students into the two programs?

4. How many students received the Barriers intervention treatment?

5. What was the mean post-reported (i.e., after intervention) building barriers score for the Barriers group? What was the corresponding mean for the control group?

6. Was the difference between the two means in your answer to Question 5 statistically significant? If yes, at what probability level?

7. Was there a difference between the Barriers group and the Wheels group on the Children's Social Distance from Handicapped Persons Scale?

Questions for Discussion

8. In lines 30–32, the researchers indicate that negative attitudes expressed by their peers may be the most difficult type of barrier encountered by children with disabilities. Would you recommend this program to educators who are looking for a tool to help reduce negative attitudes? Explain.

9. The control group also received a VR program (i.e., "Wheels"). Do you think it would be worthwhile to conduct another study in which the control group did not receive a program? Explain. (See lines 274–281.)

10. In your opinion, is the control program ("Wheels") described in sufficient detail? Explain.

11. When scores are very high (near the top of a scale) at the beginning of an experiment, there is little room for improvement. Thus, it is not possible to obtain large increases. This problem is called the "ceiling effect," which the researchers refer to in lines 423–426. Were you previously aware of this type of problem in conducting research? How important do you think it was in this study?

12. If you were conducting a study on the same topic, what changes in the research methodology, if any, would you make?

Quality Ratings

Directions: Indicate your level of agreement with each of the following statements by circling a number from 5 for strongly agree (SA) to 1 for strongly disagree (SD). If you believe an item is not applicable to this research article, leave it blank. Be prepared to explain your ratings. When responding to criteria A and B below, keep in mind that brief titles and abstracts are conventional in published research.

A. The title of the article is appropriate.

SA   5   4   3   2   1   SD

B. The abstract provides an effective overview of the research article.

SA   5   4   3   2   1   SD

C. The introduction establishes the importance of the study.

SA   5   4   3   2   1   SD

D. The literature review establishes the context for the study.

SA   5   4   3   2   1   SD

E. The research purpose, question, or hypothesis is clearly stated.

SA   5   4   3   2   1   SD

F. The method of sampling is sound.

SA   5   4   3   2   1   SD

G. Relevant demographics (for example, age, gender, and ethnicity) are described.

SA   5   4   3   2   1   SD

H. Measurement procedures are adequate.

SA   5   4   3   2   1   SD

I. All procedures have been described in sufficient detail to permit a replication of the study.

SA   5   4   3   2   1   SD

J. The participants have been adequately protected from potential harm.

SA   5   4   3   2   1   SD

K. The results are clearly described.

SA   5   4   3   2   1   SD

L. The discussion/conclusion is appropriate.

SA   5   4   3   2   1   SD

M. Despite any flaws, the report is worthy of publication.

SA   5   4   3   2   1   SD

Article 13

Project Trust: Breaking Down Barriers Between Middle School Children

MARY ELLEN BATIUK
Wilmington College

JAMES A. BOLAND
Wilmington College

NORMA WILCOX
Wright State University

ABSTRACT. This paper analyzes the success of a camp retreat weekend called Project Trust involving middle school students and teachers. The goal of the camp is to break down barriers between cliques identified as active in the school. The camp focuses on building team relationships across clique membership and incorporates elements of peace education and conflict resolution. A treatment group (campers) and comparison group (noncampers) were administered an adaptation of the Bogardus Social Distance Test and the Piers-Harris Children's Self-Concept Scale before and after the camp. Attendance was found to lower social distance scores for nine of the ten groups/cliques. Campers also had higher self-concept scores after the retreat.

From *Adolescence*, *39*, 531–538. Copyright © 2004 by Libra Publishers, Inc. Reprinted with permission.

The *Final Report and Findings of the Safe School Initiative* indicates that from 1993 to 1997, the "odds that a child in grades 9–12 would be threatened or injured with a weapon in school were 8 percent, or 1 in 13 or 14; the odds of getting into a physical fight at school were 15 percent, or 1 in 7" (Vossekuil, Fein, Reddy, Borum, & Modzeleski, 2002, p. 12). Such widespread experiences of school violence have led to what McLaren, Leonardo, and Allen (2000) call a "bunker mentality" on many school campuses. As Tompkins (2000) points out, "increased levels of security suggest to students and teachers that they learn and teach in a violent environment where students cannot be trusted and are under suspicion" (p. 65). This is doubly unfortunate, not only because positive school climates promote learning, but that they have been found to be strong predictors of the absence of school violence (Welsh, 2000).

Further, one of the ten key findings of the analysis of the Safe School Initiative is that "many attackers felt bullied, persecuted, or injured by others prior to the attack" (Vossekuil et al., 2002, p. 18). In a word, attackers felt excluded. Kramer (2000) has established that patterns of individual exclusion in school settings contribute to violence among students because exclusion separates them from the informal social control networks provided by parents, schools, and communities. This lack of informal social control has been linked to diminishing social and cultural capital (Hagen, 1985) and ultimately delinquency (Cullen, 1994; Currie, 1998; Sampson & Laub, 1993). Exclusion also preempts the kind of dialogue that can resolve conflicts (Aronowitz, 2003).

As a result, many educators have called for curricular changes incorporating programs in peace education (Caulfield, 2000; Harris, 1996; Pepinsky, 2000) and conflict resolution (Bretherton, 1996; Children's Defense Fund, 1998). For example, 10 years ago, Wilmington College collaborated with a local middle school to provide programming aimed at eliminating patterns of mistrust and exclusion fostered by student cliques. The collaboration was a natural one since Wilmington College offers extensive teacher education programs and maintains a strong tradition of conflict resolution and peacemaking tied to its Quaker heritage.

The training emphasized a mutual and reflexive process of problem solving and conflict resolution in which involved parties actively frame the understanding of both the problem and its solution. Teachers and students at the middle school overwhelmingly pointed to the ongoing problem of conflicts arising from student cliques. As a response, teachers and students designed activities that would help break down barriers among the cliques. From this collaboration emerged Project Trust—a weekend camp retreat in which student opinion/clique leaders engaged in discussions, role-playing, and noncompetitive risk-taking tasks.

The present paper focuses on a program for middle school children that incorporates principles of peace education and conflict resolution techniques to address the pervasive sources of these conflicts within networks of student cliques. It was hypothesized that by engaging student leaders in activities focused on cooperation and breaking down barriers, these same students would become more receptive to interacting with members of other cliques. It was also hypothesized that participation in the retreat weekend would lead to increased self-esteem in the participants.

Method

Project Trust

In the fall of 1990, middle school teachers and stu-

70 dents were asked to brainstorm about the kinds of cliques that were active in the school. A list of 24 groups, active within the school, emerged from these initial brainstorming sessions. Discussions with both students and teachers allowed project managers to hone 75 the list to eight, and these groups became the focal point for Project Trust. The groups included: (1) preps—smart and well dressed, well to do or at least giving the perception that they are, doing what they are told to do; (2) alternatives—baggy clothes, various 80 colors of hair, might be skaters, long hair; (3) jocks—athletes or individuals whose lives are dominated by sports interests, wearing NBA and NFL jerseys; (4) hoods/gangsters/thugs—rule-breakers, tough, like to fight, might be in a gang, wearing black; (5) dorks—85 geeks, socially awkward, nonathletic; (6) cheerleaders—attractive and active girls; (7) hicks/hillbillies—rural kids, possibly live in trailer parks, like country music; and (8) dirties—poor kids, dirty and cannot help it, poor hygiene.

90 The names of the cliques came directly from the students and teachers. Ethnic groups were not mentioned by the students but were added by the project managers after discussions with the teachers (i.e., whites and African Americans).

Treatment and Comparison Groups

95 Project Trust camp retreats include student opinion/clique leaders who are identified by teachers and invited to spend the weekend at a local camp that regularly provides team-building exercises to local civic groups and businesses. Middle school teachers receive 100 training from Wilmington College project managers in group process and team building. Both teachers and Wilmington College professors lead the retreats. Once at the camp, students and teachers are placed into Family Groups of 8–10 members designed to cut across 105 clique memberships. Students are encouraged to take ownership of the weekend agenda by developing contracts with retreat leaders. Contracting processes involve eliciting from students what they hope to "get" from the weekend (everything from food to fun activi-110 ties) and what they are willing to "give" to get those things. During the course of the weekend (Friday evening through Sunday afternoon), student family groups take part in discussions, cooperative tasks, and team building and survival exercises.

115 One team-building activity, titled Toxic Waste, involves blindfolded team members "dumping" a cupful of sludge into another cup inside of a 4 × 4 square. Unsighted family team members cannot cross into the square, have access only to 4 bungee cords, the cup of 120 sludge and a rubber band, and are given directions by their sighted team members. Another activity, called Plane Crash, involves the completion of various tasks by team members who have received several handicaps (broken bones, loss of sight) and limited supplies 125 (food, water, blankets). Also included in the retreat are an extended outdoor trust walk and a structured discussion about the harmful effects of put-downs and techniques for resolving conflicts around them. Students and teachers discuss the case study of a young girl who 130 committed suicide, leaving a note explaining the exclusion she felt because of being called a "fat hog" by her classmates.

Family groups are brought together regularly to assess how the retreat is progressing. Plenty of snacks, 135 pizza, and pop are provided to foster an environment of fun and relaxation during the time that students and teachers spend together.

In addition to this treatment group, fellow students who did not attend the camp were selected on the basis 140 of availability and assessed using the same instrument, for the purposes of comparison. Treatment group students were identified by teachers on the basis of being "opinion leaders."

Assessments

145 Assessment of Project Trust weekends relies primarily on an adaptation of the Bogardus (1933) Social Distance Scale to measure the social distances between the students and identified groups before and after the camp experience. The scale was chosen because of its 150 ease of scoring and high reliability (Miller, 1991; Owen et al., 1981). In addition, the scale has also been successfully and widely adapted for use with school-age children (Cover, 2001; Lee, Sapp, & Ray, 1996; Mielenz, 1979; Payne, 1976; Williams, 1992). On this 155 modified scale, students were asked to rate all ten groups on a scale of 0–7, with 7 representing the greatest degree of social distance: 0–be best friends with; 1–invite over to my house; 3–choose to eat lunch with; 4–say "hi" to only; 5–as a member of my homeroom only; 6–as a member of my school only; 7–exclude 160 them from my school. Both treatment and comparison groups completed this scale immediately before the retreat weekend and within one month after the camp.

In addition, treatment and nontreatment groups completed the Piers-Harris Children's Self-Concept 165 Scale (Piers, 1984). This self-report scale measures self-concept using 80 yes/no questions and is intended for use with youths aged 8–18. The scale was administered to the treatment group before and after the camp experience, and to the comparison group before the 170 camp experience.

Results

Camps have been held from 1998 through 2002 in both the fall and spring. An independent-samples *t* test (equal variances not assumed) comparing the pretest mean scores of the treatment group (*n* = 298) and com-175 parison group (*n* = 215) found significant differences between only two groups: preps (*t* = 5.058, *df* = 405, *p* < .01) and jocks (*t* = 2.654, *df* = 378, *p* < .01). In both cases, the means of the treatment group social distance scores were lower than for the comparison group: preps 180 (*M* = 2.28, *SD* = 2.06, for campers, vs. *M* = 3.34, *SD* =

2.24, for noncampers), jocks ($M = 2.07$, $SD = 2.14$, for campers, vs. $M = 2.66$, $SD = 2.43$, for noncampers). Thus, treatment and comparison students were roughly equivalent in their perceptions of social distance from their classmates with the exception of the preps and the jocks. In these two instances, the campers reported statistically significant lower social distance scores when compared to noncampers.

A paired-samples t test was calculated for both the treatment group ($n = 216$) and comparison group ($n = 80$). Table 1 reports the results for the treatment group. For all eight cliques, attendance at the camp significantly reduced perceptions of social distance. In addition, perceptions of social distance were significantly reduced for African Americans but not whites. Mean scores for whites were already low (pretest $M = .54$, $SD = 1.00$) and did fall (posttest $M = .47$, $SD = .86$), though not to a statistically significant degree. The greatest change for campers was in their perceptions of dirties, moving an average of 1.55 points on the 7-point scale (pretest $M = 5.55$, $SD = 1.40$; posttest $M = 4.00$, $SD = 1.71$); dorks, moving an average of 1.37 points (pretest $M = 4.60$, $SD = 2.10$; posttest $M = 3.23$, $SD = 1.65$); and hicks, moving an average of 1.23 points (pretest $M = 4.38$, $SD = 2.07$; posttest $M = 3.15$, $SD = 1.96$).

Table 1

Paired-Samples Two-Tailed t Test for the Treatment Group (n = 216)

Campers	t	df	p
Preps	6.816	212	.000
Alternatives	5.254	196	.000
Jocks	6.532	207	.000
Hoods	6.709	205	.000
Dorks	10.810	206	.000
Cheerleaders	3.282	213	.001
Hicks	8.608	203	.000
Dirties	11.751	204	.000
African Americans	2.500	208	.013
Whites	1.141	206	.255

Table 2 reports the results for the comparison group (noncampers). The only statistically significant shift was for preps (pretest $M = 3.18$, $SD = 2.23$; posttest $M = 2.74$, $SD = 2.37$). In all other instances, there were no statistically significant changes. However, there were two instances, for dorks and African Americans, in which social distance scores actually regressed.

On the Piers-Harris Children's Self-Concept Scale, self-concept scores also shifted for the treatment (camper) group. The mean score on the pretest was 61.37 ($SD = 12.6$) and the mean on the posttest was 66.13 ($SD = 11.32$). The difference was statistically significant ($p < .01$).

Conclusions

The results suggest that educational programs for middle school children that incorporate peace education and conflict resolution hold potential for reducing divisive student cliques built around difference, mistrust, and exclusion, that often result in the violence found in schools today. While this is only one study in a rural area of a mid-Atlantic state with a unique subculture, it does offer hope of greater validity and reliability with its longitudinal character. Obviously, the study needs to be replicated in a variety of cultural and institutional contexts and across different age groups. However, there is much to be gained by such replication in a society struggling to understand the attitudes of the "other."

Table 2

Paired-Samples Two-Tailed t Test for the Comparison Group (n = 80)

Noncampers	t	df	p
Preps	2.035	72	.046
Alternatives	0.967	63	.337
Jocks	0.150	65	.881
Hoods	0.567	61	.573
Dorks	−0.068	68	.946
Cheerleaders	0.935	72	.353
Hicks	2.264	72	.353
Dirties	1.589	67	.117
African Americans	−0.271	74	.787
Whites	0.090	206	.928

References

Aronowitz, S. (2003). Essay on violence. In *Smoke and mirrors: The hidden context of violence in schools and society* (pp. 211–227). New York: Rowman and Littlefield.

Bogardus, E. S. (1933). A social distance scale. *Sociology and Social Research, 17,* 265–271.

Bretherton, D. (1996). Nonviolent conflict resolution in children. *Peabody Journal of Education, 71,* 111–127.

Caulfield, S. L. (2000). Creating peaceable schools. *ANNALS: The American Academy of Political and Social Science, 567,* 170–185.

Children's Defense Fund. (1998). *Keeping children safe in schools: A resource for states.* Available: http://www.childrensdefense.org.

Cover, J. D. (1995). The effects of social contact on prejudice. *The Journal of Social Psychology, 135,* 403–405.

Cullen, F. T. (1994). Social support as an organizing concept for criminology: Presidential address to the Academy of Criminal Justice Sciences. *Justice Quarterly, 11,* 527–559.

Currie, E. (1998). *Crime and punishment in America.* New York: Metropolitan Books.

Hagen, J. (1985). *Modern criminology: Crime, criminal behavior and its control.* New York: McGraw-Hill.

Harris, I. M. (1996). Peace education in an urban school district in the United States. *Peabody Journal of Education, 71,* 63–83.

Kramer, R. (2000). Poverty, inequality, and youth violence. *ANNALS: The American Academy of Political and Social Science, 567,* 123–139.

Lee, M. Y., Sapp, S. G., & Ray, M. C. (1996). The Reverse Social Distance Scale. *The Journal of Social Psychology, 136,* 17–24.

McLaren, P., Leonardo, Z., & Allen, R. L. (2000). Rated "cv" for cool violence. In S. U. Spina (Ed.), *Smoke and mirrors: The hidden context of violence in schools and society* (pp. 67–92). New York: Rowman and Littlefield.

Mielenz, C. C. (1979). Non-prejudiced Caucasian parents and attitudes of their children toward Negroes. *The Journal of Negro Education, 1979,* 12–21.

Miller, D. (1991). *Handbook of research design and social measurement.* Newbury Park, CA: Sage Publications.

Owen, C. A., Eisner, H. C., & McFaul, T. R. (1981). A half century of social distance research: National replication of the Bogardus studies. *Sociology and Social Research, 66,* 80–98.

Payne, W. J. (1976). Social class and social differentiation: A case for multidimensionality of social distance. *Sociology and Social Research, 61,* 54–67.

Pepinsky, H. (2000). Educating for peace. *ANNALS: The American Academy of Political and Social Science, 567*, 157–169.

Piers, E. V. (1984). *Piers-Harris Children's Self-Concept Scale revised manual 1984*. Los Angeles: Western Psychological Services.

Sampson, R. J., & Laub, J. H. (1993). *Crime in the making: Pathways and turning points through life*. Cambridge, MA: Harvard University Press.

Tompkins, D. E. (2000). School violence: Gangs and a culture of fear. *ANNALS: The American Academy of Political and Social Science, 567*, 54–71.

Vossekuil, B., Fein, R. A., Reddy, M., Borum, R., & Modzeleski, W. (2002). *The final report and findings of the Safe School Initiative: Implications for the prevention of school attacks in the United States*. Washington, DC: U.S. Secret Service and U.S. Department of Education.

Welsh, W. N. (2000). The effects of school climate on school disorder. *ANNALS: The American Academy of Political and Social Science, 567*, 88–107.

Williams, C. (1992). The relationship between the affective and cognitive dimensions of prejudice. *College Student Journal, 26*, 50–54.

About the authors: *Mary Ellen Batiuk*, Department of Social and Political Studies, Wilmington College. *James A. Boland*, Department of Education, Wilmington College. *Norma Wilcox*, Department of Sociology, Wright State University.

Address correspondence to: Mary Ellen Batiuk, Department of Social and Political Studies, Wilmington College, Wilmington, OH 45177. E-mail: mebatiuk@wilmington.edu

Exercise for Article 13

Factual Questions

1. What resulted from the brainstorming sessions?

2. On the Social Distance Scale, what does a rating of "3" represent?

3. On the Social Distance Scale, does a high rating (e.g., "7") represent the greatest degree of social distance *or* does it represent the least degree of social distance?

4. In terms of social distance, the greatest change for campers from pretest to posttest was in their perceptions of what group?

5. In Table 1, all differences are statistically significant except for one group. Which group?

6. Was the treatment group's pretest to posttest difference on self-concept statistically significant? If yes, at what probability level?

Questions for Discussion

7. Keeping in mind that this is a research report and not an instructional guide, is the description of the treatment in lines 95–137 described in sufficient detail so that you have a clear picture of it? Explain.

8. For the comparison group, fellow students who did not attend the camp were selected on the basis of availability. How much stronger would this experiment have been if students had been randomly assigned to the treatment and comparison groups? Explain. (See lines 138–143.)

9. In your opinion, is the Piers-Harris Children's Self-Concept Scale described in sufficient detail? Explain. (See lines 163–170.)

10. The researchers state that "the study needs to be replicated in a variety of cultural and institutional contexts and across different age groups." In your opinion, are the results of this study sufficiently promising to warrant such replications? Explain. (See lines 228–230.)

11. What changes, if any, would you suggest making in the research methodology used in this study?

Quality Ratings

Directions: Indicate your level of agreement with each of the following statements by circling a number from 5 for strongly agree (SA) to 1 for strongly disagree (SD). If you believe an item is not applicable to this research article, leave it blank. Be prepared to explain your ratings. When responding to criteria A and B below, keep in mind that brief titles and abstracts are conventional in published research.

A. The title of the article is appropriate.

   SA   5   4   3   2   1   SD

B. The abstract provides an effective overview of the research article.

   SA   5   4   3   2   1   SD

C. The introduction establishes the importance of the study.

   SA   5   4   3   2   1   SD

D. The literature review establishes the context for the study.

   SA   5   4   3   2   1   SD

E. The research purpose, question, or hypothesis is clearly stated.

   SA   5   4   3   2   1   SD

F. The method of sampling is sound.

   SA   5   4   3   2   1   SD

G. Relevant demographics (for example, age, gender, and ethnicity) are described.

   SA   5   4   3   2   1   SD

H. Measurement procedures are adequate.

   SA   5   4   3   2   1   SD

I.   All procedures have been described in sufficient detail to permit a replication of the study.

SA   5   4   3   2   1   SD

J.   The participants have been adequately protected from potential harm.

SA   5   4   3   2   1   SD

K.   The results are clearly described.

SA   5   4   3   2   1   SD

L.   The discussion/conclusion is appropriate.

SA   5   4   3   2   1   SD

M.   Despite any flaws, the report is worthy of publication.

SA   5   4   3   2   1   SD

Article 14

The Effects of a Parent–Child Paired Reading Program on Reading Abilities, Phonological Awareness, and Self-Concept of At-Risk Pupils

ALAIN CADIEUX
Université du Québec en Outaouais

PAUL BOUDREAULT
Université du Québec en Outaouais

ABSTRACT. There is a body of literature suggesting that involving parents in their children's education is an effective strategy for children at risk of reading failure. In a pretest/posttest control group design, parents in an experimental group received reading materials and were trained on techniques to stimulate their child during paired reading at home, while a control group only received materials. Reading and general academic abilities were pre- and posttested, as well as phonological awareness and self-concept. The results show statistically significant gains in general academic abilities and phonological awareness in favor of the experimental group, while no significant gains were noted in reading abilities and self-concept. This report discusses the factors which could explain those results.

From *Reading Improvement*, 42, 224–237. Copyright © 2005 by Project Innovation, Inc. Reprinted with permission.

The prevention of academic failure has become an increasing concern for those who aim to ensure the success of the greatest number of pupils possible (Leslie & McMillan, 1999; Snow, Burns, & Griffin, 1998; Torgesen, 2002). In many Western countries, the alarming number of pupils dropping out or failing has incited many researchers, educators, and parents to mobilize their efforts to redress this concerning situation. Over the last few years, the increasing number of pupils experiencing difficulties in normal classes combined with budgetary cuts, which limit services available to students, have led policy makers and education specialists to put more emphasis on a better cooperation between schools and parents in order to prevent academic failure, particularly in reading (Cadieux & Boudreault, 2003). Reading is at the center of learning activities at the beginning of a child's schooling. Among other things, reading permits access to culture and facilitates learning many other school subjects. Early failure in reading often has disastrous impacts on the academic future of children. However, the number of children failing can be significantly reduced when parents cooperate actively in their children's school education right from the start (Purcell-Gates, 2000). Among other things, many researchers have highlighted the positive effects of parent–school cooperation programs on the performance of at-risk pupils, including those at risk of failure in reading (Fitton & Gredler, 1996; Hoover-Dempsey & Sandler, 1997; McCarthey, 2000; Sanacore, 1990; Vadasy, Jenkins, & Pool, 2000; Wasik, 1998). Paired reading, which is one of those programs that necessitate an active cooperation between a child's family and school (Topping, 1995; Topping and Lindsay, 1991), was introduced in the 1970s and was based mostly on the research of K. J. Topping. This method is simple to learn and is effective with parents who do not have a high level of education or who have poor reading abilities. It includes essentially a simultaneous reading phase and an independent reading phase. In the first phase, the parent and the child read out loud together a short text previously chosen by the child. The parent follows the same reading speed as his/her child, acts principally as a model and pays attention to the child's pronunciation during reading. In the second phase, the child gives a certain signal that indicates to the parent that he/she is ready to continue reading on his/her own. The parent praises his/her child and lets him/her read alone until he/she makes a mistake or hesitates for more than four seconds. When this occurs, the parent reads the word with the child and starts reading simultaneously with his/her child again until the child signals that he/she is ready to start reading alone again, and so on (Topping, 1995).

Several literature reviews analyzed the results of primary studies that explored the effects of paired reading on reading ability (Fitton & Gredler, 1996; Toomey, 1993; Topping, 1995; Topping & Lindsay, 1991; Topping & Wolfendale, 1985). Topping (1995) identified 18 studies that focused on the effects of paired reading. In these studies, the age of participants varied between 5 and 13 years, with groups of 3 to 33 children participating in a 4- to 39-week intervention.

Twelve studies used the biological parents of the children, and six used peers or volunteer parents. The
65   measures used as dependent variables included comprehension scale scores, such as the Neale Analysis of Reading Ability, or results obtained on other tests that generated a single reading accuracy score. Most studies obtained results expressed in "reading age" and in-
70   cluded an analysis of "ratio gains," corresponding to the reading age gain achieved by a subject on a standardized reading test divided by the subject's chronological age (Topping, 1995). The ratio gain of participants varied from 0.94 to 9.75 in accuracy and from
75   0.96 to 9.27 in comprehension, while the ratio gains of control groups ranged from –0.43 to 4.88 in accuracy and from –0.13 to 7.11 in comprehension. In follow-up studies, the results varied generally from one child to another. Topping (1995) suggested that the duration of
80   the intervention period and the acceleration of learning do not particularly affect the results but that nothing indicated that the gains were not sustained.

Overett and Donald (1998) also provided data on the effects of paired reading. In six training sessions,
85   they trained 29 parents from low socioeconomic backgrounds to use the paired reading technique, then compared their results with those of a control group composed of 32 parents. The results indicated a statistically significant increase only for the experimental group in
90   scores obtained on the Neale Analysis of Reading Ability for accuracy and comprehension. The authors also reported that the level of communication and enthusiasm of the education specialists during the training phase and the level of cooperation of parents had bene-
95   ficial impacts. On the other hand, Law and Kratochwill (1993) as well as Miller and Kratochwill (1996) suggested that paired reading does not produce statistically significant gains in reading performance. It is worth noting, however, that Topping (1997) pointed out some
100   inconsistencies, notably in the description of the paired reading method and the measurement of reading gains.

Topping (1995) indicated that the results of many studies are somewhat limited, for example, at the level of the reading process, which pertains to how parent
105   tutors controlled their behaviors following their training on paired reading. In studies that experimentally assess paired reading, it is imperative to ensure that the tutors make their behaviors compliant with the paired reading method in order to reduce any variation when
110   the independent variable is introduced. Topping (1997) noted that only a few studies reported detailed information on the behaviors of tutors following their training. Among those few studies who did, Bushnell, Miller, and Robson (1982) evaluated the behaviors of tutors
115   during home visits with the parents using a checklist that included items pertaining directly to paired reading and other independent items. The results revealed that only four aspects of the paired reading technique were significantly correlated, but only slightly, with the
120   gains observed in reading accuracy. In addition, Winter

(1988) conducted a study of tutor behaviors with audio recordings. His results suggested that full and rigorous compliance with the paired reading technique had little direct impact on the tutees' reading outcomes. Winter
125   also concluded that when participants received home visits, the degree of compliance with the technique increased.

Few studies assessed the effects of paired reading on self-concept and phonological awareness and their
130   results are inconsistent (Topping, 1995). In a longitudinal study, Chapman, Tunmer, and Prochnow (2000) found that young children with negative self-concepts at the beginning of their schooling had poorer phonological awareness and performed at a lower level in
135   reading compared to children with positive self-concepts. Since the relationship between negative self-concept and poor reading achievement is established early and is maintained over the first years of schooling, Chapman et al. (2000) suggested that it is crucial
140   to reverse this process in order to avoid long-term negative effects on reading performance.

In short, paired reading appears to be an effective means of improving reading performance, and nothing proves that reading gains cannot be sustained over
145   time. Those studies that examined processes demonstrated variable levels of compliance with the paired reading technique, but this factor does not seem to be closely linked with reading gains. More studies are needed to further describe the sources of variation as-
150   sociated with the individual characteristics of participants, the measurement method, and the treatment. Accordingly, the hypothesis that we attempted to verify through our research project was whether a parent–child paired reading intervention would increase gen-
155   eral academic skills and, more specifically, reading skills. Moreover, we analyzed the effects of paired reading on phonological awareness and self-concept on an exploratory basis.

Methodology

Our research methodology consisted of using a
160   nonequivalent control group quasi-experimental design. The goal of our research program was to reduce the risks of reading delay among children who were identified as at-risk pupils in kindergarten. The experimental group received all the necessary materials
165   and preparatory reading training over the school year (10 months) and was supervised by research assistants, while the control group only received the materials and received attention from members of the research group without any instruction or specific training.

Participants

170   The participants were selected among 632 kindergarten pupils attending schools that were part of the same school board in the Outaouais region of the province of Quebec. They were identified in May 2000 using screening tools that were proven by several studies
175   to predict school delays (Boudreault, Laberge,

84

Cadieux, & Rodrigue, 1996; Cadieux & Boudreault, 2002; Cadieux, Boudreault, & Laberge, 1997). These tools included the Otis-Lennon School Ability Test [OLSAT], Level 1, as well as a checklist completed by teachers. This checklist was developed and validated with effective predictors of school delays in reading (Cadieux & Boudreault, 2002). In a Cadieux et al. (1997) study, the predictive value of the OLSAT in relation with general school performance was of 0.49 for the first grade and of 0.50 for the second and third grades. In addition, Cadieux and Boudreault (2002) reported the results of a validation of the checklist completed by kindergarten teachers to predict later school performance in French (reading and writing) of their pupils. These results indicated correlations of 0.63 and 0.66 between the total score of the checklist and later performance in the first and second grades, respectively.

The scores of the OLSAT and the checklist were integrated into a single score. Each measure was weighed based on its predictive value as reported in previous validation studies (Cadieux & Boudreault, in press). The critical threshold applied to select the students was based on statistics from the Education Ministry of Quebec with regard to the percentage of pupils experiencing difficulties in the Outaouais (i.e., children among the 13.9% of students who are deemed to have the poorest performance). After considering the number of parents who accepted to participate during the entire experimentation period and for whom complete and valid data could be gathered, the final total number of participants was 54 pupils. In order to divide them between the experimental and control groups, the participating schools were assigned at random to one of these two groups. Therefore, pupils in one particular school all received the same treatment condition. The number of pupils in the experimental group was 32, while 22 pupils were assigned to the control group.

With regard to the gender variable, the experimental group had 17 boys and 15 girls, whereas the control group included 15 boys and 7 girls. At the beginning of the project, the average age of the pupils was 71.0 months (S.D.: 3.7) and there was no statistically significant difference ($F_{(1,52)}$ = 2.18; n.s.) between pupils of the experimental and control groups. The socioeconomic level of participants was assessed based on the father's occupation or the education level of the parents on a scale of 1 to 5 (1 = unemployed or without any diplomas; 2 = manual or unskilled worker or secondary/professional diploma; 3 = technical job or CEGEP diploma (pre-university level); 4 = professional or undergraduate university degree; 5 = senior executive or graduate university degree). The results indicated that the socioeconomic level of participants was generally low (average = 2.3; standard deviation = 1.0), but did not indicate a statistically significant difference between the experimental and control groups ($F_{(1,52)}$ = 0.2; n.s.). Approximately 70% of pupils lived in urban areas while 30% lived in rural communities. Also, at the beginning of the project, none of the students had received any formal teaching in reading, and most of them (92.6%) were in kindergarten for the first time.

With regard to maternal language, 41 children spoke French at home while 13 spoke another language (English, Spanish, or Arabic). The students whose maternal language was not French were divided almost equally among the experimental (n = 6) and control groups (n = 7); a Chi^2 test did not reveal any statistically significant difference between the two groups (χ^2 = 0.81; n.s.).

Dependent Variables

Academic Ability

The OLSAT-Level 1 (Otis-Lennon, 1995), which was used to screen students, was also administered during the posttest phase. This instrument measures several general academic abilities, such as the ability to follow instructions, attention, discrimination, and number representation. The version used was a translated and adapted French language version with adequate psychometric properties (Sarrazin, Vaillancourt, & McInnis, 1986). An analysis of internal consistency among participants of the research study revealed Cronbach's alpha coefficients of 0.80 at the pretest and 0.82 at the posttest.

Reading Ability

Reading ability was measured with five reading development scales from the Brigance Inventory of Early Development (for children aged between 0 and 7 years) (Brigance, 1995) (i.e., color naming, number naming, reading common signposts, auditory discrimination, and initial consonant sounds). The metrological qualities, assessed with a group of francophones from the Outaouais region, indicated acceptable properties. With regards to internal consistency, Cronbach's alpha coefficients from 0.79 to 0.85 were found. As for validity, a correlation of 0.79 was noted between the total score at the posttest (average of the five Brigance scales) and the reading accuracy scale measured by the Neale Analysis of Reading Ability. Since the results from the Neale Analysis of Reading Ability were taken only at the posttest, they were not included under this pretest/posttest design.

Phonological Awareness

Phonological awareness was assessed with the French Auditory Analysis Test (Test d'analyse auditive en français, TAAF) proposed by Rosner and Simon (1971). The test was translated and adapted by Gignac (1997) with the collaboration of Cormier from the University of Moncton. This is a test administered exclusively orally where the pupil is invited to play with sounds. Generally, the test consisted in making a child repeat a word, then asking him/her to say it again by removing a particular sound (omission of a syllable or phoneme). For example, the examiner asked the child

to repeat the word "flying," then asked him to repeat it again but without the "ing" sound at the end of the word. The child then had to say the word "fly" in order to pass that item. The test was divided in eight catego-
290 ries in which the pupil had to repeat a word by elimi-nating a syllable or phoneme either at the beginning, in the middle, or at the end of the word. In the first, sec-ond, and seventh categories, the child had to remove a syllable at the end, at the beginning, and in the middle
295 of a word, respectively. In the third category, the pupil had to remove a phoneme at the end of a word, whereas in the fourth and fifth categories, he/she had to remove a phoneme at the beginning of a word. Finally, for the sixth and eighth categories, the child had to
300 remove a phoneme placed in the middle of a word. The test ended when two consecutive categories were en-tirely failed. Each category included eight items, and scores ranged from 0 to 8. The total score was the av-erage of the eight categories.
305   An analysis of internal consistency for each cate-gory indicated Cronbach's alpha coefficients from 0.77 to 0.83. These results were fairly similar to those re-ported by Cormier, MacDonald, Grandmaison, and Ouellette-Lebel (1995), who validated a similar version
310 of the TAAF. In their study, Cronbach's alpha coeffi-cients varied from 0.68 to 0.91. As for validity, Cormier et al. (1995) found statistically significant links between scores on the TAAF and performance on reading and spelling subtests, which is consistent with
315 the results of other studies on the relations between phonological awareness and academic performance (Blachman, 2000).

Self-Concept

Self-concept was measured with a translated and adapted version of the Pictorial Scale of Perceived
320 Competence and Social Acceptance for Young Chil-dren (PSPCSA) (Harter & Pike, 1983). Even though the original instrument includes four dimensions, only three of them were used for our study: school self-concept, social self-concept, and physical self-concept.
325 These dimensions were translated and adapted in French. Their factorial structure and other psychomet-ric data are reported in Cadieux (1996). The instrument includes a total of 18 pairs of images, and a short story is told to the child for each of those pairs. One of the
330 images describes an ability in positive terms while the other describes this same ability in negative terms. The pupil must choose which image is the most like him/her and must write an "X" in one of two circles: in the small circle if the image is "a little like him/her," or
335 in the big circle is the image is "really like him/her." A four-point measurement scale was used (1 being the most negative and 4 being the most positive). The met-rological qualities of the instrument were tested with learning disabled students and proved to be adequate
340 (Cadieux, 1995, 1996). In this study, Cronbach's alpha coefficients ranging from 0.71 to 0.93 were obtained for the three self concept dimensions at the pretest and posttest phases.

Independent Variables

Wasik (1998) identified eight components to ensure
345 the effectiveness of a tutoring program. These compo-nents were integrated in the control of the independent variable.

1) *Training of the tutors by a specialist.* Two re-search assistants who were completing their final year
350 in a remedial teaching program acted as reading spe-cialists for this research project. They received thor-ough instructions on how to train parents on using the paired reading technique and on how to supervise them. The assistants' training included learning the
355 principles and features of the paired reading technique, practical training sessions to allow them to experiment with the technique and integrate its particularities, and assessment of the tutors and tutees. Three two-hour theoretical training sessions and four or five practical
360 training sessions with a child allowed the assistants to master perfectly all the elements of the program. In order to evaluate their competencies, a checklist in-spired by Bushnell et al. (1982) was used. The two assistants both had scores of 5 out of 5 on all items of
365 the list. The assistants were supervised throughout the entire year to ensure that they maintained a proper level of knowledge of the paired reading technique.

2) *Supervision of the tutors.* The tutors were trained and received regular feedback from the research assis-
370 tants. To ensure that parents properly applied the method, particular emphasis was put on the following instructions. First, when the child made a mistake, the parent had to wait four seconds to allow the child to correct himself/herself. If after four seconds the child
375 was not able to read the word, the parent was instructed not to let the child struggle any longer with the word but to simply read it, then ask the child to repeat the word. Second, the parent was instructed not to give the right answer when the child went silent, but wait four
380 seconds to allow the child to find the answer. Third, when the child was reading well, the parent had to rein-force his/her efforts by smiling or giving praise. Fourth, if the child skipped some words, the parent was encouraged to point out each word while reading. Fifth,
385 when the child showed signs of being tired or lacking attention, the parent was invited to stop the session and to show that he/she was proud of the child's efforts.

3) *Structure of the program.* Tutoring sessions were structured and used rich reading materials. Paired read-
390 ing is a simple method for nonprofessionals that can be adapted and takes into consideration the interests of the pupils. This technique is divided in two stages: simul-taneous reading and independent reading. Before be-ginning the reading session, the child chooses a book
395 and discusses the story or the subject with his/her par-ent. Then, the child and the parent begin with simulta-neous reading. During this phase, the child reads out

loud at the same time as the parent. The parent corrects the child's mistakes only by modeling. During the in-
400 dependent reading phase, the child gives a signal to the parent to indicate that he/she is ready to read alone. The parent praises the child for taking this initiative and encourages him/her regularly. When the child makes a mistake, the parent corrects him/her, making
405 sure that the child repeats exactly the same thing, and then starts reading out loud with the child again.

4) *Consistency and intensity of the program.* Tutoring is intensive and consistent. During each reading activity, the child chose by himself/herself the material
410 before beginning reading with one of his/her parents. The length of the reading session was at least five minutes each day, five days a week. The parents were instructed not to go beyond 15 minutes per day unless the child stated that he/she wanted to continue. The loca-
415 tion chosen for reading varied from one child to another (bedroom, kitchen table, living room), but had to be a calm and comfortable location. Parents were instructed to turn off the television or the radio. It was also suggested to parents and children to read in close
420 physical proximity to make the experience more intimate and enjoyable.

5) *Quality of the material.* Good quality materials were used with all subjects to ensure a certain uniformity and enjoyment of reading. Since the reading materi-
425 als available to each child at home were different, we gave a standard material package to all participants. This package included 50 flash cards (26 letters, 16 consonant–vowel syllables, and 8 consonant–vowel–consonant syllables) and 32 small first-grade books
430 from a popular series of child literature in Quebec. The flash cards were used for letter reading and syllable recognition activities, while the small books were introduced to practice reading with proselike materials. The stories included in the books were adapted to the
435 reading level of the pupils and followed the progression of materials received in school. The children received two or three books at each tutoring session. These books contained illustrations and were interesting from the children's perspective. They were adapted
440 to the level of the reading abilities of the child and parent.

6) *Assessment of the students on a regular basis.* The progress made by each child was assessed regularly. Within each home visit, the parent and the re-
445 search assistant discussed the progress of the tutee by evaluating the number of errors made during reading sessions. This discussion helped the research assistant adapt the material and the parent's behavior with their child.
450 7) *Assessment of the tutors on a regular basis.* To verify the frequency of reading sessions, a calendar was provided to parents and their children. Each reading session was recorded by putting an "X" or the number of a book in the space corresponding to a par-
455 ticular day on the calendar following each session.

Moreover, a short reading activity was proposed to parents and children for each day of the calendar. Parents could do this activity with their child in an informal way in order to have fun while reading. Also, a
460 booklet was provided to parents for them to write down any question or comment. However, most parents did not use this booklet. Since there were regular follow-up visits, parents preferred to ask their questions as the weeks went along, without noting the difficulties they
465 may have had in between visits. Moreover, the goal of the home visits was to assess compliance with the paired reading technique and correct the parents to ensure they achieved an acceptable level of understanding. During these visits, the parent and the child prac-
470 ticed reading while the assistant observed them. Afterward, the assistant made comments by focusing first on positive aspects, then by discussing other aspects that needed improvement. With a checklist inspired by Bushnell et al. (1982), the parents had to obtain a score
475 of 4/5 or 5/5 on all items of the list. During all home visits, the parents were evaluated and corrected immediately until all the criteria that applied to simultaneous reading and independent reading were mastered. At the beginning of the parents' training, most visits lasted
480 about an hour, and in some cases even required two hours. After one or two visits, the assistants rarely needed to correct the parents anymore since most of them mastered the features of the technique. From time to time, however, it was necessary to remind parents
485 that they needed to praise their child during reading.

8) *Coordination of tutoring with classroom instruction and materials.* A questionnaire was completed by the teachers of all participating children to assess the reading materials and instruction received in school.
490 The results revealed that the reading program and materials used in the paired reading study were similar to those used in school.

Results

Table 1 presents the means, standard deviations, and two-tailed t tests of the pre- and posttest scores for
495 all dependent variables. The results indicate that pupils from the experimental group made gains that were statistically more significant compared to children of the control group in their general academic abilities and phonological awareness. With regard to reading abili-
500 ties, the results indicate that pupils of both the experimental and control group made important gains between the pretest and posttest, but differences between scores of the experimental and control group were not statistically significant. The experimental group
505 reached the level of 0.05 ($t = 2.04$; d.f. = 52; $p < .05$) only on Brigance's fourth subtest, the auditory discrimination test. With regard to self-concept, the three scales did not reveal any significant differences between pretest and posttest scores obtained by the ex-
510 perimental and control groups.

87

Table 1
Pre- and Posttest Means of All Dependent Variables

Dependent variables	Pretest Mean	Pretest SD	Posttest Mean	Posttest SD	Mean diff. Mean	Mean diff. SD	t	p
OLSAT								
Experimental[a]	19.9	4.6	38.5	8.0	18.6	7.6	2.1	< .05
Control[b]	18.1	5.9	32.8	11.9	14.7	9.8		
Phonological awareness								
Experimental	2.5	1.3	4.5	1.8	2.0	1.8	4.3	< .001
Control	1.8	1.4	2.5	1.5	0.7	0.9		
Reading								
Experimental	65.9	16.6	84.1	12.3	18.2	15.8	0.9	n.s.
Control	67.9	15.8	80.2	17.9	12.3	9.7		
School self-concept								
Experimental	3.4	0.6	3.6	0.6	0.2	0.6	−0.4	n.s.
Control	3.5	0.5	3.7	0.5	0.2	0.4		
Social self-concept								
Experimental	3.7	0.6	3.6	0.6	0.0	0.7	−0.8	n.s.
Control	3.7	0.5	3.8	0.4	0.1	0.5		
Physical self-concept								
Experimental	3.7	0.4	3.8	0.3	0.1	0.3	1.4	n.s.
Control	3.4	0.5	3.6	0.4	0.2	0.4		

Note. Score range: Otis-Lennon School Ability Test (OLSAT) (0–60); Phonological awareness (0–8); Reading (0–100); Self-concept (1–4).
Degree of freedom for all *t* values is 52.
[a]n = 32.
[b]n = 22.

Discussion and Conclusion

The results obtained following this study are consistent with follow-up studies conducted by Topping (1995), who noted positive gains when the paired reading technique was used. The results are also consistent with other research studies that demonstrated the positive impact of tutoring programs on reading (Elbaum, Vaughn, Hughes, & Moody, 2000; Burns, Senesac, & Symington, 2004). However, while some results are statistically significant, the extent of the gains made was not very considerable and further research must be conducted among groups of at-risk pupils.

With regard to the OLSAT, results suggest that pupils of the experimental group improved slightly compared to pupils of the control group. Since this tool measures general academic abilities, the results suggest that paired reading produces effects on areas other than reading ability. Thus, it is possible that implicating the parent in this process had radiating effects that were generalized in other learning areas. These results suggest that the active cooperation of parents in paired reading produces gains at the level of school adaptation in general. As an example of ratio gains, represented by the standardized OLSAT age divided by the chronological age multiplied by 1.00, participants of the experimental group went from 77 to 95, while participants in the control group went from 75 to 84. These results suggest that the academic abilities of at-risk pupils who received the paired reading treatment were able to reach normal levels (e.g., 88–111), like other pupils who were not at risk or did not experience any particular difficulty.

The results on the auditory discrimination subtest and the phonological awareness test suggest that paired reading has a positive impact on the degree of awareness that the pupils possessed regarding the sounds that make up their language. These results can be explained by the fact that during simultaneous reading, the child has to make an association between a letter or a group of letters and the corresponding sound. During simultaneous reading, the child can compare the sounds that his/her parent makes with the sounds that he/she produces and can make letter–sound associations. This aspect becomes a sort of "sonority game" between the child and the parent. In addition, when the child was reading independently, he/she could practice and be corrected rapidly when he/she had difficulties.

Another factor that might explain these results is the characteristics of the participants. In fact, in most studies reviewed, children who did not have any major difficulty with regard to their readiness to learn were among the participants. Our study included only children at risk of school delays who showed very little prereading abilities at the end of kindergarten. When they started the first grade, most of these pupils did not yet know the alphabetical system. This situation created some difficulties when it came to reading books made up of complete sentences. Thus, it was difficult to apply rigorously the paired reading technique during the first four months of the intervention due to the difficulties that the children were experiencing. However, the activities carried out with the flash cards were organized in a way to respect the principles of the paired reading technique as well as the specific behaviors tutors had to display during paired reading sessions. For example, the parent laid out on a table 10 "letter" flash cards and ten "syllable" flash cards. The child and the parent then started by naming the letters together from left to right, and from top to bottom, until the child signaled that he/she was ready to continue alone. When a mistake was made followed by a four-second delay, the parent provided the right answer, made the child repeat the name of the letter or syllable, then started naming the next letters with the child, and so on. Consequently, the fact that phonological awareness gains were more significant than reading ability gains can be explained in part by the fact that participants made improvements according to their own characteristics, that is at the level of pre-reading.

The use of parents as tutors is also a factor that may explain the size of the effect. None of the parents was a reading specialist. The research staff was instructed to train and help parents to master only one technique (paired reading). We deliberately chose only one technique because one of the purposes of the study was to make all parents comfortable with the use of paired reading. Other gains that were not reported in this study include the increased motivation and satisfaction of parents who were trained to help their child. They were feeling more competent and were more receptive in school situations that dealt with learning difficulties.

As for self-concept, the absence of gains is not surprising since children of that age do not differentiate their own self-concept with the perception of others and see themselves more in an absolute manner than in a relative manner (Harter, 1986; Cadieux, 1996). Moreover, a ceiling effect due to the measurement instrument was noted for participants, which made it virtually impossible to observe any differences.

This study has certain limits. One of those pertains to the behaviors of tutors. While we employed control mechanisms and made regular home visits, we cannot certify that all parents rigorously followed instructions given with the original technique devised by Topping (1995) outside of those visits. Also, the small number of participants limits our ability to make generalizations with the results. Finally, the data obtained on the psychometric properties of the reading abilities tested with the Brigance Development Inventory were limited to a population of at-risk pupils and results must be interpreted with caution. The correlation of 0.79 obtained between scores of reading accuracy from the Neale Reading Analysis of Ability and the total scores of the five subscales of the Brigance Development Inventory indicated a satisfactory but medium-low level of validity. Data regarding test and retest coefficient were not available. Other reading and prereading ability tests would have been necessary to verify more accurately the effects of the paired reading program on reading ability.

References

Blachman, B. (2000). Phonological awareness. In M. L. Kamil, P. B. Mosenthal, P. D. Pearson & R. Barr (Eds.), *Handbook of reading research: Vol. III* (pp. 483–502). Mahwah, NJ: Lawrence Erlbaum Associates.

Boudreault, P., Laberge, J., Cadieux, A., & Rodrigue, A. (1996). Élèves de maternelle à risque de difficulté d'apprentissage: Un outil de dépistage. *Apprentissage et Socialisation, 17*, 127–131.

Brigance, A. H. (1995). *Brigance: Inventaire du développement de l'enfant entre 0 et 7 ans.* (A.-M. Mayotte & D. Lalonde, Trans.). North Billerica, MS: Curriculum Associates Inc.

Burns, M. K., Senesac, B. V., & Symington, T. (2004). The effectiveness of the HOSTS Program in Improving the Reading Achievement of Children At-Risk for Reading Failure. *Reading, Research and Instruction, 43*, 87–103.

Bushnell, R., Miller, A., & Robson, D. (1982). Parents as remedial teachers: An account of a paired reading project with junior school failing readers and their parents. *Journal of the Association of Educational Psychologists, 5*, 7–13.

Cadieux, A. (1995). Concept de soi d'élèves en difficulté d'adaptation scolaire et sociale: Validation d'instruments de mesure. Paper presented at the 63rd congress of the Association Canadienne pour l'Avancement des Sciences (ACFAS), Chicoutimi, Quebec, Canada.

Cadieux, A. (1996). Psychometric properties of a pictorial self-concept scale among young learning disabled pupils. *Psychology in the Schools, 33*, 221–229.

Cadieux, A., & Boudreault, P. (2002). Psychometric properties of a Kindergarten Behavior Rating Scale to predict later academic achievement. *Psychological Reports, 90*, 687–698.

Cadieux, A., & Boudreault, P. (2003). Effets d'une intervention parentale en lecture sur la connaissance du nom et des sons des lettres et la sensibilité phonologique d'élèves à risque. *Revue des sciences de l'éducation, 29*, 545–563.

Cadieux, A., Boudreault, P., & Laberge, J. (1997). The Otis-Lennon School Ability Test as a predictor of grade repetition and academic performance. *Psychological Reports, 81*, 223–226.

Chapman, J. W., Tunmer, W. E., & Prochnow, J. E. (2000). Early reading-related skills and performance, reading self-concept, and the development of academic self-concept: A longitudinal study. *Journal of Educational Psychology, 92*, 703–708.

Cormier, P., MacDonald, W., Grandmaison, E., & Ouellette-Lebel, D. (1995). Développement d'un test d'analyse auditive en français: Normes et validation de construit. *Revue des sciences de l'éducation, 21*, 223–240.

Elbaum, B., Vaughn, S., Hughes, M., & Moody, S. (2000). How effective are one-to-one tutoring programs in reading for elementary students at risk for reading failure? A meta-analysis of the intervention research. *Reading Research Quarterly, 92*, 605–619.

Fitton, L., & Gredler, G. (1996). Parental involvement in reading remediation with young children. *Psychology in the Schools, 33*, 325–332.

Gignac, M. (1997). Effet du mode de présentation sur la performance à un test d'analyse auditive. Unpublished manuscript, University of Moncton, Moncton, New Brunswick, Canada.

Harter, S. (1986). Processes underlying the construction, the maintenance, and enhancement of the self-concept in children. In J. Suls & A. Greenwald (Eds.), *Psychological perspectives on the self: Vol. 3* (pp. 137–181). Hillsdale, NJ: Lawrence Erlbaum Associates.

Harter, S., & Pike, R. (1983). *The pictorial scale of perceived competence and social acceptance for young children.* Denver, CO: University of Denver.

Hoover-Dempsey, K. V., & Sandler, H. M. (1997). Why do parents become involved in their children's education? *Review of Educational Research, 67*, 3–42.

Law, M., & Kratochwill, T. R. (1993). Paired reading: An evaluation of a parent tutorial program. *School Psychology International, 14*, 119–147.

Leslie, M., & McMillan, G. (1999). Early intervention in the prevention of reading difficulties. *Educational and Child Psychology, 16*, 14–21.

McCarthey, S. J. (2000). Home-School Connections: A review of the literature. *The Journal of Educational Research, 93*, 145–153.

Miller, B. V., & Kratochwill, T. R. (1996). An evaluation of the paired reading program using competency-based training. *School Psychology International, 17*, 269–291.

Otis, A. S., & Lennon, R. T. (1981). *Test d'habileté scolaire Otis-Lennon* (G. Sarrazin, C. E. McInnis, R. Vaillancourt & L. Dayhaw, Trans.). Montréal: Institut de Recherches psychologiques Inc. (Original work published 1979).

Overett, J., & Donald, D. (1998). Paired reading: Effects of a parent involvement programme in a disadvantaged community in South Africa. *British Journal of Educational Psychology, 68*, 347–356.

Purcell-Gates, V. (2000). Family Literacy. In M. L. Kamil, P. B. Mosenthal, P. D. Pearson et R. Barr (Eds.), *Handbook of reading research: Vol. III* (pp. 853–870). Mahwah, NJ: Lawrence Erlbaum Associates.

Rosner, J., & Simon, D. (1971). The auditory analysis test: An initial report. *Journal of Learning Disabilities, 4*, 40–48.

Sanacore, J. (1990). Independent reading for remedial and at-risk students: The principal can make a difference. *Reading Research and Instruction, 30*, 59–65.

Sarrazin, G., Vaillancourt, R., & McInnis, C. E. (1986). *Test d'habileté scolaire Otis-Lennon. Manuel de normes pour les écoles de langue française de l'Ontario.* Montréal: Institut de Recherches Psychologiques Inc.

Snow, C. E., Burns, M. S., & Griffin, P. (1998). *Preventing reading difficulties in young children.* Washington, DC: National Academy Press.

Toomey, D. (1993). Parents hearing their children read: A review. Rethinking the lessons of the Haringey Project. *Educational Research, 35,* 223–236.

Topping, K. (1987). Peer tutored paired reading: Outcome data from ten projects. *Educational Psychology, 7,* 133–145.

Topping, K. (1995). *Paired reading, spelling and writing. The handbook for teachers and parents.* New York: Cassell.

Topping, K. (1997). Process and outcome in paired reading: A reply to Winter. *Educational Psychology in Practice, 13,* 75–86.

Topping, K., & Lindsay, G. A. (1991). Parental influence in reading: The influence of socioeconomic status and supportive home visiting. *Children & Society, 5,* 306–316.

Topping, K. J., & Wolfendale, S. W. (1985). *Parental involvement in children's reading.* New York: Nichols.

Torgesen, J. K. (2002). The prevention of reading difficulties. *Journal of School Psychology, 40,* 7–25.

Vadasy, P. F., Jenkins, J. R., & Pool, K. (2000). Effects of tutoring in phonological and early reading skills on students at risk for reading disabilities. *Journal of Learning Disabilities, 33,* 579–590.

Wasik, B. A. (1998). Volunteer tutoring programs in reading: A review. *Reading Research Quarterly, 33,* 266–292.

Winter, S. (1988). Paired reading: A study of process and outcome. *Educational Psychology, 5,* 135–151.

Exercise for Article 14

Factual Questions

1. What was the hypothesis that the researchers attempted to verify?

2. The researchers state that they used what type of experimental design?

3. What was done in order to divide the 54 students into experimental and control groups?

4. On the OLSAT, how many points did the experimental group gain on average (mean difference)? How many did the control group gain?

5. Is the difference between the two mean differences referred to in Question 4 statistically significant? If "yes," at what probability level?

6. Was the difference between the two mean differences for school self-concept statistically significant? If "yes," at what probability level?

Questions for Discussion

7. The researchers use the headings "dependent variables" and "independent variables." How would you define these terms? (See the headings between lines 245–246 as well as between lines 343–344.)

8. Is the self-concept measure described in sufficient detail? Explain. (See lines 318–343.)

9. Is the independent variable described in sufficient detail? Explain. (See lines 344–492.)

10. For a future study on this topic, would you recommend assigning individual students (not schools) at random to the experimental and control groups? Explain.

11. Does it surprise you that the mean differences for physical self-concept were not statistically significant? Explain. (See Table 1.)

12. In your opinion, are the results of this study sufficiently promising to warrant conducting large-scale studies on this topic? Explain.

Quality Ratings

Directions: Indicate your level of agreement with each of the following statements by circling a number from 5 for strongly agree (SA) to 1 for strongly disagree (SD). If you believe an item is not applicable to this research article, leave it blank. Be prepared to explain your ratings. When responding to criteria A and B below, keep in mind that brief titles and abstracts are conventional in published research.

A. The title of the article is appropriate.

SA   5   4   3   2   1   SD

B. The abstract provides an effective overview of the research article.

SA   5   4   3   2   1   SD

C. The introduction establishes the importance of the study.

SA   5   4   3   2   1   SD

D. The literature review establishes the context for the study.

SA   5   4   3   2   1   SD

E. The research purpose, question, or hypothesis is clearly stated.

SA   5   4   3   2   1   SD

F. The method of sampling is sound.

SA   5   4   3   2   1   SD

G. Relevant demographics (for example, age, gender, and ethnicity) are described.

SA   5   4   3   2   1   SD

H. Measurement procedures are adequate.

SA   5   4   3   2   1   SD

I. All procedures have been described in sufficient detail to permit a replication of the study.

SA   5   4   3   2   1   SD

J. The participants have been adequately protected from potential harm.

SA   5   4   3   2   1   SD

K. The results are clearly described.

SA   5   4   3   2   1   SD

L. The discussion/conclusion is appropriate.

SA   5   4   3   2   1   SD

M. Despite any flaws, the report is worthy of publication.

SA   5   4   3   2   1   SD

Article 15

Academic Achievement and Between-Class Transition Time for Self-Contained and Departmental Upper-Elementary Classes

CAROLE J. MCGRATH
Lincoln County Schools

JAMES O. RUST
Middle Tennessee State University

ABSTRACT. This study investigated the relationship between elementary school classroom organizational structure (i.e., self-contained versus departmental formats) and standardized achievement scores, transition time between classes, and instruction time. Participants included 103 fifth-grade and 94 sixth-grade students from one school district. Based on previous findings, students from self-contained classes were predicted to achieve significantly more than comparable students from departmentalized classes, take significantly less time to change classes, and spend more time in instruction. Results indicated that the self-contained group gained significantly more on Total Battery, Language, and Science subtests compared to the departmentalized group. Departmentalized classes took significantly longer to transition from subject to subject than did the self-contained classes. No differences were evident for instructional time. Findings were consistent for fifth and sixth grades. The results are limited because of using only one school district.

From *Journal of Instructional Psychology*, 29, 40–43. Copyright © 2002 by *Journal of Instructional Psychology*. Reprinted with permission.

Educators have debated elementary school organizational structure since the beginning of the twentieth century (Gibb & Matala, 1962; Lamme, 1976). One aspect of organizational structure involves the number
5 of subject areas covered by each teacher. In the self-contained approach, the teacher acts as a generalist and carries responsibility for the curriculum all day. The other extreme is the departmentalized approach. Here, students change teachers for instruction in different
10 subjects. Thus, teachers cover fewer subject areas (Roger & Palardy, 1987; Mac Iver & Epstein, 1992). Advocates for a self-contained organizational pattern argue that it promotes instruction that is children-centered rather than subject-centered. Self-contained
15 classrooms allow the teacher and students the opportunity to become well acquainted. Moreover, self-contained teachers know their students' strengths, weaknesses, and personality traits, enabling better accommodation of the students' individual learning styles
20 (Squires, Huitt, & Segars, 1983). Additionally, self-contained classes allow for greater flexibility in scheduling. Elkind (1988) argues that the time students spend gathering books and papers and moving to other departmental classes cuts into valuable instruction
25 time.

On the other hand, some educators have found that departmentalized organizational approaches offer distinct advantages for the student (e.g., Culyer, 1984). Anderson (1962) presented a strong case for specializa-
30 tion when he reported that only 4 of 260 teachers considered themselves well prepared in all subject areas. Walker (1990) noted greater emphasis on curriculum matters in departmentalized elementary schools.

This paper is similar to one by Garner and Rust
35 (1992), which found that fifth-grade students in self-contained rooms scored significantly higher on group achievement tests compared to their departmentalized peers. The present study added measures of transition time and actual instruction time.

Method

Participants

40 The participants included 197 students (103 fifth graders and 94 sixth graders) from two kindergarten–sixth-grade schools in rural Tennessee. There were 109 students from School A. Of these students, 58 fifth graders (30 boys and 28 girls) and 51 sixth graders (23
45 boys and 28 girls) attended departmentalized classes. School B's participants included 88 students. Of these students, 45 fifth graders (20 boys and 25 girls) and 43 sixth graders (21 boys and 22 girls) attended self-contained classrooms. All of the participants attended
50 self-contained classrooms in the fourth grade. School A used departmentalized fifth- and sixth-grade classes. School B maintained self-contained classes through grade 6. The social class compositions of Schools A and B were similar, with 27% of the students at each
55 school getting free or reduced-fee lunch.

Apparatus

The scale scores and normal curve equivalents of the norm-referenced component of the Tennessee Comprehensive Assessment Program (TCAP) were

dependent variables. The primary aim of the instrument
is to provide a measure of achievement of basic skills
in reading, spelling, language, mathematics, study
skills, science, and social studies. The Tennessee Department of Education considers the scale scores obtained on the TCAP useful for measuring growth of
students or groups of students from year to year (Tennessee Comprehensive Assessment Program, 1993).
Scores range from 0 to 999. Parents, students, and
teachers can monitor annual progress up the scale in
each subject from 0 toward 999. McWherter and Smith
(1993) refer to year-to-year scale score comparisons as
value-added assessment. The TCAP also supplies traditional normal curve equivalents (NCEs), which have
many of the characteristics of percentile ranks, but
have the additional advantage of being based on an
equal-interval scale. NCEs have a mean of 50 and a
standard deviation of 10 (Bock & Wolfe, 1996).

Transition time was recorded by direct observation.
Each group was observed for two full days, not consecutively, and not the same day of the week. Actual
time was recorded and rounded to the nearest minute
from the closing of one subject until the beginning of
the next. Instruction time was recorded during the same
days. Subject matter was noted. The first author made
these observations.

Results

Normal curve equivalents (NCEs) and scale scores
from the TCAP Total Battery and subtests (reading,
language, mathematics, science, and social studies)
were analyzed in six separate 2 (Grades: 5, 6) × 2 (Organizational Structure: Self-contained and Departmental) × 2 (Male, Female) analyses of variance. The mean
gains were calculated by subtracting the difference
between TCAP pretest scale scores from posttest scale
scores (see Table 1). School A implemented a departmentalized organizational structure, and School B implemented a self-contained structure.

Table 1
Mean Value-Added Scores

	Departmentalized		Self-contained	
Test	5th	6th	5th	6th
Total battery	7.62	19.60	16.24	27.88
Reading	16.24	14.51	18.04	21.49
Language	2.15	12.87	20.00	18.94
Mathematics	4.98	30.90	9.49	44.47
Science	−5.60	8.16	13.28	28.22
Social studies	23.82	5.53	21.62	19.93

Significant effects were found for gain scores using
the TCAP scale scores. Self-contained students gained
significantly more than departmentalized students in
total battery, language, and science in fifth and sixth
grades (see Table 1). No differences were found in
reading, mathematics, or social studies. Inspection of
Table 1 reveals wide differences in gain scores. One of
the fifth-grade classes lost points in science. All of the

other groups improved compared to the previous year's
scores. The gain scores found here are more variable
and more modest than those presented in a longitudinal
study of the TCAP (Bock & Wolfe, 1996).

In the NCE analyses, there were no significant main
effects or interactions for organizational structure.
Transition time was significantly more efficient in the
self-contained classes compared to the departmentalized school (average transition time was 3.27 minutes
for the self-contained groups compared to 4.55 minutes
for the departmental groups). However, there was no
significant difference in actual instruction time. Departmentalized classes averaged 48 minutes of instruction time per hour while self-contained classes were
engaged in instruction an average of 46 minutes. That
difference was not significant. Anecdotal observations
revealed that teachers in self-contained classes offered
instruction in academically oriented areas that were not
included in the study. Computer lab, creative writing,
and journal writing are some examples.

Discussion

Implications for practice resulting from this study
include some support for self-contained instruction for
fifth- and sixth-grade children. As hypothesized, significantly higher gains were found in three academic
areas. These findings support those of Garner and Rust
(1992).

There were two additional measures in the present
study: transition time and instruction time. Transition
time findings agree with those of Culyer (1984) and
Elkind (1988) that students spend more time transitioning from class to class in schools that follow a departmental structure compared to those organized in self-
contained groups.

One would logically assume, as Culyer (1984) did,
that the self-contained structure would increase time-
on-task because of the reduced time required to organize materials and change classrooms. Elkind (1988)
posited also that the extra time spent changing classes
would cut into valuable instruction time. However, the
present study did not find that to be the case. The present study found no meaningful differences between
departmental and self-contained situations for instruction time. Despite the longer transition time, the departmental teachers allotted a similar amount of instructional time in the five major subject areas compared to self-contained teachers. The reason for the
nonsignificant difference of instruction time appeared
to be that the self-contained teachers included time for
computer lab, creative writing, and art. The study included some support for self-contained instruction for
these children. As hypothesized, significantly higher
gains were found in language, science, and total battery. However, no differences were evident in reading,
mathematics, and social studies.

The study was limited by the small number of
classes used in one small southern town. Observation

160 lasted only two days for determining transition and instruction time. Future studies will need to expand this database to allow for generalization.

References

Anderson, R. C. (1962). The case for teacher specialization in the elementary school. *Elementary School Journal, 62,* 253–260.

Bock, R. D., & Wolfe, R. (1996). Audit and review of the Tennessee value-added assessment system (TVAAS): Preliminary report (Technical Report, pp. 1–35). Tennessee Office of Education Accountability, Comptroller of the Treasury, Nashville, TN.

Culyer, R. C. (1984). The case for self-contained classroom. *Clearing House, 57,* 417–419.

Elkind, D. (1988). Rotation at an early age. *Principal, 36,* 11–13.

Garner, S. S., & Rust, J. O. (1992). Comparison of fifth-grade achievement in departmentalized and self-contained rural schools. *Tennessee Educational Leadership, 19,* 32–37.

Gibb, E. G., & Matala, D. C. (1962). Studies on the use of special teachers of science and mathematics in grades 5 and 6. *School Science and Mathematics, 62,* 565–585.

Lamme, L. L. (1976). Self-contained to departmentalized: How reading habits changed. *Elementary School Journal, 76,* 208–218.

Mac Iver, D. J., & Epstein, J. L. (1992). Middle grades education. In M. Alkin (Ed.) *Encyclopedia of educational research* (6th ed., pp. 834–844). New York: MacMillan/American Educational Research Association.

McWherter, N., & Smith, C. E. (1993). *21st Century Schools Value Added Assessment.* Nashville: Tennessee Department of Education.

Roger, J. S., & Palardy, J. M. (1987). A survey of organizational patterns and grouping strategies used in elementary schools in the southeast. *Education, 108,* 113–118.

Squires, D. A., Huitt, W. G., & Segars, J. K. (1983). *Effective schools and classrooms: A research-based prospective.* (ASCD No. 611–83298). Alexandria, VA: Association for Supervision and Curriculum Development.

Tennessee Comprehensive Assessment Program: Guide to test interpretation. (1993). Monterey, CA: CTB, Macmillan/McGraw-Hill.

Walker, D. (1990). *Fundamentals of Curriculum.* San Diego, CA: Harcourt Brace Jovanovich.

Address correspondence to: James O. Rust, Box 533, MTSU Station, Murfreesboro, TN 37132. E-mail: jorust@mtsu.edu

Exercise for Article 15

Factual Questions

1. In the literature review, the results by Anderson (1962) were cited to support which type of organizational approach?
   A. Departmentalized
   B. Self-contained

2. How many of the participants in School A were girls? How many of the participants in School B were girls?

3. TCAP is an acronym for the name of what test?

4. What term do McWherter and Smith (1993) use to refer to year-to-year scale score comparisons?

5. The departmentalized sixth graders gained how many points on language?

6. Which group lost points in science?

7. Was the difference between the two averages for transition time significant?

Questions for Discussion

8. Is it important to know that the social class compositions of the two schools were similar? Explain. (See lines 53–55.)

9. Apparently, individual students were *not* assigned at random to attend one of the two schools (i.e., random assignment was not used). In your opinion, if it were possible to assign the students at random, would the study be improved? Why? Why not?

10. Observations of transition time were done on two different days of the week. Speculate on why the researchers used two days instead of one (e.g., both on Mondays). (See lines 78–79.)

11. Instruction time was determined by observations made by one of the researchers. In your opinion, would it be an important improvement to use more than one observer? Explain. (See lines 83–84.)

12. In your opinion, are the anecdotal observations described in lines 119–123 important? Explain.

13. The researchers indicate that their results include "some support" for self-contained instruction. In your opinion, how strong is this support? Explain. (See lines 124–126.)

14. The researchers state that "The study was limited by the small number of classes used in one small southern town." Do you think that this is an important limitation? Explain. (See lines 158–159.)

Quality Ratings

Directions: Indicate your level of agreement with each of the following statements by circling a number from 5 for strongly agree (SA) to 1 for strongly disagree (SD). If you believe an item is not applicable to this research article, leave it blank. Be prepared to explain your ratings. When responding to criteria A and B below, keep in mind that brief titles and abstracts are conventional in published research.

A. The title of the article is appropriate.
   SA   5   4   3   2   1   SD

B. The abstract provides an effective overview of the research article.
   SA   5   4   3   2   1   SD

C. The introduction establishes the importance of the study.

SA   5   4   3   2   1   SD

D. The literature review establishes the context for the study.

SA   5   4   3   2   1   SD

E. The research purpose, question, or hypothesis is clearly stated.

SA   5   4   3   2   1   SD

F. The method of sampling is sound.

SA   5   4   3   2   1   SD

G. Relevant demographics (for example, age, gender, and ethnicity) are described.

SA   5   4   3   2   1   SD

H. Measurement procedures are adequate.

SA   5   4   3   2   1   SD

I. All procedures have been described in sufficient detail to permit a replication of the study.

SA   5   4   3   2   1   SD

J. The participants have been adequately protected from potential harm.

SA   5   4   3   2   1   SD

K. The results are clearly described.

SA   5   4   3   2   1   SD

L. The discussion/conclusion is appropriate.

SA   5   4   3   2   1   SD

M. Despite any flaws, the report is worthy of publication.

SA   5   4   3   2   1   SD

Article 16

Pilot Study of Telephone Tutoring
in Reading Skills

JOSEPH M. STRAYHORN, JR.
Drexel University College of Medicine

ABSTRACT. This study tested the feasibility of tutoring children in reading via telephone sessions. Ninteen children received tutoring from any of 6 tutors for an average of 7.6 hr. per month. Initially, these children were an average of 10.4 yr. old, in average grade 4.8, and averaged 2.9 grade levels behind their grade expectations on the Slosson Oral Reading Test. Before tutoring, the children had progressed on the Slosson at an average of 0.44 grade levels per year (95% CI = 0.30 to 0.57). The children participated in telephone tutoring for an average of 1.5 yr. During tutoring, the students progressed at an average of 2.0 grade levels per year (95% CI = 1.2 to 2.8). The rate of progress during tutoring was significantly greater than that before tutoring ($p < .001$). The relations between tutors and students appeared to be positive and pleasant. Telephone tutoring seems to be a practical and feasible service delivery method which should be tested further.

From *Perceptual and Motor Skills*, *101*, 505–509. Copyright © 2005 by Perceptual and Motor Skills. Reprinted with permission.

There is growing consensus that individual tutoring is the most effective method for helping struggling readers. In the words of Allington (2004), "There is no evidence that classroom instruction of any sort can come close to meeting the needs of the readers who struggle the most. Research *does* show that expert, individual tutoring produces on-level reading achievement with many struggling readers" (p. 22). Many educators perceive one-on-one instruction as an essential intervention for students who are not learning to read (Vaughn, Hughes, Moody, & Elbaum, 2001). Wasik and Slavin (1993) reviewed five programs for one-to-one reading instruction and found all of them highly effective, despite quite different methods and theories behind them. The challenge posed by Bloom (1984) termed the "2 Sigma Problem: The search for methods of group instruction as effective as one-to-one tutoring," may need to be reframed as "the search for practical, cost-effective structures for delivering one-to-one tutoring."

The structure that is very likely the most frequently used for delivering individual instruction is the "pull-out" program, where children leave the classroom to go for individual instruction. This was the method in an individual tutoring program reported by Strayhorn and Bickel (2003), which contained many of the elements that seem to be useful, if not crucial, for success: frequent instruction, teaching of phonemic awareness, teaching of right–left discrimination or spatial awareness, teaching of letter–sound correspondence, sounding and blending of words in word families, and reading of text that over time gradually becomes more complex in accord with the student's skill. This intervention resulted in 1.5 grade levels per year progress in struggling readers.

But pull-out programs have problems. A student's participation in regular classroom work is interrupted. There is distress when the student misses a classroom test or a crucial or a very pleasant classroom activity. The public exit from the classroom by a student for individual tutoring can lead to stigmatization of that child or to distress in other children who would love some individual attention themselves. Teachers may reasonably find it irritating when tutors arrive to take the child to individual instruction. But the greatest limiting factor of all for pull-out programs is space: where will individual tutoring occur? In the Strayhorn and Bickel (2003) project, space was rented in a church located next door to the school and whose leadership was willing to offer suitable tutoring rooms at a low price. But most schools, if offered an army of expert tutors, would have to turn them away for lack of space. Thus, it is no surprise that individual tutoring has been infrequently used for students with learning disabilities, and when implemented, tutoring sessions have usually been quite brief (Vaughn, Moody, & Schumm, 1998).

Out of the frustration of searching for time in the school day and space in the school building was born the alternative service structure described here: telephone tutoring. After school hours, the tutor connects with the student by telephone to escape the logistic problems of transportation; both tutor and child are in their own homes. They each look at their own copies of identical instructional materials, getting on the same page and the same place on the page through verbal instruction rather than pointing. At the beginning of this trial, most educators with whom the investigator spoke, like the investigator himself, had great doubts as to whether such a structure could be successful. This pilot thus tested its feasibility.

Method

Measures

The measure of reading skill for this study was the Slosson Oral Reading Test, Revised (Slosson & Nicholson, 1990). For descriptions of the sample, we collected behavior ratings from parents and teachers using the ADHD Symptom Checklist 4 (Gadow & Sprafkin, 1997), and verbal ability scores using the WISC-III Verbal subscale (Wechsler, 1991). Since some of the Slosson tests were administered by telephone with the assistance of the child's parents, we checked the validity of such testing by also administering at preintervention the Test of Word Reading Efficiency (Torgesen, Wagner, & Rashotte, 1999). The correlation between the grade level scores for the Slosson test and for the Test of Word Reading Efficiency's Sight Word Efficiency subscale was .81 ($n = 14$).

Participants

Students were recruited without fixed exclusion criteria; we stated we were searching for those who were "substantially behind in reading." Recruitment was done by speaking with several principals and making flyers available in schools and by posting a notice on an Internet bulletin board. Telephone tutoring was offered to all participants. The sample was composed of 19 students—12 boys and 7 girls. The tutoring was continued for lengths of time that varied according to the child's need, with the average student receiving tutoring for 1.5 yr. We administered measures before and after the telephone tutoring intervention. The primary research question was how the rate of progress in reading skill during the intervention compared with the student's rate of progress before the intervention.

The average student at the beginning of tutoring was 10.4 yr. old, at school grade 4.8, with a mean WISC-III Verbal IQ of 93. All the students in the sample were at least 0.7 yr. behind age or grade expectations according to the norms of the Slosson Oral Reading Test. The average student was 2.9 grade levels behind.

At preintervention, parent ratings of ADHD symptoms were available for 17 children. An average of 5.7 out of 18 symptoms was reported to be presented "often" or "very often."

Intervention

Because this was viewed as a pioneering venture, heterogeneity was deemed desirable for tutors as well as students. Tutors included two former administrative assistants, a former lawyer, a preschool teacher, a grade school teacher's aide, and a 10-yr. old elementary school child. Only one tutor had a teaching certification. All tutors were women. Tutors followed the directions given in Manual for Tutors and Teachers of Reading (Strayhorn, 2002). The intervention usually began with instruction in phonemic awareness, letter–sound correspondence, and or left–right discrimination, which we called spatial awareness. From there it progressed to sounding and blending of lists of words in word families, and reading of progressively more demanding text. The text reading included Programmed Readings for Psychological Skills (Strayhorn, 2001) and other readings meant to model positive psychological functioning. Examples of the behavior in such "modeling stories" included siblings negotiating a solution to a conflict over which television show to watch, a child choosing to ignore a peer who tries to provoke him by shoving him, a child helping a hurt animal, people warning other people of danger, children using relaxation strategies to reduce performance anxiety, a child returning money that someone had dropped, an adolescent stopping the bullying of a young child at a swimming pool and giving that child a swimming lesson, a group of people ending warfare between two tribes on a distant planet, and hundreds of others. These stories are arranged in order of reading difficulty, so the tutor can choose text appropriate for the student's current skill. The student and tutor connected by phone at an appointed time, and the same page in their identical books, and carried out the approximately half-hour session over the phone.

The average student in the study received 7.6 hr. of tutoring per month in approximately 15 30-min. sessions. Thus, tutoring sessions occurred on approximately half of the days of the month. The intervention was continued for an average of 1.5 yr. per student.

Analysis

To obtain the rate of progress before the intervention, the preintervention grade level of the student of the Slosson Oral Reading Test was divided by the number of years of the child's education thus far, expressed to the nearest tenth. The result gave the number of reading grade levels the child had gained per year of school experience thus far.

To obtain the rate of progress during the intervention, the preintervention reading grade level was subtracted from the postintervention level. This increase in reading grade level was divided by the duration of tutoring for that child, yielding a grade level per year progress rate during tutoring.

One-sample t tests were used to obtain the 95% confidence intervals for rates of progress and to test significance of the difference in rates of progress before and during tutoring.

Results and Discussion

Table 1 summarizes study participants' reading grade levels. Before tutoring, the children had progressed on the Slosson test at an average of 0.44 grade levels per year (95% CI = 0.30 to 0.57). During the average of 1.5 yr. of tutoring per student, the students progressed at an average of 2.0 grade levels per year (95% CI = 1.2 to 2.8); these mean rates of progress were significantly different ($t = 4.50$, $p < .001$, $N = 19$). The difference in rates of progress during and before tutoring was about 1.5 grade levels per year (95% CI =.82 to 2.3).

Table 1
Grade Levels and Reading Progress for Participants at Preintervention and During Tutoring (N = 19)

Variable	M	SD
Preintervention		
School grade	4.8	2.4
Reading grade level	1.8	1.2
Reading grade levels behind	2.9	2.4
Grade levels per year progress	0.4	0.3
Tutoring		
Grade levels per year progress	2.0	1.7

180   The investigator, who started researching this service delivery method with a great deal of doubt as to how many children would be able to benefit from it, now believes that it may be very helpful to large numbers of children. In addition to producing improvement
185 in reading, telephone tutoring seemed, in our experience, to permit the development of close and positive relationships between tutors and students.

This initial study has limitations. The samples of both students and tutors are convenience samples not
190 representative of any population. Larger sample sizes and more samples will allow greater generalizability. But if telephone tutoring continues to prove effective, this service delivery method could eliminate very important barriers to individual tutoring. With the use of
195 this method, the total pool of available tutors can be matched with the pool of children in need without regard for physical location. The number of children who could feasibly receive individual tutoring—and, thus, the number who can become successful readers—can
200 be vastly increased.

References

Allington, R. L. (2004). Setting the record straight. *Educational Leadership, 61*, 22–25.

Bloom, B. S. (1984). The 2 sigma problem: The search for methods of group instruction as effective as one-to-one tutoring. *Educational Researcher, 13,* 4–16.

Gadow, K. D., & Sprafkin, J. (1997). *ADHD Symptom Checklist-4 manual.* Stony Brook, NY: Checkmate Plus.

Slosson, R. L., & Nicholson, C. L. (1990). *The Slosson Oral Reading Test, Revised.* East Aurora, NY: Slosson Educational Pub., Inc.

Strayhorn, J. M. (2001). *Programmed readings for psychological skills.* Wexford, PA: Psychological Skills Press.

Strayhorn, J. M. (2002). *Manual for tutors and teachers of reading.* Wexford, PA: Psychological Skills Press.

Strayhorn, J. M., & Bickel, D. D. (2003). A randomized trial of individual tutoring for elementary school children with reading and behavior difficulties. *Psychological Reports, 92,* 427–444.

Torgesen, J. K., Wagner, R. K., & Rashotte, C. A. (1999). *Test of Word Reading Efficiency.* Austin, TX: PRO-ED.

Vaughn, S., Hughes, M. T., Moody, S. W., & Elbaum, B. (2001). Instructional grouping for reading for students with LD: Implications for practice. *Intervention in School and Clinic, 36,* 131–137.

Vaughn, S., Moody, S., & Schumm, J. S. (1998). Broken promises: Reading instruction in the resource room. *Exceptional Children, 64,* 211–226.

Wasik, B. A., & Slavin, R. E. (1993). Preventing early reading failure with one-to-one tutoring: A review of five programs. *Reading Research Quarterly, 28,* 179–200.

Wechsler, D. (1991). *Wechsler Intelligence Scale for Children—Third Edition.* San Antonio, TX: The Psychological Corp.

Address correspondence to: Joseph M. Strayhorn, Jr., M.D., 11676 Perry Highway, Suite 1200, Wexford, PA 15090. E-mail: joestrayhorn@juno.com

Acknowledgments: This work was partially supported by a grant from the Heinz Endowment. The author is grateful to the tutors for this project: Kathleen Burd, Elizabeth Macken, Margaret Hertweck, Catherine Holmes, Andrea Obusek, and Jillian Strayhorn.

Exercise for Article 16

Factual Questions

1. At the beginning of this study, did the researcher feel confident that the telephone tutoring would be successful?

2. What was the correlation between the grade level scores for the Slosson test and for the Test of Word Reading Efficiency's Sight Word Efficiency subscale?

3. The average student received tutoring for how many years?

4. What was the "primary research question"?

5. Were the mean rates of progress significantly different? If "yes," at what probability level?

6. What "limitations" does the researcher mention?

Questions for Discussion

7. Is the recruitment method described in sufficient detail? Explain. (See lines 86–91.)

8. Is the intervention described in sufficient detail? Explain. (See lines 112–151.)

9. What is your understanding of the meaning of the term "95% CI"? (See lines 170–179.)

10. This study did not have a control group. Would you recommend using one in future studies on telephone tutoring? Why? Why not?

11. In your opinion, are the results of this study sufficiently promising to warrant conducting large-scale studies on this topic? Explain.

12. If you were to conduct an experiment on the same topic, what changes, if any, would you make in the research methodology?

Quality Ratings

Directions: Indicate your level of agreement with each of the following statements by circling a number from 5 for strongly agree (SA) to 1 for strongly disagree (SD). If you believe an item is not applicable to this research article, leave it blank. Be prepared to explain your ratings. When responding to criteria A and B below, keep in mind that brief titles and abstracts are conventional in published research.

A. The title of the article is appropriate.

SA   5   4   3   2   1   SD

B. The abstract provides an effective overview of the research article.

SA   5   4   3   2   1   SD

C. The introduction establishes the importance of the study.

SA   5   4   3   2   1   SD

D. The literature review establishes the context for the study.

SA   5   4   3   2   1   SD

E. The research purpose, question, or hypothesis is clearly stated.

SA   5   4   3   2   1   SD

F. The method of sampling is sound.

SA   5   4   3   2   1   SD

G. Relevant demographics (for example, age, gender, and ethnicity) are described.

SA   5   4   3   2   1   SD

H. Measurement procedures are adequate.

SA   5   4   3   2   1   SD

I. All procedures have been described in sufficient detail to permit a replication of the study.

SA   5   4   3   2   1   SD

J. The participants have been adequately protected from potential harm.

SA   5   4   3   2   1   SD

K. The results are clearly described.

SA   5   4   3   2   1   SD

L. The discussion/conclusion is appropriate.

SA   5   4   3   2   1   SD

M. Despite any flaws, the report is worthy of publication.

SA   5   4   3   2   1   SD

Article 17

Improving Textbook Reading in a Middle School Science Classroom

RICH RADCLIFFE
Southwest Texas State University

DAVID CAVERLY
Southwest Texas State University

CYNTHIA PETERSON
Southwest Texas State University

MATT EMMONS
Prairie Lea Independent School District

ABSTRACT. Ineffective approaches for teaching with print may prevent textbook reading from being a useful learning resource in middle school. University faculty mentored a middle school science teacher as he implemented a textbook study-reading approach, PLAN (Caverly, Mandeville, & Nicholson, 1995), in 2 classes (*n* = 33). PLAN orchestrates 4 strategies through student-created mapping. After 3 months of strategy use, students gained in a self-report of strategic reading and in comprehension as reflected by maps. Post-assessment interviews revealed that the teacher had changed his instructional routine, moving through stages of strategy awareness, understanding, and adaptation. The teacher changed his expectation that students would complete textbook reading and that it increased student learning. The students changed their expectation that they could read and learn from the textbook.

From *Reading Improvement*, *41*, 145–156. Copyright © 2004 by Project Innovation, Inc. Reprinted with permission.

Although educators have long debated the role of the textbook for learning, in middle school the science textbook appears to be an important learning resource. According to the National Assessment of Educational Progress (2000), 80% of eighth-grade science teachers reported using the textbook regularly. It may play a stronger instructional role in the classroom when student prior knowledge or the teacher's relative familiarity with the topic is low (Driscoll, Moallem, Dick, & Kirby, 1994).

Weaknesses in textbook content and ineffective approaches for teaching with print may prevent textbook reading from being effective. The American Association for the Advancement of Science (2002) reported that science textbooks do a poor job of following standards-based principles for concept learning, a reason science teachers might avoid assigning textbook reading. In a case study of a middle school science classroom (Driscoll et al., 1994), the teacher presented textbook reading as the learning option for "book people," a style claimed by few students, according to the study results. In this classroom, other sources of learning, such as hands-on activities, seemed more valued. The textbook was used for definitional-level learning while hands-on activities were used for problem solving. The students' low average score (59%) on a unit test of facts and vocabulary suggested that using the textbook as a dictionary was not effective.

To address some of these issues, Haury (2000) recommended that science teachers help students adopt a purposive stance and a questioning attitude for textbook reading. This stance and attitude can be operationalized in the classroom as strategies for content area reading.

The Effectiveness of Reading Strategy Instruction

A substantial body of research documents the effectiveness of strategic reading instruction for middle school students on their comprehension of text (Trabasso & Bouchard, 2002). Explicit strategies prompt students to engage their prior knowledge and to monitor their comprehension. Despite evidence of the effectiveness of these strategies, a number of studies (reviewed by Pressley, 2002) report that few teachers use them in their instruction. To change their instructional routines, teachers likely need added support.

Teachers looking to follow Haury's (2000) recommendation for the science classroom will find little research to recommend the most popular strategy specific to study–reading with textbooks, SQ3R, as it has not shown advantages over traditional studying or students' existing approaches (Graham, 1982). A newer strategy for comprehending and studying textbooks called PLAN has been demonstrated to be effective with middle school students (Caverly, Mandeville, & Nicholson, 1995). It orchestrates a repertoire of strategies that have been validated with upper elementary and middle school students: relating the text to prior knowledge, questioning, summarizing (Pressley, Johnson, Symons, McGoldrick, & Kurikta, 1989), and using imagery and setting a purpose for reading (Brown, 2002). Specifically, PLAN begins with an assessment of the reading task demand, such as taking a chapter test or writing a paper. With the task for reading in mind, students *predict* (P) the content of the text and construct a tentative map; *locate* (L) on the map what is known by placing checkmarks and what is not known by placing question marks; *add* (A) notes during the reading of the textbook to confirm checkmarks and to address the question marks; and *note* (N) a reformulated understanding by revising the map, writing a summary, or performing any other task that might be aligned with the purposes for reading. In utilizing mapping, PLAN improves upon other strategic approaches to textbook reading. The value of student construction of concept maps has been well documented for the science classroom (Al-Kunified & Wandersee, 1990).

The purpose of this research was to examine the effects of introducing the PLAN study–reading strategy into two middle school science classrooms taught by one of the authors of this study [Caverly], a middle school science teacher subsequently referred to as the teacher. First, we asked how this middle school science teacher would change his instruction over a school year as he was mentored in teaching with the PLAN strategy. Second, we asked whether his students were able to learn using PLAN. Finally, we wanted to know how students perceived their use of the strategy.

Methods

The study followed a single-group pretest-posttest design that included multiple post assessments. This multiple posttest approach was used to strengthen the single-group design and because we expected a time delay between implementing the strategic reading strategies and generating benefits.

Participants

Participants were the science teacher from a small, rural middle school and the 15 seventh-grade and 18 eighth-grade students in his two science classes. The teacher held a master's degree in biology and had more than three years of teaching experience. As the only science teacher for the school, he taught the same students for both fall and spring semesters. Students' scores on the district's recently administered STAR test of reading ability (Advantage Learning Systems, 1998) indicated mixed-ability classes. Four students who scored third grade or below on the STAR test were eliminated from the data analyses, as they lacked basic decoding skills. The 29 students included in the analyses were categorized in roughly equal groups by gender and ethnicity (Anglo and Hispanic, though a few students were African American).

Data Sources

Three instruments were administered before and after four weeks of PLAN instruction by the teacher: (a) reading comprehension tests, (b) reading strategy checklists, (c) student-created concept maps. After nine months of strategy implementation, semi-structured interviews of the teacher and students were conducted and transcribed.

Textbook chapter reading comprehension tests. The teacher followed his regular instructional routine for creating chapter tests by selecting six questions from the textbook publisher's test bank. The test for one chapter served as the pretest and a test for a different chapter was the posttest. Each test balanced multiple choice, true-false, and matching questions. The purpose of the tests was to assess students' comprehension of the textbook chapters.

Concept maps. The students created concept maps based upon the science chapters that they were reading. These pretest and posttest assessments provided a second measure of reading comprehension and revealed information about the students' reading processes. The rubric to score these maps (see Appendix at the end of this article) was adapted from one developed by Stoddart, Abrams, Gaspar, and Canaday (2000).

Reading strategy checklist. We adapted a checklist developed by a colleague who had used it for many semesters with developmental college readers. Ten true-false questions asked students about which strategies they used for reading a textbook chapter and for monitoring comprehension (see Appendix at the end of this article).

Field notes. A notebook documented the conversations with the teacher and observations held throughout the nine months of the study.

Teacher and student interviews. The teacher and four of the students were interviewed nine months after the teacher introduced the PLAN strategy into the classroom. Using parallel sets of 12 open-ended questions, one of us (who had not worked with the teacher during the nine months) conducted an hour-long interview with the teacher while another of us conducted shorter, individual interviews with the students. The teacher selected these students because their performance fell in the middle of the range of student performance in the classes. These students were very willing to be interviewed. Questions to the teacher focused on his expectations of students and his instructional routines. Questions to the students focused on their expectations of the textbook and their perceptions of learning from it. The transcriptions of the taped interviews were analyzed using a constant comparative method for identifying themes.

Procedures

The study proceeded in three phases: (a) a preparation phase during which the teacher gained strategy awareness; (b) an implementation phase during which the teacher gained contextual strategy knowledge; and (c) an adaptation phase during which the teacher gained strategy control.

Preparation. The teacher had completed a summer graduate course taught by one of us [Peterson] that focused on integrating reading strategies into content-area teaching. The course included the modeling of specific comprehension strategies for content learning and practice by class members in small groups. PLAN for study–reading was modeled during one class session and practiced by students using a chapter from the course textbook. After expressing interest in trying out the PLAN strategy in his classroom, the teacher was invited to participate in this study.

Implementation. During three months of the fall semester, the teacher met weekly, a total of over 15 hours, with two of us [Caverly and Radcliffe] subsequently referred to as the mentors. During the meetings, the mentors and the teacher held in-depth discussions of the processes of strategic textbook reading and the challenges of implementing it in a middle school classroom. Concurrently, the teacher taught the PLAN strategy in his seventh- and eighth-grade science classes through the following major steps: (a) PLAN was introduced as a new way for students "to read hard material in the science textbook," (b) the teacher illustrated how to create concept maps on the board, (c) the students created concept maps in groups and then individually, and (d) the students individually completed the four steps in the PLAN strategy based on content in their science textbook. The instruction followed Pearson and Gallagher's (1983) steps of explicit instruction by modeling the strategy for students, providing scaffolding during guided practice, and structuring time for independent strategy use for students to internalize the processes.

Adaptation. In the spring semester, the teacher did not meet with the mentors, but remained in email contact. At this point, the teacher focused on integrating PLAN into his instructional routine and on promoting in students the idea of adapting it to be an individual "plan" for strategic textbook reading.

Findings

Changes in the Teacher's Perception of the Textbook

The field notes recorded the teacher's perceptions of textbook readings. Before his participation in the study, the teacher doubted the effectiveness of textbooks for science learning. His own experience had not been positive: "When I was in school, the word 'textbook' was like a four-letter word" and he did not know how to teach well with it: "I hadn't realized that I had no experience with someone teaching me how to read and understand a science textbook." Compounding these doubts about the relative importance of the textbook was his preparation for teaching science: "Doing experiments is what science is all about." This preparation was supported by his teaching experience: "Before I taught here, I taught at a project-based learning school and textbooks were completely forbidden."

Changes in the Teacher's Instruction

Three findings emerged from analysis of the transcript of the interview conducted at the end of the study. In comparing his teaching of a unit the previous spring with the teaching of the same unit with the PLAN strategy, these changes were evident at the adaptation phase.

1. The teacher had integrated the PLAN strategy into his instructional routine. "I will begin [the unit] with the PLAN strategy... Near halfway in the first period [I'll say] 'Your assignment is to read the first section. I want you to do the P, the L, and at least get started on the A.' We kind of got in the routine." In class, he leads a discussion of what students already know. Students then have about 20 minutes to get started. They take their books home to complete their PLAN maps and return with them the next day for a grade.

2. He modified the strategy in three ways. First, he used PLAN as a way for students to build background knowledge from the textbook: "The textbook now has become a background knowledge thing." The background knowledge increased student preparation for unit activities: "They come to class ready to discuss and learn things." His second modification was to allow students to choose a mapping format: "Some of the seventh-graders like *Inspiration* (2003), a mapping program with the concept maps on the computer. So some of them have moved on to that while others like doing it by hand." His third modification was that in the "N" step he assigned students to answer the comprehension questions at the end of the section. "Part of the thing I did with the note thing was to ask yourself, did you get out of the reading what the author wanted you to get? And the way to do that is to look at your concept map and look at the question and [ask] do you have the information the author is trying to get you to get."

3. His expectations of his students had changed. "The things that I teach are the same and I use the same materials but my expectations are different."

Effectiveness of Strategy for Student Learning

Comprehension tests. Students' scores on comprehension tests and reading strategy checklists were analyzed using a paired t test statistic (two-tailed). Differences in the students' scores on the 10-point reading comprehension pretest $(M = 4.9)$ and posttest $(M = 3.9)$ were not statistically significant, $t(22) = 1.427$, $p = .167$. Although the slight drop in scores was not statistically significant and too small to be practically significant, this result was unexpected and inconsistent with other findings in this study. The small number of test questions and possible differences in student prior knowledge of the chapter topics may have confounded the results.

Concept maps. Beginning with the first PLAN map, students were able to accurately represent the major headings and subheadings of the chapter. Content accuracy remained stable from the first to the final PLAN maps, with an average of 98% of the propositions recorded correctly. What did increase was the percentage of propositions that reflected paraphrasing of content and higher order thinking (a growth of 9% to 14%). There was also a decline in the percentage of propositions that were simply copied from the text (a decline from 91% to 86%).

Reading checklists. Comparison of the students' performance on the 10-item reading strategy checklist revealed a statistically significant difference, $t(22) = -2.102$, $p = .047$, between the pretest *(M = 5.5)* and posttest *(M = 6.4)* scores. This small gain in reading strategy scores was supported by the teacher's and students' responses in interviews that investigated the expanded use of reading strategies.

Teacher interview. Analysis of interview transcripts revealed four findings from the teacher's perspective on the effectiveness of PLAN.

1. He saw improvement in his students' learning. "They were coming in with more understanding of the material." He saw that "mean grades of the class increased" because students were better prepared for the labs. At the same time, he came to believe that the publisher-provided chapter tests were inadequate measures of student learning: "By talking to them on what they learned, I know they have learned more than what they can write on a test."

2. His students moved from needing group support with strategic reading to being independent in their strategy use and able to do the reading as homework. "First, I was teaching group concepts but by February they could do them individually."

3. He believed the benefits to students in using PLAN developed over time: "I use 12 weeks [in the fall] teaching it. [After winter break], we do a refresher PLAN strategy. That is actually where I really started seeing the benefits of it, after we came back and reviewed it again. They had some time to absorb it and think about it and to see."

4. At the end of the Adaptation phase, he observed that students were more willing to complete the textbook reading. In discussing his teaching of the same unit during the previous academic year, he stated: "I assigned it but it wasn't getting done." In discussing his teaching this spring, he said: "We stand outside the classrooms in between classes and students will run up to you and ask you if they need their textbooks today. [It's] the way they ask [the] question, "Do we have to have our textbooks today?" versus "Do we need our textbooks today?" I think that portrays the kind of attitude shift away from it is your enemy...[when they get an assignment] instead it's I can do that, I understand that, I can answer those questions."

Student interviews. Analysis of interview transcripts revealed three findings from the students' perspectives on the effectiveness of PLAN.

1. The students saw PLAN as part of the classroom routine. They said the teacher prompted them to use the PLAN strategy when they took their science books home to read, and when they created concept maps. All students reported that they took their books home to read twice a week. Some days they were assigned to read a whole chapter at home, other times to read a chapter that was started in class using PLAN. One student said: "We have our PLAN thing [to do]; [we] do the webs." In some cases, the concept maps were completed in class, other times the students prepared them while reading at home. A student explained one of the steps: "I start out looking at the main titles in the chapter, and then I break it off into subtitles, and then I will read each paragraph to put information [into the concept map]."

2. The students emphatically reported an increase in their reading since implementing the PLAN strategy: "I have read a lot more this year." Consistently, the interviewed students explained that they had become better readers. "I think I am a lot better, better reader." They elaborated, sharing that they understood more of what they read and that they were using elements of the PLAN strategy. One student explained: "I can understand it a lot better because doing concept maps helped me." In response to an inquiry about changes in reading, another student shared that she used to be scared to read textbooks and did not have any confidence, but now "I like to read." She reported that in addition to reading more in her science book than a year ago, she now reads more in social studies and other subjects.

3. Consistent with the teacher's description, the four interviewed students reported that they were doing well in science; two students explained that their grades had improved during the academic year. Strategic reading appeared to be contributing to their success. Three students explained that they liked to read and that it was helpful: "I like reading the chapters, I like understanding where I got it," "It helps me learn," and "I feel like I get a lot from reading my textbook."

Discussion

This study reveals how a middle school science teacher implemented strategic reading instruction through a collection of strategies for study–reading called PLAN. It reports the subsequent gains in his students' willingness and ability to learn from textbook reading. Consistent with the case study of Driscoll et al. (1994), this teacher was reluctant to rely on textbooks for learning and did not expect his students to be successful in reading a science textbook. More than adding a teaching strategy to his repertoire, he had to overcome his negative perceptions and experiences related to using textbooks to teach science. The short chapter tests, only six questions from the publisher test bank, may have reflected his low expectation that students would read the text or that the test would be a valuable assessment.

Consistent with the research of Caverly, Mandeville, and Nicholson (1995), the middle school students in the current study benefited from their use of PLAN as documented by the concept maps. Their posttest scores on the reading strategy checklist indicated that they also engaged in additional reading strategies, such as summarizing what they had read. The students interviewed reported that reading their science textbook helped them to learn science.

A major finding in this study was that adopting this strategic reading strategy in a middle school science classroom involved substantial time and effort by the teacher to modify his instructional routine. He had to develop skills in strategic reading instruction and gain confidence that students would learn from *his* delivery of it. Over a nine-month period, he progressed through three stages as he implemented PLAN: (a) awareness of the strategy, (b) a deeper knowledge and understanding of both why and how to teach it, and (c) control of it to meet his students' needs for learning science content. Scaffolds in this process included a summer graduate course in reading strategies and 15 meetings with two mentors during the fall school term. Consistent with Pressley (2002), this teacher developed in his ability to teach students effective study–reading strategies from simply being aware of the need to teach them, to understanding how to teach them, to the control of teaching them as demonstrated by both his choice to continue to teach them and his willingness to adapt them to fit his needs.

A second major finding in this study was that the benefits of learning the strategies for textbook reading took time to develop. After four weeks of strategy instruction and implementation, the students did not gain on the textbook chapter test, but did improve in their ability to represent the details and to translate the content into their own words through concept maps. They also reported that they were reading more strategically. The teacher believed the students needed more than four weeks to internalize the processes. During the following semester (with the same students in class), he observed that they understood more than what was on the chapter test, as they were better prepared for lab work and better able to use science vocabulary. At the end of the nine months, he saw increases in his students' science grades, which he attributed to their better performance in the lab work.

The students reported that they read more often than in the previous school year and they found reading more enjoyable. PLAN engages students in taking responsibility for reading skills by requiring concrete evidence of their reading in the form of a map. In contrast, SQ3R prompts in-the-head operations that may

be difficult for the student and teacher to monitor. The teacher reported that students shifted from initially relying on his instruction about PLAN to relying on small-group support, and finally to independent use of the strategy. This sequence follows Pearson and Gallagher's (1983) steps of explicit instruction.

Finally, this study documents the process of strategy control by the teacher. In the spring semester, after mentoring had ended, the teacher revised the "Note" step in PLAN. (Recall, the Note step is map revision or content reformulation.) Instead, the teacher assigned students to read and answer the comprehension questions at the end of the chapter. Yet, the teacher presented this traditional assignment in a way that prompted students' metacognition: He asked them to compare their maps to what the textbook author saw as most important, as expressed in the chapter questions. A second modification was his focus on using the strategy for building background knowledge in preparation for lab work. This modification shows that the teacher redefined his purpose for having students read the textbook based upon his observations of what they were learning by using the strategy.

Conclusions

Textbook reading in this middle school science classroom changed from being an assignment that students were not expected to complete to one that students completed and from which they learned science content. The teacher's expectations of students moved from doubt to confidence that they would read the textbook. Over a period of nine months, the teacher's classroom routine changed to include strategic reading instruction for the use of textbooks through a study–reading strategy called PLAN. Students changed their learning strategies by completing concept maps at home on textbook chapters. The teacher moved through three stages: (a) strategy awareness, (b) understanding, and (c) control, while the students progressed from observing the teacher model PLAN to using it in small groups, to individual classroom practice and homework.

After four weeks of strategy implementation, an evaluation of the students' concept maps indicated an increase in the use of higher order thinking. They gained in their self-reported use of reading strategies. The teacher observed deeper improvement after several months of implementation. At the end of the year, students reported that they were reading their textbooks more often and were understanding more of what they read. Consistent with prior studies, such as Trabasso and Bouchard (2002), we concluded that strategic reading instruction helped students learn from their textbooks.

In this study, the teacher modified the strategy to suit his instructional needs. We believe that this adaptation phase is important, specifically that strategic reading instruction must be integrated into the teacher's instructional routine. For example, using PLAN as a vehicle for students to develop general knowledge and concepts served to link textbook reading and the hands-on activities that are often preferred in teaching science.

Although these findings support and extend prior research about PLAN (Caverly et al., 1995), they are limited by several factors. First, some of the findings are based on the teacher's and students' perceptions of the implementation. The four-week time span between pre- and posttests likely was not enough time to show the full benefit of the strategy adoption and adaptation. The study is also limited because the approach was to compare the same students' performance over time; the use of a quasi-experimental research design is recommended for future investigation.

Implementation took considerable time and effort, a year's commitment, and a combination of graduate course work and mentor support. Therefore, teacher-educators need to evaluate whether reading workshops or a single reading strategy course are sufficient to enable participants to implement complex new strategic reading routines, such as the PLAN strategy.

References

Al-Kunified, A., & Wandersee, J.H. (1990). One hundred references related to concept mapping. *Journal of Research in Science Teaching. 27*(10), 1069–1075.

American Association for the Advancement of Science (2002). *AAAS Project 2061: Middle grades science textbooks: A benchmarks-based evaluation.* Retrieved May 19, 2003, from http://www.project2061.org/tools/textbook/mgsci/mgbooks.htm

Caverly, D., Mandeville, T., & Nicholson, S. (1995). PLAN: A study reading strategy for informational text, *Journal of Adolescent and Adult Literacy. 39*(3). 190–199.

Driscoll, M. P., Moallem, M., Dick, W., & Kirby, E. (1994). How does the textbook contribute to learning in a middle school science class? *Contemporary Educational Psychology, 19,* 79–100.

Graham, S. (1982). Comparing the SQ3R method with other study techniques for reading improvement. *Reading Improvement, 19*(1), 45–47.

Haury, D. L. (2000). *High school biology textbooks do not meet national standards.* (ERIC Document Reproduction Service No. ED 463949)

Inspiration Software, Inc. (2003). Inspiration 7.0. Retrieved Jul 24, 2003, from http://www.inspiration.com

Pearson, P. D., & Gallagher, M. (1983). The instruction of reading comprehension. *Contemporary Educational Psychology, 8,* 317–344.

Pressley, M., Johnson, C. J., Symons, S., McGoldrick, J. A., & Kurikta, J. A. (1989). Strategies that improve children's memory and comprehension of text. *Elementary School Journal, 90,* 3–32.

Pressley, M. (2002). Comprehension strategies instruction: A turn-of-the-century report. In C. C. Block & M. Pressley (Eds.). *Comprehension instruction: Research-based best practices* (pp. 11–27). NY: Guilford Press.

Stoddart, T., Abrams, R., Gaspar, E., & Canaday, D. (2000). Concept maps as assessment in science inquiry learning — A report of methodology. *International Journal of Science Education, 22,* 1221–1246.

Trabasso, T., & Bouchard, E. (2002). Teaching readers how to comprehend text strategically. In C. C. Block & M. Pressley (Eds.). Comprehension instruction: *Research-based best practices* (pp. 176–200). NY: Guilford Press.

U.S. Department of Education. Office of Educational Research and Improvement. National Center for Education Statistics. (2001) *The Nation's Report Card: Science Highlights 2000,* NCES 2002–452, by National Center for Education Statistics. Washington, DC.

Address correspondence to: Rich Radcliffe, Department of Curriculum and Instruction, 214 Commons Hall, Southwest Texas State University, San Marcos, TX 78666.

Appendix

Concept Map Rubric

	Accuracy							Depth		Complexity	
Proposition #	Accurate	Partially accurate	Common knowledge	Inaccurate	Affective	Question	Don't know	Basic description	Higher order description	Simple elaboration	Complex elaboration
1.											
2.											
3.											

Each map was scored by categorizing map nodes and links into proposition units, formed by two nodes (bubbles on the concept map) connected by a link. Each proposition was numbered starting with first-level links from the superordinate node, then second-level, and so on. If partially illegible, the text was rewritten. If completely illegible, the proposition was classified as "Don't Know."

Each proposition was scored using the following categories (adapted from Stoddart et al., 2000).

I. Content Accuracy

1. *Accurate*: Correct statement confirmed by text and expert
   • for example, – "acceleration equals net force divided by mass"
2. *Partially accurate*: Correct statement but only partially correct
   • for example, – "Newton's law states a net force changes the velocity of an object"
3. *Common knowledge*: Common or popular knowledge not stated in the text
   • for example, – "Newton's Apple" (TV show)

4. *Inaccurate*: Misconception or confusion
   • for example, – "the lower the mass the greater the inertia"
   or, inappropriately linked
   • for example, – linked to superordinate when should be linked to coordinate concept
5. *Affective*: Statements that express emotions, feelings, or personal thoughts
   • for example, – "boring!"
6. *Question*: Proposition in form of question that cannot be judged
   • for example, – "mass vs. acceleration?"
   (Also, don't classify in the Depth of Explanation or Complexity categories)
7. *Don't know*: Cannot be scored because the meaning of the proposition is unclear or scorer has insufficient knowledge
   • for example, – "Newton developed"
   Cannot be scored because unintelligible due to handwriting or spelling
   • for example, – "dsjalf dasfa werter"
   (Also, do not classify in the Depth of Explanation or Complexity categories)

II. Depth of Explanation
   1. *Basic description*: Statements copied directly from the text
      • for example, – "a force that resists motion between two surfaces that are in contact"
   2. *Higher-order description*: Explanations that paraphrase the text or add function or purpose, such as "how" or "why"
      • for example, – "the rougher the surfaces the greater the friction"

III. Complexity
   1. *Simple elaboration*: The proposition is a single subject-object clause
      • for example, – "Newton's Laws of Motion" are "First Law," "Second Law," "Third Law"
   2. *Compound elaboration*: contains one or more dependent clauses as explanations
      • for example, – "An object will not change its motion unless a force is acted upon it"

Reading Strategy Checklist

_____   _____
code   **date**

Directions: Carefully read the following statements and honestly respond to them using the scale below. Circle either A or B.

A. = Yes, I did this in preparation for this quiz.

B. = No, I did not do this in preparation for this quiz.

A. B.	1.	I made predictions about what the author would say next or what would happen next.
A. B.	2.	I connected ideas from my own experience to what I read.
A. B.	3.	I figured out new words by the ones around them.
A. B.	4.	I created a map of the ideas from the reading.
A. B.	5.	I created examples from my own experience to help my understanding.
A. B.	6.	I memorized key terms.
A. B.	7.	I reviewed the passage after reading to make sure I understood.
A. B.	8.	I skipped parts I didn't understand.
A. B.	9.	I tried to put the important ideas in my own words.
A. B.	10.	I identified the purpose the author had for writing.

Exercise for Article 17

Factual Questions

1. Who used PLAN in this study?

2. On what basis were four students eliminated from the data analyses?

3. How many students were included in the analyses?

4. Was the difference between the pretest and posttest scores on the reading comprehension test statistically significant?

5. What was the mean score on the reading checklist at the pretest? What was it at the posttest?

6. What is the name of the statistical test used to test the significance of the difference between pretest and posttest means on the reading checklist?

Questions for Discussion

7. In your opinion, are the steps in PLAN described in sufficient detail? Keep in mind that this is a research article. (See lines 60–75.)

8. Are the results of this experiment sufficiently promising that you would recommend conducting additional research on PLAN?

9. In your opinion, was interviewing four students sufficient in light of the purposes of this study? (See lines 144–161.)

10. In your opinion, is a 10-point reading comprehension test adequate for a study of this type? (See lines 263–275.)

11. To determine effectiveness in terms of student learning, the researchers used a variety of measures. Is this an important strength of this experiment? Explain. (See lines 263–382.)

12. Is the absence of a control group an important weakness of this study? Explain.

Quality Ratings

Directions: Indicate your level of agreement with each of the following statements by circling a number from 5 for strongly agree (SA) to 1 for strongly disagree (SD). If you believe an item is not applicable to this research article, leave it blank. Be prepared to explain your ratings. When responding to criteria A and B below, keep in mind that brief titles and abstracts are conventional in published research.

A. The title of the article is appropriate.

SA   5   4   3   2   1   SD

B. The abstract provides an effective overview of the research article.

SA   5   4   3   2   1   SD

C. The introduction establishes the importance of the study.

SA   5   4   3   2   1   SD

D. The literature review establishes the context for the study.

SA   5   4   3   2   1   SD

E. The research purpose, question, or hypothesis is clearly stated.

SA   5   4   3   2   1   SD

F. The method of sampling is sound.

SA   5   4   3   2   1   SD

G. Relevant demographics (for example, age, gender, and ethnicity) are described.

SA   5   4   3   2   1   SD

H. Measurement procedures are adequate.

SA   5   4   3   2   1   SD

I. All procedures have been described in sufficient detail to permit a replication of the study.

SA   5   4   3   2   1   SD

J. The participants have been adequately protected from potential harm.

SA   5   4   3   2   1   SD

K. The results are clearly described.

SA   5   4   3   2   1   SD

L. The discussion/conclusion is appropriate.

SA   5   4   3   2   1   SD

M. Despite any flaws, the report is worthy of publication.

SA   5   4   3   2   1   SD

Article 18

Baby Think It Over: Evaluation of an Infant Simulation Intervention for Adolescent Pregnancy Prevention

DIANE de ANDA
University of California

ABSTRACT. In an intervention aimed at showing students the amount of responsibility involved in caring for an infant, 353 predominantly ninth-grade and Latino students carried the Baby Think It Over simulation doll in an intervention and completed matched pre- and posttest measures. Statistically significant gains were found on the total score and the impact of having a baby on academics, social life, and other family members; emotional risks; understanding and handling an infant's crying; and apprehension of the amount of responsibility involved in infant care. On a posttest-only measure, 108 participants reported statistically significant differences before and after carrying the doll with regard to the age at which they wished to have a child, their career and education plans, and the perceived interference of an infant with those education and career plans and their social life.

From *Health & Social Work, 31*, 26–35. Copyright © 2006 by the National Association of Social Workers. Reprinted with permission.

To alter adolescents' perception of the effort involved in caring for a baby and successfully increase their intent to avoid pregnancy in adolescence, students at a Los Angeles County high school participated in an
5 intervention using a life-size infant simulation doll known as "Baby Think It Over" (BTIO). The participating high school is in one of the 10 poorest cities in the nation (United Way of Greater Los Angeles, 1998–1999) and has been designated one of the adolescent
10 pregnancy "hot spots" in California because of its high rates of adolescent pregnancy (California Department of Health Services, 2001). The intervention places the tangible consequences of pregnancy before adolescent participants rather than offering only the abstract mes-
15 sages about pregnancy risks often presented in other programs.

Adolescent Pregnancy in the United States

The steady rise in adolescent pregnancy rates became a significant concern among social service and health professionals, legislators, and the general public
20 during the 1970s and 1980s. The rates increased from 95.1 per 1,000 for 15- to 19-year-olds and 62.4 per 1,000 for 15- to 17-year-olds in 1972 to an all-time high of 117.1 (in 1990) and 74.4 (in 1989), respectively. Following a variety of intervention efforts, a
25 slow decline in the rates was noted in the first half of the 1990s, followed by a more rapid decrease to below the 1972 rate by 1997: 93.0 for 15- to 19-year-olds and 57.7 for 15- to 17-year-olds (Alan Guttmacher Institute, 1999a). This period included a 20% drop in the
30 pregnancy rate among African American adolescents and a 16% reduction among white adolescents. The pregnancy rate for Latina adolescents, however, increased between 1990 and 1992 and by 1996 decreased by only 6% (Alan Guttmacher Institute, 1999b), result-
35 ing in the birth rate of 149.2 per 1,000 for Latino adolescents—the highest among the total adolescent population (National Center for Health Statistics, 2000). Inasmuch as 54.1% of Latino high school youths report they have had sexual intercourse, and only slightly
40 more than half of those who are sexually active report using protection or birth control, Latino adolescents represent a population at high pregnancy risk (Kann et al., 2000).

As early as 1967, Elkind (1967) posited the impor-
45 tance of cognitive development in understanding adolescent risk-taking behavior, including pregnancy risks. Based on empirical research, the author and colleagues also proposed that adolescent pregnancy resulting from the risk taking of unprotected sexual intercourse might
50 be significantly related to cognitive development. Specifically, this behavior might reflect a lack of full attainment of formal operations and "the sense of invulnerability—described by Elkind as the 'personal fable'" (Becerra, Sabagh, & de Anda, 1986, p.136). For-
55 mal operations refer to the individual's ability to engage in abstract and hypothetical–deductive thinking (Piaget, 1972; Piaget & Inhelder, 1958) and, in this case, project the potential for pregnancy and ultimately becoming a parent. Adolescence typically includes a
60 period of transition from concrete to formal operations, at the beginning of which recognizing oneself as a sexual being is relatively easy because it is in the present and very concrete. By contrast, considering oneself

fertile can be a rather abstract concept for a young adolescent, and the consequences of fertility can be distant and hypothetical. Others have offered similar explanatory frameworks with regard to risk taking and adolescent pregnancy (e.g., Gordon, 1990; Kralweski & Stevens-Simon, 2000; Out & Lefreniere, 2001).

Interventions have been developed to accommodate these cognitive factors by creating simulated parenting experiences to provide a concrete learning situation that will make the hypothetical risks and consequences of adolescent pregnancy more real to the adolescent participants. Some past interventions have involved caregiving situations not directly analogous to caring for an infant, involving, for example, carrying a sack of flour or an egg. More recent interventions have used a simulation more directly analogous to caring for an infant—a computerized infant simulation doll that requires attention to its demands in the form of intermittent periods of crying.

BTIO: The Intervention

BTIO is an intervention using a computerized infant simulation doll to offer adolescents experiences similar to those involved in attending to an infant. The doll is programmed to cry at random intervals and to stop crying only when the adolescent "attends" to the doll by inserting a key into a slot in the doll's back until it stops crying. An examination of participant logs indicated that most crying periods ranged between 10 and 15 minutes, and the frequency between eight and 12 times in 24 hours (including the early A. M. hours). The key is attached to a hospital-style bracelet, which is worn by the participant 24 hours a day to ensure that the adolescent provides the caregiving responsibilities during an entire two-and-a-half-day study period. The bracelets are designed so that an attempt to remove the bracelet is detectable. "Babysitting" of the doll by another student with a key or by the health class teacher who has extra keys is permitted only in certain situations—to take an examination, for example. The doll records data, including the amount of time the adolescent takes to "attend" to the infant (insert the key) and any form of "rough handling," such as dropping or hitting the doll. The term "rough handling" is used rather than abuse because there is no way to determine intentionality. Students whose records indicate neglect and rough handling receive a private counseling session with the health class teacher and have mandatory participation in a parenting class.

The purpose of carrying the infant simulation doll is to provide the students with an understanding of the amount of time and effort involved in the care of an infant and how an infant's needs might affect their daily lives and the lives of their family and significant others. This experience is augmented by presentations and group discussions led by staff from a local social services agency, covering such topics as the high incidence of adolescent pregnancy in the community, the factors that increase risk of adolescent pregnancy, and the costs of adolescent pregnancy and parenthood, with particular emphasis on the limitation of education and career opportunities and achievement. The health class teacher also offers a pregnancy prevention education program in preparation for carrying the doll and a debriefing discussion period after everyone in the class has carried the doll.

BTIO in Previous Research

A relatively small amount of research has been conducted on the effectiveness of BTIO. A literature search produced eight published research articles evaluating BTIO interventions aimed at modifying attitudes, perceptions, and behaviors related to pregnancy risk. Six studies examined whether the program affected the adolescents' view of parenthood and child-rearing responsibilities: two found their objectives met in this respect, but four determined no change in perception. In a study conducted by Divine and Cobbs (2001) with 236 eighth-grade students in nine Catholic schools in a midwestern city, a greater number of BTIO students than control group students ($p < .05$) indicated a change on two of seven items: the amount of effort and cost involved in infant care, and the feeling that they have enough knowledge about what taking care of a baby entails. The majority (63% of the male adolescents, 75.5% of female adolescents) felt carrying the doll was effective in "helping me know the challenges of infant care" (p. 599). In Out and Lafreniere's (2001) sample of 114 Canadian students in the 11th grade, BTIO participants reported significantly ($p < .01$) more examples of child-rearing consequences and responsibilities than did control group students.

In contrast to these limited positive findings, Kralewski and Stevens-Simon's (2000) sample of 68 sixth-grade and 41 eighth-grade female Hispanic students from a middle school in a lower socioeconomic status Colorado neighborhood revealed no significant differences between anticipated difficulty and the actual difficulty in caring for the BTIO doll. In addition, BTIO did little to change the girls' desire to have a baby during adolescence, with 13 expressing this intent before BTIO and 16 after carrying the doll. Somers and Fahlman (2001) used a quasi-experimental design with a predominantly white, middle-class sample drawn from three high schools in the Midwest; MANCOVA performed on the posttest scores using the pretest scores as the covariate found no differences between the 151 students in the experiment group and 62 students in the control group on perceptions regarding childcare responsibilities. Somers, Gleason, Johnson, and Fahlman's (2001) study in two Midwest high schools found no change in participants' understanding of the responsibilities involved in child rearing. Strachan and Gorey (1997) did not find a change on their Parenting Attitude Scale measuring "realistic par-

175 enting expectations" (p. 175) in their sample of 48 African American and white youths ages 16 to 18.

Only one of the studies found any significant difference or change in attitudes or behavior related to sexuality. Out and Lafreniere (2001) found that "ado-
180 lescents in the intervention group…rated themselves as being significantly more susceptible to an unplanned pregnancy compared with adolescents in the comparison group" (p. 577). However, they found no differences between the groups in attitudes toward absti-
185 nence and contraceptive use. In studies conducted by Somers and Fahlman (2001) and Somers et al. (2001), no significant change from pretest to posttest in attitudes and behaviors related to sexual behavior, contraception, and pregnancy was detected. Out and La-
190 freniere found no changes from pretest to posttest in attitudes toward abstinence and contraceptive use. Finally, Divine and Cobbs (2001) found no differences between experimental and control groups in attitudes regarding contraception, abstinence, and sexuality.
195 Although no differences were found between their 245 BTIO participants and 186 control group participants, Tingle (2002) found the majority of parents reported that the intervention had increased both their children's perceptions of the difficulties involved in
200 caring for an infant and parent–child communication regarding sexuality and parenting. Moreover, the great majority (92%) indicated they would recommend the program to a friend; 82% for use in middle schools and 97% for use in high schools. Similarly, the majority of
205 the 89 parents in a rural Ohio sample felt that the program was successful in teaching their children that a baby was a considerable responsibility (85%), time consuming (79%), and a barrier to achieving their life goals (71%), and 90% indicated they would recom-
210 mend the BTIO program to friends (Price, Robinson, Thompson, & Schmalzried, 2000).

Of the 22 teachers in Tingle's (2002) study, 59% evaluated BTIO as "somewhat effective" in preventing pregnancies and 45% said it was effective in initiating
215 communication between parent and child. In Somers and colleagues' (2001) study, few of the 57 teachers felt that BTIO reduced sexual intercourse (5%) or the number of sexual partners (7%). However, the majority (91%) believed that students learned about the respon-
220 sibilities of parenthood and recommended that BTIO be continued in the school (86%) and be adopted in other schools (84%).

There were serious methodological limitations and flaws in the preceding studies. Many of the samples
225 were small and not random, thereby limiting generalizability. In addition, volunteers were also used in a number of the studies; for example, Out and Lafreniere's (2001) intervention group consisted of students from elective courses on parenting and the con-
230 trol group from geography and physical education classes at the same schools. Additional research with larger samples, greater control of confounds (especially

selection bias), and more rigorous research designs and methodology are needed, preferably with replication,
235 before any conclusions can be drawn regarding the effectiveness of this intervention as a model for reducing the risk of adolescent pregnancy.

Objectives

The present Baby Think It Over intervention had seven major objectives. The first four posited an in-
240 crease in the degree to which the adolescent recognized: (1) that caring for a baby affects an adolescent's academic and social life; (2) that other family members are affected by having an adolescent with a baby in the family; (3) that there are emotional risks for each par-
245 ent in having a baby during adolescence; and (4) that there are family and cultural values related to having a baby during adolescence. The remaining three proposed an increase in the number planning to postpone parenthood: (5) until a later age (for the majority until
250 graduation from high school); (6) until education and career goals were met; or (7) until marriage.

Research Design and Method

Program objectives and additional constructs were measured with two main instruments: BTIO-1 and BTIO-2. A repeated-measures design was used, with
255 the BTIO-1 measure as the pretest and posttest. To increase validity, participants were used as their own controls through paired pretest-posttest comparisons, with all data entered anonymously. Moreover, confounds related to history and maturation were elimi-
260 nated because the intervention was conducted sequentially and continuously across the academic year with multiple individuals as their own controls. A posttest-only evaluation measure (BTIO-2) also was used to obtain self-report data on the impact of the program.

Measures

265 *BTIO-1.* The four main program objectives were measured using a 25-item, closed-ended instrument with a four-point Likert-type scale, ranging from 4 = strongly agree to 1 = strongly disagree. Total score and scores for each of the first four objectives were created
270 by summing the scores of the relevant items. Two separate scores were also calculated for items pertaining to understanding and dealing with a crying infant and those related to overall infant care. A higher score indicated a higher level of agreement consonant with
275 the program objectives and greater accuracy in their evaluation of the statements. The measure demonstrated good internal consistency ($\alpha = .84$).

In addition, the youths were asked to indicate *when* they would "like to have children": (1) never, (2) right
280 now, (3) when I finish junior high school, (4) when I'm in high school, or (5) after I graduate from high school. Students also checked items they would like to do "before having a baby": (1) have a good paying job, (2) go to college, (3) graduate from a junior college, (4)
285 graduate from a four-year college, (5) go to a trade or

110

technical school, (6) get married, (7) have a career, and (8) "other" write-in responses. Multiple responses were possible.

BTIO-2. The Baby Think It Over-2 measure is a post hoc, self-report measure indicating whether the experience changed what participants thought it would be like to have a baby; when they thought they would like to have a baby in terms of age and educational and career achievements; beliefs regarding the use of birth control or protection; and how much time and work are involved in taking care of a baby. Perceptions before and after carrying the BTIO doll were indicated along Likert-type scales for use of birth control or protection, amount of effort involved in caring for a baby, and the interference of infant caregiving with education goals, career goals, and social life.

Data Analysis

Paired *t* tests were performed on the summated scores for the total number of items on the Likert-type scale, the summated scores for each of the first four objectives, and the scores for crying and overall care. ANCOVAs, using the pretest as the covariate, were also conducted to determine whether there were differences in responses based on gender. Chi-square analyses were performed on the nominal data for the last three objectives on postponing pregnancy and parenthood.

Findings

Demographic Data

A total of 353 of the students who carried the infant simulation doll completed matched pre- and posttest measures: 140 male participants and 204 female participants. Nine students did not report gender. The overwhelming majority (94.3%, $n = 333$) of the participants were in the ninth grade, with the remaining five (1.4%) in the 10th and three (.9%) in the 11th grade; 12 students (3.4%) did not indicate grade level. Correspondingly, most of the participants were 14 (48.2%, $n = 170$) to 15 (47.9%, $n = 169$) years old. Reflecting the demographics of the community, 92.9% of the participants in the sample were Latino (70.8% Mexican American, $n = 250$; 5.1% Central American, $n = 18$; 17.0% other Latino, $n = 60$). The remaining participants included one African American, five American Indian, three Asian/Pacific Islander, nine white, and two multiethnic youths; five students did not provide this information.

BTIO-1

On the BTIO-1 measure, statistically significant gains from pretest to posttest were found on all but one of the paired analyses (Table 1). The statistically significant increase in the means from pretest to posttest indicates that Objective 1 was met: a greater recognition of the impact of caring for a baby on academic and social life. The posttest mean approached 20, equivalent to "agree" and edging closer to the "strongly

agree" point on the scale. When items related to the students' academic and social life were summed separately, the gains were also found to be statistically significant: academics [$t(352) = 7.893$, $p < .001$]; social life [$t(352) = 9.862$, $p < .001$].

The gain from pretest to posttest for Objective 2 was also statistically significant, indicating a greater recognition of the effect of adolescent parenthood on other family members. However, the gain was modest (from 10.8 to 11.24 in a range of possible scores from four to 16), and the mean at posttest did not quite reach the point of "agree" (12.0) on the scale. An examination of the responses to the various items provides clarification. Most participants "agreed" or "strongly agreed" on items that recognize how adolescent parenthood affects the adolescent's family: 93.8% that an infant's crying or illness might disturb other family members' sleep and 70.8% that a baby's needs would reduce money available for the needs of others in the family. The mean was reduced by the 25% to 30% who disagreed on two items that indicated that other family members would share care and responsibility for the baby.

On Objective 3, a statistically significant increase in the recognition of emotional risks accompanying adolescent parenthood was found, with the posttest mean corresponding to "agree."

Objective 4—regarding cultural and family values on adolescent parenthood—was not met. The increase was minimal (.14); however, the mean of 8 (in a range of possible scores of three to 12) is equivalent to "agree" on the four-point scale. High pretest scores may have resulted in a ceiling effect, and it is likely that cultural and family values are relatively stable.

Responses to items related to understanding why a baby cries and what actions should be taken in response were calculated into a summated score. The gain from pretest ($M = 14.18$) to posttest ($M = 15.98$) achieved statistical significance [$t(352) = 12.266$, $p < .001$], moving the mean beyond a score of 15 (range five to 20) or "agree" on the scale. The individual items clearly reflect aspects of the experience of carrying the BTIO doll: 92.6% ($n = 327$) disagreed or strongly disagreed that it was "easy to ignore a fussy, crying baby"; 86.1% ($n = 304$) disagreed or strongly disagreed that babies would not cry if they were loved and loved the parent in return. Moreover, the majority appeared to understand why infants cry and refrained from making inaccurate and judgmental appraisals of both infant and parent behavior: 85.3% ($n = 301$) did not view a baby who "cries a lot" as "spoiled," 65.7% ($n = 232$) did not attribute the crying to insufficient care by parents, and 94.6% ($n = 334$) saw crying as a form of communication (trying "to tell you something").

Three questions ascertained the participants' views regarding overall care of an infant. The increase in the mean (from 9.24 to 10.28) was statistically significant [$t(352) = -9.471$, $p < .001$], indicating an increase in

Table 1

Paired t Test Results on Objectives 1 to 4 of the Baby Think It Over Program (N = 353)

	M	SD	df	t
Objective 1: Academic and social			252	−10.633***
Pretest	18.08	3.52		
Posttest	19.99	2.48		
Objective 2: Impact on family members			352	−3.935***
Pretest	10.80	1.65		
Posttest	11.24	1.59		
Objective 3: Emotional risks			352	−6.951***
Pretest	14.50	2.25		
Posttest	15.46	2.11		
Objective 4: Family and cultural values			352	−1.593***
Pretest	8.44	1.40		
Posttest	8.58	1.36		

***$p \leq .001$.

the recognition of the substantial time and effort involved in caring for an infant. A high percentage concurred regarding the 24-hour caregiving required for the BTIO doll: 89.8% ($n = 317$) agreed or strongly agreed that, for adolescent parents, taking care of a baby might be "too much for them to handle"; 88.7% ($n = 313$) disagreed or strongly disagreed that taking care of a baby was "fun and easy"; and 96.1% ($n = 339$) agreed or strongly agreed that "taking care of a baby takes a lot of time and hard work."

The difference between the pretest ($M = 72.2$) and posttest ($M = 78.27$) means for the total score on the 25 items was statistically significant [$t(352) = −12.655$, $p < .001$], demonstrating an increase in agreement with the objectives of the program. With a range of 25 to 100, the posttest mean is equivalent to beyond "agree" (75.0) on the four-point scale.

To determine whether there were any differences in outcomes based on gender, ANCOVA was conducted using the pretest as the covariate. Female participants demonstrated greater gains on the total score [$F(1, 352) = 6.446$, $p < .012$]; Objective 1 (academic and social life) [$F(1, 352) = 4.411$, $p < .05$]; Objective 3 (emotional risks) [$F(1, 352) = 10.619$, $p < .001$]; and crying [$F(1, 352) = 9.290$, $p < .01$]. Male participants showed greater gains on Objective 4 (family and cultural values) [$F(1, 352) = 4.679$, $p < .05$], with gains negligible for both (males: 8.44 to 8.79; females: 8.42 to 8.43).

Objective 5 posited an increase in the length of time the adolescents planned to postpone parenthood. There was only a 1.4% increase (72.5% to 73.9%) in the number of those intending to wait until after graduating from high school to have children. However, the number of those wanting children before graduating from high school decreased dramatically, from 8.7% ($n = 31$) to 1.5% ($n = 5$). Perhaps the BTIO experience was extremely negative for some participants, as the number never wanting children increased from 15.9% ($n = 56$) to 23.8% ($n = 84$).

Objective 6 was met with a statistically significant increase on every item related to postponing pregnancy

to achieve academic and career goals (Table 2). Financial stability was the highest priority, as job and career had the highest frequency at both pretest and posttest. For the majority of the youths, college aspirations took precedence over having a child. Although there was minimal increase in those who desired parenthood within a marital relationship after the BTIO experience—an additional 12 adolescents—the majority of the youths (71%; $n = 251$) had already indicated this preference at pretest.

BTIO-2

The BTIO-2 measure was completed by 108 participants, 60 female and 48 male, with most ages 14 to 15 (94.4%, $n = 102$), in the ninth grade (99.1%, $n = 107$), and Latino (92.6%, $n = 100$).

To obtain the adolescents' own view of the changes they experienced in perceptions and behavior as a result of carrying the BTIO doll, they were asked to indicate their thoughts, desires, or behavior "before BTIO" and "after BTIO/Now." Paired t test analyses found statistically significant differences in the desired direction on all items (Table 3).

Students reported that carrying the BTIO doll delayed the age at which they desired to have a child, from a mean of 23 to 25 years. A dramatic drop occurred in those indicating an age of 24 years or less (67% to 32.3%). Moreover, the majority (58.3%, $n = 63$) responded "yes," that carrying the BTIO doll had helped them change their mind regarding the age to have a child.

More than three-quarters of the BTIO-2 respondents indicated that they wanted to complete college and have a job or career before becoming parents. The already high "before" rate of 72.2% ($n = 78$) increased to 77.8% ($n = 84$) "after." There was an increase in those indicating that having a baby would interfere with their education (from 65.7%, $n = 71$ to 83.3%, $n = 90$); getting a good job or career (from 54.6%, $n = 59$ to 77.8%, $n = 84$); and their social life (from 58.3%, $n = 63$ to 73.1%, $n = 79$).

Table 2

Frequency of Response Selected by Participants in the Baby Think It Over Program

| | Pretest | | Posttest | | χ^2 |
Factor	f	%	f	%	$(df = 1)$
Good paying job	298	84.4	318	89.2	65.62***
Go to college	270	76.5	296	83.9	71.02***
Graduate from junior college	108	30.6	106	30.0	80.33***
Graduate from four-year college	173	49.0	183	51.8	89.17***
Technical school	102	28.9	112	31.7	59.75***
Career	288	81.6	303	85.8	92.95***
Married	251	71.1	263	74.5	61.02***

***$p < .001.$

Table 3

t Test Results BTIO-2: Before and After BTIO

	N	M	SD	df	t
Age want to have first baby				86	−7.210***
Before	87	23.16	3.55		
After	87	25.36	3.49		
School/job prior to having baby				91	−4.061***
Before	92	5.11	1.21		
After	92	5.51	1.08		
Amount of time it takes to care for baby				96	−5.821***
Before	97	3.24	.998		
After	97	3.78	.616		
How much baby interferes with education				102	−3.966***
Before	103	4.43	.986		
After	103	4.77	.675		
How much baby interferes with job/career				103	−4.984***
Before	104	4.16	1.18		
After	104	4.63	.827		
How much baby interferes with social life				100	−3.287***
Before	101	4.29	1.061		
After	101	4.60	.873		

Note. BTIO = Baby Think It Over

***$p \leq .001.$

More than half of the respondents (55.6%, $n = 60$) answered affirmatively that BTIO changed their perceptions of what having a baby would be like. In the open-ended questions, the most frequently cited reason
480 was that it was much harder work to care for a baby than they had previously thought (39.8%, $n = 43$). Many students chose not to respond to the open-ended questions.

Nearly two-thirds (58.3%) reported that BTIO
485 helped change their minds about using birth control or protection to prevent unwanted pregnancies. Reported use of birth control or protection increased from 22.2% ($n = 24$) to 28.7% ($n = 31$). Few "never" used protection, and the number dropped slightly from 13.9% ($n =$
490 15) to 11.1% ($n = 12$). The remaining either indicated that they had never had sexual intercourse or left it blank, as the item was supposed to be skipped if not applicable.

495 Among the varied responses to the open-ended question regarding what they thought of the program in general, a few appeared with greater frequency including comments describing the program as "good" or "effective" (61.1%, $n = 66$), and that BTIO helped them learn how hard taking care of a baby actually was
500 and that they did not want a child at this time (39.9%, $n = 43$).

Discussion

The Baby Think It Over program appears to be a well-designed intervention that has multiple educational components, a well-controlled simulation ex-
505 perience, debriefing procedures, a stable position in the school's curriculum, support from the school faculty and administration, and a working collaboration with the staff from a local social services agency that funds the program through a state grant. Both the results of
510 the data analyses and the adolescents' own evaluation confirm the effectiveness of the Baby Think It Over

intervention in changing perceptions regarding the time and effort involved in caring for an infant and in rec-
515 ognizing the significant effect having a baby has on all major aspects of one's life. Participants increased their awareness of how caring for an infant would interfere with future plans and goals with regard to both educa- tion and career. The majority aspired to a college edu- cation, and the BTIO experience intensified this desire
520 to further their education. Pregnancy prevention was increasingly recognized as important to ensure their future. Furthermore, the adolescents began to have a more realistic understanding of the demands of adoles- cent parenthood, acknowledging the loss to their social
525 life along with loss of sleep and the freedom to use their time as they desired. The effect on other family members was also noted as well as the emotional stress created by the responsibility for an infant.

Most of the youths were surprised by how labor-
530 intensive taking care of the BTIO doll was, by the fre- quency with which they had to attend to the doll's needs (crying), and the disruption this caused in their lives. For most, this ended their romanticized view of having a baby—for a few, to the point of never wanting
535 to have a baby. In general, the youths appeared to be more realistic about how much time and work is in- volved in caring for a baby. The majority responded by adjusting the timeframe within which they desired to have a child, opting for parenthood at a later age and
540 after important educational and career achievements. In summary, the program appears to have been eminently successful in achieving its immediate objectives.

It should be noted, however, that these are all changes in perceptions and intention rather than longi-
545 tudinal measures of actual behavior. Nevertheless, per- ceptions and intentions are important antecedents of behavior. From a social learning theory perspective, perception and intention increase or decrease the prob- ability that a behavior will occur. Moreover, the per-
550 ceived consequences of behavior and one's perceived self-efficacy in determining the outcome of the behav- ior affect the likelihood that the behavior will occur (Bandura, 1995). In this case, the students appeared to have made a strong connection between unprotected
555 sexual intercourse and what they now evaluate as a negative outcome: having to care for a demanding in- fant and the subsequent social, emotional, and aca- demic costs. Most of the respondents wished to have financial stability, an established career, and a marital
560 relationship before parenthood.

The quantitative analyses as well as the students' own comments testify to the importance of the "hands on," simulated experience. Given that most of these youths were 14 and 15 years old, still making the tran-
565 sition from concrete to formal operations, the use of a concrete mechanism that offers direct experiential learning appears to be extremely appropriate.

The program appears to be successful in changing perceptions and intentions; however, to increase the

570 likelihood of its effectiveness in preventing adolescent pregnancy in the long term, an intervention that also provides the adolescents with methods for dealing with situations that involve pregnancy risk is needed. A comprehensive program that covers methods from ab-
575 stinence to birth control methods and access would provide adolescents with the knowledge and skills needed to actualize their intentions and the opportunity for choice in the means to accomplish this.

Finally, a number of strengths in the design of the
580 program should also be noted. First, the intervention was offered to both male and female adolescents. Sec- ond, the mechanism (BTIO) ensured that all partici- pants received the same intervention experience. Third, the process was a mandatory part of a required class, so
585 that all students participated, thereby eliminating selec- tion bias within the school sample. Fourth, the inter- vention was used sequentially throughout the school year with different participants each time used as their own controls so that there was control of confounds,
590 particularly related to history and maturation. Fifth, the program was not simply a two-day intervention, as the simulation is part of a complex educational program that involves both preparation for the experience, group and individual discussion of the experience, and addi-
595 tional intervention for those students who experienced difficulty during the simulation.

It would be ideal to assess the long-term effects of the program by obtaining data on the pregnancy rates of the participants over the subsequent three years.
600 However, an accurate count is questionable as preg- nancies are not necessarily reported to the school, and adolescents who become pregnant may drop out of school, transfer, or have a miscarriage or abortion without the school ever knowing they were pregnant.
605 Moreover, because all students in a single grade re- ceive the experience, no long-term control group will be available.

In the short term, students in the educational plan- ning course, which runs parallel with the health course,
610 can be used as controls to improve the validity of the evaluation because assignment to the courses is on a relatively random basis; that is, determined by fit within the student's schedule. Because the students switch classes the second semester, the controls will
615 then also receive the intervention, thus eliminating any ethical questions regarding the withholding of the in- tervention. Furthermore, to ascertain the effects of the BTIO doll alone, a comparison group who receives all the educational components except the doll could be
620 used.

The findings offer a number of implications for so- cial work practice with adolescents, particularly regard- ing pregnancy prevention. It appears that an intensive, realistic experience can effect a rapid and significant
625 amount of attitude change about sexual behavior and adolescent parenthood in a relatively short amount of time. Therefore, even if funds are limited, because the

experience is only two-and-a-half days long, a small number of the simulation dolls might suffice to bring about a change. However, it is important to note that the experiential intervention was supported by an educational component that included didactic instruction and peer discussion. It cannot be assumed that merely allowing an adolescent to carry the doll for a couple of days will have the same effect. It is also possible that the memory of the experience may decrease in intensity over time, so that a repeated experience in the later grades might be necessary to reinforce and maintain the long-term effects of the intervention. Moreover, the social worker needs to make sure that the experience is a balanced one, so that infants are not seen primarily as a source of annoyance and frustration. Finally, the findings suggest that an experiential learning component can alter perspectives and behavior, so that simulation, because it makes the situation very concrete, might be a powerful intervention tool in general with youths who are transitioning to formal operations.

References

Alan Guttmacher Institute. (1999a). *Teenage pregnancy: Overall trends and state-by-state information*. New York: Author.

Alan Guttmacher Institute. (1999b). *U.S. teenage pregnancy statistics: With comparative statistics for women aged 20–24*. New York: Author.

Bandura, A. (Ed.) (1995). *Self-efficacy in changing societies*. New York: Cambridge University Press.

Becerra, R., Sabagh, G., & de Anda, D. (1986). *Sex and pregnancy among Mexican American adolescents: Final report to the Office of Adolescent Pregnancy Programs, Department of Health and Human Services*. Washington, DC: U.S. Department of Health and Human Services.

California Department of Health Services, Maternal and Child Health Branch, Epidemiology and Evaluation Section. (2001). *Teen birth rate hot spots in California, 1999–2000: A resource developed using a geographic information systems approach*. Sacramento: Author.

Divine, J. H., & Cobbs, G. (2001). The effects of infant simulators on early adolescents. *Adolescence, 36*, 593–600.

Elkind, D. (1967). Egocentrism in adolescence. *Child Development, 38*, 1025–1034.

Gordon, D. E. (1990). Formal operational thinking: The role of cognitive-developmental processes in adolescent decision-making about pregnancy and contraception. *American Journal of Orthopsychiatry, 60*, 346–356.

Kann, L., Kinchen, S. A., Williams, B. I., Ross, J. G., Lowry, R., Grunbaum, J., & Kolbe, L. J. (2000). Youth risk behavior surveillance—United States, 1999. *Morbidity and Mortality Weekly Report Surveillance Summaries, 49*, 1–96.

Kralewski, J., & Stevens-Simon, C. (2000). Does mothering a doll change teens' thoughts about pregnancy? [electronic edition], *Pediatrics, 105*, e. 30.

National Center for Health Statistics. (2000). *Health, United States, 2000*. Hyattsville, MD: Author.

Out, J. W., & Lafreniere, K. D. (2001). Baby Think It Over: Using role-play to prevent teen pregnancy. *Adolescence, 36*, 571–582.

Piaget, J. (1972). Intellectual evolution from adolescence to adulthood. *Human Development, 15*, 1–12.

Piaget, J., & Inhelder, B. (1958). *The growth of logical thinking from childhood to adolescence* (A. Parsons & S. Seagrin, Trans.). New York: Basic Books.

Price, J. H., Robinson, L. K., Thompson, C., & Schmalzried, H. (2000). Rural parents' perceptions of the Baby Think It Over Program—A pilot study. *American Journal of Health Studies, 16*, 34–40.

Somers, C. L., & Fahlman, M. M. (2001). Effectiveness of the "Baby Think It Over" teen pregnancy prevention program. *Journal of School Health, 71*, 188–195.

Somers, C. L., Gleason, J. H., Johnson, S.A., Fahlman, M. M. (2001). Adolescents and teachers' perceptions of a teen pregnancy prevention program. *American Secondary Education, 29*, 51–66.

Strachan, W., & Gorey, K. (1997). Infant simulator lifespan intervention: Pilot investigation of an adolescent pregnancy prevention program. *Child Adolescent Social Work Journal, 14*, 1–5.

Tingle, L. R. (2002). Evaluation of North Carolina "Baby Think It Over" project. *Journal of School Health, 72*, 178–183.

United Way of Greater Los Angeles. (1998–1999). *State of the county report, 1999–1999*. Los Angeles: Author.

About the author: *Diane de Anda*, Ph.D., is associate professor, Department of Social Welfare, School of Public Affairs, University of California, 3250 Public Policy Building, Box 951656, Los Angeles, CA 90095. E-mail: ddeanda@ucla.edu

Exercise for Article 18

Factual Questions

1. According to the researcher, is the previous research on the effectiveness of the BTIO intervention extensive?

2. According to the researcher, do the previous studies have serious methodological limitations and flaws?

3. Was the BTIO-2 measure administered as both a pretest *and* as a posttest?

4. According to the researcher, was the gain from pretest to posttest for Objective 2 very large?

5. For Objective 3, was the increase from pretest to posttest statistically significant? If yes, at what probability level?

6. On the pretest, what percentage of the participants desired parenthood within a marital relationship? On the posttest, what percentage desired it?

Questions for Discussion

7. In your opinion, is the experimental intervention described in sufficient detail? Explain. (See lines 83–127.)

8. Is it important to know that the participants responded anonymously? Explain. (See lines 255–258.)

9. In a future study of the intervention, would you recommend a longitudinal follow-up? Explain. (See lines 543–549 and 597–604.)

10. Is it important to know that participation was a mandatory part of a required class? Explain. (See lines 583–586.)

11. In a future experiment on this topic, would you recommend the use of a control group? Explain. (See lines 605–620.)

12. Based on this experiment, do you regard the intervention as promising? Would you recommend funding to extend the program to additional schools? Explain.

Quality Ratings

Directions: Indicate your level of agreement with each of the following statements by circling a number from 5 for strongly agree (SA) to 1 for strongly disagree (SD). If you believe an item is not applicable to this research article, leave it blank. Be prepared to explain your ratings. When responding to criteria A and B below, keep in mind that brief titles and abstracts are conventional in published research.

A. The title of the article is appropriate.

SA 5 4 3 2 1 SD

B. The abstract provides an effective overview of the research article.

SA 5 4 3 2 1 SD

C. The introduction establishes the importance of the study.

SA 5 4 3 2 1 SD

D. The literature review establishes the context for the study.

SA 5 4 3 2 1 SD

E. The research purpose, question, or hypothesis is clearly stated.

SA 5 4 3 2 1 SD

F. The method of sampling is sound.

SA 5 4 3 2 1 SD

G. Relevant demographics (for example, age, gender, and ethnicity) are described.

SA 5 4 3 2 1 SD

H. Measurement procedures are adequate.

SA 5 4 3 2 1 SD

I. All procedures have been described in sufficient detail to permit a replication of the study.

SA 5 4 3 2 1 SD

J. The participants have been adequately protected from potential harm.

SA 5 4 3 2 1 SD

K. The results are clearly described.

SA 5 4 3 2 1 SD

L. The discussion/conclusion is appropriate.

SA 5 4 3 2 1 SD

M. Despite any flaws, the report is worthy of publication.

SA 5 4 3 2 1 SD

Article 19

A Pilot Intervention to Promote Walking and Wellness and to Improve the Health of College Faculty and Staff

DANELL J. HAINES
The Ohio State University

LIZ DAVIS
The Ohio State University

PATRICE RANCOUR
The Ohio State University

MARIANNE ROBINSON
The Ohio State University

TRISH NEEL-WILSON
The Ohio State University

SUSAN WAGNER
The Ohio State University

ABSTRACT. There is a need to investigate novel interventions that promote worksite physical activity and wellness. *Objective*: The authors' purpose in this study was to evaluate the effectiveness of a 12-week walking program supplemented with a pedometer, computer educational program, and weekly e-mails. *Methods*: College faculty and staff participated in a one-group pre-posttest study to determine whether the 12-week walking intervention had an effect on body mass index (BMI), blood pressure, blood glucose, and cholesterol. The authors also determined participant-perceived wellness effects. *Results*: The authors observed differences between baseline and follow-up in BMI ($p = .024$), blood glucose ($p = .06$), and total cholesterol ($p = .09$). The program had a moderate effect on fitness, mood, health awareness, nutrition, and health. *Conclusions*: It is incumbent that experts develop innovative worksite physical activity and wellness programs. A pedometer-monitored walking program is one way that a worksite health initiative can improve the health and wellness of its employees and simultaneously reduce health-care costs.

From *Journal of American College Health*, 55, 219–225. Copyright © 2007 by Heldref Publications. Reprinted with permission.

By the year 2000, approximately 90% of all workplaces with 50 or more employees had some form of health promotion program.[1] Worksite health promotion programs originated from employees requesting disease prevention programs, health education, and

5 screening, and from employers wanting the potential cost savings associated with positive health behavior change. Excess weight and a sedentary lifestyle have affected health care in the United States at a direct cost

10 of more than $90 billion a year.[2]

The cost savings that result from positive health behavior change are usually associated with a reduced number of primary care patient visits and with increased employee productivity, as measured by a de-

15 crease in work absenteeism owing to illness.[3] Researchers examining the relationship between participation in a facility-based fitness program and the number of reported absences from work because of illness found a significant relationship between fitness pro-

20 gram participation and decrease in absences.[4] According to a U.S. Department of Health and Human Services (DHHS) report, worksite health promotion programs have been shown to improve employee health, increase productivity, and yield a significant return on

25 investment for the employer, ranging from $1.49 to $4.91 (median of $3.14) in benefits for every dollar spent on the program.[5]

Of interest to us were the health benefits associated with a novel physical activity intervention, specifically

30 a worksite virtual (computer-based) walking and wellness program monitored by pedometers. Researchers have repeatedly found that health benefits are experienced when inactive people become moderately active.[6] Even though the benefits of physical activity

35 have been well publicized, the physical activity habits of people in the United States have remained relatively unchanged over the past decade.[7] There is therefore a continued need to provide physical activity incentives for employees and to test novel worksite physical ac-

40 tivity interventions to determine their efficacy and degree of participant satisfaction. In brief, we set out to determine whether the "Virtual Walking & Wellness Program" made a difference in faculty and staff health status and whether the participants perceived that the

45 program made a difference in various aspects of their physical and psychological well-being.

A secondary aim of the study was to provide the Office of Human Resources on a college campus with data that would support providing incentives for faculty

50 and staff who participate in campus physical activity programs.

Our main purpose was to determine whether a "Virtual Walking & Wellness Program" for faculty and staff had an effect on body mass index (BMI), physical

55 activity habits, blood pressure, blood sugar level, and total cholesterol level, as determined by biometric tests

we administered before and after a 12-week program. We chose these health indicators because of their effect on hypertension, hypercholesterolemia, and type 2 dia-
60 betes—health conditions that lead to heart disease and frequently require pharmacotherapy and additional physician visits. The perceived effect of the Program on wellness components, such as fitness level, health awareness, nutritional habits, health status, anxiety
65 level, happiness, weight loss, and work productivity, was self-reported by participants, using an instrument we designed.

Methods

Participants

We recruited participants (*N* = 125) from a large midwestern college campus faculty/staff wellness pro-
70 gram and on-campus Weight Watchers classes. Partici-pants were required to attend a study orientation and to complete consent and Health Insurance Portability and Accountability Act (HIPAA) forms, Physical Activity Readiness Questionnaire (PAR-Q),[8] and the Godin
75 Leisure Time Exercise Questionnaire[9] to determine their present physical activity status. Participants then underwent biometric tests: finger stick to determine total blood cholesterol and blood glucose, height and weight measurements to determine BMI, and sphyg-
80 momanometer and stethoscope measurement to deter-mine blood pressure. Exclusion criteria included symp-tomatic coronary heart disease, immobility that restricts walking, a current systolic blood pressure higher than 160 mm Hg and a diastolic blood pressure higher than
85 95 mm Hg, and pregnancy. In addition, if participants answered "yes" to any of the questions on the PAR-Q,[8] they were required to obtain a signed physician clear-ance letter. The University's Institutional Review Board for human subject research approved our study.
90 Of the 125 participants who registered for the program, 120 were deemed eligible and included 117 staff mem-bers (97.5%) and 3 faculty members (2.5%).

As shown in Tables 1 and 2, the participants in this study (*N* = 120) were predominantly women (92.5%),
95 middle-aged (*M* = 44.27, *SD* = 10.00), and Caucasian (85.0%). The mean BMI (29.96, *SD* = 6.00) was con-sidered almost obese. There was variability in the physical activity habits of the participants, evident by a mean of 24.59 and a standard deviation of 19.28 on the
100 Godin Leisure Time Physical Activity Questionnaire.[9] More than half (59.2%) of the participants were pre-hypertensive or hypertensive. Overall, blood glucose and total cholesterol were somewhat high, with mean scores and standard deviations of 101.48 (*SD* = 23.19)
105 for blood glucose and 188.53 (*SD* = 35.88) for blood cholesterol.

Measures

We measured BMI, blood pressure, blood glucose, and cholesterol at baseline and after 12 weeks. Using the participant's height and weight, we calculated BMI
110 to determine whether the participant was overweight or obese. We used a mercury sphygmomanometer and stethoscope to test blood pressure and obtained blood glucose and total cholesterol from a random single fin-ger stick using a Cholestech® (Hayward, CA). We han-
115 dled blood samples according to Cholestech LDX rec-ommendations and guidelines[10] and the Clinical Labo-ratory Improvement Amendments (CLIA) licensure.[11]

Participants used a pedometer (Omron, Tokyo, Ja-pan) to determine baseline physical activity status,
120 which we used to develop the subject's walking pro-gram. Participants logged their pedometer steps daily during the 12-week program. Using a 5-point Likert scale (0 = no improvement to 5 = significant), partici-pants rated their perceived degree of improvement in
125 the following areas of well-being; fitness level, mood, health awareness, nutrition habits, health status, anxiety level, happiness, weight loss, work productivity, and work absenteeism.

Intervention

We administered the 12-week intervention, "Virtual
130 Walking & Wellness Program," between June and Oc-tober 2004; it consisted of a 10-unit virtual (computer-based) educational program that focused on physical activity and wellness. Daily pedometer readings were logged and a weekly e-mail message, consisting of
135 walking and wellness tips, was e-mailed to participants. Unit 1 of the educational program provides information on the importance of physical activity, how to use a pedometer, and how to determine baseline daily steps. Unit 2 focuses on designing a personal walking pro-
140 gram. The remaining units include topics such as nutri-tion, stress reduction through physical activity, and other wellness-related topics. All units include an in-troduction explaining the importance of the unit, learn-ing objectives, recommended learning activities, and
145 review questions. We based subjects' personal walking programs on their baseline pedometer readings. Each week, we instructed subjects to increase their daily steps by 10% until reaching the Center for Disease Control and Prevention's (CDC) recommended 10,000
150 steps a day. To supplement a CD created by the pri-mary author to go along with the program, we gave each participant a subject manual that included a walk-ing log, information on walking safety, and emergency phone numbers.
155 According to Israel and Schurman,[12] program feed-back is vital to behavior change. We gave each partici-pant a pedometer as a way to provide feedback, pro-mote physical activity, determine participant compli-ance and progress, and to motivate the participant to
160 walk. This popular 2-inch by 2-inch device, worn on the waistband, is a relatively simple electronic device that estimates mileage walked or the number of steps taken over a period of time. Researchers have shown that pedometers are accurate, and studies with their use
165 have shown favorable validity and reliability.[13] Ap-proximately 500 steps equal .25 miles. According to

Table 1
Frequencies and Percentages: Participant Demographics and Baseline Characteristics

Characteristic	Baseline graduates and dropouts[*]		Baseline graduates[†]		Baseline dropouts[†]		
	f	%	f	%	f	%	p
Gender							
Male	9	7.5	7	11.7	2	3.3	
Female	111	92.5	53	88.3	58	96.7	
NR	0	0.0	0	0.0	0	0.0	
Age							
20–29	9	7.5	5	8.3	4	6.7	
30–39	20	16.7	14	23.3	6	10.0	
40–49	37	30.8	18	30.0	19	31.7	
50–59	45	37.5	17	28.3	28	46.7	
60–69	7	5.8	5	8.4	2	3.3	
NR	2	1.7	1	1.7	1	1.7	
Ethnicity							
Caucasian	102	85.0	55	90.0	48	80.0	
African American	15	12.5	5	8.3	10	16.7	
Asian American	2	1.7	1	1.7	1	1.7	
NR	1	0.8	0	0.0	1	1.7	
BMI							.456
Underweight	1	0.8	1	1.7	0	0.0	
Normal	27	22.5	19	31.7	8	13.3	
Preobese	38	31.7	18	30.0	20	33.3	
Obese stage 1	24	20.0	10	16.7	14	23.3	
Obese stage 2	21	17.5	10	16.7	11	18.3	
Obese stage 3	6	5.0	2	3.3	4	6.7	
NR	3	2.5	0	0.0	3	5.0	
BP							.465
Normal	48	40.0	23	38.3	25	41.7	
Prehypertension	50	41.7	29	48.3	21	35.0	
Hypertension stage 1	18	15.0	7	11.7	11	18.3	
Hypertension stage 2	3	2.5	1	1.7	2	3.3	
NR	1	0.8	0	0.0	1	1.7	

Note. BMI = body mass index; BP = blood pressure; NR = no response.
[*]$N = 120$.
[†]$n = 60$.

Table 2
Mean Values: Participant Demographics and Baseline Characteristics

Characteristic	Baseline graduates and dropouts[*]		Baseline graduates[†]		Baseline dropouts[†]		
	M	SD	M	SD	M	SD	p
Age (yr)	44.27	10.00	42.88	10.67	45.67	9.16	.156
Godin Questionnaire	24.59	19.28	23.69	18.57	25.53	20.11	.775
Blood glucose	101.48	23.19	96.71	17.58	106.48	26.29	.371
Blood cholesterol	188.53	35.88	184.68	34.74	192.02	36.94	.498
BMI	29.96	6.00	29.06	6.02	30.91	5.87	.456

Note. BMI = body mass index.
[*]$N = 120$.
[†]$n = 60$.

Bassett et al.,[13] the advantages of using a pedometer to gauge physical activity are that they: (1) are inexpensive and noninvasive; (2) have the potential for use in a variety of settings; (3) are easy to administer to large groups; and (4) have the potential to promote behavior change. The selected pedometer recorded total steps, time of day, and walking total time and archived 7 days of walking data.

To maintain contact with the participants, we sent a weekly walking and wellness tip via e-mail. With 2 weeks left in the program, we contacted participants to schedule a follow-up appointment. The follow-up consisted of participants repeating the biometric tests,

180 completing a program effects survey, and submitting their walking logs. Participants who did not return for the follow-up after notifications were phone interviewed or participated in a focus group to determine program compliance and the reasons for the follow-up
185 no-show. Following the study, we gave each program "graduate" a thank-you letter and their baseline and follow-up biometric test results.

Analysis

We analyzed baseline and follow-up scores using SPSS (Statistical Package for Social Sciences, Version
190 11.5, SPSS Inc., Chicago, IL). We observed a significant difference at $p < .05$. We expected significant differences in biometric baseline and follow-up scores using a chi-square analysis.

Results

Baseline Characteristics

We deemed 120 participants eligible for the study,
195 and they completed all baseline biometrics and surveys. Half (50%) of the participants, noted as graduates, completed the follow-up biometric tests after the 12-week program, and half did not and were noted as dropouts. The program attrition rate was 50%. As Ta-
200 ble 2 shows, the program dropouts ($M = 45.67$) were slightly older than were the program graduates ($M = 42.88$). Baseline physical activity levels, as determined by the Godin Leisure Time Questionnaire,[9] were similar between the groups ($p = .775$).

205 Table 2 shows the mean baseline BMI of the program dropouts (30.91) as slightly higher than that of the program graduates (28.76) ($p = .456$). However, when we classified the BMIs according to the National Heart, Lung, and Blood Institute BMI classifications,[14]
210 31.7% of the program graduates had a normal BMI (18.5 to 24.9) on the pretest, whereas only 13.3% of the program dropouts had a normal BMI (see Table 1).

As shown in Table 1, we classified blood pressures using the DHHS (JNC 7) classification.[15] At baseline,
215 slightly more program dropouts (41.7%) than program graduates (38.3%) had a normal blood pressure reading. Comparison of participants with stage 1 or 2 hypertension shows that 13.4% of the baseline program graduates fell into this classification, whereas 21.6% of
220 the program dropouts did.

According to the American Diabetes Association, a person with fasting plasma glucose from 100–125 mg/ml has prediabetes.[16] Mean baseline blood glucose readings were 96.71 ($SD = 17.58$) for the program
225 graduates and 106.48 ($SD = 26.29$) for the program dropouts ($p = .371$). A total blood cholesterol less than 200 mg/ml is desirable; 200 to 238 mg/ml is borderline high. Overall, baseline total cholesterol readings for graduates and dropouts were high-normal, with read-
230 ings of 184.68 mg/ml ($SD = 34.74$) and 192.02 ($SD = 36.94$; $p = .498$), respectively.

Outcome Measures

The mean number of steps recorded by participants increased 27% from week 1 to week 12. There were weeks within the study when the increase in pedometer
235 steps was more pronounced, as in week 4 (see Figure 1). Other peak periods in mean number of steps occurred during weeks 10 and 12. Evident by the high standard deviation, especially in week 4, there was considerable variability among participants in the
240 number of steps walked each week. After the 12-week program, 33.3% of the program graduates had a normal BMI, an increase of 4.8%, and the mean BMIs decreased from 29.06 to 28.76 ($p = .024$).

Of the program graduates, there was a 3.4% de-
245 crease in the number of participants in the Stage 1 or 2 hypertensive categories between baseline and followup. However, the percentage of program graduates who were in the normal range decreased from baseline-tofollow-up, whereas the percentage of graduates in the
250 prehypertensive range increased.

Table 3 indicates that blood glucose means of participants who completed the study decreased 5.27 mg/ml to 91.44 ($SD = 23.07$; $p = .06$), whereas the mean total blood cholesterol decreased from 184.68 to
255 178.81 mg/ml ($SD = 30.90$; $p = .09$) for the program graduates.

Program Effects

To evaluate the participants' perceived walking and wellness program effects, we asked participants to complete a survey on 10 health and wellness aspects,
260 as they relate to themselves, using a Likert scale (0 = no effect, 5 = significant effect). We scored 5 wellness aspects as having a greater than moderate effect on the health and wellness aspects: fitness level, mood, health awareness, nutritional habits, and health status (see
265 Table 4).

Comment

Worksite health promotion programs that involve physical activity have shown positive effects on health status, decreased health care visits, and work absenteeism. We aimed to investigate the effect of a college
270 faculty and staff "Virtual Walking & Wellness Program" on health status and the perceived effect on physical activity and wellness components. To our knowledge, no other researchers to date have attempted to study the effects of a worksite virtual physical activ-
275 ity program.

Results

Of the 120 participants who completed baseline requirements, half ($n = 60$) completed the postbiometric tests and evaluations, accounting for a 50% attrition rate. Improvements in health measures for this group
280 were noted from the beginning to the end of the study and included a 27% increase in mean number of pedometer recorded walking steps, a reduction in mean BMI from 29.06 to 28.76 ($p = .024$). The number of

Week	Mean Steps/Week	SD
1	42,797	23,203
2	52,537	26,582
3	55,742	24,021
4	63,470	63,904
5	55,496	25,641
6	55,872	23,388
7	55,502	25,959
8	55,947	23,719
9	58,168	24,031
10	59,057	28,041
11	54,836	26,502
12	58,859	27,775

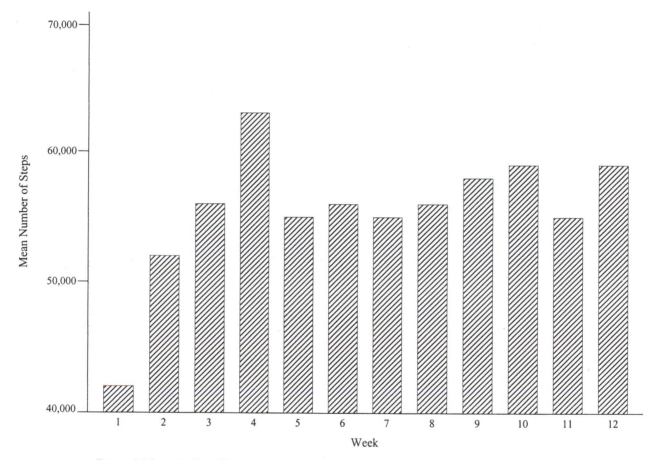

Figure 1. Mean number of steps taken by subjects per week.

participants we categorized as Stage 1 or Stage 2 hypertension decreased by 3.4%; however, the percentage of participants in the normal range of blood pressure decreased from pre- to posttest. Mean fasting glucose levels decreased 5.27mg/ml, 96.41 to 91.44 ($p = .06$), and mean total blood cholesterol levels dropped from 184 mg/dl to 178.81 ($p = .09$).

We evaluated perceived health and wellness effects using a Likert scale. Participants who completed follow-up testing reported experiencing a greater than moderate effect on the following health and wellness subcategories: fitness level, mood, health awareness, nutrition habits, and health status.

In follow-up of participants who did not complete postbiometric tests, program dropouts ($n = 60$), we conducted a focus group and phone survey to help us determine the barriers associated with participation and to gain information for future studies and programs. Information obtained from the focus group ($n = 5$) and the phone surveys ($n = 28$) indicated that participants experienced typical barriers associated with adopting healthy behaviors, which included time, motivation, job commitments, and physical problems. One participant quit the walking program after the first week because of moderate hip and knee pain. We also identified challenges with pedometer use and maintenance of

Table 3
Program Graduate Outcome Measures from Baseline to Follow-up

Outcome measure	Baseline graduate[*]				Follow-up graduate[*]				
	f	%	M	SD	f	%	M	SD	p
BMI			29.06	6.02			28.76	5.95	.024
Underweight	1	1.7			0	0.0			
Normal	19	31.7			20	33.3			
Preobese	18	30.0			19	31.7			
Obese stage 1	10	16.7			10	16.7			
Obese stage 2	10	16.7			9	15.0			
Obese stage 3	2	3.3			2	3.3			
NR	0	0.0			0	0.0			
BP									.098
Normal	23	38.3			16	26.7			
Prehypertension	29	48.3			37	61.7			
Hypertension stage 1	7	11.7			5	8.3			
Hypertension stage 2	1	1.7			1	1.7			
NR	0	0.0			1	1.7			
Blood glucose			96.71	17.58			91.44	23.07	.06
Blood cholesterol			184.68	34.74			178.81	30.90	.09

Note. BMI = body mass index; BP = blood pressure; NR = no response.
[*]$n = 60$

Table 4
Self-Reported Effect of the Walking & Wellness Program

Health and wellness aspects	M	SD
Fitness level	3.29	1.26
Mood	3.28	1.38
Health awareness	3.65	1.23
Nutritional habits	3.10	1.37
Health status	3.12	1.32
Anxiety level	2.79	1.44
Happiness	2.94	1.41
Weight loss	2.27	1.67
Work productivity	2.29	1.58
Work absenteeism	1.98	1.95

Note. Results derived from a 5-point Likert scale, in which: 5 = significant effect, 3 = moderate effect, 1 = little effect, 0 = no effect.

310 a walking log as barriers. We recommend that a "steps only" pedometer be used in future studies because pedometers with multiple capabilities requiring calibration can be difficult for participants to operate. The 50% attrition rate noted in this exercise study is consistent 315 with rates cited in the literature.[17,18] Furthermore, the lopsided representation of women to men in the study is common for walking programs, as noted by Siegel et al.[19]

Of significance, a number of participants reported unanticipated positive effects. For example, partici-320 pants indicated an increased health awareness, which led to diet improvements, increased physical activity (walking and other types of exercise), and the initiation of health care to manage physical problems that were identified as barriers to exercise. Participants reported 325 that significant others joined them in their health improvement efforts through walking and diet improvement. Two participants reported losing 35 pounds. Six participants (10% of the program dropouts) said they 330 completed all components of the study program except the follow-up tests and survey.

The results of this study demonstrate that a health promotion program using novel motivation tools has a positive impact on the health of employees and, in turn, 335 may also have a positive impact on the financial burden of health care for the employee and employer, as demonstrated in other studies.[3,4] In addition, we found that increased health awareness associated with a health promotion program can result in health benefits and is 340 not completely dependent on the employee completing the postprogram biometric tests. As evident by the participants' perceived impact of the program on increased work productivity and decreased work absenteeism and the improvements in health status, we surmise that the 345 program indirectly provided financial gains for the employer.

Limitations

In conclusion, it is important to note the study limitations. Participants were self-selected, and the program took place during the summer, possibly causing increased program compliance. During the biometric testing phase of the study, not all participants fasted prior to the blood test or rested for 5 minutes prior to having their blood pressure taken. In addition, we took 1 blood pressure reading instead of taking 3 and recording the median reading. Also, BMI is not completely accurate in determining whether participants are overweight or obese. According to the National Institutes of Health, distribution of excess fat in the abdominal area may be more of the risk factor for cardiovascular disease than a BMI near 30.[14] Future studies should include determination of body composition, rather than the use of BMI, to determine a healthy body weight. Furthermore, researchers need to replicate this study with a larger randomized controlled sample, using a power analysis to determine an adequate sample size and better representation of men and minority groups. In conclusion, because of the increase in physical activity and positive health outcomes of the "Virtual Walking & Wellness Program" with college faculty and staff, we recommend that it be adapted for use by college students, providing students with another physical activity option.

Researchers should consider the study limitations along with suggestions provided by participants who did not complete the follow-up tests in planning future research of the use of novel motivational tools to provide physical activity and wellness worksite promotional programs. It must be remembered that inactivity is only half of the lifestyle equation for health and weight control. Nutrition and diet must also be considered.

References

1. Association for Worksite Health Promotion. US Dept. of Health and Human Services, William M. Mercer Inc. *1999 National Worksite Health Promotion Survey.* Northbrook, IL: Association for Worksite Health Promotion and William M. Mercer, Inc.;2000.
2. Colditz GA. Economic cost of obesity and inactivity. *Med Sci Sports Exerc.* 1999;31:S663–S667.
3. Bertera RL. The effects of behavioral risks on absenteeism and health-care costs in the workplace. *J Occup Med.* 1991;33:1119–1123.
4. Lynch WD, Golaszewski TJ, Clearie AF, Snow D, Vickery DM. Impact of a facility-based corporate fitness program on the number of absences from work due to illness. *J Occup Med.* 1990;32:9–12.
5. US Department of Health and Human Services. Prevention Makes Common "Cents." Available at: http://aspe.hhs.gov/health/prevention/. Accessed February 27, 2004.
6. Pate RR, Pratt M, Blair SN, et al. Physical activity and public health. A recommendation from the Centers for Disease Control and Prevention and the American College of Sports Medicine. *JAMA.* 1995;273:402–407.
7. Pratt M, Macera CA, Blanton C. Levels of physical activity and inactivity in children and adults in the United States: Current evidence and research issues. *Med Sci Sport Exerc.* 1999;31:S526–S533.
8. Thomas S, Reading J, Shephard RJ. Revision of the physical activity readiness questionnaire. *Can Sport Sci.* 1992;17:338–345.
9. Godin G, Shephard RJ. A simple method to assess exercise behavior in the community. *Can J Appl Sport Sci.* 1985;10:141–146.
10. Cholestech. Cholestech LDX, results when and where you need them: Test procedure. Available at: http://www.cholestech.com/products/dp.asp#. Accessed April 14, 2006.
11. Current CLIA Regulations. Available at: http://www.phppo.cdc.gov/clia/regs/toc.aspx. Accessed April 14, 2006.
12. Israel BA, Schurman SJ. Social support, control, and the stress process. In: Glanz K, Lewis FM, Rimer BK, eds. *Health Behavior and Health Educa-*

tion: Theory, Research, and Practice. San Francisco, CA: Jossey-Bass Publishers; 1990:187–215.
13. Bassett DR, Ainsworth BE, Leggett SR et al. Accuracy of five electronic pedometers for measuring distance walked. *Med Sci Sports Exerc.* 1996;28(8):1071–1077.
14. National Institutes of Health, National Heart, Lung, and Blood Institute. *Classification of Overweight and Obesity by BMI, Waist Circumference, and Associated Disease Risk.* Available at http://www.nhlbi.nih.gov/health/public/heart/obesity/lose_wt/bmi_dis.htm. Accessed January 27, 2005.
15. US Dept. of Health and Human Services. National High Blood Pressure Education Program. JNC 7 Express. *The Seventh Report of the Joint National Committee on Prevention, Detection, Evaluation, and Treatment of High Blood Pressure.* Available at: http://www.nhlbi.nih.gov/guidelines/hypertension/jncintro.htm. Accessed February 21, 2005.
16. American Diabetes Association. *All About Diabetes.* Available at: http://www.diabetes.org/about-diabetes.jsp. Accessed January 27, 2005.
17. Dishman RK. Determinants of participation in physical activity. In: Bouchard C, Shephard RJ, Stephens T, Sutton, JR, McPherson BD, eds. *Exercise, Fitness, and Health: A Consensus of Current Knowledge.* Champaign, IL: Human Kinetics Publishers: 1990:78–101.
18. Dishman RK. Overview. In: Dishman RK ed. *Exercise Adherence: Its Impact on Public Health*, Champaign, IL: Human Kinetics Press; 1988:1–9.
19. Siegel PZ, Brackbill RM, Heath GW. The epidemiology of walking for exercise: Implications for promoting activity among sedentary groups. *Am J Public Health.* 1995;85(5):706–710.

About the authors: *Danell J. Haines* is the director of the National Research Institute for College Recreational Sports & Wellness in the Department of Recreational Sports at The Ohio State University. *Liz Davis* is the associate director of the Department of Recreational Sports at The Ohio State University. *Patrice Rancour* is the prospective health care manager for OSU Faculty/Staff Wellness Program. *Marianne Robinson* is a health educator with OSU Faculty/Staff Wellness Program. *Trish Neel-Wilson* is the program director for the Center for Wellness at The Ohio State University. At the time of the study, *Susan Wagner* was the coordinator of research and development for Managed Health Care Systems at The Ohio State University. She is now in veterinary medicine private practice.

Address correspondence to: Dr. Danell J. Haines, Department of Recreational Sports, The Ohio State University, B177, 337 W. 17th Ave., Columbus, OH 43210. E-mail: haines.2@osu.edu

Exercise for Article 19

Factual Questions

1. Did participants complete a consent form?

2. Of the 120 participants who were deemed eligible, how many were faculty members?

3. Were the majority of the participants "men" *or* "women"?

4. The mean number of steps recorded by participants increased by what percentage from week 1 to week 12?

5. How many of the participants participated in the focus group?

6. How many of the participants participated in the phone surveys?

Questions for Discussion

7. The participants (faculty/staff) were recruited from a wellness program and Weight Watchers class. In a follow-up study, would you recommend using a sample of the general population of faculty and staff? Explain. (See lines 68–70.)

8. Is the intervention described in sufficient detail to allow a replication in a future study? Explain. (See lines 129–187.)

9. In the Contents in this book, this study is classified as an example of "pre-experimental research." Do you agree with this classification? Why? Why not?

10. In a future study on this intervention, would you recommend the use of a control group? Explain.

11. The researchers discuss the limitations of their study. Do you think that the limitations are important? Explain. (See lines 347–381.)

12. In the title of the report, the researchers refer to this as a "pilot" study. Do you agree? Explain.

Quality Ratings

Directions: Indicate your level of agreement with each of the following statements by circling a number from 5 for strongly agree (SA) to 1 for strongly disagree (SD). If you believe an item is not applicable to this research article, leave it blank. Be prepared to explain your ratings. When responding to criteria A and B below, keep in mind that brief titles and abstracts are conventional in published research.

A. The title of the article is appropriate.

    SA   5   4   3   2   1   SD

B. The abstract provided an effective overview of the research article.

    SA   5   4   3   2   1   SD

C. The introduction establishes the importance of the study.

    SA   5   4   3   2   1   SD

D. The literature review establishes the context for the study.

    SA   5   4   3   2   1   SD

E. The research purpose, question, or hypothesis is clearly stated.

    SA   5   4   3   2   1   SD

F. The method of sampling is sound.

    SA   5   4   3   2   1   SD

G. Relevant demographics (for example, age, gender, and ethnicity) are described.

    SA   5   4   3   2   1   SD

H. Measurement procedures are adequate.

    SA   5   4   3   2   1   SD

I. All procedures have been described in sufficient detail to permit a replication of the study.

    SA   5   4   3   2   1   SD

J. The participants have been adequately protected from potential harm.

    SA   5   4   3   2   1   SD

K. The results are clearly described.

    SA   5   4   3   2   1   SD

L. The discussion/conclusion is appropriate.

    SA   5   4   3   2   1   SD

M. Despite any flaws, the report is worthy of publication.

    SA   5   4   3   2   1   SD

Article 20

Effects of Team Competition versus Team Cooperation in Classwide Peer Tutoring

LEASHER DENNIS MADRID
Colorado State University, Pueblo

MADELINE CANAS
Colorado State University, Pueblo

MONA ORTEGA-MEDINA
Colorado State University, Pueblo

ABSTRACT. Sixteen Hispanic Spanish/English bilingual children (6 boys and 10 girls) participated in a single-subject design study. Their chronological ages ranged from 8 to 9.5 years. The classroom teacher identified all the children as *academic at risk* on the basis of a history of poor academic performance in spelling and low scores on the Metropolitan Achievement Tests (G. Prescott, I. Balow, T. Hogan, & R. Farr, 1978). The teachers assigned the students to each instructional condition according to a randomly selected sequence of instructional order. The 3 instructional interventions were (a) competitive team peer tutoring, (b) cooperative team peer tutoring, and (c) standard teacher-led instruction. The results of the study showed that although team competition and team cooperation resulted in higher levels of correct responding relative to the standard teacher-led condition, cooperative team peer tutoring resulted in the highest rate of correct responding. Practical implications of the findings are discussed.

From *The Journal of Educational Research*, *100*, 155–160. Copyright © 2007 by Heldref Publications. Reprinted with permission.

Within the past 25 years, the general nature of the child population in the U.S. public school system has changed dramatically (Greenfield, Keller, Fuligni, & Maynard, 2003). Children vary according to socioeconomic status (SES), language background, learning style, and ethnicity (Turnbull, Rothstein-Fisch, Greenfield, & Quiroz, 2001). In addition, Quay and Jarrett (1986) showed that the school experiences of children vary considerably. For example, Hispanic children are far more likely than are white non-Hispanic children to be enrolled in remedial classes and in special education programs (Fuligni, 1997). Also, Hispanic bilingual children experience a significantly higher level of academic failure and grade retention than do white non-Hispanic children (Reyes, 1990). Overall, it appears that the academic performance of Hispanic bilingual children continues to decline each year that the child spends in school (Meece & Kurtz-Costes, 2001).

The reasons why Hispanic bilingual children do poorly in school are not clearly understood. The traditional explanatory models of academic performance have generally been focused on internal characteristics to explain achievement, including bilingualism, negative self-concept, negative cultural attitudes toward education, low intelligence, and apathy. However, a careful analysis of the literature reveals little support for those explanations (Madrid, Canas, & Watson, 2003). Ornstein (1982) argued that such concepts as self-concept, bilingualism, culture, and intelligence are too vague and undefined. Other researchers, such as Valencia, Henderson, and Rankin (1981) and Greenwood, Delquadri, and Hall (1984), supported that conclusion. Those findings highlight the importance of studying the external or environmental correlates of academic performance for low-achieving Hispanic bilingual children.

On the basis of their investigations of classwide peer tutoring, Arreaga-Mayer and Greenwood (1986) suggested that rather than focusing on broad demographics and internal characteristics of Hispanic bilingual children, researchers must focus on the way that teachers interact with students. Their work showed clearly that improved academic scores resulted from tasks that students performed in the classroom and the manner in which instructional tasks were organized. The findings of Arreaga-Mayer and Greenwood stressed the importance of (a) sustained practice on academic tasks, (b) continuous opportunities for verbal responding, and (c) rewards (points) for correct academic responding.

Arreaga-Mayer and Greenwood (1986) emphasized that a critical consideration related to the issue of environmental correlates of academic performance with Hispanic bilingual children is the need for researchers to investigate empirically the contribution of cultural practice. Kagan (1980) showed that from a social psychological perspective, Hispanic bilingual children tend to be more cooperative and affiliative relative to white, non-Hispanic children, who tend to be more competitive and individualistic. The generality of those differences occurs across age (Knight & Kagan, 1977), SES, and geographical region (Knight & Kagan, 1982). Reese, Balzano, Gallimore, and Goldenberg (1995) showed that cooperative learning formats among Hispanic bilingual children result in strong academic gains. Also, Kagan (1980) provided evidence that cooperative instructional formats produce superior academic gains for Hispanic bilingual children relative to competitive instructional formats. In addition, Madrid and colleagues (2003) measured the effects of a team approach to instruction relative to teacher-led instruction on the spelling performance of 12 low-achieving third-grade Hispanic bilingual students. The results clearly showed the benefits of a team-oriented model of instruction relative to the more competitive and individualistic traditional teacher-led model.

Although researchers who studied Hispanic bilingual children found that a team instructional format is superior to a standard teacher-led format, the relationship between cooperative and competitive team formats has not been investigated empirically. Following studies by Madrid et al. (2003) and Greenwood, Dinwiddie et al. (1984), we used a team peer-tutoring model in the present research to compare achievement outcomes that differed in their instructional context (competition vs. cooperation). We defined *team peer tutoring* as two tutoring teams, consisting of four pairs of students in each team. One student (the tutor) dictated the spelling words to the other student (the tutee) who wrote the spelling response. The tutor awarded points for correct responses or modeled the correct response if an error was made. Tutoring teams competed for the highest point total (Greenwood, Dinwiddie et al.). We defined *standard teacher-led procedures* as (a) teacher tasks (teacher–student discussion, use of worksheets, readers, media, etc.); (b) teacher positions (in front of students, among students, at desk); and (c) students' behavior (passive attention, writing, and reading workbooks; Greenwood, Dinwiddie et al.).

Our objective was to compare the effects of a competitive team peer-tutoring procedure with the effects of a cooperative team peer-tutoring procedure on Hispanic bilingual children. A standard teacher-led procedure served as the control condition. Because of the emergence of increasingly large populations of Hispanic children in the United States, Montgomery (2001) emphasized the need for empirically based instructional procedures that respond to Hispanic children's cultural variations to enhance their academic performance.

Method

Participants and Setting

The participants were 6 boys and 10 girls in the third grade who were bilingual in Spanish and English; their ages ranged from 8.0 to 9.5 years. They attended a local elementary school located in a low-income area of a southwestern city of 100,000 residents. Students at the school received federally supported lunches and compensatory education programs. The participants in the third-grade classroom were selected randomly on the basis of a cluster sampling technique from a group of third-grade classrooms. The teacher identified them because of their history of poor spelling performance

and below-average scores on the Metropolitan Achievement Tests (Prescott et al., 1978). The participants had a mean composite score of 26; the mean composite score of the nonparticipating third-grade students was 51. One teacher and her assistant were present in the classroom during the entire school day.

The 16 children received one condition for 1 week, a second condition the next week, and a third condition the following week, totaling 15 weeks. (All participants received each of three conditions five times.) The order of instructional conditions was alternated randomly. The alternated instructional conditions were (a) competitive team peer tutoring, (b) cooperative team peer tutoring, and (c) standard teacher-led instruction.

Bilingual Proficiency

DeAvila and Duncan (1984) defined *bilingual proficiency* according to the Language Assessment Scales I. This measure provided an overall index of oral linguistic proficiency based on a child's performance across four linguistic subsystems (speaking, oral reading, writing, and language comprehension). A *proficient bilingual* (high proficiency in English and Spanish) produced a score of 4 or 5 on the Language Assessment Scales I (5 was the maximum score) in both languages. A *nonproficient bilingual* produced a score of 1, 2, or 3 in one of the languages and 4 or 5 in the other language. In some cases, children scored 1, 2, or 3 in both languages. For purposes of the present study, all 16 participants scored 1, 2, or 3 in English and were considered to be nonproficient in English. In addition, all 16 participants scored 4 or 5 in Spanish and were considered proficient in Spanish. That method of language grouping was based on previous research methodology in which researchers examined qualitative differences in English-language constructions across age level in relation to Spanish/English bilingual development (Madrid & Garcia, 1981, 1985).

Curriculum

The teacher drew 150 spelling words (10 words for each of 15 weeks) randomly from the basal fourth grade-level spelling text. We used the fourth grade-level text because we were concerned that participants might have had previous classroom exposure to the spelling words at the third-grade level, thereby biasing the results. It was possible that correct spelling scores obtained from a fourth-grade text may have been lower than correct spelling scores achieved by using a third-grade text.

Probes

The teacher administered pretest probes to the children prior to training and following each weekly posttest session each Friday. The teacher asked the children to put all books away and to have only a clean sheet of paper and a pencil on their desks. The teacher presented each spelling word aloud, used it in a sentence, then repeated the word once. A 10-s period of teacher silence followed to allow each student to write the word. The procedure continued with the next word until the teacher pronounced the 10 pretest words. All pretest and posttest probes consisted of 10 words.

Design

180   We used a single-subject, alternating-treatments design to compare the three instructional approaches (Barlow & Hersen, 1984). We randomly determined the order of presentation of the three instructional approaches to control for order of effects. The teacher

185   presented each of the three conditions for 1 week, five times during the 15-week experimental period.

Procedures

In this research, we compared three procedures: (a) competitive team peer tutoring, during which team members worked to accumulate points for their team;

190   (b) cooperative team peer tutoring, during which team members worked to accumulate points for all participants (across teams); and (c) standard teacher-led instruction, during which each student worked to accumulate his or her own individual points. The standard

195   teacher-led instruction format focused on the entire class during teacher–student discussions and included the use of videotapes, audiotapes, and paper-and-pencil worksheets. The classwide format minimized all one-to-one peer interaction during spelling instruction ses-

200   sions. The three procedures, randomly alternated on a weekly basis, provided an experimental comparison of two variations of team peer tutoring with a teacher-led control condition.

Competitive team peer tutoring. Each Friday, the

205   teacher introduced 10 new fourth grade-level spelling words to the students. She pronounced each word, then asked the children to echo each word aloud and in unison (Delquadri, Greenwood, Stretton, & Hall, 1983). On the following Monday, and for the remainder of the

210   week, the teacher began the spelling session by saying, "We are going to play a game with spelling words. The purpose of the game is to learn as many new spelling words as you can and for your team to make more points than the other teams." The teacher divided the

215   class randomly into two teams. Each team of 8 students was paired into four dyads. The teacher told the team members that they would work with their teammate as a pair for that week. Each day, dyad teams flipped a coin to determine who would be the tutor and who

220   would be the tutee. The tutor was the person who read each spelling word from the spelling list. The tutee wrote each word while simultaneously spelling the word aloud. If the tutee misspelled the word, then the tutor slowly spelled the word correctly. The tutee was

225   asked to write the word consecutively three times on the answer sheet. At that point, the tutor gave verbal reinforcement to the tutee, whether or not the response was the correct spelling (e.g., "Thank you for writing the word three times"). If a dyad completed the entire

230   list before the allotted 20 min, then the tutor started

over at the top of the list. Tutees were instructed to stop writing at the sound of the 20-min timer.

Cooperative team peer tutoring. Each Friday, the teacher introduced 10 new fourth grade-level spelling

235   words to the students. She pronounced each word and asked the children to echo each word aloud and in unison (Delquadri et al., 1983). On the following Monday, and for the remainder of the week, the teacher began the spelling session by saying,

240   > We are going to play a game with spelling words. The purpose of the game is to learn as many new spelling words as you can and the team with the most points will give the other team some of their points so that everybody has the same amount of points.

245   The teacher randomly divided the class into two teams. Each team of 8 students was paired into four dyads. The team members worked with their teammate as a pair for that week. Each day, dyad members flipped a coin to determine who would be the tutor and who

250   would be the tutee. The roles of tutor and tutee were identical in the competitive and cooperative peer-tutoring conditions. Also, the verbal reinforcement procedure was the same in both conditions.

Standard teacher-led instruction. Each Friday, the

255   teacher introduced 10 new fourth grade-level spelling words. She pronounced each word and asked the children to echo each word aloud and in unison (Delquadri et al., 1983). On the following Monday, and for the remainder of the week, the teacher began the spelling

260   session by saying, "We are going to play a game with spelling words. The purpose of the game is to learn as many words as you can and to make as many points for yourself as you can." Each child worked individually, and the teacher divided the class randomly into teams

265   to replicate the peer-tutoring classroom structure. The teacher pronounced each word and asked the children to echo each word aloud and in unison. The teacher then used each of the 10 new words in a complete sentence. On Tuesday, the teacher asked the children to

270   write each of the 10 spelling words three times as she carefully and slowly read each word. On Wednesday, the children completed a spelling workbook page. On Thursday, each child wrote the 10 spelling words in alphabetical order. The teacher administered posttest

275   probes during the Friday sessions. Following a 2-min break, the teacher administered the pretest for the next week's set of training words.

Tutor Training

Students received training in each condition prior to the experiment. The teacher began the tutoring training

280   sessions by explaining that the objective was to provide a clear idea of how to play the peer tutoring games. The tutor (teacher) supervised the work of the tutee (student).

During 5 consecutive school days, in 20-min ses-

285   sions each, the teacher taught the children the correct tutoring procedures. On Day 1, the teacher demon-

strated the peer-tutoring procedures—the teacher's assistant was the tutee, the teacher was the tutor. On Day 2, the teacher randomly selected a student to join
290 her in front of the group. Using a word list prepared for use with an overhead projector, the teacher and the student demonstrated how the tutoring games worked, including how to perform the reinforcement procedure. On Day 3, the teacher randomly selected 2 students to
295 demonstrate the tutoring procedures in front of the group. As the procedure was modeled, the teacher gave the students feedback for correct tutoring behaviors and for proper use of the reinforcement procedure.

On Days 4 and 5, the teacher asked the children to
300 sit with a partner, and the entire group practiced peer tutoring for 20 min both days. A timer signaled starting and ending times. As the group practiced tutoring, two experimenters simultaneously but independently observed child-tutoring behaviors. To calculate interob-
305 server reliability, we divided the total number of observer agreements by the total number of observer agreements plus disagreements and multiplied by 100. The percentage of observer agreement (100%) was high.

Recording and Reliability

310 The experimenters scored student responses and noted *correct* and incorrect responses. A correct answer was a word written in response to a teacher or tutor prompt that contained only the required letters that composed that word, according to Morehead and
315 Morehead's (1995) *The New American Webster Handy College Dictionary*. An incorrect response was a word written in response to a teacher or tutor prompt that contained additional letters (e.g., "lookk"), substitutions (e.g., "kar"), or omissions (e.g., "grl"). In addi-
320 tion, the experimenters recorded an incorrect response when the tutee did not write the word in response to a teacher or tutor prompt. During each session when the students implemented each of the instructional approaches, the experimenters observed independently
325 each tutoring pair to check for appropriate tutoring behaviors and proper use of the reinforcement procedure. The procedure confirmed that students were reliably exhibiting the trained tutoring behaviors.

Results

The findings showed differences in correct spelling
330 responses that resulted from two team peer-tutoring procedures and the teacher-led instructional procedure. Figure 1 shows the mean percentage pre- and postspelling scores for each instructional condition. The mean percentage gain scores for competitive team peer tutor-
335 ing increased from 13% during pretests to 80.2% during posttests. The mean percentage gain scores for cooperative team peer tutoring increased from 12% during pretests to 92.8% during posttests. During the standard teacher-led sessions, the mean percentage gain
340 scores increased from 14% during pretests to 36.2% during posttests.

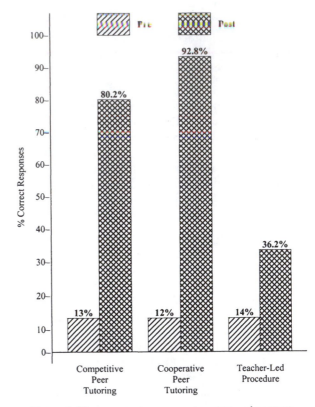

Figure 1. Mean percentage correct pretest and posttest spelling scores.

Figure 2 shows the mean correct posttest scores for each instructional intervention across 15 weeks. The data show that the standard teacher-led condition re-
345 sulted in the lowest level of mean correct responses (33%, 40%, 39%, 37%, and 32%). Weekly posttest means for correct responses for the competitive peer-tutoring condition were 80%, 75%, 80%, 82%, and 84%. Weekly posttest means for correct responding for
350 the cooperative peer-tutoring condition were the highest of all three instructional conditions: 90%, 89%, 95%, 94%, and 96%.

Discussion

Both tutoring conditions exceeded the teacher-led condition. Over all of the students and of the tutoring
355 sessions, the size of the gains made by students in the team-tutoring conditions compared favorably with those obtained in prior studies of peer tutoring (Greenwood, Arreaga-Meyer, Utley, Gavin, & Terry, 2001). It is particularly noteworthy that the mean level of correct
360 responding in the cooperative team peer-tutoring condition increased 80.8%, compared with a mean increase of 67.2% in the competitive team peer-tutoring condition. Lockheed and colleagues (1981) noted that instructional practices in the United States emphasize a
365 format in which students perceive themselves as individuals who compete with others in the classroom. Children seldom have the opportunity to interact as part of a cooperative group in their classrooms. U.S. students are taught within a system of competition and

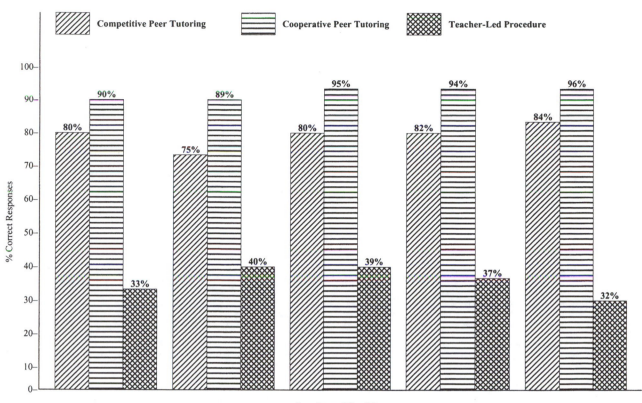

Figure 2. Mean percentage correct posttest spelling scores for each condition across 15 weeks.

370 individualism, not cooperation (Slavin, 1983). Knight and Kagan (1977) showed that Hispanic bilingual students are comparatively more socially cooperative than are non-Hispanic white children.

The findings of this study are consistent with the 375 idea that the competitive nature of instructional programs in the United States may be related to lower levels of academic achievement among Hispanic bilingual children. Although Greenwood and colleagues (2001) found that team peer-tutoring procedures are more ef- 380 fective than are standard teacher-led procedures, culturally sensitive cooperative team peer-tutoring strategies may further enhance the correct responses of students from diverse backgrounds. Our findings demonstrate the increased effectiveness of team-tutoring pro- 385 cedures that are sensitive to students' cultural orientation.

The increased effectiveness of cooperative team peer tutoring relative to competitive team peer tutoring and teacher-led procedures for Hispanic bilingual stu- 390 dents must be considered from educational and social perspectives. From an educational perspective, Delquadri and colleagues (1983) have shown that minority children learn best when they are given the opportunity to learn within a group context. However, 395 peer-tutoring researchers have not yet defined culturally responsive tutoring strategies that focus on the cultural and experiential backgrounds of Hispanic bi-

lingual children. From a social perspective, cultural influences have a direct impact on the academic per- 400 formance of bilingual children within our current system of instruction (Padilla & Alva, 1987).

Group and family affiliation and social cooperation (traditional Hispanic cultural values) form the foundation for achievement, family socialization, and group 405 identification among Hispanics (Knight & Kagan, 1982). Conversely, Hispanic bilingual children appear to have a more cooperative social orientation than do white non-Hispanic children; the structure of the traditional classroom tends to focus on individually oriented 410 competition (Kagan, 1980). Therefore, competitive team peer-tutoring strategies may not provide an instructional strategy that maximizes the achievement gains of Hispanic bilingual children.

Our findings must be viewed within the context of 415 certain cautions. Although we extended the focus of previous peer-tutoring research to incorporate team cooperation, the small sample size limits the extent to which conclusions can be generalized. Also, the focus of analysis in only one subject area (i.e., spelling) 420 raises questions as to the generality of the findings to other subject areas. Researchers may address the generality of the present findings by incorporating other subject areas and by using a larger sample of children.

With respect to teaching strategies, one should con- 425 sider the interaction between tutoring strategy and cul-

tural sensitivity. We observed effects that were most positive within a team peer-tutoring context in which the teacher emphasized cooperation. Traditional tutoring formats reward students for competing against each
430　other for the most rewards (Delquadri et al., 1983), and rewards are distributed to the most competitive children; however, this is inconsistent with the traditional values of Hispanic bilingual children. An intriguing implication of our findings is that teachers who tutor in
435　classrooms with groups of academic at-risk Hispanic bilingual children may consistently provide opportunities for cooperative team work in which all students can benefit.

References

Arreaga-Mayer, C., & Greenwood, C. (1986). Environmental variables affecting the school achievement of culturally and linguistically different learners: An instructional perspective. *NABE Journal, 1*, 113–135.

Barlow, D., & Hersen, M. (1984). *Single case experimental designs: Strategies for studying behavior change* (2nd ed.). New York: Pergamon Press.

DeAvila, E., & Duncan, S. (1984). *Language Assessment Scales I* (3rd ed.). Corte Madera, CA: Linguametrics Group.

Delquadri, J., Greenwood, C., Stretton, K., & Hall, V. (1983). The peer tutoring spelling game: A classroom procedure for increasing opportunity to respond and spelling performance. *Education and Treatment of Children, 6*, 225–239.

Fuligni, A. (1997). The academic achievement of adolescents from immigrant families: The roles of family background, attitudes, and behavior. *Child Development, 68*, 351–363.

Greenfield, P., Keller, H., Fuligni, A., & Maynard, A. (2003). Cultural pathways through universal development. *Annual Review of Psychology, 54*, 461–490.

Greenwood, C., Arreaga-Mayer, C., Utley, C., Gavin, K., & Terry, B. (2001). Classwide peer tutoring learning management system: Applications with elementary-level English language learners. *Remedial and Special Education, 22*, 34–47.

Greenwood, C., Delquadri, J., & Hall, R. (1984). The opportunity to respond and student academic performance. In W. Heward, T. Heron, J. Trap-Porter, & D. Hill (Eds.), *Focus upon behavior analysis in education* (pp. 58–88). Columbus, OH: Merrill.

Greenwood, C., Dinwiddie, G., Terry, B., Wade, L., Stanley, S., Thibadeau, S., et al. (1984). Teacher versus peer-mediated instruction: An ecobehavioral analysis of achievement outcomes. *Journal of Applied Behavior Analysis, 17*, 521–538.

Kagan, S. (1980). Cooperation-competition, culture, and structural bias in classrooms. In S. Sharan, P. Hare, C. Webb, & R. Hertz-Lazarowitz (Eds.), *Cooperation in education.* Provo, UT: Brigham Young University Press.

Knight, G., & Kagan, S. (1977). Development of prosocial and competitive behaviors in Anglo American and Mexican American children. *Child Development, 48*, 1385–1394.

Knight, G., & Kagan, S. (1982). Siblings, birth order, and cooperative–competitive social behavior: A comparison of Anglo American and Mexican American children. *Journal of Cross-Cultural Psychology, 13*, 239–249.

Lockheed, M., Amarel, M., Finkelstein, K., Harris, A., Flores, V., Holland, P., et al. (1981). *Year one report: Classroom interaction, student cooperation, and leadership.* Princeton, NJ: Educational Testing Service.

Madrid, D., Canas, M., & Watson, D. (2003). A comparative study of effective instructional strategies with low-achieving Hispanic bilingual children. *Research for Educational Reform, 8*, 25–37.

Madrid, D., & Garcia, E. (1981). The development of negation in bilingual Spanish/English and monolingual English speakers. *Journal of Educational Psychology, 5*, 624–631.

Madrid, D., & Garcia, E. (1985). The effect of language transfer on bilingual proficiency. In E. Garcia & R. Padilla (Eds.), *Advances in bilingual education* (pp. 53–70). Tucson, AZ: The University of Arizona Press.

Meece, J., & Kurtz-Costes, B. (2001). Introduction: The schooling of ethnic minority children and youth. *Educational Psychologist, 36*, 1–7.

Montgomery, W. (2001). Creating culturally responsive, inclusive classrooms. *Teaching Exceptional Children, 33*, 4–9.

Morehead, A., & Morehead, L. (Eds.). (1995). *The new American Webster handy college dictionary* (3rd ed.). New York: Penguin Press.

Ornstein, A. (1982). The education of the disadvantaged: A 20-year review. *Educational Research, 24*, 197–211.

Padilla, A., & Alva, S. (1987, March). *Factors affecting the academic performance of Mexican-American students.* Paper presented at the University of California President's Office, Linguistic Minority Conference, Los Angeles.

Prescott, G., Balow, I., Hogan, T., & Farr, R. (1978). *Metropolitan Achievement Tests: Basic Survey Battery.* San Antonio, TX: The Psychological Corporation.

Quay, L., & Jarrett, O. (1986). Teacher's interactions with middle and lower-SES preschool boys and girls. *Journal of Educational Psychology, 78*, 495–498.

Reese, L., Balzano, S., Gallimore, R., & Goldenberg, C. (1995). The concept of education: Latino family values and American schooling. *International Journal of Educational Research, 23*, 57–81.

Reyes, P. (1990). Factors affecting the commitment of children at risk to stay in school. In J. Lakebrink (Ed.), *Children at risk.* Chicago: Anderson.

Slavin, R. (1983). *Cooperative learning.* New York: Longman.

Turnbull, E., Rothstein-Fisch, C., Greenfield, P., & Quiroz, B. (2001). *Bridging cultures between home and school.* Mahwah, NJ: Erlbaum.

Valencia, R., Henderson, R., & Rankin, R. (1981). Relationship of family constellation and schooling to intellectual performance of Mexican American children. *Journal of Educational Psychology, 73*, 524–532.

Address correspondence to: Leasher Dennis Madrid, Department of Psychology, Colorado State University, Pueblo, 2200 Bonforte Boulevard, Pueblo, CO 81001-4901. E-mail: leasher.madrid@ colostate-pueblo.edu

Exercise for Article 20

Factual Questions

1. What served as a control condition in this experiment?

2. Did the researchers select a third-grade classroom at random *or* individual third-grade students at random?

3. All participants received each of the three conditions how many times?

4. The mean percentage gain scores for cooperative team peer tutoring increased from 12% during pretests to what percentage during posttests?

5. The researchers state some "cautions" for the interpretation of their results. What is the first one they state?

Questions for Discussion

6. The researchers state that the order of the instructional conditions was alternated randomly. Is this an important feature of this experiment? Explain. (See lines 132–133 and 182–184.)

7. What is your opinion of the researchers' decision to use a fourth-grade-level text? (See lines 161–168.)

8. At various points, the researchers refer to this study as an "experiment." (See, for example, lines 278–279.) Speculate on why it is considered an "experiment" and not a "survey."

9. Is the cooperative team peer tutoring condition described in sufficient detail? Explain. (See lines 233–253.)

10. In a future experiment, would you recommend using a separate group of students to serve as the control group (receiving standard teacher-led instruction)? Why? Why not?

11. Has this experiment convinced you that the cooperative team peer tutoring technique is especially superior for Hispanic bilingual students? Explain. (See lines 387–413.)

Quality Ratings

Directions: Indicate your level of agreement with each of the following statements by circling a number from 5 for strongly agree (SA) to 1 for strongly disagree (SD). If you believe an item is not applicable to this research article, leave it blank. Be prepared to explain your ratings. When responding to criteria A and B below, keep in mind that brief titles and abstracts are conventional in published research.

A. The title of the article is appropriate.

SA   5   4   3   2   1   SD

B. The abstract provides an effective overview of the research article.

SA   5   4   3   2   1   SD

C. The introduction establishes the importance of the study.

SA   5   4   3   2   1   SD

D. The literature review establishes the context for the study.

SA   5   4   3   2   1   SD

E. The research purpose, question, or hypothesis is clearly stated.

SA   5   4   3   2   1   SD

F. The method of sampling is sound.

SA   5   4   3   2   1   SD

G. Relevant demographics (for example, age, gender, and ethnicity) are described.

SA   5   4   3   2   1   SD

H. Measurement procedures are adequate.

SA   5   4   3   2   1   SD

I. All procedures have been described in sufficient detail to permit a replication of the study.

SA   5   4   3   2   1   SD

J. The participants have been adequately protected from potential harm.

SA   5   4   3   2   1   SD

K. The results are clearly described.

SA   5   4   3   2   1   SD

L. The discussion/conclusion is appropriate.

SA   5   4   3   2   1   SD

M. Despite any flaws, the report is worthy of publication.

SA   5   4   3   2   1   SD

Article 21

Effects of Explicit Timing on Elementary Students' Oral Reading Rates of Word Phrases

GARY L. CATES
Illinois State University

KATRINA N. RHYMER
Central Michigan University

ABSTRACT. An ABAB withdrawal design was used to investigate the effects of explicit timing on accurate oral reading rate of sight word phrases of four elementary students demonstrating difficulty with reading. During baseline, the students were exposed to flash cards with sight word phrases and asked to read them out loud and were not made aware that they were being timed. The explicit timing condition was conducted the same except students were told that their performance was going to be timed and to do the best that they could. Students were told how many phrases they read correctly at the end of 3 minutes in both conditions. Results demonstrated that explicit timing increased accurate response rates. Discussion focuses on directions for practice and future research.

From *Reading Improvement*, *43*, 148–156. Copyright © 2006 by Project Innovation, Inc. Reprinted with permission.

The Problem

The majority of students receiving special education services are students with specific Learning Disability Diagnoses (U.S. Department of Education, 2001). Of these students, a majority demonstrate difficulties specific to reading (U.S. Department of Educa-
5 tion, 2001). Due to this abundance of reading problems that are likely referred to school psychologists, it is not surprising that reading has become of paramount concern among lawmakers and is a focal issue in the No
10 Child Left Behind Act and the anticipated reauthorization of the Individuals with Disabilities Education Act. Specifically, such legislation is increasingly focusing on prevention and treatment of reading problems as opposed to simply labeling a student as specific learn-
15 ing disability in reading.

Research in monitoring student progress for the purposes of early identification and remediation of reading problems has suggested that reading fluency (i.e., the rate at which a student reads accurately and
20 quickly) is the most sensitive measure for measuring changes in student reading achievement (e.g., Shapiro, 2004). By measuring the number of words a student reads correctly per minute, an educator can have a brief assessment that is highly predictive of reading
25 achievement. Because reading rate is correlated with reading achievement, many practitioners have focused on reading rate as a primary dependent variable when attempting to improve reading achievement.

Previous Research

Academic Fluency

The focus on reading rate as an important variable
30 is supported by other research related to learning. In general, research has suggested that increasing accurate response rates results in increased learning rates (see Skinner, Fletcher, & Henington, 1996 for a review of this topic). By increasing words read correctly per
35 minute, a student may also increase overall reading achievement.

Explicit Timing As a Means of Increasing Academic Fluency

One method that has been demonstrated to result in increased response rates across a variety of academic skills is explicit timing. By simply telling students that
40 their academic performance will be timed, students have demonstrated increased response rates (e.g., Miller, Hall, & Heward, 1995; Rhymer, Dittmer, Skinner, & Jackson, 2000; Rhymer, Henington, Skinner, & Looby, 1999; Rhymer, Skinner, Henington, D'Reaux,
45 & Sims, 1998; Rhymer, Skinner, Jackson, McNeill, Smith, & Jackson, 2002; Van Houten, 1979; Van Houten, Morrison, Jarvis, & McDonald, 1974; Van Houten, Hill, & Parsons, 1975; Van Houten & Thompson, 1976).

50 In likely the earliest study on explicit timing, Van Houten et al. (1974) asked students in one second-grade classroom and two fifth-grade classrooms to write as long a composition as possible regarding a topic that was written on the board. This baseline ses-
55 sion was 10 minutes in length; however, students were not told of this time limit. The intervention consisted of explicit timing with immediate feedback, public posting of individual performance, and instructions to students to try to beat their best performance. During the
60 intervention sessions, students not only wrote more words in their compositions, but the quality of the written compositions increased. Simply informing students of time limits, providing performance feedback, and setting goals produced longer compositions and better
65 compositions without requiring any additional class-

room resources (Van Houten, 1979; Van Houten et al., 1974; Van Houten et al., 1975).

Explicit timing has been shown to not only be effective for writing, but also for mathematics (e.g., Miller et al., 1995; Rhymer et al., 1999; Rhymer et al., 1998; Rhymer et al., 2002; Van Houten & Thompson, 1976). In addition, explicit timing has been shown to increase rates of responding independently without immediate feedback, public posting, and instructing students to try to beat their best performance (Miller et al., 1995; Rhymer et al., 1999; Rhymer et al., 1998; Rhymer et al., 2002; Van Houten & Thompson, 1976). Furthermore, the explicit timing procedure has been shown to be effective for ethnically and educationally diverse classrooms of students (e.g., Miller et al., 1995; Rhymer et al., 1999; Rhymer et al., 1998; Van Houten & Thompson, 1976). However, two studies have suggested that students must have high accuracy levels for a skill before explicit timing will be effective and more difficult academic skills may not be conducive to explicit timing (Rhymer et al., 1998; Rhymer et al., 2002). Therefore, practitioners may need to examine students' accuracy on the academic skill and the level of difficulty of the academic skill before recommending the explicit timing intervention.

Given the numerous research studies suggesting that explicit timing is an empirically validated intervention for increasing rates of responding for writing and mathematics, it has yet to be applied to reading. Furthermore, the majority of the literature regarding explicit timing has employed an experimental model in which all students in intact classrooms have participated in the study. Lacking in the literature is an actual application of the explicit timing intervention for students *referred* to the school psychologist because of slow reading rates.

The Solution

It is one thing for an intervention to work in a classroom with a researcher and quite another when a school psychologist recommends the intervention to a teacher who applies the intervention with an actual child referred for an academic skill deficit that has not been tested in the literature. Therefore, the purpose of this study was twofold. First, this study examined whether the explicit timing intervention would increase rates of responding for reading. Second, this study examined how well the explicit timing intervention could be applied to *referred* students presenting with reading rate deficits. Specifically, the effects of explicit timing were assessed with one second-grade student and three third-grade students who were referred to a school psychologist for low rates of oral reading of sight word phrases.

Evidence for Effectiveness

Participants and Setting

Participants included four elementary students in a rural midwestern elementary school referred to a school psychologist for difficulty with reading sight words. Keith was a male in the second grade, Mike and Russell were males in the third grade, and Anu was a female in the third grade. None of the students was receiving special education services at the time of their referral. All sessions were conducted in a traditional elementary school classroom environment and were carried out by the students' teacher.

Materials

Dolch word phrases from a deck of Dolch sight phrase cards (Dolch, 1981) were used as target reading stimuli. These phrase cards included three word phrases such as "by the house" and "has run away." The teacher used a wristwatch (during baseline) and a stopwatch (during explicit timing) to keep track of time, and a pencil to record overall session response rates. The digital wristwatch was on the same hand that presented the flash card so that the teacher could covertly time the session. A stopwatch was used for the explicit timing phase to increase the saliency of the timing for the student.

Design and Procedures

An ABAB design was used with Mike, Russell, and Anu. An ABA design was used with Keith due to Keith moving out of the school district after the second baseline phase. Sessions were 3 minutes in length and were conducted once per day in the students' respective classroom. Prior to each session, the teacher shuffled approximately 100 word phrases. The same word phrases had equal opportunity to be presented in any one session in either the baseline or intervention phases.

During baseline sessions, students were told to do the best that they could. The teacher then said "Ready? Go!" The teacher then started keeping time on the wristwatch (covertly) and presented the first phrase word card. Students were given three seconds to initiate responding. If they did not initiate responding, the teacher read the phrase aloud and said, "Now you read it." If they did initiate responding and the reading was incorrect, the teacher said, "No, the card says…" and modeled the correct reading of the card and then said, "Now you read it." The correction procedure was repeated until the student responded correctly. Once the student responded correctly, 1) the student was provided positive feedback (e.g., "Good job!" "Right!"), 2) the card was placed facedown on the table, and 3) the next word phrase was presented. At the end of each session, the student was told "Good job" and told how many phrases they read correctly. A phrase was considered read correctly only if it was read correctly on the first attempt.

Procedures during the explicit timing sessions were identical to baseline sessions with one exception. Students were shown a stopwatch and told that the teacher was going to see how fast they could read, but they were to be sure to read accurately. At the end of each

175 session, the teacher counted the number of phrases read correctly and divided that number by three to obtain the number of Dolch word phrases per minute.

Interscorer Agreement

An assistant also independently scored whether phrases were read correctly or incorrectly for each ses-
180 sion for each student. Interscorer agreement was calculated for the number of correct phrases read across 100% of the sessions for all participants by dividing the number of agreements (both the teacher and the independent observing assistant agreeing that the word was
185 read correctly or incorrectly) by the number of agreements plus disagreements (the teacher and the assistant not agreeing whether the phrases were read correctly or incorrectly) and multiplying by 100%. Interscorer agreement was 100% for all four students.

Results

190 Table 1 displays the mean word phrases read correctly per minute across all phases for all four participants. Figure 1 displays the number of correctly read sight word phrases on the *Y* axis and sessions across the *X* axis for Mike, Russell, Anu, and Keith. For all
195 four participants, immediate changes in level of performance were observed as a function of implementation and removal of the explicit timing intervention. Following stable baseline performance with no trend for Mike, Russell, and Keith, an immediate increase in
200 level of performance with no change in trend was observed. For Anu, following a stable baseline with slight decreasing trend, her performance immediately increased upon implementation of the explicit timing intervention. Upon removal of the explicit timing in-
205 tervention, all four participants demonstrated levels of performance comparable to their respective initial baseline performance. When explicit timing was reintroduced, Russell and Anu demonstrated performance comparable to their respective initial intervention
210 phases while Mike demonstrated higher levels of responding than the previous baseline phases with a stable increasing trend during his final intervention phase. These data suggest that the explicit timing intervention increased rates of accurate oral responding to Dolch
215 sight word phrases.

Discussion

The results of the current study support earlier findings of research on the effects of explicit timing on student response rate (e.g., Miller et al., 1995; Rhymer et al., 1999; Rhymer et al., 1998; Rhymer et al., 2002;
220 Van Houten, 1979; Van Houten et al., 1975; Van Houten et al., 1974; Van Houten & Thompson, 1976). In addition to replication, the results of the current study extend previous research on explicit timing in two ways. First, this study was conducted with multiple
225 individuals as an applied intervention procedure in a classroom with students who were actually referred to a school psychologist. This study was conducted by the

teacher through consultation with a school psychologist for the purposes of identifying an instructional proce-
230 dure that could increase the rate of accurate responses. Second, this study extended research on explicit timing by focusing on a form of reading sight word phrases. No other studies have yet investigated explicit timing on sight word phrase reading.

235 Although the current study extended research on explicit timing, it is not without limitation. First, because the study did not assess generalization, the data do not indicate whether increased reading rates for Dolch word phrases may transfer to classroom curricu-
240 lum reading passages. Future research should investigate the extent to which increased reading speed associated with explicit timing transfers to passages with and without content overlap (i.e., with and without the target reading passages).

Table 1

Mean Word Phrases Read Correctly Per Minute Across All Phases for All Four Participants

Participant	Baseline 1	Explicit Timing 1	Baseline 2	Explicit Timing 2
Mike	13.67	20.33	16.00	25.33
Russell	13.00	20.00	15.67	21.33
Keith	16.33	28.33	18.67	N/A
Anu	17.00	21.00	18.00	21.00

245 Second, the current study was conducted with a relatively small homogenous sample. Future research should investigate such procedures with individuals with problems concomitant with reading problems (e.g., attention deficit hyperactivity disorder, mental
250 retardation, behavior disorders, learning disabilities).

Third, because of the applied nature of the study, the primary dependent variable of the current study was phrases read per minute. A more sensitive measure of increased performance may have been words read
255 correctly per minute of instructional time (e.g., Cates, Skinner, Watson, Meadows, Weaver, & Jackson, 2003). Although this may be listed as a limitation, it should be pointed out if it is a more sensitive measurement, the visual inspection of the data would only
260 become more pronounced. In addition, because students were presented a phrase and required to answer correctly before the phrase was discarded, there was no indication of accuracy on a student's first attempt. However, because students were required to make a
265 correct response before it was discarded, students always completed a phrase successfully before moving on. Finally, the current study was not designed to assess the effects of such a procedure on another important dependent variable, comprehension. Because pre-
270 vious research on reading rates and reading comprehension suggest that the two variables are related (e.g., Carver, 1982; Carver, 1990; Dee-Lucas, 1979; Himelstein & Greenberg, 1974; Samuels, 1979), future research should assess the effects of explicit timing on
275 both factual and inferential comprehension.

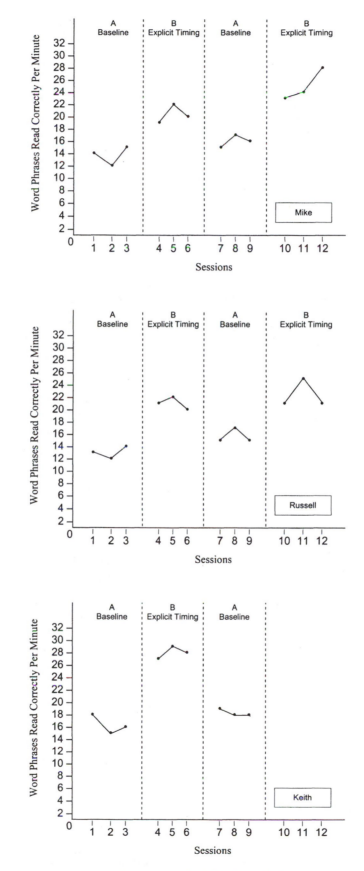

Figure 1. Number of Dolch word phrases read correctly per minute for Mike, Russell, Keith, and Anu. (*continued on next page→*)

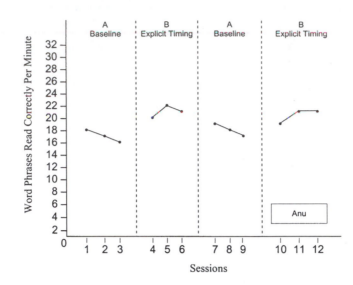

Figure 1 (continued). Number of Dolch word phrases read correctly per minute for Mike, Russell, Keith, and Anu.

Further research on explicit timing is needed to answer more specific questions regarding the utility of the intervention. First, research should be conducted to investigate explicit timing in conjunction with other
280 intervention components, such as reinforcement and feedback. Research that has focused on providing incentives for increased reading rates provides conflicting results. While some research has not resulted in increased reading performance (e.g., Daly, Witt, Mar-
285 tens, & Dool, 1997; Daly, Witt, Martens, Dool, & Hintz, 1998), other research has suggested that incentives can affect reading (e.g., Lahey, McNees, & Brown, 1973; Noell et al., 1998). The discrepancy across these research studies could be related to
290 whether students were made aware of being timed; therefore, research should investigate the effects of explicit timing with and without incentives. Second, the causal mechanisms for why explicit timing is an effective intervention in increasing academic response
295 rates should also be investigated. To date, no studies have attempted to isolate the causal mechanisms and few hypotheses have been presented.

Despite these limitations and the need for further research, explicit timing appears to be a promising
300 method for the treatment for response rate related deficiencies associated with a number of academic tasks, including reading. The application of this intervention with referred students along with a teacher completing the intervention provide further utility for the explicit
305 timing intervention as a useful tool for school psychologists.

References

Carver, R. P. (1982). Optimal rate of reading prose. *Reading Research Quarterly, 18,* 56–88.

Carver, R. P. (1990). *Reading rate: A review of research and theory.* San Diego, CA: Academic Press, Inc.

Cates, G. L., Skinner, C. H., Watson, T. S., Meadows, T. J., Weaver, A., & Jackson, B. (2003). Instructional effectiveness and instructional efficiency as considerations for data-based decision making: An evaluation of interspersing procedures. *School Psychology Review, 32,* 601–616.

Daly, E. J., Witt, J. C., Martens, B. K., & Dool, E. J. (1997). A model for conducting a functional analysis of academic performance problems. *School Psychology Review, 26,* 554–574.

Daly, E. J., Witt, J. C., Martens, B. K., Dool, E. J., & Hintz, J. M. (1998). Using brief functional analysis to select interventions for oral reading. *Journal of Behavioral Education, 8,* 203–218.

Dee-Lucas, D. (1979). Reading speed and memory for prose. *Journal of Reading Behavior, 11,* 221–233.

Dolch, E. W. (1981). *Dolch sight phrase cards.* Champaign, IL: Garrard Publishing Company.

Himelstein, H. C., & Greenberg, G. (1974). The effect of increasing reading rate on comprehension. *The Journal of Psychology, 86,* 251–259.

Lahey, B. B., McNees, M. P., & Brown, C. C. (1973). Modification of deficits in reading for comprehension. *Journal of Applied Behavior Analysis, 6,* 475–480.

Miller, A. D., Hall, S. W., & Heward, W. L. (1995). Effects of sequential 1-minute time trials with and without inter-trial feedback and self-correlation on general and special education students' fluency with math facts. *Journal of Behavioral Education, 5,* 319–345.

Noell, G. H., Gansle, K. A., Witt, J. C., Whitmarsh, E. L., Freeland, J. T., Lafleur, L. H., Gilberston, D. N., & Northup, J. (1998). Effects of contingent reward and instruction on oral reading performance at differing levels of passage difficulty. *Journal of Applied Behavior Analysis, 31,* 659–663.

Rhymer, K. N., Dittmer, K. I., Skinner, C. H., & Jackson, B. (2000). Effectiveness of a multicomponent treatment for improving mathematics fluency. *School Psychology Quarterly, 15,* 40–51.

Rhymer, K. N., Henington, C., Skinner, C. H., & Looby, E. J. (1999). The effects of explicit timing on mathematics performance in second-grade Caucasian and African American students. *School Psychology Quarterly, 14,* 397–407.

Rhymer, K. N., Skinner, C. H., Henington, C., D'Reaux, R. A., & Sims, S. (1998). Effects of explicit timing on mathematics problem completion rates in African-American third-grade elementary students. *Journal of Applied Behavior Analysis, 31,* 673–677.

Rhymer, K. N., Skinner, C. H., Jackson, S., McNeill, S., Smith, T., & Jackson, B. (2002). The 1-minute explicit timing intervention: The influence of mathematics problem difficulty. *Journal of Instructional Psychology, 29,* 305–311.

Samuels, S. J. (1979). The method of repeated readings. *The Reading Teacher, 32,* 403–408.

Shapiro, E. S. (2004). *Academic Skills Problems 3rd edition.* New York: Gulford Press.

Skinner, C. H., Fletcher, P. A., & Henington, C. (1996). Increasing learning rates by increasing student response rates: A summary of research. *School Psychology Quarterly, 11,* 313–325.

U.S. Department of Education. (2001). *Twenty-third annual report to Congress on the implementation of the Individuals with Disabilities Education Act.* Washington DC: Author.

Van Houten, R. (1979). The performance feedback system: Generalization of effects across time. *Child Behavior Therapy, 1,* 219–236.

Van Houten, R., Hill, S., & Parsons, M. (1975). An analysis of a performance feedback system: The effects of timing and feedback, public posting, and praise upon academic performance and peer interaction. *Journal of Applied Behavior Analysis, 8*, 449–457.

Van Houten, R., Morrison, E., Jarvis, R., & McDonald, M. (1974). The effects of explicit timing and feedback on compositional response rate in elementary school children. *Journal of Applied Behavior Analysis, 7*, 547–555.

Van Houten, R., & Thompson, C. (1976). The effects of explicit timing on math performance. *Journal of Applied Behavior Analysis, 9*, 227–230.

About the authors: *Gary L. Cates*, Ph.D., is assistant professor of psychology, Psychology Department, Illinois State University. *Katrina N. Rhymer*, Ph.D., is assistant professor of psychology, 138 Sloan Hall, Central Michigan University, Mt. Pleasant, MI 48859. E-mail: Katrina.N.Rhymer@cmich.edu

Address correspondence to: Gary L. Cates, Ph.D., 436 DeGarmo Hall, Psychology Department, Normal, IL 61790-4620. E-mail: glcates@ilstu.edu

APPENDIX

Implementation Guidelines

1. Be sure to select academic tasks that are at a fluency building stage. The procedure is not intended for academic skills that are at an acquisition stage.

2. Shuffle a predetermined number of flash cards with sight words or sight word phrases on them. Tell the student(s) that you are going to time their performance for three minutes and then graph how well they did. They should also be informed that they are to work as quickly as they can without making errors and to simply do their best reading. You will then show them the stopwatch and say, "Ready? GO!"

3. Present one flash card at a time. Allow the student 3 seconds to begin reading. If she does not begin reading or makes an error, read the entire phrase for her and then tell her to read it.

4. Place all incorrect responses in an "incorrect pile" and place all of the correct responses in a "correct pile." A correct response is defined as an accurately read word phrase on the first attempt.

5. After a specified time period (in this study, we used 3 minutes), you will stop the timer and count up how many cards are in the "correct pile." This number should be graphed and shown to the student. These procedures should be administered daily. It is important to maintain the same scale of measurement. If a time interval of three minutes is used on the first day, the same three minute time interval should be used.

6. Educators may wish to advance research on this procedure by determining if the rate of reading Dolch word phrases translates into higher reading fluency and/or comprehension for reading passages by determining words read correctly per minute for reading fluency and assessing reading comprehension in some manner (e.g., Maze, close, questions, etc.).

Exercise for Article 21

Factual Questions

1. In previous studies, has explicit timing been validated for improving reading?

2. The students in this study were referred to a school psychologist for what?

3. For all four students, what was the interscorer agreement (expressed as a percentage)?

4. Was this study designed to assess the effects of timing on comprehension?

5. What was the "primary dependent variable" in this study?

Questions for Discussion

6. At various points, the researchers use the term "baseline." What do you think this means? (See, for example, lines 132 and 150.)

7. The researchers use the term "ABAB design." What do you think this means? (See line 140.)

8. How important is the first limitation discussed by the researchers? (See lines 235–240.)

9. Do the results convince you that explicit timing improves performance? Explain.

10. How important are the graphs in Figure 1 in helping you understand the results of the study? Explain.

11. Would you recommend the use of a separate control group in a future study on this topic? Explain.

Quality Ratings

Directions: Indicate your level of agreement with each of the following statements by circling a number from 5 for strongly agree (SA) to 1 for strongly disagree (SD). If you believe an item is not applicable to this research article, leave it blank. Be prepared to explain your ratings. When responding to criteria A and B below, keep in mind that brief titles and abstracts are conventional in published research.

A. The title of the article is appropriate.

    SA   5   4   3   2   1   SD

B. The abstract provides an effective overview of the research article.

    SA   5   4   3   2   1   SD

C. The introduction establishes the importance of the study.

    SA   5   4   3   2   1   SD

D. The literature review establishes the context for the study.

  SA   5   4   3   2   1   SD

E. The research purpose, question, or hypothesis is clearly stated.

  SA   5   4   3   2   1   SD

F. The method of sampling is sound.

  SA   5   4   3   2   1   SD

G. Relevant demographics (for example, age, gender, and ethnicity) are described.

  SA   5   4   3   2   1   SD

H. Measurement procedures are adequate.

  SA   5   4   3   2   1   SD

I. All procedures have been described in sufficient detail to permit a replication of the study.

  SA   5   4   3   2   1   SD

J. The participants have been adequately protected from potential harm.

  SA   5   4   3   2   1   SD

K. The results are clearly described.

  SA   5   4   3   2   1   SD

L. The discussion/conclusion is appropriate.

  SA   5   4   3   2   1   SD

M. Despite any flaws, the report is worthy of publication.

  SA   5   4   3   2   1   SD

Article 22

The Effects of Self-Management in General Education Classrooms on the Organizational Skills of Adolescents with ADHD

SAMMI GUREASKO-MOORE
Lehigh University

GEORGE J. DuPAUL
Lehigh University

GEORGE P. WHITE
Lehigh University

ABSTRACT. Self-management procedures have been used in school settings to successfully reduce problem behaviors, as well as to reinforce appropriate behavior. A multiple-baseline across participants design was applied in this study to evaluate the effects of using a self-management procedure to enhance the classroom preparation skills of secondary school students with attention-deficit/hyperactivity disorder (ADHD). Three male students enrolled in a public secondary school were selected for this study because teacher reports suggested that these students were insufficiently prepared for class and inconsistently completed assignments. The intervention involved training in self-management procedures focusing on the improvement of classroom preparation skills. Following the intervention, the training process was systematically faded. Results were consistent across the 3 participants in enhancing classroom preparation behaviors. Implications for practice and future research are discussed.

From *Behavior Modification*, 30, 159–183. Copyright © 2006 by Sage Publications. Reprinted with permission.

Attention-deficit/hyperactivity disorder (ADHD) is the most prevalent diagnosed behavior disorder in childhood (Charatan, 1998), affecting 3% to 7% of the school-aged population, with males nearly 3 times more likely to manifest the disorder than females (American Psychiatric Association, 2000; Szatmaria, 1992). Those with ADHD experience chronic and pervasive difficulties with inattention, impulsivity, and/or hyperactivity across various situations and settings (Barkley, 1998). These characteristics typically appear early in life and place individuals with the disorder at risk for a variety of collateral problems, including academic underachievement, poor social relationships, and increased aggression and noncompliance.

Students diagnosed with ADHD are typically served in general education settings. Only about 50% of students with ADHD receive some form of special education services under the Individuals with Disabilities Education Act (IDEA), and of these students, at least 80% of their instructional time is spent in general education classrooms (Reid, Maag, Vasa, & Wright, 1994). Because of the high prevalence rate of ADHD among school-aged individuals, coupled with the placement of such students in general education settings, applied research in general education environments regarding attention disorders is a necessity (Mathes & Bender, 1997).

Although ADHD has received an abundance of attention in recent years, little of that attention has been specifically directed at classroom interventions. DuPaul and Eckert (1997) found that less than 100 methodologically reliable studies have investigated school-based interventions for this population. Furthermore, classroom teachers desire training in intervention approaches that would assist them in effectively working with students with ADHD (Reid et al., 1994). One setting in which this training would be particularly beneficial is in an inclusive learning environment where the majority of students with ADHD are educated.

Current classroom management strategies used to facilitate adjustment for students with ADHD focus on psychostimulant medications (i.e., methylphenidate) and teacher-based contingency management programs (i.e., token reinforcement and response cost; DuPaul & Eckert, 1997). Although these interventions have demonstrated positive behavior changes for various students, limitations should be noted, and research investigating alternative strategies should be conducted (Pelham & Murphy, 1986).

Pharmacological interventions have produced beneficial effects for some individuals with ADHD; however, psychostimulant medications, the class of drugs most frequently used to treat the symptoms of ADHD, have not been demonstrated to enhance the academic productivity for many students with ADHD (Rapport, Denney, DuPaul, & Gardner, 1994). Furthermore, psychostimulant drugs, as with other pharmacological treatments, have potential short- and long-term adverse effects, the most frequently reported being appetite reduction (Gittelman & Kanner, 1986) and insomnia (Barkley, 1977). Other limitations with the use of stimulant medications include a relatively short duration of action on behavior (Greenhill, 1995, 2001) and

65 that drugs are not educative, and therefore, individuals are not taught skills to ameliorate symptoms (O'Leary, 1980).

Teacher-based contingency management strategies are another commonly used intervention used to man-
70 age individuals' symptoms of ADHD. Although these techniques show promise in promoting academic improvement among students who exhibit behavioral disorders and learning problems (e.g., Abroamowitz & O'Leary, 1990; Abroamowitz, O'Leary, & Futtersak,
75 1988; Madsen, Becker, & Thomas, 1968; Thomas, Becker, Armstrong, 1968), they also have shortcomings. Behavioral techniques have been demonstrated to minimize some classroom behavior problems, but they do not fundamentally enhance academic performance
80 (DuPaul & Eckert, 1997), are reactive in nature (Cole & Bambara, 1992), and require an external agent (i.e., classroom teacher) to deliver consequences to manage the target behavior (Hoff & DuPaul, 1998). The demands on teachers' time and effort to implement con-
85 tingency management procedures reduce available instructional time (Cole, 1992). Considering the limitations of the current literature regarding intervention strategies to enhance the behavioral and academic functioning of individuals with ADHD, further re-
90 search is warranted to examine alternative approaches.

Instructional time during the secondary years is invaluable though limited, particularly when teachers are attempting to educate students while implementing effective classroom-based interventions. In middle and
95 high schools, teachers expect their students to behave appropriately during instructional time; they are often not inclined to make classroom modifications or specifically teach classroom preparation skills for those who require assistance (i.e., students with ADHD). The
100 organizational structure of middle school requires students to change classrooms and teachers for different academic subjects. Middle school students no longer have one individual school desk or classroom in which to place their academic materials and personal belong-
105 ings as they likely did in their elementary setting. These organizational demands imposed by the secondary school environment require students to assume more autonomy and responsibility than previously with respect to their own academic management. Students
110 are expected to arrive for classes punctually, prepare for academic instruction, bring the appropriate academic materials to class, and complete class and homework assignments on time.

In general education settings, especially at the sec-
115 ondary level, classroom preparation skills are required to attain success (Snyder & Bambara, 1997). Classroom preparation skills are preacademic behaviors that enable students to meet everyday classroom demands, such as attending classes daily, arriving for classes
120 promptly, being prepared for class, paying attention during instruction, sufficiently completing teacher-assigned tasks, and handing in work on time. At the

secondary level, these skills are particularly salient because teachers expect that students will exhibit these
125 behaviors and therefore do not directly teach these skills (Zigmond, Kerr, & Schaeffer, 1988). Students with attention problems may be at an increased risk for failure due, at least in part, to the inconsistent application of classroom preparation skills.

130 A strategy that has been used in school settings to successfully remediate problem behaviors displayed by adolescents is self-management (Cole, 1992). A number of studies have demonstrated positive effects of self-management interventions applied in school envi-
135 ronments among students with mild disabilities (Fantuzzo & Polite, 1990; Hughes, Korinek, & Gorman, 1991; Hughes, Ruhl, & Misra, 1989). Self-management interventions offer teachers, particularly at the secondary level, several advantages (Cole, 1992). One bene-
140 fit of self-management is that it centers on the students taking responsibility for their own actions. Another advantage of self-management approaches is that students are in control of the intervention; therefore, there is less demand placed on teachers. A third benefit con-
145 cerning self-management procedures is that this type of intervention has the potential to promote generalization across classroom settings (Cole, 1992).

The available literature regarding self-management procedures and ADHD focuses on the effects of these
150 procedures in treatment facilities and laboratory settings rather than in classrooms where these interventions will primarily be used (e.g., Hall & Kataria, 1992; Hinshaw & Melnick, 1992). It has been reported that out of 137 intervention studies regarding ADHD, only
155 21 were conducted within public school settings (Fiore, Becker, & Nero, 1993). This is a concern because generalization may not occur from the laboratory setting to the classroom.

This study replicated the procedures of Snyder and
160 Bambara (1997) who evaluated the effects of a comprehensive self-management intervention on secondary students with learning disabilities, without ADHD, in both a learning support classroom and a mainstream classroom. This study employed a multiple baseline
165 across settings design to evaluate the effectiveness of a self-management intervention on student classroom preparation skills. Specifically, the self-management procedures involved instruction by the students' learning support teacher of several intervention elements
170 such as problem identification, goal setting, self-monitoring, self-evaluation, and self-reinforcement. This study attempted to provide support for self-management as an acceptable and effective intervention for adolescent students with ADHD in the general
175 education setting. It was hypothesized that this intervention package would increase specific classroom preparation skills of three secondary students in three of their academic classes relative to typical classroom procedures.

Method

Participants and Setting

180   Three seventh-grade male students (Barry, Seth, and Kevin), diagnosed with ADHD, who attend a public middle school in northeastern Pennsylvania, participated in this study. Students, all 12 years old, were selected for this study on the basis of teacher reports
185 that suggested they were insufficiently prepared for class (e.g., did not have a pencil or notebook, did not hand in completed homework assignments) and did not complete assigned tasks consistently. Written consent from the students' parents and oral assent from
190 students were obtained prior to initiating the study.

To confirm the students' diagnoses of ADHD, ratings of inattention, impulsivity, and hyperactivity were obtained from the students' parents and teachers using the Inattention and Hyperactivity-Impulsivity sub-
195 scores from the home and school versions of the ADHD-IV Rating Scale (DuPaul, Power, Anastopoulos, & Reid, 1998), as well as the Attention Problems subscales of the Child Behavior Checklist (CBCL) (Achenbach, 1991) and the Teacher Rating Scale
200 (TRF) (Achenbach, 1991). In addition to these rating scales, diagnostic interviews were conducted by the first author, individually, with each of the students' parent(s). The students who were selected to participate in the current study met criteria on the diagnostic inter-
205 view of symptoms consistent with the *Diagnostic and Statistical Manual of Mental Disorders (4th ed.)* (American Psychiatric Association, 1994) criteria for the combined subtype of ADHD as reported by their parent(s). In addition, each participant had clinically
210 significant scores on (a) the Inattention or Hyperactivity/Impulsivity subscales of the ADHD-IV Rating Scale (home and school versions) at or beyond the 93rd percentile for the child's age and gender, and (b) the CBCL and TRF Attention Problems subscale, *T*-score
215 of 70 or greater.

The self-management training sessions were conducted in a small room located within the school's office area during students' homeroom periods. Observations of the students' classroom preparation skills were
220 made during targeted academic classes. For Barry and Kevin, classroom preparation behaviors were observed in language arts, whereas Seth's observations were conducted during his mathematics class.

All of the participants included in the investigation
225 received methylphenidate to help alleviate the symptoms of ADHD. Each adolescent received 10 mg of methylphenidate in the morning prior to arriving at school, as well as an additional 10 mg taken in the school nurse's office following his lunch period. These
230 participants, however, were still reported by their teachers as having problems with classroom preparation behaviors. During the course of this study, the participants' doses of methylphenidate remained constant. No changes in medication were made 3 months
235 prior to the collection of baseline data or throughout the course of the intervention phases of the study for all 3 participants. Observations in each student's target classroom were conducted following the students' lunch period, immediately after the ingestion of his
240 second daily dosage of methylphenidate.

Primary Dependent Measure and Recording Procedure

The percentage of classroom preparation skills that were demonstrated in the targeted academic classrooms was the primary dependent measure used in this study. This percentage was calculated using a checklist, com-
245 pleted by the students' teachers, that identified classroom preparation behaviors (revised from Snyder & Bambara, 1997; see Appendix A). The students used the same checklist as the means to self-record their behavior; however, the participants were not informed
250 that their teachers were completing the checklist. A list of the six classroom preparation behaviors and their operational definitions may be viewed in Table 1.

The teachers within the participants' targeted classrooms, who were not informed of the nature of the stu-
255 dents' disorders or the intervention, collected data on a daily basis for each student. The occurrence or nonoccurrence of behaviors was recorded according to the classroom preparation behaviors on each specific student's checklist. To obtain interobserver agreement
260 data, an observer who was also uninformed of the intervention procedures and the students' disorder collected data on randomly selected days for each student. The percentage of classroom preparation skills was computed by dividing the number of observed behav-
265 iors by the number of required behaviors for the day and multiplying the result by 100.

Interobserver Agreement

Interobserver agreement was measured for 31% of the total observational sessions for all students in their targeted academic classroom (26 of 83 sessions). The
270 interobserver sessions were selected randomly across all experimental phases. Data were collected independently by one observer and the teacher. The percentage of agreement (point-by-point) was computed by dividing the number of agreements by the number of agree-
275 ments added to the number of disagreements and multiplying the result by 100. Agreements were recorded when both the observer and the teacher recorded either an occurrence or a nonoccurrence of behavior as shown on the classroom preparation skills checklist. Agree-
280 ment was 100% across all sessions.

Procedural Integrity

Procedural integrity was checked once a week. An individual trained in the procedures of this study observed the training session in which the primary investigator trained the students. A checklist was established
285 incorporating all the steps of the intervention. The number of steps that were instructed correctly was summed, and a percentage was calculated by dividing

Table 1

Classroom Preparation Behaviors and Their Operational Definitions

Behavior	Operational definition
Arrives on time for class instruction	Is in seat when the class bell rings
Is ready and prepared to begin class	Has eye contact with the teacher and terminates other activities such as talking when the teacher initiates class instruction
Has paper/notebook	Has notebook or paper on desktop
Has pen/pencil	Has pen/pencil (cap off) on desktop and open prepared for instruction
Hands in sufficiently completed homework on time	Homework is turned in as requested by the teacher
Completes homework	Responds (correctly or incorrectly) to each item in homework assignment

the number of correctly trained steps by the total number of steps and multiplying the result by 100. Procedural integrity during the training, monitoring, fading, and maintenance phases was very high (100% on all occasions).

Experimental Design and Procedures

A multiple-baseline across participants design was employed to evaluate the effects of self-management of classroom preparation skills on adolescents with ADHD. Classroom preparation skills were the targeted behaviors of the self-management intervention. After stable responding had been demonstrated in baseline conditions in Barry's targeted classroom, the intervention was introduced for him while baseline conditions remained in effect for the other two students. After Barry displayed behavior change in his targeted Language Arts class, the intervention was delivered to Seth. Once a stable intervention response was maintained for Seth, the intervention was applied for Kevin.

Baseline

Baseline data were collected until a minimum of three data points were established in which the participant was engaged in less than 70% of the six identified classroom preparation behaviors. During baseline, teachers followed their customary routine. Teachers prompted students, when necessary, to follow classroom requirements and intervened in their typical fashion (e.g., provided verbal reminders) during problematic situations.

Self-Management

The self-management intervention incorporated two primary components: (a) student training of self-management skills and (b) monitoring the students' use of their newly acquired skills.

Training. Students met individually with the first author (hereafter referred to as the experimenter) during their homeroom period, in a small room located within the general office area, for 20 minutes on 3 consecutive days. During the first day of training, the experimenter gave the student an explanation and rationale for self-management. This provided students with (a) a description of their current classroom functioning based on observation results, (b) an explanation of the importance of responsibility for one's own behavior,

and (c) the specific responsibilities one must maintain to be considered prepared for class instruction.

The self-management plan was taught to the students to be used specifically in their targeted academic classroom. The students were instructed to begin self-managing their behavior on the second day of the training phase. The students were provided with two forms of the self-management plan: (a) the student log and (b) the self-monitoring checklist (Appendix A). Following the distribution of the log and the checklist, the experimenter guided the students through the process of self-management. First, the experimenter had the students identify their present problems with class preparation and write this information in their student log. If necessary, the experimenter aided the students in identifying their current problems by discussing specific incidences of inappropriate behaviors attained through teacher consultations. The next issue the experimenter addressed with students was setting goals. Students verbally stated their goals regarding their compliance with the six classroom preparation behaviors (i.e., I will complete at least four of the six preparation behaviors each day of the school week) and then wrote these goals down on their self-monitoring form. The students were then taught to self-monitor their behavior by indicating the behaviors on the classroom preparation skills checklist that they have engaged in during their targeted class. Students were also required to specify the times on the form that they self-monitored.

In addition to identifying current classroom preparation problems and goal setting, the student log served the purpose of self-evaluation and self-reinforcement. Self-evaluation obligated the students to calculate the number of behaviors they had complied with on the self-monitoring form. The students also were required to write down what they did to accomplish their goals, what they did not do to achieve their goals, and what they could do to be more effective. This helped the students both recognize problematic areas and problem-solve how to correct and improve on these areas (Snyder & Bambara, 1997). A Likert-type scale (ranging from 0 = *no effort/total dissatisfaction* to 5 = *best effort/total satisfaction*) was used for the students to evaluate the satisfaction they had with their effort. This evaluation of effort was the self-reinforcement component of the self-management procedure. A procedural

375 integrity checklist used by the experimenter during the training may be viewed in Appendix B.

Monitoring. During the monitoring phase of the classroom implementation of the self-management skills, the experimenter met with students daily to
380 monitor and assess the students' implementation of their skills. These sessions required the students to critique their self-monitoring forms and write in their student log. After students completed writing in their log, the experimenter commended students on compliance
385 with met goals and assisted them in areas in which their goals had not been met. The experimenter also commented on students' conformity to preparation skills using the data collected by the students' teachers. The intervention continued individually until the stu-
390 dent demonstrated 100% of the behaviors on the checklist for 4 out of 5 consecutive days in his targeted class.

Each week the students established new goals for themselves. Weekly goal setting and daily monitoring continued until 100% of classroom preparation skills
395 were met for 4 out of 5 consecutive days. A procedural integrity checklist used by the experimenter during the monitoring phase may be viewed in Appendix C.

Fading. The fading phase required the students to continue using the self-management plan. However,
400 the students were now only required to meet with the experimenter every other day during their homeroom. During these meetings, the experimenter continued to provide students with feedback regarding their performance in their targeted class. After the student ex-
405 hibited 100% of the classroom preparation behavior for at least 4 out of 5 consecutive days, he began the maintenance phase.

Maintenance. During this phase, the student proceeded to engage in self-management. However, dur-
410 ing this phase, the student only met with the experimenter one time per week. Once the student engaged in 100% of the classroom preparation behavior for at least 4 out of 5 consecutive school days, he was given the choice to cease the writing portion of the self-
415 management plan.

Social Validation and Recording Procedures

Peer comparison. The first measure of social validation included behaviors of "average" peers (student not diagnosed with ADHD). During 20 randomly selected opportunities, the students' teachers recorded the
420 behavior of an average student in each of the targeted students' general education classrooms. During each observational session, the teacher randomly selected a different student in the classroom to observe. To compare the average students' behaviors with the targeted
425 students' behaviors, the same checklist was used to record behavior. Interobserver agreement was established by having the teacher record the average students' performance simultaneously with the observer.

Consumer satisfaction. The second measure of so-
430 cial validity encompassed an evaluation of teacher and student satisfaction of the intervention package. Following the maintenance phase, the experimenter provided the participants with the Children's Intervention Rating Profile (CIRP) (Elliot, 1986). This question-
435 naire evaluated whether the students were satisfied with the intervention and believed the intervention to be effective. The participants responded to this seven-item questionnaire by circling a number between 1 (indicating *complete disagreement*) and 6 (denoting
440 *complete agreement*). Of the seven questions, four were phrased positively, and thus a rating of 4 or higher would indicate that the intervention was deemed acceptable. The remaining questions were worded in a negative manner; therefore, a rating of 3 or lower was
445 considered to indicate acceptability.

The students' academic teachers, who were initially uninformed of the intervention that was applied, were also provided with a rating profile to assess the intervention package's effectiveness. The teachers com-
450 pleted the rating profile following a verbal explanation of the intervention that was used. An adapted version of the Intervention Rating Profile (IRP) (Martens & Witt, 1982) was used to assess the teachers' perceptions of the self-management package. The teachers
455 completed the questionnaire containing 15 questions, which are scored on a 6-point Likert-type scale, with 1 representing *complete disagreement with an item* and 6 representing *complete agreement with an item*. The satisfaction ratings were estimated by calculating a
460 mean score for all 15 responses. An average score of greater than or equal to 4 indicated that the intervention was acceptable to the teacher.

Results

The percentages of classroom preparation behaviors across baseline and intervention phases for the 3 par-
465 ticipants are displayed in Figure 1. The percentage of classroom preparation behaviors during baseline was moderately variable for each of the 3 participants, ranging from 33% to 67% ($M = 50\%$) for Barry, 33% to 67% ($M = 53\%$) for Seth, and 0% to 67% ($M = 40\%$)
470 for Kevin.

Barry. There was a decreasing trend during the baseline phase for Barry. The effects of the self-management training were slightly delayed, as indicated by the change in intercept from baseline to train-
475 ing. The first data point during the training phase indicated the same percentage of preparation behaviors as the last day of baseline. The second and third days of training demonstrated increases in preparation behaviors to 75%, indicating an accelerating trend in the
480 training phase. A difference in the level of functioning was evidenced immediately following the change from the training phase into the monitoring phase. During the last day of the training, Barry engaged in 75% of classroom preparation behaviors. This percentage

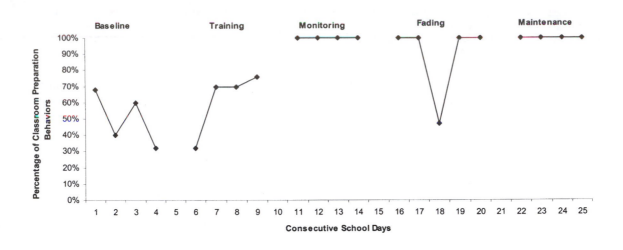

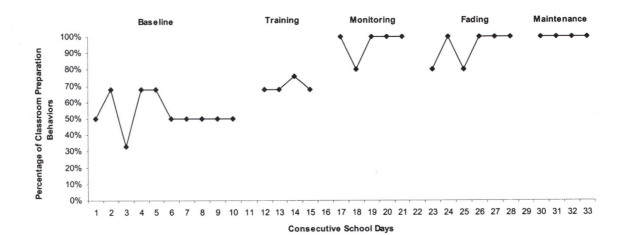

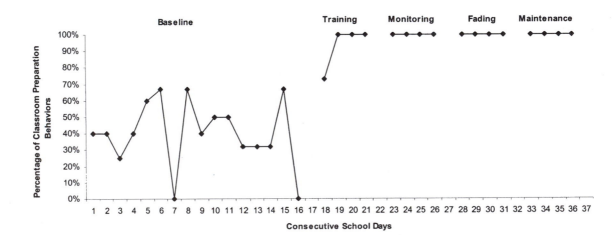

Figure 1. The percentage of classroom preparation behaviors exhibited by three adolescents with attention-deficit hyperactivity disorder (ADHD) across experimental phases.

485

increased by 25%, reaching 100% beginning the first day of the monitoring phase. Continuous performance at 100% was maintained for 4 consecutive days, the entire duration of the monitoring phase. The progression from the monitoring phase into the fading phase did not indicate a difference in level, as Barry continued at 100% performance. One hundred percent performance during the fading phase was maintained for 4 out of 5 consecutive school days. Barry's 100% performance was maintained throughout the maintenance phase.

Seth. Similar positive effects of the intervention were demonstrated by Seth. However, a primary distinction between Barry's and Seth's performances was the somewhat more immediate effects of the self-management training for Seth. Seth's performance indicated a moderate increase in the baseline to the training phase as demonstrated in the change in intercept from 50% in baseline to 67% in the training phase. The baseline and training phase data for Seth had flat trends; however, there was a 16% increase in the means from baseline to training phases (M_{bl} = 53% to $M_{training}$ = 69%). On entering into the monitoring phase, Seth was performing at an average of 69% in the training phase. The phase change from training to monitoring resulted in an immediate increase from 67% on the last day of training to 100% performance on the first day of the monitoring phase. During the monitoring phase, Seth maintained criterion, with performance falling below 100% on one occasion. Seth was performing at 100% for the 3 final days of the monitoring phase. The first data point within the fading phase indicated a slight reduction in Seth's performance to 83%, which is a 17% decrease from that in the previous session. However, over the next 4 days of the fading phase, Seth's performance only dropped below 100% on one occasion. The final 3 days of the fading phase demonstrated consistent performance at 100%. Seth's perfect performance was maintained for 4 consecutive days during the entire maintenance phase.

Kevin. The baseline data for Kevin were somewhat more variable than the data for the other participants, ranging from 0% to 67%. The initial change from baseline to the training phase indicated immediate effects. Kevin's performance increased from 0% on the last day of baseline to 75% performance on the first day of the training phase. The mean percentage of classroom preparation behaviors increased from 40% in baseline to 94% during the training phase. Following the first day of the self-management training, a completely flat trend of 100% performance occurred throughout each of the subsequent intervention phases.

Social Validation

Peer comparison. There were no occasions in which the average students' classroom preparation behavior fell below 100%. The average students' performance was collected simultaneously by the teacher and another observer for the purpose of interobserver agreement. Interobserver agreement data were collected for all 20 sessions when peer comparisons were observed. Agreement was 100% across sessions. Classroom preparation behaviors of the students with ADHD compared favorably with peers' performance during the monitoring, fading, and maintenance phases of the intervention.

Consumer satisfaction. The acceptability of the self-management package was measured at the conclusion of the intervention by requesting that both the students themselves and the teachers respond to brief questionnaires. All 3 students indicated that the self-management method was fair and suggested that they liked the intervention. Students did not record that this intervention resulted in problems with their peers. All 3 students strongly agreed that the intervention would be a good one to use with other students, and they indicated that they believed the self-management strategy helped them do better in school.

Table 2 contains the results from the scores on the IRP completed by the participants' teachers. The average score on the 15-item questionnaire was above 4 for each of the participants' teachers, indicating that they consistently believed that the self-management strategy was, in general, acceptable for the students' behaviors. Specifically, the teachers reported that the students' behavior problems were severe enough to warrant the use of the self-management intervention. The participants' teachers asserted that they would suggest the use of the intervention package to other teachers and that the intervention was appropriate for a variety of students. In addition, the teachers indicated that they would be willing to use the current intervention in their classroom again. The teachers noted that the intervention did not result in negative side effects for the students and was consistent with other interventions that they had previously used.

Discussion

This investigation evaluated the efficacy of a self-management intervention package used to enhance the classroom preparation behaviors of 3 adolescents diagnosed with ADHD. Treatment integrity scores were found to be high, demonstrating that the self-management training, monitoring, fading, and maintenance procedures were implemented as intended. A multiple baseline across participants design demonstrated positive results, indicating that the self-management intervention was successful in improving classroom preparation behaviors. Furthermore, the participants' classroom preparation skills were maintained as the intervention was systematically faded over time. Measures of social validation indicated that following the implementation of the self-management intervention, the participants performed as well as their "typical" classmates. In addition, the students and teachers

145

Table 2
Responses from the Intervention Rating Profile

Statement	Barry's teacher	Seth's teacher	Kevin's teacher
1. Self-management was an acceptable intervention package for the student's problem behaviors.	5	4	4
2. Most teachers would find this intervention package appropriate for behavior problems in addition to the one described.	5	4	4
3. This intervention package was effective in changing the student's problem behaviors.	5	4	5
4. I would suggest the use of this intervention package to other teachers.	6	4	6
5. The student's behavior problem is severe enough to warrant the use of this intervention.	6	5	6
6. Most teachers would find this intervention package suitable for the behavior problems described.	6	4	6
7. I would be willing to use this intervention package in the classroom setting.	6	5	6
8. This intervention did not result in negative side effects for the student.	6	5	6
9. This intervention package was appropriate for a variety of students.	6	4	6
10. This intervention is consistent with those I have used in classroom settings.	6	5	5
11. This intervention was a fair way to handle the student's problem behaviors.	4	4	5
12. This intervention is reasonable for the problem behaviors described.	6	5	5
13. I liked the procedures used in this intervention strategy.	6	5	5
14. This intervention was a good way to handle this student's behavior.	6	4	5
15. Overall, this intervention was beneficial for the student.	6	4	6

Note. Judgments were made on a 6-point Likert-type scale (1 = *strongly disagree*, 6 = *strongly agree*).

rated the intervention to be acceptable and effective in enhancing the participants' classroom behavior.

The results of this study are consistent with the findings of Snyder and Bambara (1997), who evaluated the effects of a self-management intervention on secondary students with learning disabilities in a learning support environment and one mainstream classroom. Both studies indicate that the self-management procedures were effective in enhancing classroom preparation behaviors.

This study extended the literature on ADHD by positing self-management as a potential intervention technique to alleviate symptoms of the disorder. Previous research regarding self-management procedures and ADHD has emphasized the efficacy of these procedures in treatment facilities and laboratory settings rather than in classrooms where these interventions will primarily be used (Hall & Kataria, 1992; Hinshaw & Melnick, 1992). This study, however, evaluated the self-management intervention within the general education classroom setting (i.e., the most common placement for children with ADHD). In addition, this study differed from prior studies evaluating self-management on adolescents with ADHD by targeting classroom preparation skills and preparation behaviors rather than self-control.

Although this study determined that the self-management intervention produced positive effects, limitations exist. The 3 students that participated in this study had combined type ADHD; therefore, the use of this intervention with other subtypes (e.g., predominantly inattentive type and predominantly hyperactive-impulsive type) is open to question. Prospective investigations should include participants with other subtypes of ADHD to evaluate the efficacy of this intervention across variants of this disorder. This study was also limited by the fact that academic productivity was not evaluated. Future researchers may consider extend-

ing this study by examining the intervention effect on the amount of classwork completed, as well as the accuracy of work completed. This investigation was also limited in that a school-based resource (i.e., school psychologist) did not implement the intervention. Ideally, students would be trained to use this intervention by school personnel, such as a school psychologist, with education and training in behavior management techniques. Although the experimenter was not specifically affiliated with the school, the intervention training and implementation, as well as the classroom observations, were conducted within the school environment. Thus, the experimenter was acting in the role of a school-based clinician in terms of the intervention training, organization of meetings, and monitoring treatment efficacy.

The self-management procedures applied in this investigation served as an adjunctive intervention strategy representing the effects of pharmacological treatment combined with a cognitive–behavioral technique. Therefore, it remains unclear as to whether the self-management procedures would be effective if used with individuals not on medication. Future studies should select participants not receiving pharmacological therapy to evaluate the efficacy of the self-management procedures in isolation.

Although the intervention in this study was intended to teach students to assume complete responsibility for their behavior without involving any significant environmentally controlling factors, it is possible that the nature of the intervention, involving meetings with the experimenter, did create some external influence. In a critical review paper of self-management interventions used with adolescents, Gross and Wojnilower (1984) concluded that most studies purporting to demonstrate the success of self-management strategies did, in fact, have external contingencies that may have affected the outcomes. This study may have reduced peripheral contingencies by continuing to collect data following the cessation of the experimenter/student meetings. Prospective research should consider evaluating the effectiveness of self-management procedures while minimizing environmental factors.

Self-management interventions, such as the one used in this study, may encourage generalization, which is especially important during junior high school and high school when students change teachers and classrooms for different academic subjects. Secondary students may apply self-management skills in all classes to enhance preparation behaviors. In addition, these strategies require students to be accountable for their actions, which again is important at the secondary education level. During junior high school and high school, teachers' expectations of student behavior most often include classroom preparation skills.

Training in the self-management procedures used in this study may be conducted by school personnel, such as school psychologists, school counselors, or teachers who have knowledge of behavior management techniques. Instructing students in self-management skills initially requires time for the instructor to train, monitor, and evaluate the intervention to promote successful outcomes. Subsequent to initial efforts and time requirements, the instructor's responsibilities for managing the intervention are diminished, placing accountability on the student. A school psychologist is well suited to assume the role of training students in self-management procedures. In addition, school psychologists may consult with teachers, providing them with the necessary instruction to train students in the application of these skills.

This study demonstrated that the self-management intervention package improved the classroom preparation behaviors of the 3 adolescents identified with ADHD who participated in this study. The results lend support for the use of self-management as an intervention in secondary classrooms for students who exhibit organization and classroom preparation difficulties. Further research is required to more specifically delineate the scope and limitations of this intervention for addressing the organizational skills of students with ADHD.

References

Abroamowitz, A. J., & O'Leary, S. G. (1990). Effectiveness of delayed punishment in an applied setting. *Behavior Therapy, 21,* 231–239.

Abroamowitz, A. J., O'Leary, S. G., & Futtersak, M. W. (1988). The relative impact of long and short reprimands on children's off-task behavior in the classroom. *Behavior Therapy, 19,* 243–247.

Achenbach, T. M. (1991). *Manual for the Teacher's Report Form and 1991 Profile.* Burlington: University of Vermont Department of Psychiatry.

American Psychiatric Association (1994). *Diagnostic and statistical manual of mental disorders* (4th ed.). Washington, DC: Author.

American Psychiatric Association (2000). *Diagnostic and statistical manual of mental disorders* (4th ed., text rev.). Washington, DC: Author.

Barkley, A. (1977). The effects of methylphenidate on various measures of activity level and attention in hyperkinetic children. *Journal of Abnormal Child Psychology, 5,* 351–369.

Barkley, R. A. (1998). *Attention-deficit hyperactivity disorder: A handbook for diagnosis and treatment* (2nd ed.). New York: Guilford.

Charatan, F. (1998). U.S. panel calls for research into effects of Ritalin. *British Medical Journal, 317,* 1545–1555.

Cole, C. L. (1992). Self-management intervention in the schools. *School Psychology Review, 21,* 188–192.

Cole, C. L., & Bambara, L. M. (1992). Issues surrounding the use of self-management interventions in the schools. *School Psychology Review, 21,* 193–201.

DuPaul, G. J., & Eckert, T. (1997). The effects of school-based interventions for attention deficit hyperactivity disorder: A meta-analysis. *School Psychology Review, 26,* 5–27.

DuPaul, G. J., Power, T. J., Anastopoulos, A. D., & Reid, R. (1998). *AD/HD Rating Scale-IV: Checklists, norms, and clinical interpretation.* New York: Guilford.

Elliot, S. N. (1986). Children's ratings of the acceptability of classroom interventions for misbehavior: Findings and methodological considerations. *Journal of School Psychology, 24,* 23–35.

Fantuzzo, J. W., & Polite, K. (1990). School-based, behavioral self-management: A review and analysis. *School Psychology Quarterly, 5,* 180–198.

Fiore, T. A., Becker, E. A., & Nero, R. C. (1993). Educational interventions for students with attention deficit disorder. *Exceptional Children, 60,* 163–173.

Gittelman, R., & Kanner, A. (1986). Psychopharmacotherapy. In H. Quay & J. Werry (Eds.), *Psychopathological disorders of childhood* (3rd ed.). New York: John Wiley.

Greenhill, L. (1995). Attention-deficit/hyperactivity disorder: The stimulants. *Child and Adolescent Psychiatric Clinics, 14,* 123–168.

Greenhill, L. (2001). ADHD and medication management. *Drug Benefit Trends, 13,* 7–10.

Gross, A. M., & Wojnilower, D. A. (1984). Self-directed behavior change in children: Is it self-directed? *Behavior Therapy, 15,* 501–514.

Hall, C. W., & Kataria, S. (1992). Effects of two treatment techniques on delay and vigilance tasks with attention deficit hyperactivity disorder (AD/HD) children. *The Journal of Psychology, 126,* 17–25.

Hinshaw, S. P., & Melnick, S. (1992). Self-management therapies and attention-deficit hyperactivity disorder: Reinforced self-evaluation and anger control interventions. *Behavior Modification, 16,* 253–273.

Hoff, K. E., & DuPaul, G. J. (1998). Reducing disruptive behavior in general education classrooms: The use of self-management strategies. *School Psychology Review, 27,* 290–303.

Hughes, C. A., Korinek, L., & Gorman, J. (1991). Self-management for students with mental retardation in public school settings: A research review. *Education and Training in Mental Retardation, 26,* 271–291.

Hughes, C. A., Ruhl, K. L., & Misra, A. (1989). Self-management with behaviorally disordered students in school settings: A promise unfulfilled? *Behavioral Disorders, 14,* 250–262.

Madsen, C. H., Becker, W. C., & Thomas, D. R. (1968). Rules, praise, and ignoring: Elements of elementary classroom control. *Journal of Applied Behavior Analysis, 1,* 139–150.

Martens, B. K., & Witt, J. C. (1982). *The intervention rating profile.* Lincoln: University of Nebraska–Lincoln.

Mathes, M. Y., & Bender, W. N. (1997). The effects of self-monitoring on children with attention-deficit/hyperactivity disorder who are receiving pharmacological interventions. *Remedial and Special Education, 18,* 121–128.

O'Leary, D. (1980). Pills or skills for hyperactive children. *Journal of Applied Behavior Analysis, 13,* 191–204.

Pelham, W. E., & Murphy, H. A. (1986). Attention deficit and conduct disorders. In M. Hersen (Ed.), *Pharmacological and behavioral treatment: An integrative approach* (pp. 108–148). New York: John Wiley.

Rapport, M. D., Denney, C., DuPaul, G. J., & Gardner, M. J. (1994). Attention deficit disorder and methylphenidate: Normalization rates, clinical effectiveness, and response prediction in 76 children. *Journal of the American Academy of Child and Adolescent Psychiatry, 33,* 882–893.

Reid, R., Maag, J. W., Vasa, S. F., & Wright, G. (1994). An analysis of teachers' perception of attention-deficit hyperactivity disorder. *Journal of Research and Development in Education, 27,* 185–191.

Snyder, M. C., & Bambara, L. M. (1997). Teaching secondary students with learning disabilities to self-manage classroom survival skills. *Journal of Learning Disabilities, 30,* 534–543.

Szatmaria, P. (1992). The epidemiology of attention-deficit hyperactivity disorders. In G. Weiss (Ed.), *Child and adolescent psychiatry clinics of North America: Attention deficit hyperactivity disorder* (pp. 361–372). Philadelphia: W. B. Saunders.

Thomas, D. R., Becker, W. C., & Armstrong, M. (1968). Production and elimination of disruptive classroom behavior by systematically varying teacher's behavior. *Journal of Applied Behavior Analysis, 1,* 35–45.

Zigmond, N., Kerr, M. M., & Schaeffer, A. (1988). Behavior patterns of learning disabled and non-learning disabled adolescents in high school academic classes. *Remedial and Special Education, 9,* 6–11.

About the authors: *Sammi Gureasko-Moore is an advanced doctoral student in the School Psychology Program at Lehigh University. While at Lehigh, she participated in a leadership training grant from* the U.S. Department of Education, affording her a subspecialization in pediatric school psychology. She completed her doctoral internship at the Virginia Beach City Public Schools, in the public health track. She has extensive experience working with children and adolescents with attention-deficit hyperactivity/disorder (ADHD). Currently, she is finishing her dissertation, which will further investigate the effects of self-management interventions for adolescents with ADHD. *George DuPaul* is a professor and coordinator of the School Psychology Program at Lehigh University. He received his Ph.D. in school psychology from the University of Rhode Island in 1985. He has extensive experience providing clinical services to children with ADHD and their families as well as consulting with a variety of school districts regarding the management of students with ADHD. He has been an author or a coauthor on more than 100 journal articles and book chapters related to ADHD. He has published two books and two videos on the assessment and treatment of ADHD. Dr. DuPaul serves on the editorial boards of several journals and is section editor of the Research Design and Methodology section of

School Psychology Quarterly. Currently, he is investigating the effects of early intervention and school-based interventions for students with ADHD. *George White* is a professor and coordinator of the Educational Leadership Program at Lehigh. While at Lehigh, Dr. White has been responsible for the development of specialized programs to prepare individuals for leadership roles in urban school districts and international schools. He directs the Lehigh University Middle Level Partnership, a venture designed to assist schools in improving the education of preadolescent students. Dr. White is a nationally recognized consultant, having worked with more than 60 school districts, educational organizations, and colleges and universities in addressing the issues associated with organizational development and change, partnership development, strategic planning, and on topics relating to middle-level education. He has published numerous articles on these topics and has recently authored a book that deals with the issue of implementing community service into the school curriculum.

APPENDIX A

Self-Monitoring Checklist

Classroom preparation behaviors	Yes	No
Was I in my seat when the bell rang?	_____	_____
Did I have eye contact with my teacher and stop my other activities when the teacher began class instruction?	_____	_____
Did I have my pen/pencil (cap off) on my desk?	_____	_____
Did I have my notebook or paper and textbook on my desk and open at the beginning of the lesson?	_____	_____
Did I turn in my homework as requested by my teacher?	_____	_____
Did I respond to each item in my homework assignment?	_____	_____

Day: _____

Time: _____

APPENDIX B

Procedural Integrity Checklist for the Training Phase

_____ 1. Gave the student an explanation and rationale for self-management.

_____ 2. Told student their current classroom functioning and the results of their functioning.

_____ 3. Told student salience of self-responsibility of action.

_____ 4. Informed students of their specific responsibilities that they must maintain for class preparation.

_____ 5. Taught students to use procedures in their targeted classroom.

_____ 6. Provided students with two forms of the self-management plan: (a) the student log and (b) the self-monitoring checklist (see Appendix A).

_____ 7. Had students identify their present problems with class preparation.

_____ 8. If necessary, aided students in identifying their current problems by discussing specific incidences of inappropriate behaviors.

_____ 9. Had students verbally asserting their goals regarding behaviors concerning classroom preparation.

_____ 10. Told students to write these goals down on their self-monitoring form.

_____ 11. Taught students to self-monitor their behavior by checking off the behaviors on the self-monitoring checklist.

_____ 12. Taught students to specify the times on the form that they self-monitored.

_____ 13. Told students to write down what goals they accomplished.

_____ 14. Told students to write down what they did that caused them not to achieve their goals.

_____ 15. Told students to write down ideas that would be effective in achieving their goals.

_____ 16. Taught students to evaluate the satisfaction they had with their effort to attain their goals in their log using a Likert-type scale (ranging from 0 = *no effort/total dissatisfaction* to 5 = *best effort/total satisfaction*).

APPENDIX C

Procedural Integrity Checklist During Monitoring Session

After students have completed writing in their log:

_____ 1. Commended students on compliance with met goals.

_____ 2. Assisted students in areas where they have not met their goals.

According to the data teachers collect:

_____ 3. Commented on students' conformity to targeted classroom skills.

_____ 4. When a new week began, students were told to establish a new behavioral goal.

Exercise for Article 22

Factual Questions

1. What is the researchers' explicit hypothesis?

2. How many of the participants in this study were receiving medication to help alleviate the symptoms of ADHD?

3. What was the "primary dependent measure" in this study?

4. How often were the participants required to meet with the experimenter during the "fading" phase?

5. At baseline, were any of the participants at 100% on classroom participation behaviors?

6. Do the researchers call for further research on this topic?

Questions for Discussion

7. Is the information on interobserver agreement important? Explain. (See lines 267–280.)

8. How helpful are the operational definitions of classroom preparation behaviors in helping you understand this study? Explain. (See Table 1.)

9. What is your understanding of the meaning of the term "baseline" as used by these researchers? (See lines 306–314 and Figure 1.)

10. Is the self-management intervention described in sufficient detail? (See lines 315–415.)

11. How helpful is Figure 1 in helping you understand the results of this study? Explain.

12. In your opinion, is this study worthwhile even though only three students were studied? Explain.

Quality Ratings

Directions: Indicate your level of agreement with each of the following statements by circling a number from 5 for strongly agree (SA) to 1 for strongly disagree (SD). If you believe an item is not applicable to this research article, leave it blank. Be prepared to explain your ratings. When responding to criteria A and B below, keep in mind that brief titles and abstracts are conventional in published research.

A. The title of the article is appropriate.

SA   5   4   3   2   1   SD

B. The abstract provides an effective overview of the research article.

SA   5   4   3   2   1   SD

C. The introduction establishes the importance of the study.

SA   5   4   3   2   1   SD

D. The literature review establishes the context for the study.

SA   5   4   3   2   1   SD

E. The research purpose, question, or hypothesis is clearly stated.

SA   5   4   3   2   1   SD

F. The method of sampling is sound.

SA   5   4   3   2   1   SD

G. Relevant demographics (for example, age, gender, and ethnicity) are described.

SA   5   4   3   2   1   SD

H. Measurement procedures are adequate.

SA   5   4   3   2   1   SD

I. All procedures have been described in sufficient detail to permit a replication of the study.

SA   5   4   3   2   1   SD

J. The participants have been adequately protected from potential harm.

SA   5   4   3   2   1   SD

K. The results are clearly described.

SA   5   4   3   2   1   SD

L. The discussion/conclusion is appropriate.

SA   5   4   3   2   1   SD

M. Despite any flaws, the report is worthy of publication.

SA   5   4   3   2   1   SD

Article 23

Drug Use Patterns Among High School Athletes and Nonathletes

ADAM H. NAYLOR
Boston University

DOUG GARDNER
ThinkSport® Consulting Services

LEN ZAICHKOWSKY
Boston University

ABSTRACT. This study examined drug use patterns and perceptions of drug intervention programs among adolescent interscholastic athletes and nonathletes. In particular, it explored the issue of whether participation in high school athletics is related to a healthier lifestyle and decreased use of recreational drugs and ergogenic aids. One thousand five hundred fifteen Massachusetts high school students completed a 150-item survey that assessed illicit and nonillicit substance use. Chi-square analyses revealed that athletes were significantly less likely to use cocaine and psychedelics, and were less likely to smoke cigarettes, compared with nonathletes. Conversely, nonathletes were less likely to use creatine than were athletes. There was no difference in the use of anabolic steroids and androstenedione between athletes and nonathletes. Descriptive analyses appear to indicate that drug interventions for athletes are falling short of their objectives. This study suggests that athletes have a healthier lifestyle and that the efficacy of intervention programs must be further examined.

From *Adolescence*, 36, 627–639. Copyright © 2001 by Libra Publishers, Inc. Reprinted with permission.

Drug use by athletes has made newspaper headlines, sport governing body rulebooks, and doctors' waiting rooms on a regular basis. Despite this, the relationship between drug use and participation in athletics
5 is not yet a clear one. On one hand, it has been suggested that participation in athletics leads to a healthier lifestyle and wiser decisions about substance use (Anderson, Albrecht, McKeag, Hough, & McGrew, 1991; Shephard, 2000; Shields, 1995). Conversely,
10 others have suggested that drug use is inherent in sports and its culture (Dyment, 1987; Wadler & Hainline, 1989). In between these two perspectives, one is left wondering if there is any difference in the substance use patterns of athletes and the general public (Adams,
15 1992; Anshel, 1998).

One way to begin clarifying this issue is to differentiate between recreational substances and ergogenic aids. Recreational substances are typically used for intrinsic motivates, such as to achieve altered affective
20 states. Examples of such drugs are alcohol, tobacco, marijuana, psychedelics, and cocaine. Ergogenic substances are used to augment performance in a given domain. In sports, such drugs are typically used to assist athletes in performing with more speed and
25 strength, and to endure more pain than normal. Examples of ergogenic aids are creatine, androstenedione, anabolic steroids, major pain medication, barbiturates, and amphetamines. The categorization of specific substances is debatable in some cases (Adams, 1992). For
30 instance, although marijuana is traditionally viewed as a recreational substance, it recently has been banned by the International Olympic Committee for its performance-enhancing potential (i.e., lowering of physiological arousal) (H. Davis, personal communication, Octo-
35 ber 4, 1999). Similarly, amphetamines have been used for recreational purposes. Nevertheless, the attempt to label substances as either recreational or ergogenic assists in clarifying differences between athletes and nonathletes in their drug use patterns.

Recreational Drugs

40 It has been traditionally believed that participation in athletics leads to a healthier lifestyle and less use of recreational drugs. Increased physical activity not only creates a physically healthier person, but also may lead to changes in overall lifestyle, highlighted by "a pru-
45 dent diet and abstinence from cigarette smoking" (Shephard, 2000). Some research has supported the popular notion that substance use is negatively correlated with healthful activities. In the university setting, athletes have self-reported less alcohol and drug use
50 than their peers (Anderson et al., 1991), providing further evidence that the high-level physical and mental demands of sports are incompatible with recreational drug use. Shields (1995) indicated that high school athletic directors perceived that students who partici-
55 pated in athletics were less likely to smoke cigarettes, consume alcohol, chew tobacco, and smoke marijuana than were students who did not participate in extracurricular athletic activities. These findings, while encouraging, ought to be verified through confidential self-
60 reports of high school students themselves. Nonetheless, these findings offer support for the notion that participation in sports promotes health and wellness.

Conversely, Wadler and Hainline (1989) have suggested that athletes may be more likely to experiment
65 with recreational and ergogenic aids than individuals

not participating in athletics. Physically, athletes might use recreational drugs to cope with the pain of injury rehabilitation. Mentally, stress (arising from the competitive demands of sports) and low self-confidence are issues that might lead athletes to recreational drug use. Furthermore, the "culture" of the particular sport might socialize athletes into drug use (e.g., baseball and smokeless tobacco) (Anshel, 1998). However, there is little evidence to suggest that recreational drug use is higher for athletes than nonathletes.

Ergogenic Aids

Unlike recreational substances, use of ergogenic aids is more likely in competitive athletic settings (Dyment, 1987). Wadler and Hainline (1989) have pointed out five instances that might lead athletes to utilize performance-enhancing pharmacological aids: (1) athletes who are at risk for not making a team or achieving the level of performance they desire; (2) athletes who are approaching the end of their career and are striving to continue to compete in their sport; (3) athletes who have weight problems and are seeking a means to increase or decrease weight; (4) athletes who are battling injuries and are trying to find ways to heal quicker; and (5) athletes who feel external pressure, such as from teammates, coaches, and parents, to use performance-enhancing drugs. Little research has contradicted the notion that those participating in sports are more disposed to use ergogenic aids. However, the findings of Anderson and colleagues (1991) did not support the notion that there is an anabolic steroid epidemic in collegiate athletics. Although their study did not examine whether athletes more frequently use anabolic steroids than do nonathletes, Anderson et al. concluded that steroid use by intercollegiate athletes did not increase over a four-year span. However, the prevalence of ergogenic aids a decade later has multiplied, with the advent of over-the-counter supplements (Hendrickson & Burton, 2000).

Educational Interventions

While the relationship between drug use and participation in organized athletics is still unclear, few disagree that early identification of, and education about, drug use is necessary. Andrews and Duncan (1998) have noted that cigarette smoking that begins during adolescence proceeds to more frequent use in the two years following high school. Furthermore, onset of drug use has been found to be a major determinant of adolescent morbidity and failure to perform age-related social roles (Grant & Dawson, 1998). In light of these facts, identification of substance use patterns during the high school years is important for preventing and curbing at-risk behaviors that might arise later in an individual's life.

Sports organizations have made it their mission to deter substance use by athletes. In 1986, the National Collegiate Athletic Association implemented a national drug education and drug-testing program for its member institutions (Anderson et al., 1991). Other organizations at various levels of sports have also adopted programs to monitor and police drug use behaviors in athletes (Shields, 1995). The Massachusetts Interscholastic Athletic Association (MIAA) has initiated one such program for high school athletic programs in the state (Massachusetts Interscholastic Athletic Association, 1999). The cornerstone of this intervention is the MIAA Chemical Health Eligibility Rule.

> During the season of practice or play, a student shall not, regardless of the quantity, use or consume, possess, buy/sell or give away any beverage containing alcohol; any tobacco product; marijuana; steroids; or any controlled substance.... The penalty for the first violation is that a student shall lose eligibility for the next two (2) consecutive interscholastic events or two (2) weeks of a season in which the student is a participant, whichever is greater. If a second or subsequent violation occurs, the student shall lose eligibility for the next twelve (12) consecutive interscholastic events or twelve (12) consecutive weeks, whichever is greater, in which the student is a participant.

It is the desire of the MIAA that this rule will not only be effective during the athletic season, but lead to an overall healthier lifestyle. High school coaches and athletic directors are responsible for implementing this rule and levying punishments as infractions occur. Adams (1992) found that students favored the eligibility rule and would like to see it strictly enforced. Furthermore, student athletes supported the notion of mandatory/random drug testing in high school athletics. Although drug intervention programs have been supported by both administrators and athletes, their efficacy must still be determined.

Purpose of the Present Study

The purpose of this study was to examine the incidence of drug use by interscholastic high school athletes, and to see if participation in interscholastic athletics is related to a healthier lifestyle, and specifically decreased use of recreational drugs and ergogenic aids year-round. Exploring possible differences in drug use patterns between athletes and nonathletes was a central element. This study sought to replicate previous high school drug use and abuse surveys conducted in the state of Massachusetts (Adams, 1992; Gardner & Zaichkowsky, 1995).

Besides the desire to update the findings on substance use habits since 1991, two other issues motivated this research. First, drug use by athletes has received a great deal of media attention. For example, the supplement androstenedione came to wide public attention during the baseball season in which Mark McGwire broke the home run record. Second, the governing bodies of state high school athletics have instituted wellness programs, drug education, and specific rules to prevent drug use. This study examined descriptive data relating to the effectiveness of these rules and programs.

Method

Participants

One thousand five hundred fifteen students, representing 15 high schools within the state of Massachusetts, were surveyed. Male students represented 51% of the sample ($n = 773$), while female students accounted for 49% ($n = 742$). Thirty-five percent were freshmen, 24.6% were sophomores, 23.4% were juniors, and 17% were in their senior year of high school. Seventy-four percent reported they had participated in one or more formally sanctioned interscholastic sports within the past 12 months.

The 150-item questionnaire used in this study was based on previous studies that have examined drug use patterns among high school students and student athletes (Adams, 1992; Anderson & McKeag, 1985; Johnston, O'Malley, & Bachman, 1999; Gardner & Zaichkowsky, 1995; Zaichkowsky, 1987). It included questions about students' drug use within the past 12 months, and made "nonuse" as stringent a classification as possible. Consistent with previous studies, both recreational and ergogenic substance use was self-reported. Recreational substances included alcohol, cigarettes, smokeless tobacco, marijuana, cocaine, and psychedelic drugs. Ergogenic aids included major pain medications, anabolic steroids, barbiturates, amphetamines, androstenedione, and creatine. A final section of the questionnaire asked students to address the effectiveness of the Massachusetts Interscholastic Athletic Association's substance use rules and educational interventions.

Table 1

Drug Use Patterns Among High School Athletes and Nonathletes

	Athletes (%)	Nonathletes (%)	Total (%)
Alcohol	68.8	68.4	68.7
Cigarettes**	36.1	44.0	38.4
Smokeless tobacco	8.0	7.7	7.9
Marijuana	37.5	42.9	39.1
Cocaine**	3.1	7.2	4.3
Psychedelics***	9.8	18.1	12.3
Creatine**	10.4	4.4	8.6
Androstenedione	2.3	2.1	2.2
Anabolic steroids	2.5	3.4	2.8
Pain medication	29.3	31.9	30.1
Barbiturates	3.7	6.1	4.4
Amphetamines	6.8	9.6	7.6

**Significant difference between athletes and nonathletes at the .01 level.
***Significant difference between athletes and nonathletes at the .001 level.

Procedure

Permission to conduct the study was obtained from the principals of 15 randomly selected public high schools in Massachusetts. Each principal agreed to allow between 100 and 180 students to participate in the study, and assigned a school athletic director or wellness coordinator to be the primary contact person for the researchers.

Each contact person was asked to select students who were representative of the school's gender, ethnic, and athletic demographics to participate in the study. Students were categorized as athletes if they participated on any state-sanctioned interscholastic athletic team. Upon creating the sample, the principal investigator and each school's contact person selected a class period and date in which to administer the questionnaire.

The principal investigator and two research assistants visited the 15 schools over a period of a month and a half. Students were administered the questionnaire in the school auditorium or cafeteria. They were assured that they would remain anonymous, that their responses would be viewed only by researchers, and that all information would be kept confidential. The questionnaire took approximately 30 minutes to complete.

Data Analysis

The frequencies of all variables were calculated. Descriptive statistics and chi-square analyses were conducted using the Statistical Package for the Social Sciences (SPSS).

Results

Athlete/Nonathlete Differences

Chi-square analyses indicated statistically significant differences between athletes and nonathletes in reported use of 4 of the 12 substances (see Table 1). In terms of recreational drugs, significantly more nonathletes than interscholastic athletes have smoked cigarettes, $\chi^2(1, N = 520) = 7.455, p < .01$. Nonathletes also reported using cocaine, $\chi^2(1, N = 59) = 11.491, p < .01$, and psychedelics, $\chi^2(1, N = 171) = 18.382, p < .001$, with greater frequency. One ergogenic aid, creatine, was used significantly more by athletes than nonathletes, $\chi^2(1, N = 115) = 7.455, p < .01$. Athletes were less likely to use marijuana, amphetamines, and barbiturates than were nonathletes, although the differences fell just short of being statistically significant.

Interscholastic Drug Intervention Feedback

The Massachusetts Interscholastic Athletic Association's Chemical Health Eligibility Rule seeks to discourage the use of recreational and ergogenic substances by high school athletes. Sixty-eight percent of the student athletes were aware of this rule (see Table 2). Thirty-eight percent reported having violated the rule; only 12% of these student athletes reported having been punished by school officials. Thirteen percent of those caught breaking the rule said they had not been punished. Seventy-one percent believed that some of their teammates had violated the Chemical Health Eligibility Rule.

Not only does the MIAA set drug use rules for student athletes, but it also seeks to implement intervention programs. Fifty-seven percent of the athletes stated that their coaches further this mission by discussing the issue of drug use and abuse. Thirty-one percent of the athletes expressed interest in drug education programs provided by the athletic department, while 48% stated that they would submit to random drug testing.

Table 2
Interscholastic Athletes' Perceptions of Drug Intervention Effectiveness

Topic	Yes	No
Do you know the Chemical Health Eligibility Rule?	68%	32%
Have you violated this rule during the season?	38%	62%
Have you received a penalty if you violated this rule?	12%	88%
Have you been caught and not been penalized?	13%	87%
Have any of your teammates violated this rule?	71%	29%
Does your coach discuss the issue of drugs?	57%	43%
Would you submit to voluntary random drug testing?	48%	52%
Are you interested in drug prevention programs from the athletic department?	31%	69%

Discussion

270   The results of this study appear to reflect current trends in substance use by high school students when compared with national averages (see Johnston et al., 1999). One encouraging finding was that cigarette smoking in Massachusetts was lower than national
275   averages. Roughly 38% of the students surveyed here reported smoking at least one cigarette as compared with the lowest estimate of 51% of the adolescents surveyed by the National Institute on Drug Abuse (Johnston et al., 1999). Massachusetts has engaged in
280   an aggressive antitobacco campaign over the last decade, which might account for this finding.

Previous research suggests three possible reasons for adolescent drug use: experimentation, social learning, and body image concerns (Anshel, 1998; Collins,
285   2000). Experimentation with drugs has been associated with boredom and is often supported by adolescents' belief that they are impervious to the harmful side effects of dangerous substances. Social learning theory states that individuals will take their drug use cues
290   from others in the environment. Modeling of parents' and friends' behavior is a prime example of social learning. Last, individuals have been found to use certain drugs to improve their appearance.

Recreational Substances

It has been suggested that recreational drug use
295   does not differ for athletes and nonathletes (Adams, 1992; Anshel, 1998; Dyment, 1987; Wadler & Hainline, 1989). The results of the present study were mixed in regard to student athlete and nonathlete substance use differences. There were no significant dif-

300   ferences for three of the six recreational drugs: alcohol, marijuana, and smokeless tobacco.

It is clear that alcohol use is socially accepted (Bailey & Rachal, 1993; Bush & Iannotti, 1992; Reifman et al., 1998), which might explain the high percentage of
305   students who consumed alcohol and the lack of difference in alcohol use between athletes and nonathletes. Further, the media provide opportunities for high school students to model the drinking behaviors of their professional and collegiate counterparts (Collins,
310   2000). Although the peer group influences the use of most substances, the culture of sports has also promoted alcohol use.

Slightly over 37% of the athletes reported smoking marijuana in the last year as opposed to about 43% of
315   the nonathletes. This is similar to the pattern for cigarette smoking, although the difference between athletes and nonathletes for marijuana was not significant ($p <$ .052). Even though marijuana and cigarettes are two different types of drugs, it seems that the athletes were
320   more aware of the negative impact smoking any kind of substance has on athletic performance.

Conversely, the lack of conclusive difference in marijuana use may reflect the availability of marijuana, the rising social acceptability of the drug, and the de-
325   sire to experiment (Johnston et al., 1999). In addition, athletes might not perceive marijuana as being as harmful as cocaine or psychedelics, and therefore may be more inclined to try the perceived lesser of two evils.

330   Marijuana has often been labeled a "gateway" drug to more addictive substances (Bush & Iannotti, 1992), yet the present study does not support this contention. Perhaps participation in athletics acts as a barrier to the use of more addictive substances. The significantly
335   lower use of cocaine and psychedelics by athletes can possibly be explained by the commitment necessary to participate in high school athletics. Seasons are year-round for some athletes, and others may be multisports athletes. After-school practices and weekend competi-
340   tions leave student athletes with less time for drug use/experimentation and less time to recover. Thus, organized athletics might reduce the desire of youth to indulge in more addictive and socially unacceptable drugs.

Ergogenic Aids

345   There was no significant difference between athletes and nonathletes for most ergogenic aids (anabolic steroids, androstenedione, pain medication, barbiturates, and amphetamines), which is a positive finding. This suggests that the culture of high school athletics in
350   Massachusetts does not encourage widespread use of these illicit substances. However, it should be noted that the lack of differences might reflect body image issues, specifically in regard to nonathletes who take steroids. Steroids increase an individual's muscle mass,
355   thus increasing self-confidence (Anshel, 1998). Addi-

tionally, muscle-building substances provide the opportunity for individuals to live up to societal standards for physical appearance. Similarly, amphetamines may be used to lose weight and help an individual achieve the 360 "ideal" figure. These substances may not necessarily be utilized to improve athletic performance, but rather to help students improve their body image (Anshel, 1998).

The lack of differences for most of the ergogenic 365 aids might further be explained by the skill level of the typical high school athlete. Wadler and Hainline (1989) have pointed out that few adolescents compete at "elite" levels. In light of this fact, there is little need for illicit performance-enhancing substances in the average 370 high school athlete's competitive endeavors. As the competitive demands get greater and the opposition tougher, one might expect the usage levels of ergogenic aids to increase (Wadler & Hainline, 1989).

The sole difference in the use of ergogenic aids by 375 athletes and nonathletes was for creatine, a nutritional supplement. High school athletes were more than twice as likely to use creatine than were nonathletes. The legality and availability of creatine are perhaps the greatest reasons for the higher level of use among ath- 380 letes, who are likely trying to gain a competitive edge (Dyment, 1987).

Intervention

Can the differences in illicit drug use behaviors between student athletes and nonathletes be explained by interscholastic chemical health programs? While it 385 would appear that the eligibility rule has helped in policing the substance use of interscholastic athletes, many are still unaware of this rule or ignore it. Seventy-one percent of the athletes reported that teammates have violated the Chemical Health Eligibility 390 Rule. Furthermore, almost 40% of the athletes admitted to having broken this rule, with 13% having not been penalized after being caught. These figures bring the effectiveness of the rule and its enforcement into question. Only 57% reported that their coaches addressed 395 the issue of substance use and abuse, which indicates that this is an educational opportunity that needs to be strengthened.

Educating this population is not an easy feat. A majority of the students were not interested in any further 400 drug interventions. Over half said they would not submit to voluntary random drug testing, and 69% were not interested in drug prevention programs provided by their athletic departments. These findings indicate a change in student attitudes over the last decade. Adams 405 (1992) found that a majority of student athletes were receptive to the idea of random drug testing and additional substance abuse programming through their athletic departments. One reason for the change might be that students have been saturated with drug education. 410 Alternatively, the fact that athletes generally used fewer illicit substances than nonathletes might suggest

that athletes felt they had already acquired healthful behaviors. Furthermore, recent studies have suggested that drug education programming needs to begin early 415 (Faigenbaum, Zaichkowsky, Gardner, & Micheli, 1998), and interventions aimed at high school athletes might be too late for high success rates.

Conclusion

Despite this study's large sample size, one must be cautious regarding generalization of the findings. The 420 high school and sports cultures examined here might only be representative of Massachusetts or the northeastern United States. Because the social circumstances of adolescents and their athletic participation greatly influence their substance use behaviors, more must be 425 done to understand the social climate of high school athletics.

Nevertheless, the present study suggests that participation in athletics is related to a healthier lifestyle. It also reveals that marijuana and alcohol are the two 430 primary substances where more education and intervention are necessary. Furthermore, this study suggests that coaches and administrators must assess the efficacy of their drug prevention programs and their efforts to enforce rules and regulations.

435 Athletic activities provide many opportunities to promote healthful behaviors. Therefore, sports organizations ought to assess the needs of their athletes and provide effective interventions in a timely manner.

References

Adams, C. L. (1992). *Substance use of Massachusetts high school student athletes.* Unpublished doctoral dissertation, Boston University.

Anderson, W. A., Albrecht, R. R., McKeag, D. B., Hough, D. O., & McGrew, C. A. (1991). A national survey of alcohol and drug use by college athletes. *The Physician and Sportsmedicine, 19,* 91–104.

Anderson, W. A., & McKeag, D. B. (1985). *The substance use and abuse habits of college student athletes* (Report No. 2). Mission, KS: The National Collegiate Athletic Association.

Andrews, J. A., & Duncan, S. C. (1998). The effect of attitude on the development of adolescent cigarette use. *Journal of Substance Abuse, 10,* 1–7.

Anshel, M. H. (1998). Drug abuse in sports: Causes and cures. In J. M. Williams (Ed.), *Applied sport psychology: Personal growth to peak performance* (pp. 372–387). Mountain View, CA: Mayfield Publishing Company.

Bailey, S. L., & Rachal, J. V. (1993). Dimensions of adolescent problem drinking. *Journal of Studies on Alcohol, 54,* 555–565.

Bush, P. J., & Iannotti, R. J. (1992). Elementary schoolchildren's use of alcohol, cigarettes, and marijuana and classmates' attribution of socialization. *Drug and Alcohol Dependence, 30,* 275–287.

Collins, G. B. (2000). Substance abuse and athletes. In D. Begel & R. W. Burton: (Eds.), *Sport psychiatry.* New York: W. W. Norton & Company.

Dyment, P. G. (1987). The adolescent athlete and ergogenic aids. *Journal of Adolescent Health Care, 8,* 68–73.

Faigenbaum, A. D., Zaichkowsky, L. D., Gardner, D. E., & Micheli, L. J. (1998). Anabolic steroid use by male and female middle school students. *Pediatrics, 101,* p. e6.

Gardner, D. E., & Zaichkowsky, L. (1995). *Substance use patterns in Massachusetts high school athletes and nonathletes.* Unpublished manuscript.

Grant, B. F., & Dawson, D. A. (1998). Age of onset of drug use and its association with DSM-IV drug abuse and dependence: Results from the National Longitudinal Alcohol Epidemiologic Survey. *Journal of Substance Abuse, 10,* 163–173.

Hendrickson, T. P., & Burton, R. W. (2000). Athletes' use of performance-enhancing drugs. In D. Begel & R. W. Burton (Eds.), *Sport psychiatry.* New York: W. W. Norton & Company.

Johnston, L. D., O'Malley, P. M., & Bachman, J. G. (1999). *National survey results on drug use from the Monitoring the Future study, 1975–1998: Volume 1. Secondary school students* (NIH Publication No. 99–4660). Rockville, MD: National Institute on Drug Abuse.

Massachusetts Interscholastic Athletic Association. (1999). *Massachusetts Interscholastic Athletic Association wellness manual*. Milford, Massachusetts.

Mayer, R. R., Forster, J. L., Murray, D. M., & Wagenaar, A. C. (1998). Social settings and situations of underage drinking. *Journal of Studies on Alcohol, 59*, 207–215.

Nurco, D. N. (1985). A discussion of validity. In B. A. Rouse, N. J. Kozel, & L. G. Richards (Eds.), *Self-report methods of estimating drug use: Meeting current challenges to validity* (NIDA Research Monograph No. 57, DHHS Publication No. ADM 85–1402). Washington, DC: U.S. Government Printing Office.

Reifman, A., Barnes, G. M., Dintscheff, B. A., Farrell, M. P., & Uhteg, L. (1998). Parental and peer influences on the onset of heavier drinking among adolescents. *Journal of Studies on Alcohol, 59*, 311–317.

Shephard, R. J. (2000). Importance of sport and exercise to quality of life and longevity. In L. Zaichkowsky & D. Mostofsky (Eds.), *Medical and psychological aspects of sport and exercise*. Morgantown, WV: FIT.

Shields, E. W., Jr. (1995). Sociodemographic analysis of drug use among adolescent athletes: Observations–perceptions of athletic directors–coaches. *Adolescence, 30*, 849–861.

Wadler, G. I., & Hainline, B. (1989). *Drugs and the athlete*. Philadelphia: F. A. Davis Company.

Zaichkowsky, L. (1987). *Drug use patterns in Massachusetts high school athletes and nonathletes*. Unpublished manuscript.

Acknowledgments: The researchers would like to thank the Massachusetts Governor's Committee on Physical Fitness and Sports for the grant that supported this study, and Bill Gaine and the Massachusetts Interscholastic Athletic Association for their assistance and support.

Address correspondence to: Adam H. Naylor, School of Education, Boston University, 605 Commonwealth Avenue, Boston, Massachusetts 02215. E-mail: adamnaylor@juno.com

Exercise for Article 23

Factual Questions

1. Barbiturates are classified as
   A. a recreational drug.   B. an ergogenic drug.

2. According to a study reported in the literature review, do student athletes support the notion of mandatory/random drug testing in high school athletics?

3. Male students represented what percentage of the sample?

4. Permission to conduct the study was obtained from whom?

5. What percentage of the athletes reported using cocaine? What percentage of nonathletes reported using cocaine?

6. Was the difference between the two percentages in your answer to Question 5 statistically significant? If yes, at what probability level?

7. What percentage of the student athletes reported that their coaches discussed the issue of drugs?

8. Which drug often has been labeled a "gateway" drug?

Questions for Discussion

9. In this study, a relatively large number of schools (15) was represented. To what extent does this increase your confidence in the results? Explain. (See lines 178–180.)

10. The students were asked to report on their drug use during the past 12 months. Do you think that this is an appropriate time interval? Explain. (See lines 193–195.)

11. The contact person at each school was asked to select students who were representative of the school's gender, ethnic, and athletic demographics to participate in the study. In your opinion, was this a good way to select the sample? (See lines 214–216.)

12. The students were assured that they would remain anonymous, that their responses would be viewed only by researchers, and that all information would be kept confidential. In your opinion, how important were these assurances? Do you think that some students might still deny their illicit drug use even though they were given these assurances? Explain. (See lines 226–229.)

13. The researchers mention the northeastern United States as an area to which these results "might only be representative." Do you agree? Explain. (See lines 419–422.)

14. The researchers state that "the present study suggests that participation in athletics is related to a healthier lifestyle." Do you agree? Do you also think that this study provides evidence that participation in athletics *causes* a reduction in students' substance use? Explain. (See lines 427–428.)

Quality Ratings

Directions: Indicate your level of agreement with each of the following statements by circling a number from 5 for strongly agree (SA) to 1 for strongly disagree (SD). If you believe an item is not applicable to this research article, leave it blank. Be prepared to explain your ratings. When responding to criteria A and B below, keep in mind that brief titles and abstracts are conventional in published research.

A. The title of the article is appropriate.

SA   5   4   3   2   1   SD

B. The abstract provides an effective overview of the research article.

SA 5 4 3 2 1 SD

C. The introduction establishes the importance of the study.

SA 5 4 3 2 1 SD

D. The literature review establishes the context for the study.

SA 5 4 3 2 1 SD

E. The research purpose, question, or hypothesis is clearly stated.

SA 5 4 3 2 1 SD

F. The method of sampling is sound.

SA 5 4 3 2 1 SD

G. Relevant demographics (for example, age, gender, and ethnicity) are described.

SA 5 4 3 2 1 SD

H. Measurement procedures are adequate.

SA 5 4 3 2 1 SD

I. All procedures have been described in sufficient detail to permit a replication of the study.

SA 5 4 3 2 1 SD

J. The participants have been adequately protected from potential harm.

SA 5 4 3 2 1 SD

K. The results are clearly described.

SA 5 4 3 2 1 SD

L. The discussion/conclusion is appropriate.

SA 5 4 3 2 1 SD

M. Despite any flaws, the report is worthy of publication.

SA 5 4 3 2 1 SD

Article 24

A Comparison of American and Taiwanese Students: Their Math Perception

YEA-LING TSAO
Taipei Municipal Teachers College

ABSTRACT. The major purpose of this study was to attempt to understand some of the reasons for mathematics perception of Taiwanese children compared to American children. The study was conducted with elementary schools in the Denver metropolitan area and Taipei, Taiwan, in which fifth graders in each city (21 and 37, respectively) were selected as target subjects in the study. To determine if attitudes and beliefs have a profound effect on American students' performance in mathematics, researchers believe that it may be helpful to compare American students to Chinese students. By providing comparative data, the researcher found marked differences in the beliefs of American and Taiwanese students in three areas under investigation: how to do well in mathematics, what math solutions should be, and motivation. The present study makes a potentially important contribution to our understanding of child development and education in two cultures.

From *Journal of Instructional Psychology*, *31*, 206–213. Copyright © 2004 by Project Innovation, Inc. Reprinted with permission.

Poor performance by American students on tests of mathematics and science has reached the level of a national crisis. Why is this? Study after study has reported on one or another facet of the low standing of
5 Americans in international competition. For example, in a recent cross-national study of mathematics achievement, American students in the eighth and twelfth grades were below the international average in problem solving, geometry, algebra, calculus, and other
10 areas of mathematics. In contrast, Japanese eighth graders received the highest average scores of children from 20 countries, and, at the twelfth-grade level, Japanese students were second only to Chinese students in Hong Kong (Garden, 1987). We must ask why
15 this is the case. Why are Chinese students consistently among the top scorers in cross-national studies of achievement and American students consistently below the international average?

The primary purpose of this research project was to
20 attempt to provide some answers to this question. The researcher was interested in exploring cross-cultural differences in mathematics perception and attitudes of younger children. The major concern was to describe the context in which different levels of achievement
25 occur in these two cultures. The researcher sought to identify not only contexts that appear to be important in explaining differences observed in the early years but also those that might be related to the cross-cultural differences in achievement that have been found
30 among older children and youth. What effect does it have on our children's performance in mathematics? The researcher hopes these questions can be answered in further research.

Literature Review

Logically, children's academic achievement is related to three major factors: their intelligence, their
35 experiences at school, and their experiences at home. With regard to the first factor, it seems unlikely that cross-national differences in academic achievement among Chinese, Japanese, and American children can
40 be accounted for by differences in general intelligence. There is no evidence that Chinese and Japanese children are more intelligent than American children.

According to Schoenfeld (1989), the way people engage in mathematical activities is shaped by their
45 conception of mathematics. There have been many studies that confirm that affective factors shape how students behave. For instance, perceived personal control (Lefcourt, 1982), and perceived usefulness of mathematics (Fennema & Sherman, 1978) are all posi-
50 tively correlated with achievement in mathematics (Schoenfeld, 1989). However, it is unclear if there is a cause-and-effect relationship between affective factors and achievement in mathematics. It is interesting to note that Schoenfeld (1989) found that the strongest
55 correlation was between mathematical performance and perceived mathematical ability.

Children's academic achievement is given a more central role in some cultures than in others. In developing countries such as Taiwan, personal advancement is
60 closely linked to academic achievement, and there is great emphasis on education. In Japan, where natural resources are limited, progress in technology and science is essential for the nation's economic health, and such progress is highly dependent on having a well-
65 educated work force. Other cultures have different goals. Some value experiences that stimulate children

to think and build up a broad fund of knowledge, regardless of whether such experiences result in higher school grades; others stress the importance of children developing a sense of self-worth. The goal of education in these societies is not only the acquisition of specific types of knowledge but also the development of children who feel good about themselves and their capabilities; self-confidence is believed to facilitate later learning. In other words, while some cultures value activities that help a child master prescribed skills, others, such as that in the United States, value experiences that will make a child more creative and confident (Stevenson, Lee, Chen, Stigler, Lee, Hsu, & Kitamura, 1990).

Chinese students must go through a series of rigorous entrance exams in order to get into a top university. Forty percent of Chinese students will make it to one of these universities. It is clear that these exams provide intense motivation for students in China to perform well. It would appear that the teachers in China put a great emphasis on teaching in preparation for these national exams. They do in fact do this, but they emphasize conceptual understanding and applications of math to the real world instead of just computations.

Reynolds and Walberg (1992) found that motivation and home environment have a strong indirect effect on achievement. They also found that motivation appeared to be a stronger indicator of mathematics attitude than home environment. This would suggest that the students are responsible for changing their attitude toward mathematics and that their home environment is less influential. However, this could be very difficult for students in the United States if they are consistently hearing that it is okay to not be good in mathematics.

American teachers spent twice as much time on educating students in language arts than they did on mathematics (Stevenson, Lee, & Stigler, 1986). Chinese teachers spent equal amounts of time on language arts and mathematics. Furthermore, teachers in the U.S. are allowed to organize their classrooms according to their own desires, not to a national standard (Stevenson, Lee, & Stigler, 1986). Also, Stevenson, Lee, and Stigler (1986, 1987) found that American teachers only spent about 22% of their time in the classroom imparting information, whereas Chinese teachers spent about 60% of classroom time imparting information. Chinese students spent 240 days a year in school, whereas American students only spent 178 days in school (Stevenson, Lee, & Stigler, 1986; 1987). Upon closer analysis of schools in China and the U.S., it has been found that students in Taiwan spend five-and-a-half days in school a week compared to only five days a week for American students. Further, children in Taiwan spend more time in the day studying mathematics than their American counterparts (Stigler, Lee, Lucker, & Stevenson, 1982; Stigler, Lee, & Stevenson, 1987).

There appear to be issues such as how teachers', parents', and society's attitudes and beliefs affect our

children. Research completed by Haladyna, Shaughnessy, and Shaughnessy (1983) found that there is a strong association between teacher quality measures and attitude toward mathematics. It is interesting to note that when teachers were asked what factors may influence students' performance in mathematics, 41% of American teachers believed that innate intelligence was more important than studying hard, which was just the opposite of Chinese teachers (Stigler, Chen, & Lee, 1993). It was also found that American mothers felt that success in school was attributed to ability and Chinese mothers felt that success was to due to effort. Stigler, Chen, and Lee (1993) found that even though Americans seem to be aware of the trouble that the American educational system is in, they still feel that the schools are doing a "good" or "excellent" job in educating their children. Parents have a high regard for their children's academic performance even though they continue to be outperformed by their Chinese counterparts.

In Taiwan, the Ministry of Education specifies the curriculum for all schools in great detail. The ministry publishes all textbooks; furthermore, every school in Taiwan uses the same textbooks (Stigler, Lee, & Stevenson, 1986). However, in the United States there is a great deal of variation among textbook series (Stigler, Lee, Lucker, & Stevenson, 1982). This is due to the fact that there is not a national curriculum in the United States. All the textbooks in both countries use a common international system of mathematical notation and Arabic numerals (Stigler, Lee, Lucker, & Stevenson, 1982). Stigler, Lee, Lucker, and Stevenson (1982) also found that the Taiwanese curriculum lagged behind the United States' curriculum when concepts and skills were introduced. Therefore, it does not appear as if only the curriculum in the United States should be blamed for American students' low scores in comparison to Chinese students.

In studies of parental evaluations of children's capabilities, the closer the match between parental evaluations and the child's ability, the better the developmental outcome (e.g., Miller, 1988). Parents whose views are realistic are more likely to adapt interactions with their child to a level appropriate to the child's abilities than are parents who overestimate or underestimate what their child is capable of doing. The same effect would be expected at the societal level: Members of some societies may generally be realistic in evaluating themselves and their children, and others may be biased and give excessively favorable or unfavorable ratings. Realistic evaluation should create a more positive environment for academic achievement (Stevenson, Lee, Chen, Stigler, Lee, Hsu, & Kitamura, 1990). Parents' perceptions of their child's capabilities are an important factor in their expectations for that child. For instance, the U.S. culture has a tendency to place a higher value on achievement in sports than in mathematics (Geary, 1996). The Asian culture, on the other hand, prioritizes mathematical learning. In fact, the elders of the culture believe that high achievement in mathematics is an important goal for the younger members of the culture (Geary, 1996). It is clear that education is highly valued in China. In fact, ongoing education is the norm.

Stevenson, Lee, Chen, Stigler, Lee, Hsu, and Kitamura (1990) stated that the degree to which parents, family, and other members of society become involved in children's development and education is likely to differ, depending on the society's conception of the individual in relation to these entities. Chinese and American children do have very different experiences at school. These differences in the cultural valuation of mathematics translate into differences in the investment of children, parents, and teachers in learning mathematics, and are likely to be the primary source of differences in mathematical ability between East Asian and U.S. children (Geary, 1996; Stevenson & Stigler, 1992). According to research by Hackett and Betz (1989), mathematics performance was significantly and positively correlated with attitudes toward mathematics. Stigler, Chen, and Lee concluded that the achievement gap is "unlikely to diminish until there are marked changes in the attitudes and beliefs of American parents and students about education" (Stigler, Chen, & Lee, 1993, p. 57).

Methodology

Participants

The study was conducted with fifth-grade children from Taipei, Taiwan, and Denver, Colorado. Taipei is a large modern city that is relatively comparable to Denver. The researcher selected one public elementary school from each city and surveyed one classroom from each school. The Taipei classroom had 37 students and the Denver classroom consisted of only 21 students as target subjects in the study.

The researcher chose elementary schoolchildren as the subjects for two reasons. First, the researcher wanted to know if cross-cultural differences in achievement emerged during these early years of schooling. If this proved to be the case, it would be difficult to account for cross-cultural differences in achievement primarily in terms of the educational practices of the schools. A second reason for focusing on elementary schoolchildren was to gain some understanding of the early antecedents of the large differences that appear later in middle and senior high school.

Instrument

A questionnaire containing 39 closed questions was developed by Alan Schoenfeld (1989) and was used with his permission in this study. All items were present in the form of a seven-point rating scale, ranging from 1 = "strongly agree" to 7 = "strongly disagree." The questionnaire contained questions related to students' perception of what mathematics is and how to do well in it, what mathematics solutions should be, how math problems can be solved, how mathematics is learned, and student motivation. The students rated each of the first 33 questions on a seven-point scale with one being strongly agree, four being neutral, and seven being strongly disagree. The last six questions were concerned with gender, grades, and perception of their parents' attitudes toward mathematics. The questionnaire was determined to be highly reliable with an alpha of 0.8468.

Procedure

In this study, the fifth-grade students were asked to answer the questionnaire. Due to the fact that the researcher was unable to go to Taipei to conduct the study, the teacher who is a friend of the researcher distributed the questionnaire at her convenience. However, the researcher was able to distribute the surveys in the Denver school. Typically, the questionnaire took only 10–15 minutes to complete.

Data Analysis

The form of the data collected contained the attitude measure from a Likert-type scale and personal information. The researcher compared the means of each question in the questionnaire and used a two-tailed t test to analyze the data. Then the researcher categorized some of the related questions to determine if there was a correlation between categories.

Result

Specific prior hypotheses were not developed because information from previous work was insufficient to allow confidence to be developed about the characteristic of each culture. Although it was not the researcher's purpose to evaluate the usefulness of the constructs that have emerged from this work explaining differences in achievement in the two cultures at issue, the researcher did use them to help organize some considerations. The researcher used a two-tailed t test to compare the mathematical perceptions between Chinese and American students. The means of each question in the questionnaire was also compared. Among the 33 items, 23 items were significantly different between American and Chinese students' answers: items 1, 3, 4, 5, 6, 7, 8, 12, 14, 15, 16, 18, 19, 20, 21, 22, 24, 25, 26, 28, 29, 31, and 33.

The following items were grouped into six categories, with the thought that some questions asked might have the same concept. Table 1 displays the six categories and the mean score of the items that were significantly different for the two cultures.

Discussion of Results

The researcher found marked differences in the beliefs of American and Taiwanese students in many of the areas under investigation. The data show significant differences in the means for the category of what mathematics is. It is interesting to note that the questions in this category suggest that mathematics are

Table 1
Six Categories: The Mean Score of the Items Shows Significant Differences in the Two Cultures

Number of category	Concept	Contained items
1	What mathematics is	1,* 2, 3,* 31*
2	How to do well in it	14,* 28*
3	What mathematics solutions should be	4,* 5,* 6,* 15*
4	How math problems can be solved	7,* 8,* 11, 12,* 13
5	How mathematics is learned	10, 27
6	Student motivation–negative	19,* 22*
	Student motivation–positive	20,* 23, 24*

$*p < .01$

mostly numbers. The Taiwanese students tended to disagree or feel neutral about these statements. However, the American children tended to agree with this perception of mathematics.

The second category of how to do well in mathematics also showed significant differences in the mean scores. The American students strongly agreed that memorization was the key to doing well in mathematics. If they could memorize all the formulas and how to do them, then they would do fine in the class, even if they did not understand what they were doing. It is hardly the most creative or logical of acts, but it also is a creative discipline in math where one can discover and learn to be logical. Their Taiwanese counterparts, on the other hand, were again more apt to disagree with this belief.

The category of what math solutions should be encompassed where there could be more than one right solution to a problem. Again a significant difference in the mean score was determined. American students believed the solution to be right answers. Taiwanese students' responses were more flexible. Taiwanese students strongly disagreed with the idea that in mathematics they are either right or wrong. However, the American students tended to strongly agree with this idea.

The category of how math problems can be solved and how mathematics is learned did not show significant differences in the two cultures. For the last category, the researcher broke up the category of motivation into two parts: negative motivation and positive motivation. There were significant differences between the two sub-categories for the two cultures. The negative motivation subcategory encompassed the idea of learning math because it was required or because of fear of punishment. The Taiwanese answers showed that they are affected by this negative motivation. They tended to agree with these statements. However, the American students strongly disagreed with these statements. Instead, the American students were more influenced by positive motivation such as wanting to do well in class or impress the teacher.

There were a few individual questions that were of interest to the researcher. Table 2 shows the mean score for each culture. There was a significant difference in the mean scores. American students believed that solving mathematics problems depended on knowing the rules. Mathematics was presumed to be more rule-bound. Taiwanese students tended to agree that good teaching practice in mathematics consisted of making sure students knew how to use the rules. On the other hand, students also thought that good teaching practice consisted of showing students lots of different ways to look at the same question. The researcher also found the reason Taiwanese students believed school math was useful in real life was that they might have been more preoccupied with learning itself rather than being concerned with self-perceptions.

What is interesting to note is that even though the Taiwanese students' perceptions of mathematics was overall more positive than their American counterparts, they seemed to be learning mathematics mainly because of the fear of punishment. This area should probably receive more attention in future research studies. Even though the Taiwanese students hinted that they learned mathematics for negative reasons, they did have a more positive perception of mathematics than their American counterparts. This is most likely due to the fact that their culture places such a high value on mathematics achievement and it in turn trickles down into the schools. The two cultures' perceptions of mathematics was clearly different, but the students did share some of the same beliefs regarding mathematics that take place inside class and mathematics that take place outside.

From past international studies of achievement, we know that Taiwan continues to outperform the United States in mathematics achievement. The researcher also found (Tsao, 2000) that there are marked differences in the attitudes and beliefs of the two cultures toward mathematics and in the students' attitudes and beliefs toward mathematics. This difference in mathematics achievement could be the effect of the Taiwanese's more positive perception of mathematics. Further, it appears that the negative attitude of the American cul-

Table 2

Question	Mean score USA	Mean score Taiwan	p value
Math is mostly facts and procedures that have to be memorized	2.3000	4.2432	0.000*
Math is just a way of thinking about space, numbers, and problems	2.2000	5.2222	0.000*
In mathematics, something is either right or wrong	1.6500	5.5833	0.000*
The best way to do well in math is to memorize all of the formulas	1.8500	4.2162	0.000*
I'll get in trouble if I don't try to learn math	4.2000	2.4324	0.003*
Different math courses cover unrelated topics	2.6500	4.8649	0.000*
Some people are good at math and some aren't	1.3500	2.9189	0.000*
When you get the wrong answer to a math problem, it is absolutely wrong—there's no room for argument	3.2105	5.1351	0.000*

*$p < .01$

ture could be one factor causing the low international achievement scores in mathematics.

These differences in the cultural valuation of mathematics translate into differences in the investment of children, parents, and teachers in learning mathematics, and are likely to be the primary source of the mathematical ability differences comparing East Asian and U.S. children (Geary, 1996). According to research by Hackett and Betz (1989), mathematics performance was significantly and positively correlated with attitudes toward mathematics. Stigler, Chen, and Lee (1993) concluded that the achievement gap is "unlikely to diminish until there are marked changes in the attitudes and beliefs of American parents and students about education" (p. 57).

There is still a great need for further investigation into the differences between the two cultures' perceptions of mathematics. In further studies, researchers should do a series of questionnaires and interviews of students from elementary school through college in order to pinpoint an age level or grade level at which students' attitudes and beliefs toward mathematics begin to change. Other studies should study the students' parents and teachers in order to get a better understanding of what their attitudes and beliefs are.

Limitations

The major limitation of this study is that they are convenience samples and small samples from each country. A larger number of samples would not only have resulted in more reliable and generalized conclusions about the effects of math perception between American and Taiwan students, but would also allow a more systematic study of the relationship between math perception and performance outcome in mathematics.

Educational Implications

The goal of education in these societies is not only the acquisition of specific types of knowledge, but also the development of children who feel good about themselves and their capabilities. Self-confidence is believed to facilitate later learning. In other words, while some cultures value activities that help a child master prescribed skills, others, such as those in the United States, value experiences that will make a child more creative and confident. The degree to which parents, family, and other members of society become involved in children's development and education is likely to differ, depending on the society's conception of the individual in relation to these entities. The firmness of boundaries separating individuals, families, and groups has important implications for children's development. In some cultures, such as that in the United States, the individual is deemed to be responsible for his or her accomplishments and difficulties; in others, such as the Chinese cultures, members of the family, teachers, or a larger group—such as pupils in the same classroom—are expected to assume some of the responsibility. As the interdependence among individuals increases, their mutual obligations to each other also increase. Individuals in such situations work hard not only to satisfy their own goals but also to meet the goals set by their families, and the success of the group is valued as highly as the success of particular individuals within the group.

The greater the cultural emphasis on effort, the more likely it is that parents and teachers will believe that they can be instrumental in aiding children in their academic achievement. This belief is transmitted to children, and they, too, come to believe that diligence will lead to success. If, however, adults believe that innate ability imposes critical limitations on children's progress in school, it seems unlikely that they would be motivated to make such strong efforts at assistance. Taiwan, like other countries influenced by the Confucian belief in human malleability, is among the cultures that place great weight on the possibility of advancement through effort.

It would be helpful if more studies that focus on af-

450 feetive issues would have stronger links to research on other topics related to the improvement of practice in mathematics education. Although little has been done to connect research on affective issues to these kinds of studies of cultural influences on mathematics learning, such connections should be able to link differences in

455 achievement to beliefs that are connected to cultural influences.

References

Fennema, E., & Sherman, J. (1978). Sex-related differences in mathematics achievement, spatial visualization, and affective factors. *American Educational Research Journal, 14.* 51–71.

Garden, R. A. (1987). The second IEA mathematics study. *Comparative Education Review, 31,* 47–68.

Geary, D. C., Salthouse, T. A., Chen, G., & Fan, L. (1996). Are East Asian versus American differences in arithmetical ability a recent phenomenon? *Developmental Psychology, 32,* 254–262.

Geary, D. C. (1996). Biology, culture, and cross-national differences in mathematical ability. In R. J. Sternberg & T. Ben-Zeev (Eds.), *The Nature of Mathematical Thinking* (pp. 145–171). Mahwah, NJ: Lawrence Erlbaum Associates, Publishers.

Hackett, G., & Betz, N. E. (1989). An exploration of the mathematics self-efficacy/mathematics performance correspondence. *Journal for Research in Mathematics Education, 20,* 261–273.

Haladyna, T., Shaughnessy, J., & Shaughnessy, J. M. (1983). A causal analysis of attitude toward mathematics. *Journal for Research in Mathematics Education, 14,* 19–29.

Lefcourt, H. M. (1982). *Locus of control.* Hillsdale, NJ: Erlbaum.

Miller, S. A. (1988). Parents' Beliefs about Children's Cognitive Development. *Child Development, 59,* 259–285.

Reynolds, A. J., & Walberg, H. J. (1992). A process model of mathematics achievement and attitude. *Journal for Research in Mathematics Education, 23,* 306–328.

Schoenfeld, A. H. (1989). Explorations of students' mathematical beliefs and behavior. *Journal for Research in Mathematics Education, 20,* 338–355.

Stevenson, H. W., Chen, C., & Lee, S. (1993). Mathematics achievement of Chinese, Japanese, and American children: Ten years later. *Science, 259,* 53–58.

Stevenson, H. W., Lee, S. Y., Chen, C., Stigler, J. W., Lee, S., Hsu, C. C., & Kitamura, S. (1990). Contexts of achievement: A study of American, Chinese, and Japanese children. *Monographs of the society for research in Children Development, 55.* (Serial No. 221.)

Stevenson, H. W., Lee, S., & Stigler, J. W. (1986). Mathematics achievement of Chinese, Japanese, and American children. *Science, 231,* 693–699.

Stigler, J. W., Lee, S., Lucker, G. W., & Stevenson, H. W. (1982). Curriculum and achievement in mathematics: A study of elementary school children in Japan, Taiwan, and the United States. *Journal of Educational Psychology, 74,* 315–322.

Stigler, J. W., Lee, S., & Stevenson, H. W. (1987). Mathematics classrooms in Japan, Taiwan, and the United States. *Child Development, 56,* 1272–1285.

Tsao, Y. L. (2000). *Do the attitudes and beliefs of a culture have an effect on students' performance in mathematics?* Unpublished manuscript. University of Northern Colorado.

Address correspondence to: Dr. Yea-Ling Tsao, Math Computer Science Education Department, Taipei Municipal Teachers College, No. 1, Ai-Guo West Road, Taipei, 100, Taiwan. E-mail: tsaoyealing@hotmail.com

Exercise for Article 24

Factual Questions

1. According to the literature review, American teachers spend about 22% of their time imparting information. What is the corresponding percentage for Chinese teachers?

2. How many children from Denver participated in this study?

3. On the seven-point rating scale used in this study, what does a "7" stand for?

4. Did the USA sample *or* the Taiwan sample have a higher mean score on "Math is mostly facts and procedures that have to be memorized"?

5. What was the mean score of the Taiwan sample on "The best way to do well in math is to memorize all of the formulas"?

6. Are all the differences between means in Table 2 statistically significant at the $p < .01$ level?

Questions for Discussion

7. How desirable would it be in a future study of this type to use students from more than two cities? Explain.

8. Do you think that this study identifies *causes* of the differences in mathematics achievement between American and Chinese students? Explain.

9. The researcher discusses a major limitation of this study in lines 399–406. Do you agree? In your opinion, is the limitation serious enough to affect the validity of the results of this study? Explain.

10. If you were conducting a study on the same topic, what changes, if any, would you make in the research methodology?

Quality Ratings

Directions: Indicate your level of agreement with each of the following statements by circling a number from 5 for strongly agree (SA) to 1 for strongly disagree (SD). If you believe an item is not applicable to this research article, leave it blank. Be prepared to explain your ratings. When responding to criteria A and B below, keep in mind that brief titles and abstracts are conventional in published research.

A. The title of the article is appropriate.

　　　　SA 5 4 3 2 1 SD

B. The abstract provides an effective overview of the research article.

　　　　SA 5 4 3 2 1 SD

C. The introduction establishes the importance of the study.

　　　　SA 5 4 3 2 1 SD

D. The literature review establishes the context for the study.

        SA   5   4   3   2   1   SD

E. The research purpose, question, or hypothesis is clearly stated.

        SA   5   4   3   2   1   SD

F. The method of sampling is sound.

        SA   5   4   3   2   1   SD

G. Relevant demographics (for example, age, gender, and ethnicity) are described.

        SA   5   4   3   2   1   SD

H. Measurement procedures are adequate.

        SA   5   4   3   2   1   SD

I. All procedures have been described in sufficient detail to permit a replication of the study.

        SA   5   4   3   2   1   SD

J. The participants have been adequately protected from potential harm.

        SA   5   4   3   2   1   SD

K. The results are clearly described.

        SA   5   4   3   2   1   SD

L. The discussion/conclusion is appropriate.

        SA   5   4   3   2   1   SD

M. Despite any flaws, the report is worthy of publication.

        SA   5   4   3   2   1   SD

Article 25

Learning to Love Reading:
Interviews with Older Children and Teens

LINDA TERAN STROMMEN
Educational Consultant

BARBARA FOWLES MATES
Long Island University

ABSTRACT. Students in sixth and ninth grades were surveyed to determine attitudes toward reading and identify factors associated with the development of a love of reading.

From *Journal of Adolescent & Adult Literacy*, 48, 188–200.

Certainly, learning to read is valued by many cultures, and the ability to read is regarded as the most fundamental goal of education. However, though most children in the United States do learn to read, many
5 leave school unable to read beyond the most basic functional level. The degree to which schools are effective purveyors of reading education and the methods used to teach reading has become the subject of controversy. However, factors that foster a child's love of
10 reading have, for the most part, been left out of the debate.

Many studies of the early stages of reading acquisition have shown that the home environment and support from a parent or other adult may be essential to
15 encouraging literacy development (Adoni, 1995; Bissex, 1980; Bloom, 1970, 1973; Cambourne, 1995; Clark, 1984; Durkin, 1966; Fader, 1983; Forester, 1986; Hall & Moats, 2000; Harste, Burke, & Woodward, 1982; Morrow, 1983; Neuman, 1980, 1986; Tay-
20 lor, 1983; Teale, 1984; Yaden, 1986). Although such studies largely focused on the acquisition of reading skills, more recently McKenna, Kear, and Ellsworth (1995) surveyed children's attitudes toward reading and concluded that children's views of recreational and
25 academic reading are tied to reading ability as well as to community norms and beliefs. Their work documented a change in children's attitudes toward reading that typically evolves from enthusiasm to comparative indifference by the end of the elementary school years.
30 A meta-analysis of research on reading (National Institute of Child Health and Human Development, 2000) listed no recent studies that address the love of reading or its relation to reading achievement.

The preponderance of research findings suggest
35 that few children, skilled readers or not, choose to de-

vote their leisure time to reading. Surveys of schoolchildren's reading practices (Anderson, Hiebert, Scott, & Wilkinson, 1985; Anderson, Wilson, & Fielding, 1988; Himmelweit & Swift, 1976; Lyness, 1952;
40 Moffitt & Wartella, 1992; Neuman, 1980, 1986, 1995) have shown that young people across all age groups devote very little time to recreational reading, and this has been true since the 1940s. While studies that survey the reading practices, leisure time use, and aca-
45 demic achievement of older children and teens (Anderson et al., 1988; Greaney & Hegarty, 1987; Greaney & Neuman, 1983; Lewis & Teale, 1980; Long & Henderson, 1973; Neuman, 1981, 1986, 1995) revealed patterns of behavior and suggested that children's percep-
50 tions about reading influenced this behavior (Neuman, 1995), they did not explain the genesis of attitudes about reading. Teens spend even less time reading than younger children (Moje, Young, Readence, & Moore, 2000), despite the fact that they also spend less time
55 watching television. Kubey and Csikzentmihalyi (1990) reported that "the average American teenager watches more than 21 hours of TV each week but devotes only 5.6 hours a week to homework and a mere 1.8 hours to pleasure reading" (p. 24). Nevertheless,
60 several investigators (Greaney, 1980; Neuman, 1986, 1995; Searls, Mead, & Ward, 1985) have failed to find a significant relationship between time spent reading and time spent watching television for any age group.

Nell's research into the psychology of reading for
65 pleasure (1988) documented factors that contribute to a book's readability and made a significant contribution to our understanding of how reading can be emotionally satisfying. Additionally, Moore, Bean, Birdyshaw, and Rycik (1999) posited that "vicariously stepping
70 into text worlds can nourish teens' emotions and psyches as well as their intellects" (p. 102). However, little in the research literature on reading addresses the factors that lead some young people to embrace the satisfactions afforded by recreational reading. This is true
75 despite the fact that a recent position paper on teen literacy (Moore et al., 1999) noted that a desire to read is an important cornerstone of adolescents' literacy achievement.

Smith (1988) has argued that we learn to read, and become literate in the process, simply by reading. In *The Power of Reading* (1993), Krashen explored research findings that supported Smith's idea and the role reading for pleasure plays in a child's literacy development. Krashen stated that

the relationship between reported free voluntary reading and literacy development is not always large, but it is remarkably consistent. Nearly every study that has examined this relationship has found a correlation, and it is present even when different tests, different methods of probing reading habits, and different definitions of free reading are used. (p. 7)

Krashen concluded that children who frequently read for pleasure

will become adequate readers, acquire a large vocabulary, develop the ability to understand and use complex grammatical constructions, develop a good writing style, and become good (but not necessarily perfect) spellers. Although free voluntary reading alone will not ensure attainment of the highest levels of literacy, it will at least ensure an acceptable level. (p. 84)

Those who do not develop the habit of reading for pleasure may have "a very difficult time reading and writing at a level high enough to deal with the demands of today's world" (p. x). With this view in mind, we sought to determine factors that contribute to and support a child's learning to love to read.

Procedure

We wished to identify older children and teens for whom reading extended texts is a significant, pleasurable, recreational activity and consistent part of daily life, hereafter identified as *Readers*, as well as a comparable group who seldom or never choose to read for pleasure, hereafter called *Not-readers*. (We chose this term rather than *Nonreaders* in order to avoid the inaccurate implication that children and teens in this group lack reading skills.) To make these identifications, we designed, pilot-tested, and distributed questionnaires to a cross-section of sixth-grade students attending a suburban middle school outside a large northeastern U.S. city and to ninth-grade students in the same school district. The questionnaire was administered by classroom teachers who followed a specific set of instructions we provided.

The students who completed the questionnaire represented the available spectrum of academic achievement, including remedial and honors students. The participants were heterogeneously grouped sixth-grade students in four core (English/social studies) classes (*n* = 65), and ninth-grade students in five homogeneously grouped English classes (*n* = 86), including one remedial and one honors group. A total of 151 students responded to the written questionnaire. A numerical identification system was used to protect the anonymity of all students. The language spoken at home, reading ability, and level of academic achievement were not controlled.

The questionnaire—presented as a survey of leisure time use by students—included, in addition to basic demographic information, a broad range of questions in the following categories:

1. Activities engaged in outside of school (students were asked to estimate time per day spent at activities such as sports, music lessons, leisure activities, media use, reading for pleasure, homework, and chores).
2. Self-perceptions and attitudes (likes and dislikes, self-description).
3. Reading practices and materials (novels, informational books, magazines; reading compared with other leisure activities; reading practices of family members and friends; availability of reading materials in the home).

We included this broad range of items to mask our specific objective and to help us place reading activities in the context of students' lives.

Embedded within the 10-page questionnaire was a seven-item Literacy Index, which was designed to identify both Readers and Not-readers. On the basis of interviews conducted as part of a pilot study, we had concluded that time spent reading books was a more reliable indicator of a love of reading than time spent reading shorter print texts. The content and scoring for these items is indicated in Table 1.

The questionnaire yielded only a small number of Readers whose answers to the index questions clearly distinguished them from the rest of the respondents. Four sixth-grade students and eight ninth-grade students (12 students in all out of a total of 151, or approximately 8% of the students) met all of the criteria as listed in Table 1 and were identified as Readers. It should be emphasized that we sought to identify those young people who read extended texts as a form of enjoyable recreation, not those characterized by excellent reading skills alone.

Of the sixth-grade Readers, three were female and one was male. One sixth-grade Reader participated in a special remedial reading program. Of the ninth-grade Readers, two were male and six were female. One ninth-grade Reader was designated as having a learning disability and two ninth-grade Readers were honors students.

The greatest number of students surveyed at both grade levels fell into our Not-reader category. Not-readers were also distributed across remedial, general, and honors classes. A small number of students gave one or two answers on the index that fell into the Reader category, but because they otherwise most resembled Not-readers they were grouped with the latter. Our primary intention was to identify a group of young people who clearly loved to read.

Table 1
Literacy Index Items

	Reader response	Not-reader response
1. I enjoy reading a good book.	Selected this item	Did not select this item
2. Favorite leisure activity.	Named reading	Named other activities
3. Books read in past three years.	20 or more	0–5
4. Novels read in past year.	Several (not school assigned)	None
5. I prefer to read.	Selected this item	Did not select item
6. Time spent reading for pleasure on a typical weekday.	30 minutes or more	No time spent
7. Describe a "perfect" day.	Included a period of reading	No reading

190   It is interesting to note that reading skill and academic achievement (as characterized by students in subsequent interviews) were not definitive factors in distinguishing Readers from Not-readers. Several Not-readers were honors students, while a few Readers 195 claimed to struggle with reading and writing assignments.

In response to items on the questionnaire, all of the students in both groups indicated that literacy materials, such as newspapers and reference books, were 200 available in their homes. Many students had computers at home, and all had access to computers in school. There were no notable differences in students' reported television viewing habits, with Readers and Not-readers alike reporting three to four hours of television 205 viewing per day (though most said the TV was often "just on" while they pursued other activities, such as completing homework, looking at magazines, or chatting online with friends). In addition, there was no noteworthy difference in the nature and number of ex-210 tracurricular activities, such as music lessons, sports, clubs, or time spent with friends. Readers did not prove to be less social or less occupied with activities than Not-readers, though general studies ninth-grade Not-readers did report being less involved in organized ac-215 tivities than their classmates.

The questionnaire proved to have validity as a tool for identifying Readers and Not-readers. In all cases, students who were later interviewed confirmed their preliminary classification as Reader or Not-reader. 220 Each readily agreed with our characterization of them as either a person who enjoys reading and does so often or as one who does not enjoy reading and never reads books for recreation.

All students identified as Readers and an equal 225 number of Not-readers were invited by letter to meet with one of the principal investigators for a one-on-one interview that focused on their leisure-time reading practices. Interviews were approved by parents and arranged by a school staff member. These took place at 230 the schools during the student's free period.

Because of scheduling difficulties, only five of the eight ninth-grade students identified as Readers could be interviewed. All four of the sixth-grade Readers were interviewed. Four sixth-grade Not-readers and five ninth-grade Not-readers were selected who, insofar 235 as possible, matched the Readers in terms of gender and academic tracking. We had anticipated some reluctance on the part of Not-readers to be characterized as such, but this did not occur.

Interviews were informal, following a protocol of 240 guided, open-ended questions. The interview questions were derived from the following research questions:

1. Are there consistent attributes of the social environment of Readers that appear to maintain reading activity? 245

2. Are there consistent early childhood and ongoing experiences that promote interest in reading?

3. Do students who identify themselves as Readers display similar ideas and attitudes about the appeal of reading? 250

4. Are these ideas and attitudes different from those of Not-readers?

All interviews were audiotaped, with the permission of the student, and transcribed in full by the interviewer. A sample of interview questions is listed in Table 2. 255

Findings

The methods we used to examine the interview data were determined by the size of the sample and the intensive nature of this research. The two investigators independently studied each recorded interview to 260 search for important features that recurred in interviews with Readers and were largely absent from those of Not-readers. The identified features were extensively discussed and clarified. The resulting list of features was then used to reexamine each interview protocol to 265 ensure that it was broadly characteristic of Readers alone. At this time, we chose examples that typified each feature among Readers as well as examples from Not-readers to help illustrate our findings.

The clear differences between Readers and Not-270 readers that were indicated in the survey data were confirmed under the closer scrutiny of one-on-one interviews. When we analyzed the interviews in light of our research questions, several significant themes emerged. Profiles of individuals who were classified as Readers 275 or Not-readers revealed unique features of each student's experiences, but also a number of clear common threads within each of the two groups. We found the

Table 2
Sample Interview Questions

Questions for Readers	Questions for Not-readers
Your responses to the questionnaire show that you enjoy reading. Do you agree? Why do you like to read?	Your responses to the questionnaire show that you dislike reading. Do you agree? Why don't you enjoy reading?
How do you decide what to read?	Do you ever feel like reading a book or magazine article? Internet info or chat? Why?
Where do you get the things you read?	What things to read are in your home?
Do you ever talk about things you read with family or friends?	Do other family members talk about things they read?
If your friends told you about a great story that was available on film and book, would you see the movie or read the book? Why?	Same as for Readers. Also: If your friends told you about a great book, would you give it a try?
What is it about reading that makes you want to spend time reading?	What is it about reading that makes you not want to read?
Is there anything that your parents did that contributed to your enjoyment of reading? What?	Is there any experience that you remember that may have contributed to your dislike of reading? What?
Do you remember any of the first books read to you? Which were your favorites?	Same as for Readers.
Do you think your parents like to read? What makes you think they do or don't?	Same as for Readers.
Do you think it's important to be a reader? Why?	Same as for Readers.
Do your friends (or a best friend) enjoy reading? Why do you think they do or do not?	Same as for Readers.
Do you think people need to be able to read well? Why?	Same as for Readers.

following commonalities to hold across the age groups. All student names are pseudonyms.

280 *Readers regularly interact around books with other members of their social circle who love to read.* All the Readers interviewed reported discussing what they read with other interested readers. These conversations, which regularly took place between the Reader and a 285 family member or close friend, were characterized by Readers as simply "what we do." Discussions about books allow young people to draw upon the reading experiences of other members of their social circle and to see reading as part of their social life.

290 Mark, a ninth-grader, was typical of the Readers interviewed. Mark recalled that when he was quite young, his mother would readily drop everything to read to him at his request. Now that he is a teen, this interaction has evolved. He and his mother and 295 younger sister, who is also an avid reader, recommend books to one another and discuss them later. Mark commented that his mother "put me on to Agatha Christie. She also reads the books I'm reading. It gets annoying sometimes. I'll put a bookmark in and come 300 back 10 minutes later and my mom'll be reading it."

All three share a love of Agatha Christie mysteries, which they swap and discuss. Mark laughingly remarked that he and his sister "use books as a threat, like 'if you don't take your plate off the table, I'll tell 305 you who did it!'—because they're usually murder mysteries—so both of us have to put our dishes in the dishwasher."

Recounting stories or talking about character and plot with another enthusiastic reader was an important 310 element of Readers' experiences. Anne, a ninth-grade Reader, described how stories from books enhanced her interest in reading and also provided her with material to share with friends and family:

> We tell each other stories [from books]. I read books and 315 then tell her [her mother], and she reads my books. She tells me stories of her books and I read hers. So we go back and forth. Sometimes, I share stories with my friends. If it has to do with a topic we're talking about, I'll bring up the book that I read and tell them the situa- 320 tion.

Though Readers extended this interaction to their peers, the pattern was always established within the family. Ken, a sixth-grade Reader, said he is most likely to talk about books with his dad, who recom- 325 mends action and mystery books, and with his two best friends. Ken told the interviewer,

> I mean, we don't set aside time to book chat like on Oprah. But we'll talk about books, and we'll see if there's anything that none of us have read before and if 330 it's just the same old. And we'll talk about mysteries where the person you least expect, like the old granny, is the one who did it.

Nicole, a ninth-grade Reader, explained how her cousins conveyed their love of reading to her and thus 335 played a role in building her own interest:

My older cousins told me about books. They'd tell me these great stories and say, "try reading this and you'll find the more detailed story." In elementary school my cousins would tell me about other novels they had read when they were my age. Also, I have some cousins who are my age and they're big readers…. They would tell me about this book and I would try to find it and read it.

Readers learned from family or other members of their social circle that reading can be an entertaining, diverting, enjoyable, sociable, and therefore worthwhile activity. Anne, a ninth-grade Reader, said that her mother's love of reading

encouraged me because also it seemed fun. She liked the books that she read, she would tell me about them, and it seemed interesting. I was just like, "Why is reading a book so much fun?" So I decide to try it, and it is fun.

Peer-group approval was not a big issue with Readers, even in adolescence. Most Readers had many friends who did not choose to read for pleasure. None were judgmental about this, but most believed that by choosing not to read their friends were missing out on a good thing.

In contrast to Readers, Not-readers' family reading experiences were more variable, did not continue beyond early childhood, and did not evolve to include discussions about the characters or events in books. The older sibling of one Not-reader had suggested books for her to read but had not done so regularly. Several Not-readers mentioned that their parents said they should read more because reading would make them smarter. Jessica, a ninth-grade Not-reader, said that talking about books was "not really a big part" of family discussions, which tended to be "about current events but not about books."

This lack of family discussions about books may account for our finding that over half of our Not-reader subjects claimed to have enjoyed reading until between 9 and 11 years of age. At this point, they told us they lost interest in childhood favorites and found no alternative reading material that appealed to them. Mary, a sixth-grade Not-reader, told the interviewer, "I read Goosebumps every night. Maybe I gave up reading because I phased out of the Goosebumps books." Jake, a ninth-grade Not-reader, commented, "I had a time— like when I was 8 or 9—when I liked Ramona Quimby and the Beverly Cleary books that I could read. And that stopped when I was about 10." Apparently, these students did not have the support of a family member who enjoyed reading to suggest and share appropriate books.

Readers see being an active member of a community of readers as an important part of their identity. An important attribute of each Reader's environment is that it includes others who read for pleasure. Mark, a ninth-grade Reader, said, "I was surrounded with it. There were always books lying around the house. They [his parents] were always reading." Both parents of

Ken (a ninth-grade Reader) are also avid readers who, according to Ken, read the newspaper "cover to cover, each day" and, by his estimate, several books a week. Ken, who sees himself as a Reader in a family of avid readers, gave this description:

It's part of my life, because that's what I do. Like, I'll go out in my tree house and I'll stay and read books like jungle and mystery and secret agent books. There's a rule in the house that I have to read a book a week, but I usually read three books a week. In the summer I have a lot of things going on, but I'll usually read a book a day.

Brian, a ninth-grade Reader who was designated as having a learning disability by his school, said he did not begin reading until he was 8 or 9. Nevertheless, Brian thinks of himself as a reading member of a reading family:

They're teachers. They just love to read. They read everything. Everyone in my house reads. Not just one person reads. Everyone. When I was smaller there was one time when everyone had to read. It was like "Reading Time!" Now I do it even at school in my free time.

Not-readers, in contrast, did not see recreational reading as an important part of their families' lives. They described parents and siblings as occasional readers who might read magazines, newspapers, and work-related material, or as people who do not enjoy reading at all. They said their parents were "too busy" to read or were involved in other activities. They did not see being a reader as an important aspect of their own identity or the identity of family members.

Parents or other family members of Readers explicitly prioritize reading as a recreational activity. Readers see reading as an activity that plays a significant and enjoyable role in the life of one or more family members or friends. Nicole, a ninth-grade Reader, recalled,

My mother likes to read these big books in Korean. When they [her parents] have free time they read, usually a few times a week. Sometimes at night I'll see the light on and they're usually reading. My mother and grandmother read books to me when I was little and taught me to read by reading to me and with me. They consider it very important. When I was young they would always say to read more. "Don't watch TV, read!" They do that with my sisters now.

Not-readers had different experiences. Several of them mentioned that a parent occasionally told them that they should read more in order to do well in school or become smarter. But Not-readers believed their parents did not see reading as a priority for themselves or for the family.

Jessica, a ninth-grade Not-reader, offered an account that differed somewhat from other Not-readers. She mentioned that her parents

read current events, and also my mother went back to school about five years ago and is starting her own practice so she's reading a lot of psychotherapy books. And my father reads a lot of fiction and nonfiction books. I guess they read mostly every day.

But, when asked if her parents encouraged her to spend time reading, Jessica said, "When I was younger they tried to get me to read; my uncle would bring me books. It's just not something I have motivation to do. My parents never really thought it was that important, basically."

Readers have access to plentiful, varied reading materials. As our survey indicated, and the interviews confirmed, basic reading materials were available at home to all of the young people with whom we met. For Readers, however, interest in reading was sustained by an involved parent or other family member who continued to provide access to a variety of books as the child matured and to guide the child's choices. For Not-readers, this type of support was far less evident, especially once the child entered school.

Stephanie, a sixth-grade Reader, told the interviewer,

> I own a lot of books. Actually, my mother and sister and my sister's friends [and I] are starting a mother–daughter book club. I thought I would announce at the first meeting that I would start a sort of library because I have so many books—at least a hundred. I have four boxes in the attic, and a whole shelf in our playroom.

Not-readers had vague memories of engaging with books during playtime or at bedtime. Only four Not-readers interviewed recalled owning books as a child. Asked if she had her own books, Jessica, a ninth-grade Not-reader, stated, "I have books in my room that have been given to me and have not been read."

Readers recalled frequent visits to a public library or bookseller, and most told us this activity continued to the present. Corinne, a ninth-grade Reader, described her experience:

> Yes, we went to the library very often. I still go often. Once every two weeks or so. I walked to the library as soon as I was old enough to go by myself. I was in a reading club on the weekend. There was story time, then a book club. You would tell about your book, then we had pizza.

Those Not-readers who recalled being taken to the library said that this practice ended, along with being read to by a parent, once they entered school, or that trips to the library were made infrequently and only for the purpose of obtaining a book for a school assignment. Samantha, a ninth-grade Not-reader, spoke of occasionally visiting a local bookseller: "I'll go with a friend and sit there and read. But I don't buy the books because I'll never get a chance to read them."

Readers love reading. Readers had vivid and fond memories of their early encounters with books and talked with great enthusiasm about specific books read to them when they were very young. Brian, a ninth-grade Reader, told the interviewer,

> There was one, I don't remember what it was called, about some boy, and he was afraid of his basement. He thought that these goblin guys were in his basement and he beat them with a broom and they got smaller and smaller at the end. I read that constantly. I still have all of my books.

Corinne, a ninth-grade Reader, recalled,

> *The Giving Tree.* I remember it's about how much a little boy uses the tree and as he gets older he uses it more and more and they have kind of a relationship. It was so sad for the tree, so upsetting. The boy is so selfish. He gives nothing back to the tree. But the tree is happy.

Readers told of having established a reading ritual (usually the bedtime story) that had never really ended. In fact, they could not imagine a day when they would not read, if only for a short while, before turning out the lights at night. Mark, a ninth-grade Reader, commented, "I like reading so much. I can't picture myself without it."

The Readers we interviewed said they love to read because reading stimulates their imagination; takes them to new places; and introduces them to new ideas, events, and elements of human emotion. Several also said that books give them a wealth of detail not available through television and film and told how they imagine a setting or the intensity of emotion in their mind's eye, something they cannot do when watching television or a movie. Brian, a ninth-grade Reader, commented,

> It's always fun to read. You're just sitting there and there's this whole other world waiting. You're reading something and the whole world stops when you close the book. And when you open it up again—okay—let's turn it back on again. It's weird when you think about it.

Anne, a sixth-grade Reader, said, "You can read and no one tells you how the picture should be. It's just your mind that's going with the words and it can be any picture you want it to be...you're making your own little story." Ken, a sixth-grade Reader, reflected,

> It takes me to places that I always wanted to be. Like, I read detective books and I feel like I'm the person trying to solve the case. Or, say I want to go to some undiscovered planet but I'm stuck in my house, I'll just read the book. I like the fact that you can be a totally different person and that you can have different abilities. It's almost like a game. In books you have the ability to see the future, or fly. On TV you don't use your imagination. It's like the TV is your imagination. In books you can determine the setting and the atmosphere of the story. Say it's a dark street. In your imagination you can have a street with dumpsters, say people on the side, dogs and garbage, and you can really get into it more and that makes the story more exciting.

Readers prefer reading to other sources of information or entertainment because they feel reading provides greater depth of understanding, more details, more insights on character, and an understanding of interpersonal relationships, as well as a basis for empa-

565 thy. Nicole, a ninth-grade Reader, commented, "Sometimes it relates to my life too, because you read about
someone who has similar problems, and other times
you just realize about other people's problems."

Readers also like the portability and companion-
570 ability of books and enjoy choosing what, when, and
where to read. Most carried a book when traveling.
With a book at hand, they knew they would never be
bored. As Mark, a ninth-grade Reader, noted, "A book
is good company." Ken, a sixth-grade Reader, de-
575 scribed the pleasure of choosing a book to read, as well
as the place to read it, in keeping with the mood created by the weather.

> Today it's nice out. I'd probably want to read a Hardy
> Boys or this book called *The Prodigal Spy*. And well, on
580 > rainy days, or just an ordinary day, I'll sit and read my
> textbook or books about early explorers and ancient civi-
> lizations.

Stephanie, a sixth-grade Reader, smiled as she said,
"You can sink into a book…or on a rainy day you can
585 always sit and read. You can have dreams about it. I
dream I'm the character. You can put aside your problems. It's another world."

Not-readers had no comparable feelings to relate.
Most recalled other activities more vividly and talked
590 about playing outside, involvement with sports, and
time spent "hanging out" with friends. However, Not-
readers, particularly those who are high-achieving,
spoke of the value of reading, an activity they see as
virtuous and admirable. In contrast, only one of the
595 Readers mentioned this self-improvement aspect of
reading: Corinne, a ninth-grade Reader, told the interviewer, "It's easier for me to understand things when
they're written down because I've read so many books.
And it's easier to write because I know how authors
600 place their words." Brian, a ninth-grade Reader, appeared at first to share this utilitarian view, but then his
thoughts took quite a different direction:

> You learn a lot from reading. Like, there's some reading
> you should do. Some people are better off without read-
605 > ing. They don't understand where the writer is coming
> from. If I've got a book to read, I want to know about the
> author. People just see things for what they are. A lot of
> people don't care for the emotional stuff and don't like
> reading and say it's a waste of time. It's a waste of time
610 > because they don't understand. It's like the arts—you
> have to be into it to understand. You have to be into the
> themes.

*School is not the critical factor, though a teacher's
enthusiasm might be.* Even though our interviews took
615 place in a school setting, the subject of school played a
minor role in all of our conversations. All of the Readers interviewed clearly connected a love of reading
with experiences provided outside of school.

None of the students interviewed mentioned read-
620 ing instruction or reading skill as something that supported their enjoyment of reading, though one Not-
reader told us that poor reading ability contributed to

his dislike of reading. Another Not-reader recalled enjoying some of the books assigned in school when he
625 was younger (through fourth grade) but could not remember even being interested enough to complete a
single assigned book since that time. In fact, only two
Readers said they truly enjoyed reading the novels assigned for classes or their textbooks. Readers tended to
630 see assigned reading as something to be accomplished
quickly in order to make time for books of their own
choice.

Samantha, a ninth-grade Not-reader, offered some
insight into an aspect of the school reading experience
635 that may diminish the pleasure of reading:

> I just don't enjoy reading books and textbooks. I mean
> they're easier to read than primary documents and it's
> better than learning from the activities we do, but I don't
> enjoy reading them. It's become a chore. It's just not
640 > pleasurable. It's so fact filled and you have to know eve-
> rything—knowing that I have to know everything for a
> test….

Readers and Not-readers in all classes told us they
scan assigned material to locate answers to questions
645 posed by teachers rather than read assignments in full.

When asked what teachers had done to contribute
to their enjoyment of reading, several Readers recalled
early grade-school teachers who invited students to
borrow books from classroom libraries or suggested
650 particular books. Brian, a ninth-grade Reader, told of a
teacher who spoke about books with real passion:

> There's a teacher who's getting a lot of people to read.
> Not me. I'm already into books, but a lot of people in our
> grade. It's like her one goal in life is to make everyone
655 > enjoy and love reading. She gets so into it. She loves it.

Though our survey did not support Brian's impression that his teacher's passion for reading had per-
suaded "a lot of people to read," this particular teacher
and a few others were praised by Readers because they
660 demonstrated an enthusiasm for books, had "lots of
books" in their classrooms, let students borrow books,
and read aloud in class frequently.

Readers read (no matter what). Readers said that
they read books for pleasure every day, or nearly every
665 day, no matter how busy they are. Several of the Not-
readers we interviewed expressed open admiration for
their friends who are voracious readers, claiming to be
baffled by how these students find the time to read
books of their choice given the pressure of school as-
670 signments and after-school activities. Over half the
Not-readers said they were "too busy" to read for
pleasure. However, all of the Readers saw distractions
from schoolwork and other activities as a nonissue.
Though some said they did not have as much time to
675 read as they would like, all Readers made time for
reading because it was enjoyable to them. Because our
original survey questions did not reveal any significant
differences in reported involvement in other activities
between Readers and Not-readers, it does not appear

680 that the demands of school assignments and activities dictate the choices young people make about reading. Rather, attitudes about reading determine these choices.

685 Readers told of reading a great variety of written material as well as almost any available print, including advertising on cereal boxes, even labels and the like. Ken, a sixth-grade Reader, commented,

> Usually, I'm late for school 'cause I'll be reading. Like, when my dad's reading the newspaper I'll usually take a
690 > section from him and start reading that. And I'll read pamphlets that my mom has, and I'll read tags on my shirt and stuff.

In contrast, Not-readers told us reading was too "tedious," "slow," or "boring" to engage their interest.
695 All but one of the Not-readers told us they do not enjoy reading novels because written material is too detailed and takes too long to get to the point, or because they do not understand what the author is trying to convey. Not-readers described reading in terms of purpose
700 rather than pleasure. They saw reading as a means to improve vocabulary or to access information (if not available from another source), and to manage one's affairs (for example, to fill out a job application). But, given the choice, all Not-readers would see the movie
705 rather than read the book. In fact, Not-readers, even those whose reading skills were excellent, avoid reading whenever possible.

All but two of the Not-readers interviewed told us they valued reading and cited not having sufficient
710 time as the principal reason for not engaging in reading as a recreational activity. Samantha, a ninth-grade Not-reader, told the interviewer, "I never feel I have enough time to read…if I had more time I would just read. Definitely." When asked what occupied her time,
715 Samantha replied that drawing takes up her time, and "flipping through magazines because I'm interested in fashion design." Clearly, Samantha and other Not-readers choose to fill leisure time with activities other than reading.

720 Like many Not-readers, Samantha told us she believed that peers who include recreational reading in their daily schedules read at a fast rate and therefore require less time for reading. This notion was commonly held by Not-readers although Nell's (1988)
725 work (which shows that reading for pleasure most often proceeds at an unhurried pace) did not support this assumption. Readers, however, saw reading as intrinsically worthwhile and something they "always" find time for.

What It Takes to Become a Reader

730 Although this research involves close study of a relatively small group of older children and teens, the profiles of Readers in our survey clearly indicate that becoming a Reader is not a simple matter of attaining fluency. The Readers we interviewed believed that
735 reading was a worthwhile way to spend leisure time

because it was pleasurable. Not-readers were of the opinion that reading was boring, tedious, and a waste of their time.

Our study suggests that when parents establish a
740 routine of reading to their young children, they foster an early interest in books that can be maintained if a variety of books is made available as children mature and their interests change. Easy access to the books that a particular Reader finds enjoyable enables reading
745 to continue as an attractive alternative to other activities for young people. All but one of the Readers in our study acknowledged that family or friends shared books or bought books for them or that visits to the library were a frequent family activity that continued to
750 be supported as they grew older. In addition, parents (or other close family members) who read for recreation provide a model for the children to emulate. Parents who schedule a time for family reading activities clearly demonstrate reading is a priority.

755 The ongoing dialogue about books that takes place between parents and children seems to have a particularly important role in the development of a child's love of reading. Discussions about books among family members demonstrate the pleasure that books inspire,
760 spark a Reader's interest, help Readers to make reading selections, and make it possible for Readers to become participants in an activity that their immediate social circle, and the wider culture, values and esteems. Adults who encourage such activity send a powerful
765 message about the pleasures of reading. This may be key to developing the perception of oneself as a Reader. In addition, because these informal conversations about books are congenial, they bring a social, refreshing, and renewing component to the reading
770 experience. Readers learn, through social interaction with other Readers, that reading is entertaining and stimulating.

Implications

If it is true, as previous research seems to indicate, that by reading for pleasure young people can attain
775 literacy competence, then encouraging a child's love of reading is a desirable goal. In addition, Readers' experiences with books, and their obvious pleasure in sharing them with us, made it clear that reading can be a wonderful, satisfying, and enriching activity for those
780 who are fortunate enough to become engaged by it.

Those who would hope to foster a young person's love of reading must acknowledge that, while students surely benefit when teachers recognize the need to motivate them to read, young people must see themselves
785 as participant readers in a community that pursues reading as a significant and enjoyable recreational activity if reading is to become a lifelong endeavor. To this end, the child's immediate culture, the family, must invest itself in the process to demonstrate the
790 pleasure reading affords by regularly reading aloud to young children, making age- and interest-appropriate

books easily available as the child matures, providing a model for children to emulate, scheduling time for family reading, and demonstrating the social nature of reading and encouraging interest through conversations about the books family members read.

795

References

Adoni, H. (1995). Literacy and reading in a multimedia environment. *Journal of Communication, 45*, 152–174.

Anderson, R., Hiebert, E., Scott, J., & Wilkinson, I. (1985). *Becoming a nation of readers: The report of the Commission on Reading*. Washington, DC: National Institute of Education.

Anderson, R., Wilson, P., & Fielding, L. (1988). Growth in reading and how children spend their time outside of school. *Reading Research Quarterly, 23*, 285–303. doi:10.1598/RRQ.23.3.2

Bissex, G. (1980). *GNYS at work*. Cambridge, MA: Harvard University Press.

Bloom, L. (1970). *Language development: Form and function in emerging grammar*. Cambridge, MA: Harvard University Press.

Bloom, L. (1973). *One word at a time*. Paris: Mouton.

Cambourne, B. (1995). Towards an educationally relevant theory of literacy learning: Twenty years of inquiry. *The Reading Teacher, 49*, 182–190.

Clark, M. (1984). Literacy at home and at school: Insights from the study of young fluent readers. In H. Goelman, A. Oberg, & F. Smith (Eds.), *Awakening to literacy* (pp. 122–130). Portsmouth, NH: Heinemann.

Durkin, D. (1966). *Children who read early*. New York: Teachers College Press.

Fader, D. (1983). Literacy and family. In R. Bailey & R. Fosheim (Eds.), *Literacy for life: The demand for reading and writing* (pp. 236–247). New York: Modern Language Association.

Forester, A. (1986). Apprenticeship in the art of literacy. In D. Tovey & J. Kerber (Eds.), *Roles in literacy learning: A new perspective* (pp. 66–72). Newark, DE: International Reading Association.

Greaney, V. (1980). Factors related to amount and type of leisure reading. *Reading Research Quarterly, 15*, 337–357.

Greaney, V., & Hegarty, M. (1987). Correlates of leisure-time reading. *Journal of Research in Reading, 10*, 3–32.

Greaney, V., & Neuman, S. (1983). Young people's view of reading: A cross-cultural perspective. *The Reading Teacher, 37*, 158–163.

Hall, S., & Moats, L. (2000, Spring). Why reading to children is important. *American Educator*, pp. 26–33.

Harste, J., Burke, C., & Woodward, V. (1982). Children's language and world: Initial encounters with print. In J. Langer & M. Smith-Burke (Eds.), *Reader meets author: Bridging the gap* (pp. 105–131). Newark, DE: International Reading Association.

Himmelweit, H., & Swift, B. (1976). Continuities and discontinuities in media usage and taste: A longitudinal study. *Journal of Social Issues, 32*, 133–156.

Krashen, S. (1993). *The power of reading: Insights from the research*. Englewood, CO: Libraries Unlimited.

Kubey, R., & Csikszentmihalyi, M. (1990). *Television and the quality of life: How viewing shapes everyday experience*. Hillsdale, NJ: Erlbaum.

Lewis, R., & Teale, W. (1980). Another look at secondary students' attitudes toward reading. *Journal of Reading Behavior, 12*, 187–201.

Long, B., & Henderson, F. (1973). Children's use of time: Some personal and social correlates. *Elementary School Journal, 73*, 193–199.

Lyness, P. (1952). The place of mass media in the lives of boys and girls. *Journalism Quarterly, 29*, 43–54.

McKenna, M., Kear, D., & Ellsworth, A. (1995) Children's attitudes toward reading: A national survey. *Reading Research Quarterly, 30*, 934–956.

Moffitt, M., & Wartella, E. (1992). Youth and reading: A survey of leisure reading pursuits of female and male adolescents. *Reading Research and Instruction, 31*, 1–17.

Moje, E., Young, J., Readence, J., & Moore, D. (2000). Reinventing adolescent literacy for new times: Perennial and millennial issues. *Journal of Adolescent & Adult Literacy, 43*, 400–407.

Moore, D., Bean, T., Birdyshaw, D., & Rycik, J. (1999). *Adolescent literacy: A position statement for the Commission on Adolescent Literacy of the International Reading Association*. Newark, DE: International Reading Association.

Morrow, L. (1983). Home and school correlates of early interest in literature. *Journal of Educational Research, 76*, 221–223.

National Institute of Child Health and Human Development (2000). *Report of the National Reading Panel: Teaching children to read: An evidence-based assessment of the scientific research literature in reading and its implications for reading instruction* (NIH Publication No. 00-4769). Washington, DC: U.S. Government Printing Office.

Nell, V. (1988). *Lost in a book: The psychology of reading for pleasure*. New Haven, CT: Yale University Press.

Neuman, S. (1980). Why children read: A functional approach. *Journal of Reading Behavior, 12*, 333–336.

Neuman, S. (1981). *Effects of television on reading behavior*. Willimantic: Eastern Connecticut State College. (ERIC Document Reproduction Service No. ED205941)

Neuman, S. (1986). Television, reading and the home environment. *Reading Research and Instruction, 25*, 173–183.

Neuman, S. (1995). *Literacy in the television age: The myth of the TV effect* (2nd ed.). Norwood, NJ: Ablex.

Searls, D., Mead, N., & Ward, B. (1985). The relationship of students' reading skills to TV watching, leisure time reading and homework. *Journal of Reading, 29*, 158–162.

Smith, F. (1988). *Understanding reading*. Hillsdale, NJ: Erlbaum.

Taylor, D. (1983). *Family literacy*. Exeter, NH: Heinemann.

Teale, W. (1984). Home background and young children's literacy development. In H. Goelman, A. Oberg, & F. Smith (Eds.), *Awakening to literacy* (pp. 173–206). Portsmouth, NH: Heinemann.

Yaden, D. (1986). Issues related to home influence on young children's print-related development. In D. Yaden & S. Templeton (Eds.), *Metalinguistic awareness and beginning literacy* (pp. 145–148). Portsmouth, NH: Heinemann.

Address correspondence to: Linda Teran Strommen, 30 Smith Street, Glen Head, NY 11545. E-mail: ltstrommen@aol.com

Exercise for Article 25

Factual Questions

1. Why did the researchers choose the term *Not-readers* instead of the term *Nonreaders*?

2. How was the anonymity of the students protected?

3. Did the researchers "mask" their specific research objective?

4. Approximately what percentage of the 151 students were identified as *Readers*?

5. How many of the *Readers* were interviewed?

6. Were the interviews audiotaped?

Questions for Discussion

7. What is your opinion of the validity of the Literacy Index Items in Table 1? Do you think that some of the items are more important than others for identifying *Readers*? (See lines 155–162.)

8. In your opinion, how important is the information in the paragraph starting with line 216 (in which the validity of the questionnaire is discussed)? Explain.

9. If you had conducted this study, would you have used open-ended questions such as those in Table 2 *or* would you have used forced-choice items (i.e., items with choices)? Explain.

10. For the interviews, the researchers attempted to match the *Readers* and *Not-readers* in terms of gender and academic tracking. Is this important? Explain.

11. In the Findings section of this research article, there are many more direct quotations of participants' responses than in most other articles in this book. Do you think that the inclusion of numerous direct quotations is a strength of this article? To what extent did the quotations help you understand the findings? Explain.

12. To what extent do you think this research has helped to identify the causes of learning to love reading? Explain. Consider the entire article when answering this question, with special attention to lines 730–772.

Quality Ratings

Directions: Indicate your level of agreement with each of the following statements by circling a number from 5 for strongly agree (SA) to 1 for strongly disagree (SD). If you believe an item is not applicable to this research article, leave it blank. Be prepared to explain your ratings. When responding to criteria A and B below, keep in mind that brief titles and abstracts are conventional in published research.

A. The title of the article is appropriate.

SA   5   4   3   2   1   SD

B. The abstract provides an effective overview of the research article.

SA   5   4   3   2   1   SD

C. The introduction establishes the importance of the study.

SA   5   4   3   2   1   SD

D. The literature review establishes the context for the study.

SA   5   4   3   2   1   SD

E. The research purpose, question, or hypothesis is clearly stated.

SA   5   4   3   2   1   SD

F. The method of sampling is sound.

SA   5   4   3   2   1   SD

G. Relevant demographics (for example, age, gender, and ethnicity) are described.

SA   5   4   3   2   1   SD

H. Measurement procedures are adequate.

SA   5   4   3   2   1   SD

I. All procedures have been described in sufficient detail to permit a replication of the study.

SA   5   4   3   2   1   SD

J. The participants have been adequately protected from potential harm.

SA   5   4   3   2   1   SD

K. The results are clearly described.

SA   5   4   3   2   1   SD

L. The discussion/conclusion is appropriate.

SA   5   4   3   2   1   SD

M. Despite any flaws, the report is worthy of publication.

SA   5   4   3   2   1   SD

Article 26

Are We Ignoring Youths with Disabilities in Foster Care? An Examination of Their School Performance

SARAH GEENEN
Portland State University

LAURIE E. POWERS
Portland State University

ABSTRACT. This study examined the extent to which the academic achievement of adolescents receiving both foster care and special education services differs from the performance of youths involved in only foster care, special education, or general education. Extant school data were collected on 327 students ages 13 through 21 who attended school in a large urban school district in Oregon. The study also collected information about students' general foster care experiences, such as length of time in care and type and number of placements. Analyses revealed that foster care youths in special education typically demonstrated lower performance on academic variables in contrast to one or more of the comparison groups. These youths also appeared to experience more restrictive special education placements than youths in special education only. Although foster care or special education status alone appears to place a student at risk of academic difficulties, the negative impact of interfacing with both systems appears multiplicative. Greater attention, commitment, and time must be given to the educational needs of foster care youths with disabilities by both education and child welfare professionals.

From *Social Work, 51*, 233–241. Copyright © 2006 by the National Association of Social Workers. Reprinted with permission.

The number of youths in foster care has nearly doubled in almost 20 years, from 276,000 in 1985 to approximately 523,000 currently (Adoption and Foster Care Analysis Reporting System, 2005). An additional 15,000 youths are in foster care through the juvenile justice system (U.S. General Accounting Office [GAO], 2000). Statistics further indicate that 30 percent to 40 percent of foster care youths receive special education services (Edmund S. Muskie School of Public Service, 1999; Goerge, Voorhis, Grant, Casey, & Robinson, 1992; McIntyre & Keesler, 1986; Richardson, West, Day, & Stuart, 1989). Despite the substantial number of foster care youths with disabilities (i.e., those receiving special education services), little is known about their educational performance.

The scant information that is available suggests that the needs of foster care youths with disabilities are too often ignored or ineffectively addressed within the educational system. For example, a survey conducted in Oregon found that although 39 percent of youths in foster care had an individualized education plan (IEP), only 16 percent actually received services (White, Carrington, & Freeman, as cited in Ayasse, 1995). The special education system emphasizes, and is compelled to a large extent, by parental advocacy and participation. Although the Individuals with Disabilities Education Act (P.L. 101–476) requires that an educational surrogate must be appointed in a timely fashion when a biological parent is unavailable, evidence indicates that for foster youths in special education, a consistent, involved advocate typically does not exist. For example, although foster parents often serve as educational surrogates, a study by the Advocates for Children of New York (2000) found that 90 percent of foster parents reported that they had no involvement in the special education process. The educational experiences of foster youths in special education are also affected by their high mobility. A change in foster placement frequently means a change in schools and when paperwork does not follow the student promptly (as is often the case), staff members of the new school have little or no information about the special education needs of the transferring foster student (Advocates for Children of New York; Ayasse). This lag often results in students being placed in inappropriate settings or programs and their IEPs not being implemented.

The education of foster care youths with disabilities may frequently be overlooked in child welfare as well. One study revealed, for example, that caseworkers underestimated the number of foster children who receive special education by sixfold (Goerge et al., 1992). The lack of awareness that caseworkers have regarding the special education needs of foster youths may reflect a pervasive lack of focus on the education of foster youths in general, regardless of disability. In a British study investigating the considerations of social workers when planning for foster youths, education was listed as a priority only 2 percent of the time (Aldgate, Heath, Colton, & Simm, 1993). Likewise, literature from the United States seems to confirm that caseworkers in the

U.S. child welfare system, who typically have caseloads twice the recommended levels (GAO 2003), must focus on immediate child protection issues for foster youths, leaving little time for educational priori-
65 ties (Goerge et al., 1992; Goren, 1996; National Association of Social Workers, 1997; Timbers, 2001).

The educational performance of foster care youths in general has been substantially investigated, and research indicates that this group of students is struggling
70 in school. For example, Joiner (2001) found that foster youths have a high rate of absenteeism; Burley and Halpern (2001) demonstrated that foster youths score 15 percent to 20 percent below their peers on statewide achievement tests. Blome (1997) found that foster
75 youths dropped out of school at twice the rate of youths not in care, and in a Maine survey, 40 percent of foster youths had repeated at least one grade (Edmund S. Muskie School of Public Service, 1999).

In contrast, little is known about the educational
80 performance of foster care youths in special education, and the few studies that have investigated this area have been limited by small samples. Weinberg (1997) conducted a case study of 12 foster care youths using interviews and records review to investigate the way
85 agencies—school, child welfare, mental health—affect the education of youths in both foster care and special education. The author found that foster youths experienced the routine lack of compliance with special education laws that affect all students with disabilities;
90 however, youths in care were more likely to experience these routine violations because they lacked the protection and oversight of a parental advocate. Smucker and colleagues (1996) compared the school-related problems of foster care students receiving special education
95 services for emotional disturbance ($n = 8$) with the behavioral and academic problems of three comparison groups: students in foster care only ($n = 8$), students in special education only ($n = 8$), and students in neither special education nor foster care ($n = 8$). Their findings
100 showed that foster care youths labeled as having an emotional disturbance experienced more school problems than the comparison groups, as indicated by interviews with school staff and a review of school records.

Although school success is a critical factor for all
105 students in achieving positive adult outcomes, educational accomplishment may be particularly important for youths in foster care, who when transitioning to adulthood may have little else to draw upon. Every year, approximately 20,000 youths are emancipated
110 from the child welfare system when they reach the age of majority (typically age 18), and frequently they enter adult life with little to no financial resources, community connections, or help from family (Carroll, 2002; GAO, 1999). The odds for successful transition into
115 adulthood are often stacked against foster youths, and research investigating the outcomes of these youths is troubling. A national study of former foster youths ages 18 to 24 who had aged out of the child welfare system found that 2.5 to four years after leaving care, 30 per-
120 cent were receiving public assistance, 50 percent had used illegal drugs, and 25 percent had been homeless at least one night (Westat, 1991). Furthermore, foster youths with disabilities (emotional, chronic health, physical, or developmental disabilities) demonstrated
125 significantly poorer outcomes than their peers in foster care who did not have identified disabilities (Westat). Perhaps most important, research investigating resilience among foster care youths has demonstrated that educational achievement (e.g., high school completion)
130 is one of the best predictors of positive adult outcomes, such as employment and postsecondary education (Jackson, 1994; Westat).

Although education may be the most important bridge that foster youths have to successful adult life,
135 many foster youths who also experience disability are stumbling before they get across, as the whipsaw effect of both foster care and special education may place them at even further risk of academic failure. The purpose of this study was to investigate the educational
140 performance of foster youths in special education. Specifically, the study examined the extent to which the educational achievement of foster youths in special education differs from the academic performance of youths in foster care alone, youths in special education
145 alone, and youths in general education (not foster care or special education).

Method

The Oregon Division of Human Services (DHS) Child Welfare (the state foster care program) and the Oregon Youth Authority (OYA, which has a separate
150 foster care program for youths involved in the juvenile justice system) identified all foster care youths ages 13 to 21 whose zip codes fell within a large urban school district in Oregon that serves approximately 57,000 students; using this selection process, 256 foster care
155 youths were identified by DHS and 22 youths were identified by OYA. All youths were currently in foster care on the day the list was formed. The names and birth dates of each youth were forwarded by the agencies to the school district. In addition, DHS provided
160 information about each youth's foster care experience, including the number of foster care placements the youth had, the type of foster care placement (e.g., non-relative or kinship care), and length of time in foster care. Using names and dates of birth, school staff at-
165 tempted to match each youth with his or her school student identification number and determine which youths received special education services. Among the 278 youth identified by DHS and OYA, the school district was able to locate identification numbers for
170 267 students, of which 222 were enrolled at the time. Sixty-four of these students attended an alternative school, and no academic data were available for these youths. Among the remaining 158 students, 88 of these foster youths were not enrolled in special education

175 and made up the foster-care-only group. Approximately 44 percent ($n = 70$) of the 158 foster care youths were enrolled in special education and assigned to the special education and foster care group. According to the school district, 29 percent of these youths had a
180 primary disability of emotional disturbance; 19 percent had a physical disability (i.e., orthopedic, hearing or vision impairment or both, or other health impaired); 44 percent had a learning disability; 4 percent had a cognitive disability (mental retardation, autism); and 4
185 percent had a communication disorder.

A comparison group of 81 students ages 13 to 21 who were in special education only (not in foster care) was also selected. The goal was to have the special-education-only group resemble the special education
190 and foster care group in terms of disability so that this could be ruled out as a factor if the analyses revealed any between-group differences. Thus, stratified sampling was used to select the comparison group, ensuring that the two special education groups had equal
195 proportions of students with emotional, physical, learning, cognitive, and communication disabilities. Specifically, students in the special-education-only comparison group were randomly selected from all special education students (ages 13 to 21, not in foster care) in
200 each disability group.

A final comparison group of 88 students in general education only (i.e., youths who were in neither special education nor foster care) was randomly selected. Thus, the study included four groups: foster care and
205 special education (group 1, $n = 70$); foster care only (group 2, $n = 88$); special education only (group 3, $n = 81$); and general education only (group 4, $n = 88$), with a total sample size of 327.

For each study participant, data were gathered by
210 school staff on the following seven academic variables: (1) cumulative grade point average (0.00 to 4.00 grading system); (2) number of days absent (year to date); (3) cumulative earned credits toward graduation (22 required); (4) number of schools attended in student's
215 career; (5) number of grades retained; (6) performance on standardized state testing in math and reading (based on a proficiency level assigned by the school district where a 1 = high performance, exceeds standards, and 5 = fails to meet standard, very low per-
220 formance); and (7) exemption rates on state testing. In addition, the school district provided basic demographic information for each student (i.e., race and ethnicity, gender, age, grade, and name of student's school). For study participants enrolled in special edu-
225 cation, data were gathered on the type and level of restrictiveness of the student's special education placement.

Participants

Among the 327 students participating in the study, 59.6 percent were boys. The study's groups varied
230 somewhat by gender; the special education groups (special education only and foster care and special education) had a larger percentage of males (Table 1). This reflects national statistics, which indicate that boys receive special education services at twice the rate of
235 girls (Rousso & Wehmeyer, 2002). In terms of race and ethnicity, 176 participants were white, 109 were African American, 16 were Hispanic, 16 were Asian, and 10 were Native American. The foster care groups (foster care only and foster care and special education) had
240 a larger percentage of African American students; this difference is consistent with the over-representation of African American youths in foster care on a national level (Adoption and Foster Care Analysis Reporting System, 2005). The average age of participants was
245 14.9, and the average grade level was 9.67. Although detailed information on the socioeconomic status of participants was not available, the school district indicated which students received free or reduced lunch at school. This included all youths in the foster care
250 groups (foster care only and foster care and special education), 22 youths in special education only, and eight youths in general education only. Among foster care youths, the median length of time in care was 133 weeks, with most youths (72 percent) experiencing one
255 to four placements. The majority of these youths (79 percent) were in a nonrelative foster care placement.

Results

Differences Among Study Groups on Academic Indicators

To investigate whether the study groups varied in terms of educational achievement, analysis of variance (ANOVA) was conducted for each academic variable.
260 In each ANOVA, the independent variable was group status (foster care and special education, foster care only, special education only, or general education only), and the dependent variable was the group performance on a particular academic indicator. When an
265 ANOVA revealed a significant difference between the study groups on a particular variable, a post hoc analysis was conducted to discover where that difference rested among the four groups. Post hoc analyses were conducted using t tests, with p values adjusted to con-
270 trol for multiple comparisons using the Bonferroni method.

Significant omnibus differences were obtained (Table 2) for cumulative grade point average [$F(3,323) = 3.77, p \leq .01$]; number of schools attended [$F(3,323) = 7.52, p \leq .0001$]; and cumulative earned credits
275 [$F(3,323) = 3.24, p \leq .05$]; performance on standardized state testing in reading [$F(3,190) = 15.19, p \leq .0001$]; performance on standardized state testing in math [$F(3,182) = 13.55, p \leq .0001$]; and exemption
280 rates on standardized state testing [$F(3,323) = 6.55, p \leq .0001$]. Follow-up analyses ($p \leq .05$) revealed that youths who were in the foster care and special education group had significantly lower grade point averages

176

Table 1
Ethnicity and Gender for Youths with Disabilities

	Foster care and special education			Foster care only			Special education only			General education only		
	Male	Female	Total	Male	Female	Total	Male	Female	Total	Male	Female	Total
Asian	0	0	0	0	2	2	3	3	6	4	4	8
Native American	1	0	1	2	0	2	4	1	5	0	2	2
African American	17	12	29	23	20	43	12	7	19	9	9	18
White	27	11	38	21	17	38	30	14	44	32	24	56
Hispanic	0	2	2	1	2	3	5	2	7	4	0	4
Total	45	25	70	47	41	88	54	27	81	49	39	88

Table 2
Summary of Statistics of Academic Variables for All Study Groups

	Foster care and special education			Foster care only			Special education only			General education only			
	M	SD	n	M	SD	n	M	SD	n	M	SD	n	F
Grade point average	1.34	1.11	70	1.49	1.27	88	1.50	1.17	81	1.96	1.44	88	3.77**
Number of days absent	8.49	8.48	70	5.35	5.83	88	8.93	13.19	81	6.97	9.20	88	2.41
Cumulative earned credits	5.35	6.83	70	7.76	8.70	88	7.73	7.60	81	9.29	8.20	88	3.24*
Number of schools attended	4.06	2.04	70	3.43	1.67	88	3.02	1.26	81	2.94	1.45	88	7.52****
Number of grades retained	.26	.47	70	.16	.55	86	.27	.57	81	.13	.40	88	.174
Exemption rate on state testing	.40	.84	70	.07	.30	88	.28	.76	81	.06	.28	88	6.55****
Performance on state testing: math[a]	3.64	1.32	33	2.74	1.19	57	3.67	1.11	45	2.39	1.11	51	13.55****
Performance on state testing: reading[a]	3.80	.90	35	2.84	.91	58	3.39	1.04	49	2.44	1.16	52	15.19****

[a]Items are reversed scored, where a 1 = exceeds standards and a 5 = fails to meet standards.
*$p < .05$. **$p < .01$. ****$p < .0001$.

(GPAs) than youths in general education only (group 4). Additionally, youths in the foster care and special education group changed schools more frequently than did youths in the special-education-only group or the general-education-only group (group 4). Youths in the foster care and special education group also earned significantly fewer credits toward graduation compared with youths in the general-education-only group. In terms of performance on state testing, the foster care and special education group and the special-education-only group had significantly lower state testing scores in reading and math. Specifically, youths in the foster care and special education group had greater difficulty than youths in the foster-care-only and general-education-only groups in both reading and math. Students in the special-education-only group demonstrated poorer performance than those in the general-education-only group in reading, and poorer performance than youths in the foster-care-only group and general-education-only group in math. Finally, youths in the foster care and special education group were significantly more likely to be exempted from standardized state testing than youths in either the foster-care-only or general-education-only groups. No other significant differences between the study groups were revealed. Thus, on all but one variable, when a significant group difference was found, the difference rested between the foster care and special education group (group 1) and one or more of the other groups. The only exception was on standardized testing, where the special-education-only group (group 3) demonstrated significantly lower performance than group 4 in reading and groups 2 and 4 on math.

Because study groups varied on important demographic characteristics, analyses of covariance (ANCOVAs) were conducted to control for possible covariates that may be contributing to the group differences described earlier. Specifically, an ANCOVA was conducted for each of the seven academic variables, where study group was the independent variable and

325 gender, race–ethnicity (minority compared with non-minority), and free-lunch status were entered as covariates. Race–ethnicity appeared to be a significant covariate for number of schools attended. However, even when it was statistically controlled for, significant group differences persisted. Thus, when race–ethnicity 330 was held constant statistically, youths in the foster care and special education group still changed schools significantly more than did youths in the special-education-only group or the general-education-only group.

Restrictiveness of Special Education Placement

335   Restrictiveness of special education placement was investigated using a series of codes used by the school district for federal reporting purposes. The school district sorts each student's special education placement into one of five categories: (1) regular class or resource 340 room, (2) separate class (self-contained classroom), (3) public separate (separate public school), (4) private separate (separate private school), and (5) hospital (residential treatment center, inpatient hospitalization). We rank ordered these five placement codes or categories 345 according to restrictiveness of placement: regular class or resource room was rated as least restrictive (1); separate class was rated as moderately restrictive (2); and public separate, private separate, and hospital were rated as most restrictive (3). Pearson chi-square was 350 used to evaluate whether the placements of youths in the foster care and special education and special-education-only groups varied by level of restrictiveness, and a significant difference was obtained [$\chi^2(2, N = 323) = 10.20, p \leq .01$]. Thirty percent of foster care 355 youths in the foster care and special education group had a special education placement that fell within the most restrictive range, compared with 15 percent of youths in the special-education-only group. In contrast, 65 percent of youths in the special-education-only 360 group had a placement that fell within the least restrictive range, compared with 44 percent of youths in the foster care and special education group.

Relationship Between Foster Care Experience and Academic Performance

    Pearson's correlation coefficient was used to evaluate whether performance on the seven academic indica-365 tors varied by length of time in foster care (days) and number of foster care placements. The results indicated that number of foster care placements was negatively correlated with GPA ($r = -.14, p \leq .05$) and positively correlated with proficiency level on state testing in 370 math ($r = .23, p \leq .05$). Thus, as the number of foster placements went up, GPA decreased. This was also the case with math. Because this item was reverse scored (where a 1 = high performance and 5 = fails to meet standards), the positive correlation indicates that actual 375 performance on state testing in math decreased as number of placements increased. No other significant results were found.

A two tailed t test was used to assess whether the foster care and special education group had a greater 380 number of placements than the foster-care-only group, and a significant difference was found ($p \leq .05$). The average number of placements for youths in both foster care and special education was 4.45 ($SD = 4.58$) compared with 3.35 ($SD = 2.80$) for youths in foster care 385 only.

    A series of t tests were calculated to evaluate whether academic performance varied by type of foster care placement (relative or kinship foster care vs. nonrelative foster care). A t test was conducted for each 390 academic variable; the results indicated that students placed in nonrelative care had significantly higher GPAs ($p \leq .05$) and a greater number of credits toward graduation ($p \leq .05$). No other differences were found for type of placement.

Discussion

395   The purpose of this study was to investigate the academic achievement of youths involved in foster care **and** special education, both in absolute terms and in comparison with their peers who experienced **only** foster care, special education, or general education. 400 Consistent with other research (e.g., Goerge et al., 1992), we found that a large percentage of youths in foster care were receiving special education services (44 percent). The results also indicated that foster care youths with disabilities performed poorly in school, 405 lagged behind their peers in a number of important indices of academic achievement, and experienced significant challenges to educational success. For example, youths in foster care with disabilities had lower GPAs than youths in general education, changed 410 schools more frequently than youths in general education and special education only, earned fewer credits toward graduation than youths in general education, had lower scores on state testing, and were more likely to be exempted from testing than youths in general 415 education and foster care only. In comparison with other students with disabilities, foster youths experienced more restrictive special education placements. In contrast to other youths in care, foster youths with disabilities had more foster home placements. With regard 420 to foster care experience, the findings indicated that as the number of youth foster placements increases, GPA and performance on state testing in math decreases. The results also suggested that youths placed in nonrelative care (compared with kinship) had higher GPAs 425 and a greater number of credits toward graduation.

Limitations

    Several limitations exist in the interpretation of the study's results. First, it is quite possible that some youths in the foster-care-only group experienced a disability but were not identified for special education 430 services; or their disability was undiagnosed or undocumented. Indeed, this likelihood may be high as the experiences of youths in foster care (e.g., lack a consistent educational advocate; frequent school changes) often result in their special education needs going unnoticed and unmet. Second, our sample involved students from one urban school district, which limits the generalizability of the findings. Third, it is important to note that the special education groups may have differed by severity of disability. For example, youths identified through the juvenile justice system may have had more severe behavioral disabilities than youths selected from the general special education population. Although the study used stratified sampling to assure that youths in the foster care and special education group and youths in the special-education-only group resembled one another in terms of disability type, unfortunately, no information about severity of disability was available from the school district. Finally, this study was not able to qualitatively explore what experiences in foster care and special education contributed to the poor educational performance of foster youths with disabilities. For example, before their placement in foster care, many youths lived in families overwhelmed by poverty, homelessness, substance abuse, illness, and poor education, and this study was not able to evaluate the impact of those experiences on a youth's current educational functioning. In addition, youths have been exposed to neglect, abuse, and separation from family, and this study did not investigate the effect of this trauma on the academic achievement of youths. It also is likely that issues related to disability—such as a foster parent's ability and training to support the unique needs of a youth with significant emotional or behavioral challenges—further contributes to the school performance, but that was not explored in this study. Like the current study, earlier research on the educational performance of foster youths (e.g., Blome, 1997; Burley & Halpern, 2001; Joiner, 2001) has not explored the impact of potentially significant variables, such as poverty, quality of foster home placement, and nature of abuse, and this is an area for future research.

Implications for Future Research

These research findings demonstrate that foster youths with disabilities lag behind their peers, including foster youths who do not receive special education services, on a number of important academic variables. Therefore, researchers who are examining the educational performance of youths in foster care should work to identify which youths are also in special education. In general, earlier research on the school performance of foster care youths has failed to do this, and it is likely that foster youths with disabilities may contribute disproportionately to the lower academic scores of foster youths in general. Given that a sizable percentage of foster care youths receive special education and that these youths appear to experience greater educational difficulties than foster youths in general, it may

not be appropriate to treat them as a homogenous group.

In addition, future research should investigate the relationship between kinship care and educational achievement for foster youths with disabilities. Our findings suggest that foster youths in special education who are placed with relatives had lower GPAs and fewer credits compared with youths placed in nonrelative care. Earlier research has suggested the opposite to be true. For example, using data from a Los Angeles county, Iglehart (1994) found that adolescents in kinship care demonstrated greater placement stability and better mental health functioning. Brooks and Barth (1998) found no relationship between relative foster home placement and grades or retention based on the reports of foster parents. Thus, the relationship between academic performance and kinship care revealed in this study should be interpreted cautiously, and more research is needed. As mentioned earlier, future research should also investigate the role of other important life experiences (such as poverty, nature of abuse, relationship with birth family and foster parents) in the educational achievement of youths in care.

Implications for Practice

The findings suggest serious cause for concern regarding the academic performance of foster care youths in general, and foster youths with disabilities in particular. Although foster care or special education status alone appears to place a student at greater risk for academic difficulties, the negative impact of interfacing with both systems is multiplicative. These youths appear to be experiencing a whipsaw effect as they simultaneously face challenges related to special education and foster care separately, as well as the interaction between the two. An example of this multiplicative effect can be found in the higher rate of foster placement turnover among foster youths with disabilities. Instability in foster care, which is typically associated with a change in schools, creates educational challenges for all foster youths, but adjusting to a new educational setting may be especially difficult for a foster youth with a disability. The new school may be unaware of his or her special education needs and fail to provide necessary educational supports as stipulated in the student's IEP. Such problems in providing appropriate special education support may become compounded over time as foster youths with disabilities are more likely to experience multiple care placements. In turn, they may be more likely to experience instability in care because their foster parents lack the training, support, and resources necessary to address their special needs.

As stated by Heath and colleagues (1994), "Average inputs are not enough for children with above-average educational needs. Clearly, the educational needs of separated (foster) children must be given much higher priority" (p. 258). This statement could not be truer for foster care youths with disabilities.

545 Greater attention, commitment, and time must be given to the educational needs of foster care youths with disabilities in general education, special education, and child welfare. At a very basic level, there is a need for timely exchange of information between systems. Our

550 sampling methodology—the child welfare agencies first identifying youths in care and transmitting this information to the school district for determination of special education status—was used because the school district and child welfare could not identify this group

555 from their own records. Educators need to know which students are foster care and child welfare professionals need to have information about a youth's disability needs and involvement in special education. Legislative barriers (such as the Family Educational Rights

560 and Privacy Act, PL. 93-380) that make this exchange of information difficult must be addressed. Limited opportunities for schools and child protection agencies to collaborate are emerging, but educators and child welfare professionals must be proactive and work to

565 engage one another if partnerships are to form. For example, as mentioned earlier, the transition planning and services that are offered through foster care independent living programs are rarely connected to the transition planning and services that occur through

570 special education. Furthermore, there is a strong need to train educators on how to support the specific education and transition needs of foster youths. As Noble (1997) pointed out, "Foster children exhibit behavior problems that are not unlike those of children living

575 with their biological or adoptive families Although these problems are also found among children not in foster care, the reasons behind them are different. Therefore, intervention must be different" (p. 26). Similarly, professionals in child welfare require educa-

580 tion and training on the disability-related needs of youths. This information is critical for caseworkers' effective planning and support for youths in care, such as in selecting the best foster care placement and in appropriately interpreting and responding to problems

585 that arise. Training should also be offered to foster parents and educational surrogates regarding how to advocate effectively for foster youths in the special education process. Foster parents and surrogates must be informed that youths are eligible for special education

590 services and of how the system works if they are to have any chance to be an ally for the youths.

References

Adoption and Foster Care Analysis Reporting System. (2005). *The AFCARS report: Preliminary FY 2003 estimates as of April 2005*. Retrieved April 6, 2006, from http://www.acf.hhs.gov/programs/cb/stats_research/afcars/tar/report10

Advocates for Children of New York. (2000). *Educational neglect: The delivery of educational services to children in New York City's foster care system*. Retrieved June 15, 2004, from http://www.advocatesforchildren.org/pubs/2005/fostercare.pdf

Aldgate, J., Heath, A., Colton, M., & Simm, M. (1993). Social work and the education of children in foster care. *Adoption & Fostering, 17*, 25–34.

Ayasse, R. H. (1995). Addressing the needs of children in care: The Youth in Care Services Program. *Social Work in Education, 17*, 207–216.

Blome, W. W. (1997). What happens to foster kids: Educational experiences of a random sample of foster care youth and a matched group of non-foster care youth. *Child and Adolescent Social Work Journal, 14*, 41–53.

Brooks, D., & Barth, R. P. (1998). Characteristics and outcomes of drug-exposed and non drug-exposed in kinship care and non-relative foster care. *Children and Youth Services Review, 20*, 475–501.

Burley, M., & Halpern, M. (2001). *Educational attainment of foster youth: Achievement and graduation outcomes for children in state care*. Retrieved April 6, 2006, from http://www.inpathways.net/edattainfy.pdf

Carroll, K. (2002). *The Foster Care Independence Act of 1999 and the John H. Chafee Foster Care Independence Program*. Reno, NV: National Council of Juvenile and Family Court Judges.

Edmund S. Muskie School of Public Service. (1999). *Maine study on improving the educational outcomes for children in care*. Baltimore: Annie E. Casey Foundation.

Goerge, R. M., Voorhis, J. V., Grant, S., Casey, K., & Robinson, M. (1992). Special education experiences of foster children: An empirical study. *Child Welfare, 71*, 419–437.

Goren, S. G. (1996). Child protection and the school social worker. In R. Constable, J. P. Flynn, & S. McDonald (Eds.), *School social work: Practice and research perspectives* (pp. 355–366). Chicago: Lyceum.

Heath, A. F., Colton, M. J., & Aldgate, J. (1994). Failure to escape: A longitudinal study of foster children's educational attainment. *British Journal of Social Work, 24*, 241–260.

Iglehart, A. (1994). Kinship foster care: Placement, service, and outcome issues. *Children and Youth Services Review, 16*, 107–122.

Jackson, S. (1994). Educating children in residential and foster care. *Oxford Review of Education, 20*, 267–279.

Joiner, L. L. (2001). Reaching out to foster children. *American School Board Journal, 188*, 30–34.

McIntyre, A., & Keesler, T. Y. (1986). Psychological disorders among foster children. *Journal of Clinical Child Psychology, 15*, 297–303.

National Association of Social Workers. (1997). A reveille for school social workers: Children in foster care need our help! *Social Work in Education, 19*, 121–127.

Noble, L. S. (1997). The face of foster care. *Educational Leadership, 54*, 26–28.

Richardson, M., West, M. A., Day, P., & Stuart, S. (1989). Children with developmental disabilities in the child welfare system: A national survey. *Child Welfare, 68*, 605–612.

Rousso, H., & Wehmeyer, M. (2002). *Gender matters: Training for educators working with students with disabilities*. Newton, MA: WEEA Equity Resource Center.

Smucker, K. S., Kauffman, J., & Ball, D. (1996). School-related problems of special education foster-care students with emotional or behavioral disorders: A comparison to other groups. *Journal of Emotional and Behavioral Disorders, 4*, 30–39.

Timbers, J. (2001). *Educating schools on behalf of children in care*. Retrieved April 6, 2006, from http://www.connectforkids.org/node/295

U.S. General Accounting Office. (1999). *Foster care: Effectiveness of independent living services unknown* (GAO/HEHS-00-13). Washington, DC: U.S. Government Printing Office.

U.S. General Accounting Office. (2000). *Foster care: HHS should ensure that juvenile justice placements are reviewed* (GAO/HEHS-00-42). Washington, DC: U.S. Government Printing Office.

U.S. General Accounting Office. (2003). *Child welfare: HHS could play a greater role in helping child welfare agencies recruit and retain staff* (GAO 03-057). Washington, DC: U.S Government Printing Office.

Weinberg, L. A. (1997). Problems in educating abused and neglected children with disabilities. *Child Abuse & Neglect, 21*, 889–905.

Westat. (1991). *A national evaluation of Title IV-E foster care independent living programs for youth: Phase 2*. Rockville, MD: Author.

Acknowledgments: This study was supported by grant #H324N010012-02 from the U.S. Department of Education. The authors are grateful to Jenny Miller, Jonathan Fields, Devon Burris, and members of the Fostering Futures Advisory Board for their assistance with this study.

About the authors: *Sarah Geenen*, Ph.D., is assistant professor, Portland State University—Regional Research Institute, P.O. Box 751, Portland, OR 97207 (e-mail: geenens@pdx.edu). *Laurie E. Powers*, Ph.D., is professor, Portland State University—Regional Research Institute.

Exercise for Article 26

Factual Questions

1. What is the researchers' stated purpose?

2. What percentage of the participants in the "special education and foster care group" had emotional disturbance as their primary disability?

3. How were the participants in the "general education only group" selected?

4. What type of information was used as an indicator of socioeconomic status?

5. Were the differences among the averages for grade-point average statistically significant?

6. What was the value of the Pearson correlation coefficient for the relationship between number of foster care placements and GPA?

Questions for Discussion

7. The researchers used participants from both the DHS and the OYA. If you had planned this study, would you have used both groups *or* used only one of the groups? Explain. (See lines 147–170 and 439–442.)

8. Stratified random sampling was used to select the comparison group. Is this important? Explain. (See lines 186–200.)

9. The researchers used analysis of covariance. What is your understanding of the purpose of this statistical test? (See lines 317–334.)

10. Do you agree that there should be further research on this topic? Explain. (See lines 473–510.)

11. Has this research convinced you that placement in foster care *causes* lower school performance? Explain.

12. Are any of the results of this study surprising? Are any especially interesting? Explain.

Quality Ratings

Directions: Indicate your level of agreement with each of the following statements by circling a number from 5 for strongly agree (SA) to 1 for strongly disagree (SD). If you believe an item is not applicable to this research article, leave it blank. Be prepared to explain your ratings. When responding to criteria A and B below, keep in mind that brief titles and abstracts are conventional in published research.

A. The title of the article is appropriate.

SA   5   4   3   2   1   SD

B. The abstract provides an effective overview of the research article.

SA   5   4   3   2   1   SD

C. The introduction establishes the importance of the study.

SA   5   4   3   2   1   SD

D. The literature review establishes the context for the study.

SA   5   4   3   2   1   SD

E. The research purpose, question, or hypothesis is clearly stated.

SA   5   4   3   2   1   SD

F. The method of sampling is sound.

SA   5   4   3   2   1   SD

G. Relevant demographics (for example, age, gender, and ethnicity) are described.

SA   5   4   3   2   1   SD

H. Measurement procedures are adequate.

SA   5   4   3   2   1   SD

I. All procedures have been described in sufficient detail to permit a replication of the study.

SA   5   4   3   2   1   SD

J. The participants have been adequately protected from potential harm.

SA   5   4   3   2   1   SD

K. The results are clearly described.

SA   5   4   3   2   1   SD

L. The discussion/conclusion is appropriate.

SA   5   4   3   2   1   SD

M. Despite any flaws, the report is worthy of publication.

SA   5   4   3   2   1   SD

Article 27

Smoking Cessation for High School Students: Impact Evaluation of a Novel Program

MEGHAN L. O'CONNELL
Yale-Griffin Prevention Research Center

MATTHEW FREEMAN
Yale University School of Medicine

GEORGIA JENNINGS
Yale-Griffin Prevention Research Center

WENDY CHAN
Yale-Griffin Prevention Research Center

LAURA S. GRECI
Yale-Griffin Prevention Research Center

IRINA D. MANTA
Yale University School of Medicine

DAVID L. KATZ
Yale-Griffin Prevention Research Center

ABSTRACT. This pilot study was designed to evaluate the feasibility and the impact of a smoking-cessation program that would meet the specific needs of high school students. Feedback from focus groups conducted with adolescent smokers at a Connecticut high school was used to develop a tailored intervention. Intervention components included commonly used behavioral strategies, with additional options to assist students to quit smoking, including use of bupropion, concomitant support for parent smoking cessation, stress management, and physician counseling. On completion, 20 of the 22 enrolled students remained committed to quitting. Twenty-seven percent of students quit smoking, and 69% of those who continued to smoke reduced the number of cigarettes smoked per day by an average of 13. Providing additional options to students and additional support for concomitant parental cessation may enhance the appeal of adolescent smoking-cessation programs. Further investigation into efficacy of bupropion use for adolescent cessation is warranted.

From *Behavior Modification, 28*, 133–146. Copyright © 2004 by Sage Publications, Inc. Reprinted with permission.

Tobacco use is the leading cause of premature (preventable) death in the United States (Centers for Disease Control and Prevention [CDC], 1994) and will result in death or disability for half of all regular users
5 (CDC, 1999). Tobacco use among teenagers is in particular an enormous public-health concern. Tobacco use onset, regular use, and dependence often begin during adolescence (CDC, 1994; Elders, Perry, Eriksen, & Giovino, 1994). Behavior patterns are set during
10 this time and often continue into adulthood (Caplan, 1995). The 1998–1999 National Youth Tobacco Survey (CDC, 2000) indicates that 63.5% of U.S. high school students have smoked cigarettes during their lifetime, with 34.8% having smoked during the past 30
15 days and 20.1% smoking on a daily basis. It is estimated that in the United States alone, 3,000 young people become regular smokers every day, and the proportion of youth addicted to cigarettes is growing

(Lamkin, Davis, & Kamen, 1998). There is a great
20 need for innovative tobacco-cessation programs targeting adolescents (Schubiner, Herrold, & Hunt, 1998; Sussman, Lichtman, Ritt, & Pallonen, 1999), as intervention during this life stage has the potential to reach smokers before the habit becomes well established
25 (Elders et al., 1994).

Despite frequent studies on the prevalence of cigarette smoking among adolescents and the proliferation of programs to prevent initiation of cigarette use, few studies of smoking-cessation interventions for youth
30 have been reported. Although some adolescent smoking-cessation programs have been implemented in schools, few have been evaluated (Lamkin et al., 1998). Existing cessation programs for adolescents (Dino et al., 2001; Sussman, Dent, & Lichtman, 2001)
35 aim to enhance participant problem-solving skills for managing personal barriers to quitting, help in coping with physical and psychological withdrawal symptoms, and encourage identification of situations that trigger the urge to smoke. Bupropion, a monocyclic antide-
40 pressant that may help relieve some of the anxiety associated with smoking cessation (Nichols, 1999), has been efficacious in adult programs (Hurt et al., 1997), although evidence to support its use for smoking cessation in adolescents is lacking.
45 This article reports the results of a tailored smoking-cessation program developed for students at one Connecticut high school.

Method

Focus Groups

Using methods described by Krueger (Krueger, 1994), the research team conducted focus groups with
50 11th- and 12th-grade students. Students evaluated and suggested modifications of existing smoking-cessation programs used in Connecticut, including the American Lung Association's Nicotine Challenge (American Lung Association, n.d.) and an adapted version of the
55 adult Smoke Stoppers program (Smoke Stoppers,

1998), and identified barriers to smoking cessation that had not been addressed.

Students were recruited for focus groups in April and May of 2000 by the high school nurse, the school outreach worker, and through public-address system announcements. A prescreening questionnaire identified 45 eligible students (23 males, 22 females) who were invited to participate in one of eight single-gender focus groups. Students were eligible if they were current and regular smokers (defined as smoking more than one cigarette per day) (Farkas et al., 1996). The average number of participants in each group was five.

Structured, open-ended questions were used to guide discussions, along with videotape segments and materials from the established cessation programs. Key questions related to personal experiences with smoking (e.g., addiction, interest in quitting, and friends' and parents' smoking status), likes and dislikes of former program components, and opinions of elements proposed for inclusion in the pilot program. Researchers also inquired about logistical considerations for recruiting students and about implementing the program in the school. Each focus group lasted 90 minutes and was audiotaped. The students were provided with $25, pizza, and soda for their participation.

The pilot smoking-cessation program was developed and revised based on clear consensus among focus-group participants about the inclusion or the exclusion of specific intervention components. Clear consensus was defined by researchers as total agreement or agreement among a large majority of participants, with no dissent.

Program Components

Unique program components, including pharmacotherapy, concurrent parental intervention, stress management, and physician involvement were incorporated into a tailored intervention. These components were considered complementary to the features of currently used programs. Bupropion was viewed as a possible strategy to assist students in their quitting efforts; however, focus groups did not support use of nicotine replacement. A parental-intervention component was planned to educate parents about effects of household smoke on their child's ability to quit and to increase awareness of ways they could support their teenager's efforts to quit. Cessation support for parents was also available upon request as an adjunct to the adolescent program.

In addition to the above intervention components, weekly group meetings were planned based on effective strategies used in prior cessation programs that were deemed acceptable to focus groups. Strategies employed were based principally on the transtheoretical model of change (Prochaska & DiClemente, 1983) and a recent adaptation emphasizing the importance of an individualized approach to raising motivation, and/or lowering barriers to change (Katz, 2001). This behavioral component included exercises for students to further choose personalized strategies for preparing to quit and remaining smoke free by learning skills to overcome barriers. Various techniques to deal with personal cravings, stress, and peer pressures were incorporated to encourage participants to try many strategies. Specific tips were given to help students consider and to help open dialogue about the various ways to avoid personal triggers to smoke. Discussion also served to help students identify alternate ways to relieve stress, how to seek support from family and friends, and what to say to friends who offer cigarettes. Motivational videos and contracts with students were also used.

Recruitment

Faculty, counselors, and administrators referred interested students for a 20-minute to 30-minute assessment with the school nurse; other students were self-referred. The transtheoretical model (Prochaska & DiClemente, 1983) of behavior change was used to identify appropriate candidates for the program. Students determined to be of contemplator status or greater in the stages of change were encouraged to take part. The school nurse engaged in short discussions with students in the precontemplator stage in an attempt to move them closer to the contemplator stage. These students received information about the program to encourage future participation.

Based on student opinion that lack of parental support was an important impediment to cessation, parents were addressed during school orientation in September 2000. Messages about health risks associated with adolescent smoking and the influence parents have on their child's smoking behavior were delivered. The new program was presented as an opportunity for parents to help students quit. All parents received a letter in the mail with answers to frequently asked questions and tips on how to support their children's attempts to quit smoking.

Program Implementation

Enrollment commenced following protocol approval by the pertinent Institutional Review Board (Griffin Hospital, Derby, CT). Twenty-two 11th- and 12th-grade students who had been smoking for at least 2 years and were motivated to quit enrolled in the pilot adolescent smoking-cessation intervention program. Intake assessments were completed prior to the intervention, including baseline measures of smoking habits, information on perceived impediments to smoking cessation, and students' desire to try strategies to overcome these barriers.

Participants were screened for seizure and eating disorders, as well as use of other medications before being given the option of the addition of 300 mg of bupropion per day for up to 3 months (with parental permission). Verbal and written, student and parental

Table 1

Student Ratings of the Helpfulness of Intervention Components

Program component	Extremely helpful or quite helpful			Somewhat helpful			Not helpful		
	%	Male	Female	%	Male	Female	%	Male	Female
Weekly meetings	57	7	1	29	2	2	14	2	0
Developing strategies to cut down	43	6	0	43	5	1	14	0	2
Physician involvement	29	3	1	50	5	2	21	2	1
Discussion of ways to stay smoke-free	36	5	0	50	5	2	14	1	1
Video	29	3	1	57	6	2	14	2	0
Tip sheet	21	3	0	29	3	1	50	5	2
Parent discussion with physician	14	2	0	21	2	1	64	7	2
Relaxation tape	7	1	0	21	3	0	71	7	3
Zyban* (9 out of 14 respondents used Zyban)	11	1	0	44	3	1	44	3	1
Relaxation session	0	0	0	43	5	1	57	6	2
Contract	0	0	0	21	2	1	79	9	2

Note. Ratings did not differ significantly between male and female respondents. $N = 14$ (11 males, 3 females).

*Zyban is a brand name for bupropion.

consent was obtained prior to drug dispensation by the school nurse.

Referrals to outside agencies were made for students with other chemical dependencies (determination of dependency was made by the school nurse and the outreach worker).

The program spanned November and December of 2000 and was coordinated and run by the school nurse and the school outreach worker, with support from the research team. Smoking-cessation group sessions were held during rotating class periods. On completion of the intervention, student quit data were collected and process-evaluation questionnaires were completed.

There were no adult smoking-cessation programs available in the community. Interested parents of enrolled students were provided contact information for the study personnel and offered guidance in their quit effort. As appropriate, parents were offered bupropion and physician counseling.

Analysis

Students were asked to complete surveys to report their smoking status and to rate how helpful each program component was toward their efforts to quit or reduce smoking. Chi-square statistics and Fisher's exact tests (for analyses where expected cell-frequency counts were less than five) were used to assess associations between gender and quit or reduction rates as well as intervention component ratings. Analyses were performed to compare numbers of male and female students who quit smoking and who quit or reduced smoking. Comparisons were also made to assess frequency with which male and female students rated a program component as being helpful in their efforts to quit or reduce smoking.

Results

At the end of the program (following Week 8), 20 out of 22 students (91%) were surveyed about their experiences as members of the program, and 14 of 22 students provided feedback on the usefulness of specific program components. For analysis purposes, the two students who were lost to follow-up were considered to be smoking.

Six out of 22 students (27%) reported being smoke free. The average number of cigarettes smoked per day among students who were not able to quit decreased from 22 per day prior to the program to 9; 11 of the 16 who remained smokers (69%) had cut down on the number of cigarettes smoked per day. Overall, 17 of 22 respondents either completely quit or significantly cut down (77%) throughout the course of the program. Numbers of male and female students who quit smoking were comparable (males: 4 out of 15 [27%]; females: 2 out of 7 [29%]; $p = 0.38$). There was also no difference in the number of students who quit or reduced smoking by gender (males: 5 out of 7 [71.4%]; females: 11 out of 15 [73.3%]; $p = 0.38$). The majority (79%) of students who continued to smoke stated that they would participate in such a program again.

Eleven students (50%) whose parents provided written consent were started with a two-week supply of bupropion. More than 40% of students taking bupropion reported that it was somewhat useful as an aid for quitting. However, 7 of the 11 students using the medication reported sleep disturbance. One person each reported headache and stomach upset. Although 8 of 11 students taking bupropion reported taking the medication regularly, as directed, facilitators believed this to be untrue, as some students returned unused packets of medication.

Components of the intervention that received the highest ratings regarding their helpfulness were meeting weekly as a group, the development of personal strategies to cut down and refrain from smoking, the use of a motivational video, and talking with the physician. The majority (86%) of students rated each of these as somewhat helpful, quite helpful, or extremely helpful. Components of the program that were considered helpful by smaller percents of students included bupropion, relaxation techniques, and the physician's conversation with parents. Comparison by chi-square testing revealed no significant differences in male and female students' ratings of each component (see Table 1).

Sixty percent (12 out of 20) of participants reported having at least one smoking parent or other family member. Among these participants, 75% viewed the smoking habits of a family member as an impediment to their own quitting. Some students reported that more parental involvement would be beneficial; however, 55% did not believe that their parents would be interested in learning about ways to support students' efforts.

Discussion

Student recruitment into the smoking-cessation program following the focus groups was greater by a factor of three than that experienced during previous years at the same school. Whether this resulted from school presentation and focus-group participation or the lessons learned from them is unclear; however, modifications made to the prior promotion and the enrollment process clearly enhanced student interest in the program. Methods for maintaining interest and maintaining contact with the students were effective, as indicated by the 13% dropout rate. The specific components of this program, preprogram focus groups, or both may have value for all schools sponsoring smoking-cessation interventions.

The 27% quit rate among participants in this pilot program is relatively high compared to prior programs with adolescents, the previously highest recorded quit rate being approximately 22% (Dino et al., 2001). Quit rates did not differ significantly between males and females. Differences in the degree of difficulty experienced by males and females while attempting to quit were not determined; however, a recent study suggests that male and female adolescents may require gender-specific intervention (Dino et al., 2001). Therefore, preferences among this student population for gender-specific programs will be ascertained at a 12-month follow-up and considered for future study.

Inclusion of pharmacotherapy was considered acceptable by more than half of the participants. Willingness to try pharmacological therapies as an aid to smoking-cessation efforts may have important implications for future treatment of nicotine addiction among adolescents. Efficacy of this approach for adolescent smokers is as yet uncertain; the strong student support for making bupropion available demonstrated in this study may be important to consider in the design of future programs. Use of bupropion for smoking cessation has been found to increase the probability of successful quitting among adult smokers (Holm & Spencer, 2000; Hurt et al., 1997) and may produce similar results in adolescents if taken correctly. Parental supervision may be necessary to ensure bupropion is taken regularly and at recommended intervals to maximize helpful effects and avoid side effects such as sleeplessness.

Acceptance of the use of bupropion by 11 of the 13 parents contacted suggests that they are willing to consider this approach to smoking cessation in their children. Further, the process of obtaining informed parental consent for use of bupropion may have engaged parents in a complementary quit effort of their own—an ancillary benefit.

Successful adolescent smoking cessation may require efforts to increase parental awareness of the benefits of expressing concerns about smoking and ways to support family members who are trying to quit. Provision of communication-skills training for parents and their teenagers may also be beneficial. A study examining parental influences on adolescents' transitions from nonsmoker to experimenter and from experimenter to established-smoker status demonstrated that lack of perceived parental concern about smoking distinguished experimenters who progressed to regular smoking from those who did not; problem-solving communication with parents was found to be protective (Distefan, Gilpin, Choi, & Pierce, 1998). Concurrent smoking-cessation programs for parents of teenagers attempting to quit are also likely to be of profound importance. This study attempted to encourage parents who smoke to consider quitting. However, no programs were available in the community to meet the needs of adults who desired assistance. More work is required to determine effective ways to engage parents in efforts to support their teenager's quit attempts, regardless of whether they are willing to make personal quit attempts. Without parental support, it seems unlikely that adolescents will be successful in their attempts to quit smoking.

There is evidence to suggest that the average smoker requires multiple quit attempts before quitting for good (Hymowitz, Sexton, Ockene, & Grandits, 1991; Zhu, Sun, Billings, Choi, & Malarcher, 1999). Many participants in this study who have not quit smoking have reduced the number of cigarettes smoked per day. Cutting down on number of cigarettes smoked not only reduces health risks associated with smoking but also may lessen the difficulty experienced in attempting to quit in the future. Results of this experience support available evidence suggesting that adolescents are aware of the dangers associated with cigarette smoking and are often motivated to quit (Engels,

Knibbe, de Vries, & Drop, 1998; Houston, Kolbe, & Eriksen, 1998) but find quitting prohibitively difficult (CDC, 1994; Lamkin et al., 1998).

350   Research indicates that tailoring health messages and interventions to individual needs may enhance smoking-cessation outcomes (Juszczak & Sadler, 1999; Strecher et al., 1994). It is well recognized that disease-prevention efforts targeting adolescents must be con-
355 sidered in the context of adolescent development. Therefore, timing and tailoring of interventions to suit adolescent target groups is recommended (Juszczak & Sadler, 1999), particularly to support behaviors throughout each stage of change (Damrosch, 1991).
360 Students emphasized the desire for a program that is not rigid but offers various options for different needs. Thus, making options such as pharmacotherapy, physician contact, and parental involvement available may enhance the appeal of smoking-cessation programs
365 even for students who may not be interested in these particular intervention components.

    Limitations of the study should be noted. The 27% quit rate is promising; however, long-term evaluation data are not yet available. Conclusions as to efficacy of
370 the program in terms of sustained-quit and smoking-reduction rates are premature. Students participating in this study are part of a fairly homogeneous group made up of predominantly white teenagers with moderate to high socioeconomic status, and the study sample is
375 quite small. Therefore, population-based generalizations cannot be made, and further research is needed to determine if the proposed program components are relevant for other adolescent groups. It is unclear to what extent participation in focus-group interviews by
380 some program members influenced interest in the program. Therefore, replication of the program may require alternate methods to establish similar rates of participation. Sophisticated methods to verify self-reported quit and smoking-reduction rates were not
385 available due to financial constraints.

Conclusions

    Student demand for and commitment to this smoking-cessation program as well as the promising quit rate warrant further investigation into school-based methods of assisting adolescents to quit smoking. Pre-
390 intervention focus groups may add independent value by conferring a sense of local ownership and thereby attract program participants. Pharmacological intervention as part of a comprehensive program represents a possible additional means of overcoming certain resis-
395 tances to change; however, further study is required, and a controlled means of monitoring compliance may be necessary. Parental involvement and support is recommended and further research into appropriate and effective ways of engaging parents in efforts to assist
400 their teenagers to quit smoking (and to consider quitting themselves) is encouraged. Finally, refinements in the process of identifying individual impediments to

smoking cessation and to offering strategies tailored to an individual's impediment profile offer the promise of
405 greater success and warrant increased attention.

References

American Lung Association. Connecticut Chapter (n.d.). Nicoteen Challenge. Retrieved from www.lungusa.com

Caplan, D. (1995). Smoking: issues and interventions for occupational health nurses. *AAOHN Journal*, *43*, 633–644.

Centers for Disease Control and Prevention. (1994). Guidelines for school health programs to prevent tobacco use and addiction. *Mortality and Morbidity Weekly Report*, *43*, 1–18.

Centers for Disease Control and Prevention. (1999). *Best practices for comprehensive tobacco control programs—August 1999*. Atlanta, GA: U.S. Department of Health and Human Services, Centers for Disease Control and Prevention, National Center for Chronic Disease Prevention and Health Promotion, Office on Smoking and Health.

Centers for Disease Control and Prevention. (2000). Youth tobacco surveillance—United States, 1998–1999. *Mortality and Morbidity Weekly Report*, *49*, vi–94.

Damrosch, S. (1991). General strategies for motivating people to change their behavior. *The Nursing Clinics of North America*, *26*, 833–843.

Dino, G., Horn, K., Goldcamp, J., Maniar, S., Fernandez, A., & Massey, C. (2001). Statewide demonstration of not on tobacco: A gender-sensitive teen smoking cessation program. *Journal of School Nursing*, *17*, 90–97.

Distefan, J. M., Gilpin, E. A., Choi, W. S., & Pierce, J. P. (1998). Parental influences predict adolescent smoking in the United States, 1989–1993. *Journal of Adolescent Health*, *22*, 466–474.

Elders, M. J., Perry, C. L., Eriksen, M. P., & Giovino, G. A. (1994). The report of the surgeon general: Preventing tobacco use among young people. *American Journal of Public Health*, *84*, 543–547.

Engels, R. C., Knibbe, R. A., de Vries, H., & Drop, M. J. (1998). Antecedents of smoking cessation among adolescents: Who is motivated to change? *Preventive Medicine*, *27*, 348–357.

Farkas, A., Pierce, J., Zhu, S., Rosbrook, B., Gilbin, E., Berry, C., et al. (1996). Addiction versus stages of change models in predicting smoking cessation. *Addiction*, *91*, 1271–1280.

Holm, K., & Spencer, C. (2000). Bupropion: A review of its use in the management of smoking cessation. *Drugs*, *59*, 1007–1024.

Houston, T., Kolbe, L. J., & Eriksen, M. P. (1998). Tobacco-use cessation in the '90s—Not "adults only" anymore. *Preventive Medicine*, *27*(5 Pt 3), A1–A2.

Hurt, R. D., Sachs, D. P., Glover, E. D., Offord, K. P., Johnston, J. A., Dale, L. C., et al. (1997). A comparison of sustained-release bupropion and placebo for smoking cessation. *New England Journal of Medicine*, *337*, 1195–1202.

Hymowitz, N., Sexton, M., Ockene, J., & Grandits, G. (1991). Baseline factors associated with smoking cessation and relapse: MRFIT Research Group. *Preventive Medicine*, *20*, 590–601.

Juszczak, L., & Sadler, L. (1999). Adolescent development: Setting the stage for influencing health behaviors. *Adolescent Medicine*, *10*, 1–11.

Katz, D. (2001). Behavior modification in primary care: The pressure system model. *Preventive Medicine*, *32*, 66–72.

Krueger, R. (1994). *Focus groups: A practical guide for applied research* (2nd ed.). London: Sage.

Lamkin, L., Davis, B., & Kamen, A. (1998). Rationale for tobacco cessation interventions for youth. *Preventive Medicine*, *27*(5 Pt 3), A3–A8.

Nichols, M. (1999). The use of bupropion hydrochloride for smoking cessation therapy. *Clinical Excellence for Nurse Practitioners*, *3*, 317–322.

Prochaska, J. O., & DiClemente, C. C. (1983). Stages and processes of self-change of smoking: Toward an integrative model of change. *Journal of Consulting and Clinical Psychology*, *51*, 390–395.

Schubiner, H., Herrold, A., & Hunt, R. (1998). Tobacco cessation and youth: The feasibility of brief office interventions for adolescents. *Preventive Medicine*, *27*(5 Pt. 3), A47–A54.

Smoke Stoppers. (1998). Smoke stoppers participant kit—Adult group program. West Chester, PA.

Strecher, V. J., Kreuter, M., Den Boer, D. J., Kobrin, S., Hospers, H. J., & Skinner, C. S. (1994). The effects of computer-tailored smoking cessation messages in family practice settings. *Journal of Family Practice*, *39*, 262–270.

Sussman, S., Dent, C. W., & Lichtman, K. L. (2001). Project EX: Outcomes of a teen smoking cessation program. *Addictive Behaviors*, *26*, 425–438.

Sussman, S., Lichtman, K., Ritt, A., & Pallonen, U. (1999). Effects of thirty-four adolescent tobacco use cessation and prevention trials on regular users of tobacco products. *Substance Use & Misuse*, *34*, 1469–1503.

Zhu, S. H., Sun, J., Billings, S. C., Choi, W. S., & Malarcher, A. (1999). Predictors of smoking cessation in U.S. adolescents. *American Journal of Preventive Medicine*, *16*, 202–207.

Acknowledgments: This study was supported financially by a tobacco mini grant from the Connecticut Southwest Area Health Education Council and the Connecticut Orange Drug and Alcohol Action Council. We gratefully acknowledge the participation of Amity High School's students and staff, the support of the Connecticut American Lung Association and of St. Vincent's Hospital, Bridgeport, CT, and the technical assistance of Michelle LaRovera.

About the authors: *Meghan L. O'Connell*, M.P.H., is currently a project coordinator at the Yale-Griffin Prevention Research Center. Her research focuses on adult- and adolescent-tobacco-use prevention, as well as the prevention and control of obesity. She has a particular interest in adolescent health. She earned her M.P.H. from Curtin University in Perth, Australia. *Matthew Freeman* earned his M.P.H. in chronic-disease epidemiology from the Yale University School of Medicine. He is currently in the nurse-practitioner program at The Ohio State University. His field of interest is adolescent and college health. *Georgia Jennings*, M.P.H., is the deputy director of the Yale-Griffin Prevention Research Center, where her primary interest is modifying health-risk behaviors through community-based participatory research. She is currently engaged in a yearlong project in Spain related to her interest in developing international collaborations to address the growing list of common public health challenges, especially those related to cardiovascular disease. She received her M.P.H. from the Yale University School of Medicine. *Wendy Chan*, M.P.H., is a biostatistician in the Community and Preventive Medicine Department of the Mount Sinai School of Medicine. She is currently performing statistical analysis for association studies to understand the role of genetic polymorphisms on chronic disease, disease progression, nutrient processing, metabolism of environmental contaminants, and pubertal development. She received her M.P.H. from Emory University. *Laura S. Greci*, M.D., M.P.H., completed her residency in internal medicine/preventive medicine at Griffin Hospital/Yale University in June 2002 and has recently finished her M.P.H. degree requirements from the Yale University School of Public Health. She is participating in research projects involving adult vaccination usage in the inpatient setting, the application of laboratory tests for disease diagnosis (e.g., diabetes), and race and ethnic differences in motor-vehicle fatality rates. After her residency, she plans to continue to research interests in clinical preventive medicine and health promotion in New Mexico, where she attended medical school at the University of New Mexico. *Irina D. Manta* is a research assistant at the Yale-Griffin Prevention Research Center. *David L. Katz*, M.D., M.P.H, F.A.C.P.M., is an associate clinical professor of epidemiology and public health and medicine and the director of medical studies in public health at the Yale University, School of Medicine. A board-certified specialist in both internal medicine and preventive medicine and public health, Katz earned his B.A. from Dartmouth College, his M.D. from the Albert Einstein School of Medicine, and his M.P.H. from the Yale University School of Medicine. Recipient of the American College of Preventive Medicine's Rising Star award in 2001, Katz is a former preventive-medicine residency director, founder and director of an Integrative Medicine Center in Derby, CT; and director of the Centers-for-Disease-Control-funded Yale-Griffin Prevention Research Center, where he oversees a research staff of more than 20. In his role as director, Katz serves as principal investigator for numerous studies related to obesity prevention and control, nutrition effects on health, behavior change, and chronic-disease prevention.

Address correspondence to: Meghan L. O'Connell, Yale Griffin PRC, 30 Division Street, Derby, CT 06418.

Exercise for Article 27

Factual Questions

1. The pilot smoking-cessation program for this research was developed and revised on what basis?

2. How were the participants recruited?

3. How many students enrolled in the program?

4. Who coordinated and ran the program?

5. Why did the facilitators believe that some students did not take bupropion as directed?

6. The quit rate in this program was 27%. According to the researchers, what is the previously highest reported quit rate in the literature?

Questions for Discussion

7. What is your opinion on the use of focus groups to plan this program? Do you think that it would be better to rely on expert opinion instead of students' opinions? Explain. (See lines 48–87.)

8. In your opinion, are the program components described in sufficient detail? Explain. (See lines 88–125.)

9. Does the fact that Table 1 includes only three females affect your interpretation of the data in it? Explain.

10. The data on the effectiveness of the program are based on self-reports by students. Are there advantages and disadvantages to using self-reports for such data? Explain.

11. The researchers describe limitations in lines 367–385. In your opinion, are all the limitations important? Are some more important than others?

12. Based on the information in this article, would you be in favor of using public funds to support additional evaluations of this program? Explain.

Quality Ratings

Directions: Indicate your level of agreement with each of the following statements by circling a number from 5 for strongly agree (SA) to 1 for strongly disagree (SD). If you believe an item is not applicable to this research article, leave it blank. Be prepared to explain your ratings. When responding to criteria A and B below, keep in mind that brief titles and abstracts are conventional in published research.

A. The title of the article is appropriate.

SA 5 4 3 2 1 SD

D. The abstract provides an effective overview of the research article.

    SA   5   4   3   2   1   SD

C. The introduction establishes the importance of the study.

    SA   5   4   3   2   1   SD

D. The literature review establishes the context for the study.

    SA   5   4   3   2   1   SD

E. The research purpose, question, or hypothesis is clearly stated.

    SA   5   4   3   2   1   SD

F. The method of sampling is sound.

    SA   5   4   3   2   1   SD

G. Relevant demographics (for example, age, gender, and ethnicity) are described.

    SA   5   4   3   2   1   SD

H. Measurement procedures are adequate.

    SA   5   4   3   2   1   SD

I. All procedures have been described in sufficient detail to permit a replication of the study.

    SA   5   4   3   2   1   SD

J. The participants have been adequately protected from potential harm.

    SA   5   4   3   2   1   SD

K. The results are clearly described.

    SA   5   4   3   2   1   SD

L. The discussion/conclusion is appropriate.

    SA   5   4   3   2   1   SD

M. Despite any flaws, the report is worthy of publication.

    SA   5   4   3   2   1   SD

Article 28

Evaluation of a Standards-Based Supplemental Program in Reading

DUANE INMAN
Berry College

LESLIE MARLOW
Berry College

BENNIE BARRON
Northwestern State University

ABSTRACT. This pilot descriptive study examined expressed perceptions of a diverse group of teachers who, in the 2002–2003 school year, piloted implementation of a new standards-based supplemental program in reading/language arts, EduSTRANDS. Over 600 teachers in 153 schools using a supplemental, standards-based reading/language arts program were surveyed on their impressions of the features and effectiveness of the program. Standard assessment scores from the schools were compared for the year immediately preceding the use of the materials and for the first year of use of the materials. Overall, teacher evaluations of the program were positive. Scores increased at all tested levels except in sixth grade.

From *Reading Improvement*, *41*, 179–187. Copyright © 2004 by Project Innovation, Inc. Reprinted with permission.

Political, sociological, and educational changes hallmarked the school atmosphere in the United States at the opening of the 21st century. The enactment of the No Child Left Behind Act of 2001, signed on January 8, 2002, provided the impetus for educators to take a closer look at classroom practices and subsequent student outcomes. The ultimate goal is to instruct in a manner which results in the highest possible student performance on standardized achievement measures, thus addressing the demand for stronger accountability for results (www.ed.gov/nclb). Within the next decade "...2013–2014, all students will reach high standards, at a minimum attaining proficiency or better in reading/language arts." Where student performance is found to be at less-than-desirable levels, measures must be taken to implement sound, research-based methodology. Students must be provided with advantageous education programs which address mandated standards and which have been found to be correlated with increased student performance on measures of their standards-based outcomes (NCLBA, 2002). The high standards on which student performance is to be based will come from the professional educational organizations. Specifically, national guidelines established by the International Reading Association (IRA) and by the National Council of Teachers of English (NCTE) for reading and language arts will play a primary role in student evaluation.

In response to the demand for students to achieve at high levels and to meet specified standards, all states have mandated a statewide testing program for all of their students. For example, yearly in Louisiana, students at specific grade levels are tested using the Louisiana Statewide Norm-Referenced Testing Program in order to ascertain their levels of achievement in comparison with national results (Louisiana State Education Progress Report, 2001–2002). The results of this test provide a standard measure for student achievement and can provide an indication of school progress on a year-to-year basis.

This pilot descriptive study examined expressed perceptions of a diverse group of teachers who, in the 2002–2003 school year, piloted implementation of a new standards-based supplemental program in reading/language arts, EduSTRANDS. The EduSTRANDS materials address each of the standards set forth by IRA/NCTE and include multiple activities and strategies to introduce, reinforce, and evaluate student performance. Content examples and practice are provided for each identified skill. Lessons are arranged vertically between grades as well as horizontally within grades for grades 1–8. Well-designed instructional approaches support effective reading instruction. According to the American Federation of Teachers (2003), the following components are needed to effectively teach reading: comprehension strategies, vocabulary instruction, systematic and explicit instruction regarding written English, decoding skills, and phonemic/phonics instruction. The EduSTRANDS materials which address these components were developed in response to numerous teacher requests for a coherent way to ensure all reading/language arts standards could be adequately and thoroughly addressed. Extant basal texts and available curricula often were limited in their consideration of the entire set of standards at particular grade levels.

Over 20 years ago reading research specialists investigated and identified primary instructional areas which were critical to students' success in reading (Share, Jorm, Maclean, & Matthews, 1984; Miller & Ellsworth, 1985). This research continued into the mid-1990s when studies began to emphasize the need for teachers to adapt and supplement lessons in order to

189

meet the unique needs of individual students (Turner, 1995; Snow, Burns, & Griffin, 1998; Pressley, 1998; Pressley, Rankin, & Yokoi, 1996). More recently, the findings of the National Reading Panel (2000), a re-examination of the findings of the National Reading Panel (Camilli, Vargas, & Yurecko, 2003) and research by Farstrup and Samuels (2002) re-emphasized the importance of a comprehensive reading program that allows for specific skill instruction in a variety of areas.

There are a number of programs which have been developed which claim to meet the criteria set forth by these research programs. However, limited independent research is available on the effectiveness of these programs.

Support for the approach taken in this evaluative project was supplied by the IRA (2002) Position Statement on Standards Based Reading Instruction which identifies specific questions to be addressed when reviewing instructional materials:

- Does this program or instructional approach provide systematic and explicit instruction in the particular strategies that have been proven to relate to high rates of achievement in reading for the children I teach?
- Does the program or instructional approach provide flexibility for use within the range of learners in the various classrooms where it will be used? Are there assessment tools that assist teachers in identifying individual learning needs? Are there a variety of strategies and activities that are consistent with diverse learning needs?
- Does the program or instructional approach provide a collection of high-quality literary materials that are diverse in levels of difficulty, genre, topic, and cultural representation to meet the individual needs and interests of the children with whom it will be used?

As an outgrowth from the IRA (2002) Position Statement, the following research questions were addressed by this study:

1. What is the nature of the population of teachers currently using the EduSTRANDS materials?
2. What are the expressed teacher opinions of the materials?
3. What is the nature and direction of change in student scores on the Louisiana Statewide Norm-Referenced Testing Program instrument in the schools using the EduSTRANDS program?

Population

Nineteen school systems within Louisiana participated in this pilot study. Six hundred twelve teachers from 153 schools cooperated in the implementation and assessment of the EduSTRANDS program. The schools ranged from fewer than 200 to over 500 total enrollment, grades K thru 12, and were located in diverse settings including rural, suburban, and urban with a wide diversity of ethnicities and economic levels represented by the 77,000 students using the program. Although some of the schools served grades K–12, only teachers actively engaged in teaching grades K–8 or using the EduSTRANDS materials for remediation in higher grades were surveyed.

Instrument

The EduSTRANDS Teacher Opinion Survey is composed of two major sections: Section One, containing seven items related to demographic information of the teachers and their classrooms, and Section Two containing 14 items. The 14 items assessed expressed teacher perceptions regarding EduSTRANDS materials organization, practical aspects for using the materials, alignment with standards, and preparation for standard evaluation instruments. The instrument was developed by a panel of university professors specializing in reading, research, and education. The materials were peer reviewed and piloted for clarity by classroom teachers, and revised multiple times prior to being disseminated to the target population.

Information concerning student performance within the schools was obtained from the Louisiana school report cards, available as public domain information.

Limitations

Survey research, when conducted through the mail, typically results in respondent participation of less than 20% (Losh, 2003; Zhu, 2001). Generally, these respondents have strong feelings regarding the topic, either positive or negative, which influences their decision to participate (Gall, Gall, & Borg, 2003).

This descriptive study does not attempt to demonstrate a causal effect for the program as indicated by student performance, although information regarding student performance for the year immediately prior to using EduSTRANDS and for the first year of the use of EduSTRANDS is included for comparison purposes. To reach definite conclusions within the first year of implementation would be premature as both students and teachers needed some time to become familiar with the materials, not only with how to use them but how to most effectively integrate them into each instructional/curricular program.

Data Analysis and Procedures

All data were tabulated and analyzed using the SPSS-x program running in the Windows XP environment.

In early spring of 2003, survey packets were sent to each of the participants. Each packet contained a letter of explanation, a survey form, and a self-addressed, stamped envelope for return. The return was anonymous with no identifiers for teacher, school, or school system included on either the envelope or the response form. There was no follow-up on the initial mailing. Approximately 30% of the completed surveys were returned, a rate which is well in excess of the 20% ex-

Table 1
Demographic Information

Teaching assignment	K–4	5–8	8–12	Other	
	54%	22%	9%	12%	
Years' experience	1–3	4–10	11–20	> 20	
	9%	32%	25%	31%	
Education level	Bachelor's	Master's	Master's +	Some college	
	57%	15%	21%	3%	
School enrollment	< 200	200–300	300–400	400–500	> 500
	25%	8%	23%	19%	24%
Class size	< 15	15–20	21–25	26–30	30+
	12%	48%	30%	9%	0%

pected response rate for one-wave mail surveys (Losh, 2003; Zhu, 2001).

Results

Demographics

Respondent demographics are summarized in Table 1. The majority of the teachers (76%) taught in grades 185 1–8 with only 9% at higher grades. Twelve percent expressed that their assignment was "other," which probably indicates that their teaching assignments were multiple levels or special classes not specified on the questionnaire. This was an experienced group of teach- 190 ers with only 9% having fewer than four years of teaching experience. They taught in a wide variety of school sizes and 79% had a class size of 15–25 students. Fifty-seven percent of the respondents had a bachelor's degree, with an additional 36% having at 195 least a master's degree. The remaining 3% indicated "some" college.

Program Opinions

In looking at the individual components of the satisfaction section of the survey, there is strong support from the teachers regarding the usefulness of the materials in the three categories—practical aspects of use 200 (Table 2), alignment with standards (Table 3), and materials organization (Table 4). Noteworthy are the items in which there was over 85% agreement or strong agreement. These items were: well-organized materials, ease of use, alignment with content standards, 205 alignment with state benchmarks, usefulness for enrichment, and usefulness for extended practice. In looking for items of agreement between the 80% and 85% levels, teachers expressed agreement that the materials were ready for immediate use, complemented the read- 210 ing and language arts programs, provided a variety of formats, and accommodated student needs. There were two remaining items with which at least 75% of the respondents agreed: The materials complement the 215 basal in use, and the materials provide ease of lesson modification.

Table 2
Practical Aspects of Use

	Strongly agree/agree	Strongly disagree/disagree	Neither
Ready for immediate use	80.8%	5.5%	9.3%
Ease of use of all materials	88.5%	2.8%	8.2%
Ease of lesson modifications	76.4%	2.8%	19.9%
Accommodates for student needs	82.3%	1.7%	10.4%
Use as enrichment	85.2%	2.8%	11.0%
Use for extended practice	89.6%	.6%	8.8%

Table 3
Alignment with Standards

	Strongly agree/agree	Strongly disagree/disagree	Neither
Aligned with content standards	88.5%	1.1%	9.9%
Aligned with state benchmarks	85.2%	1.1%	13.2%
IOWA test	66.5%	3.9%	29.1%
LEAP test	67.6%	3.3%	28.6%

Table 4
Materials Organization

	Strongly agree/agree	Strongly disagree/disagree	Neither
Well-organized materials	85.7%	2.2%	8.8%
Complements basal	74.7%	2.2%	20.3%
Complements reading/language arts curriculum	82.4%	2.8%	14.3%
Variety of lesson formats	81.3%	4.8%	13.7%

Thus, there was agreement by more than 3/4 of the teachers with the usefulness of all the features of the program. When looking at the portion of the population which disagreed with the 14 items, there were no items with which there was disagreement at greater than 5.5%.

Outcomes

An examination of the progress of test scores within the schools using EduSTRANDS reveals that there were higher scores at all levels (Table 5) on the Louisiana Statewide Norm-Referenced Testing Program between spring 2002 and spring 2003 results except at grade 6. All differences were significant at the $p > .05$ level. While this does not necessarily indicate a causal relationship between the use of the program and test scores, it does indicate that significant progress is being made in almost every grade where the program is in effect.

Table 5
Comparison of Mean Scores, 2002–2003

Grade level	Mean scores	
	2002	2003
3	48.31	52.22
5	46.13	51.75
6	48.50	41.98
7	46.17	47.14

Discussion

It is necessary to provide appropriate reading instruction to all students beginning in the early grades of elementary school and extending throughout middle and high school. To become good readers, students must develop an awareness of the skills needed for decoding as well as the ability to read text accurately and fluently and the ability to apply comprehension strategies as they read. Research included in the report from the National Reading Panel (2002) emphasized that teachers needed to adjust the instruction in these areas in order to meet the specific needs of their students. The program examined through this survey has materials that incorporate this component so that students receive instruction and support that integrates with the current classroom materials to supplement learning endeavors in reading. The results of the teacher satisfaction survey indicate that teachers are highly in agreement that the features of the program meet the requirements for an effective, research-based set of materials. According to the respondents, the versatility of the EduSTRANDS program provides teachers with the tools that are critical to the teaching of reading.

Additionally, an examination of the test scores indicates gains at almost all levels. Based on test score results and teacher evaluations, there appears to be no discernable distinction between the effectiveness of this program in grades K–8 and its use in specific remedial instruction at the high school level. It is strongly recommended that additional research be done with respect to student progress for the populations using the program, and comparisons be made with non-participant peers to discover if the change in scores is indeed causal.

References

American Federation of Teachers (2003). www.aft.org/edissues/reading/

Camilli, G., Vargas, S., & Yurecko, M. (2003). Teaching children to read: The fragile link between science and federal education policy. *Education Policy Analysis Archives, 11*(15). Retrieved [Dec. 2003] from http://epaa.asu.edu/epaa/v11n15

Farstrup, A., & Samuels, S. (Eds.) (2002). *What research has to say about reading instruction.* Newark, Delaware.

Gall, M., Gall, J., & Borg, W. (2003). *Introductory Statistics.* Boston, Allyn and Bacon.

International Reading Association (2002). *What is evidence-based reading instruction?* Newark, Delaware.

Losh, S. C. (2003). http://edf5481-01.fa02.fsu.edu/Guide5.html.

Louisiana Department of Education (2003). *2001–2002 Louisiana State Education Progress.* Baton Rouge, Louisiana.

Miller, J., & Ellsworth, R. (1985). The evaluation of a two-year program to improve teacher effectiveness in reading instruction. *Elementary School Journal, 85.*

National Reading Panel (2000). *Teaching children to read: An evidence-based assessment of the scientific research literature on reading and its implications for reading instruction.* Washington, DC.

Pressley, M. (1998). *Reading instruction that works: The case for balanced teaching.* New York: Guilford Press.

Pressley, M., Rankin, J., & Yokoi, L. (1996). A survey of instructional practices of primary teachers nominated as effective in promoting literacy. *Elementary School Journal, 96,* 363–384.

Share, D., Jorm, A., Maclean, R., & Matthews, R. (1984). Sources for individual differences in reading acquisition. *Journal of Educational Psychology, 76,* 1309–1324.

Snow, C., Burns, M., & Griffin, P. (Eds.) (1998). *Preventing reading difficulties in young children.* Washington, DC.: National Academy Press.

Turner, J. (1995). The influence of classroom contexts on young children's motivation for literacy. *Reading Research Quarterly, 30,* 410–441.

U. S. Department of Education (2002). Executive summary. The No Child Left Behind Act of 2001. http://www .ed.gov.offices/OESE/esea/execsumm.html.

Zhu, Y. (2001). http://biostat.coph

About the authors: Drs. *Duane Inman* and *Leslie Marlow,* Charter School of Education/Human Sciences, Berry College, Mount Berry, GA. *Dr. Bennie Barron,* Teacher Education Center, Northwestern State University, Natchitoches, LA.

Address correspondence to: Dr. Duane Inman, Charter School of Education/Human Sciences, 2277 Martha Berry Hwy. NW, Mount Berry, GA 30149.

Exercise for Article 28

Factual Questions

1. Who developed the instrument used in this program evaluation?

2. Was the instrument pilot tested?

3. Do the researchers claim that this evaluation shows a causal effect (i.e., the effect of the program on student performance)?

4. The researchers cite a study suggesting that when survey research is conducted through the mail, the typical respondent participation is less than what percentage?

5. What percentage of the responding teachers taught in grades higher than 8th grade?

6. Were all the differences in mean student performance from 2002 to 2003 statistically significant? If yes, at what probability level?

Questions for Discussion

7. The researchers state that this is a pilot descriptive study. Do you agree? If yes, what could be done to make it a more definitive study? (See line 41.)

8. Does the description of the EduSTRANDS program give you an adequate overview of it? Explain. (See lines 41–65.)

9. The response rate was approximately 30%. In your opinion, is this a serious limitation of this program evaluation? (See lines 179–182.)

10. In your opinion, how important would it be to include a control group in a future study of student outcomes resulting from the EduSTRANDS program? Explain. (See lines 223–233.)

11. This evaluation focuses on teachers' perceptions of a program. Do you think that this is equally important to student outcomes when evaluating an educational program? Explain.

Quality Ratings

Directions: Indicate your level of agreement with each of the following statements by circling a number from 5 for strongly agree (SA) to 1 for strongly disagree (SD). If you believe an item is not applicable to this research article, leave it blank. Be prepared to explain your ratings. When responding to criteria A and B below, keep in mind that brief titles and abstracts are conventional in published research.

A. The title of the article is appropriate.

SA   5   4   3   2   1   SD

B. The abstract provides an effective overview of the research article.

SA   5   4   3   2   1   SD

C. The introduction establishes the importance of the study.

SA   5   4   3   2   1   SD

D. The literature review establishes the context for the study.

SA   5   4   3   2   1   SD

E. The research purpose, question, or hypothesis is clearly stated.

SA   5   4   3   2   1   SD

F. The method of sampling is sound.

SA   5   4   3   2   1   SD

G. Relevant demographics (for example, age, gender, and ethnicity) are described.

SA   5   4   3   2   1   SD

H. Measurement procedures are adequate.

SA   5   4   3   2   1   SD

I. All procedures have been described in sufficient detail to permit a replication of the study.

SA   5   4   3   2   1   SD

J. The participants have been adequately protected from potential harm.

SA   5   4   3   2   1   SD

K. The results are clearly described.

SA   5   4   3   2   1   SD

L. The discussion/conclusion is appropriate.

SA   5   4   3   2   1   SD

M. Despite any flaws, the report is worthy of publication.

SA   5   4   3   2   1   SD

Article 29

Program to Reduce Behavioral Infractions and Referrals to Special Education

JAY GOTTLIEB
New York University

SUSAN POLIRSTOK
Lehman College of the City University of New York

This article reports the results of a professional development program using positive behavioral interventions designed to reduce the number of behavioral infraction reports and referrals to special education and
5 to improve academic achievement. Clinical personnel participated in all of the training sessions and were encouraged to explore how their interactions with teachers could support the "positive intervention" program. Not only can clinical personnel offer caring and
10 support for teachers who are committed to examining their management practices and making changes, they also can serve as resources when discussing students who present with severe physical, behavioral, or social-emotional challenges. From a clinical perspective,
15 helping teachers meet the individual and more specialized intervention needs of students with special challenges can begin only when classroom climate, organization, and structure have been addressed. The importance of these broad issues has been noted by Pollo-
20 way, Patton, and Serna (2001), who maintained that classroom organization and management are essential "precursors to teaching."

Intervention Sites

Three elementary schools from an inner-city school district, schools A, B, and C, were chosen for interven-
25 tion on the basis of requests to the district superintendent for assistance with classroom management and concerns about the rate of referral to special education. All three schools had similar student populations—primarily low-income racial and ethnic minority stu-
30 dents. On average, 40.3 percent of the schools' student populations were African American, 55.7 percent were Latino, 3.2 percent were Asian, and .8 percent were white. The proportion of students receiving free lunch across the three schools ranged from 91 percent to 99
35 percent. All three schools had characteristics commonly found in inner-city elementary schools: high teacher turnover, poor staff morale, low academic achievement, and substantial poverty and social fragmentation in the community.

40 In the first school selected for training, school A (a K–8 school with about 550 students, of whom approximately 300 were in grades K–5), teachers forwarded to the principal 625 anecdotal reports of behavioral infractions by students in grades K–5. This was
45 42 percent more than the 360 reports forwarded to the principal during the preceding school year for the elementary-level students. School A also had an extremely high rate of special education referrals, which was of great concern to the school district administra-
50 tion; 11.2 percent of the school's K–5 population was referred, compared with an average of 4.7 percent for the whole school district. The referral rate of 11.2 percent placed this school in the upper 5 percent of all 811 primary and middle schools in the city for which data
55 were available. In schools B and C, trained during the following school year, student referrals to special education represented 8 percent of the enrollment in each school, almost double the average district special education referral rate.

Schoolwide Training Program

60 At the request of the district superintendent and the principals of schools A, B, and C, a training program for all administrators, clinical personnel, teachers, and paraprofessionals in these three schools was initiated. The training focused on behavior management proce-
65 dures using positive behavioral interventions to increase the level of teacher praise and reinforcement of students and reduce the use of punishment and negative teacher comments. This is in keeping with trends in behavioral intervention, which stress positive interven-
70 tions over negative and punitive strategies (Smith, Polloway, Patton, & Dowdy, 2004).

Careful crafting of classroom rules, contingent teaching, use of teacher praise, development of hierarchies of no-cost or low-cost tangible reinforcers, and
75 selective ignoring were among the techniques taught. These techniques have been widely documented in the literature as effective in promoting student learning (Lloyd, Forness, & Kavale, 1998). The program sought to empower teachers to create high-approval class-
80 rooms that children would find emotionally safe to take

Table 1
Professional Development Program Results Compared with the Preceding Year

Target outcomes	Preceding year comparison data *n*	After professional development program *n*	Percent improvement %
Behavioral infractions reports for school A	625	246	−61
Special education referrals for school A	30	11	−63
Special education referrals for schools B and C	32	22	−31
Students reading at grade level in school A (%)	27	35.3	8.3†
Students reading at grade level in schools A, B, and C (%)	28.8	32.2	3.5‡

Notes. †Overall school district performance showed a 3.5 percent increase across all 15 elementary schools in the district compared with the 8.3 percent increase in school A. ‡Overall school district performance showed a 1.5 percent decline across all 15 elementary schools in the district compared with the 3.5 percent increase for schools A, B, and C.

the necessary risks to tackle difficult academic tasks and change inappropriate behaviors.

An overriding intent when developing the training program was to minimize demands on teachers. Steps were taken to ensure that teachers did not have to do things that were overly demanding of their time. The rationale was that if teachers were asked to do things that were too taxing or foreign to their normal routines, they would not attempt the required activities, an outcome often evident when new programs are initiated.

In school A, training began immediately before school opened for the academic year and the last session occurred in mid-January. The seven half-days that were available between September and January for training were the entire allotment of contractually mandated professional development days through mid-year. In late March, a 45-minute follow-up session was provided to review key points that were covered during the seven sessions; this refresher session took place during the monthly faculty meeting. Schools B and C were trained jointly during the following year; only five half-day sessions were available for the professional development program between September and January. Similarly, a follow-up refresher session in March was held for both schools at their regular monthly faculty meetings.

The 150-minute professional development sessions typically began with a question and answer period, during which teachers raised questions about problems they encountered in their classes. The trainer encouraged group discussions to address these problems. Another portion of each session focused on a specific behavior management technique and how that technique could be used in classrooms.

The techniques taught in the professional development program were the following:

1. How to develop classroom rules that are behaviorally specific (that is, few in number and stated positively)
2. How to teach classroom rules to foster student ownership of academic and behavioral performance (that is, increase locus of control through self-monitoring)
3. How to increase teacher consciousness about language used with students to praise or reprimand and whether teacher comments were appropriate given classroom rules (that is, how to be a contingent teacher in the use of approval and disapproval)
4. How to increase the number of positive statements made by teachers to individual students and to the whole class compared with the number of negative statements (that is, how to be a high-approval teacher and change the approval-disapproval ratio in the classroom)
5. How to develop reinforcement systems that were "user-friendly" in terms of time and record keeping (that is, limit the complexity of the system)
6. How to use selective ignoring while trying to "catch students being good" (that is, change the focus from "catching students being bad")
7. How to work with high-frequency disruptive behaviors by reducing them gradually over time (that is, set realistic behavior change goals that recognize that change is often a slow process).

Time was allotted during each training session for participants to meet in small groups, usually by grade level taught, to discuss how the techniques presented could be applied in their classrooms in a developmentally appropriate way. Clinical personnel were integrated into these small-group discussions and provided a developmental perspective about what strategies might work with particular grades. Group members' collective sharing during training sessions led to other discussions outside the program. Participants were learning how to collaborate and support each other with respect to general classroom management issues, as well as issues related to the special needs of individual children.

Outcomes

The evaluation of outcomes varied slightly according to the data available in individual schools (see Table 1). Standardized achievement tests and referrals for special education were available in all three schools. Other data, such as the number of behavioral infraction reports forwarded to the principal, were available only for school A.

Information on behavioral infractions in school A was provided by the principal. The number of behav-
170 ioral infraction reports that the principal received from the teachers was recorded monthly. The number of referrals to special education and reasons for the referrals were obtained from the clinical team responsible for processing special education referrals for each of
175 the schools. Members of the clinical team assigned to each school received the referrals and accompanying documentation, conducted the multidisciplinary assessments, and determined eligibility and placement recommendations. Information on referrals from each
180 clinical team was gathered in mid-June.

Behavioral Infraction Reports

In the year preceding the training, 625 behavioral infraction reports were sent to the principal in school A, a significant increase over the 360 reports submitted the year before. During the school year in which the
185 professional development program was offered, 246 behavioral infraction reports were forwarded, a reduction of 61 percent over the preceding year and 32 percent over the year before that.

Referrals to Special Education

Special education referrals to the clinical team for
190 behavioral problems were collected in schools A, B, and C. In school A, data on referrals to special education declined from 30 the preceding year to 11 during the training year, a 63 percent reduction. Referral rates for special education in schools B and C dropped 31
195 percent during the training year compared with the preceding year.

Academic Achievement

School achievement data on standardized reading tests administered to all schools in the city were used as measures of academic achievement. During the
200 school year preceding the professional development program, 27 percent of the students in school A scored at or above grade level on the California Test of Basic Skills, which was administered annually to all students in city school systems beginning in the third grade. In
205 the year immediately following the training, 35.3 percent of the students in school A scored at or above grade level. The increase of 8.3 percent of children reading at or above grade level was substantially higher than the 3.5 percent average increase for that inner-city
210 school district as a whole across its 15 elementary schools. It was also the first time in six years that reading scores in school A had improved.

Reading scores for schools A, B, and C at the end of the second training year were compared with the
215 other 12 elementary schools in the district. The percentage of children reading at or above grade level in the three schools that received the professional development program increased from 28.8 percent to 32.3

percent. During the same period, scores for the other 12
220 schools declined from 39.2 percent reading at or above grade level to 37.7 percent. Although the district had allocated the same level of resources for literacy development in all 15 elementary schools, the three schools that received the professional development program
225 improved five percentage points beyond the other schools. Only two of the 12 schools in the comparison group improved their performance during the same time period.

School Climate

As a consequence of the professional development
230 program, tangible changes in school climate were noted in schools A, B, and C. Observational data supplied by the principals characterized the nature of these changes:

- Teachers treated children with greater respect.
235 - There was less "backbiting" among teachers than in previous years.
- The faculty seemed less stressed.
- Teacher-paraprofessional teams functioned more consistently and more effectively with regard to
240 classroom management. Itinerant teachers saw positive changes in the school environment.
- Clinical staff interacted with teachers in a broader context as resource personnel.

Changes in school climate occurred even though
245 not every teacher had adopted the program. Principals reported that about one-third of the teachers attempted the program and dropped it within a day or two, claiming that it was not effective. Another third attempted to implement the behavioral program, stopped, and then
250 resumed it, sometimes for several iterations. The final third of the teachers implemented the program and stuck with it for the duration of the school year. Asked why some teachers believed that the program was unsuccessful, the principals responded that teachers who
255 saw the program as a failure were seeking total and immediate elimination of the inappropriate behaviors they were trying to improve. When the behaviors were not eliminated immediately, the teachers concluded that the program was not viable. Teachers who kept
260 coming back to the program were more willing to accept a gradual reduction in inappropriate behavior as a criterion for success. Changing classroom behavior of whole classes or individual students requires that teachers courageously examine their use of reinforce-
265 ment and punishment and the provision of incentives to foster engagement of students in the change process. For teachers who had the patience to work with the program, results were evident.

Implications

This professional development program confirmed
270 what researchers and teachers typically say about classrooms—that successful behavior management is a

196

critical prerequisite for successful academic instruction. Less time spent on managing behavior translates into more time available for instruction. This finding is supported in the literature: "Effective classroom management is required if students are to benefit from any form of instruction, especially in inclusive classrooms where students display a wide range of diversity (Jones & Jones, 2001)" (Smith et al., 2004, p. 42).

As a result of this professional development program, behavioral infraction reports and conduct-related special education referrals declined substantially. When teachers were provided with the skills to manage disruptive behavior, they referred fewer students for special education. In reviewing the referrals to special education over the intervention period, we noted that the nature of these referrals shifted from primarily conduct-related referrals to more academic referrals that were skill specific. Overall, all three schools improved on the variables targeted for intervention. However, school A showed greater improvement than schools B and C. This may be due in part to the fact that school A was trained by itself over seven half-day sessions, whereas schools B and C were trained together over five half-day sessions. The differences in the number of half-day training sessions that were available each year were a function of mandated professional development time from which the district could not deviate. Moreover, training two schools together could have affected the teachers' comfort level when sharing concerns regarding their teaching and management. Finally, the role and reputation of the principal as a leader and respected colleague could have affected the performance of each of these schools. School A's principal was highly regarded by the staff and attended all training sessions and actively participated throughout the program, whereas the principals of schools B and C supported the program and encouraged the staff but did not actively participate in the sessions. This suggests that the active participation of the principal in this type of schoolwide intervention may be a critical variable.

This schoolwide approach to improving behavior significantly affected school climate and highlighted the roles clinical personnel can play in supporting school change. Clinical personnel met more often with groups of teachers to discuss reinforcement programs for whole classes as well as individual students with special needs. The gap between "in-classroom personnel" (teachers and paraprofessionals) and "out-of-classroom personnel" (clinical psychologists and social workers) was bridged by this positive intervention program.

The professional development program highlighted in this article recognizes the importance of creating school communities rich with approval and opportunities for success. Interactions between teachers and students that are characterized by high approval can contribute to a successful instructional program and a positive school climate, which can yield the types of academic and behavioral gains described in this work.

References

Lloyd, J. W., Forness, S. R., & Kavale, K. A. (1998). Some methods are more effective than others. *Intervention in School and Clinic, 33*, 195–200.

Polloway, E. A., Patton, J. R., & Serna, L. (2001). *Strategies for teaching learners with special needs* (7th ed.). Columbus, OH: Merrill.

Smith, T. E., Polloway, E. A., Patton, J. R., & Dowdy, C. A. (2004). *Teaching students with special needs in inclusive settings* (4th ed.). Boston: Pearson.

Acknowledgment: This work was supported by a grant from the New York Community Trust to New York University.

About the authors: *Jay Gottlieb*, Ph.D., is professor of special education, Department of Teaching and Learning, New York University, New York, NY. *Susan Polirstok*, Ed.D., is associate dean, Department of Specialized Services in Education, and professor of special education, Lehman College of the City University of New York.

Address correspondence to: Dr. Susan Polirstok, Lehman College of the City University of New York, 250 Bedford Park Boulevard West, Bronx, NY 10468. E-mail: susan.polirstok@lehman.cuny.edu

Exercise for Article 29

Factual Questions

1. The three schools were selected for this program based on requests to the district superintendent for assistance with what?

2. How did the professional development sessions typically begin?

3. Were the clinical personnel (trainers) integrated into the small-group discussion sessions?

4. What was the percent improvement in behavioral infraction reports for school A?

5. What percentage of the students in school A was reading at or above grade level after the professional development program?

6. Who supplied the observational data on school climate?

Questions for Discussion

7. The professional development session lasted 150 minutes. In your opinion, is this long enough for the implementation of a program such as this one? (See line 107.)

8. Keeping in mind that this is a research report and not a professional development guide, is the implementation of the program described in sufficient detail to provide you with a clear understanding of it? (See lines 107–160.)

9. In your opinion, is the observational process used by the principals to collect data on school climate described in sufficient detail? Explain. (See lines 229–268.)

10. Does it surprise you that one-third of the teachers attempted the program and dropped it within a day or two, claiming that it was not effective? Explain. (See lines 244–248.)

11. Do the data in this report convince you that this program deserves to be explored in further research? Explain.

Quality Ratings

Directions: Indicate your level of agreement with each of the following statements by circling a number from 5 for strongly agree (SA) to 1 for strongly disagree (SD). If you believe an item is not applicable to this research article, leave it blank. Be prepared to explain your ratings. When responding to criteria A and B below, keep in mind that brief titles and abstracts are conventional in published research.

A. The title of the article is appropriate.

    SA   5   4   3   2   1   SD

B. The abstract provides an effective overview of the research article.

    SA   5   4   3   2   1   SD

C. The introduction establishes the importance of the study.

    SA   5   4   3   2   1   SD

D. The literature review establishes the context for the study.

    SA   5   4   3   2   1   SD

E. The research purpose, question, or hypothesis is clearly stated.

    SA   5   4   3   2   1   SD

F. The method of sampling is sound.

    SA   5   4   3   2   1   SD

G. Relevant demographics (for example, age, gender, and ethnicity) are described.

    SA   5   4   3   2   1   SD

H. Measurement procedures are adequate.

    SA   5   4   3   2   1   SD

I. All procedures have been described in sufficient detail to permit a replication of the study.

    SA   5   4   3   2   1   SD

J. The participants have been adequately protected from potential harm.

    SA   5   4   3   2   1   SD

K. The results are clearly described.

    SA   5   4   3   2   1   SD

L. The discussion/conclusion is appropriate.

    SA   5   4   3   2   1   SD

M. Despite any flaws, the report is worthy of publication.

    SA   5   4   3   2   1   SD

Article 30

Efficacy of Alternative Teacher Certification Programs: A Study of the Florida Model

JO LYNN SUELL
Sul Ross State University

CHRIS PIOTROWSKI
University of West Florida

ABSTRACT. Alternative certification teacher programs have been gaining in popularity in recent years. Yet the efficacy of such programs remains in question, and empirical data on such programs are urgently needed. The current study compared confidence in instructional skills designated in the Florida Educator Accomplished Practices in a sample of alternative certification program first-year graduates and traditional teachers. No significant differences between the two groups were noted. These results support prior research findings regarding equivalence in teacher competency in graduates of alternative programs versus traditionally trained teachers.

From *Education*, *127*, 310–315. Copyright © 2006 by Project Innovation, Inc. Reprinted with permission.

Introduction

Alternative certification (AC) programs give instructors a fast-track avenue to obtain certification while working in the classroom as a teacher. Candidates usually have bachelor's degrees or advanced degrees in other areas of specialization. Alternative certification programs vary widely in purpose, content, and structure from state to state, but the majority of the programs require training, licensure exams, coursework, and mentoring while the individual is working in the classroom (U.S. Department of Education, 2002, 2003). The major goals of AC programs are to increase the quantity and quality of teachers and to increase the number of male and minority teachers. Moreover, programs attract individuals who are committed to staying in the teaching profession. Morris (2002) conducted a study of different AC programs and found that the age and academic major of the individual have a major impact on teacher retention, with older individuals more likely to stay in teaching.

Florida Alternative Certification Programs

Florida faces a teacher shortage similar to states in the West and in the rest of the South. In fact, Florida will need more than 162,000 new teachers and paraprofessionals by the year 2010. It is estimated that the state will need 16,000 new teachers every year for the next 8 years as a result of the high teacher retirement rates, attrition in the field, and lack of interest in recent graduates of college teacher preparation programs. Bonuses are frequently offered to new teachers who agree to work in high-poverty districts at schools whose students have low grades on state tests. Florida has three ways for individuals to meet specialization requirements and two ways to meet the professional requirements to enter the teaching profession (Richard, 2003).

Section 231.17(b) of the Florida Statutes authorizes every school district to develop its own AC program to allow individuals to obtain the professional preparation for certification without earning college degrees. Individuals must meet the state certification requirements in subject areas or have 30 hours of coursework in the field to participate in this program. The district plan must have approval by the Florida Department of Education. The participant must also pass all state certification examinations, demonstrate professional education competence, and satisfy credit requirements. Seven school systems have approved alternative certification programs; these include Hillsborough, Orange, Manatee, Broward, Escambia, Santa Rosa, and the Florida State University Research School. The Bureau of Educator Certification works with each district to obtain pass rates and data on all candidates (Florida State Report, 2002).

The Florida Alternative Certification Program (2002) is based on 12 competencies referred to as the "Educator Accomplished Practices," which were adopted by the Florida State Board of Education in November of 1996. These include (a) assessment, (b) communication, (c) continuous improvement, (d) critical thinking, (e) diversity, (f) ethics, (g) human development and learning, (h) knowledge of subject matter, (i) learning environment, (j) planning, (k) role of the teacher, and (l) technology. This is part of Florida's A+ Plan for improvement and accountability in school throughout the state for student learning and teacher competency.

The state provides a comprehensive set of tasks that includes products and performance practices. The 12 practices are assessed by a set of 2 to 5 tasks and observations. The Florida teacher may use computer programs, online classes, in-service workshops, or college courses to master the material. The teacher is provided a trained mentor and support in the school while teaching and working toward certification (Florida Alternative Certification Program, 2002).

75 The primary purpose of the current study was to compare two teacher education preparation programs. The two programs included teachers who had recently graduated from a traditional program of teacher education and a group who had entered the teaching field through an alternative certification program designed
80 and administered by a local university.

Alternative Program in Northwest Florida

The University of West Florida (UWF) is working with local school districts to provide opportunities for individuals to participate in an alternative certification (AC) program. The university entered into a contract
85 with the local school district for the 2002–2003 school year to develop 12 pedagogic modules to instruct AC candidates using the Florida Department of Education's 12 Educator Accomplished Practices. The university also agreed to provide support and evaluation,
90 collect program fees, and report and collaborate with the director of staff development.

The UWF alternative program commenced on July 25, 2003. Two counties contracted with the University regarding this program for the 2003–2004 school year.
95 Two professors from the university and a coordinator from one of the counties presented an orientation program to explain the basics of the program to principals, mentors, and participants. Information on classes, schedules, and the importance of mentors was stressed.
100 Mentors are teachers who have completed clinical educator training and are teaching similar subjects or grade levels as the participants. The mentor serves as an adviser to the participant and helps locate information and media resources.
105 The AC program begins with a preassessment of skills within 3 weeks of employment. This preassessment consists of (a) a self-assessment by the participant of his or her competency in each of the accomplished practices, (b) informal observations, and (c) the district
110 formal assessment system. This preassessment establishes a baseline and allows experienced participants to omit modules that they have already mastered.

A 3-day course provides training in (a) basic classroom management techniques, (b) strategies for the
115 start of the school year, and (c) rules and procedures. It was developed by the local school district and is comparable to what the state of Florida Department of Education calls Survival Training in its program. If participants are hired after the first of the year, they take this
120 course using a compact disk and workbook. Monthly support group meetings were a new feature introduced during the 2003–2004 school year. These were completely voluntary and intended to help participants by allowing them to share experiences and talk with staff.
125 Classes for the county AC participants were Tuesday nights and some Saturday mornings. The participants

earned 15 hours of graduate credit. The courses included Human Development and Learning, Knowledge of Subject, Role of the Teacher, Lesson Planning, and
130 Assessment.

Traditional Programs in Florida

The UWF program for a traditional undergraduate education degree in middle school education includes 36 hours of education courses. These include courses in (a) psychology, (b) foundations, (c) curriculum, (d)
135 technology, (e) assessment, (f) inclusion, (g) diversity, (h) instruction, (i) management, and (j) reading. These courses are correlated to competencies referred to as Florida Educator Accomplished Practices that were adopted by the state of Florida in 1996 and specify
140 what every teacher should know and be able to do in the classroom.

Method

Site and Participants

This study was conducted in Escambia County in northwest Florida. The Escambia County school system is the 17th largest in Florida and employs over
145 2,500 teachers. All first-year teachers in the county school system, including teachers enrolled in the alternative certification program and teachers who had graduated from traditional college teacher preparatory programs, were included in this study. The selection
150 was limited to first-year teachers with no previous teaching experience and those enrolled in the UWF alternative certification program or certified through traditional methods. A total of 43 alternative and traditional teachers met the qualifications for the study as:
155 (a) not having any previous teaching experience and (b) being either in the university alternative program or certified through a traditional program.

Instrumentation

The instrument used was a Likert scale rating form based on Florida's Accomplished Practices Survey.
160 This scale is currently used as a self-assessment in order to provide the level of competency on basic skills for the Florida Alternative Program to determine areas of strength and weakness. The scale is composed of 44 items and is divided into the 12 areas of accomplished
165 practices. The areas are (a) assessment, (b) communication, (c) continuous improvement, (d) critical thinking, (e) diversity, (f) ethics, (g) human development and learning, (h) knowledge of subject matter, (i) learning environment, (j) planning, (k) role of the teacher,
170 and (l) technology. The 43 participants were asked to rate their comfort level for each of these areas on a scale that ranged from (1) *strongly disagree*, (2) *disagree*, (3) *agree*, to (4) *strongly agree*.

Results and Discussion

The sample population included all first-year teachers in the alternative program group ($n = 25$) and the
175 traditional teacher group ($n = 18$). Based on two-tailed

Table 1

Teachers' Mean Scores on the Educator Accomplished Practices Survey

Practice areas	Alternative ($n = 25$)		Traditional ($n = 18$)	
	M	*SD*	*M*	*SD*
Assessment	3.16	0.54	3.21	0.42
Communication	3.27	0.70	3.31	0.37
Continuous improvement	3.37	0.63	3.42	0.40
Critical thinking	3.21	0.77	3.19	0.43
Diversity	3.35	0.74	3.37	0.40
Ethics	3.39	0.67	3.16	0.52
Human development	3.09	0.72	3.17	0.37
Knowledge of subject	3.20	0.90	3.32	0.48
Learning environment	3.21	0.58	3.19	0.41
Planning	3.24	0.61	3.28	0.44
Role of teacher	3.14	0.77	3.12	0.55
Technology	2.81	0.84	3.08	0.60

Note. Items were measured on a 4-point Likert scale, 1 = *strongly disagree*, 2 = *disagree*, 3 = *agree*, and 4 = *strongly agree*; total *n* = 43.

independent sample *t* tests ($p < .05$), there were no significant differences between the teacher groups on any of the 12 Florida Educator Accomplished Practices areas. The means and standard deviations for each practice area, based on teacher group, are presented in Table 1.

These findings corroborate the work of Stone (2000) and Wayman et al. (2003), who found that teachers trained via alternative approaches express similar levels of competencies as teachers from traditional degree programs. Furthermore, the current findings support similar studies in Texas and Georgia, which concluded that teachers in alternative programs tend to be satisfied with the skills acquired in their training (Chen, 2003; Lohmeier, 2000; Thompson, 2003; Viveros, 2002).

The UWF alternative certification program seems to be providing teachers in Florida with the pedagogical knowledge needed in the 12 areas of Florida Educator Accomplished Practices. In addition, participants in the AC program acknowledged the importance of mentors and in-service support functions. On the other hand, the traditional teachers noted that their internship experience enhanced their sense of teaching proficiency across the 12 practice areas. Future research should include comparative studies on different types of alternative programs and the efficacy of certification programs in other states.

References

Chen, A. L. (2003). The effects of alternative teacher certification programs in Texas on the teacher shortage. (Doctoral dissertation, Texas A&M University, 2003.) *Dissertation Abstracts International, 64,* 3913.

Florida Alternative Certification Program. (2002). *School district implementation resources.* Kit provided to the University of West Florida by Florida Department of Education: Author.

Florida Department of Education. (2000). Critical teacher shortage areas. Retrieved June 11, 2003, from http://www.firn.edu/doe/bin00065/ctstrfactsheet.htm

Florida State Report. (2002). Florida plan for Title II. Retrieved July 18, 2003, from http://www.title2.org

Lohmeier, H. P. (2000). Alternatively certified and traditionally certified novice teacher: An evaluative comparison. (Doctoral dissertation, University of Georgia, 2000.) *Dissertation Abstracts International, 61,* 3012.

Morris, A. L. (2002). Teacher retention: A comparison of alternate route, special alternate route and approved program route licensure in Mississippi. *Dissertation Abstracts International, 63,* 2069. (UMI No. 3058215)

Richard, A. (2003). Quality counts 2003: The teacher gap: Florida. *Education Week.* Retrieved June 19, 2003, from http://edweek.org/sreports/qc03/templates/state.cfm?slug=17qcfl.h22

Stone, M. (2000). Are we adequately preparing teachers for California's class-size reduction? In J. McIntyre & D. Byrd (Eds.), *Research on effective models for teacher education* (pp. 203–217). Thousand Oaks, CA: Corwin.

Thompson, T. M. (2003). Candidate perception of training and self-efficacy in traditional versus alternative teacher preparation programs. *Dissertation Abstracts International, 64,* 2048, A.

Title II. (2004). Meeting the highly qualified teachers challenge: The secretary's annual report on teacher quality, 2003. (2004). Retrieved on August 1, 2004, from http://www.title2.org/2002_2003files.htm

U.S. Department of Education. (2002). *Meeting the highly qualified teacher challenge: The secretary's annual report on teacher quality.* Washington, DC: Author.

Viveros, M. (2002). Alternative versus traditional certification: Comparing experiences of first-year teachers in Kansas City, Kansas (Doctoral Dissertation, University of Kansas, 2002). *Dissertation Abstracts International, 64,* 471.

Wayman, J. C., Foster, A. M., & Mantale-Bromley, C. (2003). A comparison of the professional concerns of traditionally prepared and alternatively licensed new teachers. *The High School Journal, 86,* 35–40.

Exercise for Article 30

Factual Questions

1. What was the "primary purpose" of the study?

2. Did the teachers in this study have previous teaching experience?

3. The alternative program group consisted of how many teachers?

4. What is the mean score for the competency of Assessment for the alternative program group?

5. The scores on the Accomplished Practices Survey could range from a low score of 1 to what high score?

6. Were any of the differences between the means in Table 1 statistically significant?

Questions for Discussion

7. In your opinion, is the alternative program described in sufficient detail? (See lines 81–130.)

8. What is your opinion on using "self-assessment" to measure the teachers' competencies? Are there other ways competencies could be measured? (See lines 158–173.)

9. What is your understanding of the meaning of the term "independent sample *t* tests"? (See line 177.)

10. Do you agree that additional research should be conducted on this topic? Explain. (See lines 201–204.)

11. Do you think that this study has important implications for training teachers? Why? Why not?

12. In a future study, would it be desirable to randomly assign the participants to the two types of programs? Explain.

Quality Ratings

Directions: Indicate your level of agreement with each of the following statements by circling a number from 5 for strongly agree (SA) to 1 for strongly disagree (SD). If you believe an item is not applicable to this research article, leave it blank. Be prepared to explain your ratings. When responding to criteria A and B below, keep in mind that brief titles and abstracts are conventional in published research.

A. The title of the article is appropriate.

SA 5 4 3 2 1 SD

B. The abstract provided an effective overview of the research article.

SA 5 4 3 2 1 SD

C. The introduction establishes the importance of the study.

SA 5 4 3 2 1 SD

D. The literature review establishes the context for the study.

SA 5 4 3 2 1 SD

E. The research purpose, question, or hypothesis is clearly stated.

SA 5 4 3 2 1 SD

F. The method of sampling is sound.

SA 5 4 3 2 1 SD

G. Relevant demographics (for example, age, gender, and ethnicity) are described.

SA 5 4 3 2 1 SD

H. Measurement procedures are adequate.

SA 5 4 3 2 1 SD

I. All procedures have been described in sufficient detail to permit a replication of the study.

SA 5 4 3 2 1 SD

J. The participants have been adequately protected from potential harm.

SA 5 4 3 2 1 SD

K. The results are clearly described.

SA 5 4 3 2 1 SD

L. The discussion/conclusion is appropriate.

SA 5 4 3 2 1 SD

M. Despite any flaws, the report is worthy of publication.

SA 5 4 3 2 1 SD

Article 31

Beginning to Write with Word Processing: Integrating Writing Process and Technology in a Primary Classroom

CHARLENE A. VAN LEEUWEN
University of Prince Edward Island, Canada

MARTHA A. GABRIEL
University of Prince Edward Island, Canada

In a state of organized chaos, students return from their outdoor recess, grab their snacks, and retrieve their notebooks and pencils for writing workshop. One student approaches the teacher asking, "Whose turn is it to use the computers?" Although Sarah (all names are pseudonyms) is disappointed that it is not her turn today, she quickly finds Alex, one of the students chosen to work with the word processor, and shares the good news with him. This information galvanizes Alex into action as he packs his remaining snack away and darts over to the computer corner, anxious to begin his new piece of writing.

This scene might occur in many elementary schools throughout North America today. As federal, state, and provincial governments provide substantial monies for placement of computer technologies in schools, the question remains how best to use this resource in the context of 21st-century classrooms. The purpose of this article is to explore one focused use of these computer technologies and, in particular, to describe the writing behaviors demonstrated by a group of grade 1 students who used word processors to support their writing.

What Does the Literature Say?

Educators have responded to new conceptions of student learning and the emergence of digital technologies with continual searches for effective teaching and learning strategies to meet the needs of 21st-century learners (Leu, 2001; McKenzie, 2000; Turbill, 2002). The integration of the new literacies of information and communication technologies (ICTs) and the curriculum has become a goal for literacy educators (International Reading Association, 2001; International Reading Association & National Council of Teachers of English, 1996; International Society for Technology in Education, 1998; Kinzer, 2003). The integration of ICTs at the classroom level includes the use of word processors as tools supporting the writing process—the focus of this study.

Sociocultural theories of literacy recognize and acknowledge the importance of the social context along with the background experience and skills of students (Bruner, 1996; Vygotsky, 1978). Much of the research on writing, computers, and young children is grounded in the work of these social and cultural theories of language and classroom interaction (Bigge & Shermis, 1999; Cochran-Smith, 1991; Daiute, 1988). Research has demonstrated that communication patterns among students in classrooms change when word processors are introduced as writing tools (Dickinson, 1986; Fisher, 1994; Kumpulainen, 1994; Shilling, 1997). Leu (2002) has pointed out that literacy learning has become increasingly social as technologies and classrooms are integrated. Using a word processor may facilitate meaning making as students and teachers interact within the context of a process writing approach. Student talk and reflection can facilitate sharing and construction of knowledge in a social setting such as a primary classroom.

There are effects on educators as well. Teachers' philosophy, pedagogy, and instructional practices with regard to ICT use directly influence outcomes (Russell, Bebell, Cowan, & Corbelli, 2002). If there is a shift to a more collaborative approach in the environment of a classroom, then the role of the teacher supporting the writing process is also transformed (Cochran-Smith, Paris, & Kahn, 1991; Mercer & Fisher, 1992). The teacher becomes facilitator, guide, and participant in a learning community when engaged in computer-based activities (Labbo, 2004; Snyder, 1993). Even greater transformations of the role of classroom teachers may be emerging. Although Cuban (2001) argued that despite increased access to ICTs, meaningful changes in the instructional practices of teachers have not occurred. Leu, Karchmer, and Leu (1999) proposed that "just as new technologies change literacy, literacy also changes new technologies within a transactional relationship" (p. 638). These researchers suggested that in order to keep pace with the changing role of technologies in literacy classrooms, reflective teachers will increasingly determine and share effective ICT integration in the classroom.

Integrating ICTs frequently requires modification of teaching strategies employed by educators. The use of computers not only affects classroom culture and the social interactions of students and teachers, but it also introduces a new technology (Baker, 2000; Sandholtz, Ringstaff, & Dwyer, 2000). The use of a different tool—a computer with word-processing software—to complete a task traditionally completed with pencil and paper introduces a new realm of possible differences in attitudes, interactions, instructional strategies, and written products (Wood, 2000). In doing so, use of a new tool raises questions with regard to best practices for students at all levels of writing development.

This case study sought to examine the impact that different writing tools had on the writing of beginning writers in the primary grades. The study focused on a class of grade 1 students, including aspects such as the physical environment, classroom culture, instructional goals of the teacher, interactions among students, teacher–student interactions, and the development of student writing while using a word processor. This work is a component of a larger study that included students from three primary classrooms (grades 1–3).

Methods

This research was conducted in a grade 1 class in a rural school in a province on the east coast of Canada. The purpose of the case study (Stake, 1994) was to develop greater understanding of the multiple factors involved in the use of word processing by beginning writers, as well as the effect of integrating ICTs on the classroom environment and on the teacher. The first author (Van Leeuwen) spent hours observing in the classroom, examining variations in student writing behavior, the classroom culture, and communication about writing projects (Patton, 2002). Six boys and seven girls in grade 1 participated in this study; all of them had previous computer experience either at home or through their kindergarten program.

Data Collection and Analysis

Information was collected from classroom observations, informal conversations with the teacher during field visits, interviews with students and the teacher, and student writing samples (Marshall & Rossman, 1999). Observation sessions and interviews were audiotaped and transcribed to capture oral-language interactions of students with peers, the teacher, and the researcher.

Classroom visits occurred every three weeks throughout the school year for 40 to 90 minutes per visit. Students were observed to see how they used the two writing media, word processing, or pencil and paper. During classroom visits, samples of handwritten and word-processed texts produced by the children were collected, and informal conversations were held with the teacher. Short interviews, lasting about 10 minutes, were conducted with four students to further explore their approaches to writing with the two media. These four students were representative of a range of characteristics such as gender, kindergarten attendance, and computer experience. Students were asked how they prepared to write, where they found their ideas for writing, and whom they approached for help. Field notes written after each visit captured as many of the activities and actions of the students in the classroom as possible.

The perspective of the classroom teacher was explored through informal conversations during field visits and through a semistructured interview. Topics discussed in the interview included the following:

- aspects of student behavior,
- qualities of student interactions,
- observations of students during writing sessions,
- professional experiences, and
- the teacher's approaches to writing and technology.

The field notes were annotated to compile information from the notes, audiotapes, and writing samples. Student writing samples were collected and assessed using criteria developed by Alberta Education, Student Evaluation Branch (1997). This information was coded by one coder, using themes identified in the literature such as attitudes toward writing and the teacher's writing instruction (Clements, 1987; Cochran-Smith et al., 1991; Mercer & Fisher, 1992) as well as emerging themes. Emerging themes included interactions with peers, skill transfer, and classroom dynamics. An iterative coding process was used until all annotated notes were reviewed and coded (Miles & Huberman, 1994).

The Grade 1 Class

In Robin Neville's grade 1 classroom, students' desks were arranged in small groups in the center. Around the periphery of the room were a music corner with piano, chairs, and couch; the teacher's work area and desk; low shelving filled with children's books, math manipulatives, and other art supplies; and the computer corner. The three computers in the classroom were older Apple machines. In contrast, the school's computer lab contained 18 new computers, with 3 other computers located outside the lab in the nearby resource center.

The culture in Robin's classroom reflected a focus on productive and enthusiastic activity. Helping her grade 1 students become readers and writers was a high priority. Children were involved daily in a process writing approach as they worked on prewriting, drafting, revising, editing, and publishing the various texts they produced. Expectations were clearly communicated at the start of writing time and were reviewed at the end. During writing workshop, three students in the class were allowed to work at the computers for the duration of the session. The entire class rotated through these three computers so that each child wrote using a word processor every one and one-half weeks.

Technology and Teaching Experiences

Robin frequently encouraged students who made a discovery on the computer to extend their understanding of that discovery. The following exchange is one example:

Robin: I want you to put your name "Nicholas" in between quotes.

Nicholas: Quotes? These?

Robin: These things...and I want a capital "N." So do that.

Nicholas has discovered the shift key and some of the things that it can do. He begins to experiment. Robin notices and encourages him to try a few things. The teacher then asks him to use this newfound option in another sentence (observation notes).

Students were encouraged to experiment and discover things for themselves in this classroom. They were also asked to apply what they had discovered to other circumstances. Problem solving and responsibility were qualities this teacher sought to develop in students.

Teaching experiences play a significant role in what goes on within a classroom, and experiences with technology are no exception. Robin's approach to integrating ICTs and process writing was constantly changing and evolving:

This is my fourth year teaching grade 1, and as each year goes by, I'm surprised how quickly they catch on to technology...when it comes to writing. I think time spent in the lab or developing skills with individuals in the classroom [is time well spent].... Some kids actually write better on a computer or...compose faster using a keyboard than pen and paper.... So my use [of] computers is probably expanding as I go along with grade 1 (teacher interview).

Robin believed that integrating ICTs was important for students and brought old computers in from home to set up in the classroom. These provided the opportunity for grade 1 students to have consistent access to a word processor to support their writing.

Findings

Student Attitudes Toward Writing and Computers

For the most part, students' attitudes toward the writing they did in their classroom were positive. When engaged in writing tasks, students were generally focused. They were enthusiastic writers both on and off the computer. Students were often observed counting the number of sentences they had written. Their body language demonstrated excitement with their progress. Students' enthusiasm to share their finished work (both handwritten and computer generated) was equally intense.

Robin placed a high value on writing and found that students in the class were very motivated when involved in writing. She described how students spoke about writing: Are we having writing time today? When is our writing time? Can we go into the computer lab to finish up a story? Can I share it with the class? Using the computers was something the students enjoyed. Robin said that "even with the ancient technology in my room, there's still...novelty in...using the computer to write" (teacher interview).

Of the four students interviewed about their writing tool preference for composing the first draft of a story, three indicated their preference was for a word processor, and one student preferred to use paper and pencil. Students expressed their concern with the mechanics of writing and the efforts involved with letter formation, spelling words, typing on the computer, and creating pictures to illustrate their story. This is expressed in the following conversation:

Researcher: Why do you like the computer more?

Nicholas: Because, like, we don't have to draw the shapes, all you have to do is just press the buttons.

Researcher: Now, when you say "draw the shapes," do you mean making the shape of the letter?

Nicholas: Yeah (observation notes).

The effort involved in writing with paper and pencil was a major challenge; students spoke of their hands tiring when they wrote that way. In contrast, students enjoyed hunting for letters on the keyboard. Classroom observations confirmed students' stated preferences related to different writing tools—pencil and paper or keyboard—when composing a story.

Teacher Instruction

Robin indicated that developing keyboarding skills and some familiarity with basic word-processing functions were among the primary goals for word-processor use in this classroom. To accomplish this, a variety of instructional strategies were used, such as

- encouraging students to continue their efforts,
- helping students focus on the important details, and
- supporting students as they developed problem-solving strategies.

Most writing skill instruction was a mixture of large-group teaching, followed by individual student–teacher conferences focused on a piece of the student's writing. In contrast, instruction in word-processing skills was approached differently. Large-group lessons were not often used. Word-processing instruction was frequently embedded in lessons designed to teach both writing and word-processing skills, followed by an opportunity for practice. The following is from a lesson on capital letters and punctuation, and it provides a sense of how this was accomplished:

Robin has students sit on the floor near a monitor so that they all can see what is happening. A group lesson on capital letters and punctuation is the focus. A file with the "daily message" is called up. Students are instructed to read the message and then correct the missing capital letters and punctuation. Robin demonstrates several ways to make capital letters. Two students are asked to help demonstrate the tasks, and they come over to the keyboard to do this (observation notes).

Often, word-processing instruction took the form of short mini-lessons slipped into the middle of a writing session. Mini-lessons were not often planned in advance of the session. They were a response to student questions or emerging student needs, or they were presented when Robin wished to share strategies helpful for the entire class. While circulating to observe students' writing, Robin provided advice or guidance on writing skills or conventions to individual students. This one-to-one coaching was extended to include word-processing functions when students wrote with word processors.

Another aspect of instruction was the writing conference. While Robin conducted writing conferences with individual students in the classroom, this was not the situation in the computer lab. In the computer lab, students requiring help with word-processing functions or hardware problems were competing with students who needed guidance about their writing. Conferences in the lab generally took place at the computer, were of shorter duration, and were focused on smaller segments of text.

Interactions

Interactions between teacher and students, and among students themselves, occurred frequently in the writing-process classroom, as well as in the computer lab. The audiotapes from many of the observation sessions revealed the constant hum from conversation when students were writing. There were differences observed in the amount of talk among students depending on where they were writing; the amount of talk in the computer lab was consistently higher than in the classroom.

Students were blatant eavesdroppers. Many times they would enter into an interaction by volunteering information or assistance:

Kayla looks at me and asks, "How do you spell once?" I ask her how it would start and she says "O-U-C." Maria, sitting at the next computer listening to our conversation says, "I know how to spell it." She points to her screen. Kayla scoots around the computer table to see how to spell "once." She returns then to her computer and resumes typing (observation notes).

These interactions may also have begun with students narrating their own actions as they were faced with a task on the computer. Something that frequently emerged from these exchanges between students was the discovery of another word-processor function. In this way, students became peer coaches. It did not matter who taught the students a skill—teacher or peer. If the children wanted to know how to do something, they were satisfied as long as their question was answered.

Robin constantly interacted with students concerning their writing in the classroom and in the computer lab. Aside from regular editing conferences, she helped students with a variety of revisions to their work. The focus tended to be on writing conventions and skills taught to the class. Robin also pointed out differences in student–teacher interactions in the computer lab; students did not need as much attention and developed skills in working independently. Robin speculated that these observed differences might be the result of students' high level of concentration on typing words.

The last form of interaction occurred with the revision of computer-based writing, when students read the text displayed on a classmate's monitor. Students sometimes offered comments on writing they had just read. Students were never observed doing this with a classmate's handwritten work.

Writing Behaviors

Students' writing behaviors using paper and pencil or word processing revealed some intriguing differences in the amount of focused writing time, reading and rereading behaviors, and planning of their writing. Students with strong writing skills working in a notebook with a pencil were frequently able to sustain their focus on a writing task longer than when they worked on the computer. Almost all students with poorer keyboarding skills seemed to slow down in terms of text production after 10 or 15 minutes, whether students were composing new pieces or transcribing their writing.

Reading and rereading handwritten work appeared to be for reflection and for determination of what should come next regarding story development and content. On the computer, reading and rereading was for assessment of what students had typed and of whether the correct keys had been used. Rereading appeared more frequently during word processing and occurred in short bursts. In contrast, students reviewing handwritten work revealed longer, more sustained rereading of their piece of writing. This was particularly obvious during composition of a first draft.

When students were asked how they prepared to write, they reported using a variety of strategies. Some stated that they first prepared their writing tools. Others reported that "thinking" was their starting point. Some students read or reread a book they had enjoyed in preparation for writing, and others sat down to consider which of their personal experiences they wanted to write about. All of these strategies were used in the classroom during traditional writing process sessions, but fewer strategies were used when beginning to write with a word processor.

Writing Sample Analysis

The quality of each of the writing samples was assessed on three criteria: ideas and order, words and sentences, and conventions of language. Analysis of the writing samples revealed that word processors did not reduce the quality of writing of these grade 1 students; that is, word-processed and handwritten pieces were of similar quality. However, there was a difference in the length of the texts. Writing samples composed with pencil and paper were generally longer than those composed with a word processor. There was a range from 73 to 305 words and a mean of 163 words for handwritten work, compared with 37 to 116 words and a mean of 71 words for pieces composed with a word processor.

Discussion

Teacher Instruction

As the integrated use of computers becomes more commonplace in primary-grade curricula, developing a greater understanding of the computer's impact on instruction is increasingly important. Tailoring writing instruction to the context is an important aspect of effective instruction (Cochran-Smith et al., 1991; Mercer & Fisher, 1992; Sandholtz et al., 2000; Snyder, 1993). One challenge of group lessons in the computer lab stems from the students' desire to begin to use the computers. They are not easily engaged by a demonstration lesson that is not hands-on for them. Lesson timing may need to be a more important consideration based on the finding that almost all students with poor keyboarding skills started slowing in their production of text after 10 or 15 minutes. If students start to lose focus, teachers need to consider different ways to break up keyboarding time so the final portion of the writing period is used effectively. The midpoint of a writing session with word processors may be better timing for a mini-lesson than at the beginning, when students are eager to use the computers.

Classroom Interactions

The types of interactions observed, comments by the teacher, and responses drawn from the student interviews reveal the power and frequency of peer interactions. Observations revealed that students relied on one another for help with spelling and word-processing functions. This is similar to findings by Labbo (2004); Lomangino, Nicholson, and Sulzby (1999); and Philips (1995). The help that students provide one another redirects some of the demands on the teacher's attention, enabling the teacher to focus on higher-level questions and problems. Such help also enhances students' problem-solving skills. Most help provided by students to their peers was in the form of direction and generally did not incorporate explanation. This confirms the importance of peer interactions while recognizing the limitations of such assistance.

Classroom observations revealed that the teacher was more tolerant of student talk in the computer lab setting. Increased talk among peers suggests that teachers need to accept a greater degree of interaction in a computer lab. This increased tolerance of student interactions while using the computer may have encouraged students to help their peers. Some research into collaborative writing has found improvements in the quality of writing when students engage in metacognitive talk about their text (Dickinson, 1986; Jones & Pellegrini, 1996). This suggests the possibility that allowing greater task-related interaction among students when they are writing with word processors may result in improved writing quality.

The one-on-one interaction of a writing conference was different when conducted in a computer lab as compared to the classroom. Content was different because various word-processing skills or keyboard issues were frequently addressed. Conferences were shorter in the computer lab because the teacher and student did not work through the entire text in one sitting but addressed one or two issues, and then the student returned to writing. This may be due to challenges in redirecting the student's attention from the computer to the text. This could also be the result of students' demands for speedy assistance with word-processor-related functions in order to continue with their writing task.

Writing conferences generally took place at the student's computer workstation where constraints of the physical environment may have played a role. The teacher and student did not move to a separate table or area of the room to signal to others that a writing conference was in progress. This seemed to give other students greater license to interrupt the conference, given the more diverse demands for assistance in the computer lab. The physical effects of standing bent over a computer screen for several minutes to conduct a writing conference may also have an impact.

Writing Behaviors

In this study, observations of students writing with computers reveal that they rarely create a story web or plan. One reason for this may be that making changes with a word processor is easier, and writers count on the revision process to refine their work. Previous research has not determined how reduced planning affects the quality of grade 1 students' stories. There has been speculation that writers compensate for this reduction in planning by reading and rereading their work (Haas, 1989). The current study did find differences in the reading behavior of participants when composing, with short, more frequent reading of word-processed text. This shift in reading patterns was also found in a study of slightly older students in Australia (Sutherland-Smith, 2002).

Frustration and reluctance were more frequently observed in students when they were transcribing, a less interesting task compared to composing. This is also a finding in studies with older students (Cochran-Smith et al., 1991; Mumtaz, 2001; Seawel, Smaldino, Steele, & Lewis, 1994). The keyboarding skills of younger students did not appear to interfere with their composing because very beginning writers have a slower composing and inscribing rhythm (Cochran-

Smith et al., 1991). Incorrect finger positioning did not seem to impede students' success or enthusiasm in using a keyboard, an observation also noted by Gemmell (2003). Even students who expressed a preference for handwriting stories still had strong interest in using the computers. No participant ever said that he or she would rather not use the computer.

Writing behaviors observed in the computer lab might also result from students' differing levels of concentration when typing words. Alternative explanations for these differences in behavior may be that students are more autonomous in this environment, or more motivated to try invented spelling on the computer because editing is easier. Another potential explanation is that they are more absorbed with the technology and, as a result, are less involved with the adults around them. Students may have been helping one another more frequently because there was a higher tolerance of talk among students in the lab. The combination of influences at work within the environment and how they shape one another, and the understanding and practices of the teacher, are likely the source of the observed changes. This finding is in agreement with Cochran-Smith et al. (1991), Jones and Pellegrini (1996), and Snyder (1994).

Considerations for Classroom Practice

A number of implications for classroom practice emerged from the findings of this study. When integrating word processing and the writing program, teachers should consider the following:

- Develop realistic expectations when implementing a word-processing component in the process writing program. When teachers plan to integrate word processing in their writing workshop, a number of questions must be addressed. What role will the teacher play? Facilitator, guide, or provider of direct instruction? When should keyboarding be introduced to children? What word-processing skills should be introduced to grade 1 students?

- Plan to adjust current instructional strategies. Teachers need to develop and adjust instructional strategies in order to assist students in carrying out all aspects of the writing process, from prewriting to final revisions. Working with the technology brings a new set of decisions that must be made: Who will write with the word processor today? How much work will students do in pairs? Individually? How much peer mentoring will be allowed? Will students be encouraged to assist their peers?

- Schedule feedback times for students. Writing conferences play a critical role in the writers' workshop. Teachers must consider how to ensure that appropriate feedback is given to students when they write with a word processor. Will writing conferences happen at computer terminals? At a table away from the bank of computers? Will teacher and student be able to sit down together? Should the student print the piece of writing to be discussed?

- Be prepared for students to focus on the computers—not on a lesson—in the computer lab. In-class preparations before going to the computer lab may need to take on a new focus to address the students' impatience to begin using computers as soon as they arrive. Teachers could give students minimal instruction before leaving the classroom and let them begin working on the computers immediately. A lesson could then be timed to provide a break for students from keyboarding when those with weaker skills begin to lose their focus, probably at the 10- to 15-minute mark.

- Teach students skills in working collaboratively. Peer teaching can be a powerful tool; however, students need instruction in how to work effectively with one another. What roles will students assume? Which team member should find the next letter? Who could work on checking the spelling? Would peer help be more effective if the peer teacher dictated the next letter or word?

Summary

This study affords an exploration of how beginning writers learn to write using different instruments, and it also provides further information about the relationships among students, teachers, the writing process, and the use of word processors as tools. The dynamic interplay of influences on classroom culture and on the interactions among individuals within a grade 1 classroom is described. From the observations in this study, it is clear that no one composing tool is able to serve all the needs of beginning writers. Word processors are tools that can complement the range and type of writing activities in elementary school classrooms. The leadership role played by the classroom teacher in implementing word processing in the writing curriculum is a critical component in determining the felicitous use of this tool.

References

Alberta Education, Student Evaluation Branch. (1997.) *Classroom assessment materials project (CAMP) grades 1 & 2.* Edmonton, AB: Education Advantage.

Baker, E. A. (2000). Instructional approaches used to integrate literacy and technology. *Reading Online.* Retrieved August 15, 2006, from http://www.readingonline.org/articles/art_index.asp?HREF=baker

Bigge, M. L., & Shermis, S. S. (1999). *Learning theories for teachers* (6th ed.). New York: Longman.

Bruner, J. (1996). *The culture of education.* Cambridge, MA: Harvard University Press.

Clements, D. H. (1987). Computers and young children: A review of research. *Young Children, 43,* 34–44.

Cochran-Smith, M. (1991). Word processing and writing in elementary classrooms: A critical review of related literature. *Review of Educational Research, 61,* 107–155.

Cochran-Smith, M., Paris, C. L., & Kahn, J. L. (1991). *Learning to write differently: Beginning writers and word processing.* Norwood, NJ: Ablex.

Cuban, L. (2001). *Oversold and underused: Computers in the classroom.* Cambridge, MA: Harvard University Press.

Daiute, C. (1988). The early development of writing abilities: Two theoretical perspectives. In J. L. Hoot & S. B. Silvern (Eds.), *Writing with computers in the early grades* (pp.10–22). New York: Teachers College Press.

Dickinson, D. K. (1986). Cooperation, collaboration, and a computer: Integrating a computer into a first–second grade writing program. *Research in the Teaching of English, 20*, 357–378.

Fisher, E. (1994). Joint composition at the computer: Learning to talk about writing. *Computers and Composition, 11*, 251–262.

Gemmell, S. (2003). A study of keyboarding instruction and the acquisition of word processing skills. (*ERIC* Document Reproduction Service No. ED477756.) Unpublished master's thesis, Chestnut Hill College, Philadelphia, PA.

Haas, C. (1989). How the writing medium shapes the writing process: Effects of word processing on planning. *Research in the Teaching of English, 23*, 181–207.

International Reading Association (2001). *Integrating literacy and technology in the curriculum* (Position statement). Newark, DE: Author. Retrieved September 15, 2006, from http://www.reading.org/downloads/positions/ps1048_technology.pdf

International Reading Association & National Council of Teachers of English (1996). *Standards for the English language arts.* Newark, DE; Urbana, IL: Authors. Retrieved September 6, 2006, from http://www.ncte.org/print.asp?id=110846&node=204

International Society for Technology in Education (1998). *National educational technology standards for students.* Eugene, OR: Author. Retrieved September 15, 2006, from http://cnets.iste.org/students/s_stands.html

Jones, I., & Pellegrini, A. D. (1996). The effects of social relationships, writing media, and microgenetic development on first-grade students' written narratives. *American Educational Research Journal, 33*, 691–718.

Kinzer, C. K. (2003). The importance of recognizing the expanding boundaries of literacy. *Reading Online.* Retrieved September 11, 2006, from http://www.readingonline.org/electronic/elec_index.asp?HREF=kinzer

Kumpulainen, K. (1994). Collaborative writing with computers and children's talk: A cross-cultural study. *Computers and Composition, 11*, 263–273.

Labbo, L. D. (2004). Author's computer chair. *The Reading Teacher, 57*, 688–691.

Leu, D. J., Jr. (2001). Internet project: Preparing students for new literacies in a global village. *The Reading Teacher, 54*, 568–572. Retrieved September 6, 2006, from http://www.readingonline.org/electronic/elec_index.asp?HREF=rt/3-01_column/index.html

Leu, D. J., Jr. (2002). Internet workshop: Making time for literacy. *The Reading Teacher, 55*, 466–472. Retrieved September 6, 2006, from http://www.readingonline.org/electronic/elec_index.asp?HREF=electronic/RT/2-02_Column/index.html

Leu, D. J., Jr., Karchmer, R. A., & Leu, D. D. (1999). The Miss Rumphius effect: Envisionments for literacy and learning that transform the Internet. *The Reading Teacher, 52*, 636–642. Retrieved September 6, 2006, from http://www.readingonline.org/electronic/elec_index.asp?HREF=rt/rumphius.html

Lomangino, A. G., Nicholson, J., & Sulzby, E. (1999). *The nature of children's interactions while composing together on computers* (CIERA Report #2-005). Ann Arbor, MI: Center for the Improvement of Early Reading Achievement (*ERIC* Document Reproduction Service No. ED447477).

Marshall, C., & Rossman, G. B. (1999). *Designing qualitative research* (3rd ed.). Thousand Oaks, CA: Sage.

McKenzie, J. (2000). *Beyond technology: Questioning, research, and the information literate school.* Bellingham, WA: FNO.

Mercer, N., & Fisher, E. (1992). How do teachers help children to learn? An analysis of teachers' interventions in computer-based activities. *Learning and Instruction, 2*, 339–355.

Miles, M. B., & Huberman, A. M. (1994). *Qualitative data analysis: An expanded sourcebook* (2nd ed.). Thousand Oaks, CA: Sage.

Mumtaz, S. (2001). Children's enjoyment and perception of computer use in the home and the school. *Computers & Education, 36*, 347–362.

Patton, M. Q. (2002). *Qualitative research & evaluation methods* (3rd ed.). Thousand Oaks, CA: Sage.

Philips, D. (1995). *Evaluation of exploratory studies in educational computing. Study 6: Using the word processor to develop skills of written expression. Final report* (*ERIC* Document Reproduction Service No. ED387820).

Russell, M., Bebell, D., Cowan, J., & Corbelli, M. (2002). *An AlphaSmart for each student: Does teaching and learning change with full access to word processors?* Paper presented at the 23rd National Educational Computing Conference, San Antonio, Texas (*ERIC* Document Reproduction Service No. ED475950).

Sandholtz, J. H., Ringstaff, C., & Dwyer, D. C. (2000). The evolution of instruction in technology-rich classrooms. In R. Pea (Ed.), *The Jossey-Bass reader on technology and learning* (pp. 255–276). San Francisco: Jossey-Bass.

Seawel, L., Smaldino, S. E., Steele, J. L., & Lewis, J. Y. (1994). A descriptive study comparing computer-based word processing and handwriting on attitudes and performance of third- and fourth-grade students involved in a program based on a process approach to writing. *Journal of Computing in Childhood Education, 5*, 43–59.

Shilling, W. A. (1997). Young children using computers to make discoveries about written language. *Early Childhood Education Journal, 24*, 253–259.

Snyder, I. (1993). The impact of computers on students' writing: A comparative study of the effects of pens and word processors on writing context, process and product. *Australian Journal of Education, 37*, 5–25.

Snyder, I. (1994). Writing with word processors: The computer's influence on the classroom context. *Journal of Curriculum Studies, 26*, 143–162.

Stake, R. E. (1994). Case studies. In N. K. Denzin & Y. S. Lincoln (Eds.), *Handbook of qualitative research* (pp. 236–247). Thousand Oaks, CA: Sage.

Sutherland-Smith, W. (2002). Weaving the literacy web: Changes in reading from page to screen. *The Reading Teacher, 55*, 662–669.

Turbill, J. (2002). The four ages of reading philosophy and pedagogy: A framework for examining theory and practice. *Reading Online.* Retrieved September 6, 2006, from http://www.readingonline.org./international/iner_index.asp?HREF=turbill4/index.html

About the authors: *Charlene A. Van Leeuwen* and *Martha A. Gabriel* teach at the University of Prince Edward Island in Canada.

Address correspondence to: Martha A. Gabriel, 550 University Avenue, Charlottetown, Prince Edward Island, C1A 4P3, Canada. E-mail: mgabriel@upei.ca

Exercise for Article 31

Factual Questions

1. How many boys participated in this study?

2. Did the students in this study have previous computer experience?

3. How was the perspective of the classroom teacher explored?

4. How many computers were in the classroom?

5. The researchers explicitly state a number of implications. What is the first one?

Questions for Discussion

6. The researchers identify this study as a "case study." What is your understanding of the meaning of this term? (See lines 94 and 106.)

7. The observation sessions and interviews were audiotaped and transcribed. Is this an important strength of this study? Explain. (See lines 122–125.)

8. What is your opinion on interviewing only four of the participants? (See lines 133–138.)

9. In your opinion, is the process for coding student writing samples described in sufficient detail? (See lines 156–166.)

10. Are any of the findings of this study especially interesting? Are any surprising? (See lines 229–416.)

11. In your opinion, is the case study method an important scientific tool? If "yes," does this study illustrate its importance? Explain.

Quality Ratings

Directions: Indicate your level of agreement with each of the following statements by circling a number from 5 for strongly agree (SA) to 1 for strongly disagree (SD). If you believe an item is not applicable to this research article, leave it blank. Be prepared to explain your ratings. When responding to criteria A and B below, keep in mind that brief titles and abstracts are conventional in published research.

A. The title of the article is appropriate.

    SA   5   4   3   2   1   SD

B. The abstract provides an effective overview of the research article.

    SA   5   4   3   2   1   SD

C. The introduction establishes the importance of the study.

    SA   5   4   3   2   1   SD

D. The literature review establishes the context for the study.

    SA   5   4   3   2   1   SD

E. The research purpose, question, or hypothesis is clearly stated.

    SA   5   4   3   2   1   SD

F. The method of sampling is sound.

    SA   5   4   3   2   1   SD

G. Relevant demographics (for example, age, gender, and ethnicity) are described.

    SA   5   4   3   2   1   SD

H. Measurement procedures are adequate.

    SA   5   4   3   2   1   SD

I. All procedures have been described in sufficient detail to permit a replication of the study.

    SA   5   4   3   2   1   SD

J. The participants have been adequately protected from potential harm.

    SA   5   4   3   2   1   SD

K. The results are clearly described.

    SA   5   4   3   2   1   SD

L. The discussion/conclusion is appropriate.

    SA   5   4   3   2   1   SD

M. Despite any flaws, the report is worthy of publication.

    SA   5   4   3   2   1   SD

Article 32

Looking for a Struggle: Exploring the Emotions of a Middle School Reader

CHERI FOSTER TRIPLETT
Virginia Polytechnic Institute and State University

ABSTRACT. Struggling readers often feel alienated from teachers and frustrated by social comparisons. However, it is possible to create contexts in which struggling readers experience success and begin to redefine themselves.

From *Journal of Adolescent & Adult Literacy*, *48*, 214–222. Copyright © 2004 by International Reading Association. Reprinted with permission.

The purpose of this case study was to explore a middle school student's emotions in the tutoring context in order to better understand the "struggles" facing a struggling reader. The study revolved around a sixth grader, Mitchell; his mother, Joan (both names are pseudonyms); and me—his reading tutor. When we first talked about the possibility of tutoring for Mitchell, Joan's eyes welled up with tears. She reported that Mitchell had struggled with reading since the early grades but had learned some compensatory strategies that had helped him. Now in the sixth grade, Mitchell was reading at a third-grade level, and according to Joan, reading had become increasingly frustrating for him.

The terms *struggling*, *frustrated*, and *tears* immediately brought to mind an array of negative emotions. As a tutor, I was interested in exploring the emotions of this struggling reader. Could Mitchell's emotions offer clues about how to help him? After reading literature in cognitive psychology explaining that emotions are a result of our individual interpretations of particular situations or contexts, I was convinced that studying a student's emotions could provide clues about how that student is interpreting the tutoring context. I was also convinced that understanding the emotions of a struggling reader could benefit other tutors and teachers as well.

A Cognitive Explanation of Emotions

According to research in cognitive psychology, emotions emerge from a conceptual appraisal process in which an individual infers and interprets to make sense of a situation. Initial or primary appraisals are made concerning the personal relevance of the situation, followed by secondary appraisals concerning perceived control over the situation (Lazarus, 1991; Smith, 1991). Emotions such as happiness or pride are linked to primary appraisals that a situation is beneficial to the individual. Emotions such as anger or fear are linked to primary appraisals that a situation is harmful to the individual. Differentiations between challenge and frustration, pride and gratitude are distinguished by secondary appraisals. For instance, pride and gratitude have identical primary appraisals of personal benefit, but they are distinguished by the secondary appraisal of accountability. Pride is a result of perceived self-accountability. Gratitude is a result of perceived "other-accountability" (Parkinson, 1994; Smith, 1991).

This appraisal process may help to explain some of the emotions encountered in previous literacy research. For example, Oldfather (1994) discovered a range of feelings associated with students' experiences when not motivated for literacy learning. Students openly expressed anger and helplessness. Some students' statements were direct appraisals that learning situations were out of their control and that they were not accountable for their frustrations. For instance, one angry student explained, "Teachers kind of get on your back and everything. I really get mad" (p. 13). If we use the appraisal process to interpret this student's anger, we know he perceives the learning context as somehow harmful or not beneficial (primary appraisal), and that he perceives another as accountable for the situation (secondary appraisal). Also, in Allen, Michalove, and Shockley (1993), one student's pride was evidenced in his comments: "I'm learning to read!... Want me to show you?... Want me to read it to you?...Ooh, this is my favorite part!" (p. 71). Another student was grateful to those around her for their assistance: "I read big words. Ms. Willis and Ms. Shockley read books and I read and they tell it when I don't know a word. I learn if I read. Ms. Shockley, Ms. Willis, and my sister, my eleven-year-old sister, will help" (p. 105). In their quotes, these students revealed that the ability to read is personally relevant and beneficial (primary appraisals), but they differed in their secondary appraisals of accountability. The first student saw himself as accountable; he expressed the confidence and excitement that often accompany feelings of pride. The second student consistently mentioned

those who helped her; she expressed gratitude toward
80 her teachers and her sister.

A Social Explanation of Emotions

These cognitive explanations of emotion did help me to understand our tutoring interactions; however, they only seemed to scratch the surface of the emotional issues surrounding Mitchell's struggle to be a
85 successful reader. Thus, after analyzing data for only a short period, I realized that there were themes that were better explained by social theories. In essence, I realized that Mitchell's struggle was not just a result of his individual interpretation of one particular context—
90 Mitchell's struggle was being socially constructed in a variety of contexts and in numerous relationships.

Social constructionism emphasizes that knowledge is formulated between participants in a social relationship (Hruby, 2001). This theory is somewhat different
95 from the social *constructivism* attributed to Vygotsky, in that constructivism can be considered a cognitive description of knowledge and *constructionism* can be considered a social description of knowledge. Emotions have likewise been described from a social con-
100 structionist perspective. Scheff (1997) explained that emotions are created within our social relationships. He described feelings of enjoyment and pride as associated with relationships of solidarity. He described feelings of shame, fear, anger, and indifference and associated
105 them with alienating relationships. By situating thoughts and feelings within social contexts, social constructionism provides a framework for understanding how interactions in a classroom can influence a student's emotional responses and how a student's
110 struggle can be socially constructed.

Literacy research framed by social constructionism (Hinchman, Bourcy, Thomas, & Olcott, 2002; McCarthey, 2001; Moje, 2000) has detailed how particular contexts and particular relationships help to
115 construct students' literacy identities, including notions of struggle. McCarthey (2001) concluded that students who identify well with school and with teachers tend to be more successful in school literacy practices and those who find their identities defined by other aspects
120 of their lives may not be as successful in school literacy practices.

Procedures and Methods

This qualitative study took place in the context of tutoring during four months of biweekly, one-hour sessions. All data collection took place in and around the
125 tutoring context or in the small university snack shop, where parents often waited to pick up their children. Written retrospective narratives and interviews informed me of what took place in Mitchell's reading history before I began to tutor. Other data sources in-
130 cluded field notes (i.e., theoretical, methodological, tutorial, and personal), artifacts, and ongoing taperecorded interviews. Triangulation of perspectives was an important aspect of this case study. The emic per-

spectives of parent and student, or what may be termed
135 *lay theories*, provided a richer, more intersubjective explanation of the emotions in this context (Mathison, 1993).

Constant comparative methods (Glaser & Strauss, 1967; Strauss & Corbin, 1990) were used for data
140 analysis. Although constant comparative analysis originated in the context of grounded theory (Glaser & Strauss), it has been used in a variety of educational studies as an analytic induction method—even in studies not intending to develop grounded theory (Merriam,
145 1998). In this study, constant comparative methods were not used for the purpose of developing theory but for their systematic approach. This approach involves closely attending to data sources and noticing what patterns emerge (open coding), noting categories or
150 themes, and then beginning to describe the properties that exemplify each category by comparing and contrasting subsequent data.

Constant comparative analysis provides an opportunity to recognize and use the recursiveness of the
155 research process. As categories are identified, a type of theoretical sampling takes place in which emerging concepts influence subsequent data collection. At the same time, data are revisited in order to clarify the categories and subcategories. The findings are then
160 discussed in relation to theories from the original literature review and in relation to new theories to explain unfamiliar categories (Strauss & Corbin, 1990). For example, one category or theme that emerged during data collection was Mitchell's socioemotional relation-
165 ship with teachers. I sought other explanations because this category was not best explained by the literature in cognitive psychology. Visiting the social constructionist literature provided a richer, more colorful and thus more credible interpretation of the data (Lather, 1991).

170 Other measures were also taken to provide credibility. Triangulation of perspectives, triangulation of data sources, and member checks (LeCompte & Preissle, 1993; Merriam, 1998) validated emerging categories. Member checks consisted of open-ended interviews in
175 which I asked for feedback or clarification regarding emerging concepts, as well as informal conversations throughout to share my own thoughts about what I was interpreting.

Findings and Discussion

Cognitive Explanations: Looking for a Struggle

As I began to notice particular patterns of emotion
180 in the tutoring context, I was perplexed when I did not see or hear any evidence of a struggle. I assumed I would hear negative emotions expressed, such as frustration, anger, or disappointment because of Mitchell's reading history. Joan explained that Mitchell had al-
185 ways struggled with reading and that he had worked with many tutors. She said, "He is always falling apart when he works on his reading, writing, and spelling.... He often cries." Even during our first meeting together,

190 when some students seem apprehensive about working with a new person, Mitchell seemed relaxed and somewhat relieved that our initial meeting was focused on conversation instead of testing. Likewise, throughout our semester together, Mitchell expressed positive emotions about tutoring:

195   Mitchell: [interview] I like funny books like this, and like *Matilda* [Dahl, 1998, Puffin], they make me laugh!

      Cheri: [field notes] Mitchell and I laugh a lot! We both love this book!

200   Joan: [interview] I've noticed that I hear you both laughing when I pass by your office…. I thought, well, they sound like they are having a good time!

Fun, laughter, and enjoyment were expressed in the
205 context of tutoring. For example, one afternoon as Joan and I were discussing Mitchell's progress over a cup of coffee, I told her how much I enjoyed getting to know Mitchell and that "he is fun, interesting, and thoughtful." She said that "he always really enjoyed tutoring"
210 and that "he looked forward to it!" These contextual responses of fun, laughter, and enjoyment indicate primary appraisals of personal benefit.

All three case study participants also consistently commented on Mitchell's obvious pride and success in
215 reading tasks. During one session, I recorded my thoughts as Mitchell reacted to his obvious success on a spelling assessment:

[Mitchell is pleased. I can tell as we go along by his expression…he is obviously excited!]

220   Cheri: What do you think about that? You spelled 17 out of 20 words correctly and distinguished between the short vowel *a* and short vowel *e*!

Mitchell: [with a coy grin on his face] I'm good!

      Cheri: Yes, indeed!

225 Mitchell also began to experience some pride in his successes at school. He came to my office a little early one day and excitedly reported, "When I have reading or spelling at school, I've noticed that I am reading the big words a lot better! I have also noticed when I am
230 spelling…that I am not getting mixed up." According to the emotion appraisal process, pride and success can be linked to secondary appraisals of self-accountability.

Emotions and Motivation in Literacy Contexts

What aspects of tutoring may have influenced Mitchell's appraisal of personal benefit, resulting in
235 feelings of fun, laughter, and enjoyment? What aspects of tutoring may have influenced Mitchell's appraisal of self-accountability, resulting in feelings of pride and success? Several aspects of tutoring contributed to Mitchell's positive feelings, such as having opportuni-
240 ties to make choices, participating in activities that were personally relevant, working within his instructional level, and having opportunities to experience

success. These aspects were apparent in my notes from our first meeting:

245 We spent the first 20 minutes talking about Mitchell's upcoming soccer trip…. We talked about the kinds of books Mitchell likes to read. He mentioned *Matilda*, so we discussed Roald Dahl and compared the movie *Matilda* with the book…. The last 30 minutes, Mitchell read aloud three
250 different passages from the Qualitative Reading Inventory—second-, third-, and fourth-grade passages. He seemed relieved that I asked him to read "easy stuff" before we moved on to the passages that were more difficult.

I continued to focus on choice and personal rele-
255 vance throughout the semester. Each book that we read together was a book that Mitchell chose to read, based on his own interests. We spent a lot of time laughing over books like *There's a Boy in the Girls' Bathroom* (Sachar, 1988, Yearling), *The Mouse and the Motorcy-*
260 *cle* (Cleary, 1990, HarperTrophy), and *Matilda* because Mitchell liked funny books. We also spent time reading soccer magazines and newspaper articles about World Cup Soccer. Writing opportunities came from these readings, such as writing predictions about what would
265 happen in the next chapter or writing about a favorite soccer player. Writing opportunities also arose from personal narratives such as a fishing trip in which Mitchell caught a huge shark. Personal letter writing and letter reading were a natural part of Mitchell's de-
270 sire to keep in touch with his friends and family—these were a vital part of our concentration on reading, writing, and spelling. For example, Mitchell wrote a letter to his mother. We looked for spelling errors in his first draft, circling a few obvious mistakes. We then used
275 those particular spelling patterns to create a word sort together by writing words in columns, cutting them apart, and sorting them again into appropriate columns.

Oldfather and Wigfield (1996) explained that students feel motivated for literacy learning when they

280 experience learning environments as places to pursue personal interests, as places in which they can achieve at least some degree of self-determination and participation in shaping aspects of their own learning agenda, as places in which their ideas and their literate actions are taken se-
285 riously. (p. 101)

Unfortunately, Mitchell perceived most of his experiences of reading, writing, and spelling at school as "not very interesting." He reported a literacy history of boredom, anxiety over testing, competition for points
290 and grades, rarely getting to choose what he read, and always reading "hard stuff."

Reading, writing, and spelling within Mitchell's instructional level certainly benefited his feelings of success. Through ongoing assessment, such as running
295 records, spelling inventories, and writing samples, I was able to be attentive to his growth so that tasks were challenging but not frustrating. Morris (1996) identified "diligent, unrelenting attention to instructional level" as essential to success in tutoring. I also realized
300 early on that Mitchell had difficulty recognizing and

213

celebrating his own successes. Each week I asked him to focus on what he did well, such as reading with expression, breaking down big words by looking at syllables, or sorting numerous words into the correct word-pattern column. Asking Mitchell to be attentive to his successes no doubt contributed to his feelings of pride—for once, he had an opportunity to think of himself as a successful reader.

Social Explanations: Contexts and Relationships of Struggle

Social relationships were very important to Mitchell, and his mother and I both noticed that he had unique socioemotional strengths. Joan commented, "Mitchell will make it in this world…. He always has good friends, he's often the leader of his social group, [and] he's very popular with the other kids." Comments like these from his mother and my ongoing notes about Mitchell's emphasis on social relationships caused me to query, "Mitchell talks about his friends a lot: playing with friends, wanting to finish his work so he can talk with friends, how he hopes to have good friends when he moves to Alabama. Do most kids talk about their friends this much?" When we were able to use this strength through writing letters to friends and family, writing personal stories, and reading books that highlighted relationships (e.g., *There's a Boy in the Girls' Bathroom*), Mitchell flourished.

Social comparisons at school. Mitchell's socioemotional strengths were often portrayed in his ability to empathize with his peers. Throughout our four months together, Mitchell expressed concerns about the social comparisons made in his literacy experiences. He expressed concern for himself but also for his peers. For example, Mitchell reported "feeling bad" in years past when he "never got the prizes" offered by Accelerated Reader. However, he also reported that he "felt bad for his friends" from other classes who were not good readers because they never got their points and they "hated Accelerated Reader." Mitchell relayed a history of concerns over Accelerated Reader. He was happy to finally have a teacher who treated students "fair" when it came to Accelerated Reader points. In an informal, audiotaped interview he explained that he was really happy that his teacher set goals that everyone could reach:

Mitchell: Other classes have to do more. I think they have to read a bunch of books for points to get…like cameras and other big prizes like that…and some kids can't read that many and they don't get prizes.

Cheri: Does everybody get the points they need in your class?

Mitchell: Yeah, last time we all got the points we need…we all got [an ice cream] bar!

Mitchell also reported some embarrassment about the color codes that were used on Accelerated Reader books to mark their level. He said his friends always know when he got a third-grade book, and that sometimes he checked out "books that are really too hard" because his friends were reading them. Unfortunately, other social comparisons plagued Mitchell's reading history as well. When I asked him to tell me more about reading third-grade books, Mitchell immediately reported frustration over always being in the "low reading group." He seemed to be angry about this issue when he talked about it. When I asked Mitchell to explain how these reading groups made him feel, he replied, "I just…I really don't know what to say…it just made me feel dumb."

Although there have been studies reporting positive effects (McGinn & Parrish, 2002; Topping & Paul, 1999), Accelerated Reader has also been criticized for its competitive reward system (Biggers, 2001; Stevenson & Camarata, 2000). Extrinsic rewards and incentive programs like those offered by Accelerated Reader have also been criticized for decreasing students' intrinsic motivation to read (Carter, 1996; Gambrell, 1996; Pavonetti, Brimmer, & Cipielewski, 2003). Likewise, ability grouping has received a wide range of criticisms, from lack of effectiveness to negative emotional effects on students (Allington, 1983; Slavin, 1986). Although teachers and researchers in the early 1990s (Allington, 1992; Berghoff & Egawa, 1991; Flood, Lapp, Flood, & Nagel, 1992) suggested an alternative to ability grouping with the use of flexible groupings, teachers and researchers continue to debate the issue (Pallas, Entwisle, Alexander, & Stluka, 1994; Wilkinson & Townsend, 2000; Worthy & Hoffman, 1996).

Socioemotional relationships. One-on-one tutoring gave Mitchell and me the time to develop a positive and supportive socioemotional relationship. This was essential to Mitchell's success in tutoring. We began each tutoring session by catching up on our daily lives and recording our personal thoughts in our notebooks. He shared stories about fishing trips and soccer matches. I shared stories about hiking trips and books I was reading.

Mitchell had positive and supportive socioemotional relationships with his friends, his family, his coach, and his tutor. Mitchell described talking with these people in a relational and personal way. For instance, Mitchell said his coach was "like a friend 'cause he's nice and jokes around with me and my friends…and talks with me and my friends." He likewise described his mother as his friend. Joan and Mitchell continuously expressed pride in each other's accomplishments. It is interesting that enjoyment, fun, laughter, and pride were expressed about these relationships. Scheff (1997), explaining the importance of our socioemotional relationships from a social constructionist perspective, relayed that feelings of enjoyment and pride in relationships evidence solidarity and interdependence.

Scheff (1997) described a type of "We-ness" associated with relationships of interdependence. Unfortunately, the relationships that could not be defined by this "We-ness" were Mitchell's relationships with most teachers. The talk that Mitchell associated with many teachers was directive in nature but not relational. When I asked Mitchell to explain the difference between his coach and his teachers, he poignantly replied, "The teachers that like you as a person...they also think you are smart. They talk and laugh and talk to you in the hallways and stuff. Then there are ones who don't really talk to you at all. You don't know what they think of you." Mitchell's interpretation of his interactions with most teachers involved anger, fear, and indifference. Mitchell shared with me that he was often afraid to ask his teachers for help because "they'll get mad like you didn't listen or something." Joan concurred that relationships with teachers had been "a constant battle."

As I tried to make sense of Mitchell's thoughts about certain relationships with adults, I began an open-ended interview to make sure I was getting the message straight. Even after four months of developing camaraderie, I was jarred by his candor.

Cheri: Mitchell, I wanted to ask you some questions today because I want to see if I'm getting the message straight here, OK? [Mitchell nods.] You've told me a lot about your coach and your teachers. How is your coach like your teachers? Or how is he different from your teachers?

Mitchell: [He pauses and seems to be thinking about it.] I have seven teachers, right? Only one, my third-period teacher, he's the only one that I can remember ever joking around with me and my friends and stuff. That teacher is like my coach—then all the other teachers, they just don't like teaching so they don't kid around and stuff...that's different from my coach.

Cheri: So, are you saying that your coach likes coaching soccer, but most of your teachers don't like teaching?

Mitchell: Well, they are always in a bad mood...getting mad...and yelling at kids...like they don't like being around you.

Cheri: So, your third-period teacher is like your coach? [Mitchell nods.] How else are they alike?

Mitchell: They joke around and talk...and they try to make it fun.

Cheri: Are they trying to be friends with you?

Mitchell: Yeah and like, the sixth-period teacher, she definitely doesn't want to be friends. She doesn't care if all the kids hate her!

Cheri: Well, does your coach like what he is coaching? I mean, does he like soccer? [Mitchell nods.] But what about your teachers...do they—

Mitchell: [Mitchell interrupts with an answer before I finish the question.] They don't like what they teach and they don't like teaching.

Social constructionism and literacy identity. Mitchell's anger and fear evidenced his alienation from school literacy contexts. Similar to McCarthey's (2001) findings, Mitchell did not identify with school or with teachers and had not experienced success in school literacy contexts or in relationships with teachers. Although Mitchell did not see himself as a successful reader or writer, he saw himself as a successful soccer player. McCarthey (2001) concluded "teachers need to provide students with opportunities to connect their literate selves with other aspects of their identity" (p. 145). When Mitchell's interests (i.e., soccer, socioemotional relationships, humor) were incorporated into our reading and writing activities, Mitchell began to redefine himself as a reader and writer.

McCarthey and Moje (2002) further highlighted how contexts can influence our identities, including the way we are positioned by people and practices. The social comparisons made in school literacy contexts made Mitchell feel dumb. He expressed anger, embarrassment, and frustration associated with reading groups and Accelerated Reader. Because there were no social comparisons in our one-on-one tutoring context, Mitchell was able to focus on his own successes and recognize his own improvements. Likewise, a one-on-one context gave us the opportunity to develop a positive and supportive socioemotional relationship.

Because Mitchell made meaning through relationships, he perceived the amount of and nature of verbal interaction between himself and teachers to be a key factor in his understanding of who he was as a learner. It is possible that teachers differentiated their feedback to Mitchell because he has had difficulty in school. There is research supporting the fact that teachers respond differently to those who are struggling, including more directives and less relational feedback (Allington, 1983). Phelps and Weaver's (1999) research, exploring the public and personal voices of adolescents in literacy classrooms, revealed that relationships with teachers have a major influence on students' willingness to participate in classroom dialogue. These researchers discovered that students did not speak up when they feared ridicule from the teacher. Qualitative accounts of successful literacy instruction include descriptions of teachers who take time to build personal relationships with individual students (Dillon, 1989; Ladson-Billings, 1994; Oldfather, 1994).

Create a Context for Success

This study offers insight into the context-specific and relationship-specific emotions of a literacy learner. A student's feelings of enjoyment tell us that he interprets his experience as personally beneficial. Feelings of pride tell us that he sees himself as accountable for his successes. Feelings of anger and frustration signal that he sees that someone else is responsible for his lack of success. If a reader is feeling a struggle, then he or she interprets the situation as not beneficial, and the reader interprets that someone else is accountable for 530 the experience. Likewise, this study identifies the specific aspects of tutoring that contributed to Mitchell's feelings of enjoyment and pride, such as having opportunities to make choices, participating in activities that were personally relevant, working within his instruc535tional level, and focusing on his successes. As a tutor, I was able to create a context in which Mitchell did not experience feelings of struggle.

Also, this look at one middle school reader's emotions helps us to understand how feelings related to 540 struggle, such as anger, frustration, and fear, can be socially constructed in particular contexts and in particular relationships. It is unfortunate that Mitchell experienced a literacy struggle at school and with teachers. The social comparisons made through reading 545 groups and Accelerated Reader made Mitchell feel dumb. Lack of personal relevance in reading and writing activities made Mitchell feel unmotivated. Relationships with teachers made Mitchell feel fearful, angry, and alienated.

550   This study questions the notion of struggle and our practice of labeling students as struggling readers. If we consider that Mitchell was a successful literacy learner in one context and a struggling reader in another context, then we are challenged to create contexts 555 in which a student experiences success. According to McCarthey and Moje (2002), "When we consider identities to be social constructions, and thus always open for change and conflict depending on the social interaction we find ourselves in, we open possibilities for re560 thinking the labels we so easily use to identify students" (p. 230).

References

Allen, J., Michalove, B., & Shockley, B. (1993). *Engaging children: Community and chaos in the lives of young literacy learners*. Portsmouth, NH: Heinemann.

Allington, R. (1983). The reading instruction provided readers of differing reading abilities. *Elementary School Journal, 83*, 548–559.

Allington, R. (1992). Reconsidering instructional groupings. *Reading Horizons, 32*, 349–355.

Berghoff, B., & Egawa, K. (1991). No more "rocks": Grouping to give students control of their learning. *The Reading Teacher, 44*, 536–541.

Biggers, D. (2001). The argument against Accelerated Reader. *Journal of Adolescent & Adult Literacy, 45*, 72–75.

Carter, B. (1996). Hold the applause!: Do Accelerated Reader and Electronic Bookshelf send the right message? *School Library Journal, 42*, 22–25.

Dillon, D. (1989). Showing them that I want them to learn and that I care about who they are: A microethnography. *American Educational Research Journal, 26*, 227–259.

Flood, J., Lapp, D., Flood, S., & Nagel, G. (1992). Am I allowed to group? Using flexible patterns for effective instruction. *The Reading Teacher, 45*, 608–616.

Gambrell, L. (1996). Creating classroom cultures that foster reading motivation. *The Reading Teacher, 50*, 14–25.

Glaser, B. G., & Strauss, A. L. (1967). *The discovery of grounded theory: Strategies for qualitative research*. Chicago: Aldine.

Hinchman, K., Bourcy, L., Thomas, H., & Olcott, K. (2002). Representing adolescents' literacies: Case studies of three white males. *Reading Research and Instruction, 3*, 229–246.

Hruby, G. (2001). Sociological, postmodern, and new realism perspectives in social constructionism: Implications for literacy research. *Reading Research Quarterly, 36*, 48–62. doi: 10.1598/RRQ.36.1.3

Ladson-Billings, G. (1994). *The dreamkeepers: Successful teachers of African American children*. San Francisco: Jossey-Bass.

Lather, P. (1991). *Getting smart: Feminist research and pedagogy within the postmodern*. New York: Routledge.

Lazarus, R. S. (1991). *Emotion and adaptation*. Oxford, UK: Oxford University Press.

LeCompte, M., & Preissle, J. (1993). *Ethnography and qualitative design in educational research*. New York: Academic Press.

Mathison, S. (1993). From practice to theory to practice. In D. Flinders & G. Mills (Eds.), *Theory and concepts in qualitative research: Perspectives from the field* (pp. 55–67). New York: Teachers College Press.

McCarthey, S. (2001). Identity construction in elementary readers and writers. *Reading Research Quarterly, 36*, 122–151. doi: 10.1598/RRQ.36.2.2

McCarthey, S., & Moje, E. (2002). Conversations: Identity matters. *Reading Research Quarterly, 37*, 228–238. doi: 10.1598/RRQ.37.2.6

McGinn, J., & Parrish, A. (2002). Accelerating ESL students' reading progress with Accelerated Reader. *Reading Horizons, 42*, 175–189.

Merriam, S. (1998). *Qualitative research and case study applications in education*. San Francisco: Jossey-Bass.

Moje, E. (2000). "To be part of the story": The literacy practices of gangsta adolescents. *Teachers College Record, 102*, 651–690.

Morris, D. (1996). A case study of middle school reading disability. *The Reading Teacher, 49*, 368–377.

Oldfather, P. (1994). *When students do not feel motivated for literacy learning: How a responsive classroom culture helps*. Athens, GA: National Reading Research Center.

Oldfather, P., & Wigfield, A. (1996). Children's motivations for literacy learning. In L. Baker, P. Afflerbach, & D. Reinking (Eds.), *Developing engaged readers in school and home communities* (pp. 89–113). Mahwah, NJ: Erlbaum.

Pallas, A., Entwisle, D., Alexander, K., & Stluka, M. F. (1994). Ability group effects: Instructional, social or institutional? *Sociology of Education, 67*, 27–46.

Parkinson, B. (1994). Emotion. In B. Parkinson & A. M. Colman (Eds.), *Emotion and motivation* (pp. 1–21). New York: Longman.

Pavonetti, L., Brimmer, K., & Cipielewski, J. (2003). Accelerated Reader: What are the lasting effects on the reading habits of middle school students exposed to Accelerated Reader in the early grades? *Journal of Adolescent & Adult Literacy, 46*, 300–311.

Phelps, S., & Weaver, D. (1999). Public and personal voices in adolescents' classroom talk. *Journal of Literacy Research, 31*, 321–354.

Scheff, T. (1997). *Emotions, the social bond, and human reality*. Cambridge, MA: Cambridge University Press.

Slavin, R. (1986). *Ability grouping and student achievement in the elementary schools* (Synthesis Report No. 1). Baltimore: Center for Research on Elementary and Middle Schools.

Smith, C. A. (1991). The self, appraisal and coping. In C. R. Snyder & D. R. Forsythe (Eds.), *Handbook of social and clinical psychology: The health perspective* (pp. 116–137). Elmsford, NY: Pergamon.

Stevenson, J., & Camarata, J. (2000). Imposters in whole language clothing: Undressing the Accelerated Reader program. *Talking Points, 11*, 8–11.

Strauss, A., & Corbin, J. (1990). *Basics of qualitative research: Grounded theory procedures and techniques*. Newbury Park, CA: Sage.

Topping, K., & Paul, T. (1999). Computer-assisted assessment of practice at reading: A large scale survey using Accelerated Reader data. *Reading and Writing Quarterly, 15*, 213–231.

Wilkinson, I. A. G., & Townsend, M. A. R. (2000). From Rata to Rimu: Grouping for instruction in best practice New Zealand classrooms. *The Reading Teacher, 53*, 460–471.

Worthy, J., & Hoffman, J. (1996). Critical Questions: Is ability grouping in first grade a negative? *The Reading Teacher, 49*, 65–67.

Address correspondence to: Cheri Foster Triplett, College of Human Resources and Education, 318 War Memorial Hall, Virginia Tech, Blacksburg, VA 24061-0313. E-mail: ctriplet@vt.edu

Exercise for Article 32

Factual Questions

1. What is the explicitly stated purpose of this study?

2. This study took place in the context of tutoring that lasted how long?

3. How was the researcher "informed" of Mitchell's reading history before the researcher began to tutor?

4. In addition to the "tutoring context," where else were the data collected?

5. What did "member checks" consist of?

6. Did the student express positive emotions about tutoring?

Questions for Discussion

7. This is a case study of a single student. Before reading this article, to what extent did you believe that case studies are useful sources of information? Has reading it changed your belief? Explain.

8. In your opinion, how important is the discussion of social theories in lines 81–121 for establishing a framework for this study? Explain.

9. In line 122, the researcher refers to this as a "qualitative study." Do you agree with this classification? If yes, what features of this research study distinguish it from a quantitative study?

10. To what extent is the use of multiple data sources a strength of this study? (See lines 127–132.)

11. Before reading this article, how familiar were you with "constant comparative methods"? To what extent does the material in lines 138–169 better inform you of these methods?

12. In your opinion, is the dialogue in lines 437–472 an important part of the Findings and Discussion section of this research article? Explain.

13. Do you think that this study has important implications for tutors who work with struggling readers? Explain.

Quality Ratings

Directions: Indicate your level of agreement with each of the following statements by circling a number from 5 for strongly agree (SA) to 1 for strongly disagree (SD). If you believe an item is not applicable to this research article, leave it blank. Be prepared to explain your ratings. When responding to criteria A and B below, keep in mind that brief titles and abstracts are conventional in published research.

A. The title of the article is appropriate.

   SA   5   4   3   2   1   SD

B. The abstract provides an effective overview of the research article.

   SA   5   4   3   2   1   SD

C. The introduction establishes the importance of the study.

   SA   5   4   3   2   1   SD

D. The literature review establishes the context for the study.

   SA   5   4   3   2   1   SD

E. The research purpose, question, or hypothesis is clearly stated.

   SA   5   4   3   2   1   SD

F. The method of sampling is sound.

   SA   5   4   3   2   1   SD

G. Relevant demographics (for example, age, gender, and ethnicity) are described.

   SA   5   4   3   2   1   SD

H. Measurement procedures are adequate.

   SA   5   4   3   2   1   SD

I. All procedures have been described in sufficient detail to permit a replication of the study.

   SA   5   4   3   2   1   SD

J. The participants have been adequately protected from potential harm.

   SA   5   4   3   2   1   SD

K. The results are clearly described.

   SA   5   4   3   2   1   SD

L. The discussion/conclusion is appropriate.

   SA   5   4   3   2   1   SD

M. Despite any flaws, the report is worthy of publication.

   SA   5   4   3   2   1   SD

Article 33

Urban School Principals and Their Role As Multicultural Leaders

MARY E. GARDINER
University of Idaho, Boise

ERNESTINE K. ENOMOTO
University of Hawaii at Manoa

ABSTRACT. This study focuses on the role of urban school principals as multicultural leaders. Using cross-case analysis, the authors describe what 6 practicing principals do in regard to multicultural leadership. The findings suggest that although multicultural preparation was lacking for these principals, some did engage in work that promoted diversity in their daily activities. All principals dealt with multicultural issues, usually focusing on individual students or specific programs to accommodate immigrants or refugees. Although some principals held high expectations for all, others were less aware of the connection between affirming diversity and student achievement. Recommendations are made to support principals in their work.

From *Urban Education*, *41*, 560–584. Copyright © 2006 by Corwin Press, Inc. Reprinted with permission.

American school students have always been culturally diverse. Regardless of whether they are schooled in the midwestern United States or the southwestern border states, or whether they are from a predominant

5 racial-ethnic group or a variety of cultural groupings, students are diverse in age, gender, sexual orientation, socioeconomic status, religion, physical and mental ability, language, and ethnicity. Although some schools might have greater challenges with diversity than other

10 schools, all must recognize an increasing diversity within their respective communities, districts, and states and the nation as a whole. According to Marx (2002), by the year 2050, the United States will become a "nation of minorities," with less than half of the

15 population being non-Hispanic white. At present, more than half of the students attending urban schools are members of minority groups (Orfield, 2001).

Standards and educational leadership practices are often focused on managerial, instructional, and partici-

20 patory leadership. Within these areas of competence, administrators and their staff need to be knowledgeable about diversity to provide education that is culturally sensitive to difference, is free from discrimination and prejudice, and promotes educational equity. School

25 principals have a critical role. For example, they can ensure that inclusive teaching and learning are encouraged or that culturally relevant teaching practices are

explored (Riehl, 2000). Principals can maintain high expectations for all while advocating for appropriate

30 pedagogical approaches for each student (Lomotey, 1993). School principals are also challenged by their specific school needs and issues related to serving diverse student groups that might be at odds with local communities.

35 In this study, we examined the real-world experiences of practicing principals as they dealt with the multicultural issues facing their schools. We defined multicultural leadership broadly in terms of that which enables principals to address diversity within a school

40 setting through affirming cultural pluralism and educational equity (Bennett, 2001). Our aim in this study was to critically examine the role of urban principals as multicultural leaders.

Our data sources in this study consisted of case

45 studies of 6 school principals in one urban school district (four elementary schools and two secondary schools). For analysis, we used traditional methods of qualitative analysis with a to-and-fro process between the field data, the researchers' experiences, and key

50 theoretical points from the research literature. Riehl's (2000) framework, which she developed from a literature review, was useful to compare against themes arising from our own field data. It is described in the next section of this article. We also examined the principals'

55 background, education, experiences, and challenges in their respective schools by writing case studies on each school principal. Finally, we considered each principal's views of his or her leadership preparation. In conclusion, we offer recommendations for supporting edu-

60 cational administrators in the multicultural dimensions of their leadership.

A Multicultural Leadership Framework

Scholars have written much about multicultural education and leadership for social justice (see Arredondo & Perez, 2003; Banks & Banks, 2001; Capper,

65 1993; Cochran-Smith, 2001; Delpit, 1995; Gay, 2001; Henze, Katz, Norte, Sather, & Walker, 2002; Hollins, 1996a, 1996b; Ladson-Billings, 1995; Marshall, 1993; Nieto, 2000; Nuri-Robins, Lindsey, Lindsey, & Terrell, 2002; Robins, Lindsey, Lindsey, & Terrell, 2002;

70 Sleeter, 2001; Sleeter & Grant, 1987; Wallace, 2000).

According to Bennett (2001), multicultural education rests on four broad principles, namely,

> (a) cultural pluralism; (b) ideals of social justice and the end of racism, sexism, and other forms of prejudice and discrimination; (c) affirmations of culture in the teaching and learning process; and (d) visions of educational equity and excellence leading to high levels of academic learning for all children and youth (p. 173).

Theorizing about the practice of educational administration, Riehl (2000) identifies three key tasks in determining whether administrators would be adequately prepared to respond to diversity and demonstrate multicultural leadership. The first task is fostering new meanings about diversity. For example, do principals maintain high expectations for all while providing support for diverse groups of students? To what extent do they attempt to institute and sustain school reform? How do they support dialogue and discussion among groups that might be culturally different? The second task involves promoting inclusive instructional practices within schools by supporting, facilitating, or being a catalyst for change. To what extent do principals demonstrate instructional leadership that promotes inclusion, awareness of pedagogical practices, or concern for appropriate assessments? The third task relates to building connections between schools and communities. Are principals engaged with parents and families to encourage success for their children? Do they encourage community involvement and partnering with social service agencies? To what extent do they endeavor to bridge cultural clashes between diverse groups within their school-communities? These tasks are grounded in the values of multicultural education, advocating for cultural pluralism and honoring difference while ensuring social justice and equity among all students. As such, they offer a useful means to frame what is meant by multicultural leadership and how to consider its enactment.

Research Methods, Data Sources, and Analysis

Our aim in this study was to critically examine multicultural leadership through in-depth qualitative case studies of practicing administrators in 6 urban schools (four elementary, two secondary) through the course of a school year. Pseudonyms were used for the administrators and schools in this study to provide for confidentiality. The school district housed 53 public schools in grades PreK-12, with a total of approximately 27,000 students. The majority of the students were Caucasian with a small percentage of minority youngsters, some of whom were relocated refugees (Afghans, Bosnians, Slovaks, Somali Bantu, Rwandan Tutsi, Hutu). The district's English Language Learner (ELL) program accommodated 56 different languages. Although there were a number of Hispanic and other ethnic minority students, there was little diversity in the teaching or administrative staff, who were predominantly Caucasian.

Criteria for selecting the principals were the following: (a) that the principal was an administrator in an urban school undergoing demographic changes with an increasingly diverse student population in terms of ethnic and cultural background and/or socioeconomic status (SES); and (b) that the principal had been an administrator for at least 3 years with some leadership experience. We compiled a list of potential participants and purposively selected individuals who were in schools where they were likely to be dealing with multicultural issues because the student population was becoming increasingly diverse. Thus, the increasing diversity of the school student population, rather than the principal's own background, guided principal selection. In one case, we purposefully selected the assistant principal because he had a reputation at the district level as a "hands-on" administrator with students and families and was likely to be information rich in knowing about multicultural issues. He was recommended by one of the district-level personnel, and during the course of the study, he became the principal.

All 6 administrators in this study were Caucasian. There were 3 women and 3 men, ranging in age from 42 to 51 years. All the participants were married, with adult or high school-aged children. One of the 6 participants held a doctoral degree in education; the other participants held master's degrees with principal certification. Their years as principal varied from as few as 1 to as many as 15, with years at the school being as many as 7 years. See Table 1 for information on the principals.

Initial fieldwork, observation, and collection of documents were aimed at learning the social, political, historical, and cultural context of each school and community (Rossman & Rallis, 2003). The goal was to understand how school leaders were conceptualizing and engaging in their roles as multicultural leaders to serve the diverse populations in their schools and communities. Learning the context was followed by in-depth interviews with each school principal. Interviews were conducted on-site in the principals' offices. These interviews were conducted in a conference room at the district office complex. Interviews focused on learning what principals were doing with regard to multicultural leadership and included their views of multicultural education and leadership, particular issues they had faced in school, and their preparation for the work. The interview guide for principals is included in the Appendix. A similar guide was used for the district administrators, with the questions focused on their work as district administrators in supporting principals. All the interviews were transcribed and the field notes were written. School-based documents were also collected, which composed an extensive research record.

The Researchers

Qualitative research relies on the researchers engaging in self-awareness and reflexivity throughout the

Table 1
Information on Principals

	1	2	3	4	5	6
Principal	Kroll	Sanders	Caruthers	Brown	Garrison	Andrews
Years as principal	15	5	15	6	4[a]	7
Years at school	3	1	1	5	2[a]	7
Race or ethnicity	Caucasian	Caucasian	Caucasian	Caucasian	Caucasian	Caucasian
Gender	Female	Female	Female	Male	Male	Male
Age	51	48	50	42	41	51
Education	BA, special education	BA, special education	BS, education	BA, elementary education	BA	BA, sociology and history
	MA, special education	MEd	MS, education	MEd	MEd	MA, anthropology
	Principal credential	PhD	Principal credential	Principal credential	Principal credential	Principal credential

[a] Started as an assistant principal and became the principal during the study.

research process. As individuals, the authors both have an interest in well-qualified school administrators lead-
185 ing diverse schools. Mary has two sons: one African American and one Caucasian. She lives with the joys and the heartache of a biracial family in a predominantly white school district. Ernestine is a third-generation Japanese American who has studied schools
190 and school systems struggling with issues of diversity. Our commitment to this topic meant that we needed to be constantly aware of our points of view in relation to the research and writing and to be clear where we are stating our own positions. Collaboration aided the re-
195 search process by enhancing accountability. Simply stated, the point of view that we both share and that we brought to this study is that principals who are multicultural leaders will value diversity; hire teachers and staff of color when possible; and find ways to integrate
200 curriculum that reflects multicultural ideas and music, literature, and activities that will lead to improved student outcomes. Above all, we see great principals as those who believe in students, relate to them and their families, and are able to support teachers to educate
205 students to be caring, lifelong learners who live meaningful and connected lives.

Data Collection and Analysis

The qualitative methods used in this study relied on a cross-case analysis (Creswell, 1998; Merriam, 1998, 2002) that involved four stages and ongoing discus-
210 sions and reflection throughout the process. Case studies were written on each principal and district-level administrator in the first stage. Data were primarily obtained from in-depth interviews conducted at the schools in the principals' offices and observations of
215 the principals at work. In addition, school Web sites, school self-reports, catalogs, brochures, and school publications were obtained. Information was gathered on school mission, context, organization and aims, student enrollment, staffing, curriculum, pedagogy, and
220 parent–school relationships. See Table 2 for information on the characteristics of the schools. The second stage involved the process of seeking answers to ques-

tions regarding the principal's conceptualization of his or her role as multicultural leader and the dilemmas
225 and challenges he or she faced in the school. As a third stage, we used the three tasks from the multicultural education framework outlined above and examined the data from the separate case studies. In addition, we considered the preparation of each administrator and
230 the extent to which his or her background and experience informed praxis. After categorizing the data according to skills and preparation, the fourth stage was to write about the analysis in narrative form, drawing out the similarities and differences in the principals'
235 leadership.

Findings

The principals in this urban school district reported that they had little preparation in the multicultural dimensions of leadership. Principal Caruthers did complete one semester of urban internship as part of her
240 undergraduate teacher preparation. Principal Andrews argued that his master's degree in cultural anthropology prepared him "very well." Three of the principals had educational backgrounds in special education, which might have better prepared them for inclusive
245 educational practices. However, not one administrator recalled focusing on multicultural issues during his or her principal credentialing. Their programs were oriented toward traditional business management (e.g., planning, finance, management, human factors, and
250 public relations). Currently, most administrator preparations programs require at least a course in multicultural diversity or social justice leadership, but the principals in this study were prepared years ago when such a requirement did not exist.

255 All 6 principals dealt with problems as they occurred, focusing on individual students or handling specific concerns with the ELL program. Some administrators tried to provide basic needs for students who were refugees and seemed to be busy with regular edu-
260 cation youngsters. In general, diversity issues were not the focus. As an example, Principal Sanders, although a caring principal, noted that multicultural leadership

Table 2
Data on School Characteristics from School Performance Report 2002–2003

	1	2	3	4	5	6
Name	Republic	Colton	Wakefield	Lowen	Valley View	Boyd
Grades	K–6	K–6	K–6	K–6	7–9	10–12
Enrollment	441	225	326	338	680	1,154
English-language learners	13.6%	3.1%	40.6%	11.4%	12.8%	1.5%
Gifted and talented program (elementary) or advanced placement (secondary) participants	2.0%	3.0%	1.0%	10.0%	—	84.8%
Free or reduced lunch participants	72.0%	40.6%	94.5%	53.7%	41.3%	15.6%
Special education participants	13.6%	9.8%	18.0%	13.2%	12.8%	9.3%
Average daily attendance	94.4%	97.6%	97.0%	96.2%	95.1%	91.4%
Average class size	20.6	19.7	21.7	23.9	20.2	22.2

was not one of her priorities: "At this school, diversity is pretty limited. The teachers have just had limited exposure. Would they be willing to learn? Sure. But I don't think the need has been there." She stated that only one of her teachers "did some activities on Martin Luther King Day."

At the other end of the spectrum, Principals Caruthers, Brown, and Kroll were committed to becoming multiculturally proficient. For example, Principal Caruthers, who led a school populated by low-income students and refugees stated it this way: "It's what we do here on a daily basis. How can you teach the students if you don't know them, where they are coming from, who they are, what they value?" She viewed herself as an instructional leader and a learner, constantly learning from her students and their families and guiding her teachers to apply relevant multicultural curriculum and instruction. Between these two extremes, other principals could be described as transitional or emergent multicultural leaders.

In the next section, we describe in detail what practicing principals did related to demonstrating multicultural leadership based on Riehl's (2000) three key tasks.

Multicultural Task 1: Fostering New Meanings About Diversity

High expectations for all. Principals who demonstrated multicultural leadership were able to embrace a position where they and their teachers and staff were learners who challenged stereotypes and conventional wisdom. For instance, despite having "impoverished" ELL or low-income students as well as "talented" high-SES students, Principal Kroll at Republic Elementary School set about raising expectations for all learners (also see Okagaki & Moore, 2000). Reframing perceptions and valuing differences were accomplished by celebrating ELL and low-income learners and, where appropriate, placing them in enrichment and advanced programs. Principal Caruthers's mantra was that all students can succeed, regardless of home background,

given that they have well-educated teachers who hold high expectations: "Your life at home may be in the pits. It may be terrible. But you're at school now. What can we do to make you more successful?" Principal Caruthers noted, "We have gifted and talented students in this school, and that wasn't always the expectation. Why wouldn't students from low-income homes be gifted and talented? Some people are surprised by that."

Changing the cultural deficiency perspective. Principals Caruthers and Kroll saw the need for cultural change in their schools. They felt that too many teachers held a deficit perspective toward students from low-SES backgrounds and that teachers needed to be guided toward a new view of believing in the capabilities of all students. Principal Kroll put it this way:

> The school had a huge impact from transience, homelessness, and a population, unfortunately, in our old way of thinking, that had too many challenges to be academically successful.... You can't feel sorry for yourself and the kids. You just need to get on with the business of putting all your energy into student success.... When you're a new parent, the baby is your first priority. For schools, the baby is student success.

Principal Kroll engaged in a school improvement plan that fundamentally altered the way her staff viewed the students—a shift to high expectations. The new school culture was accomplished in conjunction with a district initiative based on teacher collaboration, instructional focus, frequent observations, administrative observations, and team time. Team time involved student grouping following frequent assessments according to instructional need. Some students were retaught in new ways until they were proficient, and others were given enrichment activities. More important than the districtwide program, however, was the principal's instructional leadership in insisting that all teachers cast off old doubts and begin to believe that all students can learn. The old class-based model of focusing on the high-SES students and neglecting low-income students was no longer tolerated.

In contrast, other principals seemed to be focusing on basic needs. An example is the way one principal spoke of refugee camps in which students had lived prior to coming to the United States:

> We have some students out of Africa right now that have basically been raised in a tent camp and don't know how to flush a toilet, how to go through a cafeteria line. Our goal is to socialize [the students] to our educational system, as well as teach them some English skills.

The camps seemed to define the students as lacking rather than this being a challenging experience that these amazing students had overcome, thus demonstrating their potential. Another example is one principal's negative view of a low-income neighborhood: "The highest crime rate, highest number of released felons, they reside there…in the quadrant that goes to this particular school."

With so few teachers of color in the schools and so few culturally proficient administrators, the burden of multicultural leadership sometimes fell on the few Hispanic ELL teachers. Principal Sanders described a situation when she was principal at Wakefield Elementary School:

> The ELL teacher was Hispanic—natively. So she was able to bring that firsthand to the teachers and she had to explain—I can remember a situation with, I'll call it abuse, we were very concerned [about] the discipline that was being used at home and we had some pretty heart-to-heart talks. In the Hispanic culture, the father is the head of the house and he does spank and he may be the disciplinarian, and we had to kind of know where to draw the line on that between abuse and just this is their way and it is none of our business. That was very difficult for a lot of us; she was masterful at helping us understand that being very soft-spoken and knowing that when the parents came in that we addressed the dad and that sort of thing. So that was a learning experience.

Some principals also referred to the disruptive home lives of Hispanic students in their schools. Many of these families were legal or illegal immigrants who labor in the state's agricultural industry. During the winter months when work is scarce or not available, families take their children along when they seek work in southern states, such as Texas, or when they return home to Mexico. Some principals criticized these families for interrupting their children's education and saw this action as burdensome to the school. Principal Brown spoke of the tendency "in the past" of some other school principals to classify students by the SES of their parents and then neglect those students. Principal Brown stated,

> What I've heard is that you would take a school with, say, a predominant Hispanic culture, and there would be a whole bunch of them in a school that had been there for a lot of years. And people just kind of ignored them. You're a migrant worker. You can't learn anything.

Understanding through communication. Noticing gang problems in his junior high school, Principal Garrison acted as a learner rather than the all-knowing professional. "We had a real concern with local gang issues, so we spent a lot of time with the community resources, families, and students, working on gang-related issues." To begin to address these issues, he attended the National Latino Conference and served on a district committee examining Latino dropout rates. He then conducted staff development meetings with his teachers to talk about validating student identity, raising expectations, and communicating those expectations to students and families. He explained, "We met with individual students as issues arose and laid out our expectations. Once we began to communicate what our needs were, the students responded and our discipline issues really declined—really dropped." Education, learning about and from Latinos, connecting with families, and then working with school resource officers and several police department gang units helped this principal work with his staff to assess the situation. They considered whether the students were being unfairly identified as gang members simply because they looked and dressed differently. The principal noted that teachers previously could not distinguish between friendship groups and gang formation. Communication was enhanced when the principal adopted a learner stance in relation to the school community, and he encouraged his teachers to do the same.

Socializing new immigrants into U.S. schools. Many of the principals in the study were involved in socializing new immigrant students to an American way of life and to U.S. school practices. Some of these principals knew little about the history, culture, or languages of Bosnia, Somalia, Afghanistan, Iran, and Iraq until they were presented with new immigrant and refugee students. Interpreters in Farsi and Dharsi were brought in to assist in one elementary school. Principals sought to learn about the unfamiliar religions, cultures, and ethnicities of their new students. However, the priority was socializing and teaching these students the English language, not learning their languages and cultures.

Principal Garrison at Valley View Junior High School noted that one multicultural issue he was dealing with involved "interactions between our male students that come from diverse cultures and our female students, and teaching them the proper ways that the dating game is played in America." In this particular case, the "male students from diverse cultures" were refugee students from Africa, Afghanistan, and so forth, and "our female students" were Caucasian. It was not apparent the extent to which Principal Garrison was aware of his actions in socializing students given their diverse backgrounds and experiences. Nor was it apparent that he and other principals viewed new immigrants as a rich resource. New knowledge, languages, cultures, and/or ethnicities were present in all six schools and could have been brought into the center of the learning in the classrooms and schools.

Multicultural Task 2: Promoting Inclusive Instructional Practices Within Schools

Hiring practices. Principals in this study bemoaned
the fact that they "had to let teachers go [teachers who
460 were Hispanic, ethnically diverse, or bilingual] due to
budget cuts." From one principal, we heard the argument, "I am a firm believer that one should hire the
best person for the job, regardless of race, sexual orientation, or ethnicity. I do not believe that a person
465 should be hired to increase the diversity of the population." At Valley View Junior High School, diversity in
staffing occurred in the kitchen staff, some of whom
were of minority background or were immigrants.
Kitchen staff would, on their own initiative, occasion-
470 ally hold multicultural days, featuring menus from their
own ethnic cuisine to honor students' special holidays
and backgrounds.

Multicultural display. At Republic, Wakefield, and
Lowen elementary schools, there was evidence of mul-
475 ticulturalism in the posters and student work displayed
in hallways and classrooms. Different languages, skin
colors, and cultural norms were visible in these displays, although multiculturalism did not appear to be a
central focus that was celebrated. Principals argued that
480 multiculturalism and pluralism were addressed some
time ago in textbooks and that any texts adopted by the
school district would be representative of diversity. Yet
one of the district administrators noted that the curriculum was only "somewhat multicultural," and in our
485 view, attention to multiculturalism in classrooms was
less than optimal. Boyd High had numerous Native
American artifacts displayed, celebrating the Braves
mascot of the school, but multicultural representations
were not readily apparent. (For a discussion of the
490 American Psychological Association position on Native American mascots, see American Psychological
Association, n.d.)

Peer tutoring and inclusive educational practices.
A useful practice, the strategy of peer tutoring was es-
495 tablished for students who were ELLs at Lowen, Republic, and Wakefield elementary schools. Students for
whom English is a first language were paired for short
lessons with students for whom English is their second
language. Student outcomes were positively affected
500 by the focus on learning and the inclusive school culture created.

In contrast to the inclusion at the elementary level,
ELL instruction at the secondary academy was separated from the general education students. Principal
505 Garrison at Valley View Junior High School recognized that the school had a problem in its separation of
both teachers and students divided along ELL and SES
lines because many of the ELL students were also low-
income students. The school housed the district's ELL
510 secondary program, with students enrolled from ages
12 to 21 years. However, there was little interchange or
collaboration between ELL teachers and general educa-

tion teachers and students. Principal Garrison explained,

515 > The other thing that we really have to pay attention to is
> the inclusion of our ELL population. We have high
> school students here, and so it's different than a junior
> high mentality and trying to mix them so they can be-
> come friends and meet at school.... We try to run intra-
520 > mural activities so that the ELL and general populations
> are intermingling with one another.... When they begin
> to segregate if there is an issue, it becomes peer group
> against peer group...and some of those lines are drawn
> the ELL versus the general population.

525 The principal was able to identify the problem. He was
searching for ways to close the gaps of misunderstand-
ing between the students in the ELL program and the
general student body but did not feel he had the knowledge or skills to institute necessary policy and practices
530 to address the problem.

Multiculturally proficient instruction. When asked
whether the school or curriculum was multicultural,
principals commented that they left that up to the
teachers. Several principals asked the researcher to
535 explain what she meant by culturally proficient instruction. When asked why there was no student work in the
halls pertaining to Martin Luther King Jr. Day, the
Colton elementary school principal said, "I had a
teacher once who did all kinds of neat things. But she
540 had adopted some black children and was attuned to it
[multiculturalism]." When it was suggested that teachers could be assessed for their multicultural skills,
Principal Garrison at Valley View Junior High reflected, "I don't know [if] I've ever evaluated my
545 teachers on whether they are culturally proficient.... It
is kind of an expectation, since we have the [ELL]
academy here." Principals had little knowledge of culturally proficient instruction beyond basic learning-
styles information. They had gained some knowledge
550 through practice. For instance, Principal Kroll explained how the Bosnian students in her school are
physically active and how close interpersonal proximity is the norm. Most of the principals expressed an
interest in learning more.

Multicultural Task 3: Building Connections Between Schools and Communities

555 *Early educational opportunities and intervention.*
Principals who demonstrated multicultural leadership
in this task were able to work with parents to achieve
necessary changes in schools despite initial opposition.
For instance, noting the large proportion of low-income
560 youngsters in the area because of changing demographics, one principal worked with district administrators to
offer quality preschool programs and all-day kindergarten programs for low-income students. This all-day
kindergarten is offered at an affordable tuition rate.
565 One of the elementary schools with a declining enrollment became an inclusive preschool, which is free,
based on academic need or income guidelines, and

currently funded through federal grants. The benefits provided to families strengthened the relationship between school and community. By partnering with Head Start, the district plans to eventually extend preschool and all-day kindergarten programs to other schools.

Parent involvement. Those principals who saw their role as multicultural leaders were able to foster parent pride and involvement in nontraditional ways. Principal Caruthers's school, Wakefield Elementary, is a low-income school with a 94.5% free or reduced lunch participation, which contrasts with the district's average of 41.3%. The school has the reputation in the city as a tough school with failing students. Recently, a local resident was quoted in the newspaper as saying that it was an "alarming" prospect that his daughter might be transferred to this school because of the proposed closing of a neighborhood school. Principal Caruthers was visibly concerned the morning that the article ran in the newspaper. Her parents were also upset and mobilized to counter the negative perception. Encouraged by their efforts, Caruthers said, "I love that the parents care that this [is] happening. I've got a mom that has e-mailed me already her letter to the editor."

Community involvement. Many of the principals sought out and encouraged community groups to use school facilities and to view the school as their own. For instance, at Lowen Elementary, prayers during Ramadan were held in the gym. A Jewish Passover Seder was held at the high school. Gospel singing from the Black Baptist Church could be heard from the neighborhood school.

Partnerships with social service agencies. Principals, in caring for the needs of the children in their schools, partnered with numerous community and social service agencies. In Republic Elementary School, for example, Principal Kroll worked with Operation School Bell to fund school supplies, clothing, and books for youngsters in need. A neighborhood church sponsored a whole grade level of youngsters. The local television broadcast network ran an essay contest. Schools were supported by community resource workers, police officers, YMCA, Boys and Girls Clubs, and relief agencies that provided services to students, especially the refugees. Speaking of the challenges with 55 ELL youngsters in his school, Principal Brown of Lowen acknowledged the help received from the Agency for Americans and World Relief. "I am so grateful for them and would like to see them do more. However, I know they are stretched thin…. Are their services adequate? Absolutely not. Is it their fault? I don't think so." Social service organizations provided a start, and energetic principals took advantage of these services. More assistance to students and their families in urban schools seems to be needed.

Discussion

In this study, the role of the principals as multicultural leaders was evolving as principals learned on the job. Generally, principals learn in actual situations and glean information from other principals. This finding is consistent with research on professional socialization. (For literature on principal socialization, see Browne-Ferrigno, 2003; Hart, 1993; Heck, 1995; Leithwood, Steinbach, & Begley, 1992; Parkay, Currie, & Rhodes, 1992; Saks & Ashforth, 1997.) However, university preparation programs could also provide support, and participants noted that professional development on the multicultural dimensions of leadership was needed. As principals credentialed many years ago, these men and women had achieved principal certification in programs with no attention to issues of diversity, social justice, or multicultural education.

All 6 principals had roles as multicultural leaders in dealing with diversity issues in their respective schools. All principals were generally empathetic with new immigrants, attempting to demonstrate cultural sensitivity and appreciating the cultural diversity brought to the school by students from as near as Mexico and as far away as Afghanistan. But although some administrators held high expectations for all youngsters, others maintained deficit views about certain groups of students. For the junior high school principal, socializing the refugees was a challenge. Likewise, Principal Sanders, who did not see herself as a multicultural leader, stated early on in the study, "I feel that the mission of schools is learning. I will leave the issue of pursuing social justice to others as I work with my students, parents, and community." She did value and try to include her parents and community in her school. But she appeared to be unaware of the negative impact that a monocultural assimilation environment can have on student learning, and she initially was not prepared to be a learner in multicultural education herself. During the course of this study, her views changed. She later stated, "Diversity is a worthy cause."

Of the three multicultural leadership tasks, the second one, promoting inclusive instructional practices, seemed to be the least evident. Principals were not sure what was meant by "culturally proficient instruction" and tended to rely on their teachers. With the challenges of second-language learners and recent immigrants, Principal Brown suggested that good teaching was simply good teaching:

> If a child doesn't understand because of a language barrier, that's not necessarily different than a child who doesn't understand because they have a learning disability. You've got to look at other ways to get the information across.

But we would counter the notion that all students should be acculturated to a single way of knowing and behaving. In research on effective schooling, Rosenholtz (1991) proposes that principals need to support teachers in learning ways to better instruct, guide, and mentor youngsters from diverse ethnic, linguistic, social, and economic backgrounds. As well, superintendents can support principals by providing learning opportunities "to refine and expand their pedagogical repertoires, opportunities for critical inquiry, rigorous discourse and analysis" (p. 188).

685 As noted earlier, some principals in this study commented, "I don't see color. I teach children." We appreciate that they are trying to be impartial in this statement. However, in not seeing diversity, they are denying their students the beauty and richness of the 690 backgrounds, heritage, and cultural treasures that the students bring to the classroom (see Gardiner, 2005, for a personal account). Ferguson (2000) showed that educators who are ethnocentric and view their students as "culturally disadvantaged" simply because of their eth- 695 nicity have a devastating effect on students' willingness to learn. In contrast, other studies indicate positive effects of teachers holding high expectations for students and appreciation for their ethnic diversity. Test scores are likely to rise when the focus is not on the 700 tests but instead on a lively and engaging educational environment that validates and encourages all students. (For more on the fallacy of color blindness, see Bell, 2002; Frankenberg, 1993; Marx, 2004; Thompson, 1998; Williams, 1997.)

705 Principals who are multicultural leaders help raise test scores by ensuring that teachers are including multicultural knowledge in the curriculum and in their pedagogy. Evaluation of teachers (and principals) could include multicultural proficiency as a dimension 710 of evaluation. In predominantly white schools, there is a need for school administrators to be attentive to issues of racism, intolerance, and prejudice. It may be even more important in seemingly nondiverse settings to have administrators who value diversity. All stu- 715 dents, including Caucasians, are better educated when they are able to communicate cross-culturally and are prepared for the pluralistic societal and work environments that characterize our nation and world.

Placement of students in special programs such as 720 ELL can be helpful, but principals noted the lack of integration between students in ELL and the mainstream student body. Questions for further research might review whether such an interchange promotes better learning and inclusion, or whether a separate 725 ELL academy supports individualized student growth and development, especially for those who are older. Consideration might be given to offering ELL at neighborhood schools rather than centralizing services in a few selected elementary schools and one secon- 730 dary ELL academy. A bilingual school with a sufficient population of both native Spanish speakers and native English speakers could be beneficial to both groups of students. We encourage continued research on the effectiveness of two-way bilingual education and other 735 bilingual education programs (see Nieto, 2000, for analysis of several types of program) and the sheltered English language immersion that is currently used in this particular school district.

Conclusions and Recommendations

This exploratory qualitative study has illustrated 740 how 6 urban school principals enact leadership in facing numerous multicultural challenges. Professional development, particularly when requested by principals themselves, could be helpful. Principals, together with university faculty, might work with their staff to con- 745 sider how educational law and policy have marginalized certain groups of students. Or they might look at the curriculum of their schools to determine whether there is still bias and stereotyping and offer recommendations for reform. Principals and their staff could also 750 connect research with practice concerning instructional strategies that work successfully with particular groups of students. Practices would then need to be adapted for unique contexts and individual students.

Second, as issues of equity, excellence, and social 755 justice are addressed in the schools, principals are more likely to be successful if they receive consistent reinforcement and support from their district-level administrators. Multiculturalism or social justice values must be clearly written in district and school mission state- 760 ments and core values to serve students effectively. Mission statements articulate a vision and communicate values, standards, and evaluation expectations for all employees. It is not enough for culturally proficient instruction to be "kind of an expectation" (Principal 765 Garrison). Multicultural leadership could be an explicit expectation tied to staff and administrators' evaluations.

Finally, to integrate multicultural leadership principles within one's practice, school principals can be 770 encouraged to be self-reflective and to critique their own school sites and context. Urban school principals who are aware of themselves and the social–cultural milieu in which they live and work will be more effective in reaching their students. Adopting a mental 775 framework of listening and learning from oneself and one's own school and community is critical. For instance, administrators in the school district could examine their own ethnic background, traditions, and values. Then they could engage in professional devel- 780 opment to learn about the history, cultures, and languages of the Native American tribes in the region and learn to speak Spanish if there is a significant Hispanic population. Principals cannot possibly be prepared for all the ethnic, linguistic, cultural populations they may 785 serve. In Boyd School's district, with more than 56 languages spoken, it is unrealistic to expect principals to know all those languages. Yet learning one new language and a willingness to listen and learn would be appreciated. As one reviewer of this article noted, there 790 is much to be said for a position of silence. As Principal Andrews of Boyd High noted when he explained that most of his teachers were Caucasian and monolingual in English, "We have communication problems here. It is definitely a disadvantage." For administrators 795 who argue that they "have always treated everyone equally," the realization that equality does not necessarily mean identical treatment but treatment that listens to, recognizes, and affirms unique student needs and backgrounds can be powerful.

References

American Psychological Association. (n.d.). *Resolution recommending the immediate retirement of American Indian mascots, symbols, images, and personalities by schools, colleges, universities, athletic teams, and organizations.* Retrieved February 10, 2006, from http://www.apa.org/releases/ResAmIndianMascots.pdf

Arredondo, P., & Perez, P. (2003). Expanding multicultural competence through social justice leadership. *The Counseling Psychologist, 31,* 282–289.

Banks, J., & Banks, C. (Eds.). (2001). *Handbook of research on multicultural education.* San Francisco: Jossey-Bass.

Bell, L. (2002). Sincere fictions: The pedagogical challenges of preparing white teachers for multicultural classrooms. *Equity & Excellence in Education, 35,* 236–244.

Bennett, C. (2001). Genres of research in multicultural education. *Review of Educational Research, 71,* 171–217.

Browne-Ferrigno, T. (2003). Becoming a principal: Role conception, initial socialization, role-identity transformation, purposeful engagement. *Educational Administration Quarterly, 39,* 468–503.

Capper, C. (1993). *Educational administration in a pluralistic society.* Albany: State University of New York Press.

Cochran-Smith, M. (2001). Multicultural education: Solution or problem for American schools. *Journal of Teacher Education, 52,* 91–93.

Creswell, J. (1998). *Qualitative inquiry and research design: Choosing among five traditions.* Thousand Oaks, CA: Sage.

Delpit, L. (1995). *Other people's children: Cultural conflict in the classroom.* New York: New Press.

Ferguson, A. (2000). *Bad boys: Public schools in the making of black masculinity.* Ann Arbor: University of Michigan.

Frankenberg, R. (1993). *White women, race matters: The social construction of Whiteness.* Minneapolis: University of Minnesota Press.

Gardiner, M. (2005). Through the eyes of a Black child in White Idaho: CMCD principles of multicultural leadership. *Inland, 26,* 4–7.

Gay, G. (2001). *Culturally responsive teaching: Theory, research, and practice.* New York: Columbia University, Teachers College.

Hart, A. W. (1993). *Principal succession: Establishing leadership in schools.* Albany: State University of New York.

Heck, R. H. (1995). Organizational and professional socialization: Its impact on the performance of new leaders. *The Urban Review, 27,* 31–49.

Henze, R., Katz, A., Norte, E., Sather, S., & Walker, E. (2002). *Leading for diversity: How school leaders promote positive interethnic relations.* Thousand Oaks, CA: Corwin.

Hollins, E. (1996a). *Culture in school learning: Revealing the deep meaning.* Mahwah, NJ: Lawrence Erlbaum.

Hollins, E. (1996b). *Transforming curriculum for a culturally diverse society.* Mahwah, NJ: Lawrence Erlbaum.

Ladson-Billings, G. (1995). But that's just good teaching! The case for culturally relevant pedagogy. *Theory Into Practice, 34,* 159–165.

Leithwood, K., Steinbach, R., & Begley, P. (1992). Socialization experiences: Becoming a principal in Canada. In F. W. Parkay & G. E. Hall (Eds.), *Becoming a principal: The challenges of beginning leadership* (pp. 284–307). Boston: Allyn & Bacon.

Lomotey, K. (1993). African-American principals: Bureaucrat administrators and ethnohumanists. *Urban Education, 27,* 395–412.

Marshall, C. (1993). The new politics of race and gender. In C. Marshall (Ed.), *The new politics of race and gender* (pp. 1–6). Washington, DC: Falmer.

Marx, G. (2002, spring). Ten trends: Educating children for tomorrow's schools. *Journal of School Improvement, 3.*

Marx, S. (2004). Regarding Whiteness: Exploring and intervening in the effects of White racism in teacher education. *Equity & Excellence in Education, 37,* 31–43.

Merriam, S. (1998). *Qualitative research and case study applications in education.* San Francisco: Jossey-Bass.

Merriam, S. (2002). *Qualitative research in practice: Examples for discussion and analysis.* San Francisco: Jossey-Bass.

Nieto, S. (2000). *Affirming diversity: The sociopolitical context of multicultural education.* New York: Addison Wesley Longman.

Nuri-Robins, K., Lindsey, R., Lindsey, D., & Terrell, R. (2002). *Culturally proficient instruction: A guide for people who teach.* Thousand Oaks, CA: Corwin.

Okagaki, L., & Moore, D. (2000). Ethnic identity beliefs of young adults and their parents in families of Mexican descent. *Hispanic Journal of Behavioral Sciences,* 139–162.

Orfield, G. (2001). *Schools more separate: Consequences of a decade of segregation.* Cambridge, MA: Harvard University, The Civil Rights Project.

Parkay, F. W., Currie, G. D., & Rhodes, J. W. (1992). Professional socialization. *Educational Administration Quarterly, 28,* 43–75.

Riehl, C. (2000). The principal's role in creating inclusive schools for diverse students: A review of normative, empirical, and critical literature on the practice of educational administration. *Review of Educational Research, 70,* 55–81.

Robins, K., Lindsey, R., Lindsey, D., & Terrell, R. (2002). *Culturally proficient instruction: A guide for people who teach.* Thousand Oaks, CA: Corwin.

Rosenholtz, S. J. (1991). *Teachers' workplace: The social organization of schools.* New York: Columbia University, Teachers College.

Rossman, G., & Rallis, S. (2003). *Learning in the field* (2nd ed). Thousand Oaks, CA: Sage.

Saks, A. M., & Ashforth, B. E. (1997). Organizational socialization: Making sense of the past and present as a prologue for the future. *Journal of Vocational Behavior, 51,* 234–279.

Sleeter, C. (2001). Preparing teachers for culturally diverse schools: Research and the overwhelming presence of Whiteness. *Journal of Teacher Education, 52,* 94–106.

Sleeter, C., & Grant, C. (1987). An analysis of multicultural education in the United States. *Harvard Educational Review, 57,* 421–444.

Thompson, A. (1998). Not the color purple: Black feminist lessons for educational caring. *Harvard Educational Review, 68,* 522–554.

Wallace, B. (2000). A call for change in multicultural training at graduate schools of education: Educating to end oppression and for social justice. *Teachers College Record, 102,* 1086–1111.

Williams, P. (1997). *Seeing a color-blind future: The paradox of race.* New York: Noonday.

Note: An earlier version of this article was presented at the annual meeting of the American Educational Research Association, April 15, 2004.

Acknowledgments: We would like to thank Carolyn Hondo and Emmy Olmstead for transcribing the interview transcripts. The six school principals and three district level administrators who gave freely of their time and ideas are also very much appreciated. Their job is a difficult one, and it is easy for armchair theorists to develop solutions to problems. Thank you, David Mueller (Mary's husband), for the many conversations throughout the fieldwork enterprise that helped the analysis to develop. And finally, our thanks to the reviewers for their thoughtful critique of the article.

About the authors: *Mary E. Gardiner*, Ph.D., is a professor in the Department of Counseling and School Psychology, Special Education and Educational Leadership, at the University of Idaho, Boise. She is the author of several books reflecting her research interests: *School Cultures* (1993, Ablex), *Parent–School Collaboration* (1996, SUNY), and (as coauthor with Ernestine Enomoto and Margaret Grogan) *Coloring Outside the Lines: Mentoring Women Into School Leadership* (2000, SUNY). *Ernestine K. Enomoto*, Ed.D., is an associate professor in the Department of Educational Administration at the University of Hawaii at Manoa. Her research interests include educational leadership and organizational culture and contexts, especially those serving multiethnic student populations.

APPENDIX

Interview Guide for Principals

Information on Participant

Number of years served as principal_____

Number of years principal at current school_____

Cultural, racial, or ethnic identity_____

Gender: Female Male

Age_____

Educational degrees and credentials_____

1. Tell me about this particular school. What is it like and what makes it unique or similar to other schools?

2. Describe the student demographics of this school. Who are the various socioeconomic, social, racial, ethnic, religious and ability groups that make up this school? How representative is the school of the district as a whole?

3. What multicultural dilemmas and challenges have you faced recently in your school?

4. Tell me about a specific multicultural problem or issue that you have faced as a principal. What did you do? What would you have done differently, if anything?

5. With regard to diversity, what changes have you made or plan to make in the school?

6. What instructional methodologies or pedagogical approaches are employed in this school?

7. What is the content of the curriculum? Is it multicultural? How so?

8. To what extent are your teachers "culturally proficient instructors"?

9. How do you teach, support, and mentor your teachers to succeed in diverse school settings?

10. What faculty development has occurred over the past few years with regard to teaching diverse learners?

11. Please describe the social, cultural, ethnic, or other communities that your school serves.

12. As principal, how do you go about making connections between the school and its community (e.g., networking with community members to provide services for students and their families)?

13. To what extent were you prepared for the social, cultural, economic, and political challenges of serving a diverse school community? If well prepared, what enabled you? If not, what areas were lacking?

14. How might school leaders be better prepared in terms of knowledge, skills, and attitudes to serve culturally diverse schools?

15. Is there anything you can add about the process of becoming a multicultural leader? Is there anything else I should have asked? Any final comments? Thank you very much.

Exercise for Article 33

Factual Questions

1. The principals in this study were drawn from how many school districts?

2. Why did the researchers use pseudonyms for the administrators and schools?

3. Did the diversity of the school student population *or* the principal's own background guide selection of the principals for this study?

4. What was the age range of the principals?

5. What percentage of the students in School 6 were English language learners?

Questions for Discussion

6. In a future study, would you use a sample that consists only of Caucasian principals? (See line 148.)

7. Did the inclusion of the Appendix at the end of this article help you understand this study? Explain.

8. Is the information on the researchers' backgrounds important? (Note that in qualitative research, such information is sometimes referred to as "self-disclosure.") Explain.

9. Are the direct quotations from principals important in helping you understand the results of this study? Explain. (For example, see lines 317–324.)

10. If you were to conduct another study on this topic, would you use qualitative *or* quantitative research methodology? Explain.

11. Are any of the results of this study particularly interesting or surprising? Explain.

Quality Ratings

Directions: Indicate your level of agreement with each of the following statements by circling a number from 5 for strongly agree (SA) to 1 for strongly disagree (SD). If you believe an item is not applicable to this research article, leave it blank. Be prepared to explain your ratings. When responding to criteria A and B below, keep in mind that brief titles and abstracts are conventional in published research.

A. The title of the article is appropriate.

SA   5   4   3   2   1   SD

B. The abstract provides an effective overview of the research article.

SA   5   4   3   2   1   SD

C. The introduction establishes the importance of the study.

SA   5   4   3   2   1   SD

D. The literature review establishes the context for the study.

SA   5   4   3   2   1   SD

E. The research purpose, question, or hypothesis is clearly stated.

SA   5   4   3   2   1   SD

F. The method of sampling is sound.

SA   5   4   3   2   1   SD

G. Relevant demographics (for example, age, gender, and ethnicity) are described.

SA   5   4   3   2   1   SD

H. Measurement procedures are adequate.

SA   5   4   3   2   1   SD

I. All procedures have been described in sufficient detail to permit a replication of the study.

SA   5   4   3   2   1   SD

J. The participants have been adequately protected from potential harm.

SA   5   4   3   2   1   SD

K. The results are clearly described.

SA   5   4   3   2   1   SD

L. The discussion/conclusion is appropriate.

SA   5   4   3   2   1   SD

M. Despite any flaws, the report is worthy of publication.

SA   5   4   3   2   1   SD

Article 34

Factors of a Low-SES Household: What Aids Academic Achievement?

ALLISON MILNE
Wenatchee School District

LEE A. PLOURDE
Central Washington University, Wenatchee

ABSTRACT. The home factors of low-SES primary students, having high academic achievement, were investigated. Six second-grade students were identified as living in low-SES homes and qualifying for free and reduced lunch, while also having high academic achievement. Their primary caretakers were interviewed in order to investigate the factors within their homes that aided academic achievement. The results of this qualitative study exhibited that none of these high achieving second-grade students had home factors that were typical of low-SES home environments. Information was gathered through interviews, observations, and various documents. The interviews were semi-structured and evolved throughout the study. After the audio-recorded interviews were transcribed and examined, four common themes emerged: (a) educational resources/influences, (b) the mother's education, (c) relationships, and (d) causes of child's success. The results of this study have implications for all educators.

From *Journal of Instructional Psychology, 32*, 183–193. Copyright © 2006 by Project Innovation, Inc. Reprinted with permission.

The role of the teacher has taken on many descriptors over the past 100 years. Today, the job of the teacher is not simply to facilitate learning, but often includes being a nurse, social worker, parent, referee,
5 advocate, and much, much more. This is due to many changes in society that have taken place. One of those changes has been the number of children living in poverty. The U.S. Bureau of Census reports that the poverty rates of children are currently higher than they
10 have ever been (Bureau of Census, 2002). This in turn leads to a larger percentage of students in the classroom who come from low socioeconomic households. Why is this increase significant? There has been a tremendous amount of research done that shows that a
15 child's socioeconomic status (SES) affects his/her overall cognitive ability and academic achievement (Bradley & Corwyn, 2002; Bracey, 1996; Ram and Hou, 2003; Duncan, Yeung, Brooks-Gunn, & Smith, 1998). According to Vail (2004), "[children] from high
20 poverty environments enter school less ready to learn, and they lag behind their more-affluent classmates in their ability to use language to solve problems" (p. 12).

It has also been found that SES seems to affect the consistency of a student's attendance, as well as how many
25 years of education he/she ultimately completes (Bradley & Corwyn, 2002). Many researchers agree that there is usually a positive correlation between SES and academic achievement.

But what about those students who come from low-
30 SES homes and are still able to succeed academically? In fact, not only are many of them succeeding, some tend to be well above the academic achievement standards for their determined grade level. "While low-SES is highly correlated with low achievement, some low-
35 SES students *are* academically successful" (Caldwell & Ginther, 1996, p. 142). Research has also found discrepancies within the correlations between SES and achievement (Molfese, DiLalla, & Bunce, 1997; Caldwell & Ginther, 1996). The issues have therefore be-
40 come less of looking at the correlations between SES and academic achievement, and more of looking at what factors of low-SES are contributing to success in school.

Statement of the Problem

Why is the child reared in a low-SES household
45 still able to succeed in school? Molfese, DiLalla, & Bunce (1997) found that home environment measures were the single most important predictor of differences in children's intelligence at ages 3 through 8. In one study, Duncan, Yeung, Brooks-Gunn, & Smith (1998)
50 found that "...children in families with incomes less than one-half of the poverty line were found to score between 6 and 13 points lower on the various standardized tests" (p. 408). However, even as many researchers have found that low-SES is a determining factor in
55 how a child will succeed in school, many still agree that the effects of SES on learning achievement vary from case to case. In a study that investigated the role of environment in the development of reading skills, Molfese, Molfese, & Modglin (2003) were able to con-
60 clude that while SES scores of children between the ages of 3 and 10 were consistently correlated with reading achievement, the correlations were not high. In fact, some of their results indicated that SES scores were weak or insignificant correlates of reading scores.
65 Where is the discrepancy coming from? Why are some

students so clearly affected by their home situation, while others are seemingly unaffected?

Significance of the Study

Just knowing that students come from low-SES homes is not enough. There is first a need to know and understand what constitutes a low-SES household. Once this is established, researchers have found that while some students come from low-SES backgrounds, that doesn't necessarily predict that they will not succeed in school (Molfese, Molfese, & Modglin, 2003; Caldwell & Ginther, 1996). By understanding what type of home environment students of low-SES are coming from, teachers can better predict and understand student achievement in class.

Purpose of the Study

There is much research that exists to support the theory that SES affects students' learning achievement (Caldwell & Ginther, 1996; Battle, 2002; Duncan, Yeung, Brooks-Gunn, & Smith, 1998). What remains unclear is what factors of SES determine if students will succeed or not. The purpose of this study was to examine, in second-grade students who come from low-SES homes, the factors of low-SES that affect students' overall academic achievement. The research was guided by two main questions: (1) what are the common factors of low-SES homes from which children are able to achieve academic success, and (2) do some low-SES children succeed simply because they are resilient and would succeed no matter what type of home they were in?

Research Question

Some students coming from low-SES homes are able to maintain high levels of success in school while others cannot. Therefore, the main question to be researched was: What are the home factors of low-SES second-grade students in a Central Washington school that contribute to their achieving academic success?

Review of Related Literature

History of Socioeconomic Status

Poverty rates of children in the United States are the highest they have ever been. According to the U.S. Census Bureau, some 28.7 million children are living in poverty across the United States (U.S. Bureau of Census, 2003). This is significantly more than in 1995, when about 15.3 million children lived with families that were stricken with poverty (U.S. Bureau of Census, 1995). As the rising of poverty rates has continued in the United States, so has the debate on the effects of socioeconomic status (SES) on children. It is clear that children coming from low-SES households endure trials and unpleasant circumstances that are much more severe than those of middle or high-SES households. However, to what extent does their socioeconomic status play a role in their cognitive abilities and academic achievement?

In order to come to any conclusions, it is important to clarify how SES is measured. There has historically been considerable debate on what factors determine SES. "The most common debate of the proponents of SES has been between economic position and economic social status" (Bradley & Corwyn, 2002, p. 371). In considering these proponents, however, psychologists have agreed that looking at the idea of capital may be a better way of measuring SES. "Capital (resources, assets) has become a favored way of thinking about SES because access to financial capital (material resources), human capital (nonmaterial resources such as education), and social capital (resources achieved through social connections) are readily connectable to processes that directly affect well-being" (Bradley & Corwyn, 2002, p. 371). Therefore, capital is summed up as being determined by household income, occupation, and parent education.

Changes in family structure should also be considered in measuring SES. Ram & Hou (2003) found in a recent study that "[compared] with children in families with two original parents, those in lone-parent and stepparent families are at a disadvantage on every measure of child outcome, even when their initial disadvantages and socioeconomic background are taken into account" (p. 309). Studies show that divorce or separation will inevitably lead to a severe drop in family income and standard of living, and this often will lead to families being forced to move into poor neighborhoods (Hetherington & Stanley-Hagan, 1999). When a marriage ends, more likely than not the result will be that the lone parent must work extended hours outside of the home to make up for severe financial drops; therefore, spending less time with the children (Ram & Hou, 2003).

In sum, the majority of researchers agree that income, education, and occupation together best represent SES, while some others feel that changes in family structure should also be considered. Bradley (1994) concludes that "the choice of how to measure SES remains open. Part will be determined by the question being examined, part by the practical considerations concerning the acquisition of data, and part by the population from whom the data are collected" (p. 242).

Effects of SES on Students' Abilities

With the definition of SES more clearly defined, it is now important to discuss the effects of SES on students' cognitive abilities and academic success. Several researchers have found that SES affects students' abilities. In a recent study that looked at the effects of childhood poverty on the life chances of children, results revealed that correlations were the highest between family income and children's ability and achievement. "Children in families with incomes less than one-half of the poverty line were found to score between 6 and 13 points lower on the various standardized tests" (Duncan, Yeung, Brooks-Gunn, & Smith,

1998, p. 408). The researchers in this article also cite the comprehensive study by Haveman & Wolfe (1995), in which they found that family income is positively 175 associated with educational attainment.

In another study, Caldwell & Ginther (1996) found that students from a low socioeconomic background constitute the largest population of individuals considered to be at-risk of not graduating from high school. 180 They cite that the lack of academic achievement is the best predictor of dropping out of school. Therefore, they reason that if dropout rates are going to be lowered, strategies to improve academic achievement of at-risk students must be formulated.

185 While there is some research that disputes, or at the very least finds inconsistencies within the fact that SES affects students' academic achievement, most researchers agree that children are affected by SES. Perhaps most alarming are the findings that while SES 190 seems to affect all children in their academic achievement and cognitive abilities, it tends to be most detrimental in the earliest years of development. Study after study reveals that children are hardest hit by family economic conditions during their early years (Ram & 195 Hou, 2003; Bradley & Corwyn, 2002; Lindjord, 2002).

Low-SES Factors

As the research has been conducted, there has been a considerable amount of time spent on trying to find out why SES affects students' achievement. Bradley & Corwyn (2002) found that the children from poor fami- 200 lies have less access to educational resources available to children coming from higher SES families. They have less chances of visiting local libraries or museums, less chances of visiting any educational centers in their communities or theatrical events. Constantino 205 (2005) also found that children from high-SES homes have more books in their homes than those of low-SES environments.

Children from low-SES homes also tend to live in environments that are overcrowded, with many siblings 210 and many overall needs that must be met by their parents. This leads to less time for their parents, usually their mothers, to spend quality time working with them to teach them the basics needed for attending schools.

Bradley & Corwyn (2002) also found that high-SES 215 parents talk with their children more, engage them in more meaningful and deeper conversations, read to them more, and provide many more teaching experiences. These parents generally try to get their children to talk more, they encourage them to be engaged in 220 conversations with adults, and they tend to use richer vocabulary with their children. Low-SES parents are less likely to purchase educational materials such as reading books or workbooks for their children. They also fail to regulate the amount and quality of televi- 225 sion their children watch. Children from these homes are typically expected to sit for longer periods of time

quietly, and are encouraged to not interrupt adults who are conversing (Bradley & Corwyn, 2002).

Adding to the issues of low-SES is the problem of 230 changes in family structure and its effect on the home environment of children. Ram & Hou (2003) have found that parents' marital conflict will often lead to less involvement in their children's school activities and inconsistencies in their style of supervision. Par- 235 ents who are going through a separation or divorce tend to inconsistently supervise, control, and discipline their children. They also found that the situations will most likely not be better off once the lone parent is in charge of the family. "There is evidence to suggest that lone 240 parents make fewer demands on children, do not adequately monitor their behavior, and utilize less effective disciplinary strategies" (Ram & Hou, 2003, p. 311). These parenting behaviors tend to be caused by longer work hours to make up for large financial drops. 245 All of these behaviors tend to have a negative effect on the academic achievement of children. There has been some research, however, that disputes the effects of divorce on academic achievement (Battle, 1997). In his research, Battle (1997) suggests that once the marriage 250 dissolves and the conflict is no longer inside the home, the stress of the household goes down. With less conflict at home, students are able to achieve more at school.

In sum, nearly all of the researchers agree that SES 255 does affect students' overall cognitive development and academic achievement. Where the literature is lacking, however, is in the discussion of students who come from low-SES homes that tend to have high academic achievement. Research is needed in understand- 260 ing why these students succeed in school when so many of their peers are unable to. Specifically, research is needed in identifying any common factors within the homes of the academically successful students.

Methodology

Introduction

The method of research in this study was qualita- 265 tive. The study was designed to investigate the different factors of low-SES homes contributing to academic success in second-grade students of a Central Washington elementary school. In order to discover these factors, the researcher needed to first identify the students 270 who were living in low-SES homes. The researcher then needed to use interviews of the primary caretaker(s) of these children as a means of ascertaining the factors of each home that may or may not be contributing to the academic success of the participants. By rec- 275 ognizing the factors that aid high academic achievement in the homes of students, educators will have a better understanding of what children from low-SES situations are truly lacking in their homes that are affecting their academic achievement.

Participants

280 The participants of this study were a purposive

sample of six second-grade students who were all between the ages of seven and eight and their parents. All of the students were in the same second-grade classroom. The school in which they attended was located
285 in Central Washington. At the time of the study, the school served approximately 450 students in which 52% came from low-SES homes. The participants were initially selected because the school had identified them as being qualified for the free and reduced lunch
290 program. All six of these participants were selected for this study due to their high academic success, as they were all at least one trimester above the second-grade standard. Three of the participants were females. Five of the six participants came from homes in which Eng-
295 lish was the primary language spoken. One of the participants came from a home in which Spanish was the primary language spoken. The researcher felt that this would have little bearing on the study for two reasons. The first reason was that the participant had received
300 his education in English starting in kindergarten and had high academic achievement in English in all academic areas. The other reason was that the researcher was bilingual/biliterate in Spanish and would not have any difficulties communicating with the participant's
305 primary caretaker.

The persons interviewed for this study were the primary caretakers of the participants. For the purpose of this study, however, due to previous findings in research, the researcher was particularly interested in
310 interviewing the mothers of the participants. Once the participants were selected, the researcher found that all of the participants' primary caretakers were their mothers, with the only exception being that two of the participants had both parents who carried the load of car-
315 ing for the children. Therefore, when interviews took place, four of the interviews were conducted with just the mother as the primary caretaker. The other two interviews were with both the parents present and partaking in the interview process.

Procedures
320 In order to select the participants for this study, the researcher obtained the free and reduced lunch status of the entire second-grade class. From this list, the researcher then identified six students who could possibly participate in this study based on their academic
325 achievement in the second-grade. Once the students were identified according to their free and reduced lunch status and their academic achievement, the researcher then contacted the primary caretakers of the students to ask them if they would be willing to participate in this study by being interviewed. The re-
330 searcher did not reveal to the caretakers that their children were selected for this study due to both their SES level and high academic achievement. The researcher simply told them the purpose of the study was to see
335 what they were doing at home that was aiding their child in having such high academic success.

Once the caretakers agreed to participate in the interviews, a time and place were scheduled to have the interview. The researcher interviewed the caretakers
340 within two weeks of them being asked to participate. The caretakers were given a choice on where the interview would take place based on where they were most comfortable. Four of the six interviews took place in their child's second-grade classroom. The other two
345 took place in the participants' homes. Each interview contained several questions that led the caretakers to openly discuss different factors that may or may not be contributing to their child's academic success. Each interview lasted a minimum of 45 minutes, with most
350 of them going beyond an hour.

Research Design
This was an ethnographic study in which the researcher was able to gain perspective on the participants by interviewing their primary caretaker(s). Once the setting was established, each of the caretakers was
355 interviewed one-on-one. The caretakers were asked about twenty semi-structured questions designed to get them talking about their lives at home. Some of the questions were asked to get the caretakers talking about their relationships with their child, while others asked
360 them to describe typical routines at their homes. Even though the list of questions was the same for each interview, some of the interviews included extra questions or questions asked in different ways. Because the questions were semi-structured, sometimes the answers
365 given would lead the researcher and caretaker through territory that needed to be discussed at length, causing the researcher to ask more clarifying questions. Also, when a question was asked to the caretakers but they did not understand the language used, the researcher
370 changed the wording to make it more understandable. In order to protect the privacy of each of the participants, the researcher used pseudonyms in any written documents.

Measurement Tools
The researcher used the records kept by the school
375 in which the participants attended in order to obtain their free and reduced-lunch information. In order to qualify for free and reduced lunch in this school district, the caretakers of the students attending the school seeking to qualify for free and reduced lunch filled out
380 a form that was then reviewed for acceptance or declination of free and reduced lunch. The researcher also used her own records of her second-grade class to see which students were at least one trimester above the second-grade standard. The researcher primarily
385 looked at the students' academic achievement in reading based on their District Reading Assessment (DRA) scores. In order to be at least one trimester above grade level in reading, according to the DRA, the students needed to be at a level 24 at the time of the interview.
390 Therefore, at the time of participant selection, during the first trimester, if the students were at a level 24,

they were considered to be at least one trimester above grade level.

Interview Protocol

As participants were interviewed, they were asked about twenty semi-structured questions that were designed to get them talking about what their lives at home looked like and why their lives were the way they were. Because I was constantly monitoring the participants as they were being interviewed, some of the questions were asked in a different way in order to get the participants talking more. Throughout the interviews, it became clear that there were some questions that were being answered in similar ways by every participant.

Data Analysis

After the interviews were transcribed, the data were coded. Coding categories emerged after transcribing the information and carefully looking for commonalities in wording and phrasing. Bogden and Biklen's "Cut Up and Put Into Folders Approach" (Bogden & Biklen, 1992) was utilized. Major headings emerged during this process as well as smaller subcodes. Common themes and attributes surfaced, which led to further research and analysis.

Results

Throughout my entire research process I focused on answering two main guiding questions: (1) what are the common factors of low-SES homes from which children are able to achieve academic success?, and (2) do some low-SES children succeed simply because they are resilient and would succeed no matter what type of home they were in? In order to find some answers to these questions, I felt that the best place to look was with the parents of these successful children. What could they tell me that would reveal the common factors of a low-SES home whose kids are successful in school? I purposefully selected interview questions that, as I spoke with these children's parents, would give me insight into their home environments. If they were living in a typical low-SES home, their answers would reveal it.

On the onset of each interview, I was greeted with the caretakers expressing an uncertainty of why they may have been chosen to partake in the interview. While all the caretakers wanted to express their gratitude for being recognized for their child's academic achievement, this expression was consistently laced with an overwhelming sense of self-doubt, especially from those caretakers who were single mothers. Despite the presence of this clear self-doubt, however, I was continually amazed, and occasionally caught off guard, by the caretakers' willingness to openly share details of their home situation throughout the interview. Once I had completed all six interviews and the data were compiled, I was able to identify four common themes within the homes and attitudes of the participants' caretakers.

Conclusions

These themes were categorized accordingly: (a) educational resources/influences, (b) the mother's education, (c) relationships, and (d) causes of child's success. Under each of these major categories, several subcategories were included.

Educational Resources/Influences

As I spoke with each participant, I was truly amazed by what I heard them say about the educational resources and influences that had been made available to their children.

In each home, the participants had made sure that they had educational materials available to their children. In some homes, the materials were less than others, but they all discussed having books and writing materials available at the very least. A few of these families even had support systems who had supplied them with these materials as well, making sure that having no money could not be an option for not having educational materials around and available to their children.

The participants also all spoke of having time allotted each day for the children to do homework and other academic activities. Their homes all had a structured after-school schedule in which homework and reading could take place. The participants each discussed that they made themselves available as well to participate in the activities that their children were doing. For some, this meant supporting and guiding their child when it was needed; for others, this meant actually doing the projects with their child. However each family's system was set up, what was clear was that the parents were making sure that each day their children were spending time doing educational activities outside of school.

The amount of television watched was another area in which all of the participants had similar answers. In every household, the parents of these children had a small time set aside for their children to watch television. This time was anywhere from 30 minutes to one hour per day. The participants each talked about there not being enough time for their children to watch any more than that. Several of the participants also discussed the importance of television being monitored in order that appropriate shows were being watched.

All of the participants' children had attended preschool before entering Kindergarten. One child attended for only one year, while the rest attended preschool for two years. The participants all felt that it was important that their children were prepared before they entered school. A few of the participants had taken advantage of a preschool like Head Start, in which they did not have to pay for their children to attend, while others paid for preschool. What was most important, however, was that they took advantage of the resources made available to their children in order that they would be ready to start school.

Relationships

While the situations of each family interviewed clearly varied from case to case in many ways, there were also similarities that could not be denied. The family structure varied for all of the participants. Of those caretakers interviewed, one was a single mother who had never been married with only one child; two were single and divorced with three children; one of the caretakers was married, but with a blended family of three children; and two of the caretakers were married, one having two children and one having three. While structurally these families differed immensely, there were very clear patterns in how they related to each other, the extent of the involvement of the caretakers in their children's lives, and the support that the caretakers felt from certain individuals around them.

As I spoke with each participant about their relationship with their child, I was encouraged as they spoke about the amount of time spent together. Over and over again, I heard the words, "we do everything" together. Even though these participants each struggled with the amount of time they were away from their children due to their work schedule, they all seemed to work extremely hard at spending as much of their time outside of work with their children. They spoke about the need for quality one-on-one time, as well as wanting to do things together. Several participants described their relationship with their child as one being more like a team. Many times, this was due to the need for both child and parent to pitch in and help if they were going to make it through each day. They also discussed the importance of there being a clear definition to who was the parent and who was the child. These parents all wanted to be respected, but they also wanted to have open relationships with their children, and they wanted to be able to have fun together.

At some point during our conversations, each participant discussed with me that they spent time talking with their child. They liked having the kind of relationship in which they would seem approachable by their children, that their children would be able to talk with them about anything if they wanted to. Many times, I got the feeling that these were much more like adult-to-adult conversations in which the children were exposed to good language in the natural setting of it being their parent who was doing the talking.

All of the participants also expressed the need of having a support system. Each participant had a clearly defined support system in which they could relate. In fact, two of the participants even spoke of having mentors who they could seek advice about their parenting. The participants who were single parents all spoke of having friends who were in the same situation and who they could talk to about the challenges that they faced. Four of the six participants did not have any family nearby who could help them out, and they therefore strongly relied on their social circles to bring them that support. Whatever their specific situation, all of the participants knew that they could not make it on their own and were thankful that they had people around them whom they could lean on for support.

Mother's Education

While each of the participants differed in the area of their own education, they did have some similarities. Every participant had at least completed the tenth grade in school. Two of the participants had dropped out after tenth grade, with one going back later to get her GED; another participant was currently in college to get her A.A.; two of the participants earned a two-year degree in college; and one of them earned a bachelor's degree. While the amount of education each of the participants had differed, none of them seemed overly confident in their own accomplishments. Several of them talked about school coming easy to them but that a lack of motivation had kept them from truly succeeding. They all expressed, however, that they felt having an education was very important and they wanted their children to understand this point.

Causes of Success

When asked to discuss what they felt had been their role in helping their child to succeed in school, each answer was eerily similar. They spoke of the need for much support and guidance at home. They all seemed to speak with their children about the importance of getting an education and how it would help them in the future. They also spoke about having clear boundaries so that their children would know that doing schoolwork and other educational activities was not optional. Through their actions of always trying to keep their kids on track, they set the example to their children of how very important doing well in school was.

Implications

There are several implications of this study. The first being that if enough support is given to low-SES parents in order that they may have the resources (time, educational materials, and knowledge) that other higher SES homes have, their financial situation will not impact their child's academic achievement. The participants of this study all had enough support around them to be able to give their children exactly what they needed academically. They had the education to know that their children would do better in school if they were prepared in preschool first. They spent time with their children and helped them in their learning. They had people around them who could help them get the educational materials they needed for their children to have success. They had support that could pick up where they left off when they had to work longer hours or simply couldn't do any more. Support was crucial for these low-SES parents. They were already doing so much and doing it the best that they could. However, they needed people around them who could help carry some of the load.

610 There is a huge need to educate parents who are in low-SES households. All of the parents who participated in this study had many struggles to deal with due to their situation, but they also knew what to do to help their children have high academic achievement. This

615 really sets them apart from other low-SES home environments. It shows that if these homes can have the right factors in place, their children will be able to succeed in school. Therefore, we need to be educating those parents who are in low-SES situations and show-

620 ing them the things that they can do to set their children apart from the rest.

It is also obvious that all children truly can succeed in school despite the amount of capital that their family might have. It has been presented many, many times

625 that if a child is failing in school, the likelihood of finding their name on the free/reduced-lunch list is extremely high. All of the children from this study were selected because they were on that list, but they were also selected because they were so successful in school.

630 Their families may not have many material items, but they provide their children with all of the things they need to be successful in school.

Summary

If a child comes from a low-SES home, should we just assume that they are going to struggle and even fail

635 in school? The answer is no, and this study has proven that answer to be true. There has been so much research in the past that has led us to believe that the answer to that question is always yes. And then, each year as we have children from these homes being

640 highly successful in school, we ask ourselves how that can be possible. Why are they doing so well? Are they just special somehow? It is my conclusion that most likely, they come from a low-SES home that was described throughout this study rather than from one of

645 those described in previous research. It is beneficial for us to know what type of home environment children do come from so that we, as educators, will know how to best support them in school. It is true that all children can have success in school, but it is also true that that

650 success may only come once enough support has been given to their families.

Limitations

This study only looked at the home environments of six children from a second-grade classroom. The students all came from low socioeconomic environ-

655 ments in a Central Washington school district. Therefore, this study cannot be generalized.

As the researcher was the sole interviewer and instrument of this study, researcher bias was possible in any of the interpretations. Though the researcher

660 worked hard to keep out any personal opinions, the possibility of subjectivity was still present.

Also, it was possible that in interviewing parents of the students that they would not be willing to give accurate information about their home environment in

665 order to maintain a certain level of social dignity. These parents also had to answer interview questions from the researcher who was also the teacher of their children. This provided a certain level of uncomfortableness and uncertainty as they worried about how

670 they would be judged by their child's teacher.

References

Battle, J. (2002). Longitudinal analysis of academic achievement among a nationwide sample of Hispanic students in one- versus dual-parent households [Electronic version]. *Hispanic Journal of Behavioral Sciences, 24,* 430–447.

Bracey, G. W. (1996). SES and involvement [Electronic version]. *Phi Delta Kappan, 78,* 169–170.

Bradley, R. H. (1994). The HOME inventory: Review and reflections. In *Advances in Child Development and Behavior,* secondary source, 241–288.

Bradley, R. H., & Corwyn, R. F. (2002). Socioeconomic status and child development [Electronic Version]. *Annual Review of Psychology, 53,* 371–400.

Caldwell, G. P., & Ginther, D. W. (1996). Differences in learning styles of low socioeconomic status for low and high achievers [Electronic version]. *Education, 117,* 141–148.

Constantino, R. (2005). Print environments between high and low socioeconomic (ses) communities [Electronic version]. *Teacher Librarian, 32,* 22–26.

Duncan, D. J., Yeung, W. J., Brooks-Gunn, J., & Smith, J. R. (1998). How much does childhood poverty affect the life chances of children? [Electronic version]. *American Sociological Review, 63,* 406–424.

Lindjord, D. (2002). Families and adversity in the faltering U.S. economy: The misery goes on and on. Family review [Electronic version]. *Journal of Early Education and Family Review, 10,* 4–5.

Molfese, V., DiLalla, L., & Bunce, D. (1997). Prediction of the intelligence test scores of 3- to 8-year-old children by home environment, socioeconomic status, and biomedical risks. *Merril-Palmer Quarterly, 43,* secondary source, 219–234.

Molfese, V., Modglin, A., & Molfese, D. (2003). The role of environment in the development of reading skills [Electronic version]. *Journal of Learning Disabilities, 36,* 59–67.

Ram, B., & Hou, F. (2003). Changes in family structure and child outcome: Roles of economic and familial resources [Electronic version]. *Policy Studies Journal, 31,* 309.

Vail, K. (2004). Grasping what kids need to raise performance [Electronic version]. *The Education Digest, 69,* 12–25.

Weinberg, D. H. (2003). Press briefing on 2002 income and poverty estimates [Electronic version]. U.S. Census Bureau.

About the authors: *Allison Milne,* MEd., Wenatchee School District, Wenatchee, WA. *Lee A. Plourde,* Ph.D., Central Washington University-Wenatchee, WA.

Address correspondence to: Dr. Lee A. Plourde, Central Washington University, 213 N. Western Avenue, Wenatchee, WA 98801. E-mail: plourdel@cwu.edu

Exercise for Article 34

Factual Questions

1. What was the purpose of this study?

2. How many of the participants came from homes in which Spanish was the primary language?

3. How many of the interviews were conducted with both parents present?

4. Four of the six interviews took place where?

5. What did the researchers do to protect the privacy of the participants?

6. Students were selected based on their achievement in what academic area?

Questions for Discussion

7. The researchers state that they drew a "purposive sample." Speculate on the meaning of this term. (See lines 280–281.)

8. The researchers did not reveal to the parents that SES was considered in the selection process. Do you think this was a good idea? Why? Why not? (See lines 330–336.)

9. If you had conducted this study, would you have used a standard set of questions for all parents *or* would you have asked questions in various ways and added extra questions? Explain. (See lines 360–363 and 398–401.)

10. In your opinion, is the data analysis described in sufficient detail? Explain. (See lines 405–413.)

11. Are the implications of this study important? Explain. (See lines 589–632.)

12. The researchers discuss the limitations of their study. Are they all important? Are some more important than others? Explain. (See lines 652–670.)

Quality Ratings

Directions: Indicate your level of agreement with each of the following statements by circling a number from 5 for strongly agree (SA) to 1 for strongly disagree (SD). If you believe an item is not applicable to this research article, leave it blank. Be prepared to explain your ratings. When responding to criteria A and B below, keep in mind that brief titles and abstracts are conventional in published research.

A. The title of the article is appropriate.

   SA   5   4   3   2   1   SD

B. The abstract provides an effective overview of the research article.

   SA   5   4   3   2   1   SD

C. The introduction establishes the importance of the study.

   SA   5   4   3   2   1   SD

D. The literature review establishes the context for the study.

   SA   5   4   3   2   1   SD

E. The research purpose, question, or hypothesis is clearly stated.

   SA   5   4   3   2   1   SD

F. The method of sampling is sound.

   SA   5   4   3   2   1   SD

G. Relevant demographics (for example, age, gender, and ethnicity) are described.

   SA   5   4   3   2   1   SD

H. Measurement procedures are adequate.

   SA   5   4   3   2   1   SD

I. All procedures have been described in sufficient detail to permit a replication of the study.

   SA   5   4   3   2   1   SD

J. The participants have been adequately protected from potential harm.

   SA   5   4   3   2   1   SD

K. The results are clearly described.

   SA   5   4   3   2   1   SD

L. The discussion/conclusion is appropriate.

   SA   5   4   3   2   1   SD

M. Despite any flaws, the report is worthy of publication.

   SA   5   4   3   2   1   SD

Article 35

Class Jumping Into Academia:
Multiple Identities for Counseling Academics

MARY LEE NELSON
University of Wisconsin, Madison

SANDRA C. TIERNEY
University of Wisconsin, Madison

MATT ENGLAR-CARLSON
California State University, Fullerton

JULIE M. HAU
University of Wisconsin, Madison

ABSTRACT. Eleven counseling psychology and counselor education academics were interviewed regarding their experiences of progressing from lower- or lower-middle-class backgrounds to college and, further, to academic positions. Grounded theory method was used for data analysis, and consensual qualitative research methods were used for triangulation and data presentation. Participants described experiences of hardship as children, obstacles to advancement, resources that enabled academic pursuits, and thwarted belonging needs in academic environments and original referent group settings. Bicultural and tricultural identity development were identified as central phenomena for participants. Implications regarding social class as an important aspect of multiculturalism are discussed.

In discussing key components of multicultural psychology, numerous authors have nominated social class as one of those factors that intersect with race, ethnicity, gender, sexual identity, and other variables to influence people's identity, personality, and behavior (Fouad & Brown, 2000; Frable, 1997; Heppner & Scott, 2004; Liu, 2001; Liu, Ali, et al., 2004; Liu, Soleck, Hopps, Dunston, & Pickett, 2004). However, some psychologists have argued that the fields of counseling and counseling psychology have neglected to address social class as it relates to these phenomena or to conduct research that takes social class into account as something more salient than a demographic variable (Fouad & Brown, 2000; Liu, Ali, et al., 2004). Liu, Ali, et al. (2004) argued that early social class experiences exert as strong an influence on identity development as do other, more observable factors, such as race, ethnicity, and gender. Moreover, these authors argued that the field of psychology has paid scant attention to social class as an intrapsychic, or individual, experience.

From the standpoint of social-cognitive career theory (Lent, Brown, & Hackett, 1994), career advancement depends on the confluence of an individual's development of self-efficacy with multiple resources and obstacles, one of which is social class background. Richardson (1993) and Whiston and Keller (2004) commented on the paucity of career and vocational psychology research incorporating the experience of persons of lower socioeconomic status (SES). Richardson stated, "There is almost no acknowledgment that poor and lower class populations, regardless of race or ethnicity, are almost totally absent from this literature" (p. 426). The intent of this investigation is to examine social class-related experiences of counseling academics whose career development included advancement into the "ivory tower" from lower- or lower-middle-class beginnings.

Coleman (1990) defined *social capital* as characteristics of a social structure that support individuals so that they may profit or advance in some manner. Social capital includes wisdom about how to advance educationally or economically, social contacts that facilitate advancement, and knowledge about how to work within social systems (Bubolz, 2001). Social class is a powerful socializing agent in that it bestows or limits power (Liu, 2001; Liu, Ali, et al., 2004). When children are raised in a system such as a working-poor community, they acquire skills necessary to navigate in that particular environment. However, they probably do not learn the skills necessary to advance into more privileged classes. Indeed, many children from lower and working-class backgrounds do not benefit from the type of social capital that most middle-class children have access to—values that encourage children to pursue higher education as a means to a comfortable life (Littrell, 1999).

The process of upward mobility in the United States has been associated with the centrality of individual achievement and the Protestant work ethic (Mirels & Garrett, 1973). In the context of a capitalist economic structure, getting ahead and acquiring possessions are seen as primary life goals. Though not all people aspire to get ahead (Liu, 2001), hard work, delayed gratification, and sacrifice are all accepted means

65 of achieving the socially constructed, highly touted American dream.

Education as Access

Education is undoubtedly one of the primary avenues by which upward mobility is made possible. Van de Werfhorst (2002) argued that educational attainment
70 is the mediating link between class of origin and class of destination. Though upward mobility is not a major motivation for everyone (Liu, 2002; Liu, Ali, et al., 2004), it is a strong part of the American consciousness and the notion of access to a better life. Higher educa-
75 tion, in particular, is viewed broadly as necessary for career advancement and high achievement (Littrell, 1999; Ryan & Sackrey, 1984; Van de Werfhorst, 2002). Access to higher education, particularly in university settings, requires a certain degree of intelli-
80 gence, knowledge about how to succeed academically, a certain degree of maturity, interest in contributing to the social order, and, often, evidence of talent in a given field. High school students who benefit from enough social capital are either consciously or implic-
85 itly aware of these entrance requirements in the years before they need to apply for college admission. They learn the requirements from their family, privileged peers, and the families of their peers, and they have time to prepare themselves to meet the criteria.

90 People from less privileged classes encounter many challenges when their aspirations involve pursuit of higher education. Such challenges involve more than identifying adequate financial supports; they include appropriating enough social capital to guide the indi-
95 vidual through the mobility process. Advancing to higher education may entail making profound shifts in a person's social contexts and supports. Most important, perhaps, the challenge of upward mobility may also involve negotiating a new identity and incurring
100 the losses related to abandoning the old one.

Class Identity, Upward Mobility, and Loss

According to the social class worldview model (Liu, Soleck, et al., 2004), identity development occurs within context, as experiences within a particular social stratum become internalized. In this view, people's
105 assumptive worlds, behavioral repertoires, and perceptual sets are powerfully influenced by their social class background. People appropriate family and community social structures as they form internalized economic identities, and individuals learn to conform to the be-
110 havioral, attitudinal, and value-based expectations of their internalized class.

Little is known, however, about what people from lower or lower middle classes experience as they pursue social mobility, what motivates them to aspire to
115 break with their own class expectations and pursue a different life, what struggles they encounter as they move between classes, or the coping strategies they use as they advance. It is likely that upward class mobility is more than a simple experience of gaining desired
120 resources and status. Rather, upward mobility seems to involve alterations in identity and related stressors as well as loss of connection to one's original culture, loss of a sense of home, and other losses, such as no longer being simpatico with family members and old friends.

125 Such cultural losses may not emerge as the stuff of traditional psychotherapy or counseling, which may instead emphasize relationships with individual early caretakers or current associations. In the desire to uphold the image of our culture as egalitarian, Americans
130 have remained mute about the subject of social class and related interpersonal and intrapsychic experiences (Ryan & Sackrey, 1984). Therapists' omission of social class as a critical psychological experience is logically a natural outcome of the greater culture of silence. The
135 intent of this study, then, is to shed light on the internalized experience of social class by first going to members of our own academic culture who might be willing to assist in our effort to understand the internal experience of upward class mobility—with all of its
140 rewards and costs.

The phenomenon we have chosen to study is the life experiences of counseling academics from lower or lower middle classes. We are interested in their developmental and educational experiences, the nature of the
145 resources that allowed them to eventually pursue a doctorate, and the psychological challenges they faced as they progressed. Thus, we chose to examine the participants' experience of internalized social class as it developed over time and as it related to their eventual
150 career choice.

We are particularly interested in the experiences of counseling academics as a population for two reasons: First, we guessed that counseling and counseling psychology are fields that are not as visible to the general
155 public as other professions, such as medicine, nursing, computer science, law, or teaching, might be. We wondered how promising students from more humble neighborhoods actually discovered and committed to research and teaching in the areas of counseling and
160 counseling psychology. Second, the fields of counseling and counseling psychology have developed strong agendas that call for research, teaching, and practice in the area of multicultural phenomena and social justice. We hope to contribute to our field's understanding of
165 social class as a critical influence on the identity, prosperity, and experience of well-being of individuals from our own midst who make the journey from dirt roads to the ivory tower.

Method

Participants

Participants were 6 male and 5 female professors of
170 either counseling psychology or counselor education. Ethnicities represented were Caucasian (*n* = 5), Latino (*n* = 3), African American (*n* = 1), Native American (*n* = 1), and Southwestern Asian (*n* = 1). Three individuals had been participants in an American Psycho-

175 logical Association symposium in 2003 titled *Dirt Roads to Ivory Towers: Class Jumping Into Academia* (Englar-Carlson & Nelson, 2003) and volunteered to tell their stories again in the form of interviews. All were on the faculty of a doctoral-granting institution.
180 Seven were full professors, 2 were associate professors, and 2 were assistant professors. Seven were counseling psychologists, and 4 were counselor educators.

Five participants stated that they grew up in a lower-middle-class, blue-collar family. Six participants
185 described growing up in mild to extreme poverty as children of working-poor parents. Three were from coal-mining towns, and 3 were from farming families. Three attended country schoolhouses. The families of 2 participants sometimes grew or killed their own food to
190 survive. Only 1 of the participants had a parent who had completed college. Two had a mother who had taken a few college courses, either to benefit the family or for self-satisfaction. Two mentioned an extended family member who had completed college.

Instrument

195 We developed a structured interview schedule to tap the participants' descriptions of experiences of growing up, perceived personal strengths, perceived social resources, early social reference groups, and other barriers and facilitators to the following: entry
200 into higher education, development and fulfillment of career aspirations, current social reference groups, and social and professional aspirations as adults. We derived interview questions from constructs suggested by Liu (2001) and Fouad and Brown (2000). We also
205 drew on our understanding of multicultural theory and from our own personal experiences. Mary Lee Nelson and Matt Englar-Carlson conducted all interviews.

Interviews began with a "grand tour" question: "Tell me the story about where you began your life and
210 how you came to be an academic." Specific questions included, "How would you describe the social class of your origins?" "What resources were available to you as you progressed toward a more educated class?" and, "How would you describe the social group with which
215 you currently identify?" Interviewers used questioning strategies and a set of probes recommended by Kvale (1996). As the theoretical structure developed, we added two interview questions to the protocol to address the need to integrate ethnic or racial minority
220 experience with the social class experience. One was, "How much do you think your experience has been about minority versus majority culture and how much do you think it has been about social class?" Another was, "What do you think the field of counseling should
225 know about this intersection as it relates to your experience?"

Other Artifacts

We included as artifacts papers written for and notes taken during the *Dirt Roads to Ivory Towers* symposium (Englar-Carlson & Nelson, 2003). We also
230 included e-mailed notes sent to us by interview participants after they had participated in the interviews and memos that we made regarding our observations as we conducted interviews and discussed our findings. Three participants continued to provide input through e-mail.

Procedure

235 We began participant solicitation by posting announcements about the study on professional e-mail lists for counseling and counseling psychology professors. The posts requested participants for a study of the life stories of counseling academics who had grown up
240 in lower- or lower-middle-class contexts. Because we were interested in the subjective experience of social class, we did not attempt to verify the actual class standing of our participants' family of origin. Volunteers either read the e-mail post or heard about the
245 study by word of mouth. Interested parties contacted us by e-mail or in person, volunteering to participate. Participants from the *Dirt Roads to Ivory Towers* symposium (Englar-Carlson & Nelson, 2003) were e-mailed directly and invited to participate. Because, early on,
250 our coding process began to reveal a clear interaction between social class and ethnic and racial minority status, we made an additional effort to recruit participants whose experiences encompassed both. This decision represented the theoretical sampling process rec-
255 ommended by Strauss and Corbin (1998) as well as an effort to ensure information richness (Morrow, 2005). We stopped sampling when we realized our data were becoming saturated.

We interviewed all participants by telephone for 1
260 to 2 hr, with an average of about 80 min, and we audiotaped all interviews. We encouraged participants to e-mail us if they had additional information they would like to add to what they had discussed in the interviews. We transcribed the audiotapes and gave them all
265 to Mary Lee Nelson and Sandra C. Tierney, who served as the primary coders.

Approach to the data. For our analysis, we combined what we perceived to be the strengths of two qualitative analytic strategies—grounded theory
270 (Glaser & Strauss, 1967; Strauss & Corbin, 1998) and consensual qualitative research (CQR; Hill et al., 2005; Hill, Thompson, & Williams, 1997). With regard to data analysis itself, we believe that a grounded theory approach allows meaning to emerge from the raw data
275 in a more open fashion than does CQR. In CQR, after initial perusal of the data, researchers create major categorical domains, then subsequently code data into the major domains. In CQR, creation of conceptual domains occurs prior to deep analysis of the data. In a
280 grounded theory analysis, data are fractured—broken apart and analyzed thoroughly—before primary domains are allowed to emerge. Major conceptual categories develop near the end of the coding process, only after data are thoroughly analyzed, grouped, and rear-
285 ranged into potential meaning clusters. Thus, we pre-

ferred the grounded theory approach because it requires that researchers hold their a priori guesses about the broad meaning of their data in abeyance until they have considered all data.

290 With regard to triangulation, we selected a technique from CQR. Although many researchers currently using a grounded theory technique use researcher group consensus as a method of triangulation, we chose the consensual format of CQR recommended by Hill et

295 al. (1997) because it provides clear strategies for conducting group consensus work, including an auditing process. An auditor is a researcher who was not involved in the initial coding and group consensus-building process. The auditor independently examines

300 both the raw data and the meaning structure derived by the research group. The auditor's responsibility is to question and critique the ideas created by the initial coding group and to provide feedback. CQR typically makes use of one or more auditors.

305 *Coding process.* The coding process followed a grounded theory format (Glaser & Strauss, 1967; Strauss & Corbin, 1998). The task of coders was to create initial observations, or *open codes*, and to note them on a coding form, along with the line numbers

310 from each transcript or artifact where the codes occurred. Coders began by asking themselves, "What am I observing here?" As the coders progressed, they also began to consider broader thematic content—potential *axial codes*, or categories in which particular open

315 codes might theoretically be located. When observed, potential axial codes were noted on the coding sheet next to the open codes.

Once they had initially coded the transcripts, coders worked by telephone, over the Internet, and in person

320 to share their observations. They developed primary and secondary axial categories. Through a recursive process of developing categories (Fassinger, 2005), then returning to the raw data, comparing one category with another, and recognizing when categories seemed

325 to interact with and/or subsume each other, the coders reached consensus on the categorical structure. The final coding structure consisted of three increasingly general categorical levels.

Auditing process. The audit is conducted independ-

330 ently of the primary coders by one or more persons interested in providing perspectives on the data that, because of the social construction process, the primary coders were unable to see. The task of an auditor or auditing team is to review the data in a fashion similar

335 to the approach of the initial coders and to review the coding structure developed by the initial coders to examine its credibility. The auditor then makes observations and recommendations to the initial coders. A final thematic structure is developed as coders and auditors

340 argue the structure to consensus. Matt Englar-Carlson and Julie M. Hau served as auditors for the study. Independently from the initial coders and from each other, they read the transcripts, communicated with

345 Mary Lee Nelson about the categorical structure, and made recommendations for revision. Mary Lee Nelson then, in collaboration with the entire team, revised and formalized a final categorical structure.

Participant input. Once the coding team had agreed on a categorical structure, we provided participants

350 with the structure, along with a narrative description of the findings. We offered participants the opportunity to critique the findings, provide input, and request additions or omissions. Three participants critiqued the findings and provided additional input, 5 indicated that

355 they were comfortable with the meanings derived by the researchers, and 3 did not respond to our request for input.

We undertook this process for several reasons. First, according to the hermeneutic tradition (Rennie,

360 1998), data analysis should be recursive. Not only did we approach data analysis as a revisiting of the data as we created categories, we also wished to honor the participants' voice by involving them in the analysis. Second, *member checking* (Lincoln & Guba, 1985) is a

365 method of data triangulation (Creswell, 1998) and a means of ensuring that the analysis accurately represents the participants' experience (Morrow, 2005). Third, for ethical reasons, we wanted to give members a chance to delete any quotations or information about

370 which they felt uncomfortable.

Author Biases

Mary Lee Nelson is a professor of counseling psychology. She came from a lower middle, working-class background, was the first in her family to pursue higher education, and had many of the experiences described

375 by the research participants. This background provided her with important insights about the data. In addition, it might have biased her expectations about what participants' experiences would be. She expected to hear stories of financial hardship, social confusion, loneli-

380 ness, and challenges with personal and career identity development. Matt Englar-Carlson is a counseling psychologist and currently an associate professor of counselor education. He has a strong interest in new developments in social class theory. He comes from a mid-

385 dle-class, educated family background. He came to the study with expectations that findings might conform to the social class worldview model, as developed by Liu (2001). Sandra C. Tierney is a recent graduate of a doctoral program in counseling psychology and an adjunct

390 professor in a counseling psychology department. She comes from a middle-class, educated family background. She has a strong interest in social learning theory (Bandura, 1982) and social-cognitive career theory (Lent et al., 1994) and expected that many of the find-

395 ings would reflect these existing theories. Julie M. Hau is a doctoral student in counseling psychology with interests in both social class and social-cognitive career theory. She comes from a working-class family and is the first in her family to attend college. She also had

400 expectations that findings would reflect ideas from the social-cognitive career theory model. We worked to bracket our assumptions and examine our own biases, yet we acknowledge that biases might have operated beyond our conscious awareness.

Results

405 Our initial analysis yielded five major categories (see Table 1), which we further broke down into secondary and tertiary categories. Secondary categories indicated a level of abstraction between tertiary (most specific) and primary (most general) categories. Cate-
410 gory 1, obstacles to the pursuit of higher education, contained 12 tertiary categories; Category 2, resources, contained 3 secondary and 18 tertiary categories; Category 3, developmental experiences, contained 4 secondary and 20 tertiary categories; Category 4, current
415 social supports and valued contacts, contained 4 tertiary categories; and Category 5, personal outcomes, contained 11 tertiary categories.

For data presentation, we elected to use a variation of the classification style used by Hill et al. (1997) to
420 indicate prevalence of each phenomenon within the sample. We called a category *typical* if it was found in 9 to 11 cases, *frequent* if it was found in 4 to 8 cases, and *variant* if it was found in 1 to 3 cases.

We chose to present our data in this fashion be-
425 cause we believe that such presentation allows the reader to study the intricacies of the participants' experiences in addition to the conceptual framework suggested by their stories. In the Discussion section, we develop a more global, theoretical understanding of the
430 participants' developmental process, which we illustrate by a graphic representation. Because this report includes quotations from participants, we have changed all actual names to code names.

Obstacles to Pursuit of Higher Education

All of our participants described experiencing pro-
435 found obstacles to their pursuit of an academic career. The most common denominator was, of course, financial struggle, which characterized all of the families described in this study. All of our participants described struggles around finding funding sources for
440 their education. Frequently, hard work during the college years either took a toll on the participant's stamina or mental health or resulted in extremely stressful college experiences. As Betty described, "I didn't stop to take a breath. I think when I took my first deep breath,
445 it was at the University of X. Because when I finally started paying my bills, then I could calm down." Likewise, Marshall saw his options as limited to finding a graduate program that would allow him to work while completing his doctorate:

450 In terms of getting my doctorate, I knew I couldn't go to a school that was very expensive. And I could only go to a school where I could work…. I had to be able to pay for tuition, and in order for me to do that I needed to do that. I went on Friday night for one class and two classes on

455 Saturday all day. So I was [working full time and] taking 9 hours a semester, it was exhausting.

With the exception of 3 of our participants who described their family as being zealous about their children pursuing education and 1 participant whose par-
460 ents were supportive of whatever she wanted to do, most of our participants described a lack of family emotional or financial support for their children's educational pursuits. Some described their parents as being neutral with regard to their children's interest in higher
465 education. Two told stories of their parents expecting them to get jobs to earn money rather than to get an education.

Allied with the participants' experience of not receiving support for their educational pursuits was a
470 kind of class rigidity in the family. Frequently, participants described their family as being content to remain where they were in terms of class. Even when mothers had some aspirations for moving up, as occurred in two cases, fathers did not, and, at best, most mothers were
475 ambivalent about their children pursuing a different life. Thus, most participants received mixed messages about career advancement because of differing perspectives of their mother and father. Some participants described their parents as being resentful toward them
480 for breaking out of the class structure of the family. As Ted described,

My father, a couple of times, told me, "When you move away, son, don't be an ingrate," which I understood fully well to mean that you don't forget your family of origin.
485 And he and Mom had heard some horror stories of snobby, you know, kids from blue-collar backgrounds moving away to snobby schools and then disowning their families and so on…. So always a fear of that.

The participants' parents did not have "dreams," as
490 Betty put it, of their children transcending their upbringing and making more of themselves. Perhaps, as Betty said, the parents simply could not imagine the dreams. Perhaps they could not see pathways to lifestyles different from their own. They lacked informa-
495 tion about careers other than the blue-collar opportunities they saw in their own community. As Miguel explained when describing a conversation with an advisor,

I didn't know what was going to be required and like I
500 said I literally was more uninformed academically, personally, professionally. I was more uninformed than informed so he had to tell me what it was all about. Because I said to him, "Well I don't know anybody who's done this. What do you have to do?"

505 Miguel's words speak to an experience that was common to all of our participants: the lack of social capital (Coleman, 1990)—knowledge about how to navigate in a social system, including familiarity with language idioms and cultural practices and, most of all,
510 information about how to get ahead and succeed. Lack

Table 1

Major and Minor Categories of Class-Jumping Experiences

Major and minor category	Typical	Frequent	Variant
Obstacles to pursuit of higher education			
Economic challenges	X		
Families without dreams	X		
Lack of emotional support from family		X	
Family member resentment about participant advancing academically		X	
Family pressures to go to work early		X	
Poor early schooling		X	
Mental health problems in family		X	
Lack of social capital (e.g., knowledge about what higher education could bring, how to plan for higher education, connections)	X		
Lack of knowledge about careers	X		
Marriage, nonsupportive partners, unexpected pregnancy		X	
Needing to work long hours while in college	X		
Not knowing how to manage money			X
Resources			
Economic			
Federal grants or loans		X	
Scholarships		X	
GI Bill			X
Graduate assistantships	X		
Employment	X		
Family contribution			X
Personal characteristics			
High intelligence	X		
Extreme motivation	X		
Persistence	X		
Intellectual hunger	X		
Creative problem solvers	X		
Social–emotional			
Loving parents		X	
Parents encouraged academic pursuits		X	
Extended family nearby		X	
Strong advisers	X		
Strong mentors/role models	X		
Supportive peers			X
Supportive or challenging partners		X	
Developmental experiences			
Career development phenomena			
Work = a job rather than a career		X	
Career choice dissonance			X
Uncertain trajectory: knew little about psychology growing up	X		
Could not afford other professional schooling (medicine or law): chose the next best thing			X
Serendipity ("It just so happened…"), luck	X		
Multicultural identity development			
Ongoing identification with poor or blue-collar culture		X	
Bicultural or tricultural identity		X	
Disidentification with original culture			X
Feelings of invisibility in academic culture	X		
Ongoing sense of social isolation			
Ostracism in school	X		
Feeling misunderstood by family	X		
Not fitting in in college		X	
Exposure to racism or sexism		X	
Marginalization in school and/or college		X	
Loss of contact with racial or cultural peers		X	
Feeling like misfits	X		
Leaving home			
Needing to move far from family to realize dreams	X		
Feelings of loss of culture of origin		X	
Being the only child to leave the family fold		X	
Feelings of rejection by family for being the one who left			X
Current social supports/valued contacts			
Other academics		X	
Therapists		X	
Custodial or support staff at work		X	
Other interest-based groups	X		
Personal outcomes			
Achieved beyond imagination	X		
Feelings of being blessed	X		
Pride	X		
Sense of self-determination	X		
Ongoing resentment about early hardships		X	
Ongoing concerns about competence		X	
Ongoing sense of loss		X	
Ongoing sense of oppression		X	
Gratitude for available supports	X		
Ongoing empathy/sympathy with oppressed groups	X		
Commitment to social justice	X		

Note. Typical = 9–11 participants, Frequent = 4–8 participants; Variant = 1–3 participants.

of social capital became most salient for our participants when they reached graduate school. The stress
associated with this cultural deficit was marked for
most. Carole's description of her experience with
graduate school peers was poignant.

> These people spoke a different language. They wrote bet-
> ter than I did, and they had come from a larger experi-
> ence base and exposure. So they were talking about ex-
> periences, and I can remember sitting in class and feeling
> like they were talking over my head. And I'd go home a
> wreck…. The way the other students were maneuvering,
> I had no clue. I had no clue…. And that's when I think
> that I really…at that point I lost my confidence and was
> really scared and anxious…. That whole first year I kept
> thinking, "I have no clue what I am doing."

Lack of social capital also was evident to participants when they became academics. Some continued to
struggle; some felt more comfortable with their acculturative success. Randy eloquently voiced the senti-
ments expressed by many of our participants:

> One of my difficulties in the academy is that I very often
> find myself not having much in common with some of
> my colleagues who either came through upper-middle-
> class or privileged experiences and consider themselves
> entitled to the privileges they are enjoying. I tend to get
> along well with the custodians and the working-class
> folks sometimes more than I do with my academic col-
> leagues…. I think it is the internal recognition… that life
> is hard. And that you have to somehow through a combi-
> nation of hard work and breaks just hold your own in the
> world. People who are privileged or have an easier trail,
> can adopt an attitude of superiority pretty quickly and not
> recognize how hard it is for many people in life just to
> stay above water and achieve success.

The observation that colleagues from more privileged backgrounds seemed to assume a superior, more
competitive, or more elitist position was commonly
expressed in our sample. Whereas many struggled with
that knowledge, others found ways to cope. Sarah described an interaction with a former dean:

> He was telling me, well this year I was getting .89 or
> something of a raise, and the raises were so pathetic any-
> way. Who would give a shit? And so uh, I shrugged my
> shoulders and I said okay. And he said, "Doesn't that
> bother you?" And I said, "Well no. Why should it bother
> me?" [laughter]. And he said, "Well if there was a list of
> people put up and how much money they were getting in
> a raise and somebody got $10 more than somebody else I
> would want that someone to be me." And, I thought,
> "How strange, you know." And I said to him, "I think
> that is very male."

In this scenario, Sarah displayed how she used her
feminist philosophy and stance to cope with and disen-
gage from the competitiveness in academia that many
of our participants found oppressive. In describing how
she managed her position in a department composed
primarily of men, Eleanor, a Latina, expressed a different type of coping from a similar feminist viewpoint: "I
have just learned how to act like a white male!"

Whereas Sarah overtly rejected the male aspects of
academic culture, Eleanor found a way to work within
the culture. Nevertheless, both of these women found
that their feminist ideology helped them cope in a system that they saw as patriarchal.

Other obstacles mentioned by some of our participants were lack of knowledge about how to manage
money, poor early schooling experiences that resulted
in hardship in college, early marriages and unplanned
pregnancies that prevented the participants from pursuing their career on a typical timeline, and family mental
health problems that distracted participants from their
studies.

Resources

Three secondary categories emerged as we began to
identify the resources our participants either possessed
or discovered on their way to academia: economic supports; personal characteristics, such as motivation and
persistence; and social-emotional supports.

Economic supports. All of our participants were
able to avail themselves of financial supports for their
education. Those supports were scholarships, federal
grants and loans, the GI Bill, graduate assistantships,
and employment. Only 1 participant mentioned financial contributions from a family member—in that case,
an older brother who was employed. Most indicated
that their parents had nothing at all to contribute to
their education. Several participants who had gotten
their undergraduate degree in the 1960s and 1970s
mentioned that they were aware of having benefited
from the *cohort effect* in terms of financial aid, which
was more plentiful during those decades. Because of
that phenomenon, they recognized that they did not
amass the amount of education-related debt that their
younger colleagues have had to assume.

Personal characteristics. One of the most consistent findings of this study is that most of our participants were voracious learners and extremely hard
workers. All seemed to be of high intelligence, and
most learned at an early age that they had intellectual
gifts. They excelled in school and were identified by
school personnel as being talented. In addition, all described career trajectories marked by extreme hard
work, determination, and persistence. Though many of
their career trajectories were somewhat winding, the
motivation described by these participants was indeed
remarkable. As Randy put it,

> I knew that I was going to go into counseling and guid-
> ance; I knew that I was going to go on for my doctorate
> and become a college professor. Once I made that deci-
> sion, it was like what Maslow called your "constitutional
> destiny"—that I was called to that…. Once I knew what I
> wanted to do, I pursued it with a vengeance.

Perhaps one of the most remarkable commonalities
in this sample is the degree of intellectual hunger most
of the participants seem to have experienced throughout life. Some were insatiable readers. Several de-

scribed strong scientific interests that drove them to research and inquiry. Perhaps no one described the hunger itself better than Janet:

> I love the study and the inquiry. And that's why these books, doing these books is so exciting to me. Because that's how I really get to use my…I've always had a very inquiring mind and I loved to be around an environment where that could happen.

Janet later described the intersection of intellectual hunger and motivation:

> It was so hard getting my bachelor's degree, I thought, "I'll never go through this again." And in two years, I'm already saying, "Yep. I've got to have something more here," so there is an internal drive that's just beyond anything and everything, you know? I don't know where that comes from.

Last, every one of our participants demonstrated a capacity to creatively solve problems, to view the obstacles that they faced in terms of challenges to be overcome and devise and seek means to get past them. A phrase participants often used when describing this experience is, "OK. So I thought, 'Well,…'" words that indicate the participants' active reasoning about what the next step might need to be. Eleanor had been looking for a master's program in counseling when she learned that financial aid at the master's level was hard to come by. She resolved her dilemma in the following manner: "When I was reading up on graduate school, I read that master's programs don't really provide financial support, but doctoral programs do. So, I said, "'Well, I guess I'm going to have to get a Ph.D.!'" Having become disillusioned with law school, Jeff described a novel approach to maintaining a funding source that was unwilling to support a degree leading to an academic career:

> They said, "We would have paid for a JD, but we're not going to pay for you to get a PhD." So, I lied, I lied to them. I said, "Well what I really want to do is be a high school social studies teacher." Ah, OK, that's great—they fell for that!

Thus, both Eleanor and Jeff found novel solutions to the problem of finding funding for graduate school. Marshall, who was "place bound" because of a relationship at the time he finished his doctorate, maintained his viability as a counseling academic by saying, in effect, "'Have teaching background, will travel.' I would teach four courses per semester while having a full-time independent practice and at the same time being involved in the Career Development Association." He found such creative solutions to support his academic identity until he was able to move and pursue a tenure-line position.

Social-emotional supports. Though all of our participants struggled, they also described the sources from which they derived comfort, feelings of belonging, and encouragement. Though only 2 of our participants described parents who actively encouraged their

educational pursuits, about half expressed appreciation for a loving family that was supportive in other ways, and some described living near extended family whom they could also rely on for a sense of belonging and support. All of our participants, however, referred to experiences with strong advisers and mentors who provided guidance and education that advanced them toward their goals. As Randy put it, "There are so many angels in my life that I can't count all of them." Every participant described at least one person whose influence had a profound impact on his or her career development, and some described several. Carole described a librarian whom she had known in her country schoolhouse and who later worked in her high school:

> Well, she'd hand me books to read, "Go read this. Come back and tell me about it. Carole, read this." And that went from elementary school in fifth grade all the way through high school. I can remember her giving me Solzhenitsyn in high school and said, "Go read it." And Irving Stone, "Go read it." I mean, and she'd just, you know there are certain books, I can still remember reading this German book called *Arms of Krupp*.

From this experience, Carole developed a passion for reading and acquiring knowledge, a passion that stayed with her into her academic career.

Developmental Factors

All of our participants described the course of their personal and career developmental processes and the interplay between the two. It was clear that participants' experiences of career development were contextualized within the class-based influences of their cultures of origin. It was also clear that participants' choice of career ultimately necessitated the development of multiple cultural identities.

Career development. It is not surprising that several of our participants initially viewed the career they would eventually obtain as a job, a source of income, rather than a lifestyle or a pursuit that would sustain them in a broader sense. Two of the participants experienced what we termed *career choice dissonance*, or ambivalence about choosing a career that would result in their besting their father or mother. They feared that success would bring a loss of connection to their parents, siblings, and extended family and friend networks.

All of our participants underwent very uncertain career trajectories. None of them had initially planned or even hoped to be a counselor or therapist, and none majored in psychology as an undergraduate. Rather, they initially chose more visible careers—careers that would clearly lead to work—such as law, medicine, business, and school teaching. Two participants indicated that the switch from law or medicine as a goal was due in part to the recognition that they would not be able to afford the educational expenses of attending professional schools. So, for them, counseling was the next best thing. Some felt that the more visible careers did not offer them enough opportunity to make a difference.

Almost all of our participants viewed their career trajectory as being marked by serendipity. They described many experiences of having lucky accidents, such as being in the right place at the right time or meeting a potential role model through happenstance. One participant lost a sports scholarship because of an injury and was forced to reevaluate his college plans. Several participants learned about the field of counseling through jobs they had in or after college, such as resident assistantships in dormitories or paraprofessional counseling positions in residential treatment settings. Thus, our participants described a process of discovering their way into counseling psychology as a profession.

Multicultural identity development. Most of our participants described having developed the ability to identify with two or more cultures—learning to operate within academic culture but being more comfortable sometimes interacting with lower SES or oppressed groups. Several described warm relationships with custodians in their campus buildings. All had learned to *code switch* in some way, to speak two languages—one, the language of their ethnic or blue-collar background, with family (the language of "hillbilly," as Sarah put it), and the other, the language of academia, with colleagues—a process that can be termed *bicultural identity development* (Sadeo, 2003; Vasquez & McKinley, 1982).

In describing their early development, participants of color indicated that social class and culture of origin seemed to be indistinguishable experiences; as they matured, however, they became aware of the distinction between ethnicity and social class. Addressing the relative degrees of salience between race and social class, Carole described an aspect of her current identification thus:

I will tell you I think it's a combination, because I've met, um, blacks from high SES, who, I scare them. I mean because of the fact that I'm too direct, and they've been brought up to be less direct. So I think being black and low SES, I think adds a different piece to it. And then being black, low SES, and Appalachian! Because I've seen other blacks look at me like, "We didn't know you folks even existed in rural America."

Some participants described learning to manage three cultures as they moved up the educational ladder: their ethnic culture of origin, white culture, and the culture of higher education. Thus, these participants appeared to have developed a kind of *tricultural* identity. Only 2 of our participants indicated presently feeling so uncomfortable around people from their original cultures that they wished to avoid them. These participants disavowed any desire to interact with or identify with those cultures. We called this type of reaction *disidentification* with the original culture.

Though most of our participants felt as though they had reached or were on the way to reaching their potential in academia, most felt that their cultural selves were invisible to their colleagues. They felt that their colleagues could not see or appreciate the struggles they had been through to reach their goals. White professors, in particular, felt that because they were white, their colleagues automatically assumed they were from a privileged background.

Ongoing sense of social isolation and deprivation. Most or all of our participants described experiences of social isolation and deprivation, of feeling like social misfits in many of their contexts. Some described ostracism by peers in school because they were "nerds" or "bookish." Many described feelings of not fitting in with their family because their interests differed from those of other family members. Some described not fitting in in college because fellow students did not understand their background. As Jeff put it,

There was one guy from West Virginia, but he was from a fairly big town in West Virginia. I remember thinking, "Okay, he's from West Virginia, he must be like me." No, no. So, there were times when I felt pretty alien to all the other grad students 'cause I would talk about my grandparents for example and you know, me taking care of them as they got older and people thought that was kind of strange.

Several participants described exposure to racism and sexism. Whether participants viewed these experiences as hindering career factors varied within the group. However, all targets of "isms" described these experiences as disheartening and discouraging. Some were motivated by anger and used it as fuel to move them toward their goals. Participants of color described the experience of losing touch with many of their early racial and cultural peers because they excelled academically and were placed into more advanced tracks and classrooms. Many felt out of place in their new, more traditionally white settings.

Regardless of racial and cultural background, however, most of our participants described experiences of feeling marginalized throughout their life and in many settings, from home and neighborhood of origin to places of employment, and their identity was defined in part by their experiences as misfits. As academics, many felt either misunderstood by or invisible to their colleagues, especially colleagues outside the field of counseling. They described coping strategies such as establishing friend networks away from their university and not attending "shirt and tie" functions or college social functions where they would feel out of place and potentially exposed.

Leaving home. All of our participants described the experience of leaving home to pursue their dreams. For 1, this meant immigrating to the United States. For most, it meant moving some distance away from their family and hometown. Most were grateful to have "made it out," but some experienced feelings of loss, nostalgia, and guilt about abandoning their family. Related to their experiences of isolation were many participants' experiences of being the only child in the family to leave and thus not having other siblings with whom to discuss the challenges of the bicultural experience. A minority of the participants experienced ongoing rejection by their family for being the one to leave.

Most participants described what it was like for them to return to their place and culture of origin, and most expressed feeling uncomfortable with their original culture. Eleanor described encountering old high school friends when going home to visit:

> I don't like seeing them because they're usually working like as a cashier at a grocery store. And that's their job, and I see that, and I get really depressed that, how can we be so different that they ended up, you know, being a cashier at a grocery store (and I know how much cashiers make) and me being a professor at a major university, you know. So part of me is like, wants to hide my success in a sense? Because I don't want other people to feel bad.

Participants felt that they had grown up and away because of their changing experiences and interests, whereas most of the people in their hometown had remained the same. They described difficulties relating to their family of origin when they did return to visit and the loss they experienced because of that. Two participants described how small their original house looked to them now compared with how the house looked when they were children. Two described a strong aversion to going home and only did so for obligatory reasons.

Current Social Supports and Valued Contacts

With regard to current friendships and support systems, most participants expressed appreciation for some of their academic colleagues, who had become close friends. They seemed satisfied with these relationships and found them highly fulfilling and stimulating. Some friendship circles were composed of people with whom participants shared important interests. Many participants also described friendships with their partner's colleagues and friends, many of whom were also in the professions.

Personal Outcomes

Despite the challenges our participants faced, all described pride in their achievements and satisfaction with the career they had developed. In one way or another, all talked about being blessed with good luck and influential and supportive mentors. Most held the belief that they had achieved beyond their capacity to imagine. They recognized that they had reached their goals primarily through hard work and self-determination. It is interesting, however, that some continued to express uncertainty about professional competence—not that they felt like imposters but that they remained somewhat unclear about the strength of certain skills, such as clinical skills, research skills, or

professional networking skills. Participants frequently described an ongoing sense of oppression in and alienation from academia, with which some seemed to cope more effectively than others. Most participants expressed feelings of empathy with and sympathy toward oppressed groups in general and voiced a commitment to promoting social justice.

Discussion

Using qualitative techniques, we were able to examine the internalized experience of social class for our participants. Our analysis allowed for the examination of multiple variables impacting the experiences of these academics. Our study incorporates class in the understanding of career development (i.e., class jumping) for academics in counseling and counseling psychology. The intent of this study is to uncover some of the personal and contextual phenomena that contributed to the social mobility of our participants as well as the subjective experiences of this particular group, both as the participants progressed into academia and also as they continue their life as academics. In this discussion, we address implications for theory, for training, and for research.

For a graphic depiction of a theoretical perspective on the process of our participants' development over time, see Figure 1. Our participants overcame numerous obstacles on the way to realizing their dreams. Participants who were minorities all described having encountered behaviors that they would consider racist on the way to achieving their goals, and 3 of the 5 women described being the target of sexist behavior at some point. Some participants were stigmatized as children and derided by other children for being different. The women described sexist experiences that occurred in their interactions with male academics. Despite these encounters, none of our participants gave up on pursuing his or her goals.

Perhaps one of the most common experiences described by participants was growing apart from their family, who had no career aspirations for their children. Only a minority of our participants described parents who had dreams—who actively encouraged their children's learning and college aspirations. Allied, perhaps, with the concept of having dreams is the notion of social capital (Coleman, 1990; Liu, 2001), or access to knowledge about opportunities and collective wisdom about how to navigate one's way toward opportunity. Most of our participants did not have access to such wisdom; therefore, they were required to piece together a vision of the future. Most grew up in a community that did not place value on education and provided no educational or networking opportunities that would allow the participants to learn about career options. All of our participants revealed that they knew little about psychology during their undergraduate years and learned about it as they pursued other interests or became employed in counseling-related jobs.

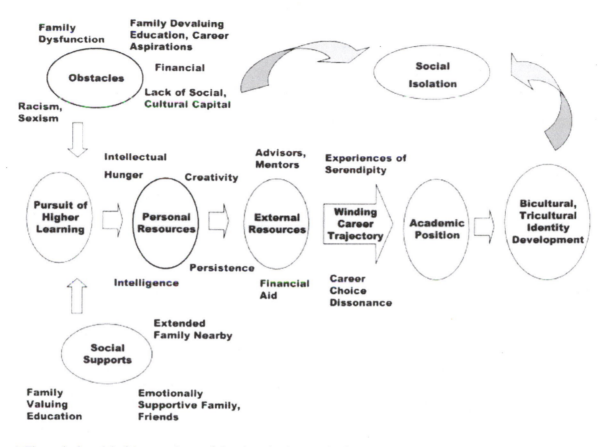

Figure 1. Theoretical model of the experience of class jumping into academia.

Most of our participants described having always had strong interests in reading and learning. Two mentioned specific adults who encouraged them to read. Yet, though a number of parents provided a loving home, only a small minority actually encouraged their children's scholarly interests. Some parents actually actively discouraged their children from pursuing lofty goals, either directly or indirectly communicating fears that they would be bested, rejected, or disrespected by their ambitious children.

Liu (2002) used the term *economic culture* to refer to the class-influenced social context in which an individual resides. He posited that the context exerts social pressure on the individual to exhibit class-consistent behaviors. Our participants described experiences of this pressure from friends as well as from family. In their community, as in most communities, fitting in requires conformity. When an adolescent in school is faced with having to choose between being bookish and being cool, it is most tempting and perhaps most fun to be cool, pursuing beauty, dating, drinking, and fast cars at the expense of learning—particularly when there is no bookish peer group in the student's school. Thus, in their original community, most of our participants experienced multiple sources of pressure to conform to class expectations.

How, then, were these participants able to break from such expectations? Another compelling finding of this study is that all of our participants possessed a high degree of intelligence, persistence, and creative problem-solving ability. Moreover, all were extremely hard workers, and most described a kind of intellectual hunger that drove them toward knowing more. Rather than express the desire to achieve beyond the norms of the culture of their beginnings, most of our participants described experiences of feeling compelled to use their natural intelligence and curiosity to learn and, eventually, to teach. In elucidating their social-cognitive career theory model, Lent et al. (1994) described career development as a process of uncovering one's direction through increasing success experiences with pursuits of interest. Through this process, the individual is thought to develop enhanced self-efficacy regarding these interests and motivation to continue to pursue them.

Our participants' stories reflect their progress from discovering a love of learning and/or helping through multiple experiences of success with these pursuits. Most were excellent students in their elementary and secondary school career, and most received advice from teachers and school counselors that they could go to college if they wanted to. The defining characteristic of our participants, however, seems to be an awareness of their own strong intelligence, curiosity, and hunger for knowledge. These findings echo those of Sadeo (2003), who studied the experiences of academics of color—their motivations, supports, and experiences. One of her participants described the motivation thus:

> Well, one [factor] is some kind of inner impetus, some kind of compelling drive; and I think it's probably genetically determined in the sense that it's inherent. I don't know which particular ancestors—I guess I have some I could say—but none of my immediate family were at that level of curiosity: wanting to know more and wanting to find out. Anyway, this is something that is constantly a part of me and I cannot suppress it. I cannot. (p. 9)

In a study of 691 youth, Whitehead (1984) found that intellectual curiosity was related to intrinsic motivation and that intrinsic motivation was independent of both parental attitude and social class influences. It may be that intellectual hunger or curiosity is an aspect of temperament that propels people toward academic achievement.

Though all participants were conscious that they were good students, the suggestion that they could achieve in college came for some as a revelation. The idea of moving away from their culture of origin to pursue an actual career was foreign and required time to process. For others, their continued success in secondary school and advice from counselors and teachers represented confirmatory information that fueled their nascent ideas of moving on to college.

We also observed that our participants had been creative problem solvers. Most entered college with either no career goals or career goals that reflected their interest in some of the most visible professions, such as law, medicine, and business. Others majored in liberal arts subjects that were also highly visible. Once in college, however, our participants began to find other interests. Through the use of creative problem solving, they were able to engage in trial-and-error processes that eventually led them to study counseling and psychology. Perhaps as they passed through and overcame challenges, the participants also developed a sense of self-efficacy about their ability to encounter the unexpected, think through the problem in a novel way, and find a solution that would move them forward. Whether they perceived a sense of efficacy about that ability, however, is unclear.

Most of our participants were somewhat humble about how they achieved what they did. They described their career path as being marked by serendipity—the chance appearance of mentors or lucky incidents that resulted in their finding the right opportunities. Bandura (1982) discussed the powerful role of chance encounters in the influence on and change of life trajectories. These encounters seemed highly salient to our participants in their assessments of what contributed to their career advancement. Bandura and Schunk (1981) found that self-efficacy related to achieving proximal goals was a better predictor of ultimate competence than self-efficacy regarding distal goals. Perhaps this is

the phenomenon we observed in our participants' stories. Achievement of successive moderate goals enhanced the participants' perception that they could accomplish the more proximal challenges they undertook, thus eventuating in the distal goal: their ultimate arrival in academia.

In a study similar to our investigation, Williams et al. (1998) described the career path of prominent women in counseling psychology as serendipitous. It may be that counseling psychology itself is not a very visible career and that students often discover it through encounters with counseling psychology professionals or role models who introduce them to counseling psychology as an option. Regardless of social class background, the route to a career in counseling psychology may, more often than not, be full of twists and turns.

It may also be that serendipity is a central phenomenon in most people's career development experiences. Krumboltz (1998) posited that serendipity is not actually as serendipitous as one may think. Serendipity may, in fact, be a career development phenomenon experienced by most of us, including those with well-developed career plans. According to Krumboltz, serendipity may be a way of describing an unplanned event that influences future events. The so-called unplanned events may, in fact, occur because people have placed themselves in situations that allow them to take advantage of opportunities that arise. Thus, because of their inherent drive and creativity, our participants might have planned to position themselves in the path of opportunity and simply opened themselves to take advantage of it.

Having grown up in contexts that reflected lower-class or blue-collar values and norms, many of our participants talked in terms of getting jobs rather than careers. Some expressed what we came to describe as career choice dissonance, ambivalence about choosing a career that would take them out of the contexts in which they were socialized. They described conflicts related to knowing that to pursue college, they would have to enter another culture. They would have to relinquish the close geographic and cultural ties with parents, siblings, and extended family whom they had known all of their life. Though they all made the decision to leave, some expressed feelings of loss and sadness that they had to make the choices they made.

Participants also described the challenges involved with learning the culture of academia—both as graduate students and as academics. All had to struggle with stresses resulting from a lack of social capital, a struggle that continued into their professional life. Most described experiences of feeling at times like an outsider in the academy.

In their book *Strangers in Paradise: Academics From the Working Class*, Ryan and Sackrey (1984) presented descriptions of isolation recounted by many professors from lower- and working-class backgrounds who felt they had no comfortable home in the academy. Ryan and Sackrey's participants described multiple challenges along with the intellectual rewards associated with their career choice. For those intellectual rewards, many of Ryan and Sackrey's participants felt that they had to sacrifice a sense of community. As one of their participants expressed,

> I do not work as hard as my father did, though I make at least five times as much money as he ever did. But I must admit that there are moments when I believe that those things have cost me the relationships, the cultural ties, the human interactions which define people most humanly. (p. 307)

Ryan and Sackrey (1984) offered a strong critique of the culture of academia, which, they argued, continues to promote and defend the social elitism of white, capitalist society at the expense of some of its most intelligent and creative members. The mores of the professoriate indeed may seem oppressive to many who, through fortune, intelligence, and determination, make it through academia's door. Though most of our participants expressed an ongoing sense of oppression in the academic environment, all found creative ways to adapt or cope. The development of the ability to interact in different cultures allowed our participants to realize their goals, though this process was often distressing.

Discomfort related to adapting to new cultures has been termed *acculturative stress* and has been linked to numerous symptoms, such as depression, anxiety, and suicidality (Joiner & Walker, 2002; Sandhu & Asrabadi, 1994). Acculturative stress was marked for all of our participants. Caucasian participants described an experience of acculturation into a more educated class, which involved learning to code switch and developing what numerous authors have termed a bicultural identity (Sadeo, 2003; Vasquez & McKinley, 1982). Nonwhites described a similar process but also addressed experiences of learning to get by in both educated culture and white culture—thus developing what might be termed a tricultural identity. For the minorities, the challenges involved having to learn two complex sets of rules. They had high regard for their original culture and many of their cultural values; however, they also wished to be skilled at operating in both white and academic cultures.

Some of our white participants described experiences of being able to pass as middle class because they were white. For some, this experience of passing resulted in their feeling invisible, misunderstood, and unappreciated. They experienced ambivalence about whether they wanted their humble beginnings to be known. On one hand, they wished to pass so that they would be accepted. On the other hand, they wished to be fully known and accepted in spite of their background. Thus, for all participants, the process of identity development was deeply interpersonal, involving both belonging and appreciation needs.

Had it not been for our participants' strong needs for achievement and intellectual engagement, they might not have been willing to incur the losses they experienced along the way. Most of our participants wanted to tell us what it was like when they went home to their community of origin, and many had profoundly mixed feelings about it. Most said they had no basis from which they could relate to their old school peers and few points of connection with parents, siblings, and extended family. Going home was a lonely and often frustrating experience for most. Thus, although our participants had learned to navigate in two or more cultural contexts, they also experienced stress and alienation related to not feeling authentic membership in any of the cultures. Ryan and Sackrey (1984) referred to a similar process of balancing class locations, which they described thus:

> What we do find is one after another of straightforward accounts of the time and effort (and talent and imagination) necessary to remain faithful to remnants of the old life while developing a growing attraction (even loyalty) to the new one. (p. 205)

Despite the sense of isolation and alienation most of our participants experienced in academia in general, many talked about some of their close colleagues in favorable terms. Many called certain colleagues their closest friends and indicated that they found support from and collegiality with their colleagues. Still, they reported feeling invisible with regard to their original culture. In general, they did not feel that they had permission to discuss or call attention to their social class experience.

Though many of our participants longed to be understood in their current settings, many talked about having participated in a culture of silence with regard to social class. Though all participants thought social class was a critical aspect of multiculturalism, several talked about feeling that their social class background had not been prioritized as an important aspect of the multicultural dialogue within the fields of counseling and psychology. Thus, they struggled in silence, wanting to be seen but fearful of being found out by a culture that does not want to talk about social class. As one of Ryan and Sackrey's (1984) participants put it,

> I doubt that anywhere on earth self-deception has been institutionalized more thoroughly than in the U.S., and above all, in higher education in this country, which accepts the middle class credo: Don't think about it, and it will go away. Don't notice it, and it won't exist. Don't talk about it, and it will never have happened. (pp. 272–273)

Implications for Theory

One of the reasons counseling psychology researchers traditionally might have been hesitant to address social class is that they fear social class might be adopted as a proxy for race or ethnicity—which would abnegate the importance of racial and ethnic experience. Racial minorities in our sample were aware of this concern, yet they were able to address the confluence between their race and class experiences, expressing the conviction that the social class experience was extremely important and that the profession had neglected it. Thus, our participants echoed the concerns of Liu, Ali, et al. (2004); Liu, Soleck, et al. (2004), Fouad and Brown (2000), and others that a person's identity is deeply tied to the internal experience of social class and that it should be considered an important aspect of the person's psychological and cultural makeup. Our findings suggest that researchers need to further refine multicultural theory to incorporate a deeper understanding of how class, race, and ethnicity intersect.

We examined only the experiences of the counseling academics who volunteered to participate in our study and cannot generalize our findings beyond our sample. We can, however, suggest theory. It is possible that aspects of our participants' experiences may transfer to others' experiences of class mobility. In fact, because counseling professionals are expected to be open and receptive by virtue of their training, class mobility for academics in other fields may involve greater challenges than the process we have described here. Academia, however, is only one profession. The nature of the experience likely varies according to the qualities of different professional contexts. Future research should examine the nature of these variations.

We believe that the experience of internalized social class (Liu, Ali, et al., 2004) is still poorly understood. Our findings represent a step in the direction of uncovering how social class context frames and, thus, influences a myriad of human experiences. It likely interacts with many familiar and measurable psychological phenomena, such as self-esteem, self-efficacy, experienced social support, and alienation. An important step in the refinement of our understanding of internalized social class is to define it carefully. Multiple theoretical and research efforts are needed to accomplish this goal.

Implications for Research

Future qualitative efforts could provide much information about experiences of social class and how they interact with other personal and social experiences. First, little is known about the culture of silence surrounding issues of social class. Why have theoreticians and researchers alike avoided looking at social class as an important intrapsychic and interpersonal variable? Second, what human experiences lie at the confluence of race, ethnicity, and social class? What experiences lie at the social class boundaries within racial and cultural groups? Third, how does social class impact the experiences of other types of social groups, such as children, adolescents, and older adults; gays,

lesbians, bisexuals, and transsexuals; or people with disabilities? Fourth, what is the experience of social mobility like for people of all backgrounds, and how does class mobility interact with other identity variables to shape people's experience?

Our findings suggest that class mobility requires multiple external and internal resources, that finding one's way to another class stratum may require finding important mentors, that it may involve experimentation and creativity, and that there are costs as well as rewards for making the transition. Degree of acculturative stress (Joiner & Walker, 2002; Sandhu & Asrabadi, 1994) along the way is likely to be a predictor of training processes and outcomes, such as subjective well-being, depression, career goal-setting ability, and achievement. Future research on supervision and training should examine this relation.

Implications for Training

Because experiences of internalized social class and acculturative stress are invisible, students may need assistance from advisers, teachers, and mentors to discuss and manage class-related stressors. Students and new professionals of color may be undertaking the dual task of adapting both to mainstream and to academic cultures. They may experience class-based challenges but may hesitate to mention them for fear of being disloyal to the cause of emphasizing racial and ethnic diversity. White students and new professionals may be especially vulnerable because they may feel that they are expected to pass. They may deny feelings of discomfort and alienation. Perhaps one of the most helpful things mentors and trainers can do to help is to simply break the silence about social class, integrating it more centrally into conversations about multiculturalism. Another is to prevent alienation among students and new professionals by working to provide a sense of community within academic departments.

Conclusion

This study can serve as a reminder of the multiple identities and the diversity within the field of counseling psychology, with specific acknowledgment that many of our colleagues come from lower- or lower-middle-class backgrounds. Social class has largely been overlooked in the counseling psychology (Liu, Ali, et al., 2004) and larger psychology literatures (Lott & Saxon, 2002), yet the participants in this study, from all ethnic backgrounds, all acknowledged with a resounding voice that social class was a highly salient variable for them. It appears that the path from dirt roads to ivory towers is winding, unpredictable, highly challenging, and, at times, lonely. Success seems to depend on complex contextual and personal factors—including important cultural aspects, such as race and ethnic background.

This study sheds additional light on the relation between career development and class (Brown, 2004; Heppner & Scott, 2004; Whiston & Keller, 2004). The challenges described by our participants can heighten awareness of the difficulties that current and prospective students in the field may be experiencing with regard to entering the counseling profession. Our findings also lend support to Liu's (2002) and Liu, Soleck, et al.'s (2004) notion that one's early social class experiences are deeply internalized and that they have lasting influence on one's worldview. Social class worldview appears to relate to identity and career development as well as to the experience of class mobility.

Only in folklore did ragged boys enter medieval towns and rise to become burghers clothed in gold—W. R. Manchester, *The Arms of Krupp*

References

Bandura, A. (1982). The psychology of chance encounters and life paths. *American Psychologist, 37*, 747–755.

Bandura, A., & Schunk, D. H. (1981). Cultivating competency, self-efficacy, and intrinsic interest through proximal self-motivation. *Journal of Personality and Social Psychology, 41*, 586–598.

Brown, M. T. (2004). The career development influence of family of origin: Considerations of race/ethnic group membership and class. *Counseling Psychologist, 32*, 587–595.

Bubolz, M. M. (2001). Family as source, user, and builder of social capital. *Journal of Socio-Economics, 30*, 129–131.

Coleman, J. S. (1990). *Foundations of social theory.* Cambridge, MA: Belknap Press.

Creswell, J. W. (1998). *Qualitative inquiry and research design: Choosing among five traditions.* Thousand Oaks, CA: Sage.

Englar-Carlson, M. J., & Nelson, M. L. (2003, August). *Dirt roads to ivory towers: Class jumping into academia.* Symposium conducted at the 111th Annual Convention of the American Psychological Association, Toronto, Canada.

Fassinger, R. (2005). Paradigms, problems, and promise: Grounded theory in counseling psychology research. *Journal of Counseling Psychology, 52*, 156–166.

Fouad, N. A., & Brown, M. T. (2000). Role of race and social class in development: Implications for counseling psychology. In S. D. Brown & R. W. Lent (Eds.), *Handbook of counseling psychology* (3rd ed., pp. 379–408). New York: Wiley.

Frable, D. E. S. (1997). Gender, racial, ethnic, sexual, and class identities. *Annual Review of Psychology, 48*, 139–162.

Glaser, B., & Strauss, A. (1967). *The discovery of grounded theory: Strategies for qualitative research.* New York: Aldine Publishing.

Heppner, M. J., & Scott, A. B. (2004). From whence we came: The role of social class in our families of origin. *Counseling Psychologist, 32*, 596–602.

Hill, C. E., Knox, S., Thompson, B. J., Williams, E. N., Hess, S. A., & Ladany, N. (2005). Consensual qualitative research: An update. *Journal of Counseling Psychology, 52*, 196–205.

Hill, C. E., Thompson, B. J., & Williams, E. N. (1997). A guide to conducting consensual qualitative research. *Counseling Psychologist, 25*, 517–572.

Joiner, T. E., Jr., & Walker, R. L. (2002). Construct validity of a measure of acculturative stress in African Americans. *Psychological Assessment, 14*, 462–466.

Krumboltz, J. D. (1998). Serendipity is not serendipitous. *Journal of Counseling Psychology, 45*, 390–392.

Kvale, S. (1996). *InterViews.* Thousand Oaks, CA: Sage.

Lent, R. W., Brown, S. D., & Hackett, G. (1994). Toward a unifying social cognitive theory of career and academic interest, choice, and performance. *Journal of Vocational Behavior, 45*, 79–122.

Lincoln, Y. S., & Guba, E. G. (1985). *Naturalistic inquiry.* Beverly Hills, CA: Sage.

Littrell, B. (1999). The liberal arts and the working class. *Peace Review, 11*, 267–273.

Liu, W. M. (2001). Expanding our understanding of multiculturalism: Developing a social class worldview model. In D. B. Pope-Davis & H. L. K. Coleman (Eds.), *The intersection of race, class, and gender in counseling psychology* (pp. 127–170). Thousand Oaks, CA: Sage.

Liu, W. M. (2002). The social class-related experiences of men: Integrated theory and practice. *Professional Psychology: Research and Practice, 33*, 355–360.

Liu, W. M., Ali, S. R., Soleck, G., Hopps, J., Dunston, K., & Pickett, T., Jr. (2004). Using social class in counseling psychology research. *Journal of Counseling Psychology, 51*, 3–18.

Liu, W. M., Soleck, G., Hopps, J., Dunston, K., & Pickett, T., Jr. (2004). A new frame to understand social class in counseling: The social class worldview model and modern classism theory. *Journal of Multicultural Counseling and Development, 32*, 95–122.

Lott, B., & Saxon, S. (2002). The influence of ethnicity, social class, and context on judgments about U.S. women. *Journal of Social Psychology, 142*, 481–499.

Mirels, H. L., & Garrett, J. B. (1973). The protestant ethic as a personality variable. *Journal of Consulting and Clinical Psychology, 36*, 40–44.

Morrow, S. L. (2005). Quality and trustworthiness in qualitative research in counseling psychology. *Journal of Counseling Psychology, 52*, 250–260.

Rennie, D. L. (1998). Qualitative research: A matter of hermeneutics and the sociology of knowledge. In A. Kopala & L. A. Suzuki (Eds.), *Using qualitative methods in psychology* (pp. 3–13). Thousand Oaks, CA: Sage.

Richardson, M. S. (1993). Work in people's lives: A location for counseling psychologists. *Journal of Counseling Psychology, 40*, 425–433.

Ryan, J., & Sackrey, C. (1984). *Strangers in paradise: Academics from the working class.* Boston: South End Press.

Sadeo, K. C. (2003). Living in two worlds: Success and the bicultural faculty of color. *Review of Higher Education, 26*, 397–418.

Sandhu, D. S., & Asrabadi, B. R. (1994). Development of an acculturative stress scale for international students. *Psychological Reports, 75*, 435–448.

Strauss, A., & Corbin, J. (1998). *Basics of qualitative research: Grounded theory procedures and techniques.* Thousand Oaks, CA: Sage.

Van de Werfhorst, H. G. (2002). A detailed examination of the role of education in intergenerational social class mobility. *Social Science Information, 41*, 407–438.

Vasquez, M. J., & McKinley, D. L. (1982). "Supervision: A conceptual model": Reactions and extension. *Counseling Psychologist, 10*, 59–63.

Whiston, S. C., & Keller, B. K. (2004). The influences of the family of origin on career development: A review and analysis. *Counseling Psychologist, 32*, 493–568.

Whitehead, J. (1984). Motives for higher education: A study of intrinsic and extrinsic motivation in relation to academic attainment. *Cambridge Journal of Education, 14*, 26–34.

Williams, E. N., Soeprapto, E., Like, K., Touradji, E., Hess, S., & Hill, C. E. (1998). Perceptions of serendipity: Career paths of prominent academic women in counseling psychology. *Journal of Counseling Psychology, 45*, 379–389.

About the authors: *Mary Lee Nelson* and *Julie M. Hau*, Department of Counseling Psychology, University of Wisconsin, Madison. *Matt Englar-Carlson*, Department of Counseling, California State University, Fullerton. *Sandra C. Tierney*, Department of Psychiatry, University of Wisconsin, Madison.

Address correspondence to: Mary Lee Nelson, Department of Counseling Psychology, University of Wisconsin, Madison, 321 Education Building, 1000 Bascom Mall, Madison, WI 53706. E-mail: mlnelson@education.wisc.edu

Exercise for Article 35

Factual Questions

1. The researchers indicate that they are particularly interested in the experiences of counseling academics for how many reasons?

2. How many of the participants described growing up in mild to extreme poverty as children?

3. The interviews began with what "grand tour" question?

4. Did the researchers attempt to verify the actual class standing of each participant's family of origin?

5. What did the auditor independently examine?

6. A category was called "variant" if it was found in how many cases?

Questions for Discussion

7. In your opinion, is the sample size ($n = 11$) for this type of qualitative study sufficiently large? (See line 169.)

8. Is the coding process described in sufficient detail? Explain. (See lines 305–328.)

9. Does the use of an auditor increase your confidence in the validity of the results of this study? Explain. (See lines 329–347.)

10. Is the use of participant input (i.e., member checking) important? Explain. (See lines 348–370.)

11. The authors discuss their backgrounds and possible biases. Is such a discussion important? Explain. (See lines 371–404.)

12. Did you find any of the results especially interesting? Surprising? Explain.

Quality Ratings

Directions: Indicate your level of agreement with each of the following statements by circling a number from 5 for strongly agree (SA) to 1 for strongly disagree (SD). If you believe an item is not applicable to this research article, leave it blank. Be prepared to explain your ratings. When responding to criteria A and B below, keep in mind that brief titles and abstracts are conventional in published research.

A. The title of the article is appropriate.

SA   5   4   3   2   1   SD

B. The abstract provides an effective overview of the research article.

SA   5   4   3   2   1   SD

C. The introduction establishes the importance of the study.

SA   5   4   3   2   1   SD

D. The literature review establishes the context for the study.

SA   5   4   3   2   1   SD

E. The research purpose, question, or hypothesis is clearly stated.

SA   5   4   3   2   1   SD

F. The method of sampling is sound.

SA   5   4   3   2   1   SD

G. Relevant demographics (for example, age, gender, and ethnicity) are described.

SA   5   4   3   2   1   SD

H. Measurement procedures are adequate.

SA   5   4   3   2   1   SD

I. All procedures have been described in sufficient detail to permit a replication of the study.

SA   5   4   3   2   1   SD

J. The participants have been adequately protected from potential harm.

SA   5   4   3   2   1   SD

K. The results are clearly described.

SA   5   4   3   2   1   SD

L. The discussion/conclusion is appropriate.

SA   5   4   3   2   1   SD

M. Despite any flaws, the report is worthy of publication.

SA   5   4   3   2   1   SD

Article 36

"That I'll Be Killed": Pre-Service and In-Service Teachers' Greatest Fears and Beliefs About School Violence

KIMBERLY WILLIAMS
SUNY Cortland

KEN CORVO
Syracuse University

ABSTRACT. Pre-service teachers who had completed their practicum or student teaching and in-service teachers in their first 3 years of teaching ($n = 218$) completed open-ended surveys about their beliefs and fears of school violence and rated their fears for such acts as use of weapons and the likelihood of those acts about their fears about schools and school violence. There were significant differences between pre-service and in-service teachers in their rankings of fearful events and the perceived likelihood of these events using t-tests to compare the groups. The informants reported being most afraid of guns or other weapons or other forms of dangerous violence (hostage taking, an outside stranger coming in and threatening their students, and so on). These fears were significantly correlated with their beliefs in the likelihood that these events would happen. Open-ended questions revealed that pre-service teachers tended to be more afraid for their personal safety and personal failure in a crisis situation and in-service classroom teachers tended to be more afraid for their students' safety. The implications for teacher education and preparing teachers to address school violence are discussed.

From *Journal of School Violence*, 4, 47–69. Copyright © 2005 by The Haworth Press, Inc. Reprinted with permission.

Teacher Fears

As our nation continues to face a shortage of qualified teachers, particularly in high needs areas (Howard, 2003) where violence tends to be more pervasive and prevalent, we must better understand what teacher candidates (pre-service teachers) and newly trained in-service teachers fear about schools. Do fears of violence prevent students from choosing careers in teaching? Do fears of violence prevent pre-service teachers from fully joining the profession? Perhaps fears of violence drive out new in-service teachers. Is fear of violence greater or less for more experienced teachers? Once we better understand what teachers (pre-service and in-service) fear most, and how likely they think these events are to happen, we can address their fears with appropriate support and education. This study represents a contribution to our understanding of the beliefs that may drive the fears of neophyte teachers.

School violence is a national concern. Although the number of reported violent acts in schools has decreased, these violent acts have become more severe and dangerous (1999 Annual Report on School Safety). In 1996, the National Center for Educational Statistics conducted a nationwide survey of teachers' perceptions of school violence and issues related to school safety. From 1987–1988 to 1993–1994, elementary and secondary public school teachers reported that they believed that physical violence stemming from conflicts and weapon carrying increased significantly. Teachers have tended to believe that violence is becoming more problematic and pervasive in schools, even with violent acts in schools on the decline. Teacher violent victimization, although higher in urban school settings (39 out of every 1,000 versus 22 out of every 1,000 in rural and suburban settings), exists everywhere (Annual Report on School Safety, 1999). However, according to the Annual Report on School Safety (1999), teachers were more likely to be victims of theft than of violence. What we do not understand well is what fuels teachers' fears. What are teachers most afraid of? How do these fears start during their teacher education programs and how are they changed?

Price and Everett (1997) reported that most teachers were not fearful and had not personally experienced violence. Teachers in this study mostly felt that violence was something that happened at large, urban schools with high minority populations.

White and Beal (1999) examined factors that pre-service and in-service teachers included in their perceptions of school violence and the differences between these two groups. They found in their comparison of pre-service and in-service teachers that both groups were concerned about school violence, but pre-service teachers were more concerned. Young and Craig (1999) reported similar findings. Both sets of researchers speculated that media reports of school violence may be the cause of this concern, especially for pre-service teachers with little classroom experience, and that because in-service teachers have more classroom experience, they have more realistic attitudes and are therefore less afraid. White and Beal (1999) also found that both in-service and pre-service teachers blamed increased availability of firearms, increased violence in the media, lack of parental involvement, and lack of children's ability to control their anger as causes for increased violence in schools.

Ferraro (1995) in his book *Fear of Crime* analyzed a decade's worth of research and national data on perceptions and fears of criminal behavior. He claimed that consistently for decades, women have been more afraid of crime, even though they are less likely to be victims of all kinds of crime except sexual assault. Also, the age group with the highest level of fear of crime was the 18–24-year-olds (dropping dramatically in the 25–36-year age group). The population of those studying to become teachers meets this profile: overwhelmingly female and overwhelmingly in the 18–24-year age bracket.

According to Ferraro (1995, p. 45):

People typically estimate their risk of crime with limited information. They rely on the media and "secondhand sources" as well as personal experiences in developing their perceptions of crime (Tyler & Cook, 1984). As such, actors use information from the physical and cultural environment to judge their risk of victimization. Most research comparing crime rates with public estimates of risk reflects a pattern of considerable public accuracy when judging general crime risk at one point in time.

Ferraro's work suggests that some of these perceptions and demographic factors may provide insights into teachers' fears of violence.

The present study focused on pre-service and in-service teachers and examined their perceptions qualitatively and quantitatively to obtain more depth of understanding on how these informants came to hold the perceptions and attitudes that they did about school violence.

Research Questions

The present study sought to examine the following questions: Were there significant differences in the ways pre-service and in-service teachers rated their fears of different violent acts (guns, weapons, rape, suicide, etc.)? Were there significant differences in the ways pre-service and in-service teachers rated the likelihood of these events happening (guns, weapons, rape, suicide, etc.)? Were there significant correlations between fear of these acts and the perception of likelihood that these events would happen? How did pre-service and in-service teachers describe their greatest fears of school violence and their own personal experiences with violence?

Method

Data Sources and Evidence

Through a combination of qualitative and quantitative data-gathering, pre-service and in-service teachers were asked a series of open-ended and closed questions about school violence to determine how they constructed meaning about and rated their fears and beliefs of likelihood of school violence.

The survey. The survey asked general open-ended questions such as: "What is your definition of violence?" "What do you think causes children to be violent in school?" "What are you most afraid of when you think of school violence and your role as a teacher?" "Can you describe your most memorable personal experience with school violence?" "Have you ever been a victim of a violent crime and, if so, would you please explain?" Informants were also asked to rate their fears of a series of violent acts (physical fighting, verbal fighting, hostage taking, assaults, bullying, suicide, and rape) or words related to school violence (guns, knives, other weapons, or bombs). See Appendix A for copy of the survey.

Participants. Informants ($n = 218$, 78% female and 22% male; 95% white and 5% minority; mean age 26.6 years; 35% were current in-service teachers and 65% were pre-service teachers) were given the survey prior to a mandatory 2-hour workshop on school violence to students at a middle-sized university in New York State. Survey responses were anonymous.

The Quantitative Analysis: Comparing Pre-Service and In-Service Teachers and Correlations

The purpose of the quantitative analysis was twofold. First was to determine if there were significant differences in perceptions and fears of violent acts in school between in-service teachers and pre-service teachers. This was done using *t*-tests comparing the two groups' ratings of their fears of violent acts such as use of weapons, hostage taking, fighting, etc.

The second purpose was to determine if there were significant correlations between fears and likelihood of those acts occurring. If pre-service and in-service teachers are fearful of certain violent acts in school, do they believe these acts will happen?

Using SPSS 11.5 to analyze data, the aforementioned *t*-tests and correlation analyses were conducted.

The Qualitative Framework and Analysis

This study began from the premise that school violence is socially constructed, and that people have different constructed realities based on their personal experiences that help them make sense of school violence. According to the theoretical framework of symbolic interactionism, "Interpretation is not an autonomous act, nor is it determined by any particular force, human or otherwise. Individuals interpret with the help of others—people from their past, writers, family, television personalities, and persons they meet in settings in which they work and play—but others do not do it for them. Through interaction, the individual constructs meaning" (Bogdan & Biklen, 1992, p. 36).

This qualitative portion of this study began from the theoretical framework proposed by Bogdan and Biklen (1992) and used Glaser's (1978) constant comparative method of analysis in which one begins collecting data looking for key issues and emerging themes. Then the researcher collects data that give examples of these key categories: describing all the categories while trying to account for all examples, working with the data to examine social processes, sampling, coding, and writing based on the core categories of the analysis. Over 200 pre-service teachers were asked general questions about their perspectives on school violence to begin to look for key issues and emerging themes. Notes from these written descriptions to the questions were coded and themes were analyzed.

To determine best how pre-service and in-service teachers constructed meaning about school violence, this study relied primarily on narrative analysis. Narrative analysis allows informants time to reflect on challenging topics such as school violence. Previous research has yielded fruitful information on illegal topics about which many tend to be guarded in traditional interviews (Williams, 1998; Williams, 2001). Thus, allowing opportunities for narratives, including anonymous narratives such as open-ended questions, about one's attitudes and perceptions of school violence was expected to be fruitful as well.

Using a variety of qualitative research strategies—open-ended opinionnaires and observations in workshops—this study used the constant comparative method of analysis of field notes of pre-service elementary school teachers' words.

Results

Qualitative Results

Informants had a variety of personal experiences around school violence, including but not limited to sexual, physical, and verbal assault and robbery. However, these experiences rarely shaped their personal definitions of violence or what they were most afraid of when they thought of school violence. Second, what in-service and pre-service teachers were most afraid of when asked about their greatest fears of school violence were guns, hostage situations, and fears of acts that were least likely to happen in actuality. Third, pre-service teachers tended to focus on fears of harm to themselves (fears of being shot, hurt, or killed) or fears of making a mistake (missing warning signs, acting inappropriately and failing to stop a potentially violent situation) when describing their greatest fears. In-service teachers tended to describe their greatest fears as harm to students as well as fear of fear of failure to act appropriately to prevent violence. Finally, gender differences were found in the nature of descriptions of one's greatest fears. Women tended to describe their greatest fears contextually where men tended to list acts.

Fears rooted in media representations rather than reality. First, informants had a variety of experiences, yet these personal experiences rarely shaped their fears

or personal definitions of violence. Some said that they had not personally experienced any violence, yet these informants were mostly afraid of guns and hostage situations. Some admitted to seeing fights in school, but did not include fighting as a behavior they feared or included in their personal definitions of violence. Among the most dramatic examples were that one informant wrote that she had been sexually assaulted by her eleventh-grade English teacher, yet she did not include "rape" among her behaviors associated with violence or among the behaviors she most feared. One informant had seen a classmate shoot himself in middle school, yet suicide was not included in her personal definition of school violence. With the exception of the last example, none of the other informants had seen guns in school, yet many included a fear of guns or being shot and killed in schools.

Despite the national findings supporting that 3.4, 3.1, and 2.6 percent of students in grades 8, 10, and 12 respectively reported bringing guns to school in the past 12 months (Monitoring the Future Study, 1999), the overwhelming majority of elementary pre-service and in-service teachers in this project reported that they were most afraid of guns, being shot, or having their students shot. The federal government did not collect survey data on early elementary student self-reports of guns and gun carrying in school, but nonetheless, it is likely that the numbers would be smaller.

Two examples of the fear of guns and the root of this fear are from two different informants:

> When I think of violence in the schools, I am most afraid of something happening like what happened at Columbine High School. I am afraid of not recognizing the violent potential in a student.

> I think the massive massacre at Columbine has instilled the most fear in me.

Columbine was cited as having the most impact on informants' fears. One single horrifying incident has shaped the fears and perspectives of elementary pre-service teachers even more than their own experiences. Also important in the former example is the second statement: fearing failure. This fear of failure to recognize warning signs or failure to protect students was a common theme to emerge for pre-service and early in-service teachers.

Most examples of personal experiences were like this informant, who said:

> When I think of school violence, what scares me most are students who bring guns into the school. This fear has been derived from all of the recent school shootings painted all over the news. The only personal experience I have had with school violence was when I, myself, was a student in junior high and high school. There were usually fist fights every few months, and it really bothered me to see people beating on each other for petty differences. It would usually take a couple of minutes for an adult to break it up. What also bothered me was the constant bullying that I witnessed. Other than that, I can't

think of anything. Times have changed a lot since then. Now, instead of being fearful of bullying and fist fights, students and teachers have to worry about their lives being taken. It is really sad.

285 She, like many, was most afraid of guns, although she had never personally experienced any violence in school that involved guns. She did not report being afraid of fights and bullying, just "bothered." Now the fear was loss of life.

290 What was particularly intriguing was that most informants, when questioned, had experienced bomb threats; many had experienced them often. In terms of potential damage, the loss of life from one bomb explosion would be far greater than a gun, and the threats 295 are so common. Yet informants were not afraid of bombs. As one informant said,

When I was a student in high school, I experienced several bomb threat situations. I do not ever remember being scared. Like most of my classmates, I believed it was a 300 prank so that a student could get out of a test or something. The person who called in the threats eventually got caught. My sister is a student in middle school. One day during this past school year, the students were kept out of the building because a hit list was found written on a 305 bathroom door. I was terrified by that, I think maybe because I am older and can see the potential disaster. As a future teacher, I do worry about violence. I think that some children who are depressed or disturbed see violence on television and get ideas from it.

310 The informants had been saturated with bomb threats, as students and as student teachers, and did not see this as a threat. However, the "hit list," associated with the media representations of massacres such as Columbine, was terrifying for this informant. She argues that she 315 "can see the potential disaster," and yet she cannot see the "potential disaster" of a bomb. Even the mother of one elementary aged child was not as afraid of bombs as she was of guns:

As we pulled into the high school parking lot, there were 320 a number of police cars and a handful of people running out of the buildings. I asked her [the informant's daughter] what she thought was going on, and she replied casually, "Maybe drugs, maybe weapons, maybe a bomb threat, who knows…it happens all the time." Later, she 325 wrote when asked what she was most afraid of she replied, "I am most afraid of guns because I know the damage they can do."

Only a few informants mentioned bomb threats, but not as something that they were particularly afraid of 330 when they thought of school violence. In this case, as a mother, she described her children going to school with frequent bomb threats, but the mother–informant was most afraid of guns. She never mentioned herself being afraid of bomb threats, and in fact said that her children 335 accepted this as regular commonplace behavior. Student teachers talked lightly about bomb threats in workshops, but more that they were not taken seriously. What is particularly curious is why were these

340 informants afraid of bombs when the damage from one bomb could potentially be much more lethal to greater numbers of students than a gun? And these informants had experienced bomb threats, but only one had seen a gun in school. Most of the informants said they were influenced by the media reports, particularly of Columbine High School.

Also, some informants reported fearing the outside stranger coming in and placing their students at risk of harm. The outside stranger myth is even more rare than gun violence, and yet this was a fear that several informants reported.

Fears of pre-service elementary teachers seem to be grounded in media reports rather than in fact or their own personal experiences in the schools as students and student teachers. This suggests that of all the experiences pre-service teachers factor into their constructions of school violence, media reports of extreme violence carry more weight in shaping their definitions than their own personal experiences as students and student teachers. For example, statistics suggest that teachers are at higher risk of theft than any other kind of crime in schools, and yet no informant mentioned fear of theft or even experiencing theft in schools. Bomb threats are potentially more lethal than gun threats, yet informants, many of whom experienced several bomb threats as "annoying," were quite afraid of guns.

Pre-service versus in-service teachers' greatest fears. The most notable difference in the qualitative data between pre-service and in-service teachers' greatest fears was that pre-service teachers tended to focus their written description of fears on harm to themselves (fear of being shot themselves, attacked, or hurt) or fear of doing something wrong (missing warning signs or some other act that resulted in harm to themselves or students). In-service teachers, although some were fearful for their own safety, the majority tended to focus on their fears of harm to their students.

Pre-service teachers	→ → →	In-service teachers
Focus on self:	→ → →	*Focus on students:*
Self injury ("being shot, killed…")		Fear of students being hurt
Failure (failing to respond correctly or recognize warning signs)		

In-service teachers tended to use language that reflected their perception of responsibility for the safety of their students "that one of my students will be hurt." The pronoun of ownership "my" is found among many female in-service teachers (it is never mentioned by males). Obviously, pre-service teachers do not have their "own" students for whom they are primarily responsible, so this is perhaps why their greatest fears tended to focus on their own harm or their own failure. Pre-service teachers who did describe fear for or of students, still ultimately, typically returned to their fears for their own welfare or their own failure as illus-

390 trated in this example: "repercussions of students who have quit, left, or been expelled for reasons dealing with me."

Gender differences. When asked: "What are you most afraid of when you think about school violence
395 and your role as a teacher?" men in nearly every case (regardless of in-service or pre-service) listed behaviors (pain, shooting, breaking up fights, etc.), whereas many of the women (regardless of whether in-service or pre-service) described situations or contexts (e.g., "a
400 stranger coming into the school or class and threatening to hurt or hurting someone"). These findings support Noddings's (1992) assertion that: "women who speak in the different voice refuse to leave themselves, their loved ones, and connections out of their moral
405 reasoning. They speak from and to a situation, and their reasoning is contextual" (p. 21). Gilligan (1993) also theorized that women use context and relationships to help them make decisions. She wrote (p. 17), "women not only define themselves in a context of human rela-
410 tionship, but also judge themselves in terms of their ability to care." Fears were contextualized for women regardless of experience and perhaps this is driven by a judgment of themselves as Gilligan suggests in their "ability to care" for their students.

Quantitative Results

415 Similar to previous studies, this study found some significant differences between pre-service and current teachers when asked to rate their fears of guns, knives, hostage taking, bombs, etc., in school using *t*-test analysis to compare the two groups.

420 *Rankings of greatest fears: in-service versus pre-service teachers.* Pre-service teachers rated the following as acts that they feared most (from high to low based on mean from five-point scale where higher scores indicate greater fear):

425 • Guns (3.2)
• Bombs (3.08)
• Rape (3.06)
• Knives (3.02)
• Hostage taking (3.01)
430 • Suicide (3.00)
• Stranger assaults and assaults (tied 2.88)
• Other weapons (2.86)
• Physical fighting (2.4)
• Bullying (2.04)
435 • Verbal fighting (1.83)

In-service teachers rated the following acts that they feared most (from high to low based on mean from five point scale where higher scores indicate greater fear):

440 • Knives (2.82)
• Guns and stranger attacks (tied 2.78)
• Suicide (2.75)
• Other weapons (2.67)

445 • Rape (2.66)
• Assault (2.58)
• Bombs (2.52)
• Hostage taking (2.51)
• Physical fighting (2.4)
• Bullying (2.29)
450 • Verbal fighting (2.1)

t-test differences between pre-service and in-service teachers. There were significant differences using *t*-tests to compare pre-service teachers to in-service teachers on the following variables (higher means indi-
455 cate greater fear).

Pre-service versus in-service teachers' fears of certain acts. As described in the table below, pre-service teachers were significantly more fearful than in-service teachers of guns, hostage taking, bombs, and rape. In-
460 service teachers however were more fearful of verbal fights than pre-service teachers (Table 1 in Appendix C).

Pre-service versus in-service teachers' beliefs in the likelihood of certain acts. As indicated in the table
465 below, pre-service teachers believed that guns, knives, and rape were significantly more likely to happen in schools than in-service teachers did (Table 2 in Appendix C).

Correlations: Likelihood and fear. Table 3 in Ap-
470 pendix C describes the correlations between teachers' fears and the belief in the likelihood that these acts will happen.

Analysis was only used to pair variables (e.g., gun likelihood with gun fear).

475 Correlational analyses suggest that a belief in the likelihood of certain violent acts (assault, use of weapons, fighting, etc.) is significantly correlated with fear of these acts.

Discussion and Conclusions

The Role of "Experience"

Experience perhaps is responsible for the difference
480 between the self-focus of pre-service teachers and the student focus of the in-service teachers as well as their differences in fears and beliefs in the likelihood of certain acts. The quality as well as the duration of experience is different between these two groups. Pre-service
485 teachers in this study have had practicum and/or student teaching experiences, but they do not have primary responsibility or do not have "ownership" for a particular group of students. Therefore, the context of their experience is different than the in-service teachers
490 who have their own classrooms, students for whom they are primarily responsible, and more classroom experiences to shape their fears. The description of context is different, but consistently, regardless of type or nature of experience, there were still gender differ-
495 ences in the ways males and females described what they feared most. Females tended to contextualize their greatest fears, but males listed acts and behaviors with-

257

out any personal link or content or grounded in any experience.

500 As Munby and Russell (1998, p. 76) wrote: "…to the uninitiated, teaching unfolds as sets of skills; but to the initiated, teaching depends on, is grounded in, and constitutes knowledge. This knowledge is in large measure practical, and that part can only be learned in
505 practices. Equally, that part can only be studied by carefully examining practice." If the set of skills gained through experience for in-service teachers shapes their fears, then in-service teachers *should* be less fearful and ground their fears in their experience. This seemed
510 to be the case for this group of in-service teachers who were generally less fearful. The one exception was that in-service teachers were more fearful than pre-service teachers of verbal fights. Perhaps this is based on experience that in-service teachers have in which verbal
515 fights lead to escalation to more serious physical violence. Pre-service teachers have not had as many experiences to learn this, and thus tend to be less fearful of verbal fighting.

Practical, work-related experience, one would hy-
520 pothesize, would make in-service teachers more comfortable than pre-service teachers, and feel more competent and less fearful. Burstein and Sears (1998) suspected this in their research with pre-service and in-service teachers, but found the following: "It was an-
525 ticipated that with increased competency, the challenges and stress of on-the-job teachers would decrease, thus facilitating job satisfaction and retention. However, results from this study indicate that during the program, challenges and stress remained consistent
530 over time…. Teachers continue to feel exhausted, overwhelmed, and frustrated, regardless of competency…." (p. 60). The data described in this paper suggest that one could add "afraid," at least in part, to this list. Although in-service teachers were less fearful of
535 guns, hostage taking, bombs, and rape, there were still many acts that made them as *afraid* as pre-service teachers (other weapons, knives, physical fighting, stranger assaults, assaults, bullying, suicide). Also, there were no differences in the perceived *likelihood* of
540 the following acts between pre-service and in-service teachers on the following: weapon carrying (not knives or guns), fights, verbal fighting, hostage taking, stranger assaults, assaults, bullying, bombs, and suicide.

545 Perhaps experience is what explains why in-service teachers' beliefs in the likelihood of such acts as carrying guns, knives, and rape were lower than pre-service teachers. The qualitative data suggest that in the absence of a great deal of experience in the classroom,
550 pre-service teachers will default to media images to shape their fears of and feelings of likelihood of such violent acts as guns, other weapons, and rape.

The notion of a hierarchical ranking of violence for pre-service and in-service teachers. There are enough
555 similarities when looking at the rankings between in-

service and pre-service teachers that there appears to be some consistency in the acts that both groups fear. The acts that are most feared are those that are considered most physically harmful (guns, weapons, suicide). One
560 notable difference is bombs. Arguably, bombs could be the most lethal of all the choices, yet in-service teachers tend to be less afraid of bombs than pre-service teachers. Perhaps the saturation of bomb scares and threats that happen year after year has caused in-
565 service teachers to be less fearful. The bottom of the "hierarchy" is compelling as well. The similarities in verbal fights, bullying, and physical fights demonstrates some agreement in "low-level violence," with in-service teachers being more fearful of verbal fights.
570 Pre-service teachers need to understand the importance of addressing "low level" forms of violence to prevent higher forms of violence.

Implications for Policy and Practice

In an effort to address the growing concern of the dangerous nature of school violence, New York State
575 created legislation mandating that all teachers have two hours of training in the area of school violence prevention prior to certification (O'Donohue, 2000). However, prior to this project little was known about the best way to prepare pre-service teachers *before* they
580 become certified teachers or in-service teachers as they work in classrooms to deal with school violence. The two-hour program currently focuses on helping pre-service and in-service teachers identify risk factors of children likely to become violent in school. Pre-service
585 and early in-service teachers in this study reported this as a concern. However, is this the best approach for both pre-service teachers whose fears are primarily focused on harm to self and in-service teachers whose fears are contextual and based on their own students'
590 safety?

Based on the findings of this research, it is clear that the approach to teaching teachers (pre-service and in-service) needs to be developmental. There seems to be a shift when one becomes an in-service teacher to
595 focus more on students and the risk to them. It seems that the focus of these workshops or training for pre-service and in-service teachers needs to address the difference in what they fear most. Focus on personal risk and strategies for addressing this as well as statis-
600 tics on the reality of teacher victimization needs to be part of workshops for pre-service teachers. Whereas, for in-service teachers, strategies for keeping students safe and identifying warning signs grounded in their own experiences and realities in the classroom would
605 be more useful.

For both groups, some discussion about the actual statistics and acts that are most likely to result in harm should be the focus for teacher training workshops. Also, some attempt to place these examples in real-life
610 contexts would be powerful for in-service and pre-service teachers as well.

Finally, any education for teachers needs to address *their* fears. Smaller, interactive groups where individuals can share their experiences and fears with some attempt to allow time to address what drives these fears and strategies for coping with anxiety that accompanies fear would be useful as well. Burke and Harris (1996) suggested in their work with social work students that supervisors take a role. They recommended that supervisors need to play a significant role in helping students acknowledge and process their fears as well as giving them a person with whom to talk. Student teacher supervisors should be trained to understand the realities of school violence in the schools where they supervise student teachers. They need to encourage talk about fears and be prepared to address it in constructive ways.

By gathering a better understanding of what pre-service and early in-service teachers are most afraid of related to school violence, and if these fears are grounded in the likelihood of these acts occurring, we can tailor the training to address these ways and address these fears, perceptions, and misconceptions. Education programs must address these fears and help pre-service and in-service teachers realize the actual reality of numbers of school violence incidents involving a weapon and provide skills that address conflict resolution, anger management, and create a caring school environment. Instead, the New York State training currently focuses on risk factors for children at risk of violence and what to do in cases of extreme violence. When questioned about what they felt they needed to be best equipped to handle school violence, the overwhelming majority of informants in this study reported that they wanted to be able to identify children who were most likely to be violent. Thus, the New York State program of identifying risk factors is consistent with the demand of pre-service teachers that is grounded in their media-fed fears. New York and other states and education programs educating teachers and pre-service teachers in violence prevention need to adopt a more developmental approach, grounding workshops in real classroom contexts, and discussing the reality of the likelihood of different violent acts happening in school.

Teacher education should address the fears of pre-service and early in-service teachers related to school violence. We must educate pre- and in-service teachers of the realities of school violence and we must train supervisors how to systematically address the fears of their charges. Perhaps veteran teachers can be used in mentoring roles to help reduce new teachers' and student teachers' fears. If we fail to address these concerns in a systematic way, we may lose more teachers early in their careers. We cannot afford to lose good teachers to unrealistic fears and anxieties.

Recommendations for Future Study

Although the data in this study are cross-sectional, it is possible that the differences represent transitions in belief and fear are attributable to professional development, experience in the environment, and role obligations. Therefore, fears and anxieties of pre-service teachers studied here may diminish over time. Future study might involve a longitudinal analysis of this possible developmental change. Future inquiry might also include a study of interaction of severity of personal violence exposure with teachers' beliefs about likelihood of violence and fear of violence.

If recommended modifications in teacher education on school violence occur, an evaluation study of the impact of those program modifications on teachers' fears and beliefs about violence would be particularly valuable.

References

Annual Report on School Safety (1999). *Collaboration between the U.S. Department of Education and the U.S. Department of Justice*. Retrieved May 8, 2004, from http://www.hamfish.org/pub/arss99.pdf

Bogdan, R., & Biklen, S. (1992). *Qualitative research for education: An introduction to theory and methods*. Boston: Allyn & Bacon.

Burke, S. G., & Harris, R. R. (1996). Violence: A study of ways to support social work students in urban field placements. *Clinical Supervisor, 14*, 147–155.

Burstein, N. D., & Sears, S. (1998). Preparing on-the-job teachers for urban schools: Implications for teacher training. *Teacher Education and Special Education, 2*, 47–62.

Ferraro, K. F. (1995). *Fear of crime: Interpreting victimization risk*. Albany, NY: SUNY Press.

Gilligan, C. (1993). *In a different voice: Psychological theory and women's development*. Cambridge, MA: Harvard University Press.

Glaser, B. (1978). *Theoretical sensitivity: Advances in the methodology of grounded theory*. Mill Valley, CA: Sociology Press.

Howard, C. (2003). Who receives the short end of the shortage? Implications of the U.S. teacher shortage on urban schools. *Journal of Curriculum and Supervision, 18*, 142–160.

Monitoring the Future Study (1999). Retrieved May 8, 2004, from http://www.hamfish.org/data/national/csi/weapons.html

Mumby, H., & Hutchinson, N. (1998). Using experience to prepare teachers for inclusive classrooms: Teacher education and the epistemology of practice. *Teacher Education and Special Education, 21*, 75–82.

National Center for Educational Statistics (April 1996). *How safe are the public schools? What do the teachers say?* Research Brief. Retrieved May 10, 2004, from http://nces.ed.gov/pubsearch/pubsinfo.asp?pubid=96842

Noddings, N. (1992). *The challenge to care in schools*. New York: Teachers College Press.

O'Donohue, M. (2000, July 24). *Governor signs historic legislation to make schools safer*. New York State Press Release. Retrieved January 5, 2003, from http://www.state.ny.us/governor/ltgov/press99/july24_00.htm

Price, J. H., & Everett, S. A. (1997). Teachers' perceptions of violence in the public schools: The Metlife survey. *American Journal of Health Behavior, 21*, 178–86.

Tyler, T. R., & Cook, F. L. (1984). The mass media and judgments of risk: Distinguishing impact on personal and societal level judgments. *Journal of Personal and Social Psychology, 47*, 693–708.

White, B. L., & Beal, G. D. (1999). Violence in schools as perceived by pre-service and in-service teachers. *Contemporary Education, 71*, 31–39.

Williams, K. M. (2001). The importance of ethnography in understanding violence in schools. In Burstyn et al., *Preventing violence in schools: A challenge to American democracy*. Mahwah, NJ: Lawrence Erlbaum Associates, Publishers.

Williams, K. M. (1998). *Learning limits: College women, drugs, and relationships*. Westport, CT: Bergin and Garvey.

Young, B. N., & Craig, D. V. (1999, November). *Warnings from the field: A study of perceptions of violence of middle school students, middle school pre-service teachers, middle school practicing teachers, high school students, high school pre-service teachers, high school practicing teachers*. Paper presented at the Annual Meeting of the Mid-South Educational Research Association, Point Clear, AL.

About the authors: *Kimberly Williams* is associate professor with SUNY Cortland, Department of Education, Cortland, NY 13045 (e-mail: williak@cortland.edu). *Ken Corvo* is associate professor at Syracuse University, School of Social Work, Syracuse, NY 13210 (e-mail: kncorvo@syr.edu).

APPENDIX A

Perceptions of School Violence Survey

| Date:_____ | Sex:_____ | Race:_____ | Age:_____ |

Intended or current role in school:

Current teacher in (circle one):   Elementary school   Middle school   High school

Number of years teaching:_____

OR

I hope to someday teach in (circle one): Elementary school   Middle school   High school

What is your definition of violence (include the words that come to your head when you think of the word "violence")?:

What do you think causes children to be violent in school?

What are you most afraid of when you think about school violence and your role as a teacher?

Can you describe your most memorable personal experience with school violence?

Have you ever been a victim of violent crime? If so, would you be willing to explain?

Please rate your feelings about the following in school.

1 = not afraid at all
2 = somewhat afraid
3 = afraid
4 = very afraid
5 = terrified

_____ 1. Guns
_____ 2. Knives
_____ 3. Other weapons
_____ 4. Physical fighting
_____ 5. Verbal fighting
_____ 6. Hostage-taking situation
_____ 7. Stranger attack
_____ 8. Assaults
_____ 9. Bullying
_____ 10. Bombs
_____ 11. Suicide
_____ 12. Rape/sexual assault

Please rate the following according to the likelihood that you think these would happen to you or your students in school.

1 = very likely
2 = somewhat likely
3 = somewhat unlikely
4 = very unlikely

_____ 1. Attacked or threatened with a gun
_____ 2. Attacked or threatened with a knife
_____ 3. Attacked or threatened with other weapons
_____ 4. Physical fighting
_____ 5. Verbal fighting
_____ 6. Being held hostage
_____ 7. Stranger attack
_____ 8. Assaults
_____ 9. Bullying
_____ 10. Bombs
_____ 11. Suicide
_____ 12. Rape/sexual assault

APPENDIX B

Selected quotes from survey in regards to: "What are you most afraid of when you think about school violence and your role as a teacher?"

"That I'll be killed."

"I am most afraid of a stranger coming into school with a weapon. I don't think it is likely, but I wonder about it."

"I am afraid that I will be permanently harmed by a violent act."

"Getting shot dead."

"Repercussions by student(s) that have quit, left, or been expelled for reasons dealing with me."

"Being held hostage."

"Possibly getting shot."

"Being shot."

"Keeping children safe, but mostly afraid of a stranger coming into the school or class and threatening to hurt or truly hurting someone."

"Getting shot."

"Someone bringing a gun to school and threatening to use it, or taking 'hostages.'"

"Being shot by a student."

"Since I work mostly with very young children, I worry most about intruders or possibly a young child bringing a weapon to school."

"A situation like Columbine."

"Being shot."

"I'm afraid that I won't pick up on signs that one of my students might be violent. I'm also afraid because I teach in a very rural school district—many of the students hunt and have access to guns/knives."

"Shootings, bombings."

"A child (or student, or another person) coming to school with and using a gun or other deadly weapon."

"It happening in my school (bomb, guns)."

"One of my former students will reappear with weapons and do bodily harm to others and myself."

"Gun violence by students."

"Getting shot or anyone in my class."

"Incidences like Columbine and Jonesboro."

"Put simply, I am afraid of being shot point blank by a student. I am also afraid of not picking up on the warning signs."

"How shootings are increasing in today's schools."

"A child bringing in a gun and trying to harm other children with it."

"I am afraid that someday it is going to become so out of control that an elementary student is going to shoot his or her peers."

"Violence against authority—with more gangs & guns in society will we have any control over students or be afraid to show any control."

"Guns!"

"Shootings."

"A gun or knife in my classroom & how I would ensure the safety of my students."

"A student with a knife or a gun in my classroom."

"Being shot at or held against my will."

"A student bringing a weapon (gun, knife) to school."

"School shooting."

"Children bringing guns to school."

"That something will happen that I have no control over such as a Columbine type incident."

"Children entering schools w/guns & knives."

"Weapons."

"Me & my students getting caught in a crossfire—losing student's life or my own."

"Columbine."

"Strangers intruding—a custodian was shot at my school—it was a drug dealer—it was late at night (9 p.m.)."

"Being shot, stabbed, stalked, etc."

"Weapons."

"A child will come in w/a knife or gun."

"That I will be a target."

"Actually finding bombs during bomb threats, students carrying knives, guns."

"Being maimed or permanently injured."

"Physical violence with a weapon."

"Gun fire, knives, bombs."

"Kids bring weapons to school."

"If someone comes in shooting. What can one do if this happens? What if the teacher happens to be the target?"

Selected quotes from: "Victim of a violent crime."

"Suicide: 10th grade."

"Apartment robbed and vandalized."

"As a child (8 years old) I was attacked and held at knife-point."

"Mugged when I was 18. I was walking on the street and someone came up behind me knocked me down and grabbed my purse."

"Smashed car windows & valuables stolen."

"Yes, I was held at gun point and robbed at my place of work."

"Yes, child abuse."

"Yes, I was drugged and raped by someone I believed to be a close friend (9/00). I actually completed the trial a few weeks ago (6/29/01)—he was found not guilty (nice, huh?)."

"Yes, verbal & emotional abuse as a student from students & teacher. And as an adult from a boyfriend."

"Yes, grew up in NYC and was robbed at 16 in Penn Station. Also, my mom was robbed in Macy's when I was 5."

"When I got into a fist fight over a hat."

"I, personally, wasn't harmed, but my house was broken into & burglarized. I didn't shower while being home alone for weeks afterwards & I kept checking on my children in the middle of the night."

"During a soccer game in high school, I was punched in the nose."

"A girl pushed me backwards down stairs because I told on her for smoking at an indoor soccer tournament. Nothing was done to her! But I had her arrested on my own w/o school help!"

"Rape."

"Yes, held @ knifepoint by mugger in NYC. I was not hurt in the incident. "

"Yes, held up at gunpoint."

"Yes, as a 12 year old student—gang intimidation, harassment…"

"As a child—beat up."

"Yes. Sexual harassment."

"Yes. I was hit by a fellow student on the bus when I was 8. She broke my glasses. I was also a victim of date rape at 20."

"Yes. I was in 7th grade and I was being abused physically and verbally abused by a peer (not a friend) of the opposite sex. I told my parents and the teacher and nothing was done and the violence didn't stop until I left Jr. high."

"Just general fighting—guy stuff."

"I myself was victim & received a sucker punch in the face which resulted in a fractured cheekbone."

"Yes, I was seemingly punched without cause or warning."

"Yes—sorority girls surrounded my friends & I threatening us."

"Struck as a pedestrian by a drunk driver. Another man was killed and a second one got a broken back."

"$2000 damage to my new car
Life has been threatened.
Had a former student arrested for threatening to rape me.
Harm to family members.
Teacher friend punched @ work—ended up in the hospital."

"As a high school student, I was hit & molested by a male student (not a boyfriend)."

"Yes, (1) verbal assault—name calling (elementary/HS), (2) close friend (his father committed suicide when he was younger; used to be that all-American boy—popular, varsity sports, well-liked, very handsome—made the wrong decision and became hooked on drugs—his life was changed forever) who committed suicide, would demand money for drugs, from me, by making harassing phone calls to me at work, putting dents in my car by kicking, forcing me to allow him the use of my car—eventually was put in jail, then rehab (then walked out and hung himself)."

APPENDIX C

Tables

Table 1

t-Test: Pre-Service versus In-Service Teachers' Mean Fears of Certain Acts

Fear of violent acts	Pre-service teachers	In-service teachers	*t*-value
Fear of guns[a]	3.2	2.8	2.2*
Fear of verbal fights[b]	1.8	2.1	2.1*
Fear of hostage taking[c]	3.0	2.5	2.3*
Bombs[d]	3.0	2.5	2.8*
Rape[e]	3.1	2.6	2.0*

[a] = Pre-service teachers were significantly more likely than in-service teachers to fear guns.

[b] = In-service teachers were significantly more likely than pre-service teachers to fear verbal fights.

[c] = Pre-service teachers were significantly more likely than in-service teachers to fear hostage taking.

[d] = Pre-service teachers were significantly more likely than in-service teachers to fear bombs.

[e] = Pre-service teachers were significantly more likely than in-service teachers to fear rape.

* = *t*-test comparison of means were significantly different at $p < .05$.

Table 2

t-Test: Pre-Service versus In-Service Teachers' Mean Beliefs in the Likelihood of Certain Acts

Perception of likelihood	Pre-service teachers	In-service teachers	*t*-value
Likelihood of guns[a]	2.8	3.1	2.1*
Likelihood of knives[b]	2.6	3.0	2.1*
Likelihood of rape[c]	2.5	3.0	3.5*

Note. Lower means indicate higher perception of likelihood of these acts.

[a] = Pre-service teachers were significantly more likely than in-service teachers to believe that they would encounter guns in school.

[b] = Pre-service teachers were significantly more likely than in-service teachers to believe that they would encounter knives in school.

[c] = Pre-service teachers were significantly more likely than in-service teachers to believe that they would encounter rape in school.

* = *t*-test comparisons show significant differences of means at $p < .05$.

Table 3
Correlation Analysis: Pre-Service and In-Service Teachers' Perceptions of Likelihood of Violent Acts and Fear of Those Violent Acts

	Gun fear	Knife fear	Other weapon fear	Hostage taking fear	Stranger fear	Bomb fear	Suicide fear	Rape fear
Gun likelihood	*r* = .24*							
Knife likelihood		*r* = .24*						
Other weapon likelihood			*r* = .26*					
Hostage taking likelihood				*r* = .19*				
Stranger assault likelihood					*r* = .24*			
Bomb likelihood						*r* = .22*		
Suicide likelihood							*r* = .23*	
Rape likelihood								*r* = .20*

Note. There are significant correlations between fear of violent acts (guns, knives, weapons, hostage taking, strangers, bombs, suicide, and rape) and the perception of likelihood of these acts happening.
* = Significant correlations exist between variables at *p* < .01.

Exercise for Article 36

Factual Questions

1. The researchers explicitly state how many research questions?

2. What percentage of the informants were female?

3. What is the name of the test that was used to determine the significance of the differences between the two groups?

4. What did pre-service teachers rate as their greatest fear?

5. Were "in-service teachers" *or* "pre-service teachers" more fearful of verbal fights?

Questions for Discussion

6. The researchers used both open-ended and closed questions. Which type is more closely associated with qualitative research? (See lines 111–116.)

7. Did the inclusion of Appendix A at the end of this article help you understand this study? Explain.

8. Do you think it was a good idea to have the participants respond anonymously? Explain. (See line 137.)

9. Do you think that the method of qualitative analysis is described in sufficient detail? Explain. (See lines 152–197.)

10. The researchers used a combination of qualitative and quantitative methodology. In your opinion, did one method produce more interesting and useful results than the other? Explain.

11. Do you agree that a longitudinal analysis would be a good idea in a future study on this topic? Explain. (See lines 672–674.)

Quality Ratings

Directions: Indicate your level of agreement with each of the following statements by circling a number from 5 for strongly agree (SA) to 1 for strongly disagree (SD). If you believe an item is not applicable to this research article, leave it blank. Be prepared to explain your ratings. When responding to criteria A and B below, keep in mind that brief titles and abstracts are conventional in published research.

A. The title of the article is appropriate.
SA   5   4   3   2   1   SD

B. The abstract provides an effective overview of the research article.
SA   5   4   3   2   1   SD

C. The introduction establishes the importance of the study.
SA   5   4   3   2   1   SD

D. The literature review establishes the context for the study.
SA   5   4   3   2   1   SD

E. The research purpose, question, or hypothesis is clearly stated.
SA   5   4   3   2   1   SD

F. The method of sampling is sound.
SA   5   4   3   2   1   SD

G. Relevant demographics (for example, age, gender, and ethnicity) are described.

SA   5   4   3   2   1   SD

H. Measurement procedures are adequate.

SA   5   4   3   2   1   SD

I. All procedures have been described in sufficient detail to permit a replication of the study.

SA   5   4   3   2   1   SD

J. The participants have been adequately protected from potential harm.

SA   5   4   3   2   1   SD

K. The results are clearly described.

SA   5   4   3   2   1   SD

L. The discussion/conclusion is appropriate.

SA   5   4   3   2   1   SD

M. Despite any flaws, the report is worthy of publication.

SA   5   4   3   2   1   SD

Article 37

"The Teacher Said My Story Was Excellent": Preservice Teachers Reflect on the Role of the "External" in Writing

BRANDI GRIBBLE MATHERS
Geneva College

SUSAN KUSHNER BENSON
University of Akron, Ohio

EVANGELINE NEWTON
University of Akron, Ohio

From *Journal of Adolescent & Adult Literacy*, *50*, 290–297. Copyright © 2006 by the International Reading Association. Reprinted with permission.

I (Brandi Mathers, first author) started my teaching career in an elementary classroom. It was there I realized that not all students liked to write and that, although some students considered themselves successful
5 writers, many others saw themselves as failures. When I began teaching at the college level, I realized that things did not change as students grew older. I guess I should not have been too surprised by this, and yet it still dismayed me. Perhaps it was because I taught for
10 the College of Education, surrounded by students aspiring to become educators, that I assumed all my students would be confident writers. After all, it would not be long before they would be in classrooms, responsible for instructing young students of their own in the
15 intricacies of composition.

Slifkin (1997) summed up my concern, contending, "The idea of a 'nonwriter' teaching students to write well is as implausible as being taught to drive by someone who has never been behind the wheel" (p.
20 88). As troubling as it was to me, it became apparent that not all new teachers would be entering their first classrooms with high amounts of confidence in themselves as writers or as teachers of writing. So what accounted for this difference? Why was it that some pre-
25 service teachers considered themselves successful writers while others considered themselves failures?

My colleagues and I decided to go to the source and ask preservice teachers to discuss their successes and failures in writing. We did so by inviting a group of
30 192 preservice teachers to write personal literacy histories (Judy & Judy, 1983) to chronicle their development as writers. We then conducted a content analysis of their responses in hopes of gaining more insight into their beliefs regarding the reasons for their successes
35 and failures.

Theoretical Frame

An editorial in *The Reading Teacher* observed,

"Teachers sometimes admit reluctantly that they have never liked to write, find writing difficult, don't have the time to write, and in fact, are not writers" (Fawcett
40 et al., 1996, p. 358). Apparently, practicing teachers are not the only ones who feel this way about writing. Draper, Barksdale-Ladd, and Radencich (2000) lamented a similar problem when, in reference to preservice teachers, they stated, "We are confident in con-
45 cluding that preservice teacher educators cannot assume that their students are readers and writers, nor can they presume that their students hold a love of reading and writing" (p. 193).

While these student teachers may not bring a love
50 of literacy, they do bring much prior knowledge about literacy and teaching to their formal professional educations (Florio-Ruane & Lensmire, 1990). After all, they enter the college classroom with years of personal exposure to writing instruction. These personal encoun-
55 ters help shape their assumptions about literacy and their expectations regarding their own ability to perform as writers (Palmquist & Young, 1992). Additionally, their lengthy apprenticeship of observation (Lortie, 1977) provides them with a deeply ingrained, al-
60 though not necessarily accurate, perception regarding what it means to be a teacher of writing (Street, 2003).

Attribution Theory

What reasons do preservice teachers give for the assumptions and expectations they hold regarding themselves as writers? The cognitive theory known as "at-
65 tribution theory" provides a useful lens with which to examine this question. Attribution theory considers individuals' beliefs about the reasons for their successes and failures and how these beliefs influence their expectations and future behavior (Alderman,
70 2004). Attributions therefore function as a means of control because they help explain past events and predict future ones (Gedeon & Rubin, 1999).

Effort and *ability* are the two attributions most frequently cited for success and failure in achievement
75 settings (Graham & Weiner, 1993). Writing attributions can also be divided into these two categories: Some people believe writing is a "gift," likening it to

265

some kind of creative genius, others believe writing is a skill that through effort can be learned and developed (Palmquist & Young, 1992). Although effort and ability are common attributions, it is important to note that "a virtually infinite number of causal ascriptions are available" (Weiner, 1985, p. 549). For example, Weiner (1992) acknowledged that factors such as mood, fatigue, illness, and bias might also be used to explain academic performance. Work by Clifford (1986) identified learning strategies as another possible explanation, whereas work by Frieze and Snyder (1980) pinpointed interest.

Attributions can be classified according to a number of dimensions, one of which is the "locus of causality" (Weiner, 1979, 1985, 1992). This dimension considers whether a person believes the cause of an outcome results from something within himself (internal locus) or comes to pass because of the influence of an outside factor (external locus). For example, task difficulty is externally driven, whereas effort and ability both come from within an individual and are therefore considered internal.

Writing As An Internal Process

Work on the writing process by researchers including Atwell (1987), Calkins (1994), Graves (1983), and Perl (1983) has focused on the "internal" nature of writing. Central to the process approach is the notion of composition as an act of personal "meaning making," in which writing, like learning, is a meaning-making process that facilitates the learner's ability to ask questions, discover connections, and find answers (Langer & Applebee, 1987). Writers' first drafts are initial attempts to think on paper. From there, they engage in a process of elaboration and clarification as they go about making meaning. The more writers work with their ideas, the more they are able to revise, rethink, and clarify their thoughts (Murray, 1980).

The "internal" nature of writing has been discussed by other authors who elevate the importance of the personal learning process. For example, Houston (2004) used musical and sports analogies to make her point. She explained, "Playing a musical instrument cannot be taught.... My athletic friends tell me that playing a sport can only be learned as well. Writing is like these activities. It can only be learned by the writer" (pp. 6–7). Berthoff (1982) similarly reflected on the limitations of writing instruction by drawing a parallel between woodworking and writing. She contended,

> Up to a point, writing can be explained and taught as a skill. And it can be demonstrated, as dovetailing the joints of a drawer can be demonstrated...but woodcraft is not just assembling some precut forms, nor is wordcraft gluing statements together. Composing...requires more than skill (p. 11).

Purpose and Background of the Study

We used literacy histories (Judy & Judy, 1983)

written by preservice teachers as a source of information for examining their beliefs about writing. We were particularly interested in the beliefs of preservice teachers who made high or low self-assessments of their writing skills. Three questions guided this study:

1. In what ways do the literacy histories of preservice teachers reveal the belief that writing achievement depends on effort?
2. In what ways do the literacy histories of preservice teachers reveal the belief that writing achievement depends on innate ability?
3. In what ways do the literacy histories of preservice teachers reveal the belief that some other factor accounts for success or failure in writing?

Participants and Research Setting

The 192 preservice teachers who participated in this study were enrolled in sections of an introductory language arts course offered at a public university in upstate New York. There were 111 fourth-year students, 80 third-year, and 1 second-year; all but 1 were enrolled full time. Most of the students were between 19 and 22 years old, but 9 were between 23 and 26 years old, and 16 were 27 or older. There were 167 females and 25 males.

Procedures and Data Analysis

This research took place in two phases. The first phase involved an administration of Palmquist and Young's (1992) Writing Questionnaire. The validity and reliability of this questionnaire have been demonstrated in the literature (Charney, Newman, & Palmquist, 1995; Palmquist, Kiefer, Hartvigsen, & Goodlew, 1998; Palmquist & Young, 1992). The Writing Questionnaire consists of 36 items for response on a 6-point Likert scale ranging from "strongly agree" to "strongly disagree." Some items in the questionnaire required participants to make self-assessments of their own writing skills. For example, participants rated statements including "I am a good writer," "I believe I was born with the ability to write well," and "I'm no good at writing." Participants' self-assessment scores were then calculated, and extreme scores—those falling one standard deviation above or below the mean—were identified. Thirty-five preservice teachers' scores fell into these high and low self-assessment groups.

The second phase of the research involved a content analysis of these high and low self-assessment participants' literacy histories (Judy & Judy, 1983). The literacy history is a series of 14 open-ended questions that ask participants to reflect on their emergence into literacy (McLaughlin, 1994). The purpose of the history is to chronicle students' development as readers and writers. Seven of the 14 questions dealt specifically with writing, including "How did you learn to write?" "Are you a good writer?" and "Do you enjoy writing?"

An initial reading of the literacy histories revealed that these preservice teachers attributed success and failure in writing not only to effort and ability, but also to the external influence of parents, siblings, and—most often—teachers. Consequently, the attributional category of "influential others" was added to the analysis. A database was organized for all coded responses. The responses contained in the databases were read and reread, thus allowing patterns to emerge for both the high and low self-assessment groups.

Attributional Patterns of the Preservice Teachers

Content analysis revealed that the frequency of attributional references made by high and low self-assessment preservice teachers followed the same pattern. "Influential others" was cited most often, followed by "effort," with "ability" ranking third. Although the rank order of the three categories was the same for both high and low groups, a difference appeared in the tone of the two groups' comments.

Attributions Made to Ability

Of the 109 attributional statements made by the low self-assessment group, 31% referenced ability (see Table 1). The tone of these responses was predominantly negative. For example, when asked whether she considered herself a good writer, one preservice teacher wrote, "I do not believe I am a good writer. I really don't know how to structure sentences or where to use punctuation. And because of that, my opinion or point of my paper is really never understood." A second student explained, "I am not a good writer because I am a horrible speller, and I don't know my punctuation, and I am not creative when it comes to writing." Another commented,

I do not see myself as a good writer, although I do like doing it. I am not advanced when it comes to writing. I cannot think of the best words to use, I normally have incorrect grammar usage. I'm almost all-around wrong when it comes to writing.

Of the 60 attributional statements made by the high self-assessment group, 23% referenced "ability" (see Table 1). Whereas the tone of the low self-assessment participants' responses was predominantly negative, the tone of the high group was more positive. For example, to a question that asked whether respondents considered themselves good writers, responses included:

"I believe that I am a good writer. I have always done well in writing…. I can write clear and organized while being creative and interesting."

"I am a great writer. I love writing down my thoughts and feelings, and I have always done pretty well in school."

"I feel that I am a good writer because I have a lot of creative ideas."

"I consider myself to be a great creative writer, but my academic writing is not as advanced."

Table 1
Attributional References Made By Students With High and Low Self-Assessments of Their Writing Ability

Attribution category	No. (%) from high group ($n = 14$)	No. (%) from low group ($n = 21$)
Influential others	29 (48.33)	39 (35.78)
Effort	18 (30.00)	36 (33.04)
Ability	13 (22.66)	34 (31.19)

Attributions Made to Effort

Thirty-three percent of the attributions made by low self-assessment participants referenced effort (see Table 1). As was the case with their ability attributions, the majority of these participants' responses were negative in tone. For example, when asked to reflect on her worst writing assignment, one student wrote,

I tried hard and tried to fill every requirement that was in the rubric. I spent a lot of time on it, working through frustration, and then to top it all off, I got a 62 on it. I was so [angry], it was the dumbest assignment ever.

When asked about his best writing assignment, another participant commented, "No writing assignment has been good. I have a difficult time expressing myself and therefore it is always too much like work." Other respondents also connected writing with work. For instance, when asked whether she enjoyed writing, one student explained, "I do not enjoy writing because there is a lot of work involved for me to hand in a decent paper. I must go through so many revisions that it just isn't fun anymore." Another student wrote, "I do not enjoy writing because it is too much work and I can't think of things to say." One lamented her lack of ideas as well, saying,

I put off papers as long as possible when they are assigned. As much as I have tried to change this habit, I have a fear of writing. Even though I usually do well on the papers I write, I procrastinate almost every time. It is as if I think the paper will begin to write itself or that I feel some profound idea will hit me and I should wait for it. In all my years of writing, I can safely say that profound ideas are rare. Yet, I still procrastinate.

Thirty percent of the attributions made by high self-assessment participants referenced effort (see Table 1). As was the case with their ability attributions, the majority of these participants' responses were positive. In many cases, respondents made the connection between teachers' instructional choices and students' level of effort. For example, when asked to discuss best writing assignments, students recounted,

In 12th grade I had to write a paper on *The Great Gatsby*. I don't even remember what I was talking about, but the teacher allowed us to revise it after meeting with her. I put a lot of effort into that paper, and it helped me to think more about the book.

Our instructor gave us many good writing assignments that forced us to think outside the box and to write that way as well…. The thing that made this assignment so great was that it caused us to think critically about our

writing, stepping out of our comfort zones to create stories
ries that were different but that were great. He allowed us
to write many drafts, grading us on improvement rather
290   than the final product. It was a hard assignment, but it is
one of my most cherished pieces of work.

Attributions Made to Influential Others

When discussing their beliefs about writing, low
self-assessment participants referenced influential others more often than either ability or effort. Thirty-six
295   percent of the coded statements made by this group
referenced the influence of parents, siblings, and—
most often—teachers (see Table 1). Family members
were commemorated in a positive light. For instance,
one student explained, "I mostly learned how to write
300   in junior high school, but my parents had a big influence on helping me learn to write." Teachers, on the
other hand, were associated with criticism. For example, when asked to reflect on her worst writing assignment, one student explained, "The worst writing as-
305   signment was not really an assignment; it was a whole
year. It was a course at college. All that teacher did was
criticize my ideas, my writing, and told me her 5-year-
old could write better than me."

A second student commented on criticism while
310   also addressing the issue of topic choice:

> Most writing assignments I have done I have disliked.
> None really seem worse than others, but it seemed like I
> didn't like them because of the subject matter or the
> harsh criticism I received from teachers and professors.

315   Another reflected on his perception of his teachers'
personal beliefs about writing, saying, "I have never
really enjoyed the concepts of writing because I was
never particularly good, and many of my teachers presented me with the impression that it was not interest-
320   ing."

Like their low self-assessment counterparts, the
high self-assessment participants referenced influential
others more often than either ability or effort. Forty-
eight percent of the attributional references made by
325   this group referred to others (see Table 1). References
to family members and teachers were predominantly
positive. For instance, including:

> "I basically remember trying to copy my older
> brother's homework. I loved to watch him do
330   > homework when I was not in school yet. So I used
> to sit on the kitchen table and watch him write and
> try to mimic it."

> "I learned to write through my mother and father. I
> would always see them writing down the grocery
335   > list, and I would ask them what it said."

> "I learned through practice and a lot of help from
> some good teachers."

Many high self-assessment participants highlighted
the effect of other's opinions on their beliefs about
340   themselves as writers. For instance, one student explained, "I feel that I am a good writer only because

my teachers have told me that in the past and my
grades reflect on that." A second student expressed a
similar sentiment, saying, "I feel that my grades in
345   English have been a reason for me to feel that I make
up good stories and write creative essays." And finally,
another participant replied, "I think I am a good writer.
Other people have told me that I am, and my writing
has moved people immensely. People often remember
350   my stories years after reading them, telling me how
good they were."

Can Writing Skill Be Taught?

Although the low self-assessment group recounted
many negative experiences with writing in school,
when asked whether they considered writing to be a
355   skill that could be taught and learned, their answers
were optimistic. For example, one participant explained, "One just needs to have a great teacher that is
excited and enjoys teaching English, or the students
will not learn well." Likewise, another participant
360   commented, "With the correct teachers, one has a great
chance to learn to write."

When asked whether writing was a skill that could
be taught and learned, high self-assessment respondents highlighted the importance of strong role models.
365   For example, one student wrote, "You are learning
every day, and without someone to teach you the basics, you will never be successful." Another student
corroborated, "I believe writing can be taught through
the right guidance." A third student replied, "I believe
370   it can be taught and learned because there are many
teachers that know how to make writing fun for children."

Discussion

Although "a virtually infinite number of causal ascriptions are available...within the achievement do-
375   main, a relatively small number from the vast array
tend to be salient" (Weiner, 1985, p. 549). The results
of this study indicate that, with regard to writing, one
such salient factor is the role of influential others. Influential others was not an attributional category origi-
380   nally included in the content analysis, but the frequency with which participants referred to parents,
teachers, and siblings as they described their successes
and failures in writing necessitated the addition of this
category. Forty percent of the total attributions made
385   by the participants across self-assessment groups referenced influential others, while 28% and 32% of participants referenced ability and effort, respectively.

These findings highlight the importance of the external component of writing. While the internal aspects
390   of ability and effort were mentioned frequently in the
participants' explanations of their successes and failures, the frequency of the references to the external
spoke loudly. A number of preservice teachers referred
to positive writing experiences provided by their par-
395   ents and siblings; however, the majority of references
to influential others implicated teachers. These refer-

ences included everyone from elementary school teachers to college-level instructors and ranged in tone from positive to neutral to negative. Our findings also call into question the notion that "writing is more learned than taught" (Thomason, 1998, p. 7), for such language downplays the pivotal role teachers play in the creation of student authors. Houston (2004) argued that, although some writing skills and strategies can be taught, what cannot be taught is

> how to create a piece of written discourse as a holistic, global experience in which the thoughts of the writer are synthesized into a whole work that will achieve the writer's purpose when the reader creates the intended meaning.... It is not a body of knowledge. It cannot be taught (p. 7).

The discipline known as composition may not consist of memorizable facts; however, there are many academic pursuits that involve more than the mere transmission of concrete bodies of knowledge. A teacher cannot "teach," per se, the problem-solving skills needed in chemistry, the creativity needed in painting, or the ear needed for picking up the subtleties of French, but teachers still "teach" science, art, and foreign languages. Often, this "teaching" involves merely providing "external support in order to motivate all learners to keep practicing in good faith" (Kern, Andre, Schilke, Barton, & McGuire, 2003, p. 817). The results of this study point to the need for a reconsideration of what it means to "teach" writing and underscore the importance of Houston's (2004) challenge to "think of writing and teaching writing in new ways" (p. 7).

There is no need, however, to shy away from using the word *teach* in conjunction with writing instruction. Teaching, after all, does not have to include dissemination of concrete facts; rather, teachers teach through their attitudes toward writing, the value they place on writing, and the time devoted to it in the classroom. They also teach writing when their students see them engaged in writing of their own. If we limit our definition of teaching to things factual or concrete, then most of what is being taught in school would no longer be classified as teaching.

All learning endeavors—from learning to swim, to learning to sing, to learning to write—require some kind of mental and physical activity on the part of the learner and, thus, the internal aspect of learning is undeniably crucial. The results of this study point, however, to the ways in which learning can also be affected externally by influential others. For example, the positive power of a teacher's influence is found in the reflections of one participant who wrote, "I remember writing a story in 4th grade. We had to write a Halloween story, and the teacher said my story was excellent. I remember enjoying writing from then on." Conversely, the negative effect of another teacher's influence can be felt in the response of a participant who explained, "In high school, I believed I was a bad writer because [that's what] teachers told me."

Attributions made to influential others are classified not only as external but also as uncontrollable (Weiner, 1979, 1985, 1992) because students do not have any say in the kinds of teachers they will have. In this case, the control falls out of the hands of the students and into the hands of teacher training programs, for they are responsible for educating tomorrow's teachers of writing. Consequently, it becomes imperative that preservice teachers be given the opportunity during their teacher education programs to gain confidence as writers and as teachers of writing. A good place to start might be a trip through their own literacy histories. Such a trip would allow preservice teachers to examine the effect influential others have had on them as writers, as well as allow them to make a conscious choice about the type of influence they want to have on their own students some day.

References

Alderman, M. K. (2004). *Motivation for achievement: Possibilities for teaching and learning* (2nd ed.). Mahwah, NJ: Erlbaum.

Atwell, N. (1987). *In the middle: Writing, reading, and learning with adolescents*. Portsmouth, NH: Boynton/Cook.

Berthoff, A. E. (1982). *Forming, thinking, writing: The composing imagination*. Montclair, NJ: Boynton/Cook.

Calkins, L. M. (1994). *The art of teaching writing*. Portsmouth, NH: Heinemann.

Charney, D., Newman, J. H., & Palmquist, M. (1995). "I'm just no good at writing": Epistemological style and attitudes toward writing. *Written Communication, 12*, 298–329.

Clifford, M. M. (1986). The comparative effects of strategy and effort attributions. *British Journal of Educational Psychology, 56*, 75–83.

Draper, M. C., Barksdale-Ladd, M. A., & Radencich, M. C. (2000). Reading and writing habits of preservice teachers. *Reading Horizons, 40*, 185–203.

Fawcett, G., Rasinski, T., Padak, N., Church, B., Hendershot, J., Henry, J., et al. (1996). Editorial: "What's your hobby?" *The Reading Teacher, 49*, 358.

Florio-Ruane, S., & Lensmire, T. J. (1990). Transforming future teachers' ideas about writing instruction. *Curriculum Studies, 22*, 277–289.

Frieze, I. H., & Snyder, H. N. (1980). Children's beliefs about the causes of success and failure in school settings. *Journal of Educational Psychology, 72*, 186–196.

Gedeon, J. A., & Rubin, R. E. (1999). Attribution theory and academic library performance evaluation. *The Journal of Academic Librarianship, 25*, 18–25.

Graham, S., & Weiner, B. (1993). Attributional applications in the classroom. In T. M. Tomlinson (Ed.), *Motivating students to learn: Overcoming barriers to high achievement* (pp. 179–196). Berkeley, CA: McCutchen.

Graves, D. (1983). *Writing: Teachers & children at work*. Portsmouth, NH: Heinemann.

Houston, G. (2004). *How writing works: Imposing organizational structure within the writing process*. Boston: Pearson Education.

Judy, S. N., & Judy, S. J. (1983). *The English teacher's handbook: Ideas and resources for teaching English*. Boston: Little, Brown.

Kern, D., Andre, W., Schilke, R., Barton, J., & McGuire, M. C. (2003). Less *is* more: Preparing students for state writing assessments. *The Reading Teacher, 56*, 816–826.

Langer, J. A., & Applebee, A. N. (1987). *How writing shapes thinking: A study of teaching and learning* (NCTE Research Report No. 22). Urbana, IL: National Council of Teachers of English.

Lortie, D. C. (1977). *Schoolteacher: A sociological study*. Chicago: University of Chicago Press.

McLaughlin, M. (1994, November/December). *Literacy histories of preservice teachers: The effect of the past on the present*. Paper presented at the annual meeting of the National Reading Conference, San Diego, CA.

Murray, D. M. (1980). Writing as a process: How writing finds its own meaning. In T. R. Donovan & B. W. McClelland (Eds.), *Eight approaches to teaching composition* (pp. 3–20). Urbana, IL: National Council of Teachers of English.

Palmquist, M., Kiefer, K., Hartvigsen, J., & Goodlew, B. (1998). *Transitions: Teaching writing in computer-supported and traditional classrooms*. Greenwich, CT: Ablex.

Palmquist, M., & Young, R. (1992). The notion of giftedness and student expectations about writing. *Written Communication, 9*, 137–169.

Perl, S. (1983). How teachers teach the writing process. *The Elementary School Journal, 84*, 19–24.

Slifkin, J. M. (1997). Mixing memory and desire: Some reflections on student teaching and teacher education. *English Journal, 86*, 87–89.

Street, C. (2003). Preservice teachers' attitudes about writing and learning to teach writing: Implications for teacher educators. *Teacher Education Quarterly, 30*, 33–50.

Thomason, T. (1998). *Writer to writer: How to conference young authors.* Norwood, MA: Christopher-Gordon.

Weiner, B. (1979). A theory of motivation for some classroom experiences. *Journal of Educational Psychology, 71*, 3–25.

Weiner, B. (1985). An attributional theory of achievement motivation and emotion. *Psychological Review, 92*, 548–573.

Weiner, B. (1992). *Human motivation: Metaphors, theories, and research.* Newbury Park, CA: Sage.

About the authors: *Brandi Gribble Mathers* teaches in the Education Department at Geneva College. *Susan Kushner Benson* and *Evangeline Newton* teach at the University of Akron, OH.

Address correspondence to: Brandi Gribble Mathers, Education Department, Geneva College, 3200 College Avenue, Beaver Falls, PA 15010. E-mail: bgmather@geneva.edu

Exercise for Article 37

Factual Questions

1. This article states that attributions function as a means of control because they help do what?

2. How many questions guided this study?

3. The literacy history instrument consists of how many items?

4. Were the items on the literacy history instrument open- *or* closed-ended?

5. Was the pattern (rank order) of the frequency of attributional references made by the high and low self-assessment groups the same?

Questions for Discussion

6. How important is it to know the background characteristics of the participants described in lines 147–155? Explain.

7. Is the coding of the responses to the open-ended questions described in sufficient detail? Explain. (See lines 185–194.)

8. How helpful are the direct quotations from participants in helping you understand the results of this study? (See indented quotations interspersed with the discussion of results starting with line 216.)

9. In your opinion, does this study have important implications for helping preservice teachers with low self-assessments of writing ability? Explain.

10. This study was conducted with preservice teachers. Do you think it would be worthwhile to replicate it with experienced teachers? Explain.

11. Are any of the results especially interesting to you? Are any especially surprising?

Quality Ratings

Directions: Indicate your level of agreement with each of the following statements by circling a number from 5 for strongly agree (SA) to 1 for strongly disagree (SD). If you believe an item is not applicable to this research article, leave it blank. Be prepared to explain your ratings. When responding to criteria A and B below, keep in mind that brief titles and abstracts are conventional in published research.

A. The title of the article is appropriate.

SA   5   4   3   2   1   SD

B. The abstract provides an effective overview of the research article.

SA   5   4   3   2   1   SD

C. The introduction establishes the importance of the study.

SA   5   4   3   2   1   SD

D. The literature review establishes the context for the study.

SA   5   4   3   2   1   SD

E. The research purpose, question, or hypothesis is clearly stated.

SA   5   4   3   2   1   SD

F. The method of sampling is sound.

SA   5   4   3   2   1   SD

G. Relevant demographics (for example, age, gender, and ethnicity) are described.

SA   5   4   3   2   1   SD

H. Measurement procedures are adequate.

SA   5   4   3   2   1   SD

I. All procedures have been described in sufficient detail to permit a replication of the study.

SA   5   4   3   2   1   SD

J. The participants have been adequately protected from potential harm.

SA   5   4   3   2   1   SD

K. The results are clearly described.

SA   5   4   3   2   1   SD

L. The discussion/conclusion is appropriate.

SA   5   4   3   2   1   SD

M. Despite any flaws, the report is worthy of publication.

SA   5   4   3   2   1   SD

Article 38

Project D.A.R.E. Outcome
Effectiveness Revisited

STEVEN L. WEST
Virginia Commonwealth University

KERI K. O'NEAL
University of North Carolina, Chapel Hill

OBJECTIVES. We provide an updated meta-analysis on the effectiveness of Project D.A.R.E. in preventing alcohol, tobacco, and illicit drug use among school-aged youths.

METHODS. We used meta-analytic techniques to create an overall effect size for D.A.R.E. outcome evaluations reported in scientific journals.

RESULTS. The overall weighted effect size for the included D.A.R.E. studies was extremely small (correlation coefficient = 0.011; Cohen's d = 0.023; 95% confidence interval = –0.04, 0.08) and nonsignificant (z = 0.73, NS).

CONCLUSIONS. Our study supports previous findings indicating that D.A.R.E. is ineffective.

From *American Journal of Public Health*, *94*, 1027–1029. Copyright © 2004 by American Journal of Public Health. Reprinted with permission.

In the United States, Project D.A.R.E. (Drug Abuse Resistance Education) is one of the most widely used substance abuse prevention programs targeted at school-aged youths. In recent years, D.A.R.E. has been
5 the country's largest single school-based prevention program in terms of federal expenditures, with an average of three-quarters of a billion dollars spent on its provision annually.[1] Although its effectiveness in preventing substance use has been called into question, its
10 application in our nation's schools remains very extensive.[2-6]

Given the recent increases in alcohol and other drug use among high school and college students,[7] the continued use of D.A.R.E. and similar programs seems
15 likely. In a meta-analysis examining the effectiveness of D.A.R.E., Ennett et al.[3] noted negligible yet positive effect sizes (ranging from 0.00 to 0.11) when outcomes occurring immediately after program completion were considered. However, this analysis involved 2 major
20 limitations. First, Ennett et al. included research from nonpeer-reviewed sources, including annual reports produced for agencies associated with the provision of D.A.R.E. services. While such an inclusion does not necessarily represent a serious methodological flaw,
25 use of such sources has been called into question.[8]

Second, Ennett and colleagues included only studies in which postintervention assessment was conducted immediately at program termination. As noted by Lynam et al.,[6] the developmental trajectories of drug experimentation and use vary over time. Thus, if indi-
30 viduals are assessed during periods in which rates of experimentation and use are naturally high, any positive effects that could be found at times of lower experimentation will be deflated. Likewise, assessments made during periods in which experimentation and use
35 are slight will exaggerate the overall effect of the intervention.

Ideally, problems such as those just described could be solved by the use of large-scale longitudinal studies involving extensive follow-up over a period of years.
40 There have been several longer-term follow-ups, but the cost of such efforts may limit the number of longitudinal studies that can be conducted. In the present analysis, we attempted to overcome this difficulty by
45 including a wider range of follow-up reports, from immediate posttests to 10-year postintervention assessments, in an updated meta-analysis of all currently available research articles reporting an outcome evaluation of Project D.A.R.E.

Methods

50 We conducted computer searches of the *ERIC*, *MEDLINE*, and *PsycINFO* databases in late fall 2002 to obtain articles for the present study. In addition, we reviewed the reference lists of the acquired articles for other potential sources. We initially reviewed roughly
55 40 articles from these efforts; 11 studies appearing in the literature from 1991 to 2002 met our 3 inclusion criteria, which were as follows:

1. The research was reported in a peer-reviewed journal; reports from dissertations/theses, books, and
60 unpublished manuscripts were not included. We selected this criterion in an attempt to ensure inclusion of only those studies with rigorous methodologies. As noted, a previous meta-analysis of Project D.A.R.E. included research from nonre-
65 viewed sources, a fact that critics have suggested may have added error to the reported findings.[8]

2. The research included a control or comparison group (i.e., the research must have involved an experimental or quasi-experimental design).

Table 1
Primary Articles Included in the Meta-Analysis

Study (year)	Sample	r	d	95% confidence interval
Ringwalt et al. (1991)[18]	5th and 6th graders (*n* = 1270; 52% female/48% male; 50% African American/40% Anglo/10% other), posttested immediately	0.025	0.056	−0.06, 0.16
Becker et al. (1992)[19]	5th graders (*n* = 2878), posttested immediately	−0.058	−0.117	−0.19, −0.04
Harmon (1993)[20]	5th graders (*n* = 708), posttested immediately	0.015	0.030	−0.12, 0.18
Ennett et al. (1994)[21]	7th and 8th graders (*n* = 1334; 54% Anglo/22% African American/9% Hispanic/15% other), 2 years post-D.A.R.E.	0.000	0.000[a]	−0.11, 0.11
Rosenbaum et al. (1994)[22]	6th and 7th graders (*n* = 1584; 49.7% female/50.3% male; 49.9% Anglo/24.7% African American/8.9% Hispanic/16.5% other), 1 year post-D.A.R.E.	0.000	0.000[a]	−0.10, 0.10
Wysong et al. (1994)[23]	12th graders (*n* = 619), 5 years post-D.A.R.E.	0.000	0.000[a]	−0.16, 0.16
Dukes et al. (1996)[24]	9th graders (*n* = 849), 3 years post-D.A.R.E.	0.035	0.072	−0.06, 0.21
Zagumny & Thompson (1997)[25]	6th graders (*n* = 395; 48% female/52% male), 4–5 years post-D.A.R.E.	0.184	0.376	0.07, 0.68
Lynam et al. (1999)[6]	6th graders (*n* = 1002; 57% female/43% male; 75.1% Anglo/20.4% African American/0.5% other), 10 years post-D.A.R.E.	0.000	0.000[a]	−0.15, 0.15
Thombs (2000)[26]	5th through 10th graders (*n* = 630; 90.4% Anglo/5.5% African American/4.1% other), posttested at least 1 to 6 years post-D.A.R.E.	0.025	0.038	−0.15, 0.23
Ahmed et al. (2002)[14]	5th and 6th graders (*n* = 236; 50% female/50% male/69% Anglo/24% African American/7% other), posttested immediately	0.198	0.405	0.01, 0.80

Note. r = correlation coefficient; *d* = difference in the means of the treatment and control conditions divided by the pooled standard deviation. Negative signs for *r* and *d* indicate greater effectiveness of control/comparison group.
[a]Assumed effect size.

70   3. The research included both preintervention and postintervention assessments of at least 1 of 3 key variables: alcohol use, illicit drug use, and tobacco use. We chose to include only those effect sizes that concerned actual substance use behaviors,
75   since the true test of a substance use prevention effort is its impact on actual rates of use.

Using these criteria, we refined the original list of studies to 11 studies (Table 1). We calculated effect sizes using the procedures outlined by Rosenthal.[9]
80   Meta-analysis results are commonly presented in the form of either a correlation coefficient (*r*) or the difference in the means of the treatment and control conditions divided by the pooled standard deviation (Cohen's *d*).[10] Since both are ratings of effect size, they
85   can readily be converted to one another, and, if not provided in the original analyses, they can be calculated via F, *t*, and χ^2 statistics as well as means and standard deviations.[9]

We calculated both estimations for the individual
90   included studies and for the overall analysis. As discussed by Amato and Keith,[11] tests of significance used in meta-analyses require that effect sizes be independent; therefore, if 2 or more effect sizes were generated within the same outcome category, we used the mean
95   effect size. We also used the procedure for weighting effect sizes suggested by Shadish and Haddock[12] to ensure that all effect sizes were in the form of a com-

mon metric. In addition, we calculated 95% confidence intervals (CIs) for each study and for the overall
100   analysis.

Results

The average weighted effect size (*r*) for all studies was 0.011 (*d* = 0.023; 95% CI = −0.04, 0.08), indicating marginally better outcomes for individuals partici-
105   pating in D.A.R.E. relative to participants in control conditions. The fact that the associated CI included a negative value indicates that the average effect size was not significantly greater than zero at *p* < .05. According to the guidelines developed by Cohen,[13] both
110   of the effect sizes obtained were below the level normally considered small. Four of the included studies noted no effect of D.A.R.E. relative to control conditions, and 1 study noted that D.A.R.E. was less effective than the control condition.

Furthermore, the 6 reports indicating that D.A.R.E.
115   had more positive effects were for the most part small (Figure 1). The largest effect size was found in a report in which the only outcome examined was smoking. Finally, we conducted a test of cumulative significance to determine whether differences existed between
120   D.A.R.E. participants and non-D.A.R.E. participants. This test produced nonsignificant results (*z* = 0.73, NS).

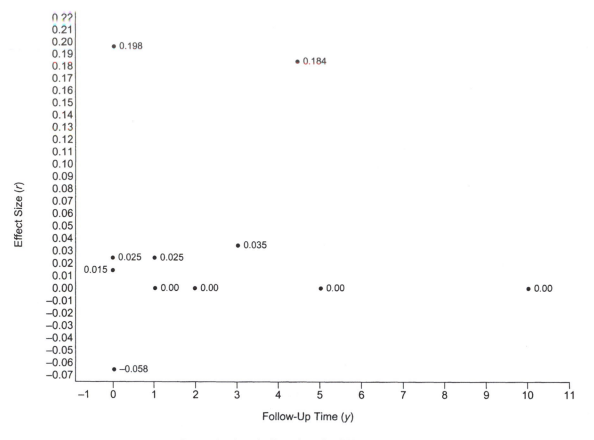

Figure 1. Plot of effect sizes, by follow-up time.

Discussion

Our results confirm the findings of a previous meta-analysis[3] indicating that Project D.A.R.E. is ineffective. This is not surprising, given the substantial information developed over the past decade to that effect. Critics of the present analysis might argue that, despite the magnitude of our findings, the direction of the effect of D.A.R.E. was generally positive. While this is the case, it should be emphasized that the effects we found did not differ significantly from the variation one would expect by chance. According to Cohen's guidelines,[13] the effect size we obtained would have needed to be 20 times larger to be considered even small. Given the tremendous expenditures in time and money involved with D.A.R.E., it would appear that continued efforts should focus on other techniques and programs that might produce more substantial effects.

Our findings also indicate that D.A.R.E. was minimally effective during the follow-up periods that would place its participants in the very age groups targeted. Indeed, no noticeable effects could be discerned in nearly half of the reports, including the study involving the longest follow-up period. This is an important consideration for those involved in program planning and development.

As noted earlier, progression in regard to experimentation and use varies over time. Use of alcohol and other drugs reaches a peak during adolescence or young adulthood and decreases steadily thereafter.[7,15] Such a developmental path would be expected of all individuals, regardless of their exposure to a prevention effort. Ideally, individuals enrolled in a program such as D.A.R.E. would report limited or no use during their adolescent and young adult years. The fact that half of the included studies reported no beneficial effect of D.A.R.E. beyond what would be expected by chance casts serious doubt on its utility.

One shortcoming of our analysis should be noted. In many of the studies we included, individual students were the unit of analysis in calculating effects. As noted by Rosenbaum and Hanson,[16] this practice tends to lead to overestimates of program effectiveness, since the true unit of analysis is the schools in which the students are "nested." Because our meta-analysis was limited to the types of data and related information available from the original articles, the potential for such inflation of program effectiveness exists. However, the overall effect sizes calculated here were small and non-significant, and thus it is unlikely that inclusion of studies making this error had a significant impact on the current findings.

An additional caveat is that all of the studies included in this analysis represent evaluations of what is commonly referred to as the "old D.A.R.E.": programs generally based on the original formulations of the D.A.R.E. model. In response to the many critiques of

the program, the D.A.R.E. prevention model was substantially revamped in 2001, thanks in part to a $13.6
180 million grant provided by the Robert Wood Johnson
Foundation.[17] The revisions to the model have since
given rise to programs working under the "new
D.A.R.E." paradigm. However, at the time of the writing of this article we were unable to find any major
185 evaluation of the new D.A.R.E. model in the research
literature, and the effectiveness of such efforts has yet
to be determined.

References

1. McNeal RB, Hanson WB. An examination of strategies for gaining con-
   vergent validity in natural experiments: D.A.R.E. as an illustrative case
   study. *Eval Rev.* 1995:19:141–158.
2. Donnermeyer J, Wurschmidt T. Educators' perceptions of the D.A.R.E.
   program. *J Drug Educ.* 1997;27:259–276.
3. Ennett ST, Tobler NS, Ringwalt CL, Flewelling RL. How effective is
   Drug Abuse Resistance Education? A meta-analysis of Project D.A.R.E.
   outcome evaluations. *Am J Public Health.* 1994;84:1394–1401.
4. Hanson WB. Pilot test results comparing the All Stars Program with seventh-grade D.A.R.E.: Program integrity and mediating variable analysis.
   Subst Use Misuse. 1996;31:1359–1377.
5. Hanson WB, McNeal RB. How D.A.R.E. works: An examination of program effects on mediating variables. *Health Educ Behav.* 1997;24:165–
   176.
6. Lynam DR, Milich R, Zimmerman R, et al. Project D.A.R.E: No effects at
   10-year follow-up. *J Consult Clin Psychol.* 1999;67:590–593.
7. Johnston LD, O'Malley PM, Bachman JG. *National Survey Results on
   Drug Use From the Monitoring the Future Study, 1975–1998. Volume 1:
   Secondary School Students.* Rockville, MD: National Institute on Drug
   Abuse; 1999. NIH publication 99–4660.
8. Gorman DM. The effectiveness of D.A.R.E. and other drug use prevention
   programs. *Am J Public Health.* 1995;85:873.
9. Rosenthal R. *Meta-Analytic Procedures for Social Research.* 2nd ed.
   Thousand Oaks, CA: Sage Publications; 1991.
10. DasEiden R, Reifman A. Effects of Brazelton demonstrations on later par-
    enting: A meta-analysis. *J Pediatr Psychol.* 1996;21:857–868.
11. Amato PH, Keith B. Parental divorce and well-being of children: A meta-
    analysis. *Psychol Bull.* 1991;110:26–46.
12. Shadish WR, Haddock CK. Combining estimates of effect size. In: Cooper
    H, Hedges LV, eds. *The Handbook of Research Synthesis.* New York. NY:
    Russell Sage Foundation; 1994:261–281.
13. Cohen J. *Statistical Power Analysis for the Behavioral Sciences.* 2nd ed.
    Hillsdale, NJ: Lawrence Erlbaum Associates; 1998.
14. Ahmed NU, Ahmed NS, Bennett CR, Hinds JE. Impact of a drug abuse
    resistance education (D.A.R.E.) program in preventing the initiation of
    cigarette smoking in fifth- and sixth-grade students. *J Natl Med Assoc.*
    2002;94:249–256.
15. Shedler J, Block J. Adolescent drug use and psychological health: A longi-
    tudinal inquiry. *Am Psychol.* 1990;45:612–630.
16. Rosenbaum DP, Hanson GS. Assessing the effects of a school-based drug
    education: A six-year multilevel analysis of Project D.A.R.E. *J Res Crime
    Delinquency.* 1998;35:381–412.
17. Improving and evaluating the D.A.R.E. school-based substance abuse pre-
    vention curriculum. Available at: http://www.rwjf.org/programs/
    grantDetail.jsp?id=040371. Accessed January 8, 2003.
18. Ringwalt C, Ennett ST, Holt KD. An outcome evaluation of Project
    D.A.R.E. (Drug Abuse Resistance Education). *Health Educ Res.*
    1991;6:327–337.
19. Becker HK, Agopian MW, Yeh S. Impact evaluation of drug abuse resis-
    tance education (D.A.R.E.). *J Drug Educ.* 1992;22:283–291.
20. Harmon MA. Reducing the risk of drug involvement among early adoles-
    cents: An evaluation of drug abuse resistance education (D.A.R.E.). *Eval
    Rev.* 1993;17:221–239.
21. Ennett ST, Rosenbaum DP, Flewelling RL, Bieler GS, Ringwalt CL, Bai-
    ley SL. Long-term evaluation of drug abuse resistance education. *Addict
    Behav.* 1994;19:113–125.
22. Rosenbaum DP, Flewelling RL, Bailey SL, Ringwalt CL, Wilkinson DL.
    Cops in the classroom: A longitudinal evaluation of drug abuse resistance
    education (D.A.R.E.). *J Res Crime Delinquency.* 1994;31:3–31.
23. Wysong E, Aniskiewicz R, Wright D. Truth and D.A.R.E.: Tracking drug
    education to graduation and as symbolic politics. *Soc Probl.* 1994;41:448–
    472.
24. Dukes RL, Ullman JB, Stein JA. Three-year follow-up of drug abuse resis-
    tance education (D.A.R.E.). *Eval Rev.* 1996;20:49–66.
25. Zagumny MJ, Thompson MK. Does D.A.R.E. work? An evaluation in ru-
    ral Tennessee. *J Alcohol Drug Educ.* 1997;42:32–41.
26. Thombs DL. A retrospective study of D.A.R.E.: Substantive effects not
    detected in undergraduates. *J Alcohol Drug Educ.* 2000;46:27–40.

Acknowledgments: Portions of this research were presented at the
Eighth Annual Meeting of the Society for Prevention Research,
Montreal, Quebec, Canada, June 2000.

About the authors: Steven L. West is with the Department of Rehabilitation Counseling, Virginia Commonwealth University, Richmond. Keri K. O'Neal is with the Center for Developmental Science,
University of North Carolina, Chapel Hill. Drs. West and O'Neal
contributed equally to all aspects of study design, data analysis, and
the writing of this article. No protocol approval was needed for this
study.

Address correspondence to: Steven L. West, Ph.D., Virginia Commonwealth University, Department of Rehabilitation Counseling,
1112 East Clay St., Box 980330, Richmond, VA 23298-0330. E-
mail: slwest2@vcu.edu

Exercise for Article 38

Factual Questions

1. To identify the articles for this meta-analysis, the
   researchers conducted computer searches of which
   three databases?

2. Which study had the largest effect size (r)? (Identify it by the name of the author and year of publication.) What was the value of r in this study?

3. What was the average weighted effect size (r) for
   all studies included in this meta-analysis?

4. The study with the largest effect size examined
   only one outcome. What was the outcome?

5. According to Figure 1, the study with the longest
   follow-up time had what effect size?

6. Were the researchers able to find any major
   evaluations of the *new* D.A.R.E. paradigm?

Questions for Discussion

7. The researchers do not describe the D.A.R.E. program components. In your opinion, would it have
   been desirable for them to do so? Explain.

8. What is your opinion of the researchers' decision
   to include only research reported in peer-reviewed
   journals? (See lines 58–66.)

9. What is your opinion of the researchers' decision
   to include only evaluations that included a control
   or comparison group? (See lines 67–69.)

10. Does it surprise you that the study by Becker et al.
    in Table 1 has negative effect sizes? Explain.

11. In Table 1, 95% confidence intervals are reported. What is your understanding of the meaning of these intervals?

12. What is your opinion on the researchers' suggestion in lines 134–138? Is your opinion based on the data in this meta-analysis? Explain.

Quality Ratings

Directions: Indicate your level of agreement with each of the following statements by circling a number from 5 for strongly agree (SA) to 1 for strongly disagree (SD). If you believe an item is not applicable to this research article, leave it blank. Be prepared to explain your ratings. When responding to criteria A and B below, keep in mind that brief titles and abstracts are conventional in published research.

A. The title of the article is appropriate.

SA   5   4   3   2   1   SD

B. The abstract provides an effective overview of the research article.

SA   5   4   3   2   1   SD

C. The introduction establishes the importance of the study.

SA   5   4   3   2   1   SD

D. The literature review establishes the context for the study.

SA   5   4   3   2   1   SD

E. The research purpose, question, or hypothesis is clearly stated.

SA   5   4   3   2   1   SD

F. The method of sampling is sound.

SA   5   4   3   2   1   SD

G. Relevant demographics (for example, age, gender, and ethnicity) are described.

SA   5   4   3   2   1   SD

H. Measurement procedures are adequate.

SA   5   4   3   2   1   SD

I. All procedures have been described in sufficient detail to permit a replication of the study.

SA   5   4   3   2   1   SD

J. The participants have been adequately protected from potential harm.

SA   5   4   3   2   1   SD

K. The results are clearly described.

SA   5   4   3   2   1   SD

L. The discussion/conclusion is appropriate.

SA   5   4   3   2   1   SD

M. Despite any flaws, the report is worthy of publication.

SA   5   4   3   2   1   SD

Appendix A

Criteria for the Evaluation of Educational Research

From Ward, A. W., Hall, B., & Schramm, C. F. (1975). Evaluation of published educational research: A national survey. *American Educational Research Journal, 12,* 109–128. Copyright © 1975 by the American Educational Research Association. Excerpt reprinted with permission of the publisher.

The set of criteria presented here was used in Hall, B. W., Ward, A. W., & Comer, C. B. (1988). Published educational research: An empirical study of its quality. *The Journal of Educational Research, 81,* 182–189.

Suggested Scale:

5—Excellent (A model of good practice.)
4—Good (A few minor defects.)
3—Mediocre (Not good, not bad.)
2—Poor (Some serious defects.)
1—Completely incompetent (A horrible example.)

Title

1. Title is well related to content of article.

Problem

2. Problem is clearly stated.

3. Hypotheses are clearly stated.

4. Problem is significant.

5. Assumptions are clearly stated.

6. Limitations of the study are stated.

7. Important terms are defined.

Review of Literature

8. Coverage of the literature is adequate.

9. Review of literature is well organized.

10. Studies are examined critically.

11. Source of important findings is noted.

12. Relationship of the problem to previous research is made clear.

Procedures

13. Research design is described fully.

14. Research design is appropriate to solution of the problem.

15. Research design is free of specific weaknesses.

16. Population and sample are described.

17. Method of sampling is appropriate.

18. Data-gathering methods or procedures are described.

19. Data-gathering methods or procedures are appropriate to the solution of the problem.

20. Data-gathering methods or procedures are used correctly.

21. Validity and reliability of data-gathering procedures are established.

Data Analysis

22. Appropriate methods are selected to analyze data.

23. Methods used in analyzing the data are applied correctly.

24. Results of the analysis are presented clearly.

25. Tables and figures are effectively used.

Summary and Conclusions

26. Conclusions are clearly stated.

27. Conclusions are substantiated by the evidence presented.

28. Conclusions are relevant to the problem.

29. Conclusions are significant.

30. Generalizations are confined to the population from which the sample was drawn.

Form and Style

31. Report is clearly written.

32. Report is logically organized.

33. Tone of the report displays an unbiased, impartial, scientific attitude.

Appendix B

Quality Control in Qualitative Research

From Patten, M. L. (2007). *Understanding research methods: An overview of the essentials* (6th ed.). Los Angeles: Pyrczak Publishing. Reprinted with permission.

This topic describes some of the specific techniques that qualitative researchers use to establish the dependability and trustworthiness of their data.[1]

One technique is to use multiple sources for obtaining data on the research topic. The technical name for this is **data triangulation**. For instance, for a qualitative study of discrimination in an employment setting, a researcher might interview employees, their supervisors, and the responsible personnel officers. To the extent that the various sources provide similar information, the data can be said to be corroborated through data triangulation.

The methods used to collect data can also be triangulated. For instance, a researcher might conduct individual interviews with parents regarding their child-rearing practices and then have the same participants provide data via focus groups. This would be an example of **methods triangulation**.

Note that in *data triangulation*, typically two or more types of participants (such as employees and supervisors) are used to collect data on a research topic. In contrast, in *methods triangulation*, only one type of participant (such as parents) is used to provide data, but two or more methods are used to collect the data.

An important technique to assure the quality of qualitative research is to form a *research team*, with each member of the team participating in the collection and analysis of data. This can be thought of as **researcher triangulation**, which reduces the possibility that the results of qualitative research represent only the idiosyncratic views of one individual researcher.

Sometimes, it is helpful to form a **team of researchers with diverse backgrounds**. For instance, for a study on the success of minority students in medical school, a team of researchers that consists of both medical school instructors and medical school students might strengthen the study by providing more than one perspective when collecting and analyzing the data.

The issue of having diversity in a research team is addressed in Example 1, which is from a qualitative research report on gender issues. The researchers point out that gender diversity in their research team helps to provide a "comprehensive view."

EXAMPLE 1
Diversity in a research team: Gender and sexuality issues were analyzed by all three researchers. That our research team included one man and two women probably helped us have a comprehensive view of the different meanings of gender issues.[2]

Oral interviews and focus groups are typically audiotaped and then transcribed. Sometimes, transcription is difficult because some participants might not speak distinctly. In addition, transcribers sometimes make errors. Therefore, checking the accuracy of a transcription helps to ensure the quality of the data. In Example 2, a sample of segments was checked.

EXAMPLE 2
Checking the accuracy of transcriptions: Each audiotaped session was transcribed verbatim. Segments of the transcriptions were checked randomly against the audiotapes for accuracy.[3]

In the analysis of data, each member of a research team should initially work independently (without consulting each other) and then compare the results of their analyses. To the extent that they agree, the results are dependable. This technique examines what is called **interobserver agreement**.[4] When there are disagreements, often they can be resolved by having the researchers discuss their differences until they reach a consensus.

The use of an outside expert can also help to ensure the quality of the research. A researcher's peer (such as

---

[1] The terms "dependability" and "trustworthiness" in qualitative research loosely correspond to the terms "reliability" and "validity" in quantitative research.

[2] Rasera, E. F., Vieira, E. M., & Japur, M. (2004). Influence of gender and sexuality on the construction of being HIV positive as experienced in a support group in Brazil. *Families, Systems, & Health, 22*, 340–351.

[3] Lukens, E. P., Thorning, H., & Lohrer, S. (2004). Sibling perspectives on severe mental illness: Reflections on self and family. *American Journal of Orthopsychiatry, 74*, 489–501.

[4] In qualitative research, this is sometimes called *intercoder agreement*. In quantitative research, this concept is called *interobserver reliability*.

another experienced qualitative researcher) can examine the process used to collect data, the resulting data and the conclusions, and then provide feedback to the researcher. This process is called **peer review**. Under certain circumstances, the peer who provides the review is called an **auditor**.

The dependability of the results can also be enhanced by a process called **member checking**. This term is based on the idea that the participants are "members" of the research team. By having the participants/members review the results of the analysis, researchers can determine whether their results "ring true" to the participants. If not, adjustments can be made in the description of the results.